The Complete Indian Dal Cookbook:

Insanely Delicious and Nutritious Recipes of Dried Beans, Lentils, and Peas from India!

Rekha Sharma

Ⓥ=VEGAN Ⓟ= QUICK PRESSURE COOKER RECIPE

About the Author _____ *1*

Introduction _____ *1*

Indian Meals _____ *2*

Using this Book _____ *3*

   Know Your Measurements _____4

Indian Spices and Seasonings _____ *5*

Indian cooking 101 _____ *12*

   Basic Techniques _____13

      Blanching Raw Nuts Ⓥ _____ 13
         Almonds (Badaam) _____ 13
         Pistachios (Pista) _____ 14
      Deep-frying the Indian Way _____ 14
      Dry-Roasting Spices, Nuts, and Flours Ⓥ _____ 15
         Spices (Masalae) _____ 15
         Nuts and Seeds (Maevae) _____ 16
         Chickpea and Other Flours (Besan aur Doosrae Aatae) _____ 16
      Reconstituting Dried Wild Mushrooms_____ 16
      Roasting and Grilling Vegetables Ⓥ _____ 17
         Eggplants (Baingan) _____ 17
         Bell Peppers (Shimla Mirch) _____ 18
      Slivering Blanched Nuts Ⓥ _____ 19
      Sprouting Beans and Seeds Ⓥ _____ 20

   Basic Ingredients _____21

      Coconut Milk Ⓥ_____ 21
      Crispy Chickpea Batter Drops Ⓥ _____ 21
      Crispy Fried Fresh Ginger Ⓥ _____ 22
      Crispy Fried Onions Ⓥ_____ 23
      Homemade Yogurt _____ 24
      Indian Clarified Butter _____ 25
      Paneer Cheese_____ 26
      Yogurt Cheese _____ 27

   Basic Spice Blends _____28

      Curry Powders _____ 28

- Basic Curry Powder Ⓥ 28
- Spiced Basic Curry Powder Ⓥ 29
- Goan Curry Powder Ⓥ 30
- Gujarati Curry Powder Ⓥ 31
- Kashmiri Curry Powder Ⓥ 32
- Marathi Curry Powder Ⓥ 33
- South Indian Curry PowderⓋ 33

Garam Masalas 34
- Basic Garam Masala Ⓥ 34
- Hyderabadi Garam Masala Ⓥ 35
- Kashmiri Garam Masala Ⓥ 36
- Mughlai Garam Masala Ⓥ 37
- Parsi Garam Masala Ⓥ 37

Savory Spice Blends 38
- Chaat Masala Ⓥ 38
- New Delhi Street Food Masala Ⓥ 39
- Bombay Bread-Snack Masala Ⓥ 40
- Cumin-Water Masala Ⓥ 41
- Griddle-Fried Bread Masala Ⓥ 42
- Stuffed Griddle-Fried Bread Masala Ⓥ 42
- Roasted Chile Pepper and Red Peppercorn Masala Ⓥ 43
- Roasted Cumin and Fenugreek Masala Ⓥ 44
- Roasted Cumin-Pepper Masala Ⓥ 45
- Punjabi Raita and Buttermilk Masala Ⓥ 45
- Kashmiri Raita Masala Ⓥ 46

Masala Blends for Special Dishes 47
- Bengali Five Whole Spice Blend Ⓥ 47
- Braised Meat Masala Ⓥ 47
- Chickpea Masala Ⓥ 48
- Grilling Masala Ⓥ 49
- Gujrati Masala Ⓥ 50
- Meat Masala Ⓥ 51
- Vindaloo Masala Ⓥ 52
- Wok Masala Ⓥ 53

Special South Indian Blends 53
- Sambar Masala Ⓥ 54
- Rasam Masala Ⓥ 54
- Chutney Coconut Masala Ⓥ 55
- Lentil Paste Ⓥ 56
- Peanut Masala Ⓥ 57

Sesame Masala (V)	58
Thenga Masala (V)	58
Dessert and Tea Masalas	59
Dessert Masala (V)	60
Tea Masala (V)	60

BASIC FLAVORING PASTES — 61

Basic Ginger Paste (V)	61
Basic Garlic Paste (V)	62
Roasted Garlic Paste (V)	62
Basic Ginger-Garlic Paste (V)	63
Almond and Poppy Seed Paste (V)	64
Basic Cashew Paste (V)	64
Basic Curry Paste with Onion (V)	65
Basic Curry Paste without Onion	65
Basic Ginger and Green Chile Pepper Paste (V)	66
Basic Onion Paste (V)	67
Boiled Onion Paste (V)	67
Chile Pepper Paste (V)	68
Fried Onion Paste	69
Goan Vindaloo Paste (V)	69
Gujarati Green Paste (V)	70
Hyderabadi Ginger-Garlic Paste (V)	71
Kerala Fried Onion Paste (V)	71
Minty Green Curry Paste (V)	72
Mughlai Curry Paste with Nuts	73
Spicy Yellow Curry Paste (V)	74
Tamarind Paste (V)	74

Chutney — 75

Green Chutneys — 76

Basic Green Chutney (V)	76
Cilantro-Lime Chutney (V)	77
Mint Chutney (V)	78
Mint-Garlic Chutney (V)	78
Scallion-Ginger Chutney	79
South Indian Cilantro Chutney (V)	80

Coconut Chutneys — 81

Fresh Coconut Chutney with Cilantro	81
Minty Coconut-Tamarind Chutney (V)	82

Roasted Coconut Chutney Ⓥ	83
Semolina-Coconut Chutney	84
Shredded Coconut Chutney Ⓥ	85

Garlic and Chile Pepper Chutneys — 86

Garlic and Fresh Red Chile Pepper Chutney Ⓥ	86
Green Garlic and Nuts Chutney Ⓥ	87
Peanut and Garlic Chutney Ⓥ	88

Bean and Legume Chutneys — 89

Classic Hyderabadi Ginger-Sesame Chutney Ⓥ	89
Roasted Black Chickpea Chutney with Peanuts Ⓥ	90
Roasted Dal and Fresh Green Chile Pepper Chutney Ⓥ	91
Sesame-Peanut Chutney Ⓥ	92

Yogurt Chutneys — 93

Yogurt Cheese Chutney with Minced Greens	93
Yogurt Chutney with Puréed Greens	94
Yogurt Chutney with Roasted Dals and Spices	95
Yogurt-Almond Chutney	96

Puréed Fruit Chutneys — 96

Puréed Fresh Mango-Ginger Chutney Ⓥ	97
Puréed Green Mango Chutney Ⓥ	97
South Indian Tomato Chutney Ⓥ	98
Tart Apple-Ginger Chutney Ⓥ	99

Preserved Chutneys — 100

Cranberry Chutney Preserve Ⓥ	100
Fragrant Mango Chutney Preserve Ⓥ	101
Red Tomato Chutney Preserve Ⓥ	102
Spicy Apple-Ginger Chutney Preserve Ⓥ	104
Spicy Apricot Chutney Preserve Ⓥ	105
Tomato Chutney Preserve Ⓥ	106

Sonth Chutneys — 107

Minty Sonth Chutney with Mango Ⓥ	107
Sonth Chutney with Dried Mango Slices Ⓥ Ⓟ	108
Sonth Chutney with Fresh and Dried Fruits Ⓥ	109
Sweet Sonth Chutney with Dates Ⓥ	111

Indian Pickles — *112*

Mango Pickles — 112

- Quick Mango Pickle (V) ... 112
- Punjabi Mango Pickle (V) ... 113
- Mango Pickle spice roast (V) ... 114
- Cooked South Indian Mango Pickle (V) ... 115
- Grated Mango Pickle (V) ... 116

Lime and Lemon Pickles ... 117
- Basic Lemon Pickle (V) ... 117
- Sweet and Sour Fresh Lime Pickle (V) ... 118
- Crushed Lemon and Fresh Red Chile Pepper Pickle (V) ... 119
- Ginger-Lemon Pickle (V) ... 120
- Minced Ginger-Lime Pickle (V) ... 121

Green Chile Pepper Pickles ... 121
- Vinegar-Marinated Green Chile Peppers (V) ... 122
- Pickled Chile Pepper with Tamarind (V) ... 122
- Fiery Green Chile Pepper Pickle (V) ... 123

Other Vegetable Pickles ... 124
- Crunchy Cucumber Pickle (V) ... 124
- Cauliflower-Carrot Water Pickle (V) ... 125
- Spicy Cranberry Pickle (V) ... 126
- Onion Pickle (V) ... 127
- Turnip Pickle (V) ... 128
- Turnip & Cauliflower Pickle (V) ... 129
- Mixed Vegetable Pickle (V) ... 130
- Eggplant and Malanga Root Pickle (V) ... 131

Snacks, Appetizers, and Street Food ... 133

Spicy Relish Mixes ... 133
- Fried Taro Chips (V) ... 133
- Gram Flour Fried Peanuts (V) ... 134
- Salted Cashews (V) ... 135
- Salty Cereal Mix (V) ... 136
- Spicy Mixed Nuts and Seeds (V) ... 137
- Spicy Pressed Rice Flake Mix (V) ... 138
- Spicy Thin Crispy Flatbreads (V) ... 139

Mathiya ... 140
- Ajwain Seed Mathiya (V) ... 140
- Mung Bean Puffed Pastries (V) ... 141
- Patty 1: Mushroom Turnovers ... 143

Patty 2: Curried Chicken or Lamb Turnovers	145
Puff Pastry Rolls	146
Puff Pastry with Ajwain Seeds	147
Red Bell Pepper-Potato Pastry Swirls	148
Salty Finger Pastries Ⓥ	149

Samosa — 150

Basic Samosa Ⓥ	151
Seven Layers Samosa	152
Sindhi-Style Samosa Ⓥ	153
Stuffed Phyllo Baked Samosa	155
Stuffed Phyllo Samosa	156
Tortilla Samosa Ⓥ	157

Fillings for Samosas — 158

Basic Potato Filling Ⓥ	158
Green Pea Filling Ⓥ	159
Meat Filling	160
Moong Dal Filling Ⓥ	161
Sprouted Green Mung Bean Filling Ⓥ	162
Vegetable Filling Ⓥ	163

Fritters (Pakorae) — 164

Frying Fritters	164
Basic Batter for Pakora Ⓥ	165
Sliced, Chopped, and Stuffed Vegetable Fritters	166
Bell Pepper Fritters Ⓥ	166
Cabbage Roll Fritters Ⓥ	166
Cauliflower Fritters Ⓥ	167
Eggplant Fritters Ⓥ	168
Fresh Green Bean Pakora Fritters Ⓥ	169
Potato Fritters Ⓥ	169
Pumpkin Fritters Ⓥ	170
Spinach Fritters Ⓥ	171
Stuffed Bread Fritters Ⓥ	171
Shredded and Minced Vegetable Fritters	172
Chopped Onion Fritters Ⓥ	172
Fenugreek Fritters Ⓥ	173
Mixed Vegetable Fritters Ⓥ	174
Rice Flour and Cashew Fritters Ⓥ	175
Rice Flour Papaya Fritters Ⓥ	176
Shredded Cabbage Fritters	177

Split Pea Fritters Ⓥ _____ 178

Cheese and Meat Fritters _____ 179
Chicken Fritters _____ 179
Fish Fritters _____ 180
Ground Meat Fritters _____ 181
Marinated Chicken Pakora Fritters _____ 182
Paneer Fritters _____ 183
Paneer Fritters with Green Chutney _____ 184
Paneer Fritters with Red Bell Peppers _____ 185
Shrimp Fritters _____ 186

Potato Snacks _____ 187
Mashed Potato Balls Ⓥ _____ 187
Chicken-Stuffed Potatoes _____ 188
Peas-Filled Bakes Potato _____ 189
Potato Fries with Tomatoes Ⓥ _____ 191

Potato Patties _____ 192
Basic Mashed Potato Tikki Ⓥ _____ 192
Basic Stuffed Potato Tikki Ⓥ _____ 193
  Fillings for Potato Patties Ⓥ _____ 194
Bread and Potato Tikki _____ 195
Potato and Cashew Tikki Ⓥ _____ 196
Potato and Tapioca Tikki Ⓥ _____ 197
Tofu and Potato Tikki Ⓥ _____ 199

Croquettes and Dumplings (Vadae) _____ 200
Coconut–Red Chile Croquettes _____ 200
Mung Croquettes Ⓥ _____ 201
Rice Croquettes Ⓥ _____ 202
Salty Croquettes Ⓥ _____ 204
South Indian Croquettes Ⓥ _____ 205
Spinach Mung Croquettes Ⓥ _____ 206
Urad Croquettes Ⓥ _____ 208

Steamed Rice Cakes (Idli) _____ 209
Basic Steamed Rice Cakes _____ 209
Quick Semolina Cakes _____ 210
Spicy Rice Cakes _____ 211

Bean and Rice Cakes (Dhokla) _____ 212
Classic Chickpea Cakes _____ 213
Chickpea Flour Rolls _____ 214

- Chickpea Flour Rolls- Stuffed _____ 215
- Chickpea Zucchini Cake _____ 217
- Steamed Chickpea Flour Cakes Ⓥ _____ 218
- Steamed Mung Cakes Ⓥ _____ 219

Indian Street Foods _____ 220
- Crispy Flour Chips Mix _____ 220
- Crunchy Puffs with Spicy Tamarind Water Ⓥ _____ 221
- Flour Chips Yogurt Mix _____ 222
- Puffed Rice Spicy Mix Ⓥ _____ 223
- Stuffed Crispy Puffs with _____ 224

Kebabs _____ 225
- Kebab and Tikka Finishing Glaze _____ 225
- Black Chickpea Kebabs Ⓥ Ⓟ _____ 226
- Chicken Drumstick Kebabs _____ 227
- Chicken Liver Kebabs _____ 228
- Cottage Cheese and Vegetable Kebabs _____ 229
- Cottage Cheese Kebabs with Pomegranate Seeds _____ 230
- Deep-Fried Mutton Kebab Patties Ⓟ _____ 231
- Egg-Stuffed Chicken Kebabs _____ 233
- Fish Kebabs _____ 234
- Green Chutney Cottage Cheese Kebabs _____ 235
- Marinated Lamb Kebabs _____ 236
- Mutton Kebab with Cardamom Seeds _____ 237
- Mutton Kebab with Nuts and Poppy Seeds _____ 238
- Mutton Kebabs with Fenugreek Leaves _____ 240
- Paneer Kebabs _____ 241
- Pan-Fried Lamb Kebabs _____ 242
- Skewered Minced Lamb Kebabs _____ 243
- Smooth Minced Chicken Kebabs _____ 244
- Vegetable Kebabs _____ 246

Tikka Kebabs and Marinades _____ *247*

Marinades _____ 247
- Chile Chicken Tikka Marinade _____ 248
- Citrus Chicken Tikka Marinade _____ 248
- Creamy Chicken Tikka Marinade _____ 249
- Garlic Chicken Tikka Marinade _____ 250
- Green Chutney Lamb Tikka Marinade _____ 250
- Grilled Fish Tikka Marinade _____ 251
- Mint Chicken Tikka Marinade _____ 252

Rosemary Lamb Tikka Marinade _____ 253
　　　Royal Lamb Tikka Marinade _____ 253
　　　Sesame Fish Tikka Marinade _____ 254
　　　Smooth Chicken Tikka Marinade_____ 255
　　　Turmeric Lamb Tikka Marinade _____ 256

Basic Tikka Recipes _____256
　　　Basic Mutton Tikka _____ 257
　　　Basic Chicken Tikka Kabaabs _____ 258
　　　Basic Fish Tikka Kabaabs _____ 259

Soups _____ 260

Basic Broths _____260
　　　Vegetarian Broth Ⓥ _____ 260
　　　Spicy Chicken Broth_____ 261
　　　Spicy Lamb Broth_____ 262

Tomato Soups_____263
　　　Creamy Tomato Soup _____ 264
　　　Tomato Soup with Curry Leaves _____ 265
　　　Tomato Soup with Mung Ⓥ _____ 266
　　　Tomato Soup with Sautéed Vegetables Ⓥ _____ 267

South Indian Soups (Rasam) _____268
　　　Classic South Indian Split Pigeon Pea Soup Ⓥ _____ 269
　　　Buttermilk Soup_____ 270
　　　Chunky South Indian Tomato Soup Ⓥ _____ 271
　　　Lemon and Mung Soup Ⓥ _____ 272
　　　Mulligatawny Soup Ⓥ_____ 273
　　　Mysore Coconut Soup Ⓥ _____ 275
　　　South Indian Ginger Soup Ⓥ_____ 276
　　　South Indian Tamarind Soup Ⓥ _____ 277
　　　South Indian Vegetable and Tamarind Soup Ⓥ _____ 278

Bean and Lentil Soups _____279
　　　Black Bean Soup Ⓟ _____ 279
　　　Black Chickpea Soup Ⓥ Ⓟ_____ 281
　　　Chickpea Chicken Soup _____ 282
　　　Chilled Chickpea Soup _____ 283
　　　Lentil, Barley, and Vegetable Soup Ⓟ _____ 284
　　　Mung and Spinach Soup Ⓥ_____ 286
　　　Sindhi Split Pigeon Pea Soup Ⓥ Ⓟ _____ 287

Vegetable Soups _____ 288
   Cabbage and Vegetable Soup Ⓥ _____ 288
   Carrot and Ginger Soup_____ 289
   Chilled Potato Soup_____ 290
   Curried Green Pea Soup _____ 291
   Goan Cauliflower Soup _____ 292
   Pumpkin Soup Ⓥ _____ 293
   Root Vegetable Soup Ⓥ Ⓟ _____ 294
   Spinach Soup_____ 296

Yogurt Soups _____ 297
   Basic Yogurt Soup _____ 297
   Almond–Poppy Seed Soup _____ 298
   Chilled Roasted Vegetable Soup _____ 299
   Mushroom Yogurt Soup _____ 300
   Spinach Yogurt Soup _____ 301
   Vegetable, Yogurt, and Coconut Soup _____ 302
   Yogurt and Roasted Eggplant Soup_____ 303

Fish and Chicken Soups _____ 304
   Cashew Corn-Chicken Broth Soup _____ 304
   Chicken and Corn Soup _____ 305
   Chicken Soup with Chayote Squash _____ 306
   Ginger and Coconut Milk Chicken Soup _____ 307
   Goan Shrimp Soup _____ 309
   Shrimp, Coconut Milk, and Tomato Soup_____ 310

Salads _____ *311*

Fresh Chopped Salads (Kachumbar) _____ 311
   Armenian Cucumber and Peanut Salad Ⓥ _____ 311
   Cucumber and Red Lentil Salad Ⓥ _____ 312
   Daikon, Mung, Peanut Salad Ⓥ _____ 313
   Gingered Tomato Cucumber Salad Ⓥ _____ 314

Tomato Salads _____ 315
   Colourful Tomato Salad Ⓥ _____ 315
   Pan-Fried Green Tomato Salad Ⓥ _____ 315
   Tomato, Scallion, Sev Salad Ⓥ _____ 316

Cabbage Salads _____ 317
   Cabbage and Broccoli Salad _____ 317
   Keral Cabbage and Red Onion Salad Ⓥ _____ 318
   Lemony Cabbage Salad Ⓥ _____ 319

Yogurt Coleslaw _____ 319

Marinated Salads _____ 320
Carrot and Cashew Salad Ⓥ _____ 321
Lemony Red Onion Rings Ⓥ _____ 321
Marinated Peanut Salad Ⓥ _____ 322
Okra and Radish Salad Ⓥ _____ 323
Zucchini Pineapple Salad _____ 324

Bean and Legume Salads _____ 325
Black-Eyed Pea Salad _____ 325
Chickpea Chaat Salad Ⓥ _____ 326
Dew Bean Salad Ⓥ _____ 327
Mixed Sprouted Bean & Potato Vermicelli Salad Ⓥ _____ 328
Parsi Sprouted Bean Salad Ⓥ _____ 329
Red Bean Salad _____ 330
Soybean-Tomato Salad Ⓥ _____ 331
Sprouted Mung and Cabbage Salad Ⓥ _____ 332

Potato and Root Vegetable Salads _____ 333
Potato Salad with Yogurt _____ 333
Potato, Sweet Potato, and Pea Salad Ⓥ _____ 334
Red Potato Chaat Salad _____ 335
Sweet Potato Salad Ⓥ _____ 336
Taro Root Salad Ⓥ _____ 337

Green Salads _____ 337
Cottage Cheese Salad with Baby Greens _____ 337
Pan-Roasted Tomato Mix Salad _____ 338
Spinach Salad _____ 339

Fruit Salads _____ 340
Savory Summer Fruit Salad Ⓥ _____ 340
Spicy Mixed Berry Salad Ⓥ _____ 341

Non-Vegetarian Salads _____ 341
Egg Salad _____ 341
Ginger-Shrimp Salad _____ 342
Minced Chicken and Lentil Wafer Salad _____ 343
Tandoori Chicken Salad _____ 344

Yogurt Raitas and Pachadis _____ 345

Basic Raitas _____ 346
Simple Salt and Pepper Raita _____ 346

Ginger and Scallion Raita	346
Iced Raita	347
Lemon Pickle Raita	347

Vegetable Raitas — 348

Beet and Scallion Raita	348
Cucumber and Radish Raita	349
Kashmiri Morel Mushroom Raita	350
Mustard Seed Raita	351
Potato and Beet Raita	351
Potato and Cumin Raita	352
Potato-Mustard Raita	353
Sprouted Beans and Vegetable Raita	354
Tomato and Mint Leaves Raita	355

Raitas with Herbs and Greens — 356

Fresh Spinach Raita with Ginger-Lime Pickle	356
Frozen Spinach Raita	356
Green Raita	357
Sautéed Spinach Raita	358
Spicy Raita with Lamb's Quarters	359
Tofu and Greens Mix Raita	360
Tofu and Mint Chutney Raita	361

Grilled or Roasted Vegetable Raitas — 361

Eggplant and Sesame Raita	361
Garlick Chinese Eggplant Raita	362
Grilled Eggplant Raita	363
Grilled Zucchini and Onion Raita	364
Roasted Bell Pepper Raita	365

Fresh and Dried Fruit Raitas — 365

Banana Raita	365
Dried Fruit Raita	366
Mandarin Orange Raita	367
Mango Chutney Raita	368
Mango-Ginger Raita	368

Dumpling Raitas — 369

Crispy Chickpea Batter Drops Raita	369
Crispy Urad Dal Croquettes in Yogurt	370
Mung Bean Croquettes Raita	371
Raita with Chickpea Flour Pancakes	372
Softened Chickpea Batter Drops Raita	373

Spicy Mung Bean Croquettes Raita with Sonth Chutney ___ 374
Urad Dal Croquettes Raita ___ 375

Meat Raitas ___ 377

Ground Lamb Raita ___ 377
Shredded Chicken Raita ___ 378

South Indian Pachadis ___ 378

Chopped Salad Yogurt ___ 378
Cucumber Pachadi ___ 379
Green Papaya and Coconut Pachadi ___ 380
Green Tomato Chutney Pachadi ___ 381
Mango and Coconut Pachadi ___ 382
Mashed Potato and Cilantro Pachadi ___ 383
Pumpkin and Tamarind Pachadi ___ 384
Rice Flakes Pachadi ___ 385
Sautéed Banana Pachadi ___ 386
Sautéed Tomatoes and Coconut Pachadi ___ 387
Tomato and Cucumber Pachadi ___ 388
Tomato, Cucumber, and Onion Yogurt ___ 389

Paneer Cheese ___ *390*

Homemade Paneer Cheese ___ 391

Paneer Cheese Appetizers ___ 392

Paneer Kebabs ___ 392
Chickpea Flour Paneer ___ 393
Lightly Seared Sour Paneer ___ 394
Onion Crunchy Paneer ___ 395
Paneer Balls ___ 396
Paneer Wraps ___ 397
Saffron Paneer ___ 398
Seared Paneer with Caper Sauce ___ 399
Spicy Peppered Paneer ___ 400

Paneer Cheese Snacks and Side Dishes ___ 402

Apple-Ginger Scrambled Paneer ___ 402
Basic Scrambled Paneer ___ 402
Chilli Paneer and Fried Ginger ___ 403
Diced Paneer with Ajwain Seeds ___ 404
Paneer with Cauliflower and Broccoli ___ 405
Paneer-Cilantro Bake ___ 406
Quick & Easy Spinach Paneer ___ 407
Sautéed Paneer with Green Chutney ___ 408

Scrambled Ginger-Lime Paneer	409
Scrambled Mushroom Paneer	410
Scrambled Paneer and Cauliflower	411
Soybeans Scrambled Paneer	412
Sun-Dried Tomato-Paneer	413
Tomato Dry Paneer	414

Paneer Cheese Main Courses and Curries — 415

Griddle-Fried Paneer	416
Nine-Jewel Paneer Curry	417
Paneer and Red Chile Pepper Curry	418
Paneer Onion Curry	419
Paneer-Coconut Curry	420
Paneer-Pea-Potato Curry	422
Paneer-Potato Curry	423
Royal Paneer Curry	424
Spinach and Fenugreek Paneer	425
Spinach Paneer	427
Stir-Fried Paneer with Onions and Bell Peppers	428
Stuffed Paneer Balls Curry	429
Coconut and Corn Paneer	431

Breads and Crepes — 432

Simple Griddle Breads — 433

Working with Whole-Wheat Dough	434
Basic Whole-Wheat Dough (V)	434
Whole-Wheat Griddle Breads (V)	435
Multi-Flour Griddle Breads (V)	436

Griddle-Fried Breads (Paranthas) — 438

Basic Parantha Breads — 438

Shaping Paranthas	438
Basic Parantha (V)	440
Green Chile Pepper Parantha (V)	441
Legume Paranthas (V)	442
Mashed Potato Parantha	443
Mint, Ajwain, and Black Pepper Parantha	444
Mughlai Parantha (V)	445
Oat and Ajwain Parantha (V)	446
Onion Parantha	447
Spinach and Red Bell Pepper Parantha (V)	448

Stuffed Griddle-Fried Flatbreads — 449
- Basic Stuffed Parantha Ⓥ — 449

Stuffings for Parantha Breads — 450
- Potato Parantha Stuffing Ⓥ — 451
- Cauliflower Parantha Stuffing Ⓥ — 452
- Ground Lamb Parantha Stuffing — 452
- Paneer Parantha Stuffing — 453
- Radish Parantha Stuffing Ⓥ — 454

Puffed Deep-Fried Breads (Pooriyan) — 454
- Basic Poori Ⓥ — 455
  - To make the Dough — 455
  - To shape and fry the poories — 456

Flavored Deep-Fried Puffed Breads — 457
- Ajwain Poori Ⓥ — 457
- Deep-Fried Bengali Breads Ⓥ — 458
- Deep-Fried Leavened Bread — 458
- Fermented Saffron Poori Ⓥ — 460
- Mint (or Fenugreek) Poori Ⓥ — 461
- Spinach Poori Ⓥ — 462
- Stuffed and Puffed Poori Ⓥ — 462

Oven-Grilled Naan and Other Breads — 463
- Basic Oven-Grilled Naan — 464

Oven-Grilled Breads with Different Flavors — 465
- Baked Semolina Breads — 465
- Cheese Naan — 467
- Dried Herb and Spice Naan — 467
- Kalonji/Sesame Naan — 468
- Oven-Grilled Garlic and Turmeric Breads — 469
- Tofu Naan — 469

Special Breads — 470
- Punjabi White Corn Flatbread Ⓥ — 471
- Basic Rajasthani Rolls — 471
- Chickpea Flour Flatbread — 473
- Fermented Leavened Flatread — 474
- Flour and Potato Flatbread Ⓥ — 475
- Gujarati Fenugreek Flatbread — 476
- Millet Flatbread Ⓥ — 477
- Opo Squash Flatbread Ⓥ — 478

Potato Baati Rolls — 479
Sorghum Flatbread Ⓥ — 480

Crepes and Pancakes — 481

Basic Rice and Bean Dosa Ⓥ — 481
Semolina Dosa — 482
Stuffed Dosa Ⓥ — 483
Chickpea Flour Crepes Ⓥ — 484
Classic Lentil Pancakes Ⓥ — 485
Mung Bean Pancakes Ⓥ — 486
Rice Flour Pancakes — 487
Stuffed Paneer Cheese Pancake Rolls Ⓥ — 488
Tomato Semolina Pancakes — 489

Rice — 491

Plain and Steamed Rice Dishes — 492

Boiled Basmati Rice Ⓥ — 492
Steamed Basmati Rice Ⓥ — 493
Steamed Green Rice Ⓥ — 493
Steamed Spicy Rice Ⓥ — 494
Steamed Tumeric Rice Ⓥ — 495

Simple Herbs and Spices Pilafs (Pullaos) — 496

Cilantro-Garlic-Pea Pilaf Ⓥ Ⓟ — 496
Ginger-Mint Pilaf Ⓥ — 497
Roasted Saffron Pilaf Ⓥ — 498
Saffron and Almond Pilaf — 499
Simple Cumin Pilaf Ⓥ — 500
Whole Spice Pilaf Ⓥ — 501

South and West Indian Vegetarian Rice Dishes — 502

Coorgi Yogurt Rice — 502
Goan Coconut Milk Pilaf Ⓥ — 503
Lemon Rice Ⓥ — 504
Madrasi Eggplant Rice Ⓥ — 505
Potato-Coconut-Yogurt Rice — 507
Roasted Peanut Rice Ⓥ — 508
Southern Mustard-Asafoetida Pilaf Ⓥ Ⓟ — 509
Southern Sesame Rice Ⓥ — 510
Southern Tamarind Rice Ⓥ — 511
Tangy Southern Rice — 513
Yogurt-Cashew Rice — 514

Vegetable Pilafs (Sabzi kae Pullao) — 515
- Cauliflower Pilaf (V) — 515
- Corn-Peas-Tomato Pilaf (V) — 516
- Cranberry Pilaf — 517
- Green Chickpea Pilaf (V) — 518
- Grilled Bell Pepper Pilaf (V) — 520
- Kashmiri Mixed Veg Pilaf (V) — 521
- Mixed Veg Pilaf — 522
- Mushroom-Pistachio Pilaf (V) — 523
- Mushrooms-Chard Pilaf (V) — 524
- Onion and Broccoli Pilaf (V) — 525
- Roasted Fenugreek Pilaf (V) — 526
- Royal Pilaf — 527
- Soybean Pilaf (P) — 529
- Spinach-Bell Pepper Pilaf (V) — 530
- Tofu/Paneer and Chickpea Pilaf (V) — 531

Non-Vegetarian Pilafs (Pullao) — 532
- Basic Lamb Pilaf — 532
- Chicken Pilaf — 533
- Ground Lamb Pilaf — 535
- Shrimp Pilaf — 536

Layered Rice Dishes (Biryanis) — 537
- Eggplant Biryani (V) — 537
- Hyderabadi Chicken Biryani — 539
- Hyderabadi Marinated Chicken Biryani — 540
- Hyderabadi Mixed Veg Biryani — 541
- Lamb Chop Biryani — 543
- Mixed Nuts and Saffron Biryani — 544
- Mutton-Apricot Biryani — 546

Khichadis (Rice and Grain Recipes) — 547
- Mung Khichadi (P) — 548
- Mixed Veg-Spinach Khichadi (P) — 548
- Tapioca Khichadi — 550
- Wheat, Rice, and Mung Khichadi (V) (P) — 551
- Wheat-Lentil-Bean Khichadi (V) (P) — 552
- Yellow Mung and Ginger Khichadi (P) — 553

Other Grain Pilafs — 554
- Asafoetida Brown Basmati (V) (P) — 554
- Peas-Potato Rice Flakes (V) — 555

Spicy Semolina Ⓥ	556
Stir-Fried Vermicelli	557
Tamarind Rice Flakes Ⓥ	559
Wild Rice Pilaf Ⓥ	560

Dried Beans, Lentils, and Peas (Dal) — 561

Know Your Dal — 562

Basics of Cooking Dal — 564

Mung Beans (Mung Dal) Recipes — 565

Yellow Mung Dal Ⓥ	565
Gujarati Green Masala Mung Dal Ⓥ Ⓟ	566
Punjabi Dry-Cooked Mung Dal Ⓥ	567
Punjabi Green Mung Dal Ⓟ	568
Rind Mung Dal Ⓥ	569
Roasted Mung and Potatoes Ⓥ	571
Sindhi Dry-Cooked Mung Dal Ⓥ	572
Southern Mung Dal Ⓥ	573
Zucchini Mung Dal Ⓥ Ⓟ	574

Lentil (Masoor Dal) Recipes — 575

Bengali Spiced Red Lentils Ⓥ	575
Dry-Cooked Red Lentils Ⓥ	576
Onion and Green Lentils Ⓥ Ⓟ	578
Roasted Green Lentils Ⓥ	579

Split Pigeon Peas (Toor Dal) Recipes — 580

Basic South Indian Sambar Ⓥ Ⓟ	580
Dry Pigeon Pea Cake Ⓥ	581
Gujarati Split Pigeon Peas Ⓥ	582
Madrasi Vegetable Sambar Ⓥ	584
Punjabi-Style Split Pigeon Peas Ⓥ	585
Sweet Split Pigeon Peas Ⓥ Ⓟ	586
Veggies Coconut Sambar Ⓥ Ⓟ	587

Urad Beans (Urad Dal) — 589

Chickpeas-Urad Dal Ⓥ Ⓟ	589
Kashmiri Black Urad Dal	590
Punjabi Black Urad Dal	591
Roasted Fenugreek Urad Dal Ⓥ	592
Slow Cooked Black Urad Dal	593

- Smoked Black Urad Dal Ⓟ ... 595
- Stir-Fried Black Urad Dal Ⓥ ... 596
- White Urad Dal Ⓥ ... 597

Split Chickpeas and Split Peas (Channa Dal and Muttar Dal) Recipes ... 599
- Dry-Cooked Green Split Pea Dal Ⓥ ... 599
- Opo Squash and Yellow Split Chickpeas Ⓥ Ⓟ ... 600
- Quick Dry Cooked Green Peas Ⓥ Ⓟ ... 601
- Spicy Dry Yellow Peas Ⓥ Ⓟ ... 602
- Spinach and Yellow Split Chickpeas Ⓥ Ⓟ ... 603

Mixed Beans and Lentils ... 605
- Five Jewels Dal Ⓥ Ⓟ ... 605
- Rajasthani Five in One Dal Ⓥ Ⓟ ... 606
- Spinach-Urad Dal Ⓥ Ⓟ ... 607
- Veggie and Legume Dal Ⓥ Ⓟ ... 609

Whole Dried Bean Dishes ... 610
- Black Rajma Curry Ⓥ Ⓟ ... 611
- Black-Eyed Peas Curry Ⓟ ... 612
- Classic Onion-Free Rajma Ⓟ ... 613
- Classic Spiced Rajma Ⓥ Ⓟ ... 615
- Kashmiri Small Rajma Ⓟ ... 615
- Punjabi Pickle Masala Raajma Ⓟ ... 617
- Roasted Adzuki Beans Ⓥ ... 618
- Spiced Adzuki Beans Ⓥ Ⓟ ... 619
- White Rajma Ⓥ Ⓟ ... 620
- Yogurt Soybeans Ⓥ ... 622
- Yogurt-Black-Eyed Peas Curry Ⓟ ... 623

Whole Chickpea Dishes ... 624
- Chickpea Chaat Masala Ⓥ ... 624
- Chickpea-Pomegranate Ⓥ ... 625
- Chickpeas in a Can Ⓥ Ⓟ ... 627
- Classic Chickpeas in Curry Ⓟ ... 628
- Dry Chickpeas, Spinach, and Potatoes ... 630
- Ginger-Cumin Black Chickpeas Ⓥ Ⓟ ... 631
- Green Chickpeas with Lentils ... 632
- Pickley Chickpeas Ⓥ ... 634
- Spiced Black Chickpeas Ⓥ Ⓟ ... 635
- Tamarind-Chickpeas Ⓥ Ⓟ ... 636

Endnote ... 638

ABOUT THE AUTHOR

Rekha Sharma was born in "Jalandhar", a small city in the Indian state of "Punjab". Her father was in the Indian army, because of which her family used to move around a lot. By a very young age, Rekha had experienced cuisines from all over India, and every time she travelled to a new area and tried new local cuisines, her passion and fascination for Indian food grew. She completed M. Phil. in English from a reputed Indian University, and then became a college professor for a few years. She got married at a young age of 23, and left her job as a college professor when she had her first child. By the age of 26, she was a mother of two- a son and a daughter, and was mostly house-bound. As she started cooking for four, her passion for cooking reignited, and she started giving cooking classes on the side. She worked as a part time cook until her kids became independent, and then she opened her own restaurant in Delhi, India. Today, she is 50+ years old, manages a restaurant, and writes Indian cookbooks on the side. She is best known for "A Taste of India", a series of Indian cookbooks.

INTRODUCTION

India is a huge landmass which contains mountains, deserts, plateaus, plains, beaches, and islands. Politically, it is divided into 28 states, and most of these states have their own languages and cultures. Even within a political state you will find multiple small villages with their own sub-languages and cultures. Needless to say, India is a land of variety, and this variety shows in its cuisine. Indian restaurants are everywhere, and if you've been through the menu of one, you know what I'm talking about.

North India is a land of flatbreads, while South India is a land of rice. India has a coastline that stretches for 7,516.6 km (4,671 miles), and you can find a wide variety of seafood here, depending on which part of the coastline you're at. Not just the ingredients, but the preparation methods also differ from region to region. If you're in the eastern state of West Bengal, you will see them prepare fish with mustard and turmeric. On the other hand, if you're in Kerala, you will watch them use coconut instead.

Majority of the people in India are Hindus, and the truly devout Hindus are usually vegetarian. Vegetarianism is especially prevalent in central India. The primary source of protein in these vegetarian dominated areas is- beans, grains, lentils, peas, etc. Indians usually refer to these as "Dal". Indian food has less meat and more vegetables, which make Indian food great for health, and also for the environment. The cooking methods used in this book make the recipes as healthy as possible without compromising the authentic Indian taste. You will find that the majority of recipes in this book are Vegan, and you can identify a vegan recipe from the "Ⓥ" symbol. Also, in India, the pressure cooker is highly popular, and hence you will find quite a few pressure cooker recipes in this book. Recipes cooked in a pressure cooker are generally very quick to make, and in this book, you can identify those recipes from the symbol "Ⓟ".

In this book, you will find delicious recipes from all over India. Most of the recipes in this book are simple, and if you're a "newbie" when it comes to cooking, this book will serve you well. You will, however, need to learn to source some of the ingredients that aren't commonly used in American cooking. If you can't find an ingredient in a local store, you can always find it on amazon.com. If there is a local Indian or ethnic market close to your home, you're in luck! Also, a pressure cooker is an indispensable tool to have in your kitchen, so invest in one if you haven't already.

INDIAN MEALS

Typically, an Indian meal contains a wet or dry dish of meat or vegetables, or both. This dish is typically eaten with an Indian flatbread, or rice. If the food is spicy, which it usually is, there is plain yogurt on the side to soothe the flavour, and also to aid with digestion. If one wishes to add a little more punch to the meal, he/she can have a pickle or chutney on the side. Salads are also quite common side dishes.

If cooking for guests, we Indians usually go for slightly "fancier" versions of the staples. Plain yogurt may be replaced by "raita" (plain yogurt with added spices and other ingredients), plain rice may be replaced by fried or seasoned rice dishes, and fried flatbreads called "paranthas" may be used. We usually offer starters and desserts to guests too.

For everyday eating, however, I will advise you to stick to the healthier low-calorie stuff. Vegetables are a staple in the Indian diet, and for good reason. A balanced meal has a good balance of carbohydrates, fiber, protein, and fat. The diet should be rich in other vitamins and minerals too, which Indian food usually is, thanks to the presence of vegetables, legumes, and grains.

Another thing you need to consider is how much spice you like. It is possible to add more later, but impossible to extract the spice once added, so it is usually a good idea to add the spice incrementally, tasting the food as you add. You will only need to do this once or twice though. Once you know what you like, and how much you can handle, go all out!

USING THIS BOOK

In this book, I will call for cooking appliances that are readily available in almost every kitchen. I understand that it is not possible to have a "tandoor" (a large cylindrical clay or metal oven used in traditional Indian cooking and baking) in your kitchen. The tandoor can be replicated by what is readily available in your kitchen, and I will clearly detail in the directions of each recipe what you need to do.

In order to prepare the recipes in this book, you will need a stove, an oven, a pressure cooker, and a microwave in a few cases. A food processor will also come in handy as it will save you a lot of hassle.

It is usually a good idea to prepare things like spice pastes, chutneys, spice powders, and other perishable basic ingredients in bulk, and in advance. These ingredients are best stored in the freezer, so if you have one, make sure you use it. Here are a few basic tips and tricks to know before you dive into the recipes:

- Read the full list of ingredients and directions before you commit to a recipe. Make sure you have all the ingredients and all the appliances used in the directions. You can make almost every spice blend used in this book easily at

- home, but you can also buy these at a store. I'll leave the decision to you. You can find almost anything online these days.
- A lot of the recipes in this book will call for ingredients like cilantro, dry-roasted cumin, sesame seeds, black peppercorns, ginger paste, garlic paste, ginger-garlic paste, green chutney, crispy fried ginger, crispy fried onions; fresh lemon juice; paneer (Cottage cheese), mango and lemon pickles, and some chutneys. If you want to add Indian recipes to your arsenal, and wish to prepare these regularly, you will do well to make these ingredients a staple in your pantry.
- Start the cooking process when you're good and ready, and have everything you need ready, and in front of you.
- It is always a good idea to add a little less salt and seasoning if you're not sure how much you will need. Taste your food as you go to hit that perfect spot. If, however, you do add more than you can handle by mistake, you have a few options. Throw in a peeled and chopped potato, or try eating the dish with yogurt on the side. You can also make some more of the dish, this time without the spice, and then add it to the over-spiced batch.

KNOW YOUR MEASUREMENTS

American cooks use standard containers, the 8-ounce cup and a tablespoon that takes exactly 16 level fillings to fill that cup level. Measuring by cup makes it very difficult to give weight equivalents, as the density plays an important role when it comes to weight. The easiest way therefore to deal with cup measurements in recipes is to take the amount by volume rather than by weight. Thus, the equation reads:

1 cup = 240ml = 8 fluid Ounces

½ cup = 120ml = 4 fluid ounces

It is possible to buy a set of American cup measures in major stores around the world.

In the States, butter is sometimes measured in sticks. One stick is the equivalent of 8 tablespoons. One tablespoon of butter is therefore the equivalent to ½ ounce/15 grams.

Liquid Measures

1 Teaspoon= 5 Millilitres

1 Tablespoon = 14 millilitres

2 Tablespoons= 1 Fluid Ounce

Solid Measures

1 Ounce= 28 Grams

16 Ounces= 1 Pound

INDIAN SPICES AND SEASONINGS

"Spicy" is the first thing that comes to mind when we think of Indian food, and for good reason. Historically, Indian spices have been one of India's greatest exported commodities. Indian spices go best with all kinds of food! Go out there and play around! In this section, we will look at a few of the most popular spices. If you cannot find a particular spice in a nearby store, you will surely find it online on amazon.com.

AJWAIN SEEDS

Ajwain, ajowan, or Trachyspermum ammi—also known as ajowan caraway, bishop's weed, or carom—is an annual herb in the family Apiaceae. Both the leaves and the seed-like fruit of the plant are fit for consumption. The name "bishop's weed" also is a common name for other plants. These tiny brown or green-brown, ridged, celery seed look-alikes seem fragrance-free at first, but when crushed, they emit an intense and highly aromatic, thyme-like aroma, which calms down once cooked. When eaten raw, they have an intensely fiery and pungent bite. *Ajwain* seeds are an amazing home remedy to relieve gas and stomachaches, and are frequently chewed raw by people with seasoned tastes.

ASAFOETIDA

Called *Hing* or *heeng* in Hindi, Asafoetida is a plant that has a bad pungent smell and tastes bitter. It is sometimes even referred to as "devil's dung." People use asafoetida resin, a gum-like material, as medicine. Asafoetida resin is produced by solidifying juice that comes out of cuts made in the plant's living roots. When cooked, however, it adds a pleasant onion-garlic flavour to the food. It also has numerous health benefits such as- it relieves flatulence, enhances digestion, acts as an antibiotic, etc. It is an indispensable part of Indian cuisine. Ground Asafoetida is used in recipes. It is usually a good idea to buy lumps or granules, and grind it before using in a recipe. Buy your asafoetida in lumps (or fine granules) and then grind them at home. If you wish to buy the already ground version from the market, remember that it might not be 100% pure.

BAY LEAVES

Called *Tejpatta, tejpat*, or *tej patra* in Hindi, the bay leaf is an aromatic leaf commonly used in cooking. It can be used whole, or as dried and ground. There are two varieties commonly available: the leaves of the bay laurel found typically in the Western world, and those of the Indian cassia tree. Both work fine, but if you can get your hands on the Indian version, it will make the recipes slightly more "Indian". Doesn't matter much, though.

BLACK SALT

Called *Kaala namak* in Hindi, black salt is a kiln-fired rock salt commonly used in South Asian regions. It has a sulphurous, pungent-smell. It is also known as "Himalayan black salt", Sulemani namak, bit lobon, kala noon, or pada loon and manufactured from the salts mined in the regions surrounding the Himalayas.

CARDAMOM PODS

Called *Elaichi* in Hindi, Cardamom (or cardamom) is a spice made from the seeds of several plants in the genera Elettaria and Amomum in the family Zingiberaceae. Both genera are native to the Indian subcontinent and Indonesia. Two variety of this are commonly available: small green ones (called hari or chhoti elaichi in Hindi), and large black ones (Called badi or kaali elaichi in Hindi). The green ones have a strong refreshing fragrance, while the big black ones have a milder woody-smoky aroma. Both are great home remedies to treat and manage gas, and also for nausea and vomiting. They also work as a healthy natural mouth freshener.

CHILES, FRESH GREEN AND DRIED RED

Called *Mirch* or *mirchi* in Hindi, chile peppers—fresh green (*hari mirch*) and dried red (*laal mirch*)—are members of the capsicum family. Green chiles are usually young, and they turn red as they age. The younger greener chilies have a much stronger hotter flavour compared to the red ones. The red chiles are dried and ground into a red powder, which is a staple ingredient in Indian dishes. If you're living in a different part of the world, look for "cayenne powder" in a nearby store or online if you cannot find pure red chile powder. Chiles are great for health too, and enhance digestion. They are used in powerful sinus, cough, and cold home remedies. Just ensure you don't touch any sensitive areas of your body if you've just handled it.

CINNAMON AND CASSIA

Called *Dalchini* or *darchini* in Hindi, Cinnamon is a common ingredient in kitchens all around the world, and is commonly available in ground, or stick form. Cinnamon adds a pleasant fragrance to foods, and is great for the digestive system.

CLOVES

Called *Laung* or *lavang* in Hindi, Cloves are the aromatic flower buds of a tree in the family Myrtaceae, Syzygium aromaticum. They have a strong aroma, and a strong sweet and sour taste. They are great for digestion, and relieving gas.

CORIANDER SEEDS AND GREENS

Called *Dhania, sookha*, and *patta* or *hara* in Hindi, Coriander is an annual herb in the family Apiaceae. It is also known as Chinese parsley, and in the United States the stems and leaves are commonly referred to as cilantro. The whole of the plant is fit for consumption, but fresh leaves and dried seeds are most commonly used in cooking. The fresh green leaves have a sweet citrus flavour, and smell absolutely fantastic. These are highly perishable so use them as soon as possible, and always store them in your fridge.

CUMIN AND BLACK CUMIN

Called *Jeera* or *zeera* in Hindi, Cumin is a flowering plant in the family Apiaceae, native to southwestern Asia including the Middle East. Its seeds – each one contained within a fruit, which is dried – are a staple in the Indian kitchen. They have a strong spicy aroma, and a bitter taste. It is great for the stomach.

CURRY LEAVES

Called *Meethineem* or *karipatta* in Hindi, Curry leaves from from the curry leaf tree, which is a tropical to sub-tropical tree in the family Rutaceae, and is native to India. Curry leaves are a staple in Indian cooking, and quite a few recipes in this book will call for this ingredient. They taste slightly bitter, but taste absolutely amazing in certain recipes.

FENNEL SEEDS

Called *Saunf* in Hindi, Fennel seeds come from Fennel, which is a flowering plant species in the carrot family. They appear long, ridged, oval or curved, and green-yellow in color. They have an aromatic pleasant taste, and are great for the digestive system.

FENUGREEK SEEDS AND GREENS

Called *Daana-methi* or *metharae* and *patta* or *hari methi* in Hindi, Fenugreek seeds are the dried, angular, yellow-brown seeds of a highly aromatic annual herb of the legume family. They are widely grown in India, and taste bitter when eaten raw. Luckily, they aren't meant to be eaten raw. When stir-fried or dry-roasted, these turn into something quite delicious.

GINGER

Called *Adrak, taaza*, and *sookha* in Hindi, Ginger needs no introduction. This juicy underground stem has a strong taste and is great for health. When buying ginger, ensure you get the fresh juicy ones. If you see any signs of dryness, shriveling, or mold, you should probably not pick that particular one.

KALONJI

You might know of these as—nigella, onion seeds, black onion seeds, black caraway seeds, or black cumin seeds. In Hindi, however, it is called *kalonji*, and that is the term commonly used outside India too, so that is what I will call it in this book. These little charcoal black triangular seeds look a lot like onion seeds. They have a light flavour like oregano, and taste bitter when raw. After cooking, however, these start to emit a nutty aroma and taste.

KOKUM

Also known as *cocum, cocamful*, and fish tamarind, *Kokum* is the sun-dried rind of a ½- to 1-inch fruit of the mangosteen-oil tree. The ripe fruits are eaten too, but the majority of them is dried into rather sticky, sour, purple-black pieces of *kokum*, a delicious spice. If a recipe calls for this ingredient, and you can't find it, Tamarind can be used instead.

MANGO POWDER

Called *Amchur* in Hindi, Mango powder is a fruity spice powder made from dried unripe green mangoes and is used as a citrusy seasoning in Indian cuisine. It is mostly produced in India, and is used as a citrus seasoning, and also to Put in the nutritional benefits of mangoes when the fresh fruit is out of season.

MINT

Called *Pudina, taaza,* and *sookha* in Hindi, Mint needs no introduction as it is one of the most popular herbs in the entire world. These are a staple in the Indian kitchen too, and when buying mint, ensure you get fresh aromatic leaves.

MIXED MELON SEEDS

Called *Char-magaz* in Hindi, this is basically a mixture of seeds from four different summer melons—cantaloupe, watermelon, cucumber, and pumpkin. The seeds are free of fragrance, and have a very mild taste similar to pumpkin. These are loaded with zinc, iron, and potassium, and are great for the brain.

MUSTARD SEEDS AND GREENS

Called *Raayi* or *rai*, and *sarson* in Hindi, Mustard is popular all over the world. The most common use of mustard seeds we see today is to make mustard oil, which is a healthy and cheap cooking oil which is a staple in kitchens all over the world. These are loaded with Vitamins A and C, Iron, and Calcium, making them a prominent health food. They have a very strong taste by themselves, but go well in quite a few Indian dishes, as you will see soon enough.

NUTMEG AND MACE

Called *Jaiphul* and *javitri* in Hindi, Nutmeg and mace are two different varieties of spices obtained from the same apricot-like fruit of a tall evergreen tree. Nutmeg is a wrinkly, medium brown, 1-inch oval nut that resides inside the thin, brittle, shiny outer shell of a ripe nutmeg seed. To obtain nutmeg, the shell has to be broken.

Mace is the lacy, web-like coating around the outside of the nutmeg shell. This dazzling coating is cautiously removed after the fruit is broken open, and is then flattened and dried to become brittle yellow-orange mace, ready to use.

They are both great for health, and vital ingredients for the pharmaceutical industry.

PAPRIKA

Called *Kashmiri degi mirch* or *rang vaali mirch* in Hindi, Indian paprika is the vivid red powder made from mild, non-pungent red chiles. Although made from red chiles, it does not taste very hot, and is primarily used for its color. It is an indispensable part of the Indian pantry.

BLACK PEPPER

Called *Kaalimirch* in Hindi, Black pepper is often called the king of all spices. It is one of the oldest and most popular spices on this planet. Naturally, it is a staple in the Indian kitchen, and can be sprinkled over pretty much any recipe in this book.

DRIED POMEGRANATE SEEDS

Called *Anaardana* in Hindi, dried pomegranate seeds are basically sun-dried or dehydrated fruity seeds and the flesh of a wild pomegranate tree. They have a sweet and fruity fragrance, and are a common ingredient in Indian cooking.

POPPY SEEDS

Called *Khas-khas* in Hindi, poppy seeds are oilseeds obtained from opium poppy. Poppy seeds come in many colors, but the Indian versions are pale yellow. If a recipe calls for poppy seeds, feel free to use any kind of poppy seeds you wish.

ROSE WATER AND ESSENCE

Called *Gulaab jal* and *ruh gulaab* in Hindi, rose water and rose essence are made from the petals of specially cultivated highly fragrant red roses. Rose water is basically water with a strong fragrance of roses. Small bottles of rose water are easily available in stores.

SAFFRON

Called *Kaesar* or *zaffron* in Hindi, Saffron is one of the priciest spices available out there, and hence should be used sparingly if you're on a budget. Almost all of Indian saffron comes from Kashmir in North India. It has an exotic flavour and imparts a yellow color to the dishes it is used in.

SCREWPINE ESSENCE

Called *Kewda* or *ruh kewra* in Hindi, screwpine is the essence made from the flowers of a tropical tree with narrow, sword-like leaves. Think of this as rose water with a different fragrance.

SESAME SEEDS AND OIL

Called *Til* or *gingelly* in Hindi, sesame seeds are the tiny, smooth, oval, flat seeds of an annual tropical herb. When raw, these have almost no aroma, but when dry-roasted, these develop a nutty flavour.

SILVER LEAVES

Called *Chandi ka verk* or *vark* in Hindi, silver leaves are primarily used as a garnish, and don't really add anything to the flavour. This is used in Indian recipes to make them look exotic.

STAR ANISE

Called *Badian, badiyan, dodhful, dodphul*, and *anasphal* in Hindi, star anise is the dried mahogany-colored, 8-pointed, star-shaped fruit of a big evergreen tree. It has a sweet flavour, and is an ingredient in quite a few Indian recipes.

TAMARIND

Called *Imli* in Hindi, tamarind has a highly sour taste, and is a staple in the Indian kitchen. It is rich in vitamin C, and good for digestion, fighting throat infections, and fighting mild colds.

TURMERIC

Called *Haldi* in Hindi, turmeric is a common ingredient in Indian curries. It has a warm and bitter taste, and one of the healthiest spices out there. It is a natural antiseptic, an anti-inflammatory agent, and a blood purifier. Turmeric is used in quite a few home remedies such as soothing aches and pains.

INDIAN COOKING 101

If you've never cooked a single Indian recipe in your life, this section is for you. Learn your basics, follow my guidance, and practice till you make it. Do I make it sound hard? Do I make it sound like a chore? I don't know, but Indian cooking is none of those things. Indian cooking is actually quite easy, once you get the hang of it.

There are a few basic techniques used in Indian cooking that you might need to learn if you're new to cooking. Luckily, you don't really need to do these things by yourself as you can easily find dry-roasted ingredients and pre-mixed spice blends in the market. If, however, you wish to make these on your own, I will teach you to do so, just in case you wish to have a little more control over your ingredients in the future. Oh, and I personally enjoy doing these things a lot, so try it out, maybe dry roasting will become your new hobby!

Most of the basic gadgets and appliances this book will call for are quite common even in the American kitchen. I will still list these basic tools below. Feel free to improvise if you don't have one of these, and don't wish to invest in one yet.

- Concave cast-iron tava griddle to make breads
- Non-stick or cast-iron
- Round-bottomed wok (called kadhai in India)
- Pressure Cooker
- Food processor

If you can't find these in a store nearby, they are easily available on amazon.com.

In this book, you can identify a vegan and a pressure cooker recipe simply by looking for the following symbols by their names:

- Ⓥ= Vegan
- Ⓟ= Quick Pressure Cooker Recipe

BASIC TECHNIQUES

In this section we will learn a few basic techniques you will need to do the most authentic Indian cooking.

BLANCHING RAW NUTS Ⓥ

This technique is called "Bhigona aur chheelna" in Hindi

Basically this technique is all about immersing the ingredients in water until their skins become soft, and then peeling them off. You can buy pre-blanched stuff in the market, but where's the fun in that? Where's the freshness? And most importantly, where's that Indian feel?

Yield: ½ cup

ALMONDS (BADAAM)

There are two ways of blanching almonds.

Traditional Method

1. Immerse ½ cup shelled raw almonds 8 to 24 hours in sufficient water to cover by minimum two inches. (This allows the nuts to absorb the water and soften.)
2. Drain and peel the skin off each one using your fingers.

Quick Method

1. Immerse and boil ½ cup almonds in water until the skins absorb the water and become loose, approximately five minutes.
2. Allow to cool, then peel.

PISTACHIOS (PISTA)

Removing the outer skin of pistachios is much easier compared to almonds.

1. Put ½ cup shelled, raw pistachios in a small stainless steel (not nonstick) saucepan, with sufficient water to cover by minimum one inch, and bring to a boil using high heat.
2. Turn off the heat and set aside to soften, approximately one hour. Drain and put them on a sanitized kitchen towel. Cover using a different towel (or fold the first one over) and rub on the towel using your hands. As you do this, the loosened skin will get removed.

DEEP-FRYING THE INDIAN WAY

This recipe is called "Talna" in Hindi

Yield: 20 to 30 pieces

Indian deep-frying is basic as it gets. You take a Chinese wok (or a "kadhaai" as we call in Hindi) and you pour in a good amount of oil, sufficient to completely submerge the ingredients you need to fry, you then heat the oil and throw the ingredients into the heated oil.

Ingredients:

- 1½ to 2 cups oil
- 20 to 30 pieces of food

Directions:

1. Heat the oil using moderate to high heat until it achieves 325°F to 350°F on a frying thermometer. At this temperature, if you throw in a small piece of food, it will take about fifteen to twenty seconds to come to the surface of

the oil. This temperature is important, as too high or too low can lead to less than ideal results.
2. Put food pieces into the wok, without overcrowding. Fry until a golden colour is achieved, approximately one minute. Using a slotted spatula, hold each piece against the edge of the wok for a few seconds, to let surplus oil to drain back into the wok. After that, move to a tray coated using paper towels.

DRY-ROASTING SPICES, NUTS, AND FLOURS Ⓥ

This technique is called "Sookha bhunna" in Hindi

Yield: Approximately ½ cup

Basically, we dry-roast dry spices, herbs, nuts, dals (legumes), and selected flours by throwing them into a skillet and browning them in absence of any cooking fat or liquid. This process filters out the unwanted raw flavour, and enhances the flavour of the essential oils, which is what we actually need. Below we will look at a few specific ingredients that we need to dry-roast in Indian cooking.

SPICES (MASALAE)

Pretty much every spice there is can be dry roasted, and a few of the most commonly dry-roasted spices are black peppercorns, coriander, mustard seeds, sesame, cumin, etc.

1. Put ½ cup of any one type of whole seeds in a small sized cast-iron skillet, saucepan, or "tava" and roast using moderate heat, stirring and swaying the pan, until smoke with a strong fragrance starts to rise and the seeds appear slightly darker, approximately two minutes.
2. Turn off the heat and allow to cool down. Using a rolling pin, the back of a big sized spoon, or using a mortar and pestle, squash them until crudely ground. Or, grind them thoroughly using a spice or coffee grinder.
3. Put inside an airtight vessel and place the vessel in a cool, dark place. Can be stored safely for approximately one month at room temperature, or six

months in a fridge. Roasted black peppercorns can be ground fresh before every use if you have a pepper mill.

NUTS AND SEEDS (**MAEVAE**)

1. Beginning with ½ cup whole, chopped, or slivered nuts, put them in a small sized cast-iron skillet, saucepan, or "tava" and roast using moderate heat, stirring and swaying the pan, until a golden colour is achieved (don't let it get brown), approximately two minutes.
2. Turn off the heat and allow to cool down.
3. Use instantly or put inside an airtight vessel and place the vessel in a cool, dark place, approximately seven days at room temperature or approximately thirty days in a fridge.

Tip: Different ingredients roast in different amounts of time, and hence it is a good idea to roast different ingredients individually.

CHICKPEA AND OTHER FLOURS (**BESAN AUR DOOSRAE AATAE**)

1. Sieve ½ cup flour and put it in a non-stick skillet or saucepan.
2. Roast using moderate to low heat until it starts to look golden and releases its fragrance, approximately three minutes. Stir continuously and shake the pan regularly to avoid lumping and burning.
3. Allow to cool, then put inside an airtight vessel and place the vessel in a cool, dark place, approximately seven days at room temperature or approximately thirty days in a fridge.

RECONSTITUTING DRIED WILD MUSHROOMS

This technique is called "Sookhi khumbon ko bhigona" in Hindi

Yield: 1 cup reconstituted mushrooms

Mushrooms are commonly available in dried form. So, you will need to rehydrate them before using in a recipe. Here's how.

Ingredients:

- 1 ounce dried wild mushrooms

Directions:

1. Rinse the mushrooms, then immerse in water to cover by minimum two inches until they absorb the water and bloat up, approximately one hour. Rinse them again under running water to eliminate all dirt that may still be sticking to them. Chop and use as required.
2. Strain the mushroom-soaking water through a coffee filter or paper towels until it seems thoroughly clean and dirt free. Use it in soups, rice pullaos (pilafs), and curries.

ROASTING AND GRILLING VEGETABLES

This technique is called "Sabziyan bhunna" in Hindi

Roasting and grilling vegetables is the first step in preparing quite a few Indian recipes, and you will need to know how it is done before you dive into the recipes. Below, we will look at how to roast a few of the most commonly roasted ingredients.

EGGPLANTS (BAINGAN)

Yield: Approximately 1½ cups of pulp from each pound of eggplant

When buying eggplants, ensure you grab the young ones. You can identify these by their weight. Young eggplants usually weigh less for their size, and have a silky smooth skin with no signs of deterioration. Also, smaller eggplants are much easier to cook than the bigger ones, for obvious reasons.

The easiest and most convenient way to roast eggplants today is to just place them directly over your gas burners. If you don't want to make a mess of your stove, use a grill too. The best way, however, is to use coals and a grill, just like the Indians have done it for centuries.

Directions to Fire-Roast Eggplants:

1. Rinse, dry, and cover your hands with a thin layer of oil, and rub them over the surface of each eggplant. Next, use a sharp kitchen knife to pierce the skin in a few places. Put over scorching coals of a grill if possible, or over the direct flame of a kitchen stove burner(coat the lowermost plate using aluminium foil), and roast, rotating using kitchen tonga as the sides turn black, until the eggplant is very soft and the skin is thoroughly charred, approximately five to seven minutes. Move to a container and allow to cool down.
2. Once cool sufficient to hold, peel off and discard the charred skin. You will have to wash your fingers multiple times as you do this. Do not rinse the eggplants. Mash the pulp using your hands or a fork until fairly smooth but still lumpy. Do not make a fully smooth purée; a little texture is required. Strain and stir in any juices that may have collected in the container. Store in the fridge for approximately five days or approximately four months in the freezer.

Directions to Oven-Roast Eggplants:

1. Slightly oil and pierce the skin in a few places using the tip of a knife and bake using an oven pre-heated to 400°F until the eggplants become soft, approximately thirty to forty minutes. You can wrap them using an aluminium foil prior to baking.

Directions to Broil Eggplants:

1. Cut into half along the length and place, skin side up, on a baking tray coated using aluminium foil.
2. Broil 8 to 10 inches from the heat source until the eggplants become soft and the skin seems charred.

BELL PEPPERS (SHIMLA MIRCH)

Yield: Approximately ⅔ cup of pulp from each pound of pepper

Bell peppers are a common ingredient in the Indian kitchen, and taste absolutely amazing when roasted.

Directions to Fire-Roast Bell Peppers:

1. Put whole bell peppers, if possible over the scorching coals of a grill or over the direct flame of the kitchen stove (coat the lowermost plate using aluminium foil) and roast, rotating using kitchen tonga as the sides turn black, until the skin is mildly charred, approximately two to three minutes. (There is no need to oil the bell peppers or poke any holes in them, or to char them completely.)
2. Move to a container, cover or seal using an air-tight bag, and allow to sit for approximately fifteen minutes. This enables the peppers to sweat and cool down, making them simple to peel. Peel the peppers, eliminating as much of the burned skin as possible. You may leave some mildly charred skin on for flavour. Do not rinse them using water. Rinse your hands as required. Eliminate the stems and seeds and chop or purée the peppers; if any juice has accumulated in the container, strain it and add it to the purée.

Directions to Oven-Roast Bell Peppers:

1. Rinse, dry, and cut each bell pepper into halves or quarters, lengthwise. Put on a baking sheet, with the cut side down. Put the sheet on the center rack of the oven, start the broiler, and roast until charred, approximately eight to ten minutes. Flip over once.
2. Put ¼ cup water on the baking sheet to dissolve most of the browned juice and use it in soups, rice, breads, or vegetables.

To Broil Bell Peppers

1. Rinse, dry, and seed the bell peppers, then cut them into 1-inch or larger pieces.
2. Put on a baking sheet coated using aluminium foil.
3. Broil 4 to 5 inches from the heat source, flipping over once or twice until the pieces are mildly charred.

SLIVERING BLANCHED NUTS

This technique is called "Mavae kaatna" in Hindi

Yield: ½ cup

You can buy slivered blanched nuts from the market, but these are done using machines. If you have some free time on your hands, then use your hands. This is a great exercise for improving your hand-eye coordination, and you will get much better and thinner shreds as compared to the mechanical versions.

1. Begin with 1 cup blanched almonds, pistachio, or other nuts.
2. Grab a paring knife in your dominant hand, and hold each nut, one at a time, between the thumb and forefinger of your other hand.
3. Scrape softly lengthwise using a sharp paring knife in tiny top-to-bottom movements.
4. As you do this, frail slivers or shavings will fall from the nut.

SPROUTING BEANS AND SEEDS

This technique is called "Sookhi dalonko phutana" in Hindi

Yield: Approximately 4 cups

Sprouted beans are one of the healthiest ingredients on the planet. Here's how to sprout beans the Indian way.

Ingredients:

- 1 cup any variety whole beans and seeds, picked over and washed
- 1 thick kitchen towel

Directions:

1. Immerse the beans overnight, in water to cover by minimum two inches.
2. Drain thoroughly, cover the container using a lid, then cover using a thick kitchen towel and put in a warm spot in the kitchen like a closet.
3. Check at least once per day and stir them a little if you wish to. Keep the beans mildly moist at all times. If the inside surface of the lid has tiny droplets of water on it, the moisture is right, and the beans should sprout in two to three days.

BASIC INGREDIENTS

Before we start with the recipes, you need to acquaint yourself with a few of the most common ingredients in Indian cooking what you might not have used before.

COCONUT MILK Ⓥ

This recipe is called "Nariyal doodh" in Hindi

Yield: 1 cup thick coconut milk

Coconut milk is different from coconut water. You can buy this in a store, or make your own. Here's how:

Ingredients:

- 1 cup hot water
- 1½ cups grated fresh coconut meat

Directions:

1. Using a food processor or a blender, combine and pulse the coconut and ½ cup of the water until thoroughly smooth. Allow the processed coconut to soak in this water for approximately half an hour. Next, pass the whole thing through the fine mesh of a food mill or a strainer.
2. Put the leftover coconut back into your food processor. Put in the rest of the ½ cup water, then process and strain once more. Combine with the first coconut milk. Add water till your desired consistency is achieved. Use instantly, or store in the fridge for approximately 4 days or freeze for no more than sixty days.

CRISPY CHICKPEA BATTER DROPS Ⓥ

This recipe is called "Boondi" in Hindi

Yield: Approximately 1½ cups

You can buy these ready-made from Indian stores, but you can also make your own. These go great with yogurt!

Ingredients:

- ¼ teaspoon salt, or to taste
- ½ cup water, or as required
- ⅔ cup chickpea flour, sifted
- 1 cup peanut oil for deep frying
- A scant pinch baking soda

Directions:

1. In a container, combine the chickpea flour, salt and baking soda. Put in the water and whisk to make a smooth and creamy batter. Let sit for about ten minutes then whisk once more.
2. Take a small wok, or saucepan, or kadhaai, pour oil into it and heat using moderate to high heat until it achieves 325°F to 350°F on a frying thermometer or until a drop of the batter surges to the surface of the oil almost instantly. Hold a round spatula with holes over the oil and progressively pour the batter through the holes, while shaking and tapping the spatula to ensure the batter falls as drops into the hot oil. Stop pouring when the wok appears to have sufficient drops.
3. Fry one batch until a golden colour is achieved, approximately forty to fifty seconds, then move the drops with another slotted spatula to a tray coated using paper towels, before you start the next batch. Keep doing it till all the batter has been used. Allow to cool, then store in an airtight vessel in the fridge for approximately three months or in the freezer about six months.

CRISPY FRIED FRESH GINGER

This recipe is called "Bhuna adrak" in Hindi

Yield: Approximately 1 cup

Ginger is a great garnish and a flavour booster!

Ingredients:

- ½ pound fresh ginger, peeled and cut into thin matchsticks
- ½ teaspoon salt, or to taste
- 1½ cups peanut oil or melted ghee for deep-frying

Directions:

1. Heat the oil in a big wok or saucepan using moderate to high heat until it achieves 325°F to 350°F on a frying thermometer. (Put a small piece of ginger into the hot oil. If it takes about fifteen to twenty seconds before it rises to the top, the oil is hot enough to proceed with the frying.) Put in the ginger in 1 or 2 batches and fry, stirring and reducing the heat if required, until rich gold in color, three to five minutes per batch.
2. Try to leave behind as much oil as you can in the wok as you take out the ginger using a slotted spoon to a container, toss with salt, and allow to sit until crunchy and cool. Move to an airtight vessel and place in your fridge for a maximum of sixty days.

CRISPY FRIED ONIONS Ⓥ

This recipe is called "Bhuna pyaz" in Hindi

Yield: Approximately 3 cups

These are great for garnish, and a great addition to the curries.

Ingredients:

- 1½ cups peanut oil for deep frying
- 6 to 8 small onions, cut in half along the length and thinly chopped

Directions:

1. Heat the oil in a big wok or saucepan using moderate to high heat until it achieves 325°F to 350°F on a frying thermometer. (Place a small piece of onion into the hot oil. If it takes about fifteen to twenty seconds before it rises to the top, the oil is hot enough to proceed with the frying.) Put in the

onions in 1 or 2 batches and fry, stirring and reducing the heat if required, until deep brown, approximately five to seven minutes per batch.
2. Try to leave behind as much oil as you can in the wok as you take out the onions using a slotted spoon to paper towels and allow to sit until crunchy and cool. Move to an airtight vessel and place in your fridge for a maximum of sixty days.

HOMEMADE YOGURT

This recipe is called "Ghar ki dahi" in Hindi

Yield: Approximately 4 cups

If you're buying all your yogurt from a store, you don't know what you're missing out. Fresh homemade yogurt tastes absolutely amazing, is more nutritious, is free of preservatives, and the feeling you get when you make yogurt is great. You just have to do it once to know what I'm talking about.

All you need to make it is some milk and a starter. The starter can be store-bought yogurt with live cultures or yogurt from a prior homemade batch. Depending on your personal taste and diet restrictions, you can choose any kind of milk too.

Ingredients:

- 1 or 2 large, thick kitchen towels
- 1 pot holder
- 2 tablespoons plain yogurt, non-fat or any kind, with active culture
- 4 cups milk

Directions:

1. Bring the milk to a boil, stirring regularly using a metal spatula in a heavy aluminium saucepan to avoid burning the milk. You can also do this using a microwave.
2. Move to a yogurt pot (if possible ceramic, though any vessel will do), and cool until the milk registers 118°F to 120°F on a thermometer.
3. Mix in the yogurt starter and cover loosely using a loosely fitting lid.
4. Place a pot holder on a shelf in a kitchen cabinet. Put the yogurt pot on top of the pot holder, fold the towels in half and cover the yogurt pot tightly on

every side. This insulates the pot and helps maintain the perfect temperature essential for the proliferation of the yogurt bacteria. You can achieve the same result by placing the yogurt pot in a deactivated gas oven using a small pilot light.
5. Let the milk rest without interruption for three to four hours.
6. Remove the lid and see if the yogurt is firm—kind of like gelatin. If you see a layer of water over the yogurt, let is be for now. You can remove it after chilling. Once the yogurt is set, place it in your fridge instantly. If you allow yogurt to sit at room temperature for too long, it will develop a sour taste.

INDIAN CLARIFIED BUTTER

This recipe is called "Ghee" in Hindi

Ghee is a class of clarified butter that originated in ancient India. It is commonly used in cuisine of the Indian subcontinent, Middle Eastern cuisine, Southeast Asian cuisine, traditional medicine, and religious rituals. Ghee has an amazing fragrance, and red chilli powder fried in ghee has an aroma out of this world. Try it out! Although delicious, it is pure fat, so use in moderation. It is easily available online and in grocery stores, but you can also make your own. Here's how:

Yield: Approximately 2 cups

Ingredients:

- 1 pound unsalted butter
- One 1-foot-square piece of fine muslin or 4 layers of cheesecloth

Directions:

1. Put the butter in a heavy, moderate-sized saucepan and simmer, stirring intermittently, using moderate to low heat until the milk solids turn golden and settle to the bottom of the pan, 15 to 20 minutes. Initially the butter will start to froth, but as it simmers, the foaming will settle. After this, pass everything through the cheesecloth or a fine-mesh strainer into a sanitized jar.
2. Do not throw away the leftover milk solids. Store them at room temperature around two days or in the fridge for approximately six months. Or mix with

whole-wheat flour to make paranthas (griddle-fried breads) or add to soups, rice, and steamed vegetables for flavour.

Feel free to add any or all of the following ingredients into the ghee to tweak its flavour.

- ¼ cup minced fresh mint leaves
- ½ cup minced fresh curry leaves plus ¼ teaspoon ground asafoetida
- 1 tablespoon crudely chopped garlic
- 1 teaspoon black peppercorns and 1 teaspoon ajwain seeds
- 1 teaspoon dried fenugreek leaves
- 2 tablespoons peeled and minced fresh ginger
- 2 teaspoons cumin seeds, 2 black cardamom pods, crushed lightly to break the skin, and 2 (1-inch) sticks cinnamon

PANEER CHEESE

This recipe is called "Paneer" in Hindi

Yield: 8 ounces or approximately 30 1¼-inch pieces

Basically, this is Indian cottage cheese. It is easily available in Indian markets, and is one of the most delicious ingredients vegetarians get to enjoy. You can easily make this at home. Here's how:

Ingredients:

- ½ gallon lowfat or whole milk
- 1 (2-foot-square) piece of fine muslin or 4 layers of cheesecloth
- 2 cups plain yogurt, non-fat or any kind, whisked until the desired smoothness is achieved, or ¼ cup fresh lemon juice, or a mixture of both

Directions:

1. Put the milk in a big and heavy saucepan and bring to a boil, stirring slowly, using high heat. Before the milk boils and the bubbles spill over, stir in the yogurt or the lemon juice, and carry on stirring until the milk curdles and separates into curds and whey, approximately a minute or two. Turn off the heat.

2. Cover a big pan using the muslin or cheesecloth and pour the curdled milk over it. The whey should drain through the cloth into the pan, and the curdled paneer cheese is left behind in the cloth.
3. While the paneer cheese is still inside it, pick up the cloth from the pan and fasten the ends of the cloth around the kitchen faucet to drain, ensuring that the cheese is a few inches over the bottom of the sink. let drain three to five minutes.
4. Take out of the faucet and carefully twist the cloth tightly around the cheese, then place the cheese between two salad-size plates (or any other flat surfaces), with the fastened cloth edges placed to one side, out of the way. Put a big pan of water on the top plate and allow the cheese to drain further, approximately ten to twelve minutes.
5. Take paneer cheese out, cut into shapes and sizes you want and use as required. Store in an airtight vessel in the fridge 4 to five days or freeze for no more than 4 months.

YOGURT CHEESE

This recipe is called "Dahi ka paneer" in Hindi

Yield: Approximately 2 cups

Yogurt cheese is basically highly condensed, almost cheese-like yogurt. Here's how we do it:

Ingredients:

- 1 (2-foot-square) piece of fine muslin or 4 layers of cheesecloth
- 1 (32-ounce) vessel non-fat plain yogurt

Directions:

1. Put yogurt in the muslin or cheesecloth, then twist the cloth tightly around the cheese and tie the ends of the cloth around the kitchen faucet, ensuring that the yogurt is a few inches above the bottom of the sink. let drain 4 to 6 hours. The cheese is now ready to be used.
2. Or, set a large colander or fine-mesh strainer into a large container (to catch the whey), and line it with muslin or 4 layers of cheesecloth. Put the yogurt in the strainer and let drain for four to six hours in a fridge.

BASIC SPICE BLENDS

Getting the seasoning right is a vital component of Indian cooking. You can buy readymade Indian spice blends in the market, and these are usually high in quality and taste. As a beginner, feel free to buy readymade spice blends. As you start to become more proficient in Indian cooking, however, you yourself will desire more control over how the final recipe tastes. You cannot tweak the amount of salt in a readymade curry powder, but if you make your own, the possibilities are endless.

So, in this section, we will take a look at a few of the most extensively used Indian spice blends. We will learn the basic ingredients used in them, and the directions you will need to follow to make these at your home. Once you get used to making these basic spice blends, feel free to play around and create your own spice blends, tailored exactly to your and your family's tastes!

CURRY POWDERS

Curries are the quintessence of Indian food. Curries are usually a blend of wet and dry ingredients. Wet ingredients are usually ground juicy ingredients like tomatoes, ginger, onions, etc. The dried ingredients are the spices, herbs, nuts, etc. These dry ingredients are the primary tastemakers, and we will take a look at these in this section.

BASIC CURRY POWDER Ⓥ

This recipe is called "Kari ka masala" in Hindi

Yield: Approximately 1½ cups

Buy this from a local Indian store, or online. However, it is more fun to make your own!

Ingredients:

- ⅓ cup ground cumin seeds
- 1 cup ground coriander seeds

- 1 tablespoon ground cayenne pepper (not compulsory)
- 1 tablespoon ground dried fenugreek leaves
- 1 tablespoon ground paprika
- 2 tablespoons ground turmeric

Directions:

1. Add all the spices to a container and stir using a spoon until they get blended.
2. Put inside an airtight vessel and place the vessel in a cool, dark place, approximately thirty days at room temperature or approximately one year in a fridge.

SPICED BASIC CURRY POWDER Ⓥ

This recipe is called "Kari ka masala" in Hindi

Yield: Approximately 2 cups

Basic curry powder we saw above, but with some extra flavour.

Ingredients:

- *1 recipe* Basic Curry Powder
- 1 tablespoon ground black cardamom seeds
- 1 tablespoon ground black peppercorns
- 1 tablespoon ground dried ginger
- 1 tablespoon ground fennel seeds
- 1 tablespoon ground fenugreek seeds
- 1 tablespoon ground green cardamom seeds
- 1 teaspoon ground cinnamon
- 1 teaspoon ground cloves
- 1 teaspoon ground nutmeg

Directions:

1. Add all the spices to a container and stir using a spoon until they get blended.

2. Put inside an airtight vessel and place the vessel in a cool, dark place, approximately thirty days at room temperature or approximately one year in a fridge.

GOAN CURRY POWDER Ⓥ

This recipe is called "Goa ka shakuti masala" in Hindi

Yield: Approximately 1½ cups

This Goan tastemaker goes perfectly with meat and chicken!

Ingredients:

- ¼ cup coriander seeds
- ¼ cup thinly chopped fresh garlic cloves
- ¾ cup grated fresh or frozen coconut or shredded unsweetened dried coconut
- 1 2-inch stick cinnamon, broken
- 1 tablespoon black peppercorns
- 1 tablespoon cumin seeds
- 1 teaspoon ajwain seeds
- 1 teaspoon black cumin seeds
- 1 teaspoon fennel seeds
- 1 teaspoon ground nutmeg
- 1 teaspoon ground turmeric
- 10 whole cloves
- 15 dried red chile peppers, such as chile de arbol, broken
- 2 tablespoons white poppy seeds
- 3 to 5 fresh green chile peppers, such as serrano, thinly chopped
- 8 to 10 green cardamom pods, lightly crushed to break the skin
- 8 to 10 quarter-size slices of peeled fresh ginger
- 8 to 10 star anise, broken

Directions:

1. In a moderate-sized cast-iron or non-stick wok or skillet, roast the coconut, stirring and shaking the skillet using moderate to low heat, until the coconut is crunchy and golden, approximately eight to ten minutes. If the coconut is

not crunchy after ten minutes, reduce the heat further to prevent browning, and cautiously watch for the next few minutes until the coconut becomes crunchy. Move to a container.
2. In the same skillet, place the garlic, ginger, and green chile peppers and dry-roast, stirring and swaying the pan using low heat until most of the moisture evaporates and the mixture is golden, approximately eight to ten minutes. Put into the coconut.
3. Put the rest of the spices in the skillet and dry-roast using moderate to low heat, stirring and swaying the pan until a golden colour is achieved and highly fragrant, approximately eight to ten minutes. Allow to cool, mix all ingredients together, and grind using a spice or coffee grinder till you get a fine powder. Store in an airtight vessel about three months in the fridge or approximately one year in the freezer.

GUJARATI CURRY POWDER (V)

This recipe is called "Dhana-jeera masala" in Hindi

Yield: Approximately 1¼ cups

A classic curry powder from North-West India!

Ingredients:

- ¼ cup cumin seeds
- 1 cup coriander seeds
- 1 tablespoon cayenne pepper

Directions:

1. In a moderate-sized cast-iron or non-stick skillet, roast the cumin seeds, stirring and swaying the pan over moderate heat until smoke with a strong fragrance starts to rise and the seeds appear slightly darker, approximately two to three minutes. Put in the coriander seeds and roast until they are just heated through, approximately one minute.
2. Allow to cool, then grind using a spice or a coffee grinder till you get a fine powder. Move the mixture to a container and stir in the cayenne pepper. Put inside an airtight vessel and place the vessel in a cool, dark place, approximately thirty days at room temperature or approximately one year in a fridge.

KASHMIRI CURRY POWDER Ⓥ

This recipe is called "Kashmiri kari ka masala" in Hindi

Yield: Approximately 2 cups

A tastemaker from the Icy state of Kashmir in North India.

Ingredients:

- ¼ cup cumin seeds
- ¼ cup fenugreek seeds
- ½ cup fennel seeds
- 1 tablespoon ground paprika
- 1 teaspoon ground cloves
- 1 teaspoon ground mace
- 1 teaspoon ground nutmeg
- 1 teaspoon saffron threads
- 10 bay leaves, crudely broken
- 2 tablespoons black cardamom seeds
- 2 tablespoons green cardamom seeds
- 2 tablespoons mustard or vegetable oil
- 2 teaspoons ground cinnamon
- 3 tablespoons ground ginger
- 4 to 5 large cloves fresh garlic, minced
- 8 to 12 dried red chile peppers, such as chile de arbol, broken

Directions:

1. In a moderate-sized cast-iron or non-stick wok or skillet, heat the oil over moderate heat and stir the red chile peppers and garlic until a golden colour is achieved, approximately one minute. Put in the fennel, cumin, fenugreek, black and green cardamom, bay leaves, and saffron, and roast, stirring and swaying the pan, until the mixture becomes slightly darker, approximately two minutes.
2. Allow to cool, then grind using a spice or coffee grinder to make a very fine powder. Put in a container and stir in the ginger, paprika, cinnamon, cloves, mace, and nutmeg. Put inside an airtight vessel and place the vessel in a cool, dark place, approximately seven days at room temperature or approximately one year in a fridge.

MARATHI CURRY POWDER Ⓥ

This recipe is called "Goda masala" in Hindi

Yield: Approximately 2 cups

A delicious curry powder from Maharashtra and Bombay, the home to Bollywood!

Ingredients:

- ¼ cup cumin seeds
- ¼ cup shredded unsweetened dried coconut
- ¼ cup white sesame seeds
- 1 cup coriander seeds
- 1 tablespoon cayenne pepper
- 1 tablespoon salt, or to taste
- 1 teaspoon black cumin seeds
- 1 teaspoon ground asafoetida
- 1 teaspoon ground turmeric
- 2 tablespoons black mustard seeds

Directions:

1. In a moderate-sized cast-iron or non-stick skillet, roast the coconut, coriander seeds, cumin seeds, white sesame seeds, black mustard seeds, and black cumin seeds, stirring constantly, initially over high and then over moderate heat until a golden colour is achieved and fragrant, approximately two to three minutes. Allow to cool, then grind using a spice or coffee grinder till you get a fine powder.
2. Put back into the skillet, stir in the cayenne pepper, salt, turmeric, and asafoetida, and stir over moderate heat until heated through, approximately one minute. Allow to cool completely and put inside an airtight vessel and place the vessel in a cool, dark place, approximately thirty days at room temperature or approximately one year in a fridge.

SOUTH INDIAN CURRY POWDER Ⓥ

This recipe is called "Kootupodi" in Hindi

Yield: Approximately 2 cups

This curry powder has a mild aroma that enhances flavour, and is great for thickening those curries and soups.

Ingredients:

- ¼ cup dried white urad beans (dhulli urad dal), sorted
- ¼ cup fenugreek seeds
- ½ cup coriander seeds
- 1 cup parboiled (converted) rice
- 10 to 12 dried red chile peppers, such as chile de arbol, broken

Directions:

1. In a moderate-sized cast-iron or non-stick skillet, roast the rice, dal, fenugreek seeds, and red chile peppers using moderate to low heat, stirring until a golden colour is achieved, approximately ten minutes. Stir in the coriander seeds and stir until heated through.
2. Allow to cool and grind using a spice or coffee grinder till you get a powder. Put inside an airtight vessel and place the vessel in a cool, dark place, approximately thirty days at room temperature or approximately one year in a fridge.

GARAM MASALAS

BASIC GARAM MASALA Ⓥ

This recipe is called "Garam masala" in Hindi

Yield: Approximately 1½ cups

"Garam" means hot in Hindi, and "Masala" means spice. So, as the name suggests, Garam Masalas are spicy hot blends, and are easily one of the most common tastemakers in India. There are many versions of this available all through India. These are easily available in stores, or you can buy them on amazon. But if you want a version that suits your personal taste, learn to make your own!

Ingredients:

- ¼ cup ground black cardamom seeds
- ¼ cup ground cloves
- ⅓ cup ground cinnamon
- ⅓ cup ground freshly black pepper
- 3 tablespoons ground green cardamom seeds

Directions:

1. In a moderate-sized cast-iron or non-stick skillet, mix and roast all the spices, stirring and swaying the pan over moderate heat until heated through, approximately two minutes.
2. Allow to cool, then put inside an airtight vessel and place the vessel in a cool, dark place, approximately thirty days at room temperature or approximately one year in a fridge.

HYDERABADI GARAM MASALA Ⓥ

This recipe is called "Hyderabad ka garam masala" in Hindi

Yield: Approximately 1½ cups

If the basic garam masala doesn't do it for you, and you want something even stronger and spicier, try this one!

Ingredients:

- ¼ cup freshly ground black pepper
- ¼ cup ground black cumin seeds
- ¼ cup ground cinnamon
- ¼ cup ground cloves
- ¼ cup ground green cardamom seeds
- 2 teaspoons saffron threads dry-roasted and ground

Directions:

1. Dry-roast and grind the saffron before you begin. Next, in a moderate-sized cast-iron or non-stick skillet, mix and roast all the spices, stirring and swaying

the pan over moderate heat until heated through, approximately two minutes.
2. Allow to cool, then put inside an airtight vessel and place the vessel in a cool, dark place, approximately thirty days at room temperature or approximately one year in a fridge.

KASHMIRI GARAM MASALA

This recipe is called "Kashmir ka garam masala" in Hindi

Yield: 1½ cups

A version of garam masala from the icy peaks of North India. Highly rich and fragrant, this version goes great with non-vegetarian dishes.

Ingredients:

- ¼ cup black cumin seeds
- ¼ cup black peppercorns
- ½ cup fennel seeds
- 1 tablespoon ground cinnamon
- 1 tablespoon ground cloves
- 1 tablespoon ground ginger
- 1 teaspoon ground mace
- 1 teaspoon ground nutmeg
- 1 teaspoon saffron threads
- 2 tablespoons green cardamom seeds

Directions:

1. In a moderate-sized cast-iron or non-stick skillet, mix and roast the fennel and cumin seeds, peppercorns, cardamom seeds, and saffron threads, stirring and swaying the pan over moderate heat until heated through, approximately two minutes.
2. Allow to cool, then grind using a spice or coffee grinder till you get a fine powder. Move to a container and stir in the cinnamon, ginger, cloves, mace, and nutmeg. Move the mixture back to the skillet and roast using moderate heat until heated through once more. Allow to cool, then put inside an

airtight vessel and place the vessel in a cool, dark place about thirty days at room temperature or approximately one year in a fridge.

MUGHLAI GARAM MASALA Ⓥ

This recipe is called "Mughlai garam masala" in Hindi

Yield: Approximately 1½ cups

This version of the garam masala was brought to India by the Mughals, Muslim dynasts who ruled India for more than 300 years!

Ingredients:

- ¼ cup freshly ground black pepper
- ¼ cup ground cumin seeds
- 1 tablespoon ground bay leaves
- 1 tablespoon saffron threads, dry-roasted and ground
- 1 teaspoon ground mace
- 1 teaspoon ground nutmeg
- 2 tablespoons ground black cardamom seeds
- 2 tablespoons ground black cumin seeds
- 2 tablespoons ground cinnamon
- 2 tablespoons ground cloves
- 2 tablespoons ground ginger
- 2 tablespoons ground green cardamom seeds

Directions:

1. Ready the saffron. Next, in a moderate-sized cast-iron or non-stick skillet, roast all the spices together, stirring and swaying the pan over moderate heat until heated through, approximately two minutes.
2. Allow to cool, then put inside an airtight vessel and place the vessel in a cool, dark place, approximately thirty days at room temperature or approximately one year in a fridge.

PARSI GARAM MASALA Ⓥ

This recipe is called "Parsi garam masala" in Hindi

Yield: Approximately 1½ cups

Parsis migrated to India from Iran, and their version of the garam masala goes perfectly with meat dishes!

Ingredients:

- ¼ cup ground black peppercorns
- ¼ cup ground cinnamon
- ¼ cup ground cumin
- ⅓ cup ground green cardamom seeds
- 2 tablespoons ground cloves
- 3 tablespoons ground star anise

Directions:

1. In a moderate-sized cast-iron or non-stick skillet, mix and roast all the spices, stirring and swaying the pan over moderate heat until heated through, approximately two minutes.
2. Allow to cool, then put inside an airtight vessel and place the vessel in a cool, dark place, approximately thirty days at room temperature or approximately one year in a fridge.

SAVORY SPICE BLENDS

CHAAT MASALA Ⓥ

This recipe is called "Chaat masala" in Hindi

Yield: Approximately 1½ cups

Chaat or chat is a savoury and spicy snack that originated in India, typically served at roadside tracks from stalls or food carts across the Indian subcontinent in India.

Ingredients:

- ¼ cup mango powder
- ⅓ tablespoons cumin seeds, dry-roasted and ground
- 1 tablespoon citric acid
- 1 tablespoon ground black salt
- 1 teaspoon ground asafoetida
- 1 to 2 tablespoons salt, or to taste
- 1 to 3 teaspoons cayenne pepper, or to taste
- 2 tablespoons ground ajwain seeds
- 2 tablespoons ground ginger
- 2 tablespoons tamarind powder
- 3 tablespoons dried mint leaves, ground

Directions:

1. Ready the cumin seeds. Next, in a moderate-sized cast-iron or non-stick skillet, mix and roast all the spices, stirring and swaying the pan over moderate heat until heated through, approximately two minutes.
2. Allow to cool, then put inside an airtight vessel and place the vessel in a cool, dark place, approximately thirty days at room temperature or approximately one year in a fridge.

NEW DELHI STREET FOOD MASALA Ⓥ

This recipe is called "Papri chaat masala" in Hindi

Yield: 1½ cups

A taste of from streets of the capital of India.

Ingredients:

- ½ cup cumin seeds
- 1 tablespoon ajwain seeds
- 1 tablespoon cayenne pepper, or to taste
- 1 tablespoon ground black salt
- 1 tablespoon ground ginger
- 1 tablespoon salt, or to taste
- 3 tablespoons ground dried mint leaves
- 3 tablespoons mango powder

- 3 tablespoons tamarind powder

Directions:

1. In a moderate-sized cast-iron or non-stick skillet, mix and roast the cumin and ajwain seeds, stirring and swaying the pan over moderate heat until the spices are seems slightly darker, approximately two minutes. Move to a container.
2. Allow to cool, then grind using a spice or coffee grinder till you get a fine powder. Return the mixture to the skillet and Put in the mango and tamarind powder, mint leaves, ginger, black salt, salt, and cayenne pepper.
3. Roast once again over moderate heat until heated through, approximately one minute. Allow to cool, then put inside an airtight vessel and place the vessel in a cool, dark place, approximately thirty days at room temperature or approximately one year in a fridge.

BOMBAY BREAD-SNACK MASALA ⓥ

This recipe is called "Pav-bhaji ka masala" in Hindi

Yield: Approximately 1½ cups

This one is from the streets of Mumbai.

Ingredients:

- ⅓ cup ground coriander seeds
- ⅓ cup ground cumin
- ½ cup freshly ground black pepper
- 1 to 2 tablespoons cayenne pepper, or to taste
- 1½ teaspoons ground asafoetida
- 1½ teaspoons ground black cardamom seeds
- 1½ teaspoons ground cinnamon
- 1½ teaspoons ground cloves
- 1½ teaspoons ground turmeric

Directions:

1. In a moderate-sized cast-iron or non-stick skillet, roast all the spices, stirring and shaking the skillet over moderate heat, until the mixture is fragrant and golden, approximately two minutes.
2. Allow to cool, then put inside an airtight vessel and place the vessel in a cool, dark place, approximately thirty days at room temperature or approximately one year in a fridge.

CUMIN-WATER MASALA Ⓥ

This recipe is called "Jeera paani masala" in Hindi

Yield: 1½ cups

This powder is commonly enjoyed mixed with water, but it can also be used as a tastemaker for various recipes.

Ingredients:

- ¼ cup ground dried mint leaves
- ⅓ cup cumin seeds
- ½ cup dried mango or tamarind powder, sifted
- 1 tablespoon black cumin seeds
- 1 tablespoon ground ginger
- 1 tablespoon salt, or to taste
- 1 teaspoon dried cayenne pepper, or to taste
- 1 teaspoon freshly ground black pepper, or to taste
- 1 teaspoon ground asafoetida
- 1 teaspoon vegetable oil
- 2 teaspoons ajwain seeds
- 2 teaspoons ground black salt

Directions:

1. In a moderate-sized cast-iron or non-stick wok or skillet, mix and roast the cumin seeds, black cumin seeds, and ajwain seeds, stirring and swaying the pan over moderate heat until heated through, approximately two minutes. Take the skillet off the heat. Allow to cool, then grind using a spice or coffee grinder till you get a fine powder.

2. Heat the oil in a small non-stick saucepan using moderate to high heat and Put in the asafoetida. It will sizzle upon contact with the hot oil. Swiftly put in the ground spice mixture and all the rest of the spices. Mix thoroughly and stir until heated through, approximately two minutes. Allow to cool, then put inside an airtight vessel and place the vessel in a cool, dark place, approximately thirty days at room temperature or approximately one year in a fridge.

GRIDDLE-FRIED BREAD MASALA Ⓥ

This recipe is called "Parantha masala" in Hindi

Yield: 1½ cups

Sprinkle this masala over griddle-fried breads or "paranthas".

Ingredients:

- ¼ cup ajwain seeds, crudely ground
- ⅓ cup black peppercorns, crudely ground
- ⅓ cup ground dried fenugreek leaves
- ⅓ cup ground dried mint leaves
- 1 tablespoon black salt (not compulsory)
- 1 tablespoon salt, or to taste

Directions:

1. In a small-sized container, combine all the spices using a spoon.
2. Put inside an airtight vessel and place the vessel in a cool, dry place, approximately thirty days at room temperature or approximately one year in a fridge.

STUFFED GRIDDLE-FRIED BREAD MASALA Ⓥ

This recipe is called "Bharvaan parantha ka masala" in Hindi

Yield: 1½ cups

Ingredients:

- ¼ cup ground dried pomegranate seeds
- ½ cup ground coriander seeds
- 1 tablespoon black salt
- 1 tablespoon cayenne pepper
- 1 tablespoon garam masala
- 1 tablespoon ground ginger
- 1 tablespoon salt, or to taste
- 1 teaspoon ground mace
- 1 teaspoon ground nutmeg
- 2 tablespoons ajwain seeds, crudely ground
- 2 tablespoons ground dried mint leaves
- 2 tablespoons mango powder

Directions:

1. In a small-sized container, combine all the spices using a spoon.
2. Put inside an airtight vessel and place the vessel in a cool, dry place, approximately thirty days at room temperature or approximately one year in a fridge.

ROASTED CHILE PEPPER AND RED PEPPERCORN MASALA Ⓥ

This recipe is called "Bhuna mirchi ka masala" in Hindi

Yield: Approximately ½ cup

This one is probably the hottest masala in this book. Use carefully.

Ingredients:

- 1 tablespoon vegetable oil
- 1 teaspoon salt, or to taste
- 15 to 20 dried red chile peppers, such as chile de arbol, broken
- 2 tablespoons red peppercorns
- 2 to 4 tablespoons ground paprika

Directions:

1. In a moderate-sized cast-iron or non-stick wok or skillet, heat the oil over moderate heat and roast the chile peppers, stirring and swaying the pan, until crunchy and seems slightly darker, approximately a minute or two. This will cause a lot of irritating smoke, so do this outdoors if possible, or when you you're alone in the house, and are willing to suffer a little by yourself. Move to a container.
2. Put in the red peppercorns and roast until heated through, without browning them. Put into the chile peppers. Allow to cool, then grind using a spice or coffee grinder till you get a fine powder. Stir in the paprika and salt and put inside an airtight vessel and place the vessel in a cool, dark place, approximately thirty days at room temperature or approximately one year in a fridge.

ROASTED CUMIN AND FENUGREEK MASALA

This recipe is called "Bhuna jeera aur methi ka masala" in Hindi

Yield: Approximately 1 cup

This one goes great in sauces!

Ingredients:

- ¼ cup cumin seeds
- 1 teaspoon ground turmeric
- 12 to 15 dried red chile peppers, such as chile de arbol, broken
- 2 tablespoons fenugreek seeds
- 2 teaspoons salt, or to taste

Directions:

1. In a moderate-sized cast-iron or non-stick skillet, mix and roast the cumin seeds, fenugreek seeds, and red chile peppers over moderate heat, stirring and swaying the pan until seems slightly darker and highly fragrant, approximately two minutes.
2. Allow to cool, then grind using a spice or coffee grinder till you get a fine powder. Stir in the salt and turmeric and put inside an airtight vessel and place the vessel in a cool, dark place, approximately thirty days at room temperature or approximately one year in a fridge.

ROASTED CUMIN-PEPPER MASALA ⓥ

This recipe is called "Bhuna jeera aur kaali-mirch ka masala" in Hindi

Yield: ½ cup

This one goes great with yogurt and salads.

Ingredients:

- ¼ cup cumin seeds
- 1 tablespoon hot red pepper flakes, or to taste
- 3 tablespoons black peppercorns

Directions:

1. In a small-sized cast-iron or non-stick skillet, roast separately the cumin seeds, the peppercorns, and the red pepper flakes, over moderate heat, stirring and swaying the pan until fragrant and seems slightly darker, approximately two minutes each for the cumin and the peppercorns, and just a few seconds for the red chile flakes.
2. Combine the roasted cumin, peppercorns and red pepper flakes. Allow to cool, then put in your pepper mill. Grind and use as needed. Or, grind crudely using a spice of coffee grinder, put inside an airtight vessel and place the vessel in a cool, dark place, approximately thirty days at room temperature or approximately one year in a fridge.

PUNJABI RAITA AND BUTTERMILK MASALA ⓥ

This recipe is called "Punjabi raita aur lussi ka masala" in Hindi

Yield: Approximately ⅓ cup

Ingredients:

- ¼ cup cumin seeds, dry-roasted and crudely ground
- 1 tablespoon black peppercorns, dry-roasted and crudely ground
- 1 tablespoon crudely ground dried mint leaves
- 1 teaspoon ground paprika
- 1 teaspoon salt, or to taste

Directions:

1. In a container, combine all the spices using a spoon.
2. Put inside an airtight vessel and place the vessel in a cool, dry place, approximately thirty days at room temperature or approximately one year in a fridge.

KASHMIRI RAITA MASALA Ⓥ

This recipe is called "Kashmir ka raita masala" in Hindi

Yield: Approximately ½ cup

Ingredients:

- ¼ cup coriander seeds
- ½ to 1 teaspoon cayenne pepper
- 1 tablespoon black mustard seeds
- 1 teaspoon salt, or to taste
- 2 rice-size pieces asafoetida
- 2 tablespoons cumin seeds
- 2 tablespoons fennel seeds
- 2 teaspoons ground ginger

Directions:

1. In a moderate-sized cast-iron or non-stick skillet, mix and roast the coriander seeds, and fennel seeds and cumin seeds, stirring and swaying the pan over moderate heat until heated through, approximately two minutes. Move to a container.
2. In the same skillet, dry-roast the asafoetida and the mustard seeds until they begin to pop, approximately one minute. (Cover pan momentarily to contain popping, if required.) Combine with the coriander-fennel-cumin mixture.
3. Allow to cool, then grind using a spice or coffee grinder till you get a fine powder. Stir in the ginger, cayenne pepper, and salt. Put inside an airtight vessel and place the vessel in a cool, dark place, approximately thirty days at room temperature or approximately one year in a fridge.

MASALA BLENDS FOR SPECIAL DISHES

BENGALI FIVE WHOLE SPICE BLEND Ⓥ

This recipe is called "Panch-phoran" in Hindi

Yield: Approximately 1½ cups

A delicious blend of five spices popular in east India that goes great with non-vegetarian curries and dishes.

Ingredients:

- ¼ cup black mustard seeds
- ⅓ cup fennel seeds
- ⅔ cup cumin seeds
- 2 tablespoons fenugreek seeds
- 3 tablespoons kalonji seeds

Directions:

1. In a moderate-sized cast-iron or non-stick wok or skillet, roast all the ingredients together, shaking and stirring the pan using moderate to high heat, until heated through, approximately two minutes.
2. Allow to cool, then put inside an airtight vessel and place the vessel in a cool, dark place, thirty days at room temperature or approximately one year in a fridge.

BRAISED MEAT MASALA Ⓥ

This recipe is called "Korma masala" in Hindi

Yield: Approximately 1½ cups

Typically used for cooking delicious "korma", which means meat braised with yogurt.

Ingredients:

- ¼ cup each: shelled and finely ground raw pistachios, almonds, and cashews nuts
- 1 tablespoon ground black cardamom seeds
- 1 tablespoon ground black pepper
- 1 tablespoon ground cinnamon
- 1 teaspoon ground cloves
- 2 tablespoons ground ginger
- 2 tablespoons ground green cardamom seeds
- 2 tablespoons white poppy seeds

Directions:

1. In a moderate-sized cast-iron or non-stick skillet, mix and roast all the ingredients, stirring and swaying the pan over moderate heat until heated through, approximately two minutes.
2. Allow to cool, then put inside an airtight vessel and place the vessel in a cool, dark place, approximately seven days at room temperature or approximately one year in a fridge.

CHICKPEA MASALA ⓥ

This recipe is called "Channa masala" in Hindi

Yield: Approximately 1½ cups

Used commonly in chickpea dishes and curries, this masala also goes great with meat dishes.

Ingredients:

- ½ cup ground coriander seeds
- ½ cup ground cumin
- ½ teaspoon ground mace
- 1 tablespoon cayenne pepper, or to taste
- 1 tablespoon freshly ground black pepper, or to taste
- 1 tablespoon ground black cardamom seeds
- 1 tablespoon ground black salt
- 1 tablespoon ground dried fenugreek leaves
- 1 teaspoon ground asafoetida

- 1 teaspoon ground cinnamon
- 1 teaspoon ground cloves
- 1 teaspoon ground ginger
- 1 teaspoon ground nutmeg
- 1 teaspoon ground turmeric
- 2 tablespoons ground dried pomegranate seeds
- 2 tablespoons tamarind or mango powder
- 2 teaspoons ground ajwain seeds

Directions:

1. In a moderate-sized cast-iron or non-stick skillet, mix and roast all the ingredients except the coriander, black salt, and turmeric, stirring and swaying the pan over moderate heat until heated through, approximately two minutes. Reduce the heat to low and stir until dark brown and fragrant, approximately three minutes.
2. Turn off the heat and stir in the coriander, black salt, and turmeric. Allow to cool completely, then put inside an airtight vessel and place the vessel in a cool, dark place, approximately thirty days at room temperature or approximately one year in a fridge.

GRILLING MASALA Ⓥ

This recipe is called "Tandoori masala" in Hindi

Yield: Approximately 1½ cups

A delicious tastemaker for pretty much any recipe right off the grill, or right out or a tandoor.

Ingredients:

- ¼ cup ground dried fenugreek leaves
- *1* cup [Mughlai Garam Masala](#)
- 1 tablespoon ground paprika
- 1 teaspoon ground turmeric
- 1 to 2 tablespoons cayenne pepper, or to taste
- 2 tablespoons ground fenugreek seeds

Directions:

1. Ready the Mughlai masala. Add all the spices to a container and stir using a spoon until they get blended.
2. Put inside an airtight vessel and place the vessel in a cool and dark place, approximately thirty days at room temperature or approximately one year in a fridge.

GUJRATI MASALA Ⓥ

This recipe is called "Dhansak masala" in Hindi

Yield: Approximately 2½ cups

Typically used with "Dhansak", a cuisine from Gujrat in West India.

Ingredients:

- ¼ cup black peppercorns
- ¼ cup cumin seeds
- ¼ cup dried curry leaves
- ¼ cup dried red chile peppers, such as chile de arbol, broken
- ¼ cup fenugreek seeds
- 1 cup coriander seeds
- 1 tablespoon black cumin seeds
- 1 tablespoon ground cinnamon
- 1 tablespoon ground cloves
- 1 tablespoon mustard seeds
- 1 tablespoon white poppy seeds
- 1 teaspoon ground mace
- 10 bay leaves, crudely broken
- 2 teaspoons ground black cardamom seeds
- 2 teaspoons ground green cardamom seeds
- 2 teaspoons ground nutmeg
- 4 star anise, broken

Directions:

1. In a moderate-sized cast-iron or non-stick skillet, mix and roast the coriander, cumin, black cumin, peppercorns, fenugreek, and chile peppers, stirring and swaying the pan over moderate heat until the mixture is seems slightly darker, approximately two minutes. Stir in the curry leaves, poppy seeds, mustard seeds, anise, and bay leaves and roast another minute. Remove from heat.
2. Allow to cool, then grind using a spice or coffee grinder till you get a fine powder. Stir in the cinnamon, cloves, black and green cardamom seeds, nutmeg, and mace. Put inside an airtight vessel and place the vessel in a cool, dark place, approximately thirty days at room temperature or approximately one year in a fridge.

MEAT MASALA Ⓥ

This recipe is called "Gosht ka masala" in Hindi

Yield: Approximately 1¼ cups

Sprinkle some of this in your meat curries for great taste!

Ingredients:

- ¼ cup shelled raw peanuts, with papery red skin removed
- 1 tablespoon black mustard seeds
- 1 tablespoon coriander seeds
- 1 tablespoon fenugreek seeds
- 1 teaspoon white poppy seeds
- 10 to 15 dried red chile peppers, such as chile de arbol, broken
- 1½ tablespoons sesame seeds
- 2 tablespoons cumin seeds
- 2 tablespoons dried yellow split chickpeas (channa dal), sorted

Directions:

1. In a moderate-sized cast-iron or non-stick skillet, roast the peanuts, stirring and swaying the pan over moderate heat until the mixture is seems slightly darker, approximately one minute.
2. Put in the chile peppers, dal, cumin seeds, and fenugreek seeds and roast until a golden colour is achieved, approximately two to three minutes. Stir in

the sesame, coriander, poppy, and mustard seeds and continue to roast until seems slightly darker, approximately two to three minutes. Allow to cool, then grind using a spice or coffee grinder till you get a fine powder. Put inside an airtight vessel and place the vessel in a cool, dark place, approximately seven days at room temperature or approximately one year in a fridge.

VINDALOO MASALA Ⓥ

This recipe is called "Vindaloo ka masala" in Hindi

Yield: Approximately 1½ cups

A delicious tastemaker from the coastal tourist state of Goa!

Ingredients:

- ¼ cup cumin seeds
- ¾ cup coriander seeds
- 1 tablespoon fenugreek seeds
- 1 teaspoon ground black cardamom seeds
- 1 teaspoon ground cinnamon
- 1 teaspoon ground cloves
- 1 teaspoon ground turmeric
- 2 tablespoons black cumin seeds
- 2 tablespoons black peppercorns
- 2 teaspoons mustard seeds
- 4 to 6 dried red chile peppers, such as chile de arbol, broken

Directions:

1. In a moderate-sized cast-iron or non-stick skillet, mix and roast the red chile peppers, coriander, cumin, black cumin, peppercorns, fenugreek, and mustard seeds, stirring and swaying the pan over moderate heat until seems slightly darker, approximately two minutes.
2. Allow to cool, then grind using a spice or coffee grinder till you get a fine powder. Move to a container and stir in the turmeric, cardamom, cloves, and cinnamon. Put inside an airtight vessel and place the vessel in a cool, dark

place, approximately thirty days at room temperature or approximately one year in a fridge.

WOK MASALA Ⓥ

This recipe is called "Kadhai masala" in Hindi

Yield: Approximately 1¼ cups

A tastemaker for recipes typically cooked in a wok or "kadhai".

Ingredients:

- ½ cup crudely ground coriander seeds
- 1 tablespoon cayenne pepper
- 1 tablespoon ground dried pomegranate seeds
- 1 tablespoon ground fennel seeds
- 1 tablespoon ground ginger
- 1 tablespoon mango powder
- 1 teaspoon ground black cardamom seeds
- 1 teaspoon ground black salt
- 1 teaspoon ground nutmeg
- 1 teaspoon ground paprika
- 2 tablespoons ground cumin seeds
- 2 tablespoons ground dried fenugreek leaves
- 2 tablespoons ground dried mint leaves

Directions:

1. Add all the spices to a small-sized container and stir using a spoon until they get blended.
2. Put inside an airtight vessel and place the vessel in a cool, dark place, approximately thirty days at room temperature or approximately one year in a fridge.

SPECIAL SOUTH INDIAN BLENDS

SAMBAR MASALA Ⓥ

This recipe is called "Sambar podi" in Hindi

Yield: Approximately 1½ cups

In South India, you will be served "Sambar" with pretty much everything. This spice blend is the lifeblood of Sambar.

Ingredients:

- ¼ cup shredded, unsweetened, dried coconut
- ⅓ cup dried curry leaves
- ½ cup coriander seeds
- 1 tablespoon each: dried yellow split pigeon peas (toor dal), dried yellow split chickpeas (channa dal), dried white urad beans (dhulli urad dal), sorted
- 1 tablespoon sesame or peanut oil
- 1 teaspoon ground asafoetida
- 1 teaspoon ground turmeric
- 10 to 15 dried red chile peppers, such as chile de arbol, broken
- 2 tablespoons fenugreek seeds

Directions:

1. In a moderate-sized cast-iron or non-stick skillet, heat the oil over moderate heat and stir-fry the red chile peppers until seems slightly darker, approximately one minute. Put in the fenugreek seeds, all the dals, and the asafoetida and stir until a golden colour is achieved, approximately two minutes.
2. Mix in the coconut and stir until a golden colour is achieved, approximately two minutes. Then Put in the coriander seeds, curry leaves, and turmeric, and stir until heated through, approximately one minute. Allow to cool, then grind using a spice or coffee grinder till you get a fine powder. Put inside an airtight vessel and place the vessel in a cool, dark place, approximately thirty days at room temperature or about an year in a fridge.

RASAM MASALA Ⓥ

This recipe is called "Rasam podi" in Hindi

Yield: Approximately 1½ cups

Rasam is the second most popular thing in South India, followed by sambar.

Ingredients:

- ¼ cup dried curry leaves
- ½ teaspoon ground turmeric
- ⅔ cup coriander seeds
- 1 tablespoon black mustard seeds
- 1 tablespoon cumin seeds
- 1 tablespoon fenugreek seeds
- 10 to 15 dried red chile peppers, such as chile de arbol, broken
- 2 tablespoons cumin seeds
- 2 tablespoons dried yellow split chickpeas (channa dal), sorted
- 3 tablespoons black peppercorns
- 3 tablespoons dried yellow split pigeon peas (toor dal), sorted
- 4 to 6 rice-size pieces asafoetida

Directions:

1. In a moderate-sized cast-iron or non-stick wok or skillet, mix and roast all the ingredients, stirring and shaking the skillet over moderate heat until it starts to look golden and releases its fragrance, approximately three minutes.
2. Allow to cool, then grind using a spice or coffee grinder till you get a powder. Put inside an airtight vessel and place the vessel in a cool, dark place, thirty days at room temperature or approximately one year in a fridge.

Variation: Mild Rasam Powder can be made by excluding or reducing the number of red chile peppers. The black peppercorns may be reduced in quantity, but do not omit, because they are essential to this blend.

CHUTNEY COCONUT MASALA Ⓥ

This recipe is called "Chutni nariyal podi" in Hindi

Yield: Approximately 1½ cups

Coconut is a staple in the South Indian kitchen, and this recipe can be used to do a lot.

Ingredients:

- ¼ cup crudely ground dried curry leaves
- 1 cup grated fresh or frozen coconut or shredded unsweetened dried coconut
- 1 tablespoon ground jaggery (gur) or dark brown sugar
- 1 teaspoon ground asafoetida
- 1 to 2 tablespoons tamarind powder
- 2 tablespoons each: dried split pigeon peas (toor dal), dried white urad beans (dhulli urad dal), dried yellow split chickpeas (channa dal), sorted
- 6 to 10 dried red chile peppers, such as chile de arbol, broken

Directions:

1. In a moderate-sized cast-iron or non-stick wok or skillet, roast the coconut, all the dals, red chile peppers, and curry leaves over moderate heat, stirring and swaying the pan until a golden colour is achieved, approximately 4 minutes.
2. Put in the asafoetida, stir for about half a minute, and remove from the heat. Stir in the tamarind powder and jaggery. Allow to cool, then grind using a spice or coffee grinder until as fine a powder as possible. Stir in the salt and put inside an airtight vessel and place the vessel in a cool, dark place, approximately seven days at room temperature or approximately one year in a fridge.

LENTIL PASTE Ⓥ

This recipe is called "Dal podi" in Hindi

Yield: Approximately 1½ cups

A delicious spice blend that adds flavour and thickens.

Ingredients:

- ¼ cup dried split pigeon peas (toor dal), sorted
- ¼ cup dried white urad beans (dhulli urad dal), sorted
- ½ cup dried yellow split chickpeas (channa dal), sorted
- ½ teaspoon ground asafoetida
- 1 tablespoon cumin seeds

- 1 tablespoon peanut oil
- 10 to 12 dried red chile peppers, such as chile de arbol, broken
- 2 teaspoons salt, or to taste

Directions:

1. In a moderate-sized cast-iron or non-stick wok or skillet, heat the oil using moderate to high heat and stir-fry the dals, cumin seeds, and red chile peppers until seems slightly darker, approximately two minutes.
2. Put in the asafoetida and stir about 30 seconds. Allow to cool, then grind using a spice or coffee grinder until a fine paste is achieved. Stir in the salt and put inside an airtight vessel and place the vessel in a cool, dark place, thirty days at room temperature or approximately one year in a fridge.

PEANUT MASALA Ⓥ

This recipe is called "Moong-phalli or nilakkadala podi" in Hindi

Yield: Approximately 1½ cups

A great seasoning for green salads, chicken, and vegetables!

Ingredients:

- ⅓ cup white sesame seeds, dry-roasted
- 1 cup roasted peanuts, papery skin removed
- 1 teaspoon ground asafoetida
- 1 teaspoon sesame or peanut oil
- 3 to 4 tablespoons dried curry leaves
- 5 to 7 dried red chile peppers, such as chile de arbol, broken

Directions:

1. Ready the sesame seeds. Next, in a moderate-sized cast-iron or non-stick wok or skillet, heat the oil using moderate to high heat and stir-fry the chile peppers until seems slightly darker, approximately one minute. Put in the curry leaves and asafoetida, and stir for about half a minute. Allow to cool, then grind using a spice or coffee grinder till you get a fine powder. Move to a container.

2. Crudely grind the peanuts and sesame seeds using a spice of coffee grinder (you will probably need to do this in 2-3 batches). Put into the ground chile pepper mixture and mix thoroughly. Put inside an airtight vessel and place the vessel in a cool, dark place, approximately seven days at room temperature or approximately one year in a fridge.

SESAME MASALA Ⓥ

This recipe is called "Til or ellu podi" in Hindi

Yield: Approximately 1½ cups

A great garnish for meat and vegetable dishes!

Ingredients:

- 1 tablespoon hot red pepper flakes, or to taste
- 1 teaspoon Asian sesame oil
- 1 teaspoon ground asafoetida
- 1¼ cups white sesame seeds
- 2 tablespoons fenugreek seeds

Directions:

1. In a moderate-sized cast-iron or non-stick wok or skillet, heat the oil using moderate to high heat, put in the fenugreek seeds, red pepper flakes, and asafoetida and stir until a golden colour is achieved, approximately one minute.
2. Put in the sesame seeds, reduce the heat to medium, and roast, stirring and shaking the skillet, until a golden colour is achieved, approximately three minutes. Allow to cool, then grind using a spice or coffee grinder to make as fine a powder as possible. Put inside an airtight vessel and place the vessel in a cool, dark place, approximately seven days at room temperature or about an year in a fridge.

THENGA MASALA Ⓥ

This recipe is called "Thenga podi" in Hindi

Yield: Approximately 1½ cups

A hot and sour tastemaker with an intense flavour.

Ingredients:

- ¼ cup dried white urad beans (dhulli urad dal), sorted
- ¼ cup grated or shredded dried coconut (kopra)
- ¼ cup ground coriander seeds
- ¼ cup ground jaggery (gur) or dark brown sugar
- ¼ teaspoon ground asafoetida
- ½ cup dried yellow split chickpeas (channa dal), sorted
- 1 teaspoon ground turmeric
- 1-inch ball of seedless tamarind pulp, broken into small bits or 1 tablespoon tamarind powder
- 2 teaspoons peanut oil
- 2 teaspoons salt, or to taste
- 7 to 10 dried red chile peppers, such as chile de arbol, broken

Directions:

1. In a moderate-sized cast-iron or non-stick wok or skillet, mix and roast the dals, stirring and shaking the skillet over moderate heat until a golden colour is achieved, approximately two to three minutes. Move to a container.
2. In the same pan, put in the oil and stir-fry the red chile peppers and tamarind until seems slightly darker, approximately two minutes. Move to the container with the roasted dal.
3. Still using the same pan, put in the coriander and coconut and roast until seems slightly darker, two to five minutes. Stir in the jaggery, salt, turmeric, and asafoetida, and roast until the jaggery melts, approximately a minute or two. Stir in the roasted dals, chile peppers and tamarind.
4. Allow to cool, then grind using a spice or coffee grinder until crudely ground. Put inside an airtight vessel and place the vessel in a cool, dark place, approximately three months in the fridge or about an year in the freezer.

DESSERT AND TEA MASALAS

DESSERT MASALA Ⓥ

This recipe is called "Mithai ka masala" in Hindi

Yield: Approximately 1½ cups

This spectacular green powder can be added to pretty much anything sweet to enhance the flavour, and is a great garnish for desserts.

Ingredients:

- ¼ cup cashews, crudely broken
- ½ cup shelled raw almonds, crudely broken
- 1 cup shelled raw pistachios
- 1 tablespoon crudely ground green cardamom seeds
- 1 teaspoon crudely ground black cardamom seeds
- 1 teaspoon saffron threads, dry-roasted and crudely crushed

Directions:

1. Ready the saffron. Next, using a spice grinder or food processor, mix together and pulse the pistachios, almonds, and cashews in one or two batches, until you get a crude powder.
2. Mix in the green and black cardamom seeds and the saffron. Put inside an airtight vessel and store, approximately three months in the fridge or about an year in the freezer.

TEA MASALA Ⓥ

This recipe is called "Chai ka masala" in Hindi

Yield: Approximately 1½ cups

An average Indian adult enjoys tea multiple times per day.

Ingredients:

- ⅓ cup green cardamom seeds
- ½ cup fennel seeds
- 1 tablespoon black peppercorns

- 1 tablespoon ground cinnamon
- 1 tablespoon ground cloves
- 1½ tablespoons ground ginger
- 2 tablespoons black cardamom seeds
- 2 tablespoons dried mint leaves

Directions:

1. Using a spice or coffee grinder, mix together and grind the fennel seeds, green and black cardamom seeds, mint, and peppercorns until a fine powder is achieved.
2. Mix in the ginger, cinnamon, and cloves, and grind one more time to combine the spices. Move to a small vessel and store in a cool, dark place, approximately thirty days at room temperature or approximately one year in a fridge.

BASIC FLAVORING PASTES

BASIC GINGER PASTE Ⓥ

This recipe is called "Pissa adrak" in Hindi

Yield: Approximately 2 cups

Ginger paste is a staple in the Indian kitchen. You can buy this store, but making your own is much more fun.

Ingredients:

- 1 pound fresh ginger, peeled and cut crosswise into thin round slices
- 1 to 3 tablespoons water, as required

Directions:

1. Add the ginger slices to a blender, as you might not get enough smoothness using a food processor. Pulse, pouring in one tablespoon of water at a time, and attain a smooth paste while adding as little water as possible.
2. Move to an airtight vessel and place in your fridge for a maximum of five days or separate into measured batches and freeze about three months. Measured batches can be used directly when you need to cook them.

BASIC GARLIC PASTE Ⓥ

This recipe is called "Pissa lussan" in Hindi

Yield: Approximately 1 cup

Garlic paste is easy to find in markets all over America, but garlic paste that has just been made from fresh garlic will always win.

Ingredients:

- 1½ cups fresh garlic cloves, peeled
- 2 to 3 tablespoons water, as required

Directions:

1. Add the garlic to a blender, as you might not get enough smoothness using a food processor. Pulse, pouring in one tablespoon of water at a time, and attain a smooth paste while adding as little water as possible.
2. Move to an airtight vessel and place in your fridge for a maximum of half a month. Since garlic paste has a strong smell, make sure you thoroughly seal it using plastic wrap below the lid. This will guarantee that the rest of your fridge doesn't smell like garlic. You can also separate into measured batches and freeze about three months. Measured batches used directly when you need to cook them.

ROASTED GARLIC PASTE Ⓥ

This recipe is called "Pissa bhuna lussan" in Hindi

Yield: Approximately 1 cup

Ingredients:

- 1½ cups fresh garlic cloves, peeled

Directions:

1. Heat your oven beforehand to 400°F. Put the garlic cloves in a small pie dish or any other baking pan and roast until a golden brown colour is achieved, approximately fifteen minutes.
2. Allow to cool, then pulse using a blender or crudely mash using a fork. Or just put the roasted cloves in an airtight vessel and place in your fridge for a maximum of thirty days or freeze for no more than six months. If you don't add any water, puréed roasted garlic can be easily separated even in its frozen form.

BASIC GINGER-GARLIC PASTE (V)

This recipe is called "Pissa adrak-lussan" in Hindi

Yield: Approximately 1½ cups

Probably the most commonly used paste in India, the ginger garlic paste is widely available in stores all over the world. However, the fresh paste you make at home will contain no preservatives and will taste much better! Oil increases the shelf life of this ingredient. Feel free to omit it if you wish to use all of it immediately.

Ingredients:

- 1 cup fresh garlic cloves, peeled
- 1 cup quarter-size slices peeled fresh ginger
- 1 to 3 tablespoons water

Directions:

1. Using a food processor or a blender, combine and pulse the ginger and garlic until a smooth paste is achieved, pouring in water as required for blending.
2. Move to an airtight container, stir in some oil (vegetable, peanut, or olive) until it forms a ⅛-inch layer on top of the paste, and place in your fridge for a maximum of half a month or freeze for no more than six months.

ALMOND AND POPPY SEED PASTE (V)

This recipe is called "Pissa badaam aur khas-khas ka masala" in Hindi

Yield: Approximately 1 cup

Used to make rich, creamy curries.

Ingredients:

- ½ cup shelled raw almonds, crudely chopped
- ½ cup warm water
- ½ cup white poppy seeds
- Seeds from 10 to 15 green cardamom pods

Directions:

1. Immerse the poppy seeds in the water for two hours.
2. Move to a blender, put in the almonds and cardamom seeds, and grind everything until a fine paste is achieved, pouring in additional water if required.
3. Move to an airtight vessel and store in the fridge four days to a week or four months in the freezer.

BASIC CASHEW PASTE (V)

This recipe is called "Pissa kaaju ka masala" in Hindi

Yield: Approximately 1 cup

Great for making rich and thick curries.

Ingredients:

- 1 cup warm water plus more for the paste
- 1¼ cups raw cashews

Directions:

1. Immerse crudely chopped cashews in the warm water to cover, approximately forty five minutes.

2. Drain and pulse using a blender adding 2 to 3 tablespoons water, as required, until a smooth paste is achieved.
3. Move to an airtight vessel and store in the fridge four days to a week or four months in the freezer.

BASIC CURRY PASTE WITH ONION Ⓥ

This recipe is called "Pyaz vaala kari masala" in Hindi

Yield: Approximately ½ cup

A basic curry paste. Feel free to play around and add ingredients you like!

Ingredients:

- ¼ cup peanut oil
- ½ cup crudely chopped fresh cilantro, including soft stems
- 1 large onion, crudely chopped
- 1 to 3 fresh green chile peppers, such as serrano, stemmed
- 2 large tomatoes, crudely chopped
- 3 large cloves fresh garlic, peeled
- 7 to 10 quarter-size slices of peeled fresh ginger

Directions:

1. Using a food processor, process the ginger, garlic, and onion until a smooth paste is achieved. Move to a container. Next, mis together and process the tomatoes, cilantro, and green chile peppers until a smooth purée is achieved.
2. Heat the oil in a big non-stick wok or saucepan using moderate to high heat, put in the ginger-onion paste and cook, using moderate to high heat the first two to three minutes and then over moderate heat until a golden brown colour is achieved, approximately five to seven minutes.
3. Mix in the puréed tomato mixture and cook, stirring until all the liquids vaporize and the oil comes to the sides. Allow to cool and store in an airtight vessel and place in your fridge for a maximum of five days or freeze for no more than three months.

BASIC CURRY PASTE WITHOUT ONION

This recipe is called "Bina pyaz ka kari masala" in Hindi

Yield: Approximately 1 cup

Al alternative to basic curry paste with onion if you don't eat onion,

Ingredients:

- ¼ cup peanut oil
- ¼ cup plain yogurt (non-fat or any kind), whisked until the desired smoothness is achieved
- ½ pound fresh ginger, peeled and thinly chopped
- 1 cup crudely chopped fresh cilantro, including soft stems
- 1 tablespoon cumin seeds
- 2 large tomatoes, crudely chopped
- 5 to 10 fresh green chile peppers, such as serrano, crudely chopped

Directions:

1. Using a food processor, combine and pulse the ginger, chile peppers, cilantro, and tomatoes until a smooth paste is achieved.
2. Heat the oil in a big non-stick wok or saucepan using moderate to high heat and cook the cumin seeds (they should sizzle upon contact with the hot oil). Swiftly put in the paste and cook over moderate heat the first two to three minutes, then using low heat until all the fluids vaporize.
3. Put in the yogurt, slowly and gradually, stirring continuously to stop it from curdling, until all of it is completely blended with the sauce. Allow to cool and store in an airtight vessel about half a month in the fridge or up to three months in the freezer.

BASIC GINGER AND GREEN CHILE PEPPER PASTE

This recipe is called "Pissi hui adrak-hari mirch ka masala" in Hindi

Yield: Approximately 1 cup

This is a decent alternative to ginger-garlic paste. I still prefer ginger-garlic paste though.

Ingredients:

- 10 to 15 fresh green chile peppers, such as serranos, crudely chopped
- 6 ounces fresh ginger, peeled and cut crosswise into thin round slices

Directions:

1. Using a food processor or blender, combine and pulse the ginger and chile peppers to make them as smooth as possible.
2. Move to an airtight vessel and place in your fridge for a maximum of ten days or freeze for no more than 4 months.

BASIC ONION PASTE Ⓥ

This recipe is called "Pyaz ka masala" in Hindi

Yield: Approximately 1 cup

A very commonly used paste in Indian cooking.

Ingredients:

- 1 large onion, crudely chopped (about 8 ounces)
- 10 to 12 quarter-size slices of peeled fresh ginger
- 2 tablespoons water
- 3 to 5 fresh green chile peppers, such as serrano, crudely chopped
- 4 large cloves fresh garlic, peeled

Directions:

1. Add to your blender the water, ginger, and garlic and pulse until the desired smoothness is achieved. Then Put in the onion and process again until the desired smoothness is achieved.
2. Move to an airtight vessel and place in your fridge for a maximum of ten days or freeze for no more than three months.

BOILED ONION PASTE Ⓥ

This recipe is called "Ublae pyaz ka masala" in Hindi

Yield: Approximately 1½ cups

This paste is great for making curries with a smooth texture.

Ingredients:

- ½ cup water
- 1 (1-inch) stick cinnamon, broken along the length into 2 pieces
- 1¼ pounds onions, crudely chopped
- 2 black cardamom pods, pounded lightly to break the skin
- 3 bay leaves
- 4 whole cloves

Directions:

1. Put all the ingredients in a moderate-sized non-stick saucepan. Cover and bring to a boil using moderate to high heat. Reduce the heat to medium-low and simmer until all the water evaporates and the onions are soft, approximately fifteen minutes.
2. Throw away the whole spices, then process the onions using a blender or a food processor until high smoothness is achieved. Move to an airtight vessel and place in your fridge for a maximum of five days or freeze for no more than three months.

CHILE PEPPER PASTE Ⓥ

This recipe is called "Pissi mirchon ka masala" in Hindi

Yield: Approximately ⅓ cup

This one is for the lovers of chile, who enjoy it when their tongue burns and eyes turn red.

Ingredients:

- ¼ cup distilled white vinegar or water
- 10 dried red chile peppers, such as chile de arbol, broken
- 2 teaspoons black peppercorns, dry-roasted and crudely ground
- 5 fresh green chile peppers, such as serrano, crudely chopped

Directions:

1. Immerse the red chile peppers in the vinegar approximately one hour to soften. Move to a blender.
2. Add the green chile peppers and the peppercorns and pulse until the desired smoothness is achieved. Move to an airtight jar and place in your fridge for a maximum of six months.

FRIED ONION PASTE

This recipe is called "Talae pyaz ka masala" in Hindi

Yield: Approximately 1 cup

This paste is used to make delicious rich-tasting curries.

Ingredients:

- ½ cup non-fat plain yogurt
- 1 cup melted ghee or vegetable oil for deep-frying
- 1 large onion, cut in half along the length and thinly chopped
- 4 large cloves fresh garlic, peeled
- 6 to 8 quarter-size slices of peeled fresh ginger

Directions:

1. Heat the oil in a big non-stick saucepan using moderate to high heat and fry the ginger and garlic until a golden colour is achieved, approximately two minutes. Put in the onion and fry until everything is thoroughly browned, approximately five minutes. Place on top of paper towels to drain and save the ghee/oil for future use.
2. Move to a blender or a food processor, put in the yogurt and pulse until a smooth and thick paste is achieved. Move to an airtight vessel and place in your fridge for a maximum of five days or freeze for no more than three months.

GOAN VINDALOO PASTE Ⓥ

This recipe is called "Goa ka vindaloo masala" in Hindi

Yield: Approximately 1 cup

Useful In making hot and tangy spicy dishes.

Ingredients:

- ¼ cup distilled white vinegar
- ½ cup Goan Vindaloo Powder (store-bought)
- 1 large onion, crudely chopped
- 2 teaspoons salt, or to taste
- 3 tablespoons peanut oil
- 3 to 4 dried red chile peppers, such chile de arbol, broken
- 30 to 40 fresh curry leaves
- 5 to 7 large cloves fresh garlic, peeled
- 8 to 10 quarter-size slices of peeled fresh ginger

Directions:

1. Immerse the red chile peppers in the vinegar, one to two hours. In the meantime, ready the vindaloo powder. Using a food processor, combine and pulse the red chile peppers, plus the vinegar, ginger, garlic, onion, curry leaves, and salt until a smooth paste is achieved. Stir in the vindaloo masala and process once more.
2. Heat the oil in a big non-stick wok or saucepan using moderate to high heat and stir-fry the paste, using moderate to high heat the first two to three minutes, and then over moderate heat until rich brown, approximately eight to ten minutes. Allow to cool, then store in an airtight vessel about thirty days in the fridge or six months in the freezer.

GUJARATI GREEN PASTE Ⓥ

This recipe is called "Gujerati hara masala" in Hindi

Yield: Approximately 1½ cups

A very hot and spicy paste from west India.

Ingredients:

- ¼ cup vegetable oil
- 4 to 6 ounces fresh green chile peppers, such as serrano, crudely chopped
- 6 ounces fresh garlic cloves, peeled

- 8 ounces fresh ginger, peeled and cut crosswise into thin round slices

Directions:

1. Using a food processor or a blender, combine and pulse all of the ingredients until high smoothness is achieved.
2. Move to an airtight vessel and place in your fridge for a maximum of 1 month, or freeze for no more than six months.

HYDERABADI GINGER-GARLIC PASTE Ⓥ

This recipe is called "Hyderabadi pissa adrak-lussan" in Hindi

Yield: Approximately 1½ cups

A Hyderabadi twist on a classic.

Ingredients:

- ¼ pound fresh garlic cloves, peeled
- ¾ pound fresh ginger, peeled and cut crosswise into thin round slices
- 1 to 3 tablespoons water

Directions:

1. You will a blander for this as a food processor just won't cut it. Mix together and pulse the ginger and garlic until the desired smoothness is achieved, pouring in water as required for blending.
2. Move to an airtight vessel and place in your fridge for a maximum of ten days or freeze for no more than six months.

KERALA FRIED ONION PASTE Ⓥ

This recipe is called "Kerala ka talae pyaz ka masala" in Hindi

Yield: Approximately 2 cups

A delicious paste with a hint of coconut.

Ingredients:

- ½ cup peanut oil
- 1 cup Coconut Milk (Homemade or store-bought)
- 15 to 20 fresh curry leaves
- 2 large onions, crudely chopped
- 5 large cloves fresh garlic, peeled
- 5 to 8 dried red chile peppers, such as chile de arbol, broken
- 6 to 8 quarter-size slices of peeled fresh ginger

Directions:

1. Heat the oil in a big non-stick saucepan using moderate to high heat and fry the red chile peppers and the onion until a golden colour is achieved, about three to four minutes. Put in the garlic, ginger, and curry leaves and fry until everything is well-browned, three to five minutes.
2. Cool, drain, and save the oil for future use. Then move to a blender or a food processor, put in the coconut milk and pulse until a smooth and thick paste is achieved. Move to an airtight vessel and place in your fridge for a maximum of five days or freeze for no more than three months.

MINTY GREEN CURRY PASTE Ⓥ

This recipe is called "Pudinae vaala hara kari masala" in Hindi

Yield: Approximately 1 cup

Great for making minty curries.

Ingredients:

- ¼ cup peanut oil
- ½ cup crudely chopped fresh mint leaves
- 1 cup crudely chopped fresh cilantro, including soft stems
- 1 tablespoon fresh lime juice
- 1 teaspoon salt, or to taste
- 1 to 3 fresh green chile peppers, such as serrano, stemmed
- 1½ teaspoons garam masala
- 4 to 5 large cloves fresh garlic, peeled
- 5 to 6 scallions, crudely chopped with greens
- 6 quarter-size slices of peeled fresh ginger

Directions:

1. Using a food processor, combine and pulse the garlic, ginger, chile peppers, and scallions until minced. Put in the cilantro, mint, and lime juice and process until a smooth paste is achieved. Move to a container and stir in the garam masala and salt.
2. Heat the oil in a big non-stick wok or saucepan using moderate to high heat, put in the green paste and cook, stirring over moderate heat for the first two to three minutes and then using moderate to low heat until thoroughly browned, approximately ten to twelve minutes. Allow to cool, then store in an airtight vessel for approximately thirty days in the fridge or six months in the freezer.

MUGHLAI CURRY PASTE WITH NUTS

This recipe is called "Korma ka geela masala" in Hindi

Yield: Approximately 1 cup

Who doesn't live cream and nuts?

Ingredients:

- *2 tablespoons* Basic Ginger-Garlic Paste
- *½ cup* Fragrant Masala with Nuts
- ¼ cup heavy cream
- ½ cup non-fat plain yogurt
- 2 tablespoons melted ghee or vegetable oil

Directions:

1. Ready the paste and then the masala. Heat the ghee in a big non-stick saucepan using moderate to high heat, put in the ginger-garlic paste and korma masala and cook, stirring, until a mild brown colour is achieved.
2. In a container, whip together the cream and yogurt using a whisk or an electric beater, then add it to the saucepan in a thin stream, stirring continuously to stop curdling, until it is thoroughly blended with the paste. Allow to cool, then store in an airtight vessel in the fridge seven to ten days or three months in the freezer.

SPICY YELLOW CURRY PASTE Ⓥ

This recipe is called "Masaladar peela kari masala" in Hindi

Yield: Approximately 1 cup

A delicious combination of turmeric and red chile.

Ingredients:

- ¼ cup peanut oil
- 1 large onion, crudely chopped
- 1 tablespoon fresh lime juice
- 1 teaspoon cayenne pepper
- 1 teaspoon garam masala
- 1 teaspoon ground turmeric
- 1 teaspoon salt, or to taste
- 1 to 3 fresh green chile peppers, such as serrano, crudely chopped
- 10 quarter-size slices of peeled fresh ginger
- 4 to 5 large cloves fresh garlic, peeled

Directions:

1. Using a food processor, combine and pulse the ginger, garlic, chile peppers, onion, lime juice, turmeric, cayenne pepper, garam masala, and salt until a smooth paste is achieved.
2. Heat the oil in a big non-stick wok or sauce-pan, put in the paste, and cook, stirring using moderate to high heat the first two to three minutes and then using moderate to low heat until thoroughly browned, approximately ten to twelve minutes. Allow to cool, then store in an airtight vessel about thirty days in the fridge or six months in the freezer.

TAMARIND PASTE Ⓥ

This recipe is called "Imli ras" in Hindi

Yield: Approximately 1½ cups

You can easily buy this from a store, but make your own for better flavour.

Ingredients:

- 1½ cups warm water
- 6 ounces shelled fresh tamarind pods with seeds or 5 ounces tamarind pulp without seeds

Directions:

1. Immerse the shelled tamarind pods or pulp in 1 cup of the water, one to two hours to soften. Using your fingers, softly rub and mash the tamarind to loosen the pulp from the fibrous parts and to isolate the seeds.
2. Throw away the seeds and pass the softened pulp through a fine-mesh strainer or a food mill until a smooth paste is achieved. Move the fibrous remains to a container, mix the rest of the ½ cup water into the pulp and mash once more. Then pass through the sieve or food mill to extract more paste. Combine with the already extracted paste. Store in an airtight vessel about 1 week in the fridge or freeze measured amounts into ice cube trays and store the cubes in zip closure bags up to six months in the freezer.

CHUTNEY

Chutneys are basically spicy Indian sauces. They go great with not only Indian food, but also western food! Next time you're enjoying a steak, try it with some chutney on the side!

Indian chutneys can be broadly classified into two categories: fresh and preserved. In the fresh, perishable category we find the tangy purées of fresh herbs, spices, fruits, and yogurt. These chutneys stay fresh for about ten days in a fridge. If the chutney doesn't contain yogurt, if is safe to freeze. The fresh purées keep well in a freezer too. To freeze, pour the chutneys in serving-size containers or in ice-cube trays. Once they freeze, move to plastic zip-closure bags and freeze for no more than six months. Thaw at room temperature, or if you are in a rush, using a microwave.

The story with the non-perishable chutneys is a little different. These can be stores safely even at room temperature for long periods of time.

Ⓥ= Vegan Ⓟ= Quick Pressure Cooker Recipe

GREEN CHUTNEYS

BASIC GREEN CHUTNEY Ⓥ

This recipe is called "Hari chutni" in Hindi

Yield: Approximately 1½ cups

One of the most common chutneys you will see in India. Can be enjoyed with pretty much everything, and tastes absolutely amazing!

Ingredients:

- ½ teaspoon freshly ground black pepper, or to taste
- 1 cup fresh mint leaves, trimmed
- 1 teaspoon salt, or to taste
- 1 teaspoon sugar
- 2 to 3 cups crudely chopped fresh cilantro, including soft stems
- 2 to 5 fresh green chile peppers, such as serrano, stemmed
- 3 to 4 tablespoons fresh lime or lemon juice
- 6 to 8 scallions, just the green parts, crudely chopped

Directions:

1. Using a food processor or blender, combine and pulse the green chile peppers and scallion greens until minced. Put in the mint and cilantro to the work container and process, stopping intermittently to scrub the inner walls using a spatula, until puréed. While processing, trickle the lime juice through the feeder tube into the work container and pulse the chutney until the desired smoothness is achieved.
2. Put in the sugar, salt, and pepper and process once more. Tweak the seasonings to your taste. Move to a container and serve instantly, place in

your fridge for approximately ten days, or freeze for no more than six months.

CILANTRO-LIME CHUTNEY

This recipe is called "Dhania chutni" in Hindi

Yield: Approximately 2 cups

A delicious chutney popular in all of India!

Ingredients:

- ½ cup fresh mint leaves
- ½ teaspoon cumin seeds, dry-roasted and crudely ground (See the Dry Roasting section in Introduction)
- 1 small green bell pepper, crudely chopped
- 1 teaspoon Chaat Masala (Homemade or store-bought)
- 1 teaspoon salt, or to taste
- 1 teaspoon sugar
- 2 to 3 tablespoons fresh lime or lemon juice
- 3 cups firmly packed, crudely chopped fresh cilantro, including soft stems
- 3 to 5 fresh green chile peppers, such as serrano, stemmed
- 4 quarter-size slices peeled fresh ginger
- 5 to 6 scallions, green parts only, crudely chopped

Directions:

1. Ready the cumin seeds and the chaat masala. Next, Using a food processor or a blender, blend together the green chile peppers, ginger, bell pepper, and scallion greens until minced. Put in the cilantro and mint to the work container and process, scraping the sides using a spatula a few times, until puréed. While processing, trickle the lime juice through the feeder tube into the work container and process to make a smooth chutney.
2. Put in the chaat masala, sugar, and salt and process once more. Tweak the seasonings to your taste. Move to a container and lightly stir in the cumin with some of it visible as a decoration. Serve instantly, place in your fridge for approximately ten days, or freeze for no more than six months.

MINT CHUTNEY (V)

This recipe is called "Pudina-anardana chutni" in Hindi

Yield: Approximately 1½ cups

This chutney is a breath of freshness. Easily one of the favourite chutneys in India.

Ingredients:

- ½ teaspoon freshly ground black pepper
- 1 cup crudely chopped fresh cilantro, including soft stems
- 1 small red onion, crudely chopped
- 1 tablespoon fresh lemon juice
- 1 teaspoon salt, or to taste
- 1 teaspoon sugar
- 2 cups fresh mint leaves
- 2 teaspoons ground dried pomegranate seeds
- 2 to 4 tablespoons water
- 3 to 5 crudely chopped fresh green chile peppers, such as serrano, stemmed

Directions:

1. Add the onion, chile peppers, lemon juice, and 2 tablespoons of water to a blender and pulse until the desired smoothness is achieved. Put in the mint and cilantro in 2 batches, putting in more once the first batch becomes smooth, and pulse until thoroughly smooth. Put in the rest of the 2 tablespoons of the water, if required.
2. Put in the pomegranate seeds, pepper, sugar, and salt and blend once more. Tweak the seasonings to your taste. Move to a container and serve instantly, place in your fridge for approximately ten days, or freeze for no more than six months.

MINT-GARLIC CHUTNEY (V)

This recipe is called "Pudina, lussan, moong-phalli aur imli ki chutni" in Hindi

Yield: Approximately 1½ cups

This chutney has a strong flavour, and goes great with fried snacks!

Ingredients:

- ⅛ teaspoon ground asafoetida
- ½ cup roasted peanuts, red skins removed
- 1 tablespoon peanut oil
- 1 teaspoon black mustard seeds
- 1 teaspoon salt, or to taste
- 1 teaspoon sugar
- 10 large cloves fresh garlic, peeled
- 2 cups packed fresh mint leaves
- 2 to 3 tablespoons Tamarind Paste
- 4 to 6 fresh green chile peppers, such as serrano, stemmed
- 5 to 6 fresh curry leaves

Directions:

1. Ready the tamarind paste. Next, Using a food processor or a blender, combine and pulse the peanuts, garlic, chile peppers, and mint until minced. Put in the tamarind paste, sugar, and salt and process once more until a smooth purée is achieved. Put in a spoonful or 2 of water if required for blending. Tweak the seasonings to your taste. Move to a serving container.
2. Heat the oil in a big non-stick wok or saucepan using moderate to high heat and Put in the mustard seeds; they should splutter upon contact with the hot oil, so reduce the heat and cover the pan until the spluttering diminishes. Put in the curry leaves and asafoetida, stir for approximately half a minute, move to the chutney and stir mildly to combine, with parts of it visible as a decoration. Move to a container and serve instantly, place in your fridge for approximately ten days, or freeze for no more than six months.

SCALLION-GINGER CHUTNEY

This recipe is called "Harae pyaz aur adrak ki chutni" in Hindi

Yield: Approximately 1½ cups

This chutney has an intense hot flavour.

Ingredients:

- 1 (2½-inch) piece fresh ginger, peeled and cut into thin quarter-size rounds
- 1 cup fresh mint or cilantro leaves
- 1 teaspoon salt, or to taste
- 1 teaspoon sugar
- 12 to 15 young scallions, with green parts included, crudely chopped
- 2 to 3 tablespoons fresh lime or lemon juice
- 2 to 3 tablespoons non-fat plain yogurt
- 2 to 4 fresh green chile peppers, such as serrano, stemmed

Directions:

1. Put the chile peppers, ginger, scallion greens, lemon juice, and yogurt into a food processor or a blender and process until minced.
2. Put in the sugar, salt, and mint or cilantro leaves, and process to a smooth purée. Tweak the seasonings to your taste. Move to a container and serve instantly, place in your fridge for approximately ten days, or freeze for no more than six months.

SOUTH INDIAN CILANTRO CHUTNEY

This recipe is called "Kothmir ki chutni" in Hindi

Yield: Approximately 1½ cups

A smooth South Indian chutney with an intense flavor.

Ingredients:

- ⅛ teaspoon ground asafoetida
- ¼ cup Tamarind Paste, or to taste
- 1 tablespoon dried white urad beans (dhulli urad dal), sorted
- 1 tablespoon peanut oil
- 1 teaspoon salt, or to taste
- 2 teaspoons black mustard seeds

- 3 cups firmly packed, crudely chopped fresh cilantro, including soft stems
- 4 to 6 dried red chile peppers, such as chile de arbol, crudely broken

Directions:

1. Ready the tamarind paste. Next, heat the oil in a small-sized non-stick saucepan over moderate heat and Put in the mustard seeds, red chile peppers, dal, and asafoetida. Cook, swaying the pan until the dal is golden, approximately one minute. Allow to cool and move to a blender and blend until as fine as possible.
2. Put in the tamarind paste and then Put in the cilantro in 2 or 3 batches, putting in more once the first batch becomes smooth. Add 2 to 3 tablespoons water, if required. Stir in the salt. Tweak the seasonings to your taste. Move to a container and serve instantly, place in your fridge for approximately ten days, or freeze for no more than six months.

COCONUT CHUTNEYS

FRESH COCONUT CHUTNEY WITH CILANTRO

This recipe is called "Nariyal aur dhania chutni" in Hindi

Yield: Approximately 2½ cups

Ingredients:

- ⅛ teaspoon ground asafoetida
- 1 cup crudely chopped fresh cilantro, including soft stems
- 1 cup plain yogurt, non-fat or any kind, whisked until the desired smoothness is achieved
- 1 fresh coconut
- 1 tablespoon coconut or peanut oil
- 1 teaspoon black mustard seeds

- 1 teaspoon salt, or to taste
- 2 tablespoons minced fresh curry leaves
- 2 to 3 tablespoons South Indian Sambar Powder (Homemade or store-bought)
- 3 quarter-size slices of peeled fresh ginger
- 3 tablespoons fresh lemon juice
- 3 to 5 fresh green chile peppers, such as serrano, stemmed

Directions:

1. Ready the sambar powder. Next, shell the coconut. Next, using a vegetable peeler, peel the brown skin off the flesh and discard. Crudely cut the coconut meat into ½- to 1-inch pieces. Using a food processor or a blender, combine and pulse the coconut, green chile peppers, and ginger until minced.
2. Put in the lemon juice, yogurt, and cilantro and process, scraping the sides of the work container a few times using a spatula until thoroughly smooth. Put in the salt and sambar powder and process once more. Tweak the seasonings to your taste, then move to a serving container.
3. Heat the oil in a small-sized non-stick saucepan using moderate to high heat and Put in the mustard seeds, curry leaves, and asafoetida; they should splutter upon contact with the hot oil, so reduce the heat and cover the pan until the spluttering diminishes. Swiftly add to the chutney and stir mildly with parts of it visible as a decoration. Move to a container and serve instantly, place in your fridge for approximately ten days, or freeze for no more than six months.

MINTY COCONUT-TAMARIND CHUTNEY Ⓥ

This recipe is called "Nariyal aur Imli ki chutni" in Hindi

Yield: Approximately 1½ cups

Ingredients:

- ¼ cup fresh mint leaves
- ¼ cup Tamarind Paste

- ½ cup crudely chopped fresh cilantro, including soft stems
- 1 fresh coconut
- 1 teaspoon crudely ground dry-roasted cumin seeds (See the dry-roasting section in Introduction)
- 1 teaspoon salt, or to taste
- 2 large cloves fresh garlic, peeled
- 3 to 5 fresh green chile peppers, such as serrano, stemmed
- 6 to 8 quarter-size slices peeled fresh ginger

Directions:

1. Prepare cumin and tamarind paste. Next, shell the <u>coconut</u>. Using a vegetable peeler, peel the brown skin off the meat and discard. Crudely cut the coconut meat into ½- to 1-inch pieces. Using a food processor a blender, combine and pulse the coconut, ginger, green chile peppers, and garlic until minced.
2. Put in the cilantro, mint, tamarind, and salt and process, scraping the sides of the work container a few times using a spatula, until the desired smoothness is achieved. Tweak the seasonings to your taste, then move to a serving container. Garnish with the cumin and serve instantly, place in your fridge for approximately ten days, or freeze for no more than six months.

ROASTED COCONUT CHUTNEY

This recipe is called "Bhunae nariyal ki chutni" in Hindi

Yield: Approximately 1½ cups

Ingredients:

- ½ teaspoon fenugreek seeds
- 1 cup shredded or grated unsweetened dried coconut
- 1 scant pinch ground asafoetida
- 1 tablespoon coconut or peanut oil
- 1 tablespoon coriander seeds
- 1 tablespoon dried white split urad beans (dhulli urad dal), sorted
- 1 tablespoon dried yellow split chickpea (channa dal), sorted
- 1 teaspoon black mustard seeds

- 1 teaspoon cumin seeds
- 2 large cloves fresh garlic, crudely chopped
- 2 to 3 tablespoons Tamarind Paste
- 5 to 7 fresh curry leaves
- 7 dried red chile peppers, such as chile de arbol, 5 broken and 2 with stems

Directions:

1. Ready the tamarind paste. Next, preheat the oven to 250°F. Spread the coconut on a baking tray and roast until a golden colour is achieved, 20 to 30 minutes (depending on the moisture content).
2. In a small-sized non-stick saucepan, dry-roast together the broken red chile peppers, urad and channa dals, garlic, coriander, cumin, and fenugreek over moderate heat until seems slightly darker, approximately two minutes. Allow to cool, then grind using a spice or coffee grinder, in two batches if necessary, until a fine powder is achieved. Remove spices to a container. In the same grinder, grind the coconut, in two batches if necessary, to make it as fine as possible. Mix with the spices.
3. Heat the oil in a moderate-sized non-stick wok or saucepan using moderate to high heat and Put in the whole red chile peppers and mustard seeds; they should splutter upon contact with the hot oil, so reduce the heat and cover the pan until the spluttering diminishes. Put in the asafoetida and curry leaves, then stir in the coconut-spice mixture. Put in the tamarind paste and the salt, and stir over moderate heat until well mixed. Move to a container and serve instantly, place in your fridge for approximately ten days, or freeze for no more than six months.

SEMOLINA-COCONUT CHUTNEY

This recipe is called "Sooji-kopra chutni" in Hindi

Yield: Approximately 1½ cups

Ingredients:

- ⅛ teaspoon ground asafoetida
- ⅓ cup fine-grain semolina
- ½ cup finely chopped fresh cilantro, including soft stems

- 1 cup non-fat plain yogurt
- 1 fresh green chile pepper, such as serrano, stemmed
- 1 tablespoon shredded or grated unsweetened dried coconut
- 1 teaspoon peanut oil
- 1 teaspoon salt, or to taste
- 15 to 20 fresh curry leaves
- 3 quarter-size slices of peeled fresh ginger

Directions:

1. Put the semolina and oil in a small-sized non-stick wok or saucepan and roast, stirring and swaying the pan using moderate to low heat, until the semolina is golden, approximately five minutes. Put in the coconut and asafoetida and cook, stirring, another two minutes.
2. Using a blender, mix together and pulse the yogurt, curry leaves, ginger, green chile pepper, and salt until the desired smoothness is achieved. Put in the roasted semolina and coconut mixture, and blend again until the desired smoothness is achieved. Allow to rest for approximately half an hour so the semolina can absorb the yogurt and expand. Move to a serving dish and refrigerate at least two hours. Stir in the cilantro and serve chilled. This chutney stays fresh in the fridge for approximately seven days. Do not freeze.

SHREDDED COCONUT CHUTNEY

This recipe is called "Kopra chutni" in Hindi

Yield: Approximately 1½ cups

Ingredients:

- ¼ to ⅓ cup water
- ½ cup crudely chopped fresh cilantro, including soft stems
- ½ teaspoon salt, or to taste
- ¾ cup fresh mint leaves
- 1¼ cups shredded or grated unsweetened dried coconut
- 2 fresh green chile peppers, such as serrano, stemmed
- 3 large cloves fresh garlic, peeled

- 3 to 4 tablespoons Tamarind Paste

Directions:

1. Ready the tamarind paste. Next, place the coconut in a medium size non-stick skillet and roast, stirring and swaying the pan over moderate heat until a golden colour is achieved, approximately two to three minutes.
2. Put all the rest of the ingredients using a blender or a food processor and process until a smooth purée is achieved. Stir in the roasted coconut and process once more until the desired smoothness is achieved. Move to a container and serve. This chutney stays fresh in the fridge for approximately ten days, or in the freezer about six months.

GARLIC AND CHILE PEPPER CHUTNEYS

GARLIC AND FRESH RED CHILE PEPPER CHUTNEY Ⓥ

This recipe is called "Lussan aur laal mirch ki chutni" in Hindi

Yield: Approximately 1½ cups

Ingredients:

- ¼ cup fresh lime juice, or to taste
- 1 tablespoon ground paprika
- 1 teaspoon cayenne pepper
- 1½ tablespoons ajwain seeds, crudely ground
- 15 to 20 fresh green chile peppers, such as serranos, crudely chopped
- 2 tablespoons black peppercorns, dry-roasted and ground (See the Dry Roasting section in Introduction)

- 2 to 3 red bell peppers, chopped
- 2 to 3 teaspoons salt, or to taste
- 6 to 8 large cloves fresh garlic, peeled
- 6 to 8 quarter-size slices of peeled fresh ginger

Directions:

1. Ready the peppercorns. Then place the garlic, ginger, red chile peppers, bell peppers, and lime juice Using a food processor or a blender and process until the desired smoothness is achieved. Put in the paprika, ajwain, 1½ tablespoons pepper, and the salt and process once more until the desired smoothness is achieved.
2. Move to a serving container, garnish with the rest of the pepper, and serve. This chutney stays fresh in the fridge for approximately thirty days or in the freezer about six months.
3. **Variation:** Make a simpler garlic chutney by processing together 2 large peeled heads fresh garlic, 2 teaspoons ground cayenne pepper, 1 small tomato, 1 teaspoon ground cumin seeds, and 1 teaspoon salt until a smooth paste is achieved.

GREEN GARLIC AND NUTS CHUTNEY

This recipe is called "Harae lussan aur nuts ki chutni" in Hindi

Yield: Approximately 1½ cups

Ingredients:

- ⅛ teaspoon ground asafoetida
- ¼ cup fresh lime or lemon juice, or to taste
- ¼ teaspoon ground paprika
- ½ cup fresh mint leaves
- ½ teaspoon black mustard seeds
- ½ teaspoon cumin seeds
- ½ teaspoon freshly ground black pepper, or to taste
- ¾ cup shelled and crudely chopped mixed raw nuts, such as walnuts, almonds, cashews, and pine nuts
- 1 tablespoon vegetable oil

- 1 teaspoon sugar
- 1½ cups crudely chopped fresh cilantro, including soft stems
- 1½ teaspoons salt, or to taste
- 3 to 5 fresh green chile peppers, such as serrano, stemmed
- 5 to 7 green garlic shoots (with bulbs), bottom 3 to 4 inches only, thinly chopped

Directions:

1. Using a food processor or a blender, combine and pulse the nuts, green chile peppers and garlic until minced. Put in the cilantro and mint to the work container and process, stopping intermittently to scrub the inner walls using a spatula, until puréed. While processing, trickle the lime juice through the feeder tube into the work container and pulse the chutney until the desired smoothness is achieved. Put in the sugar, salt, and black pepper and process once more. Tweak the seasonings to your taste. Move to a container.
2. Heat the oil in a big non-stick wok or saucepan using moderate to high heat and Put in the cumin and mustard seeds; they should splatter upon contact with the hot oil, so reduce the heat and cover the pan and reduce the heat until the splattering diminishes. Mix in the asafoetida and paprika just to blend, then move the spice mixture to the chutney and stir mildly to combine, with parts of it visible as a decoration. Move to a container and serve instantly, place in your fridge for approximately ten days, or freeze for no more than six months.

PEANUT AND GARLIC CHUTNEY

This recipe is called "Moong-phalli aur lassun ki chutni" in Hindi

Yield: Approximately 1½ cups

Ingredients:

- ¼ cup Tamarind Paste or lemon juice
- ½ cup dried shredded unsweetened coconut
- ½ teaspoon salt, or to taste
- 1 tablespoon peanut oil
- 1 teaspoon black mustard seeds

- 1¼ cups roasted unsalted peanuts, without red skin
- 2 large cloves fresh garlic, peeled
- 4 to 5 dried red chile peppers, such as chiles de arbol, broken
- 5 to 7 fresh curry leaves

Directions:

1. Ready the tamarind paste. Next, in a small skillet, dry-roast the red chile peppers until seems slightly darker. Put the peppers Using a food processor or a blender. Put in the peanuts and process until fine. Then Put in the coconut, garlic, tamarind (or lemon juice), and salt, and pulse until a smooth and thick paste is achieved, adding up to ¼ cup water, as needed.
2. Move to a serving container. Heat the oil in a small saucepan using moderate to high heat. Put in the mustard seeds and curry leaves; they should splutter upon contact with the hot oil, so cover the pan until the spluttering diminishes. Swiftly put in the spice mixture to the chutney and stir mildly to combine, with parts of it visible as a decoration. Move to a container and serve instantly, place in your fridge for approximately ten days, or freeze for no more than six months.

BEAN AND LEGUME CHUTNEYS

CLASSIC HYDERABADI GINGER-SESAME CHUTNEY Ⓥ

This recipe is called "Hyderabad ki adrak-til chutni" in Hindi

Yield: Approximately 1½ cups

Ingredients:

- ⅛ teaspoon ground asafoetida
- ¼ cup Tamarind Paste, or to taste

- 1 cup peeled and crudely chopped fresh ginger
- 1 large clove fresh garlic, peeled
- 1 tablespoon white sesame seeds
- 1 teaspoon black mustard seeds
- 1 teaspoon cumin seeds
- 1 teaspoon salt, or to taste
- 1 to 3 fresh green chile peppers, such as serrano, chopped with seeds
- 2 dried red chile peppers, such as chile de arbol, broken
- 2 tablespoons grated jaggery (gur)
- 2 teaspoons Indian sesame oil
- 8 to 10 fresh curry leaves

Directions:

1. Ready the tamarind paste. Next, heat the oil in a small-sized non-stick saucepan using moderate to low heat and cook the ginger, stirring, until a golden colour is achieved, approximately five minutes. Using a slotted spoon, remove the fried ginger to a blender jar, leaving the oil behind in the pan.
2. In the same oil, put in the garlic and the green and red chile peppers and cook, stirring, until a golden colour is achieved. Tilt the pan to gather the oil to one side and Put in the cumin and mustard seeds; they should splutter upon contact with the hot oil, so reduce the heat and cover the pan until the spluttering diminishes. Swiftly put in the curry leaves, sesame seeds, and asafoetida.
3. Move to the blender jar, put in the jaggery, tamarind paste, and the salt, and process until crudely puréed. Put in a tablespoon or 2 of hot water, if required, for blending. Move to a container and serve instantly, place in your fridge for approximately ten days, or freeze for no more than six months.

ROASTED BLACK CHICKPEA CHUTNEY WITH PEANUTS Ⓥ

This recipe is called "Kaalae channae ki chutni" in Hindi

Yield: Approximately 1½ cups

Ingredients:

- ¼ teaspoon salt, or to taste
- ½ cup crudely chopped fresh cilantro, including soft stems
- ½ cup dry-roasted unsalted peanuts, red skin removed
- ½ cup roasted black chickpeas (bhunae channae)
- ½ teaspoon sugar
- 1 to 2 fresh green chile peppers, such as serrano, stemmed
- 1 to 2 tablespoons fresh lime or lemon juice

Directions:

1. Rub off the black outer coating from the chickpeas (it comes off easily). Using a spice or coffee grinder, mix together and grind the chickpeas and peanuts until the desired smoothness is achieved.
2. Using a food processor or a blender, combine and pulse the cilantro, chile peppers, and lime juice, and then Put in the ground dal, peanuts, sugar, and salt. Process until well mixed. Move to a container and serve instantly, place in your fridge for approximately ten days, or freeze for no more than six months.

ROASTED DAL AND FRESH GREEN CHILE PEPPER CHUTNEY Ⓥ

This recipe is called "Bhel-puri ki chutni" in Hindi

Yield: Approximately 1½ cups

Ingredients:

- ¾ cup dried yellow split chickpeas (channa dal), sorted and washed in 3 to 4 changes of water
- 1½ teaspoons salt, or to taste
- 2 cups crudely chopped fresh cilantro, including soft stems
- 20 to 25 fresh green chile peppers, such as serrano, stemmed
- 3 to 4 tablespoons fresh lemon or lime juice
- 4 large cloves fresh garlic, peeled

Directions:

1. Put the dal in a small-sized cast-iron or non-stick skillet and dry-roast using moderate heat, stirring and swaying the pan until a golden colour is achieved, approximately a minute or two. Allow to cool, then grind using a spice or coffee grinder till you get a fine powder.
2. Put the cilantro, green chile peppers, garlic, and lemon juice using a blender or a food processor and process until the desired smoothness is achieved. Put in the ground dal and the salt and process once again to mix. Move to a container and serve instantly, place in your fridge for approximately ten days, or freeze for no more than six months.

SESAME-PEANUT CHUTNEY (V)

This recipe is called "Til aur moong-phalli ki chutni" in Hindi

Yield: Approximately 1 cup

Ingredients:

- ¼ cup hot water
- ¼ cup white sesame seeds
- ½ cup crudely chopped fresh cilantro, including soft stems
- ½ cup dry-roasted unsalted peanuts, red skins removed
- ½ cup Tamarind Paste
- 1 large clove fresh garlic, peeled
- 1 teaspoon salt, or to taste
- 1 to 3 fresh green chile peppers, such as serrano, stemmed

Directions:

1. Ready the tamarind paste. Next, in a small skillet, roast the sesame seeds over moderate heat, stirring and swaying the pan until a golden colour is achieved, approximately one minute. Move to a blender along with all the other ingredients and pulse until the desired smoothness is achieved.
2. Tweak the seasonings to your taste. Move to a container and serve instantly, place in your fridge for approximately ten days, or freeze for no more than six months.

YOGURT CHUTNEYS

YOGURT CHEESE CHUTNEY WITH MINCED GREENS

This recipe is called "Gaadhi dahi ki hari chutni" in Hindi

Yield: Approximately 1½ cups

Ingredients:

- ¼ cup minced fresh cilantro, including soft stems
- ¼ cup minced fresh mint leaves
- ¼ teaspoon ground paprika
- 1 (2-foot-square) piece of fine muslin or 4 layers of cheesecloth
- 1 fresh green chile pepper, such as serrano, minced with seeds
- 1 tablespoon peeled and minced fresh ginger
- 1 teaspoon Chaat Masala, or to taste (Homemade or store-bought)
- 1 teaspoon dry-roasted and crudely crushed cumin seeds (See the dry-roasting section in Introduction)
- 10 to 12 scallions, white parts only, minced
- 1½ cups non-fat plain yogurt
- 2 tablespoons fresh lemon juice

Directions:

1. Ready the cumin and the chaat masala. Next, place the yogurt in a colander or a fine-mesh strainer lined with muslin or 4 layers of cheesecloth set over a container. let drain about two hours in a fridge. Move to a serving container, then whisk with a fork until the desired smoothness is achieved.
2. Put in the scallion, cilantro, mint, ginger, green chile pepper, lemon juice, chaat masala, sugar, and half the cumin, and mix thoroughly. Tweak the seasonings to your taste. Garnish with the rest of the cumin seeds and the paprika, and serve instantly or place in your fridge for approximately seven days. Do not freeze.

YOGURT CHUTNEY WITH PURÉED GREENS

This recipe is called "Dahi ki hari chutni" in Hindi

Yield: Approximately 1½ cups

Ingredients:

- ½ teaspoon crudely ground black pepper
- 1 cup non-fat plain yogurt, whisked until the desired smoothness is achieved
- 1 teaspoon Chaat Masala, or to taste (Homemade or store-bought)
- 1 teaspoon salt, or to taste
- 1 to 3 fresh green chile peppers, such as serrano, stemmed
- 2 cups crudely chopped mixed fresh herbs in any proportion, such as cilantro, mint, parsley, dill, basil, or lemon basil
- 2 tablespoons fresh lime or lemon juice
- 4 quarter-size slices of peeled fresh ginger
- 5 to 6 scallions, crudely chopped
- Minced fresh greens of your choice (scallions, chile peppers, or herbs)

Directions:

1. Ready the chaat masala. Next, Using a food processor or a blender, combine and pulse the ginger, scallions, and green chile peppers until minced. Put in the fresh herbs and lime juice and process once more until the desired smoothness is achieved, scraping the sides of the work container using a spatula, as required. (If you need more liquid while processing, stir in some of the yogurt.) Put in the chaat masala, salt, and pepper, and process once more.
2. Put the yogurt in a serving container and Put in the puréed greens. Swirl lightly to combine, with parts of the greens visible as a decoration. Scatter the additional minced greens on top, and serve. This chutney stays fresh in the fridge for approximately seven days. Do not freeze.

YOGURT CHUTNEY WITH ROASTED DALS AND SPICES

This recipe is called "Dahi aur bhuni dal ki chutni" in Hindi

Yield: Approximately 1½ cups

Ingredients:

- ¼ cup grated fresh or frozen coconut
- ¼ teaspoon ground asafoetida
- ½ cup crudely chopped fresh cilantro, including soft stems
- 1 cup non-fat plain yogurt, whisked until the desired smoothness is achieved
- 1 tablespoon each, dried yellow split chickpeas (channa dal), split white urad beans (dhulli urad dal), yellow mung beans (dhulli mung dal), dry-roasted and ground (See the dry-roasting section in Introduction)
- 1 tablespoon vegetable oil
- 1 teaspoon black mustard seeds
- 1 teaspoon salt, or to taste
- 1 to 2 fresh green chile peppers, such as serrano, crudely chopped
- 15 to 20 fresh curry leaves
- 2 dried red chile peppers, such as chile de arbol, with stems, broken
- 2 tablespoons peeled and crudely chopped fresh ginger
- 2 teaspoons cumin seeds, dry-roasted and crudely ground (See the dry-roasting section in Introduction)

Directions:

1. Ready the dals and the cumin. Then heat the oil in a small-sized non-stick wok or saucepan using moderate to high heat and Put in the red chile peppers and mustard seeds; they should splutter upon contact with the hot oil, so reduce the heat and cover the pan until the spluttering diminishes.
2. Swiftly put in the asafoetida, curry leaves, green chile peppers, coconut, and ginger, and cook, stirring, until the coconut is golden, approximately five minutes. Put in the cilantro and stir another 5 minutes. Move to a blender or a food processor and process until a smooth paste is achieved.
3. Put the yogurt in a serving container, stir in the processed herb and coconut paste, then Put in the roasted dals, cumin (save some cumin for garnish), and

the salt, and stir to mix thoroughly. Sprinkle the reserved cumin on top and serve. This chutney stays fresh in the fridge for approximately seven days. Do not freeze.

YOGURT-ALMOND CHUTNEY

This recipe is called "Dahi-badaam ki chutni" in Hindi

Yield: Approximately 1½ cups

Ingredients:

- ¼ cup minced fresh cilantro, including soft stems
- ½ cup shelled and crudely ground raw almonds
- 1 cup non-fat plain yogurt, whisked until the desired smoothness is achieved
- 1 fresh green chile pepper, such as serrano, minced with seeds
- 1 tablespoon fresh lemon juice
- 1 tablespoon peeled and minced fresh ginger
- 1 teaspoon Chaat Masala (Homemade or store-bought)
- 1 teaspoon salt, or to taste
- Freshly ground black pepper, to taste

Directions:

1. In a serving container, combine all the ingredients except the chaat masala and chill at least 4 hours.
2. Before serving, ready the chaat masala then add it to the chutney and stir mildly to combine, with parts of it visible as a decoration. This chutney stays fresh about seven days in a fridge. Do not freeze.

PURÉED FRUIT CHUTNEYS

PURÉED FRESH MANGO-GINGER CHUTNEY Ⓥ

This recipe is called "Pakkae aam ki chutni" in Hindi

Yield: Approximately 1½ cups

Ingredients:

- ¼ cup finely chopped fresh cilantro, including soft stems
- ¼ cup fresh lime or lemon juice
- ½ teaspoon salt, or to taste
- 1 to 2 fresh green chile pepper, such as serrano, minced with seeds
- 2 tablespoons peeled and minced fresh ginger
- 3 large ripe mangoes (about ¾ pound each), washed and wiped dry
- Freshly ground black pepper

Directions:

1. Using a knife, peel the mango, then crudely cut the fruit around the center seed. Put the mango pieces in a big serving container and mash with a fork to make the fruit as smooth as possible.
2. Stir in all the rest of the ingredients. Garnish with black pepper and serve instantly, or place in your fridge for a maximum of seven days.

PURÉED GREEN MANGO CHUTNEY

This recipe is called "Harae aam ki chutni" in Hindi

Yield: Approximately 1½ cups

Ingredients:

- ⅛ teaspoon ground asafoetida
- ½ teaspoon crudely ground fenugreek seeds
- ½ teaspoon salt, or to taste
- 1 tablespoon peanut oil

- 1 teaspoon black mustard seeds
- 1 to 2 teaspoons sugar (not compulsory)
- 1 to 3 fresh green chile peppers, such as serrano, stemmed
- 15 to 20 fresh curry leaves
- 2 large unripe green mangoes (about ¾ pound each), washed and wiped dry
- 2 whole dried red chile peppers, such as chile de arbol
- 3 quarter-size slices peeled fresh ginger
- 4 scallions, crudely chopped

Directions:

1. Using a vegetable peeler, peel the mangoes, then cut the fruit around the center seed into ½- to 1-inch pieces. Put the mango pieces and the ginger, green chile peppers, scallions, curry leaves, and salt Using a food processor or a blender, and process until minced. Transfer to a serving container. Add some of the sugar if the chutney appears too tart.
2. Heat the oil in a small-sized non-stick saucepan using moderate to high heat and Put in the red chile peppers and mustard seeds; they should splutter upon contact with the hot oil, so reduce the heat and cover the pan until the spluttering diminishes. Swiftly put in the fenugreek seeds and asafoetida, stir for about half a minute, then add this seasoning mixture to the chutney, with parts of it visible as a decoration. Move to a container and serve instantly, place in your fridge for approximately ten days, or freeze for no more than six months.

SOUTH INDIAN TOMATO CHUTNEY

This recipe is called "South ki tamatar chutni" in Hindi

Yield: Approximately 1½ cups

Ingredients:

- ¼ cup peanut oil
- ½ cup finely chopped red onion
- ½ teaspoon black peppercorns
- 1 (15-ounce) can tomato sauce
- 1 tablespoon coriander seeds

- 1 teaspoon black mustard seeds
- 1 teaspoon cayenne pepper, or to taste
- 1 teaspoon cumin seeds
- 1 teaspoon dried curry leaves
- 1 teaspoon dried white urad beans (dhulli urad dal), sorted
- 1 teaspoon dried yellow split chickpeas (channa dal), sorted
- 1 teaspoon salt, or to taste
- 1 teaspoon Tamarind Paste
- 2 large cloves fresh garlic, minced
- 2 to 3 whole dried red chile peppers, such as chile de arbol

Directions:

1. Ready the tamarind paste. Next, in a spice or a coffee grinder, mix together and grind coriander and cumin seeds, dals, and peppercorns until a fine powder is achieved.
2. Heat the oil in a small-sized non-stick saucepan over moderate heat and Put in the mustard seeds, curry leaves, and red chile peppers; they should splutter upon contact with the hot oil, so reduce the heat and cover the pan until the spluttering diminishes. Swiftly put in the garlic and onion, stir a few seconds, then Put in the ground spice and dal mixture, cayenne pepper, and salt and cook, stirring, another two minutes.
3. Put in the tomato sauce and tamarind paste, cover the pan, reduce the heat to low, and cook, stirring intermittently, until the chutney is thick and fragrant and reduced to about 1 cup, approximately twenty minutes. Allow to cool, then serve instantly, place in your fridge for approximately sixty days or freeze about six months.

TART APPLE-GINGER CHUTNEY

This recipe is called "Saeb, adrak aur harae tamatar ki chutni" in Hindi

Yield: Approximately 2 cups

Ingredients:

- 1 tablespoon coriander seeds
- 1 tablespoon peanut oil

- 1 teaspoon black peppercorns, dry-roasted and crudely ground (See the Dry Roasting section in Introduction)
- 1 teaspoon salt, or to taste
- 1 teaspoon sugar
- 2 fresh green chile peppers, such as serrano, stemmed
- 2 large tart green apples, such as Granny Smith or pippin, cored and crudely chopped
- 2 small green tomatoes, crudely chopped
- 6 to 8 quarter-size slices of peeled fresh ginger
- Fresh cilantro sprigs

Directions:

1. Ready the peppercorns. Then heat the oil in a small saucepan using moderate to high heat and Put in the coriander seeds; they should sizzle upon contact with the hot oil. Swiftly put in the rest of the ingredients and cook, stirring, approximately five minutes.
2. Move to a food processor or a blender and process to make a coarse purée. Move to a container, garnish with cilantro sprigs, and serve. This chutney stays fresh in the fridge for approximately ten days, and in the freezer about six months.

PRESERVED CHUTNEYS

CRANBERRY CHUTNEY PRESERVE Ⓥ

This recipe is called "Karonda chutni" in Hindi

Yield: Approximately 4 cups

Ingredients:

- 1 tablespoon ground ginger
- 1 tablespoon vegetable oil

- 10 to 12 whole cloves
- 1½ teaspoons salt, or to taste
- 2 (12-ounce) packages fresh cranberries, washed
- 2 (1-inch) sticks cinnamon
- 2 tablespoons <u>Bengali 5-Spices</u> (Panch-Phoran), crudely ground
- 2 tablespoons peeled and minced fresh ginger
- 4 cups sugar
- 4 cups water
- 5 to 7 tablespoons distilled white vinegar
- 8 to 10 black cardamom pods, crushed lightly to break the skin

Directions:

1. Ready the 5-spices. Next, heat the oil in a big non-reactive wok or saucepan using moderate to high heat and cook the cinnamon, cardamom pods, and cloves, stirring, approximately half a minute.
2. Put in the fresh ginger and panch-phoran and cook, stirring, approximately one minute. Put in the cranberries, sugar, water, ground ginger, and salt, and bring to a boil using high heat. Cover and cook, stirring intermittently, until slightly thickened, approximately 7 minutes.
3. Reduce the heat to medium, uncover the pan, put in the vinegar, and cook until the chutney is quite thick, approximately ten minutes. (Do not make the chutney very thick; it will thicken as it cools.) Move to a container, allow to cool down, and serve at room temperature, or refrigerate at least two hours and serve chilled. This chutney stays fresh in the fridge for approximately three months, or in the freezer about 1 year.

FRAGRANT MANGO CHUTNEY PRESERVE Ⓥ

This recipe is called "Aam ki chutni" in Hindi

Yield: Approximately 4 cups

Ingredients:

- ¾ cup distilled white vinegar

- 1 tablespoon black peppercorns
- 1 tablespoon fennel seeds
- 1 tablespoon fenugreek seeds
- 1 tablespoon salt, or to taste
- 1 tablespoon whole cloves
- 10 to 12 black cardamom pods, crushed lightly to break the skin
- 10 to 12 green cardamom pods, crushed lightly to break the skin
- 1½ teaspoons kalonji seeds
- 2 (3-inch) sticks cinnamon, broken
- 4 cups sugar
- 4 large unripe green mangoes, (about ¾ pound each), washed and wiped dry

Directions:

1. Using a vegetable peeler, peel the mangoes, then cut the fruit around the center seed into thin 1½- to 2-inch long pieces. Put all the spices in a large, heavy, non-reactive saucepan and roast using moderate to high heat, stirring and swaying the pan, until heated through, approximately one minute.
2. Put in the mangoes, sugar, and salt, and bring to a boil, stirring continuously using moderate to high heat until the sugar melts and comes to a boil. Boil 1 minute, then reduce the heat to medium-low, cover the pan and cook, stirring intermittently, approximately ten minutes.
3. Uncover the pan, put in the vinegar, and cook, stirring intermittently, until the sugar caramelizes and takes on a rich honey-like color and consistency, approximately twenty minutes. (Do not make the chutney very thick; it will thicken as it cools.)
4. Allow to cool completely, then put it in sterile jars. This chutney does not need to be refrigerated. It stays fresh about six months at room temperature. The color deepens over time, but that does not affect the taste.

RED TOMATO CHUTNEY PRESERVE

This recipe is called "Tamatar-til ki chutni" in Hindi

Yield: Approximately 2 cups

Ingredients:

- ⅛ teaspoon ground asafoetida
- ¼ teaspoon ground turmeric
- 1 cup finely chopped onion
- 1 tablespoon black mustard seeds
- 1 tablespoon dried split pigeon peas (toor dal), sorted
- 1 tablespoon dried yellow split chickpeas (channa dal), sorted
- 1 tablespoon minced fresh garlic cloves
- 1 tablespoon sesame seeds, dry-roasted (See the dry-roasting section in Introduction)
- 1 teaspoon salt, or to taste
- 1 to 3 fresh green chile peppers, such as serrano, minced with seeds
- 2 large tomatoes, finely chopped
- 2 tablespoons distilled white vinegar
- 2 tablespoons minced fresh curry leaves
- 2 tablespoons peanut oil
- 2 tablespoons peeled and minced fresh ginger

Directions:

1. Ready the sesame seeds. Next, heat the oil in a medium wok or saucepan using moderate to high heat and Put in the mustard seeds; they should splutter upon contact with the hot oil, so reduce the heat and cover the pan until the spluttering diminishes. Put in the curry leaves and both the dals, and stir until the dals are golden, approximately half a minute. Put in the onion and cook, stirring, until a golden colour is achieved, approximately three minutes. Put in the ginger, garlic, and green chile peppers, stir 1 minute, then stir in the turmeric, salt, and asafoetida.
2. Put in the tomatoes and vinegar and cook until most of the fluids vaporize and the chutney is semi-thick, approximately eight to ten minutes. (It will continue to thicken as it cools.) Move to a serving dish, garnish with the sesame seeds, and serve hot or cold, or store in an airtight vessel in the refrigerator, approximately 1 year.

SPICY APPLE-GINGER CHUTNEY PRESERVE Ⓥ

This recipe is called "Saeb-adrak ki chutni" in Hindi

Yield: Approximately 4 cups

Ingredients:

- ¼ cup distilled white vinegar
- 10 whole cloves
- 1½ tablespoons salt
- 2 cups sugar
- 2 medium onions, cut in half along the length and thinly chopped
- 2 pounds tart apples, such as Pippin or Granny Smith, peeled and cut in ½-inch pieces
- 2 tablespoons Basic Ginger-Garlic Paste (Homemade or store-bought)
- 2 tablespoons fennel seeds
- 2 teaspoons crudely ground fenugreek seeds
- 2 teaspoons kalonji seeds
- 2 to 3 teaspoons cayenne pepper
- 20 to 25 dried red chile peppers, such as chile de arbol, with stems
- 3 tablespoons vegetable oil
- 4 (1-inch) sticks cinnamon
- 5 to 6 (1-inch) pieces peeled fresh ginger, cut in half along the length and thinly chopped
- 6 fresh garlic cloves, cut in half along the length and thinly chopped
- 6 to 8 black cardamom pods, crushed lightly to break the skin

Directions:

1. Ready the ginger-garlic paste. Next, heat the oil in a big non-stick wok or saucepan using moderate to high heat and cook the red chile peppers, cinnamon, cardamom pods, and cloves, stirring, approximately one minute. Put in the fennel and kalonji seeds, and stir for approximately half a minute, then Put in the onion, ginger, and garlic and cook, stirring until a golden colour is achieved, approximately ten minutes.

2. Put in the fenugreek seeds and cayenne pepper and stir 1 minute. Then Put in the apples, sugar, ginger-garlic paste, and salt, and cook over moderate heat, stirring, until the sugar melts, approximately three minutes. Increase the heat to medium-high and cook until the sugar caramelizes into a rich golden color, the apples are soft, and the chutney is thick, approximately fifteen minutes.
3. Put in the vinegar and boil using high heat approximately two minutes, or until the chutney thickens once more. (Do not make the chutney very thick; it will thicken as it cools.) Allow to cool completely and put in sterile jars. This chutney does not need to be refrigerated. It stays fresh about six months at room temperature. The color deepens over time, but that does not affect the taste.

SPICY APRICOT CHUTNEY PRESERVE

This recipe is called "Aadu ki chutni" in Hindi

Yield: Approximately 4 cups

Ingredients:

- ¼ cup Basic Ginger-Garlic Paste (Homemade or store-bought)
- ¼ to ⅓ cup distilled white vinegar
- ¾ teaspoon ground fenugreek seeds
- 1 tablespoon ground fennel seeds
- 1 teaspoon kalonji seeds
- 1½ cups sugar
- 2 pounds fresh unripe apricots, pitted and cut into wedges
- 2 tablespoons salt, or to taste
- 3 (1-inch) sticks cinnamon
- 3 small onions, cut in half along the length and thinly chopped
- 3 tablespoons vegetable oil
- 5 to 7 fresh green chile peppers, such as serrano, minced with seeds
- 6 to 8 black cardamom pods, crushed lightly to break the skin
- 8 whole cloves

Directions:

1. Ready the ginger-garlic paste. Next, heat the oil in a big non-stick wok or saucepan using moderate to high heat and cook the cinnamon, cardamom pods, and cloves, stirring, approximately one minute. Put in the onions and cook, stirring, until a golden colour is achieved, approximately 7 minutes. Put in the kalonji, fenugreek, and fennel seeds, and then stir in the ginger-garlic paste and green chile peppers and sauté approximately two minutes.
2. Put in the apricots, sugar, and salt and cook, stir-ring, over moderate heat until the sugar melts, approximately three minutes. Increase the heat to medium-high and cook until the sugar caramelizes into a rich golden color, the apricots are soft, and the chutney is thick, approximately fifteen minutes.
3. Put in the vinegar, and boil using high heat approximately two minutes, or until the chutney thickens once more. (Do not make the chutney very thick; it will thicken as it cools.) Allow to cool completely, and put in sterile jars. This chutney does not need to be refrigerated. It stays fresh about six months at room temperature. The color deepens over time, but that does not affect the taste.

TOMATO CHUTNEY PRESERVE

This recipe is called "Tamatar, kaaju aur kishmish ki chutni" in Hindi

Yield: Approximately 2 cups

Ingredients:

- ½ cup crudely chopped raw cashews
- ½ cup distilled white vinegar
- ½ cup golden raisins
- ½ teaspoon crudely crushed fenugreek seeds
- ½ teaspoon cayenne pepper
- 1 tablespoon salt, or to taste
- 1 tablespoon vegetable oil
- 1 teaspoon fennel seeds
- 1 teaspoon ground paprika
- 2 cups sugar, or more to taste
- 2 large fresh garlic cloves, minced
- 2 tablespoons peeled and minced fresh ginger

- 2 to 4 fresh green chile peppers, minced with seeds
- 3 large tomatoes, finely chopped (about 1½ pounds)

Directions:

1. Heat the oil in a big non-reactive wok or saucepan over moderate heat and cook the ginger, garlic, green chile peppers, fennel seeds and fenugreek seeds, stirring, until a golden colour is achieved, approximately one minute. Put in the cashews and raisins and stir until the raisins expand, approximately one minute.
2. Put in the tomatoes, sugar, salt, paprika, and cayenne pepper and cook, using moderate to high heat for the first two to three minutes. Then cover the pan and cook, stirring intermittently, over moderate heat until the tomatoes are very soft, approximately ten minutes. Put in the vinegar, and simmer, uncovered, until semi-thick, approximately fifteen minutes. (It will continue to thicken as it cools.) Serve instantly or allow to cool down, then store in an airtight vessel in the refrigerator, approximately 1 year.

SONTH CHUTNEYS

These are delicious sweet and sour chutneys commonly seen in Indian restaurants.

MINTY SONTH CHUTNEY WITH MANGO

This recipe is called "Pudina sonth" in Hindi

Yield: Approximately 4 cups

Ingredients:

- ½ teaspoon black salt
- ½ teaspoon ground ginger
- 1 cup crudely grated or crushed jaggery, or 1¼ cup dark brown sugar

- 1 cup mango or tamarind powder, sifted to remove any lumps
- 1 teaspoon ground paprika
- 1 to 3 fresh green chile peppers, such as serrano, stemmed
- 1½ tablespoons cumin seeds, dry-roasted and crudely ground (See the dry-roasting section in Introduction)
- 2 tablespoons <u>Chaat Masala</u> (Homemade or store-bought)
- 2 teaspoon salt, or to taste
- 20 to 25 large fresh mint leaves
- 3 to 4 cups water
- 8 quarter-size slices of peeled fresh ginger

Directions:

1. Ready the cumin seeds and chaat masala. Next, in a blender, mix together and pulse the ginger, chile peppers, mint leaves with about ½ cup of the water until a smooth paste is achieved.
2. In a large non-reactive saucepan, combine the jaggery and 3 cups of the water (disregard any lumps; they will melt when heated) and bring to a boil, stirring intermittently, until all the lumps dissolve completely, about three to four minutes. Pass through a fine-mesh strainer to filter out any impurities. Put the jaggery back into the saucepan and Put in the ginger-mint mixture, mango or tamarind powder, chaat masala, paprika, ground ginger, cumin, salt, and black salt.
3. Bring to a boil using high heat. Reduce the heat to moderate to low, and simmer, stirring intermittently, approximately five minutes. The sauce should be like a semi-thick batter. Stir in up to 1 cup of water if the sauce becomes thick too swiftly. Adjust seasoning, move to a container, then allow to cool down. Serve at room temperature. Or move to an airtight vessel and place in your fridge for approximately sixty days, or freeze about 1 year.

SONTH CHUTNEY WITH DRIED MANGO SLICES Ⓥ Ⓟ

This recipe is called "Amchur ki sonth" in Hindi

Yield: Approximately 4 cups

Ingredients:

- 1 (2-inch) piece dried ginger, crudely chopped
- 1 cup crudely grated or crushed jaggery, or 1¼ cups dark brown sugar
- 1 tablespoon Chaat Masala, or to taste (Homemade or store-bought)
- 1 tablespoon cumin seeds, dry-roasted and finely ground (See the dry-roasting section in Introduction)
- 1 teaspoon black salt
- 1 teaspoon ground paprika
- 2 teaspoons salt, or to taste
- 4 cups water
- 4 ounces dried raw mango slices
- 4 to 6 dried red chile peppers, such as chile de arbol, broken

Directions:

1. Ready the cumin seeds and chaat masala. Next, place everything (except 1 cup of the water) into your pressure cooker. Ensure that the lid is secure, and cook using high heat until the regulator shows that the pressure is high, then cook for approximately a minute more. Take the pot off the heat or turn off the heat and let the pressure release automatically, twelve to fifteen minutes. Cautiously take the lid off.
2. Pass everything through a food mill into a big container to extract a smooth sauce. Bring the reserved one cup of water to a boil in a small saucepan. Pour the boiling hot water over the fibrous residue in the food mill and collect the rest of the pulp. Mix the extra pulp into the sauce; it should be like a semi-thick batter. Tweak the seasonings to your taste, move to a container and serve at room temperature, or move to an airtight vessel and place in your fridge for approximately sixty days, or freeze about 1 year.

SONTH CHUTNEY WITH FRESH AND DRIED FRUITS Ⓥ

This recipe is called "Fallon vaali sonth" in Hindi

Yield: Approximately 4 cups

Ingredients:

- 1 cup crudely grated or crushed jaggery, or 1¼ cups dark brown sugar
- 1 cup finely chopped mixed dried fruits, such as raisins, peaches, apricots, plums, figs, and dates
- 1 cup mango or tamarind powder, sifted to remove lumps
- 1 tablespoon peeled and finely minced fresh ginger
- 1 tablespoon vegetable oil
- 1 teaspoon black salt
- 1 teaspoon cumin seeds
- 1 teaspoon ground paprika
- 1 to 2 cups chopped ripe fruits, such as bananas, mangoes, pineapple, and peaches
- 1½ cups water + 4 cups water, measured separately
- 2 tablespoons Chaat Masala, or to taste (Homemade or store-bought)
- 2 tablespoons cumin seeds, dry-roasted and ground (See the dry-roasting section in Introduction)
- 2 teaspoons ground ginger
- 2 teaspoons salt, or to taste

Directions:

1. Immerse the dried fruits overnight in 1½ cups of the water. In the meantime, ready the cumin seeds and chaat masala. When ready, drain the fruits, reserving the water.
2. In a large non-reactive saucepan, combine the jaggery and 2 cups of the water (disregard any lumps; they will melt when heated), and bring to a boil using high heat, stirring intermittently, until all the lumps dissolve completely, about three to four minutes. Pass through a fine-mesh strainer to filter out any impurities. Return to the pan. Stir in the mango or tamarind powder and up to 2 cups water, including the reserved fruit-water in this measurement. Mix thoroughly and bring to a boil using high heat.
3. Put in the drained dried fruits, fresh and dried ginger, chaat masala, salt, and black salt, reduce the heat to moderate to low, and simmer, stirring intermittently and pouring in additional water if the sauce becomes thick too swiftly, until it reaches a semi-thick batter-like consistency, approximately ten minutes. Tweak the seasonings to your taste and move to a serving container.

4. Heat the oil in a big non-stick wok or saucepan using moderate to high heat and Put in the cumin seeds; they should sizzle upon contact with the hot oil. Swiftly, take the pan off the heat, put in the paprika, and Combine with the chutney. Serve at room temperature, or move to an airtight vessel and place in your fridge for approximately sixty days, or freeze for approximately a year. Just before serving, stir in ripe fruits and serve.

SWEET SONTH CHUTNEY WITH DATES

This recipe is called "Khajjur ki sonth" in Hindi

Yield: Approximately 4 cups

Ingredients:

- ½ cup seedless tamarind pulp
- ½ to ¾ cup sugar
- 1 teaspoon salt, or to taste
- 1½ tablespoons cumin seeds, dry-roasted and crudely ground (See the dry-roasting section in Introduction)
- 2 cups chopped pitted dates
- 2 cups hot water

Directions:

1. Ready the cumin seeds. Immerse the dates and tamarind pulp in 1 cup hot water, approximately one hour to soften.
2. Using your sanitized fingers, mush the pulp to separate it from the fibrous parts of the dates and to separate any tamarind seeds that may still be present. Next, pass the softened date-tamarind pulp through a fine-mesh strainer or a food mill into a big container to extract a smooth paste. Pour the rest of the hot water over the fibrous residue in the food mill and collect the rest of the pulp and Combine with the already extracted paste.
3. Move to a small saucepan, put in the sugar, cumin, and salt, and bring to a boil using high heat. Reduce the heat to moderate to low and simmer approximately five minutes. Stir in up to 1 cup of water if the chutney

becomes thick too swiftly. Adjust the seasoning, then allow to cool down. Serve at room temperature, or move to an airtight vessel and place in your fridge for approximately sixty days, or freeze about a year.

INDIAN PICKLES

Pickles are highly popular in India. Most of the Indian households make their own pickles at home, and in bulk to last a year. Mango, lemon, and green chiles are three of the most popular pickle ingredients. Indian pickles have a long shelf life, and a few of the pickles can even last for a decade!

MANGO PICKLES

Mango pickles are the most common pickles you will find in India. It is virtually impossible to find a household where there is no mango pickle.

QUICK MANGO PICKLE (V)

This recipe is called "Aam ka achaar" in Hindi

Yield: Approximately 2 cups

The mangoes are peeled for this recipe to hasten the process.

Ingredients:

- ⅛ teaspoon ground asafoetida
- 1 cup mustard or olive oil
- 1 tablespoon salt, or to taste
- 1 teaspoon black peppercorns, crudely ground
- 1 teaspoon ground turmeric

- 2 large unripe green mangoes (about ¾ pound each), washed and wiped dry
- 2 tablespoons Bengali Five Whole Spice Blend (Panch-Phoran), crudely ground (see basic spice blends section to create your own, or buy from a store)
- 3 large cloves fresh garlic, crudely chopped

Directions:

1. Ready the 5-spices. Next, using a vegetable peeler, peel the mango, then cut the fruit around the center seed into thin ½-inch-by-2-inch pieces. Heat the oil in a big non-stick wok or saucepan using moderate to high heat and put in the garlic, panch-phoran, peppercorns, turmeric, and asafoetida. They should sizzle when they touch the hot oil.
2. Swiftly put in the mangoes and the salt, decrease the heat to medium and cook, stirring, until the mangoes absorb all the flavours, fifteen to twenty minutes. Allow to cool and let marinate at room temperature for minimum two days before you serve. Store in the fridge for approximately one month. Serve chilled or at room temperature.

PUNJABI MANGO PICKLE

This recipe is called "Punjabi aam ka achaar" in Hindi

Yield: Approximately 6 cups

A classic mango pickle from my hometown!

Ingredients:

- ¼ cup fenugreek seeds
- ½ cup fennel seeds
- ½ cup salt, or to taste
- 1 small piece of muslin or 4 layers of cheesecloth (sufficient to cover the mouth of the jar)
- 1½ to 2 cups mustard oil or olive oil
- 2 tablespoons black peppercorns
- 2 tablespoons kalonji seeds
- 2 teaspoons cayenne pepper, or to taste

- 2 teaspoons ground turmeric
- 4 large unripe green mangoes (about ¾ pound each), washed and wiped dry

Directions:

1. Cut each unpeeled mango around the center seed into 1-inch-by-½-inch pieces. Throw away the center seeds. Using a spice or coffee grinder, very crudely mix together and grind all the whole spices. Move to a container and stir in the salt, turmeric, and cayenne pepper.
2. Heat the oil in a big non-stick wok or saucepan using moderate to high heat until just smoking, and put in the spice mixture. It should sizzle when it touches the hot oil. Turn off the heat and stir, approximately half a minute. Put in the mangoes and mix thoroughly, making sure all the pieces are thoroughly coated with the spices.
3. Allow to cool and move to a big sanitized glass jar. Make sure there is minimum ½ inch of oil on the surface. (Heat and add more oil, if required.) Cover the jar with the muslin, locking it using a rubber band, and if there is a warm sunny spot in the kitchen, put it there, else put it outdoors where there it can get some sun, swaying the jar a couple of times per day until the spices are plump and soft and the mango pieces are crisp-tender, about ten to twelve days. (bring the jar indoors in the evening if you're keeping it outdoors.) This pickle can be stored safely at room temperature for approximately two years.

MANGO PICKLE SPICE ROAST

This recipe is called "Bhuna Masala aam ka achaar" in Hindi

Yield: Approximately 6 cups

Basically the same recipe as the Punjabi mango pickle, with an added punch of roasted spices!

Ingredients:

- ¼ cup fenugreek seeds
- ½ cup salt
- ⅔ cup fennel seeds

- 1 small piece of muslin or 4 layers of cheesecloth (sufficient to cover the mouth of the jar)
- 1½ cups mustard or olive oil
- 2 tablespoons black peppercorns
- 2 tablespoons kalonji seeds
- 2 teaspoons cayenne pepper, or to taste
- 2 teaspoons ground paprika
- 2 teaspoons ground turmeric
- 4 large unripe green mangoes (about ¾ pound each), washed and wiped dry

Directions:

1. Cut each unpeeled mango around the center seed into 1-inch-by-½-inch pieces. Throw away the center seeds.
2. Put the fennel, fenugreek, kalonji, and peppercorns in a heavy cast-iron skillet and dry-roast the spices, stirring and swaying the pan over moderate heat, until slightly darker and fragrant, approximately three minutes. Allow to cool and move to a spice or coffee grinder, and grind crudely. Move to a container and stir in the salt, turmeric, paprika, and cayenne pepper.
3. Heat the oil in a moderate-sized non-stick wok or saucepan using moderate to high heat until just smoking. Allow to cool until just lukewarm, then Put in the spice mixture and the mangoes and mix thoroughly, ensuring all the pieces are thoroughly coated with the spices.
4. Move to a big sanitized glass jar. Make sure there is minimum ½ inch of oil on the surface. Cover the jar with the muslin, locking it using a rubber band, and if there is a warm sunny spot in the kitchen, put it there, else put it outdoors where there it can get some sun, swaying the jar a couple of times per day until the spices are plump and soft and the mango pieces are crisp-tender, about ten to twelve days. (bring the jar indoors in the evening if you're keeping it outdoors.) This pickle can be stored safely at room temperature for approximately two years.

COOKED SOUTH INDIAN MANGO PICKLE Ⓥ

This recipe is called "Dakshini aam ka achaar" in Hindi

Yield: Approximately 2 cups

As the name suggests, this pickle is cooked, and not sun-cured like the others.

Ingredients:

- ¼ teaspoon ground asafoetida
- ⅓ cup mustard or peanut oil
- ½ teaspoon ground turmeric
- 2 large unripe green mangoes (about ¾ pound each), washed and wiped dry
- 2 tablespoons salt
- 2 teaspoons black mustard seeds, crudely ground
- 2 teaspoons fenugreek seeds
- 3 to 5 dried red chile peppers, such as chile de arbol, broken

Directions:

1. Cut each unpeeled mango around the center seed into 1-inch-by-½-inch pieces. Throw away the center seeds. Put the mango in a container, put in the turmeric, and toss to mix thoroughly.
2. In a small skillet, roast the red chile peppers and fenugreek seeds over moderate heat until a golden colour is achieved, approximately one minute. Allow to cool and grind using a spice or coffee grinder till you get a fine powder.
3. Heat the oil in a big non-stick wok or saucepan using high heat, put in the mustard seeds and asafoetida, and stir approximately one minute. Put in the mangoes, ground chile-fenugreek mixture, and salt, and cook using high heat, approximately one minute.
4. Reduce the heat to moderate to low, cover the pan and cook, stirring intermittently, until the mangoes are soft, approximately fifteen minutes. Allow to cool and move to a big sanitized jar. This pickle can be stored safely at room temperature for approximately seven days or approximately three months in a fridge. Serve chilled or at room temperature.

GRATED MANGO PICKLE Ⓥ

This recipe is called "Kaddukas aam ka achaar" in Hindi

Yield: Approximately 2 cups

Ingredients:

- ¼ teaspoon ground asafoetida
- ⅓ cup peanut oil
- 1 tablespoon black mustard seeds
- 1 teaspoon cayenne pepper, or to taste
- 1 teaspoon ground fenugreek seeds
- 3 large unripe green mangoes (about ¾ pound each), washed and wiped dry
- 5 to 7 dried red chile peppers, such as chile de arbol, broken

Directions:

1. Using a vegetable peeler, peel the mangoes, then grate the fruit around the center seed of each mango. Throw away the center seeds. Put the fenugreek and asafoetida in a small-sized cast-iron skillet and roast using moderate heat, stirring and swaying the pan, until seems slightly darker, approximately one minute.
2. Heat the oil in a big non-stick wok or saucepan using moderate to high heat, put in the red chile peppers and cook, stirring, until seems slightly darker, approximately one minute. Put in the mustard seeds; they should splutter when they touch the hot oil, so reduce the heat and cover the pan until the spluttering diminishes.
3. Put in the grated mango and cayenne pepper and cook, stirring, until a golden colour is achieved, approximately five to seven minutes. Stir in the roasted fenugreek and asafoetida, stir approximately one minute and remove from the heat. Allow to cool and move to a big sanitized jar. This pickle stays fresh approximately seven days at room temperature or approximately six months in a fridge. Serve chilled or at room temperature.

LIME AND LEMON PICKLES

BASIC LEMON PICKLE

This recipe is called "Nimboo ka achaar" in Hindi

Yield: Approximately 4 cups

Ingredients:

- ¼ cup salt
- ½ cup peeled and minced fresh ginger
- 1 small piece muslin or 4 layers cheesecloth (sufficient to cover the mouth of the jar)
- 2 tablespoons crudely crushed ajwain seeds
- 20 to 24 fresh limes (about 2 pounds)
- 4 cups fresh lime or lemon juice (from 20 additional limes)

Directions:

1. Rinse and wipe dry the limes. Cut each one into 8 wedges and place in a big sterile glass jar. Stir in the ginger, salt, and ajwain seeds, cover the jar using the palm of your hand or the lid, and shake rapidly to combine.
2. Uncover, put in the lime juice, and shake the jar once more. (The juice should cover the limes by about ½ inch; if not, add some more lime juice.) Cover the jar with the muslin, locking it using a rubber band, and if there is a warm sunny spot in the kitchen, put it there, else put it outdoors where there it can get some sun. (bring the jar indoors in the evening if you're keeping it outdoors.)
3. Sway the jar a couple of times per day, until the lime wedges are soft and light buff in color, and the juices are thick, fifteen to twenty days. This pickle can be stored safely at room temperature for more than a decade!.

SWEET AND SOUR FRESH LIME PICKLE

This recipe is called "Khatta-meetha nimboo ka achaar" in Hindi

Yield: Approximately 4 cups

Ingredients:

- ¼ cup salt
- 1 cup sugar
- 1 small piece muslin or 4 layers cheesecloth (sufficient to cover the mouth of the jar)
- 1½ to 2 tablespoons cayenne pepper, or to taste
- 2 tablespoons ajwain seeds, crudely ground
- 20 fresh limes (about 2 pounds)
- 4 cups fresh lime or lemon juice (from 20 additional limes)

Directions:

1. Rinse and wipe dry the limes. Cut each one into 8 wedges, and place in a big sterile glass jar. Stir in the sugar, salt, cayenne pepper, and ajwain seeds, cover the jar using the palm of your hand or the lid, and shake rapidly to combine.
2. Uncover, put in the lime juice, and shake the jar once more. (The juice should cover the limes by about ½ inch; if not, add some more lime juice.) Cover the jar with the muslin, locking it using a rubber band, and if there is a warm sunny spot in the kitchen, put it there, else put it outdoors where there it can get some sun. (bring the jar indoors in the evening if you're keeping it outdoors.)
3. Sway the jar a couple of times per day, until the lime or lemon wedges are soft and light buff in color, and the juices are thick, fifteen to twenty days. This pickle can be stored safely at room temperature for more than a decade!.

CRUSHED LEMON AND FRESH RED CHILE PEPPER PICKLE Ⓥ

This recipe is called "Pissa nimboo-laal mirch ka achaar" in Hindi

Yield: Approximately 2 cups

Ingredients:

- ¼ cup salt

- 1 small piece muslin or 4 layers cheesecloth (sufficient to cover the mouth of the jar)
- 1 tablespoon ajwain seeds, crudely ground
- 12 to fifteen fresh red or green chile peppers, stemmed
- 12 to fifteen thin-skinned, seedless lemons or limes (about 1 pound)

Directions:

1. Rinse and wipe dry the lemons or limes, then crudely cut them, with the rind, and remove any seeds. Move to a food processor, along with the chile peppers, and process until minced.
2. Put in the ajwain seeds and salt, and process once more until the desired smoothness is achieved. Move to a sterile glass jar. Cover the jar with the muslin, locking it using a rubber band, and if there is a warm sunny spot in the kitchen, put it there, else put it outdoors where there it can get some sun. (bring the jar indoors in the evening if you're keeping it outdoors.)
3. Sway the jar a couple of times per day, until the pickle is light buff in color and the juices are thick, approximately seven days. This pickle can be stored safely at room temperature for approximately a year.

GINGER-LEMON PICKLE (V)

This recipe is called "Adrak nimboo" in Hindi

Yield: Approximately 2 cups

Ingredients:

- ½ pound fresh ginger, peeled and cut into 2-inch matchsticks
- 1 tablespoon salt
- 1½ cups fresh lemon or lime juice (from 7 to 10 limes)
- 2 teaspoons ajwain seeds, crudely crushed

Directions:

1. Put the ginger in a big non-reactive container. Put in the salt and mix thoroughly. Let sit for about two hours at room temperature. (By then the

salt will have drawn out the juices from the ginger, and the container will have a fair amount of juice.)
2. Put in the ajwain seeds and lemon juice and set aside at room temperature until the ginger sticks are pink, 2 to four hours. Move to a sanitized glass jar and store in the refrigerator, approximately six months. Serve chilled or at room temperature.

MINCED GINGER-LIME PICKLE

This recipe is called "Pissa hua adrak nimboo ka achaar" in Hindi

Yield: Approximately 2 cups

Ingredients:

- ¼ cup salt, or to taste
- 1 cup fresh lime juice (from 5 to 7 limes)
- 1 pound fresh ginger, peeled and cut crosswise into thin round slices
- 1½ tablespoons ajwain seeds, crudely ground
- 15 to 20 fresh green chile peppers, such as serrano, crudely chopped

Directions:

1. Using a food processor or a blender, combine and pulse the ginger and green chile peppers until minced.
2. Move to a big sanitized jar and add all the rest of the ingredients. Cover the jar using the palm of your hand or the lid and shake rapidly to combine.
3. Allow to sit at room temperature about four hours. This pickle stays fresh about six months in a fridge. Served chilled or at room temperature.

GREEN CHILE PEPPER PICKLES

VINEGAR-MARINATED GREEN CHILE PEPPERS Ⓥ

This recipe is called "Sirkae vaali hari mirch" in Hindi

Yield: Approximately 1½ cups

Ingredients:

- ½ cup distilled white vinegar
- 1 tablespoon dried mint leaves
- 1 tablespoon salt, or to taste
- 1 tablespoon sugar
- 1 tablespoon Tamarind Paste
- 15 to 20 fresh green chile peppers, such as serrano, thinly chopped

Directions:

1. Ready the tamarind paste. Next, place the chile peppers in a small non-reactive container. Put in the salt and mix thoroughly. Let sit for about two hours at room temperature. (By then the salt will have drawn out the juices from the chile peppers, and the container will have a fair amount of juice.)
2. Stir in the vinegar, tamarind paste, sugar, and mint. Refrigerate at least 24 hours before using. Next, move to a sanitized glass jar and store in the fridge for approximately a year. Serve chilled or at room temperature.

PICKLED CHILE PEPPER WITH TAMARIND Ⓥ

This recipe is called "Hari mirch aur imli ka achaar" in Hindi

Yield: Approximately 1½ cups

Ingredients:

- ¼ cup white urad beans (dhulli urad dal), dry-roasted and crudely ground (See the dry-roasting section in Introduction)
- ⅓ cup Tamarind Paste
- ½ pound fresh green chile peppers, such as serranos, crudely chopped
- 1 large clove fresh garlic, chopped
- 1 tablespoon cumin seeds
- 1 tablespoon sesame seeds, dry-roasted and crudely ground (See the dry-roasting section in Introduction)
- 1 tablespoon sugar
- 1¼ cups water
- 1½ teaspoons salt, or to taste
- 2 tablespoons coriander seeds

Directions:

1. Ready the dal, sesame seeds, and tamarind paste. Next, place the green chile peppers, dal, garlic, tamarind paste, and water in a non-stick saucepan and bring to a boil using high heat. Reduce the heat to moderate to low, cover the pan and cook approximately five minutes. Put in the coriander, cumin, sugar, and salt, and continue to cook until the peppers are soft, approximately eight to ten minutes.
2. Move to a food processor or a blender and process until a smooth paste is achieved. Transfer to a serving container, lightly stir in the sesame seeds with some of them visible as a decoration, and serve. Or move to a sanitized glass jar and store in the fridge for approximately six months. Serve chilled or at room temperature.

FIERY GREEN CHILE PEPPER PICKLE

This recipe is called "Prabha ka hari mirch ka achaar" in Hindi

Yield: Approximately 1½ cups

If you like it hot, this might be the pickle for you!

Ingredients:

- ½ cup mustard or peanut oil

- ½ teaspoon ground turmeric
- 1 pound fresh green chile peppers, such as serrano, cut into ¼-inch diagonal slices
- 1 tablespoon citric acid or 2 tablespoons distilled white vinegar
- 1 tablespoon fennel seeds
- 1 to 2 tablespoons salt
- 2 teaspoons fenugreek seeds

Directions:

1. In a mortar and pestle (or a spice or coffee grinder), crudely mix together and grind the fenugreek and fennel seeds. Move to a container and stir in the turmeric.
2. Heat the oil in a big non-stick wok or saucepan using moderate to high heat. Reduce the heat to low, put in the ground spices and salt, and stir a few seconds. Put in the green chile peppers and cook until they are crisp-tender, three to five minutes. Stir in the citric acid (or vinegar) and cook another two to three minutes. Allow to cool, then move to a sanitized glass jar and store in the fridge for approximately a year. Serve chilled or at room temperature.

OTHER VEGETABLE PICKLES

CRUNCHY CUCUMBER PICKLE

This recipe is called "Kheerae ka achaar" in Hindi

Yield: Approximately 2 cups

The Indian version of a popular American pickle!

Ingredients:

- ⅛ teaspoon ground asafoetida
- ¼ cup distilled white vinegar
- 1 medium onion, cut into ½-inch pieces

- 1 tablespoon dried curry leaves
- 1 teaspoon black mustard seeds
- 1 teaspoon salt, or to taste
- 2 large cloves fresh garlic, minced
- 2 tablespoons peanut oil
- 3 to 5 dried red chile peppers, such as chiles de arbol, with stems
- 3 to 5 fresh green chile peppers, such as serrano, halved lengthwise
- 4 to 5 small seedless cucumbers (about ¾ pound), diagonally chopped

Directions:

1. In a container, toss the cucumbers with salt and allow to sweat approximately one hour.
2. Heat the oil in a big non-stick wok or saucepan over moderate heat and cook the red chile peppers about half a minute. Put in the green chile peppers and stir for about half a minute. Put in the mustard seeds; they should splutter when they touch the hot oil, so reduce the heat and cover the pan until the spluttering diminishes.
3. Mix in the asafoetida and curry leaves, then Put in the onion and garlic, and cook, stirring, until barely softened, approximately three minutes. Put in the cucumber with all the juices and cook, stirring, approximately one minute.
4. Put in the vinegar and boil using high heat approximately one minute. Turn off the heat. Allow to cool, move to a sterile glass jar, and refrigerate at least two days before you serve. This pickle stays fresh about six months in a fridge. Serve chilled or at room temperature.

CAULIFLOWER-CARROT WATER PICKLE

This recipe is called "Gobhi-gajjar ka paani wala achaar" in Hindi

Yield: Approximately 2 cups

Ingredients:

- ⅛ teaspoon ground turmeric
- ¼ teaspoon cayenne pepper, or to taste

- 1 (1-inch) piece fresh ginger, peeled, cut in half lengthwise, and thinly chopped
- 1 pound cauliflower, cut into 1½-inch florets, stems discarded
- 1 small piece muslin or 4 layers cheesecloth (sufficient to cover the mouth of the jar)
- 1½ teaspoons salt, or to taste
- 2 cups water
- 2 teaspoons black mustard seeds, ground
- 3 tablespoons distilled white vinegar
- 3 to 4 small carrots, peeled and diagonally chopped
- 8 to 10 fresh green chile peppers, such as serrano, stemmed and halved lengthwise

Directions:

1. Put the vegetables and water in a moderate-sized saucepan and bring to boil using high heat. Boil half a minute, then cover the pan and remove from the heat. Set aside approximately one minute. Move to a big sanitized glass jar with a wide mouth and stir in all the rest of the ingredients.

2. Cover the jar with the muslin, locking it using a rubber band, and if there is a warm sunny spot in the kitchen, put it there, else put it outdoors where there it can get some sun. (bring the jar indoors in the evening if you're keeping it outdoors.) Sway the jar a couple of times per day, until the vegetables are sour, two to four days. This pickle can be stored safely at room temperature for approximately seven days and about six months in the refrigerator, getting more and more pungent as time passes. Serve chilled or at room temperature.

SPICY CRANBERRY PICKLE Ⓥ

This recipe is called "Karonda achaar" in Hindi

Yield: Approximately 2 cups

Ingredients:

- ¼ cup Bengali Five Spices (Panch-Phoran) (make your own using the recipe in the spice blend section, or buy from a store)

- ½ cup mustard oil
- ½ teaspoon ground turmeric
- 1 (12-ounce) package fresh cranberries, washed
- 1 tablespoon citric acid or 2 tablespoons distilled white vinegar
- 1 tablespoon salt, or to taste

Directions:

1. In a mortar and pestle, crudely grind the 5-spices mixture. Stir in the turmeric and salt.
2. Heat the oil in a big non-stick wok or saucepan using moderate to high heat until smoking. Reduce the heat to low, put in the spices, and stir a few seconds. Put in the cranberries and cook until they are crisp-tender, approximately ten to twelve minutes. Stir in the citric acid (or vinegar) and cook another two to three minutes. Allow to cool, move to a sterile jar and store in the refrigerator, approximately a year.
3. Serve chilled or at room temperature.

ONION PICKLE (V)

This recipe is called "Pyaz ka achaar" in Hindi

Yield: Approximately 2 cups

Ingredients:

- ½ cup mustard or olive oil
- 1 pound pearl onions, peeled
- 1 small piece muslin or 4 layers cheesecloth (sufficient to cover the mouth of the jar)
- 1 tablespoon fennel seeds
- 1 tablespoon fenugreek seeds
- 1 tablespoon salt, or to taste
- 1 teaspoon cayenne pepper, or to taste
- 1 teaspoon ground turmeric
- 1½ teaspoons kalonji seeds
- 2 teaspoons black peppercorns

Directions:

1. Make a cross-cut at the base of each onion, going 75% of the way to the top. Gently open the cuts and stuff a pinch of salt in each one. Save any leftover salt for future use. Using a spice or coffee grinder, very crudely mix together and grind the fenugreek, fennel, peppercorns and kalonji. Move to a container and stir in the turmeric, cayenne pepper, and the reserved salt.
2. Heat the oil in a big non-stick wok or saucepan using moderate to high heat and put in the spice mixture; it should sizzle when they touch the hot oil. Put in the onions and cook approximately five minutes, ensuring all the onions are thoroughly coated with the spice mixture.
3. Allow to cool and move to a sterile glass jar. Cover the jar with the muslin, locking it using a rubber band, and if there is a warm sunny spot in the kitchen, put it there, else put it outdoors where there it can get some sun. (bring the jar indoors in the evening if you're keeping it outdoors.) Sway the jar a couple of times per day, until the spices are plump and soft and the onions are crisp-tender, three to five days. The onions will release some juices; that is quite normal. Store about ten days at room temperature and about six months in a fridge. The onions keep getting stronger over time.

TURNIP PICKLE Ⓥ

This recipe is called "Shalgam ka achaar" in Hindi

Yield: Approximately 4 cups

Ingredients:

- 1 small piece muslin or 4 layers cheesecloth (sufficient to cover the mouth of the jar)
- 1 tablespoon black mustard seeds, crudely ground
- 1 tablespoon salt
- 1 teaspoon cayenne pepper, or to taste
- 1½ pounds turnips, cut into 1-inch pieces (peeled or unpeeled)
- 2 to 3 cups water

Directions:

1. Bring the water to a boil in a big pot. Put in the turnips and boil approximately one minute. Drain and move the turnips to a tray coated using paper towels and air-dry them about ten minutes.
2. Move to a big sanitized glass jar with a wide mouth and put in the mustard seeds, salt, and cayenne pepper. Toss well, then cover the jar with the muslin locking it using a rubber band, and set aside at room temperature until the turnips turn sour, five to seven days. To cure faster, place in the sun during the day, bringing the pickle inside in the evening. Shake the jar once or twice a day. This pickle can be stored safely at room temperature for approximately seven days (longer in the refrigerator), getting more and more pungent as time passes.

TURNIP & CAULIFLOWER PICKLE

This recipe is called "Shalgam gobhi ka achaar" in Hindi

Yield: Approximately 8 to 10 cups

Ingredients:

- ¼ cup black mustard seeds, crudely ground
- ½ cup mustard oil
- ½ cup sugar
- 1 cup distilled white vinegar
- 1 small piece muslin or 4 layers cheesecloth (sufficient to cover the mouth of the jar)
- 1 teaspoon cayenne pepper, or to taste
- 1¼ pounds small turnips, peeled and cut into ¼-inch thick slices
- 1½ pounds cauliflower, cut into 1½-inch florets, stems discarded
- 2 ounces fresh garlic cloves, peeled
- 2 tablespoons garam masala
- 2 teaspoons ground paprika
- 3 ounces fresh ginger, peeled and cut into thin round slices
- 3 tablespoons salt
- 3 to 4 cups water

Directions:

1. Bring the water to a boil in a big pot. Put in the turnips and cauliflower and blanch approximately one minute; do not allow them to soften. Drain and move to a tray coated using paper towels and air-dry them about ten minutes. Process the ginger and garlic Using a food processor or a blender until a fine paste is achieved.
2. Heat the oil in a big non-stick wok or saucepan using moderate to high heat and put in the ginger-garlic paste. Cook, stirring, over moderate heat until rich golden in color, approximately four minutes. Put in the garam masala and stir for approximately half a minute.
3. Put in the vegetables and salt and cook, stirring, approximately two to three minutes. Put in the sugar and cook, stirring, approximately one minute. Remove from heat and stir in the mustard seeds, cayenne pepper, paprika, and vinegar. Move to a large, sanitized glass jar with a wide mouth. Cover the jar with the muslin, locking it using a rubber band, and if there is a warm sunny spot in the kitchen, put it there, else put it outdoors where there it can get some sun. (bring the jar indoors in the evening if you're keeping it outdoors.) Sway the jar a couple of times per day, until the turnips are sour, five to seven days. (Taste, and if not sour enough, cover and set aside longer.) This pickle can be stored safely at room temperature for approximately three months, getting more and more pungent over time.

MIXED VEGETABLE PICKLE

This recipe is called "Sabzi ka achaar" in Hindi

Yield: Approximately 4 cups

Ingredients:

- ½ cup distilled white vinegar
- ½ cup vegetable oil
- ½ teaspoon cayenne pepper, or to taste
- ½ teaspoon ground paprika
- ½ teaspoon ground turmeric
- 1 (15-ounce) can tomato sauce
- 1 pound carrots, finely chopped
- 1 pound cauliflower, finely chopped
- 1 tablespoon cumin seeds

- 1 tablespoon fenugreek seeds
- 1 tablespoon salt, or to taste
- 2 large heads fresh garlic, peeled and chopped
- 2 tablespoons fennel seeds
- 2 teaspoons kalonji seeds
- 5 to 7 fresh green chile peppers, such as serrano, diagonally chopped

Directions:

1. Heat the oil in a big non-stick wok or saucepan using moderate to high heat and put in the fennel, fenugreek, cumin, and kalonji seeds. They should sizzle when they touch the hot oil. Swiftly put in the turmeric, stir for approximately half a minute, and put in the vegetables, garlic, and green chile peppers. Cook, stirring, until the vegetables are lightly golden, approximately five minutes.
2. Put in the vinegar, tomato sauce, salt, paprika, and cayenne pepper, and bring to a boil using high heat. Reduce the heat to moderate to low, cover the pan, and simmer until the vegetables are crisp-tender, approximately seven minutes. Allow to cool, move to a big sanitized jar, and store in the fridge for approximately ten days. Serve chilled or at room temperature.

EGGPLANT AND MALANGA ROOT PICKLE Ⓥ

This recipe is called "Baingan-kachaalu ka achaar" in Hindi

Yield: Approximately 4 cups

Ingredients:

- 1 pound malanga root or taro root
- 1 pound small Indian eggplants or Chinese eggplants, cut into 2-inch pieces
- 1 tablespoon fennel seeds, crudely ground
- 1 tablespoon salt
- 1 teaspoon cayenne pepper, or to taste
- 1½ to 2 cups mustard oil
- 2 tablespoons black mustard seeds, crudely ground

- 2 teaspoons ground turmeric

Directions:

1. Make a cross-cut at the base of each eggplant, going 75% of the way to the top. Put in a saucepan along with 2 cups water and 1 teaspoon turmeric, and bring to a boil using high heat. Reduce the heat to moderate to low, cover the pan, and simmer until the eggplants are half cooked (crisp-tender), approximately seven minutes. Drain the eggplants over a container and reserve about ¾ cup water.
2. In the same saucepan, place the malanga root and about 4 cups of fresh water, and bring to a boil using high heat. Reduce the heat to moderate to low, cover the pan, and simmer until the malanga root is soft, pouring in additional water if it evaporates, approximately fifteen minutes. Remove from the water, allow to cool down, then peel and cut into 3/4-inch pieces. Throw away the water.
3. In a large container, combine the eggplants, malanga root, mustard and fennel seeds, salt, cayenne pepper, the rest of the 1 teaspoon turmeric, and mix thoroughly, ensuring all the vegetables are thoroughly coated.
4. Heat the oil in a small saucepan using moderate to high heat until smoking. Turn off the heat, add to the container with the vegetables, and mix once more. Allow to cool and move to a big sanitized jar. Make sure there is minimum ½ inch of oil on the surface, if not, then heat and add some more. Cover the jar with the muslin, locking it using a rubber band, and place in a warm, sunny spot in the kitchen, or outside in the sun, swaying the jar a couple of times per day for two days.
5. 5. Stir in the reserved eggplant water and shake the jar once more. Put in a warm, sunny spot in the kitchen, or outside in the sun again, swaying the jar a couple of times per day until the vegetables are very soft and tangy, about one week. This pickle can be stored safely at room temperature for approximately one month, and in the fridge for approximately six months. Serve chilled or at room temperature.

SNACKS, APPETIZERS, AND STREET FOOD

We Indians love snacks. If you take a stroll in a market in India, you will find food stalls all over the place. During peak hours, will probably get to see people waiting in lines to get their hands on the snacks being sold at these food stalls. Needless to say, India has a culture of snacks.

Now we will take a look at a few of the most popular snacks Indians enjoy. Almost every snack recipe in this section is best enjoyed with a chutney on the side. I've already listed more than 40 chutney recipes in the previous section, so make sure you go through those too.

You may or may not find a chutney recommendation in the recipes that follow, so feel free to play around and experiment.

Ⓥ= Vegan Ⓟ= Quick Pressure Cooker Recipe

SPICY RELISH MIXES

FRIED TARO CHIPS Ⓥ

This recipe is called "Tali arbi kae lacchae" in Hindi

Yield: 4 to 6 servings

Ingredients:

- ⅛ teaspoon ground asafoetida
- ½ teaspoon cayenne pepper, or to taste
- ½ teaspoon salt, or to taste

- 1 pound taro root, peeled and cut into thin julienne sticks
- 1½ to 2 cups coconut or peanut oil for deep-frying

Directions:

1. Heat the oil in a big wok using moderate to high heat until it achieves 325°F to 350°F on a frying thermometer or when a small piece of taro root dropped into the hot oil surges to the surface of the oil after fifteen to 20 seconds.
2. Put in the taro root sticks in 2 or 3 batches, adding as many as the wok can hold simultaneously. Fry, stirring and turning, until crunchy and golden, approximately one minute per batch. Move to paper towels with a slotted spatula to drain.
3. Allow to cool and remove all but 1 teaspoon of oil from the wok. Heat the oil and put in the asafoetida, cayenne pepper, and salt. Put in the taro root sticks and mix thoroughly. Serve hot.

GRAM FLOUR FRIED PEANUTS

This recipe is called "Besan-tali moong-phalli" in Hindi

Yield: Approximately 2 cups

Feel free to use any nut of your choice instead of peanuts!

Ingredients:

- ⅛ teaspoon baking soda
- ⅛ teaspoon ground asafoetida
- ½ 1 teaspoon salt, or to taste
- ½ cup chickpea flour
- ½ to 1 teaspoon cayenne pepper, or to taste
- 1 teaspoon ground ginger
- 1½ to 2 cups peanut oil for deep-frying
- 2 cups shelled raw peanuts, with or without red skin
- 3 tablespoons fresh lemon juice

Directions:

1. Put the chickpea flour into a sifter or a fine-mesh strainer and sift the flour into a moderate-sized container. Stir in the ginger, salt, cayenne pepper, baking soda, and asafoetida. Stir in the peanuts and then Put in the lemon juice and mix with clean fingers, ensuring the peanuts are coated with a thick batter (add 1 tablespoon water, if required).
2. Heat the oil in a big wok or skillet using moderate to high heat until it achieves 325°F to 350°F on a frying thermometer or until a small bit of batter dropped into the hot oil bubbles and surges to the surface of the oil instantly. Next, Put in the batter-coated peanuts, piece by piece (or by the handful), adding as many as the wok can hold simultaneously. Separate them swiftly with a fork or a slotted spatula and fry, stirring and turning, until crunchy and golden, approximately one minute. Replicate the process for the rest of the peanuts. Move to paper towels with a slotted spatula to drain. Allow to cool and serve, or store in an airtight vessel in the fridge up to half a month.

SALTED CASHEWS ⓥ

This recipe is called "Namkeen kaaju" in Hindi

Yield: Approximately 2 cups

Ingredients:

- ¼ teaspoon freshly ground black pepper, or to taste
- ¼ teaspoon salt, or to taste
- ½ cup peanut oil for deep-frying
- 2 cups raw cashews

Directions:

1. Heat the oil in a moderate-sized non-stick wok or saucepan over moderate heat and fry, stirring and turning the cashews until a golden colour is achieved, approximately one minute. Before you take them out of the wok, drain thoroughly. (The nuts will stick to paper, so don't use paper towels to drain.)
2. Move to a container and swiftly stir in the salt and pepper and toss well, ensuring the cashews are coated thoroughly.

3. Allow to cool and harden for a while before you serve, or cool to room temperature, move to an airtight vessel and store fifteen to twenty days at room temperature or approximately three months in a fridge.

SALTY CEREAL MIX Ⓥ

This recipe is called "Mila-jula namkeen" in Hindi

Yield: Approximately 8 cups

Ingredients:

- ¼ teaspoon ground asafoetida
- ¼ teaspoon ground ginger
- ½ cup crudely chopped raw cashews
- ½ cup finely chopped fresh cilantro, including soft stems
- ½ cup mixed melon seeds or shelled raw sunflower seeds
- ½ cup shelled raw peanuts, with red skins on
- ½ teaspoon cayenne pepper, or to taste
- 1 teaspoon black mustard seeds
- 1½ tablespoons Chaat Masala (Homemade or store-bought), or to taste
- 1½ teaspoons citric acid
- 2 cups canned potato sticks
- 2 cups corn flake cereal
- 2 tablespoons dried curry leaves
- 3 cups puffed rice cereal
- 3 tablespoons peanut oil

Directions:

1. Ready the chaat masala. Heat 1 tablespoon oil in a big wok or skillet and cook the peanuts and cashews over moderate heat, stirring as required, until it starts to look golden and releases its fragrance, two to five minutes. Move to a container.
2. Another way is to roast in the oven at 350°F until a mild golden colour and fragrance is achieved, ten to fifteen minutes.

3. Take the same pan again and put in the melon (or sunflower) seeds to the wok and dry-roast until a golden colour is achieved, approximately one minute. Move to the peanut container.
4. Heat the rest of the 2 tablespoons oil using moderate to high heat and put in the mustard seeds and asafoetida. They should splutter when they touch the hot oil, so cover the pan and reduce the heat until the spluttering diminishes. Stir in the cayenne pepper and ginger, and then add first the cilantro, then the curry leaves, chaat masala, and citric acid, and stir for approximately half a minute.
5. Put in the puffed rice cereal, corn flakes, potato sticks, roasted nuts, and seeds. Reduce the heat to low and cook, stirring intermittently, approximately five minutes, ensuring everything is coated thoroughly with the spices. Allow to cool completely. Move it to an airtight vessel and store at room temperature approximately sixty days.

SPICY MIXED NUTS AND SEEDS

This recipe is called "Masaledaar maevae" in Hindi

Yield: Approximately 2½ cups

Feel free to use your favourite nuts and seeds in this recipe instead of the ones I use.

Ingredients:

- ¼ teaspoon black salt (not compulsory)
- ¼ teaspoon cayenne pepper, or to taste
- ½ cup mixed shelled raw seeds, such as sunflower, pumpkin, melon
- ½ cup peanut oil for deep-frying
- 1 teaspoon cumin seeds, dry-roasted and crudely ground (See the dry-roasting section in Introduction)
- 1½ to 2 teaspoons <u>Chaat Masala</u> (Homemade or store-bought)
- 2 cups mixed shelled raw nuts, such as almonds, cashews, peanuts, pistachios

Directions:

1. Ready the cumin seeds and chaat masala. Next, in a small-sized container, combine the cumin seeds, chaat masala, cayenne pepper, and black salt.
2. Heat the oil in a medium-size non-stick wok or saucepan over moderate heat and fry the nuts until a golden colour is achieved, approximately one minute. Before you take them out of the wok, drain thoroughly. (Do not drain them on paper towels, or the spices will not adhere.) Move them to a medium container, swiftly Put in the spice mixture and toss well, ensuring that the nuts are thoroughly coated.
3. Remove all the oil from the wok, then in whatever oil remains on the wok surface, stir-fry the seeds using moderate to low heat until the seeds are fragrant and golden, approximately one minute. Put into the spiced nuts and toss together. Taste and adjust seasonings. (Keep in mind that the warm nuts will be soft, but will harden as they cool.) Allow to cool completely then serve or move to an airtight vessel and store fifteen to twenty days at room temperature or approximately three months in a fridge.

SPICY PRESSED RICE FLAKE MIX

This recipe is called "Chivda" in Hindi

Yield: Approximately 5 cups

Pressed rice flakes are easily available in Indian markets and online. It is called "poha" in Hindi.

Ingredients:

- ⅛ teaspoon ground alum
- ¼ teaspoon ground turmeric
- ½ cup dried split yellow chickpeas (channa dal), sorted and washed in 3 to 4 changes of water
- ½ teaspoon ground fenugreek seeds
- 1 (3-by-1-inch) piece dried coconut (kopra), thinly chopped (not compulsory)
- 1 cup shelled raw peanuts, with or without the red skin
- 1 teaspoon cayenne pepper, or to taste
- 1 teaspoon citric acid
- 1 teaspoon ground coriander
- 1 teaspoon ground cumin

- 1 teaspoon salt, or to taste
- 1 teaspoon sugar
- 1 to 3 fresh green chile peppers, such as serrano, minced with seeds
- 1½ tablespoons finely chopped fresh curry leaves
- 2 cups pressed rice flakes (poha)
- 2 tablespoons finely chopped fresh cilantro, including soft stems
- 2 to 3 cups peanut oil for deep-frying

Directions:

1. Put the dal in water to cover by 1 inch. Stir in the alum and soak overnight. Next, drain and spread the dal on a tray lined with several layers of paper towels or cheesecloth until completely dry, one to two hours. Stir a few times using your fingers to make sure they are thoroughly dried. (Otherwise, rest of the water will cause spluttering when the dal is deep-fried.)
2. Heat the oil in a big wok or saucepan over moderate heat until a few rice flakes dropped into the hot oil bubble and rise to the top instantly. Put the rice flakes in a big fine-mesh metal strainer (in 2 batches, if required) and place the strainer with the rice flakes in it into the hot oil. Fry, stirring the rice flakes in the strainer until they are crisp and very lightly golden, approximately one minute. Move to a container coated using paper towels. Put in the turmeric and ½ teaspoon salt to the rice flakes, and toss lightly.
3. Same way, fry the coconut slices (if using), then the dal, and finally, the peanuts. Mix each into the rice flakes. Put in the rest of the ½ teaspoon salt and toss once more.
4. Take the oil out of the wok while leaving approximately one tablespoon in it. Heat the oil on moderate to low heat and cook the green chile peppers, cilantro, and curry leaves, stirring, until a golden colour is achieved and crisp, approximately five minutes.
5. Put in the citric acid, cumin, coriander, cayenne pepper, fenugreek seeds, and sugar to the wok, and stir approximately one minute. Next, Put in the fried ingredients and mix lightly until they are coated thoroughly with the spices. Keep uncovered at all times, and cool to room temperature. Store in an airtight vessel up to sixty days.

SPICY THIN CRISPY FLATBREADS

This recipe is called "Paapad" in Hindi

Yield: 1 to 2 paapad

Ready-made paapads are easily available in Indian markets, and even online. All you need to to these pre-made paapads is fry or roast them, depending on your preference. These are extremely cheap, and in India, are a common side snacks enjoyed with rice and curry dishes. These can also be eaten just by themselves. In India, people mostly buy raw paapads and cook them immediately before eating. Try out the different brands of paapads available to you and pick your favourite one.

Ingredients:

- Raw Paapads (buy online or from Indian stores)

Directions:

1. Flame Roast using tongs: hold each paapad over the flame and roast it, starting with the edges and moving toward the center.
2. Or, put inside preheated pven until crisp—maximum 35 seconds—ensuring the edges do not burn.
3. Or, deep fry and drain thoroughly before serving.
4. Or, microwave on high power for a minute (easiest and most convenient method).

MATHIYA

Mathiya or Mathri is a West Indian snack from Rajasthan. It is a kind of flaky biscuit that is commonly enjoyed with tea.

AJWAIN SEED MATHIYA Ⓥ

This recipe is called "Ajwaini mathri" in Hindi

Yield: 16 pieces

Ingredients:

- ¼ cup canola oil
- ¼ cup semolina
- ½ cup warm water
- ½ to 1 teaspoon crudely ground black pepper + 16 black peppercorns
- 1 teaspoon crudely ground ajwain seeds
- 1 teaspoon salt, or to taste
- 1½ to 2 cups vegetable oil for deep-frying
- 2 cups all-purpose flour
- 2 tablespoons melted ghee

Directions:

1. Put the flour, semolina, oil, ghee, ajwain seeds, ground pepper, and salt in a mixing container and rub lightly with clean fingers to mix. Next, Put in the water, slowly and gradually, and mix until the dough gathers into a semi-firm ball that does not stick to your fingers. (Lightly coat your fingers with oil, if required.)
2. Split the dough into 16 identical portions and, use a rolling pin to roll out each one into a thin 3- to 4-inch disc that is approximately ⅛-inch thick. If the dough sticks to the rolling surface, coat mildly with oil; do not dust with dry flour.
3. Use the tip of a knife to poke a few holes or make ¼-inch slits all over in each round. This will ensure that the dough doesnt get puffed while frying. Put one peppercorn in the center of each mathri and push it in tightly.
4. Heat the oil in a big wok or skillet over moderate heat until it reaches 300°F to 325°F on a frying thermometer, or when a small drop of dough begins to bubble while it is still immersed. (Reduce the heat if it rises instantly or browns.) Put in the discs, as many as the wok can comfortably hold simultaneously, and fry, turning as required, until crunchy and appears mildly golden. Do not brown them and ensure the centers are crisp. Drain using paper towels. Allow to cool completely, and store in airtight containers at room temperature approximately sixty days.

MUNG BEAN PUFFED PASTRIES

This recipe is called "Mung dal kachauri" in Hindi

Yield: Approximately 30 pieces

The "kachauri" is a highly popular spicy Indian Pastry.

Ingredients:

- ¼ cup lukewarm water, or as required
- ¼ teaspoon ground asafoetida
- ½ cup vegetable oil
- ½ teaspoon black peppercorns
- ½ teaspoon ground turmeric
- ¾ cup dried yellow mung beans (dhulli mung dal), sorted and washed in 3 to 4 changes of water
- 1 tablespoon coriander
- 1 teaspoon cumin seeds
- 1 teaspoon hot red pepper flakes, or to taste
- 1½ tablespoons fennel seeds
- 2 black cardamom pods, seeds only
- 2 tablespoons chickpea flour
- 2 teaspoons salt, or to taste
- 2 to 3 cups peanut oil for deep-frying
- 3 cups all-purpose flour
- 5 whole cloves

Directions:

1. Immerse the dal in water to cover by 2 inches, and drain. Next, make the filling: Using a food processor or a blender, process the dal to make a coarse paste. In a spice or a coffee grinder, crudely mix together and grind all the whole spices (fennel to cardamom).
2. Heat ¼ cup of the vegetable oil in a big non-stick wok or saucepan using moderate to high heat and put in the asafoetida, then the ground spices, and stir for approximately half a minute. Stir in the chickpea flour and stir another half a minute.
3. Put in the dal paste and cook over moderate heat, stirring and breaking any lumps, approximately ten minutes. Put in the salt and stir to mix thoroughly. Allow to cool and divide equally into 30 portions (about 1 tablespoon each).

Make a ball of each portion and save for later. If the balls seem to fall apart, this means the filling is too dry; moisten it with 1 to 2 tablespoons hot water.

4. Make the dough: In a moderate-sized container, using clean fingers, rub together the flour, turmeric, and the rest of the ¼ cup oil until well mixed. Add sufficient water to make a soft and pliable dough, adding slowly and gradually. Put the dough on a cutting board and pound lightly with a meat mallet approximately two minutes. Turn the dough over during the two minutes to pound different sections. This makes the dough very elastic. Split the dough equally into 30 portions.
5. Assemble the kachauries: In a small-sized container, make a paste of 2 tablespoons all-purpose flour and 1 tablespoon water and keep ready. Working with one portion of the dough at a time, using your fingers press out a 3-inch patty. Brush the top surface lightly with water and place one portion of the dal filling in the center. Lift the edges over the filling, bring them together and pinch to secure. Next, softly push in the pinched edges down to make a slight depression in the center and to flatten the patty to 1-inch thick. Brush the entire kachauri lightly with the flour-water paste and save for later. Finish assembling all the kachauries. Cover with a clean, damp cotton kitchen towel and set aside.
6. Heat the oil in a wok or skillet using moderate to high heat until it achieves 300°F to 325°F on a frying thermometer, or when a small piece of the dough dropped into the hot oil surges to the surface of the oil after fifteen to 20 seconds. Reduce the heat to medium and put in the kachauries, adding as many as the wok can hold simultaneously without crowding, and fry slowly, turning only once after the bottom is golden-brown, approximately 3 to four minutes. When the other side is golden-brown, approximately 3 to four minutes more, remove from the wok with a slotted metal spatula and move to paper towels to drain. Serve instantly, or allow to cool down and place in your fridge for a maximum of half a month.

PATTY 1: MUSHROOM TURNOVERS

This recipe is called "Mushroom Patty" in Hindi

Yield: 24 pieces

"Patties" are super cheap, and highly popular among kids in India. These were practically the only food available in my school canteen back in the day.

Ingredients:

- ¼ cup finely chopped fresh cilantro, including soft stems
- ½ teaspoon salt, or to taste
- 1 (20-ounce) package frozen puff pastry sheets (2 sheets)
- 1 large egg white, beaten lightly with 1 tablespoon water
- 1 large onion, finely chopped
- 1 teaspoon minced fresh garlic
- 1 to 3 green chile peppers, such as serrano, minced with seeds
- 1½ to 2 teaspoons Basic Curry Powder (Homemade or store-bought)
- 2 tablespoons vegetable oil
- 3 cups finely chopped mushrooms
- 3 tablespoons all-purpose flour

Directions:

1. Ready the curry powder. Heat the oil in a big non-stick wok or saucepan using moderate to high heat and cook the onion, stirring, until transparent, approximately two to three minutes. Put in the garlic, green chile peppers, curry powder, and flour, and stir using moderate to low heat until the garlic and onion are golden, approximately two to three minutes. Put in the mushrooms, cilantro, and salt and cook until the mixture is completely dry, another three to five minutes. Allow to cool before using.
2. Divide the filling into two equal parts, one for each pastry sheet. Thaw the pastry sheets at room temperature, until they become a little tender but still cold to the touch, fifteen to twenty minutes.
3. Preheat your oven to 375°F. Lightly grease a baking sheet. On a mildly floured surface, working with each pastry sheet separately, unfold and softly roll it with a rolling pin to make it smooth. Next, cut each sheet into 12 squares. Roll each square to make it a little bigger. Moisten the edges with water, place 1 tablespoon of filling in the center of each square and fold one corner over the filling to the diagonal corner to form a triangle. Seal the edges by pressing with the back of a fork.
4. Brush the top of each turnover with the beaten egg and then poke a few holes with a fork so the steam can escape. Put the turnovers on the baking sheet and bake until puffed and golden, approximately twenty minutes. Move to cooling racks. Serve hot or at room temperature.

PATTY 2: CURRIED CHICKEN OR LAMB TURNOVERS

This recipe is called "Chicken/Mutton patty" in Hindi

Yield: 24 pieces

Ingredients:

- ¼ teaspoon ground turmeric
- ½ cup finely chopped fresh cilantro, including soft stems
- ½ teaspoon garam masala
- ½ teaspoon salt, or to taste
- 1 (20-ounce) package frozen puff pastry sheets (2 sheets)
- 1 large egg white, beaten lightly with 1 tablespoon water
- 1 large onion, finely chopped
- 1 pound ground chicken or lamb
- 1 tablespoon ground coriander
- 1 teaspoon dried fenugreek leaves
- 1 teaspoon ground cumin
- 1 to 3 fresh green chile peppers, such as serrano, minced with seeds
- 2 tablespoons all-purpose flour

Directions:

1. Put everything (except the flour, puff pastry, and the egg wash) in a big non-stick skillet or saucepan and cook using moderate to high heat, stirring and breaking up any lumps in the ground chicken, until a golden colour is achieved, approximately five minutes. If using lamb, cook an extra 5 to seven minutes. Reserve the pan.
2. Let the meat cool until it is safe sufficient to handle, approximately fifteen minutes, then move to a food processor, put in the flour, and process to make it as smooth as possible. Return to the pan and cook approximately five minutes to bind the filling and remove the raw taste of the flour.
3. Divide the filling into two equal parts, one for each pastry sheet. Thaw the pastry sheets at room temperature, until they become a little tender but still cold to the touch, fifteen to twenty minutes.

4. Preheat your oven to 375°F. Lightly grease a baking sheet. On a mildly floured surface, working with each pastry sheet separately, unfold and softly roll it with a rolling pin to make it smooth. Next, cut each sheet into 12 squares. Roll each square to make it a little bigger. Moisten the edges with water, place 1 tablespoon of filling in the center of each square and fold one corner over the filling to the diagonal corner to form a triangle. Seal the edges by pressing with the back of a fork.
5. Brush the top of each turnover with the beaten egg and then poke a few holes with a fork so the steam can escape. Put the turnovers on the baking sheet and bake until puffed and golden, approximately twenty minutes. Move to cooling racks. Serve hot or at room temperature.

PUFF PASTRY ROLLS

This recipe is called "Puff pastry ke rolls" in Hindi

Yield: 24 pieces

Ingredients:

- ¼ cup finely chopped fresh cilantro, including soft stems
- 1 (20-ounce) package frozen puff pastry sheets (2 sheets)
- 2 teaspoons Chaat Masala (Homemade or store-bought)
- 2 to 3 scallions, green parts only, minced
- 24 thick asparagus spears, each approximately 6 inches long

Directions:

1. Ready the chaat masala. Thaw the pastry sheets at room temperature until they become a little tender but still cold to the touch, fifteen to twenty minutes. Preheat your oven to 350°F and mildly grease a baking sheet.
2. On a mildly floured surface, unfold and sprinkle both the pastry sheets uniformly with the chaat masala, scallion, and cilantro and gently, use a rolling pin to roll each sheet, ensuring that the scallion and cilantro are pressed well into the pastry. (Drizzle with dry flour if the dough starts to become gluey.) Next, cut each sheet into 12 squares. Roll each square to make it a little bigger.

3. Working with each square separately, place one asparagus spear along the diagonal across the center with approximately 1 inch of the tip outside the pastry. Fold in half over the asparagus, then make a roll. Moisten the corner with water and press to secure. Place, 1-inch apart, on the baking sheet, with the sealed side down. Bake until crunchy and golden, fifteen to twenty minutes. Move to cooling racks. Serve hot or at room temperature.

PUFF PASTRY WITH AJWAIN SEEDS

This recipe is version of a dish commonly referred to as "Ajwain ki puff pastry" in India

Yield: 30 pieces

A popular, cheap, and insanely delicious snack commonly available I pretty much every bakery in India.

Ingredients:

- ¼ to ⅓ teaspoon crudely ground ajwain seeds
- ½ teaspoon cumin seeds, dry-roasted and crudely ground (See the dry-roasting section in Introduction)
- 1 large egg white
- 1 tablespoon all-purpose flour for dusting
- 1 tablespoon water
- Half of 1 (20-ounce) package frozen puff pastry (1 sheet)

Directions:

1. Ready the cumin seeds. Preheat your oven to 325°F. Thaw the pastry sheet at room temperature, until it is slightly softened but still cold to the touch, fifteen to twenty minutes. Lightly grease a baking sheet. On a mildly floured surface, unfold and softly roll the pastry sheet to make a smooth 14-inch square. Cut in half.
2. In a small-sized container, whisk together the egg white and water and brush it lightly over each half sheet. Sprinkle the cumin and ajwain seeds uniformly on one half, then place the second half over it, egg wash side down. Dust

lightly with flour and roll softly with a rolling pin to make a 14-by-7-inch rectangle (or larger).
3. Cut across the diagonal into approximately 30 half-inch strips. Twist and lightly stretch each strip and place, approximately 1 inch apart, on a mildly greased baking sheet. Brush with the egg wash for a shiny glaze and bake until crunchy and golden, approximately ten to twelve minutes. Serve hot or at room temperature.

RED BELL PEPPER-POTATO PASTRY SWIRLS

This recipe is called "Shimla mirch aur aalu ki Matthi" in Hindi

Yield: 48 pieces

A great snack if guests are coming over! Takes a while to prepare, but it is totally worth it.

Ingredients:

- ¼ teaspoon salt, or to taste
- ½ teaspoon garam masala
- ½ teaspoon ground cumin
- 1 (20-ounce) package frozen puff pastry sheets (2 sheets)
- 1 medium onion, crudely chopped
- 1 tablespoon vegetable oil
- 1½ tablespoons ground coriander
- 2 tablespoons peeled and minced fresh ginger
- 3 large russet (or any) potatoes
- 3 red bell peppers

Directions:

1. Preheat the broiler and mildly grease a broiler-safe baking sheet. Thaw the pastry sheets at room temperature, until they become a little tender but still cold to the touch, fifteen to twenty minutes In the meantime, cook the

potatoes in lightly salted boiling water to cover until soft, approximately twenty minutes, then peel and mash them.

2. Slice the bell peppers in half and place them, cut side down, on the baking sheet, place on the top rack of the oven or under the broiler, and broil the peppers until thoroughly charred, approximately five minutes. Take out of the oven, and reduce the oven heat to 325°F. Move the peppers to a container, then cover with a dish or a seal within a zip-closure plastic bag until cool sufficient to handle. Next, peel off and discard most of the charred skin, leaving some on for flavour. Slice thinly.

3. Heat the oil in a big non-stick wok or saucepan using moderate to high heat and cook the onion, stirring, until a golden colour is achieved, approximately two minutes. Stir in the ginger and cook another minute. Put in the mashed potatoes, coriander, cumin, garam masala, and salt, and cook stirring until a golden colour is achieved, approximately two to three minutes. Stir in the roasted bell peppers and stir approximately two minutes to blend the flavours. Allow to cool to room temperature, then split into 2 equal parts.

4. On a mildly floured surface, working with each pastry sheet separately, unfold and softly roll the sheet to make it smooth. Placing the shorter side toward you and spread one half of the potato filling uniformly over the sheet, leaving approximately a 3/4-inch border along the edges. Moisten the border with water.

5. Starting from the side closest to you, roll firmly like a jelly roll. When you reach the end, push softly on the moistened edge to secure the roll. Lightly roll back and forth to make the roll longer. Keeping the sealed side down, slice into 24 ½-inch swirls and place them 1 inch apart on a baking sheet. Replicate the process for the second pastry sheet. Bake until crunchy and golden, approximately fifteen to twenty minutes. Serve hot or at room temperature.

SALTY FINGER PASTRIES Ⓥ

This recipe is called "Namak-paarae or nimki" in Hindi

Yield: 4 to 6 servings

Ingredients:

- ½ teaspoon crudely ground ajwain seeds

- ½ teaspoon salt, or to taste
- ½ to 2 cups peanut oil for deep-frying
- 1 tablespoon cornstarch
- 1½ cups self-rising flour, plus more for dusting
- 3 tablespoons vegetable oil
- About ⅓ cup water

Directions:

1. Put the flour, cornstarch, oil, ajwain seeds, and salt into a food processor and pulse a few times to mix. Next, with the motor running, slowly and gradually pour in water and process until the dough gathers into a semi-firm ball that does not stick to the sides of the work container. Move to a container, cover, and set aside 1 to four hours. This allows the gluten to develop.
2. Slightly oil your clean hands and gather the dough into a smooth, large ball. Coat it well with the dry flour, use your hands and fingers to compress it into a disc, and roll it into a large 8- to 9-inch circle (don't worry approximately the shape) approximately ⅛ inch thick. If the dough sticks to the rolling surface, dust with more flour. (The rolling can be done on a mildly floured surface, but this is not a common practice in India.)
3. Using a knife, make diagonal cuts through the length of the rolled circle, approximately ½ inch apart. Next, make opposite diagonal cuts, separating the rolled dough into diamond-shaped bits.
4. Heat the oil in a big wok or over moderate heat until it reaches 300°F to 325°F on a frying thermometer, or when a small drop of dough begins to bubble while it is still immersed. (Reduce the heat if it rises instantly or browns.) Put in the dough bits, as many as the wok can comfortably hold simultaneously, and fry, turning as required with a slotted spatula until crunchy and appears mildly golden. Do not brown them and ensure that the centers are crisp. (Check by breaking one piece.) Move with a slotted spatula to paper towel to drain. Allow to cool completely, then store in airtight containers at room temperature, up to sixty days.

SAMOSA

Samosas are basically stuffed fried pastries, most commonly triangular in shape. The cheapest and most common stuffing you will find all across India is spicy mashed potato, but the possibilities are endless. You will find a few of the most popular samosa stuffing recipes under the next heading.

Samosas commonly enjoyed with chutneys, so feel free to randomly pick out any chutney from the chutney section to try with a samosa you prepare.

BASIC SAMOSA (V)

This recipe is called "Samosa" in Hindi

Yield: 24 pieces

The basic most commonly available triangular samosa. Use the potato filling with this if you want to enjoy the most popular samosa Indian samosa!

Ingredients:

- ½ teaspoon crudely ground ajwain seeds
- ½ teaspoon salt, or to taste
- 1 cup all-purpose flour in a moderate-sized container or a pie dish, for coating and dusting
- 1 recipe any Samosa Filling
- 1½ cups self-rising flour
- 1½ to 2 cups peanut oil for deep-frying
- 3 tablespoons vegetable oil
- About ⅓ cup water

Directions:

1. Ready the filling. Next, ready the dough: Put the self-rising flour, oil, ajwain seeds, and salt into a food processor and pulse until blended. While the motor runs, slowly and gradually pour in water and process until the flour gathers into a semi-firm ball that does not stick to the sides of the work container. Move to a container, cover using plastic wrap or a lid, and let rest at least 1 hour and up to four hours. (This lets the gluten develop.) If keeping for a longer period, place the dough in your fridge.

2. To roll and assemble: Slightly oil your clean hands (to stop the dough from sticking to them), then split into 12 1½-inch balls. Cover using aluminium foil and save for later. Work with each ball one at a time, and use your hands and fingers to compress it into a disc, cover thoroughly with dry flour, then roll using a rolling pin into a 6- to 7-inch circle of uniform ⅛-inch thickness. Use more dry flour as needed if the dough becomes sticky again.
3. Slice the circle in half and brush with water approximately ½-inch in, along the straight edge. Pick up the two corners and place one over and around the other along the straight edge, then push along the straight edge to secure, making a cone. Finally, pinch the peak of the cone to secure.
4. Another way is to fold in half, sealing the straight edge to make a simpler cone.
5. Hold the cone vertically such that the open end is on top. Fill the mouth of the cone with 2 to 3 tablespoons of filling. Brush the edges of the mouth of the cone with water and push them together to secure. You should have a stuffed triangular pastry when you're done. Cover with foil and allow to sit until ready to fry. Replicate the process for all the other balls of dough.
6. To fry: Heat the oil in a wok or skillet using moderate to high heat until it achieves 325°F to 350°F on a frying thermometer, or when a small piece of the dough dropped into the hot oil surges to the surface of the oil after fifteen to 20 seconds. Put the samosas in the wok, as many as it can hold simultaneously without crowding, and fry, turning them a few times with a slotted spatula, until crunchy and golden on all sides, about four to five minutes. (If the samosas brown too swiftly, it means the heat is too high; lower it.) Move to paper towels to drain, then serve.

SEVEN LAYERS SAMOSA

This recipe is called "Satpura samosae" in Hindi

Yield: 16 pieces

Ingredients:

- ⅛ teaspoon ground asafoetida
- ¼ teaspoon cayenne pepper, or to taste
- ¼ teaspoon salt, or to taste
- ¼ to ⅓ cup melted unsalted butter or vegetable oil

- ½ teaspoon garam masala
- 1 large russet (or any) potato
- 1 tablespoon melted ghee or vegetable oil
- 1 teaspoon cumin seeds
- 7 phyllo pastry sheets (about ¼ pound)

Directions:

1. Boil the potato in lightly salted water to cover until tender, approximately twenty minutes. Drain, allow to cool down, then peel and mash in a small-sized container. Heat the oil in a small-sized non-stick wok or saucepan using moderate to high heat and put in the cumin seeds; they should sizzle when they touch the hot oil. Swiftly put in the mashed potato, garam masala, cayenne pepper, asafoetida, and salt, and stir until a golden colour is achieved, approximately five to seven minutes. Allow to cool.
2. Moisten each phyllo sheet generously with the melted butter and stack one on top of the other on a cutting board. Using a sharp knife, cut along the length into 4 equal strips, approximately 3 inches wide, cutting through all 7 sheets. Cut each strip in half along the diagonal and then cut each half in half again to make a total of 16 rectangles, each made up of 7 layers. Cover with a damp (not wet) sanitized kitchen towel.
3. Preheat your oven to 350°F. Lightly grease a baking sheet. Using a rolling pin, lightly roll each rectangular stack of 7 layers to ensure the layers adhere to each other properly. Brush the top layer with butter and place 1 teaspoon of the filling in the center. Fold in half to, cover the filling. Press the edges well to secure in the filling. Replicate the process for the remain-ing rectangles.
4. Brush the top and bottom layers of the samosas generously with butter once again and place on the baking sheet. Bake until crunchy and golden, fifteen to twenty minutes. Move to cooling racks. Serve.

SINDHI-STYLE SAMOSA Ⓥ

This recipe is called "Sindhi samosae" in Hindi

Yield: 24 pieces

Sindh is now a part of Pakistan, but the Sindhi people and their cuisines are very much a part of India!

Ingredients:

- ¼ teaspoon salt, or to taste
- 1 cup all-purpose flour in a moderate-sized container or a pie dish, for coating and dusting
- 1 recipe any Samosa Filling of your choice
- 1½ cups self-rising flour
- 1½ teaspoons fennel seeds, crudely ground
- 2 to 3 cups peanut oil for deep-frying
- About ¾ cup water

Directions:

1. Ready the filling. Next, in a small-sized container, combine 2 tablespoons of the self-rising flour with approximately 2 tablespoons water to make a thick paste that will be used as a glue for sealing the pastries.
2. Ready the dough: Put the rest of the self-rising flour, fennel seeds, and salt into a food processor and pulse until blended. While the motor runs, slowly and gradually pour in water and process until the flour gathers into a pliable ball that does not stick to the sides of the work container. (This dough does not need to rest.)
3. To roll and assemble: Split the dough into 8 balls. Flatten each one into a 3- to 4-inch disc. Working with 4 discs at a time, brush the top surface of each thoroughly with oil then dust each one with approximately 2 teaspoons flour. Working with the rest of the 4 discs one at a time, brush with oil and place on top of one of the floured discs, oil side down, like a sandwich. Next, press each "sandwich" together to make one big disc. You will now have four large discs.
4. Working with each of the 4 discs one at a time, sprinkle mildly with the flour and roll using a rolling pin to make 8- to 9-inch circles of uniform ⅛-inch thickness. (Use more dry flour as needed if the dough becomes sticky again.)
5. Heat a griddle or a skillet over moderate heat and cook each rolled circle very lightly on both sides until it just begins to firm up but not brown, approximately half a minute per side. (You'll see the edges of the sandwiched circle starting to separate.) Transfer it to a cutting board. Cautiously pull the two sides apart to split into two paper-thin circles, and stack them. Replicate the process for the other three discs. When you're done, you should have a stack of 8 samosa skins. Slice the stack of skins into 3 equal parts, making a total of 24 long strips. Keep covered with foil.

6. Working with each strip separately, lay it along the length in front of you on the work surface and place approximately 1 tablespoon of the filling on the strip near the lower right corner. Next, fold the right corner over the filling to the left side to make a triangle. Repeatedly fold the stuffed triangle along the diagonal from one side to the other until you get to the end of the dough strip. Tuck in any spare dough to secure. When you're done, you should have a multi-folded triangle. Replicate the process for all the strips.
7. Heat the oil in a wok or skillet using moderate to high heat until it achieves 325°F to 350°F on a frying thermometer or when a small piece of dough dropped into the hot oil surges to the surface of the oil after fifteen to 20 seconds. Add as many samosas as the wok can hold simultaneously without crowding, and fry, turning them a few times with a slotted spatula, until crunchy and golden on all sides, about four to five minutes. (If the samosas brown too swiftly, lower the heat.) Move to paper towels to drain, then serve.

STUFFED PHYLLO BAKED SAMOSA

This recipe is called "Potli-samosae" in Hindi

Yield: 24 pieces

Ingredients:

- ¼ to ⅓ cup melted unsalted butter or vegetable oil
- 1 recipe any Samosa Filling of your choice
- 12 phyllo pastry sheets (about ½ pound)

Directions:

1. Brush each phyllo sheet liberally with butter and stack one on top of the other on a cutting board. Using a sharp knife, cut the sheets in half, along the diagonal, to make a total of 24 pieces. Stack once again, and cover with a damp (not wet) sanitized kitchen towel.
2. Preheat your oven to 350°F. Lightly grease a mini-muffin pan or a baking sheet. Working with each piece separately, fold in half and then in half again to make an approximately 6-by-4-inch rectangle. Put approximately 1 tablespoon of the filling in the center, then pick up the phyllo by the four

corners and pinch them together just above the filling to secure, making a little pouch.
3. Another way is to tie each one lightly with chives, scallion greens, or thin strips of carrots, or any other greens or vegetables. Replicate the process for all the pieces.
4. Brush all the pouches with the butter, and place each in one cup of the muffin pan or all of them on a baking sheet and bake until crunchy and golden, approximately 25 minutes. Move to cooling racks. Serve hot, warm, or at room temperature.

STUFFED PHYLLO SAMOSA

This recipe is called "Phyllo Ke samosae" in Hindi

Yield: 24 pieces

Ingredients:

- 1 recipe any <u>Samosa Filling</u> of your choice
- 1 to 2 tablespoons melted butter or vegetable oil
- 6 phyllo pastry sheets (about ¼ pound)

Directions:

1. Brush each phyllo sheet with melted butter and stack one on top of the other on a cutting board. Using a sharp knife, cut them along the length into 4 equal strips, each approximately 3 inches wide. You should have 24 long strips. Stack again and cover with a damp (not wet) sanitized kitchen towel.
2. Preheat your oven to 350°F. Lightly grease a baking sheet. Working with each strip separately, place it along the length in front of you on the work surface and put approximately 1 tablespoon of the filling near the lower right corner. Fold the right corner over the filling to the left side to make a triangle. Repeatedly fold the stuffed triangle along the diagonal from one side to the other until you get to the end of the phyllo. Tuck in any extra to secure. When you're done, you should have a multifolded triangle. Replicate the process for all the strips.
3. Brush the top of all the triangles with the butter, place them on the baking sheet, and bake, flipping over once midway through baking, until crunchy

and golden, approximately 25 minutes. Move to cooling racks. Serve hot, warm, or at room temperature.

TORTILLA SAMOSA Ⓥ

This recipe is called "Tortilla samosa" in Hindi

Yield: 24 pieces

A delicious combo of an Indian and Mexican snack!

Ingredients:

- 1 recipe any <u>Samosa Filling</u> of your choice
- 1½ to 2 cups peanut oil for deep-frying
- 12 (8- to 9-inch) flour tortillas

Directions:

1. 1. Stack and cut the tortillas in half to make 24 semicircles. Working with each half separately, brush with water approximately ½-inch in, along all the edges. Next, place 1½ to 2 tablespoons of the samosa filling on one side of the semi circle. Fold the other side over the filling to cover it. Press the edges well to secure in the filling. Replicate the process for the rest of the halves.
2. To roll and assemble: Slightly oil your clean hands (to stop the dough from sticking to them), then split into 12 1½-inch balls. Cover using aluminium foil and save for later. Work with each ball one at a time, and use your hands and fingers to compress it into a disc, cover thoroughly with dry flour, then roll using a rolling pin into a 6- to 7-inch circle of uniform ⅛-inch thickness. Use more dry flour as needed if the dough becomes sticky again.
3. Slice the circle in half and brush with water approximately ½-inch in, along the straight edge. Pick up the two corners and place one over and around the other along the straight edge, then push along the straight edge to secure, making a cone. Finally, pinch the peak of the cone to secure.
4. Another way is to fold in half, sealing the straight edge to make a simpler cone.
5. Hold the cone vertically such that the open end is on top. Fill the mouth of the cone with 2 to 3 tablespoons of filling. Brush the edges of the mouth of

the cone with water and push them together to secure. You should have a stuffed triangular pastry when you're done. Cover with foil and allow to sit until ready to fry. Replicate the process for all the other balls of dough.

6. To fry: Heat the oil in a wok or skillet using moderate to high heat until it achieves 325°F to 350°F on a frying thermometer, or when a small piece of the dough dropped into the hot oil surges to the surface of the oil after fifteen to 20 seconds. Put the samosas in the wok, as many as it can hold simultaneously without crowding, and fry, turning them a few times with a slotted spatula, until crunchy and golden on all sides, about four to five minutes. (If the samosas brown too swiftly, it means the heat is too high; lower it.) Move to paper towels to drain, then serve.

FILLINGS FOR SAMOSAS

BASIC POTATO FILLING (V)

This recipe is called "Samosae ka aalu ka masala" in Hindi

Yield: Approximately 4 cups

The most common Samosa filling you will find in India!

Ingredients:

- ¼ cup finely chopped fresh cilantro, including soft stems
- ½ teaspoon crudely ground fenugreek seeds
- ½ teaspoon garam masala
- ½ teaspoon salt, or to taste
- 1 teaspoon mango powder
- 1 to 3 fresh green chile peppers, such as serrano, minced with seeds
- 1½ tablespoons ground coriander
- 2 tablespoons peanut oil
- 2 tablespoons peeled and minced fresh ginger

- 2 teaspoons cumin seeds
- 4 to 5 medium russet (or any) potatoes (about 1½ pounds)

Directions:

1. Cook the potatoes in lightly salted boiling water to cover until tender, approximately twenty minutes. Drain, allow to cool down, then peel and finely chop. Heat the oil in a big non-stick wok or saucepan using moderate to high heat and put in the cumin seeds; they should sizzle when they touch the hot oil. Swiftly put in the fenugreek seeds and stir in the potatoes.
2. Stir approximately two minutes, then Put in the ginger, green chile peppers, coriander, salt, and garam masala, and stir occasionally until the potatoes are golden, approximately ten minutes.
3. Put in the cilantro and mango powder and cook another 5 minutes. Turn off the heat and allow to cool down before using.

GREEN PEA FILLING Ⓥ

This recipe is called "Samosae ka matar ka masala" in Hindi

Yield: Approximately 4 cups

Green peas are delicious and nutritious!

Ingredients:

- ⅛ teaspoon ground asafoetida
- ½ teaspoon cayenne pepper, or to taste
- ½ teaspoon salt, or to taste
- 1 cup water
- 1 large onion, finely chopped
- 1 teaspoon ground fennel seeds
- 1 teaspoon ground ginger
- 1¼ cups green split peas (muttar dal), sorted and washed in 3 to 4 changes of water
- 1½ teaspoons cumin seeds
- 2 tablespoons vegetable oil
- 2 teaspoons ground coriander

- 2 teaspoons mango powder

Directions:

1. Immerse the split peas overnight in water to cover by 2 inches, then drain. Heat the oil in a small-sized non-stick wok or saucepan using moderate to high heat and put in the cumin seeds; they should sizzle when they touch the hot oil. Swiftly put in the onion and cook, stirring, until a golden colour is achieved, approximately two minutes.
2. Put in the dal, coriander, ginger, fennel seeds, cayenne pepper, salt, and asafoetida, and cook approximately one minute. Put in the water, bring to a quick boil using high heat, then reduce the heat to low, cover the pan and cook until the split peas become soft, approximately ten minutes. Stir in the mango powder and allow to cool down before using.

MEAT FILLING

This recipe is called "Samosae ka gosht ka masala" in Hindi

Yield: Approximately 3 cups

Feel free to use any kind of meat!

Ingredients:

- ¼ teaspoon freshly ground nutmeg
- ¼ teaspoon ground turmeric
- ½ cup bread crumbs
- ½ teaspoon cayenne pepper, or to taste
- ½ teaspoon salt, or to taste
- 1 cup crudely chopped fresh cilantro, including soft stems
- 1 cup fresh fenugreek leaves
- 1 cup frozen peas, thawed
- 1 fresh green chile pepper, such as serrano, crudely chopped
- 1 pound extra lean ground meat (lamb, beef, or chicken)
- 1 tablespoon garam masala
- 2 large cloves fresh garlic, peeled
- 5 to 7 quarter-size slices peeled fresh ginger

Directions:

1. Using a food processor, combine and pulse the fenugreek leaves, cilantro, garlic, ginger, and green chile pepper until minced. Add all the rest of the ingredients, except the peas, and process once more to mix thoroughly.
2. Move to a large non-stick wok or skillet, stir in the peas, and cook, stirring, using moderate to high heat until the meat is golden and completely dry, approximately eight to ten minutes. Allow to cool before using.

MOONG DAL FILLING (V)

This recipe is called "Samosae ka mung dal ka Masala" in Hindi

Yield: Approximately 4 cups

Mung dal beans make a great filling for the samosa!

Ingredients:

- ¼ teaspoon ground turmeric
- ½ teaspoon salt, or to taste
- 1 cup finely chopped fresh spinach
- 1 cup water
- 1 fresh green chile pepper, such as serrano, minced with seeds
- 1 tablespoon ground coriander
- 1 teaspoon cumin seeds
- 1¼ cup dried yellow mung beans (dhulli mung dal), sorted and washed in 3 to 4 changes of water
- 1½ tablespoons peeled and minced fresh ginger
- 2 tablespoons vegetable oil

Directions:

1. Immerse the mung beans overnight in water to cover by 2 inches, then drain. Heat the oil in a big non-stick wok or saucepan using moderate to high heat and put in the cumin seeds; they should sizzle when they touch the hot oil. Swiftly put in the ginger, green chile pepper, and coriander, and stir for approximately half a minute.

2. Put in the spinach and stir until wilted, approximately one minute. Stir in the mung beans, turmeric, and salt, and stir approximately two minutes. Put in the water, reduce the heat to moderate to low, cover the pan and cook until all the water has been absorbed and the dal is soft, approximately ten minutes. Allow to cool before using.

SPROUTED GREEN MUNG BEAN FILLING (V)

This recipe is called "Samosae ka phooti mung dal ka masala" in Hindi

Yield: Approximately 4 cups

Ingredients:

- ½ cup finely chopped fresh cilantro, including soft stems
- ½ teaspoon ground turmeric
- 1 large onion, finely chopped
- 1 teaspoon salt, or to taste
- 1 to 3 fresh green chile pepper, such as serrano, minced with seeds
- 2 cups sprouted green mung beans (Sprout your own as shown in the "Indian Cooking 101" section, or buy in a store)
- 2 tablespoons fresh lemon juice
- 2 tablespoons ground coriander
- 2 tablespoons peanut oil
- 2 teaspoons cumin seeds
- 6 small russet (or any) potatoes

Directions:

1. Ready the mung beans in advance. Cook the potatoes in lightly salted boiling water to cover until tender, approximately twenty minutes. Drain, allow to cool down, then grate into a moderate-sized container.
2. Heat the oil in a big non-stick wok or saucepan using moderate to high heat and put in the cumin seeds; they should sizzle when they touch the hot oil. Swiftly put in the onions and cook, stirring, until a golden colour is achieved, approximately five minutes.

3. Put in the coriander and turmeric, then stir in the green chiles, sprouted dal, and salt, and cook approximately three minutes. Put in the grated potatoes, lemon juice, and cilantro, and cook using moderate to high heat, stirring, until completely dry, approximately five minutes. Turn off the heat and allow to cool down before using.

VEGETABLE FILLING

This recipe is called "Samosae ka sabziyon ka masala" in Hindi

Yield: Approximately 4 cups

Feel free to use vegetables of your choice! You don't have to follow the recipe exactly. Invent a samosa tailored exactly to your taste!

Ingredients:

- ½ teaspoon salt, or to taste
- 1 medium onion, finely chopped
- 1 tablespoon peeled and finely chopped fresh ginger
- 1 to 3 fresh green chile peppers, such as serrano, minced with seeds
- 1½ to 2 tablespoons Spicy Masala for Wok-Cooked Foods (Kadhai Masala), or store-bought
- 2 tablespoons vegetable oil
- 4 cups finely chopped mixed fresh or frozen vegetables
- Freshly ground black pepper, to taste

Directions:

1. Ready the kadaai masala. Heat the oil in a big non-stick wok or saucepan using moderate to high heat and put in the kadhai masala; it should sizzle when they touch the hot oil. Swiftly put in the onion and stir approximately two minutes.
2. Put in the green chile peppers, ginger, vegetables, salt, and black pepper, and cook over moderate heat the first two to three minutes, and then using moderate to low heat until the vegetables are soft, 5 to 7 min-utes more. Turn off the heat and allow to cool down before using.

FRITTERS (PAKORAE)

These fried treats are the first things that come to mind on a rainy day in North India. There are probably a million kinds of pakodas eaten in India as the combinations of batters and what you put in the batter are endless. These are almost always served with a chutney and served immediately after being taken out of the wok.

Even though the possibilities are endless, the most commonly used batter is chickpea flour (called "besan" in Hindi). The batter needs to be the right thickness, and that is something you will know after practice. If the batter is too thin, it won't stick to the stuff you're covering with it, and if you make it too thick, the pakora will taste a little too heavy doughy. You can do this by adjusting the amount of water. Also, it is important to sift to batter to make sure all the lumps are eliminated, and the flour stays nice and fluffy.

If you have guests coming over and you wish to pre-prepare your pakoras, it is a good idea to double fry them. Lightly fry the pakoras in advance and store in your fridge in an air-tight container. These will keep in the fridge for about five to six days. When it is time to serve, take them out of the fridge, bring them to room temperature, and refry in hot oil. If the oil, or the pakoras aren't hot enough, the pakoras will absorb more oil than they need to.

FRYING FRITTERS

This technique is called "Pakorae Talna" in Hindi

This technique will be used in all the pakora recipes that follow, so you might want to bookmark this.

Directions:

1. Heat the oil in a wok or skillet until it reaches 350°F to 375°F on a frying thermometer or a small teaspoon of batter dropped into the hot oil bubbles and surges to the surface of the oil instantly.
2. With clean hands, put the chopped or chopped vegetables (or other items) into the batter (in batches if needed) and mix lightly using your fingers. Work with each piece one at a time and shake off the surplus batter by tapping it

lightly against the sides of the batter container, then put it into the hot oil cautiously using your fingers (or with tongs) to avoid oil spluttering. Add as many pieces as the wok can hold simultaneously without crowding, and fry each batch, turning a few times with a slotted spoon, until crunchy and golden on all sides, approximately one to two minutes for small, thin pieces, approximately two to three minutes for bigger pieces. Move to paper towels to drain. Repeat the process with rest of the pieces.

BASIC BATTER FOR PAKORA

This recipe is called "Pakorae ka besan" in Hindi

Yield: 40 to 50 fritters

This is the most basic batter for pakora fritters, to which you can add as many or as few herbs and spices as you wish. With no other additions, this basic recipe forms a light, crisp coating around a large array of foods. More than anything else, it is the consistency of the batter that is really important. Thick, it will be doughy, thin it will not coat properly.

Ingredients:

- ⅛ teaspoon baking soda
- ⅓ teaspoon salt, or to taste
- ⅓ to ½ cup water
- ½ cup chickpea flour (besan)

Directions:

1. Sieve the chickpea flour into a moderate-sized container, put in the salt and baking soda and mix thoroughly.
2. Add ⅓ cup water to make a smooth batter of medium consistency. If the batter is thin, add some more chickpea flour; if it appears too thick, stir in some more water. The batter is now ready.

SLICED, CHOPPED, AND STUFFED VEGETABLE FRITTERS

BELL PEPPER FRITTERS Ⓥ

This recipe is called "Shimla mirch kae pakorae" in Hindi

Yield: Approximately 30 pieces

Ingredients:

- ½ teaspoon crudely ground ajwain seeds
- ½ teaspoon Chaat Masala (Homemade or store-bought)
- ½ teaspoon hot red pepper flakes, or to taste
- 1 recipe Basic Batter for Pakora Fritters
- 1 tablespoon Basic Ginger Paste (Homemade or store-bought)
- 1½ to 2 cups oil for deep-frying
- 2 teaspoons ground coriander
- 3 to 4 orange or red bell peppers, stemmed and seeded

Directions:

1. Ready the ginger-garlic paste and chaat masala. Cut each bell pepper along the length into 2 halves, then cross-wise into ½-inch thick half moons.
2. Ready the basic batter. Stir in the coriander, ajwain seeds, red pepper flakes, and ginger-garlic paste.
3. Put in the bell pepper slices to the batter. Heat the oil and fry the bell pepper slices as per directions under the "Frying Fritters" heading at the start of this section. Move all the fried pakoras to a serving platter, sprinkle the chaat masala on top, and serve.

CABBAGE ROLL FRITTERS Ⓥ

This recipe is called "Bundh gobhi kae pakorae" in Hindi

Yield: twelve to fifteen pieces

Ingredients:

- ½ teaspoon Chaat Masala (Homemade or store-bought)
- 1 recipe Basic Batter for Pakora Fritters
- 1½ cup any dry-cooked vegetable or meat filling (choose from Fillings for Samosa Pastries)
- 1½ to 2 cups oil for deep-frying
- Shredded cabbage to line a platter
- twelve to fifteen outer leaves Napa cabbage

Directions:

1. Ready the chaat masala and the filling, then ready the batter. Rinse and cut off the leafy top 5 inches of each cabbage leaf. Put in a microwave-safe dish, cover with the lid of the dish, and cook 3 to four minutes on high power, to wilt the leaves. (Or wilt over moderate heat in a big pan.) Allow to cool.
2. Put approximately 2 tablespoons or more of the filling on each leaf, along the diagonal at the stem end, folding it with the stem end tucked inside, to make a roll. Pinch the edges to secure the roll. Dip each roll in the batter to coat it well.
3. Fry using the directions under "Frying Fritters" at the start of this section. Move all the fried pakoras to a serving platter, sprinkle the chaat masala on top, and serve on a bed of shredded cabbage.

CAULIFLOWER FRITTERS Ⓥ

This recipe is called "Gobhi kae pakorae" in Hindi

Yield: 20 to 25 pieces

Ingredients:

- ¼ cup minced fresh cilantro, including soft stems
- ¼ cup mustard oil for deep-frying
- ¼ teaspoon garam masala
- ½ teaspoon crudely ground ajwain seeds
- ½ teaspoon hot red pepper flakes, or to taste
- ½ teaspoon salt, or to taste
- 1 large head cauliflower (about 1½ pounds), cut into 2-inch florets

- 1 teaspoon Chaat Masala (Homemade or store-bought)
- 1 to 2 tablespoons chickpea flour
- 1 to 3 fresh green chile peppers, such as serrano, minced with seeds
- 1½ recipes Basic Batter for Pakora Fritters
- 1½ to 2 cups peanut oil for deep-frying

Directions:

1. Ready the chaat masala. Put the cauliflower florets in a container and toss with salt and red pepper flakes. Set aside to let the flavours blend. Ready the basic batter. Stir in the chickpea flour, cilantro, green chile peppers, garam masala, and ajwain seeds. Put in the florets to the batter. Fry using the directions under "Frying Fritters" at the start of this section.
2. Allow to cool, then press each fritter between the palms of your hands to flatten. As you do this, the batter coating will break and reveal parts of the florets. Refry the dense florets in hot oil until the pakoras are lightly browned and crisp, approximately a minute or two. Drain using paper towels. Move all the fried pakoras to a serving platter, sprinkle the chaat masala on top, and serve.

EGGPLANT FRITTERS Ⓥ

This recipe is called "Baingan kae pakorae" in Hindi

Yield: 35 to 40 pieces

Ingredients:

- ¼ cup finely chopped fresh cilantro, including soft stems
- ¼ cup mustard oil
- ½ tablespoon Basic Garlic Paste (Homemade or store-bought)
- ½ teaspoon crudely ground ajwain seeds
- ½ teaspoon hot red pepper flakes, or to taste
- 1 recipe Basic Batter for Pakora Fritters
- 1 teaspoon Chaat Masala (Homemade or store-bought)
- 1½ to 2 cups peanut oil for deep-frying
- 2 Chinese eggplants, each 7 to 8 inches long and 2-inches in diameter, cut in ¼-inch-thick diagonal slices

Directions:

1. Ready the chaat masala and ginger-garlic paste. Next, ready the basic batter. Stir in the cilantro, garlic paste, ajwain seeds, and red pepper flakes. Put in the eggplant slices to the batter.
2. Fry using the directions under "Frying Fritters" at the start of this section. Move all the fried pakoras to a serving platter, sprinkle the chaat masala on top, and serve.

FRESH GREEN BEAN PAKORA FRITTERS (V)

This recipe is called "Hari phalliyon kae pakorae" in Hindi

Yield: 40 to 50 fritters

Ingredients:

- ½ teaspoon Chaat Masala (Homemade or store-bought)
- ½ teaspoon crushed ajwain seeds
- ½ teaspoon ground cumin
- 1 recipe Basic Batter for Pakora Fritters
- 1 tablespoon peeled and finely minced or ground fresh ginger
- 1 teaspoon ground coriander
- 1½ to 2 cups oil for deep-frying
- 40 to 50 fresh green beans (about ½ pound), trimmed from the stem end only

Directions:

1. Ready the chaat masala. Ready the basic batter. Stir in the coriander, cumin, ajwain seeds, and ginger. Put in the beans to the batter. Fry using the directions under "Frying Fritters" at the start of this section.
2. Move all the fried pakoras to a serving platter, sprinkle the chaat masala on top, and serve.

POTATO FRITTERS (V)

This recipe is called "Aalu kae pakorae" in Hindi

Yield: 25 to 30 fritters

Ingredients:

- ½ teaspoon Chaat Masala (Homemade or store-bought)
- 1 recipe Basic Batter for Pakora Fritters
- 1 teaspoon crudely ground cumin or ajwain seeds
- 1½ to 2 cups oil for deep-frying
- 2 tablespoons minced chives
- 2 teaspoons ground coriander
- 3 to 4 small russet (or any) potatoes, thinly chopped

Directions:

1. Ready the chaat masala. Ready the basic batter. Stir in the coriander, cumin (or ajwain), and chives. Put in the potato slices in the batter.
2. Fry using the directions under "Frying Fritters" at the start of this section. Move all the fried pakoras to a serving platter, sprinkle the chaat masala on top, and serve.

PUMPKIN FRITTERS Ⓥ

This recipe is called "Pethae kae pakorae" in Hindi

Yield: 24 pieces

Ingredients:

- ½ teaspoon Chaat Masala (Homemade or store-bought)
- 1 (2- by 6-inch) piece pumpkin or butternut squash, cut into ¼-inch-thick slices
- 1 recipe Basic Batter for Pakora Fritters
- 1 teaspoon sugar
- 1½ to 2 cups peanut oil for deep-frying
- 2 teaspoons Bengali 5-Spices (Panch-Phoran) or store-bought

Directions:

1. Ready the chaat masala and the 5-spices. Next, ready the basic batter and stir in the 5-spices and the sugar.

2. Put in the pumpkin slices to the batter. Fry using the directions under "Frying Fritters" at the start of this section. Move all the fried pakoras to a serving platter, sprinkle the chaat masala on top, and serve.

SPINACH FRITTERS Ⓥ

This recipe is called "Palak kae pakorae" in Hindi

Yield: 50 to 60 pieces

Ingredients:

- ½ teaspoon crudely ground ajwain seeds
- ½ teaspoon hot red pepper flakes, or to taste
- ½ to 2 cups peanut oil for deep-frying
- 1 recipe Basic Batter for Pakora Fritters
- 1 teaspoon Basic Garlic Paste (Homemade or store-bought)
- 1 teaspoon Chaat Masala (Homemade or store-bought)
- 2 teaspoons ground coriander
- 50 to 60 baby spinach leaves with stems (about ½ pound)

Directions:

1. Ready the garlic paste and the chaat masala. Ready the basic batter. Stir in the garlic paste, coriander, ajwain seeds, and red pepper flakes. Put in the spinach to the batter.
2. Fry using the directions under "Frying Fritters" at the start of this section. Move all the fried pakoras to a serving platter, sprinkle the chaat masala on top, and serve.

STUFFED BREAD FRITTERS Ⓥ

This recipe is called "Bread pakorae" in Hindi

Yield: 24 pieces

Ingredients:

- ¼ teaspoon ground asafoetida

- ¼ teaspoon ground fenugreek seeds
- ½ cup or more any Coconut Chutney
- ½ teaspoon crudely ground black mustard seeds
- ½ teaspoon Chaat Masala (Homemade or store-bought)
- 1 cup peanut oil for deep-frying
- 1 recipe Basic Batter for Pakora Fritters
- 1 tablespoon minced fresh curry leaves
- 12 thin slices packaged white or whole-wheat bread, with or without crusts removed

Directions:

1. Ready the chaat masala and the coconut chutney. Ready the batter. Put the basic batter in a flat-bottomed dish and stir in the mustard and fenugreek seeds, curry leaves, and asafoetida.
2. Spread the coconut chutney liberally on 6 of the bread slices and cover with the rest of the 6 slices. Cut each "sandwich" into 4 squares or triangles.
3. Heat the oil in a big skillet (not a wok) until it reaches 350°F to 375°F on a frying thermometer, or a piece of bread dropped into the hot oil bubbles and surges to the surface of the oil instantly.
4. Cautiously, dip each square (or triangle) into the batter and add it to the hot oil, adding as many as the skillet can hold simultaneously. Fry, turning as required, until a golden colour is achieved on both sides, approximately two minutes.
5. Drain using paper towels. Move to a serving platter. Sprinkle with the chaat masala and serve.

SHREDDED AND MINCED VEGETABLE FRITTERS

CHOPPED ONION FRITTERS Ⓥ

This recipe is called "Kattae pyaz kae pakorae" in Hindi

Yield: 25 to 30 pieces

Ingredients:

- ¼ teaspoon baking soda
- ½ cup chickpea flour
- ½ cup finely chopped fresh cilantro, including soft stems
- ½ teaspoon Chaat Masala (Homemade or store-bought)
- ½ teaspoon ground ajwain seeds
- ½ teaspoon ground cumin
- 1 small onion, finely chopped or minced
- 1 small russet (or any) potato, peeled and grated
- 1 tablespoon peeled and finely chopped fresh ginger
- 1 teaspoon dried fenugreek leaves
- 1 teaspoon salt, or to taste
- 1½ to 2 cups peanut oil for deep-frying
- 2 teaspoons coriander, crudely crushed with the back of a spoon
- 2 to 3 tablespoons water

Directions:

1. Ready the chaat masala. Sieve the chickpea flour in a moderate-sized container and stir in the onion, potato, ginger, coriander, fenugreek, cumin, ajwain seeds, baking soda, and salt. Put in the water as required to make a semi-thick mixture.
2. Heat the oil as per directions under the "Frying Fritters" heading at the start of this section. Cautiously, using your fingers or a tablespoon, drop 1-inch uneven balls of the mixture cautiously into the hot oil and fry as directed at the start of this section. Move all the fried pakoras to a serving platter, sprinkle the chaat masala on top before you serve.

FENUGREEK FRITTERS Ⓥ

This recipe is called "Hari methi kae pakorae" in Hindi

Yield: 25 to 30 pieces

Ingredients:

- ⅛ teaspoon baking soda
- ½ cup chickpea flour

- ½ teaspoon <u>Chaat Masala</u> (Homemade or store-bought)
- ½ teaspoon salt, or to taste
- 1 tablespoon ground pomegranate seeds
- 1 teaspoon mango powder
- 1 to 3 fresh green chile peppers, such as serrano, minced with seeds
- 1½ to 2 cups peanut oil for deep frying
- 2 cups finely chopped fresh fenugreek leaves, including soft stems
- 2 tablespoons crudely ground coriander

Directions:

1. Ready the chaat masala. Put the chopped fenugreek leaves in a container and add all the other ingredients, except the oil and chaat masala and mix thoroughly to make a semi-thick mixture, and set aside, approximately twenty minutes. Do not add any water; the washed leaves will be moist and the salt and spices will cause them to release more.
2. Heat the oil as per directions under the "Frying Fritters" heading at the start of this section. Cautiously, using your fingers or a tablespoon, drop 1-inch uneven balls of the mixture into the hot oil and fry as directed at the start of this section. Move all the pakoras to a serving platter, sprinkle the chaat masala on top before you serve.

MIXED VEGETABLE FRITTERS Ⓥ

This recipe is called "Milli-julli sabziyon kae pakorae" in Hindi

Yield: 25 to 30 pieces

Ingredients:

- ¼ teaspoon baking soda
- ½ cup each minced onion, red bell pepper
- ½ cup each: grated carrots, broccoli, potatoes, zucchini
- ½ cup finely chopped fresh cilantro, including soft stems
- ½ teaspoon crudely ground ajwain seeds
- ½ teaspoon crudely ground black pepper
- ½ to 2 cups oil for deep-frying
- 1 cup chickpea flour (besan), or more as required
- 1 cup finely chopped fresh spinach leaves

- 1 tablespoon peeled and minced fresh ginger
- 1 teaspoon Chaat Masala (Homemade or store-bought)
- 1 teaspoon salt, or to taste
- 1 to 3 fresh green chile peppers, such as serrano, minced with seeds

Directions:

1. Ready the chaat masala. In a container, mix everything except the oil and chaat masala together to make a semi-thick mixture, adding more chickpea flour if the batter appears too soft or some water if firm.
2. Heat the oil as per directions under the "Frying Fritters" heading at the start of this section. Cautiously, using clean fingers or a spoon, drop 1-inch balls of the mixture into the hot oil and fry as directed at the start of this section. Move fritters to a platter, sprinkle with the chaat masala before you serve.

RICE FLOUR AND CASHEW FRITTERS (V)

This recipe is called "Chaval atta aur kaaju kae pakorae" in Hindi

Yield: 15 to 20 pieces

Ingredients:

- ⅛ teaspoon baking soda
- ¼ cup chickpea flour
- ⅓ cup rice flour
- ½ cup crudely chopped fresh cilantro, including soft stems
- ½ teaspoon salt, or to taste
- 1 cup raw cashews
- 1 fresh green chile pepper, such as serrano, stemmed
- 1 small onion, crudely chopped
- 1½ to 2 cups peanut oil for deep frying
- 2 to 3 cups shredded lettuce (any kind)
- 4 to 6 quarter-size slices of peeled fresh ginger
- 8 to 10 fresh spinach leaves, with stems

Directions:

1. Using a food processor, combine and pulse the ginger, green chile pepper, onion, cilantro, and spinach until minced. Put in the cashews and pulse until the nuts are crudely chopped. Move to a container. Stir in the rice and chickpea flours, salt, and baking soda.
2. Heat the oil per directions under the "Frying Fritters" heading at the start of this section. Cautiously, using clean fingers or a spoon, drop 3/4- to 1-inch balls of the mixture into the hot oil and fry as directed at the start of this section. Move to paper towels to drain. Next, serve on a platter lined with shredded lettuce.

RICE FLOUR PAPAYA FRITTERS Ⓥ

This recipe is called "Chaval atta aur papitae kae pakorae" in Hindi

Yield: 35 to 40 pieces

Ingredients:

- ⅛ teaspoon baking soda
- ¼ teaspoon ground asafoetida
- ½ cup crudely chopped fresh cilantro, including soft stems
- ½ cup chickpea flour
- ½ teaspoon salt, or to taste
- ⅔ cup rice flour
- 1 small onion, crudely chopped
- 1 tablespoon crudely ground dried curry leaves
- 1 tablespoon vegetable oil
- 1 teaspoon mustard seeds
- 1 to 3 fresh green chile peppers, such as serrano, stemmed
- 1½ cups peeled and chopped firm unripe papaya
- 1½ to 2 cups peanut oil for deep-frying
- 2 tablespoons fresh lemon juice
- 2 to 3 cups shredded lettuce (any kind)
- 4 to 6 quarter-size slices peeled fresh ginger
- twelve to fifteen fresh spinach leaves, with stems

Directions:

1. Using a food processor, mix together and pulse the ginger, green chile peppers, onion, cilantro, spinach, and lemon juice until just minced. (Do not purée.) Put in the papaya and pulse until crudely chopped (do not mince). Move to a container. Put in the rice and chickpea flours, salt, and baking soda and mix thoroughly to make a thick, almost dough-like mixture. Add some more rice or chickpea flour, if required.
2. Heat 1 tablespoon oil in a small-sized non-stick sauce-pan using moderate to high heat and put in the mustard seeds and asafoetida. They should splutter when they touch the hot oil, so cover the pan and reduce the heat until the spluttering diminishes. Swiftly put in the curry leaves, stir for approximately half a minute, then mix the spices into the mixture.
3. Heat the peanut oil as per directions under the "Frying Fritters" heading at the start of this section. Divide the mixture into 12 identical portions and form into rolls or cylinders, each approximately 1 inch thick and 3 inches long (they don't have to be smooth). Cautiously slide them into the hot oil, adding as many as the wok can hold simultaneously without crowding, and fry, turning and moving them around as required until a golden colour is achieved, approximately two to three minutes.
4. Move with slotted spatula to paper towels to drain. Once cool sufficient to hold, pinch off approximately 1-inch pieces from each roll and refry in hot oil, drain on paper towels again, then serve on a bed of shredded lettuce.

SHREDDED CABBAGE FRITTERS

This recipe is called "Bundh gobhi kae pakorae" in Hindi

Yield: 30 to 40 pieces

Ingredients:

- ¼ cup finely chopped fresh cilantro, including soft stems
- ¼ teaspoon baking soda
- ¼ to ⅓ cup non-fat plain yogurt, whisked until the desired smoothness is achieved
- ½ teaspoon crudely ground ajwain seeds
- ½ teaspoon Chaat Masala
- 1 fresh green chile pepper, such as serrano, minced with seeds
- 1 tablespoon ground coriander
- 1 tablespoon peeled and minced fresh ginger

- 1 teaspoon dried fenugreek leaves
- 1 teaspoon salt, or to taste
- 1 to 1½ cups chickpea flour (besan)
- 1½ cups finely shredded or chopped cabbage or Brussels sprouts (or mixed)
- 1½ to 2 cups mustard or peanut oil for deep-frying

Directions:

1. **1.** Ready the chaat masala. In a container, combine all the ingredients, except the oil and chaat masala to make a semi-thick mixture, adding more chickpea flour if the mixture appears too soft or some water if it is too firm. Let sit for about fifteen to twenty minutes.
2. **2.** Heat the oil as per directions under the "Frying Fritters" heading at the start of this section. Cautiously, using your fingers or a tablespoon, drop 1-inch uneven balls of the mixture cautiously into the hot oil and fry as directed at the start of this section. Move all the fried pakoras to a serving platter, sprinkle the chaat masala on top before you serve.

SPLIT PEA FRITTERS Ⓥ

This recipe is called "Muttar dal kae pakorae" in Hindi

Yield: 20 to 25 pieces

Ingredients:

- ¼ teaspoon baking soda
- ½ cup crudely chopped fresh cilantro, including soft stems
- ½ cup green split peas (muttar dal), sorted and washed in 3 to 4 changes of water
- ½ teaspoon crudely ground ajwain seeds
- ½ teaspoon Chaat Masala or store-bought)
- ½ teaspoon ground cumin
- ⅔ cup chickpea flour, or more as required
- 1 cup crudely chopped cooking greens, your choice, such as radish, spinach, daikon, or mustard
- 1 small green bell pepper, crudely chopped
- 1 small onion, crudely chopped
- 1 small russet (or any) potato, crudely chopped

- 1 teaspoon ground dried oregano
- 1 teaspoon salt, or to taste
- 1 to 3 fresh green chile peppers, such as serrano, stemmed
- 1½ tablespoons ground coriander
- 2 small carrots, crudely chopped
- 2 to 3 cups peanut oil for deep-frying
- 5 quarter-size slices peeled fresh ginger

Directions:

1. Ready the chaat masala. Immerse the split peas in water to cover by 2 inches, approximately four hours, then drain.
2. Using a food processor, mix together and pulse the ginger, green chile and bell peppers, onion, potato, carrots, greens, and half the split peas until just minced. (Do not over-process into a purée.) Move to a container, stir in the rest of the split peas, all the spices, baking soda, and salt. Next, Put in the chickpea flour and mix thoroughly to make a semi-thick mixture. If the mixture appears too soft add more chickpea flour, and if it appears too dry add some water, and mix once more.
3. Heat the oil as per directions under the "Frying Fritters" heading at the start of this section. Cautiously, using clean fingers or a spoon, drop 1-inch balls of the mixture into the hot oil and fry as directed at the start of this section. Move to a platter, sprinkle with the chaat masala before you serve.

CHEESE AND MEAT FRITTERS

CHICKEN FRITTERS

This recipe is called "Murgh kae pakorae" in Hindi

Yield: ten to fifteen pieces

Ingredients:

- ½ teaspoon crudely ground ajwain seeds

- ½ teaspoon Chaat Masala (Homemade or store-bought)
- ½ teaspoon hot red pepper flakes, or to taste
- ½ teaspoon salt, or to taste
- 1 (2½- to 3-pound) chicken, skinned and cut into serving pieces (discard the back and wings)
- 1 recipe Basic Batter for Pakora Fritters
- 1 tablespoon ground coriander
- 1 teaspoon dry-roasted and crudely ground cumin seeds (See the dry-roasting section in Introduction)
- 1 teaspoon garam masala
- 1 teaspoon ground cumin seeds
- 1½ to 2 cups peanut oil for deep-frying
- 2 cups water
- 2 tablespoons Basic Ginger-Garlic Paste (Homemade or store-bought)
- 2 tablespoons minced fresh cilantro, including soft stems

Directions:

1. Ready the ginger-garlic paste. Next, place the chicken, water, ginger-garlic paste, garam masala, and salt in a small saucepan and bring to a boil using high heat. Reduce the heat to moderate to low, cover the pan and simmer until the chicken is tender and all the water has been absorbed, fifteen to twenty minutes. If the chicken cooks before the water dries up, uncover the pan and cook until the chicken is completely dry. Allow to cool, remove the bones and cut into smaller pieces, if you wish.
2. In the meantime, ready the chaat masala and the dry-roasted cumin seeds. Next, ready the basic batter, and stir in the cilantro, coriander, cumin, red pepper flakes, and ajwain seeds.
3. Put in the chicken to the batter. Heat the oil and fry the chicken as per directions under the "Frying Fritters" heading at the start of this section. Move to a platter, sprinkle with the roasted cumin and chaat masala.

FISH FRITTERS

This recipe is called "Macchi kae pakorae" in Hindi

Yield: twelve to fifteen pieces

Ingredients:

- ⅛ teaspoon ground asafoetida
- ½ teaspoon crudely ground ajwain seeds
- ½ teaspoon ground turmeric
- ½ teaspoon hot red pepper flakes, or to taste
- ½ teaspoon salt, or to taste
- 1 recipe Basic Batter for Pakora Fritters
- 1 teaspoon Chaat Masala (Homemade or store-bought)
- 1 teaspoon ground cumin
- 1¼ pounds halibut, salmon or sea bass fillets, approximately 1 inch thick, cut into 1½-inch pieces
- 1½ to 2 cups oil for deep-frying
- 2 large cloves garlic, finely ground
- 2 tablespoons chickpea or rice flour
- 2 tablespoons finely chopped fresh cilantro leaves
- 2 to 3 scallions, green parts only, minced
- 3 tablespoons distilled white vinegar

Directions:

1. Ready the chaat masala. Put the fish pieces in a container. Put in the vinegar, garlic, red pepper flakes, turmeric, and salt, and mix thoroughly, ensuring all the pieces are coated thoroughly. Cover and marinate at least 1 and up to 3 hours in a fridge.
2. Ready the basic batter, then stir in the flour, cumin, ajwain, asafoetida, and scallion greens. Heat the oil as per directions under the "Frying Fritters" heading at the start of this section. Dip each fish piece in the batter to cover thoroughly and fry as directed at the start of this section. Move to a platter, sprinkle with the chaat masala and cilantro before you serve.

GROUND MEAT FRITTERS

This recipe is called "Keema pakorae" in Hindi

Yield: 20 to 25 pieces

Ingredients:

- ¼ teaspoon ground turmeric
- ½ cup crudely chopped fresh cilantro, including soft stems
- ½ teaspoon Chaat Masala (Homemade or store-bought)
- ½ teaspoon salt, or to taste
- 1 large fresh garlic clove, peeled
- 1 pound extra lean ground meat (beef or lamb)
- 1 recipe Basic Batter for Pakora Fritters
- 1 small onion, crudely chopped
- 1 tablespoon dried fenugreek leaves
- 1 teaspoon garam masala
- 1 to 3 fresh green chile peppers, such as serrano, stemmed
- 1½ to 2 cups oil for deep-frying
- 2 tablespoons rice flour
- 3 to 4 slices packaged white or whole-wheat bread (crusts on or not)
- 4 to 6 quarter-size slices peeled fresh ginger

Directions:

1. Ready the chaat masala. Immerse the bread in water to cover approximately one minute. Next, squeeze out all the water and crudely crumble the bread.
2. Using a food processor, combine and pulse the crumbled bread, onion, cilantro, ginger, garlic, and green chile peppers until minced. Put in the ground meat, fenugreek leaves, garam masala, and salt, and process once more to mix thoroughly. Divide into 20 to 25 portions and shape each one into a 2-inch disc.
3. Ready the basic batter and stir in the rice flour and turmeric. Heat the oil as per directions under the "Frying Fritters" heading at the start of this section. Dip each disc in the batter to coat well, and fry as directed at the start of this section. Move to a platter, sprinkle with the chaat masala before you serve.

MARINATED CHICKEN PAKORA FRITTERS

This recipe is called "Murgh pakorae" in Hindi

Yield: 20 to 24 pieces

Ingredients:

- ¼ cup non-fat plain yogurt, whisked until the desired smoothness is achieved
- ½ small onion, crudely chopped
- ½ teaspoon Chaat Masala (Homemade or store-bought)
- ½ teaspoon salt, or to taste
- 1 large clove garlic, peeled
- 1 recipe Basic Batter for Pakora Fritters
- 1 tablespoon fresh lime or lemon juice
- 1 teaspoon garam masala
- 1 to 2 tablespoons rice flour
- 1 to 3 fresh green chile peppers, such as serrano, stemmed
- 10 to 12 chicken breast tenders, each cut along the diagonal in half
- 1½ to 2 cups peanut oil for deep frying
- 4 quarter-size slices peeled fresh ginger

Directions:

1. Using a food processor or a blender, combine and pulse the onion, ginger, garlic, and chile peppers until minced. Next, Put in the yogurt, lime juice, oil, garam masala, and salt, and process until the desired smoothness is achieved. Move to a moderate-sized container. Put in the chicken and mix until all the pieces are fully coated with the mixture. Cover and marinate at least 4 and up to 24 hours in a fridge.
2. Ready the chaat masala and the basic batter. Bring the chicken to room temperature, then mix it into the pakora batter along with the rice flour.
3. Heat the oil and fry the chicken as per directions under the "Frying Fritters" heading at the start of this section. You can fry just once, but for the best flavour and texture, allow to cool down, then refry in hot oil until heated through. Move to paper towels once more. Sprinkle with the chaat masala and serve.

PANEER FRITTERS

This recipe is called Ppaneer pakorae" in Hindi

Yield: 20 pieces

Ingredients:

- ¼ cup minced fresh cilantro, including soft stems
- ½ teaspoon crudely ground ajwain seeds
- 1 recipe
- 1 teaspoon Chaat Masala (Homemade or store-bought)
- 1 to 3 fresh green chile peppers, such as serrano, minced with seeds
- 1½ to 2 cups peanut oil for deep-frying
- 8 ounces (1 recipe) Paneer Cheese (Homemade or store-bought)

Directions:

1. Ready the paneer cheese, then the chaat masala. Slice the paneer cheese into pieces or place into a food processor and process until it begins to gather into a dough. Move it to a cutting board and shape into a large square or rectangle and cut into 20 ½-by-2-inch rectangles.
2. Ready the basic fritter batter. To the batter, stir in the cilantro, green chile peppers, and ajwain seeds. Heat the oil as per directions under the "Frying Fritters" heading at the start of this section. Dip each paneer cheese rectangle into the batter to cover thoroughly and fry as directed at the start of this section. Move to a platter, sprinkle with the chaat masala before you serve.

PANEER FRITTERS WITH GREEN CHUTNEY

This recipe is called "Paneer aur hari chutni kae pakorae" in Hindi

Yield: Approximately 30 pieces

Ingredients:

- ¼ cup rice flour, or more as required
- ½ cup Basic Green Chutney
- 1 recipe Basic Batter for Pakora Fritters
- 1 teaspoon Chaat Masala (Homemade or store-bought)
- 1½ to 2 cups peanut oil for deep-frying

- 8 ounces (1 recipe) <u>Paneer Cheese</u> (Homemade or store-bought), crudely crumbled

Directions:

1. Ready the chaat masala, paneer chese, and the green chutney. In a container, toss together the paneer cheese and the chutney and marinate one to two hours at room temperature.
2. Ready the pakora batter, stir in the rice flour, then Put in the marinated paneer cheese (plus the marinade) and 1 tablespoon of the oil to make a semi-thick mixture.
3. Heat the oil as per directions under the "Frying Fritters" heading at the start of this section. Cautiously, with your clean fingers or a spoon, drop 1-inch balls of the mixture into the hot oil and fry as directed at the start of this section. Move to a platter, sprinkle with the chaat masala before you serve.

PANEER FRITTERS WITH RED BELL PEPPERS

This recipe is called "Paneer aur laal shimla mirch kae pakorae" in Hindi

Yield: 20 to 25 pieces

Ingredients:

- ¼ cup finely chopped scallions, green parts only
- ¼ teaspoon salt, or to taste
- ½ cup large curd cottage cheese
- ½ teaspoon <u>Chaat Masala</u> (Homemade or store-bought)
- ⅔ cup chickpea flour, or more as required
- 1 red bell pepper, minced
- 1 small russet (or any) potato, grated
- 1 tablespoon peeled and minced fresh ginger
- 1 teaspoon ground coriander
- 1 to 3 fresh green chile peppers, such as serrano, minced with seeds
- 1½ to 2 cups peanut oil for deep-frying

Directions:

1. Ready the chaat masala. In a moderate-sized container, combine all the ingredients (except the oil and chaat masala) to make a thick, dough-like batter. (If the batter is too soft, add a little more chickpea flour.) Divide into 20 to 25 uneven balls.
2. Heat the oil as per directions under the "Frying Fritters" heading at the start of this section, cautiously drop the balls into the hot oil and fry as directed at the start of this section.
3. Allow to cool, then press them lightly between the palms of your hands into small discs with ragged edges. Refry them in hot oil until crisp, approximately two to three minutes. Drain using paper towels, move to a platter, sprinkle with the chaat masala before you serve.

SHRIMP FRITTERS

This recipe is called "Jhingae kae pakorae" in Hindi

Yield: 15 to 20 pieces

Ingredients:

- ¼ cup finely chopped fresh cilantro, including soft stems
- ½ teaspoon crudely ground ajwain seeds
- ½ teaspoon ground turmeric
- ½ teaspoon hot red pepper flakes, or to taste
- ½ teaspoon salt, or to taste
- 1 recipe Basic Batter for Pakora Fritters, made with yogurt instead of water
- 1 teaspoon crudely ground cumin seeds
- 1 teaspoon Chaat Masala (Homemade or store-bought)
- 1½ to 2 cups oil for deep-frying
- 15 to 20 fresh jumbo shrimp (about 1 pound), shelled and deveined, with tails on
- 2 large cloves fresh garlic, peeled and minced
- 2 to 3 tablespoons fresh lime or lemon juice

Directions:

1. Ready the chaat masala. Put the shrimp in a container. Put in the lime juice, garlic, turmeric, red pepper flakes, ajwain, and salt, and mix thoroughly, ensuring all the pieces coated thoroughly. Cover and marinate at least 1 and up to 3 hours in a fridge.
2. Ready the basic batter, using yogurt instead of water, then stir in the cumin and cilantro. Heat the oil as per directions under the "Frying Fritters" heading at the start of this section. Dip each shrimp in the batter to cover thoroughly and fry as directed at the start of this section. Move to a platter, sprinkle with the chaat masala before you serve.

POTATO SNACKS

Potato is cheap, and at the heart of inexpensive Indian Streetfood.

MASHED POTATO BALLS

This recipe is called "Aalu bhonda" in Hindi

Yield: ten to twelve pieces

Ingredients:

- ¼ teaspoon ground asafoetida
- ⅓ cup finely chopped onion
- ½ cup finely chopped fresh cilantro, including soft stems + 3 tablespoons
- ½ teaspoon salt, or to taste
- 1 recipe Basic Batter for Pakora Fritters
- 1 tablespoon dried white urad beans (dhulli urad dal), sorted
- 1 tablespoon dried yellow split chickpeas (channa dal), sorted
- 1 tablespoon minced fresh curry leaves
- 1 tablespoon peeled minced fresh ginger
- 1 teaspoon black mustard seeds
- 1 teaspoon Chaat Masala (Homemade or store-bought)
- 1 teaspoon vegetable oil
- 1 to 3 fresh green chile peppers, such as serrano, minced with seeds

- 1½ to 2 cups peanut oil for deep-frying
- 2 teaspoons rice flour
- four to five small red potatoes (about 1 pound), unpeeled but scrubbed well

Directions:

1. Ready the chaat masala. Cook the potatoes in lightly salted boiling water to cover until soft, approximately twenty minutes. Drain, allow to cool down, then crudely mash (do not peel).
2. Heat the vegetable oil in a big non-stick wok or saucepan using moderate to high heat and put in the mustard seeds. They should splutter when they touch the hot oil, so cover the pan until the spluttering diminishes. Swiftly put in the dals and cook, stirring, until a golden colour is achieved, approximately one minute.
3. Put in the curry leaves and onion and stir until a golden colour is achieved, approximately a minute or two. Stir in the green chile peppers, ginger, and asafoetida, stir momentarily, and put in the potatoes, ½ cup cilantro, and the salt. Cook over moderate heat, stirring, until a golden colour is achieved, approximately five to seven minutes. Allow to cool. Using clean hands, shape the mixture into ten to twelve round balls and set aside.
4. Ready the basic batter, then stir in the rice flour and the 3 tablespoons cilantro. Dip each potato ball into the batter to coat well.
5. Fry as per directions under the "Frying Fritters" heading at the start of this section. Move to a platter, sprinkle with the chaat masala before you serve.

CHICKEN-STUFFED POTATOES

This recipe is called "Murgh bharae aalu" in Hindi

Yield: twelve to fifteen pieces

Ingredients:

- ¼ cup finely chopped fresh cilantro, including soft stems
- ¼ cup minced scallion greens
- ¼ teaspoon salt, or to taste
- ½ cup finely chopped onion
- ½ teaspoon garam masala

- 1 cup cooked shredded chicken
- 1 fresh green chile pepper, such as serrano, minced with seeds
- 1 small clove fresh garlic, minced
- 1 tablespoon peeled minced fresh ginger
- 1 teaspoon <u>Chaat Masala</u> (Homemade or store-bought), or to taste
- 1 to 2 tablespoons fresh lime or lemon juice
- 2 tablespoons peanut oil
- ten to fifteen cherry or pear-shaped tomatoes
- twelve to fifteen medium white or purple potatoes

Directions:

1. Ready the chaat masala. Cook the potatoes in lightly salted boiling water to cover until soft but not broken, approximately fifteen minutes. Peel them if you wish, but it's not necessary. Slice off a ¼-inch cap from one end of each potato and carefully, with a paring knife and a small spoon, scoop out the insides, leaving a ¼-inch barrel-shaped shell. Reserve the insides, the shells, and the caps.
2. Heat 1 tablespoon of the oil in a small-sized non-stick wok or saucepan using moderate to high heat and cook the garlic, ginger, and onion, stirring until a golden colour is achieved, approximately two minutes. Put in the green chile pepper, cilantro, and chicken, then stir in the garam masala and salt and cook, stirring, over moderate heat until everything is golden, approximately five minutes. Stir in the reserved potatoes and stir, approximately one minute. Allow to cool.
3. Fill each potato shell with the stuffing and fit the caps on. Put in a non-stick skillet and drizzle the rest of the 1 tablespoon oil on top. Cook, turning over moderate heat until a golden colour is achieved on all sides, approximately ten minutes. Transfer to a serving platter.
4. To the skillet Put in the cherry tomatoes and cook, shaking the skillet until slightly softened, approximately one minute. Move to the potato platter as a decoration. Sprinkle the chaat masala and lime juice over everything, garnish with the scallion greens before you serve.

PEAS-FILLED BAKES POTATO

This recipe is called "Muttar bharae baked aalu" in Hindi

Yield: 20 to 24 pieces

Ingredients:

- ⅛ teaspoon ground turmeric
- ¼ cup finely chopped fresh cilantro, including soft stems
- ¼ cup grated mild cheddar or any other melting cheese
- ½ teaspoon ground cumin
- ½ teaspoon salt, or to taste
- ¾ cup frozen petite peas, thawed
- 1 fresh green chile pepper, such as serrano, minced with seeds
- 1 medium tomato, finely chopped
- 1 small clove fresh garlic, minced
- 1 small onion, finely chopped
- 1 tablespoon ground coriander
- 1 tablespoon peeled minced fresh ginger
- ten to twelve small russet potatoes (about 2 pounds), unpeeled but scrubbed well
- 2 tablespoons vegetable oil

Directions:

1. Heat your oven beforehand to 400°F. Wrap each potato in foil and bake until tender, approximately forty five minutes. Unwrap and allow to cool down, then cut each potato in half lengthwise. Using a grapefruit (or other) spoon, scoop out the insides of each potato half, leaving a ¼-inch shell. Reserve the insides. Lower oven temperature to 350°F.
2. Brush each shell with oil, inside and out. Place, cut side up, on a baking sheet and bake until crunchy and golden, approximately twenty minutes. When the potatoes are done, raise oven temperature back to 400°F.
3. To ready the stuffing, heat the oil in a small-sized non-stick wok or saucepan using moderate to high heat and cook the ginger, garlic, and onion, stirring, until a golden colour is achieved, approximately two minutes. Put in the tomato, cilantro, and chile pepper and stir, approximately two minutes. Mix in the coriander, cumin, and turmeric, then put in the peas and salt and cook, stirring a few times until the peas are soft, approximately five minutes. Stir in the reserved potatoes and cook another two minutes.

4. Divide the stuffing equally among the potato shells and fill each one. Sprinkle the cheddar cheese on top and bake at 400°F until a golden colour is achieved, approximately five minutes. Serve.

POTATO FRIES WITH TOMATOES

This recipe is called "Tamatar ke saath aalu kae chips" in Hindi

Yield: 4 to 6 servings

Ingredients:

- ½ teaspoon salt, or to taste
- 1 fresh green chile pepper, such as serrano, minced with seeds
- 1 large firm tomato, crudely chopped
- 1 teaspoon Chaat Masala (Homemade or store-bought), or to taste
- 1½ to 2 cups peanut oil for deep-frying
- four to five small russet potatoes, peeled and cut into ½-inch fingers

Directions:

1. Ready the chaat masala. Next, place the potato fingers in a moderate-sized container, toss with salt and allow to sit for approximately 30 minutes. Wash, drain, and dry well on cotton kitchen or paper towels.
2. Heat the oil in a big wok or skillet using moderate to high heat until it achieves 325°F to 350°F on a frying thermometer or, until a small piece of the potato dropped into the hot oil takes about fifteen to twenty seconds to rises to the top. Deep-fry, turning and moving the potato fingers until a golden colour is achieved and crunchy. Drain using paper towels.
3. Allow to cool and remove all but 1 teaspoon of oil from the wok. Reheat the oil using moderate to high heat and stir-fry the tomatoes and green chile pepper until just tender, approximately one minute. Put in the fried potatoes and mix thoroughly. Move to a serving platter, sprinkle with the chaat masala before you serve.

POTATO PATTIES

These fried potato discs are called "Tikki" and are easily one of the most popular and cheap street food you can find in India. In the Indian streets, these are cooked using gigantic griddles containing oil. At home, Indian cooks make these using regular griddles. If you don't have one, any old trying pan will do.

All tikkis can be made four to five days in advance then cooled completely and stored in a fridge. Reheat in a skillet or a preheated 400°F oven, approximately ten minutes.

BASIC MASHED POTATO TIKKI

This recipe is called "Aalu tikki" in Hindi

Yield: 8 to 10 pieces

Adding bread to the potato mixture greatly enhances the texture of the final product.

Ingredients:

- ¼ cup peanut or vegetable oil
- ½ teaspoon salt, or to taste
- 2 to 3 slices white bread, crusts removed
- 4 medium russet (or any) potatoes (about 1 pound)

Directions:

1. Cook the potatoes in lightly salted boiling water to cover until tender, approximately twenty minutes. Drain, allow to cool down, then peel and mash or grate. Immerse the bread in water to cover, approximately two minutes. Next, squeeze out all the water, tear the slices into tiny pieces, and place them in a big container. Put in the potatoes and salt, and with clean hands softly mix everything together. (Don't use a food processor; overmixing will result in glutinous potatoes.)
2. With mildly greased hands, divide the potatoes into 8 to 10 portions and shape each one into a smooth 1½- to 2-inch patty.

3. Heat 3 tablespoons of the oil in a large, heavy, non-stick skillet using moderate to high heat. Put the patties in the skillet in a single layer, in batches if required. Press on them lightly using a spatula, ensuring all the edges are in contact with the skillet. Let cook undisturbed approximately one minute, reduce the heat to moderate to low and continue to cook, watching cautiously until the bottom side is golden, approximately five minutes.
4. Cautiously turn each tikki over with the spatula. Add 1 to 2 tablespoons more oil (if required) and increase the heat to high approximately a minute. Next, reduce the heat to moderate to low once again and cook until the second side is golden, approximately four to five minutes. Reduce the heat and push the patties to the sides of the pan until they are thoroughly browned and a have a thick, crunchy crust. Turn a few times, as required.
5. Another way is to deep-fry the patties in hot oil and then finish cooking them on a tava-griddle. (If, when you deep-fry, the patties seem to open up or disintegrate, make a paste with ¼ cup all-purpose flour and ¼ cup water and coat rest of the patties in it before deep-frying.) Serve hot.

BASIC STUFFED POTATO TIKKI

This recipe is called "Bhari hui aalu ki tikki" in Hindi

Yield: 8 to 10 pieces

Ingredients:

- ½ teaspoon salt, or to taste
- 1 recipe Tikki Filling (Just below this recipe)
- 1½ to 2 cups peanut oil for deep-frying
- 2 large russet (or any) potatoes (about 1 pound)
- 2 slices white bread, crusts removed

Directions:

1. Cook the potatoes in lightly salted boiling water to cover until tender, approximately twenty minutes. Drain, allow to cool down, then peel and mash or grate. Immerse the bread in water to cover, approximately two minutes. Squeeze out all the water from the bread, tear it into tiny pieces and place them in a big container. Put in the potatoes and salt, and with

clean hands, softly mix everything together. (Don't use a food processor; over-mixing will result in glutinous potatoes.)

2. With mildly greased hands, divide the potatoes into 8 to 10 identical portions and do the same with the tikki filling. Working with each portion separately, flatten the potatoes into a 4-inch round. Put one portion of the tikki filling in the center of the potato round. Bring the edges together and pinch to secure, then press down the pinched top to form a smooth round or oval.
3. Heat 3 tablespoons of the oil in a large, heavy, non-stick skillet using moderate to high heat. Put the patties in the skillet in a single layer, in batches if required. Press on them lightly using a spatula, ensuring all the edges are in contact with the skillet. Let cook undisturbed approximately one minute, reduce the heat to moderate to low and continue to cook, watching cautiously until the bottom side is golden, approximately five minutes.
4. Cautiously turn each tikki over with the spatula. Add 1 to 2 tablespoons more oil (if required) and increase the heat to high approximately a minute. Next, reduce the heat to moderate to low once again and cook until the second side is golden, approximately four to five minutes. Reduce the heat and push the patties to the sides of the pan until they are thoroughly browned and a have a thick, crunchy crust. Turn a few times, as required.
5. Another way is to deep-fry the patties in hot oil and then finish cooking them on a tava-griddle. (If, when you deep-fry, the patties seem to open up or disintegrate, make a paste with ¼ cup all-purpose flour and ¼ cup water and coat rest of the patties in it before deep-frying.) Serve hot.

FILLINGS FOR POTATO PATTIES Ⓥ

This recipe is called "Tikki mein bharnae ki cheezein" in Hindi

Yield: filling for 8 to 10 pieces

Feel free to experiment with different fillings.

Ingredients:

- ¼ cup finely chopped fresh cilantro, including soft stems
- ¼ teaspoon salt, or to taste
- ⅔ cup finely chopped onion
- 1 tablespoon olive oil

- 1 tablespoon peeled minced fresh ginger
- 1 to 3 fresh green chile peppers, such as serrano, minced with seeds
- Any of the following: ⅔ cup Paneer Cheese (Homemade or store-bought), grated; ⅔ cup soaked and drained dried yellow mung beans (dhulli mung dal) or red lentils (dhulli masoor dal); ⅔ cup frozen petite peas, thawed; 1 cup minced carrots, green beans, zucchini, or cauliflower; ⅔ cup minced chicken tenders, cooked until opaque inside
- Freshly ground black pepper to taste

Directions:

1. Heat the oil in a small-sized non-stick skillet using moderate to high heat and cook the onion, stirring, until a golden colour is achieved, approximately three minutes.
2. Put in the paneer cheese or other filling, cilantro, salt, and black pepper, and cook, stirring, until a golden colour is achieved, approximately two minutes. Stir in the ginger and chile peppers and set aside to cool. The stuffing is ready to use.

BREAD AND POTATO TIKKI

This recipe is called "Aalu double-roti ki tikki" in Hindi

Yield: 15 to 20 pieces

Ingredients:

- ¼ cup finely chopped fresh cilantro, including soft stems
- ½ cup milk, heated in a pot or microwave
- ½ cup non-fat plain yogurt
- ½ cup rice flour or all-purpose flour
- ½ teaspoon salt, or to taste
- 1 fresh 4-ounce sourdough roll, cut into ½-inch dice
- 1 to 2 tablespoons plain dried bread crumbs, if required
- 1½ to 2 cups peanut oil for deep-frying
- 2 large russet (or any) potatoes (about 1 pound)
- 2 tablespoons peeled minced fresh ginger
- 2 to 3 fresh green chile peppers, such as serrano, minced with seeds

Directions:

1. Cook the potatoes in lightly salted boiling water to cover until tender, approximately twenty minutes. Drain, allow to cool down, then peel and mash. In the meantime, in a moderate-sized container, combine the bread, yogurt, and hot milk. When the bread soaks up all the liquids, put in the mashed potatoes, cilantro, ginger, green chile peppers, and salt and, with clean hands, softly mix everything together. (Don't use a food processor; over-mixing will result in glutinous potatoes.) If the mixture appears too soft, stir in 1 to 2 tablespoons bread crumbs.
2. Put the rice (or all-purpose) flour in a flat container. Divide the potato mixture into fifteen to 20 portions, shape each one into a smooth 2-inch oval or round, and coat with the flour in the container.
3. Heat the oil in a big wok or skillet until it reaches 350°F to 375°F on a frying thermometer or until a small piece of the potato mixture dropped into the hot oil bubbles and instantly rises to the top. Put in the potato ovals into the hot oil cautiously using your fingers or a spoon to avoid spluttering. Add as many as the wok can hold simultaneously without crowding and fry each batch, turning a few times with a slotted spatula, until crunchy and golden on all sides, approximately one to two minutes.
4. Move to paper towels to drain. Repeat the process with the rest of the ovals. Move to a serving platter and serve hot.

POTATO AND CASHEW TIKKI Ⓥ

This recipe is called "Aalu aur kaaju ki tikki" in Hindi

Yield: 20 pieces

Ingredients:

- ¼ teaspoon crudely ground ajwain seeds
- ¼ teaspoon cayenne pepper, or to taste
- ½ cup crudely chopped raw cashews
- ½ teaspoon salt, or to taste
- 1 tablespoon ground coriander
- 1 tablespoon peeled minced fresh ginger
- 1 teaspoon Chaat Masala (Homemade or store-bought)

- 1 teaspoon dried fenugreek leaves
- 1 teaspoon fresh green chile pepper, such as serrano, minced with seeds
- 1½ to 2 cups peanut oil for deep-frying
- 2 large eggs, lightly beaten
- 2 large russet (or any) potatoes (about 1 pound)

Directions:

1. Ready the chaat masala. Cook the potatoes in lightly salted boiling water to cover until tender, approximately twenty minutes. Cool, then peel and mash. In a large container, put in the mashed potatoes, ginger, green chile pepper, coriander, fenugreek, ajwain, cayenne pepper, and salt. With clean hands, softly mix everything together. (Don't use a food processor; over-mixing will result in glutinous potatoes.)
2. With mildly greased hands, divide the mixture into 20 portions and shape each one into a round ball, then flatten lightly to make a smooth patty or an oval.
3. Heat the oil in a big wok or skillet until it reaches 350°F to 375°F on a frying thermometer or until a small piece of the mixture dropped into the hot oil bubbles and instantly rises to the top. Dip each patty in the beaten egg, then cover thoroughly with the cashews.
4. Heat the oil in a big wok or skillet until it reaches 350°F to 375°F on a frying thermometer or until a small piece of the potato mixture dropped into the hot oil bubbles and instantly rises to the top. Put in the potato ovals into the hot oil cautiously using your fingers or a spoon to avoid spluttering. Add as many as the wok can hold simultaneously without crowding and fry each batch, turning a few times with a slotted spatula, until crunchy and golden on all sides, approximately one to two minutes.
5. Move to paper towels to drain. Repeat the process with the rest of the ovals. Drain using paper towels, garnish with the chaat masala before you serve.

POTATO AND TAPIOCA TIKKI Ⓥ

This recipe is called "Aalu-sabudana ki tikki" in Hindi

Yield: 15 to 20 pieces

Ingredients:

- ¼ cup minced fresh spinach leaves
- ⅓ cup tapioca pearls
- ½ cup boiling water
- ½ teaspoon garam masala
- ½ teaspoon ground cumin
- 1 tablespoon ground coriander
- 1 tablespoon peeled minced fresh ginger
- 1 to 2 tablespoons plain dried bread crumbs, if required
- 1½ to 2 cups peanut oil for frying
- 2 large russet (or any) potatoes (about 1 pound)
- 4 to 6 scallions, white parts only, minced

Directions:

1. In a small pan, soak 1 tablespoon of the tapioca in the boiling water for approximately half an hour. In the meantime, cook the potatoes in lightly salted boiling water to cover until tender, approximately twenty minutes. Drain, allow to cool down, then peel and mash.
2. In a small pan, cook the soaked tapioca over moderate heat until it turns glutinous, approximately five minutes. (You will still see the grain.) Allow to cool. Crudely grind the rest of the tapioca in a coffee or spice grinder. Move to a flat dish and set aside for coating the patties.
3. In a container, put in the mashed potatoes, ginger, scallions, spinach, coriander, cumin, garam masala, and the cooked tapioca. With clean hands, softly mix everything together. (Don't use a food processor; over-mixing will result in glutinous potatoes.) If the mixture appears too soft, stir in 1 to 2 tablespoons of bread crumbs.
4. With mildly greased hands, divide the potato mixture into 20 portions and shape each one into a round ball, then flatten lightly to make a smooth disc or oval. Coat each disc with the ground tapioca, then press between the palms of your hands to ensure that the tapioca adheres nicely.
5. Heat the oil in a big wok or skillet until it reaches 350°F to 375°F on a frying thermometer or until a small piece of the potato mixture dropped into the hot oil bubbles and instantly rises to the top. Put in the potato ovals into the hot oil cautiously using your fingers or a spoon to avoid spluttering. Add as many as the wok can hold simultaneously without crowding and fry each

batch, turning a few times with a slotted spatula, until crunchy and golden on all sides, approximately one to two minutes.
6. Move to paper towels to drain. Repeat the process with the rest of the ovals. Move to a serving platter and serve hot.

TOFU AND POTATO TIKKI Ⓥ

This recipe is called "Tofu-aalu ki tikki" in Hindi

Yield: 8 to 10 pieces

Ingredients:

- ¼ cup peanut or vegetable oil
- ¼ teaspoon salt, or to taste
- 1 (10½-ounce) package firm tofu, crumbled and dried well on paper towels
- 1 fresh green chile pepper, such as serrano, stemmed
- 1 large russet (or any) potato
- 2 quarter-size slices peeled fresh ginger
- Freshly ground black pepper, to taste

Directions:

1. Cook the potato in lightly salted boiling water to cover until tender, approximately fifteen minutes. Drain, allow to cool down, peel, place in a moderate-sized container, and mash.
2. Using a food processor, combine and pulse the chile pepper and ginger until minced, then put in the tofu and pulse a few times until the desired smoothness is achieved. Put in the tofu mixture to the potatoes, along with salt and black pepper and, with clean hands, softly mix everything together. (Don't use your food processor for this; over-mixing will result in glutinous potatoes.)
3. With mildly greased hands, divide the mixture into 8 to 10 portions and shape each one into a smooth 1½- to 2-inch patty.
4. Heat 3 tablespoons of the oil in a large, heavy, non-stick skillet using moderate to high heat. Put the patties in the skillet in a single layer, in batches if required. Press on them lightly using a spatula, ensuring all the edges are in contact with the skillet. Let cook undisturbed approximately one

minute, reduce the heat to moderate to low and continue to cook, watching cautiously until the bottom side is golden, approximately five minutes.
5. Cautiously turn each tikki over with the spatula. Add 1 to 2 tablespoons more oil (if required) and increase the heat to high approximately a minute. Next, reduce the heat to moderate to low once again and cook until the second side is golden, approximately four to five minutes. Reduce the heat and push the patties to the sides of the pan until they are thoroughly browned and a have a thick, crunchy crust. Turn a few times, as required.
6. Another way is to deep-fry the patties in hot oil and then finish cooking them on a tava-griddle. (If, when you deep-fry, the patties seem to open up or disintegrate, make a paste with ¼ cup all-purpose flour and ¼ cup water and coat rest of the patties in it before deep-frying.) Serve hot.

CROQUETTES AND DUMPLINGS (VADAE)

These deep fried spongy cakes are highly popular in South India and are usually served with a sauce.

COCONUT–RED CHILE CROQUETTES

This recipe is called "Ammavadai" in Hindi

Yield: 20 to 25 pieces

Ingredients:

- ¼ cup each: split pigeon peas (toor dal), yellow split chickpeas (channa dal), white urad beans (dhulli urad dal), sorted and washed in 3 to 4 changes of water
- ¼ cup finely chopped fresh cilantro, including soft stems
- ¼ teaspoon baking powder
- ¼ teaspoon ground asafoetida

- ¼ to ½ cup hot water
- ⅓ cup non-fat plain yogurt
- ½ cup rice flour
- ½ to 1 cup finely chopped onions
- 1 cup grated fresh or frozen coconut or shredded unsweetened dried coconut
- 1 teaspoon salt, or to taste
- 1 to 3 fresh green chile peppers, such as serrano, minced without seeds
- 1½ to 2 cups peanut oil for deep-frying
- 2 tablespoons peeled minced fresh ginger
- 2 to 4 dried red chile peppers, such as chile de arbol, crudely ground

Directions:

1. Immerse the dals in water to cover by 1 inch, approximately 3 hours. Drain and move to a food processor. Process until thoroughly smooth. Put in the rice flour, coconut, and yogurt, and process once more until the desired smoothness is achieved. Move to a container. Add all the rest of the ingredients (except the oil for frying) and mix thoroughly, adding the hot water as required to make a fluffy, thick batter that can be shaped.
2. Heat the oil in a big wok or skillet to 350°F to 375°F on a frying thermometer or until a pinch of batter dropped into the hot oil bubbles and instantly rises to the top.
3. With lightly moistened clean hands, shape the batter put them in carefully, one at a time, to the hot oil. Add as many as the wok can hold simultaneously without crowding, and fry, turning once in a while using tongs or a slotted spoon, until they are crisp and golden on all sides, approximately two to three minutes. (Dip your fingers in the container of water as you work.) Move croquettes to paper towels to drain. Move to a platter and serve hot.

MUNG CROQUETTES Ⓥ

This recipe is called "mungi kae laddoo" in Hindi

Yield: 18 to 20 pieces

Ingredients:

- ⅛ teaspoon baking soda
- ½ teaspoon salt, or to taste
- 1 cup dried yellow mung beans (dhulli mung dal), sorted and washed in 3 to 4 changes of water
- 1 fresh green chile pepper, such as serrano, stemmed
- 1 to 3 tablespoons hot water
- 1½ to 2 cups peanut oil for deep-frying
- 3 quarter-size slices peeled fresh ginger

Directions:

1. Immerse the dal overnight in water to cover by 2 inches. Drain. Using a food processor, combine and pulse the ginger and green chile pepper until minced. Put in the drained dal and process, adding the hot water as required to make a fluffy, semi-thick batter that can be shaped. Stir in the salt and baking soda.
2. Heat the oil in a big wok or a skillet to 350°F to 375°F on a frying thermometer or until a pinch of batter dropped into the hot oil bubbles and instantly rises to the top. Pick up approximately 2 tablespoons of the batter using clean fingers or a spoon and push it cautiously into the hot oil. (Don't worry approximately the shape when you slide it into the oil.) Add as many croquettes as the wok will hold simultaneously without crowding, and fry, turning with a slotted spoon, until they are crunchy and golden on all sides, approximately two to three minutes.
3. Using a slotted spatula, move croquettes to paper towels to drain. Repeat process with the remain-ing batter. Move to a platter and serve hot or at room temperature.

RICE CROQUETTES Ⓥ

This recipe is called "Medhu vadai" in Hindi

Yield: Approximately 20 pieces

Feel free to make a simple shape if donut shaped ones seem too hard.

Ingredients:

- ¼ teaspoon baking soda
- ¼ teaspoon ground asafoetida
- ¼ to ½ cup hot water
- ⅓ cup crudely chopped cashews
- ½ cup dried white urad beans (dhulli urad dal), sorted and washed in 3 to 4 changes of water
- ½ teaspoon salt, or to taste
- 1 cup long-grain white rice, sorted and washed in 3 to 4 changes of water
- 1 small 3-inch diameter container
- 1 tablespoon peanut oil
- 1 teaspoon crudely ground fenugreek seeds
- 1 teaspoon black mustard seeds
- 1½ to 2 cups peanut oil for deep-frying
- 2 tablespoons dried yellow split chickpeas (channa dal)
- 2 tablespoons minced fresh curry leaves
- One 10-inch square piece of plastic wrap

Directions:

1. Setting aside 2 tablespoons of the rice, soak the rice and dal in water to cover by 2 inches, approximately four hours. Drain and move to a food processor and process, adding hot water as required to make a fluffy, semi-thick batter that can be shaped. Put in the baking soda and salt, and process once more. Move to a container.
2. Heat 1 tablespoon oil in a big cast-iron or non-stick wok or a saucepan, using moderate to high heat and put in the mustard seeds. They should splutter when they touch the hot oil, so cover the pan and reduce the heat until the spluttering diminishes. Swiftly put in the reserved 2 tablespoons rice, chickpea dal, fenugreek seeds, asafoetida, curry leaves, and cashews, and cook, stirring, until a golden colour is achieved, approximately one minute. Combine with the batter. Cover and let rest in a warm, draft-free place approximately two hours.
3. Heat the oil for frying in a big wok or skillet to 350°F to 375°F on a frying thermometer, or until a pinch of batter dropped into the hot oil bubbles and instantly rises to the top.
4. In the meantime, have ready a small-sized container of water. Wrap a small piece of plastic wrap tautly around the 3-inch container and brush with a

light coating of oil. Put 1 tablespoon of the batter on the wrap and with lightly moistened, clean fingers, spread the batter into a 3-inch disc. With your forefinger, make a ½-inch hole in the center of the disc to make a doughnut shape. Gently slide each doughnut to the side and into the hot oil. (Dip your fingers in a container of water as you work.)
5. Deep-fry, adding 3 to 4 croquettes at a time and turning them using tongs 2 to 3 times until puffed and golden, approximately three minutes per batch. Move to paper towels to drain. Move to a platter and serve hot.

SALTY CROQUETTES Ⓥ

This recipe is called "Namkeen gujjia" in Hindi

Yield: ten to twelve pieces

Ingredients:

- ¼ teaspoon baking soda
- ¼ to ⅓ cup water
- ½ teaspoon ground asafoetida
- ½ teaspoon salt, or to taste
- 1 (10-inch-square) piece of muslin or 4 layers cheesecloth
- 1 (10-inch-square) piece of plastic wrap
- 1 cup dried white urad beans (dhulli urad dal), sorted and washed in 3 to 4 changes of water
- 1 small 3-inch diameter container
- 1 tablespoon shelled and crudely ground raw almonds
- 1 teaspoon cumin seeds
- 1 to 3 fresh green chile peppers, such as serrano, stemmed
- 1½ to 2 cups peanut oil for deep-frying
- 2 tablespoons chopped raisins
- 3 tablespoons shelled and crudely ground raw pistachios
- 5 to 7 quarter-size slices peeled fresh ginger

Directions:

1. Immerse the dal overnight in water to cover by 2-inches. Drain. Using a food processor, process the ginger and green chile peppers until minced. Put in

the drained dal and the water as required, and process until thoroughly smooth. Stir in the cumin seeds, asafoetida, baking soda, and salt. (The batter should be thick and slightly grainy. If it appears thin, add some chickpea flour. You should actually be able to pick up this batter using your fingers to stuff it and shape it.)
2. Move to a container, cover, and keep in a warm, draft-free place approximately eight to ten hours to ferment. Next, using a whisk or a fork, whisk the batter to that it absorbs air and becomes fluffy, approximately three minutes.
3. In a small-sized container, combine the pistachios, raisins, and almonds. Next, heat the oil in a big wok or skillet to 350°F to 375°F on a frying thermometer, or until a pinch of batter dropped into the hot oil bubbles and instantly rises to the top.
4. Have ready another small-sized container of water. Wrap a small piece of plastic wrap tautly around a 3-inch container and brush lightly with oil. Put ½ tablespoon of the batter on the wrap and, with lightly moistened clean fingers, spread it into a 3-inch semicircle. Put approximately 1 teaspoon of the nut mixture in the center of the semicircle. Cover the filling with another tablespoon of the batter and lightly press the top batter into the bottom, sealing in the filling, maintaining the shape. With your hands or a slotted spoon, slide the semicircles cautiously into the hot oil. If the batter sticks to your fingers, dip your hands in the container of water as you go along.
5. Deep-fry, adding as many semi-circles as the wok can hold simultaneously without crowding, turning once in a while until they are crisp and golden on all sides, approximately two to three minutes. Using a slotted spatula, move croquettes to paper towels to drain. Repeat the process with the rest of the batter. Move to a platter and serve hot.

SOUTH INDIAN CROQUETTES Ⓥ

This recipe is called "Vadai" in Hindi

Yield: 15 to 20 pieces

Ingredients:

- ¼ cup long-grain white rice, sorted and washed in 3 to 4 changes of water
- ¼ teaspoon baking powder

- ¼ teaspoon ground asafoetida
- ¼ to ⅓ cup hot water
- ½ teaspoon cayenne pepper, or to taste
- ½ teaspoon ground fenugreek seeds
- 1 cup dried white urad beans (dhulli urad dal), sorted and washed in 3 to 4 changes of water
- 1 teaspoon crudely ground black pepper, or to taste
- 1 teaspoon salt, or to taste
- 1½ to 2 cups peanut oil for deep-frying
- 20 to 25 fresh curry leaves
- 4 quarter-size slices peeled fresh ginger

Directions:

1. Immerse together the dal and rice overnight in water to cover by 2-inches. Drain.
2. Using a food processor, combine and pulse the ginger and curry leaves until minced. Put in the drained dal, rice, fenugreek seeds, asafoetida, and salt, and process, adding hot water as required to make a fluffy, thick batter that can be shaped. Cover and keep in a warm and draft-free place, eight to ten hours to ferment. Stir in the cayenne and black peppers, and the baking powder. Next, using a whisk or a fork, whisk the batter to that it absorbs air and becomes fluffy, approximately one minute.
3. Heat the oil in a big wok or skillet to 350°F to 375°F on a frying thermometer or until a pinch of batter dropped into the hot oil bubbles and instantly rises to the top.
4. In the meantime, have ready a small-sized container of water. With lightly moistened clean hands, form 2-inch patties from the batter and put them in carefully, one at a time, to the hot oil. Add as many as the wok can hold simultaneously without crowding, and fry, turning once in a while using tongs or a slotted spoon, until they are crisp and golden on all sides, approximately two to three minutes. (Dip your fingers in the container of water as you work.) Move croquettes to paper towels to drain. Move to a platter and serve hot.

SPINACH MUNG CROQUETTES

This recipe is called "Palak ki pakaudhiyan" in Hindi

Yield: twelve to fifteen pieces

Ingredients:

- ¼ teaspoon baking soda
- ½ small bunch fresh spinach (four to five ounces), trimmed, washed, and finely chopped
- ½ teaspoon ajwain seeds, crudely ground
- ½ teaspoon salt, or to taste
- 1 cup dried yellow mung beans (dhulli mung dal), sorted and washed in 3 to 4 changes of water
- 1 large onion, finely chopped
- 1 tablespoon coriander, crudely ground
- 1 tablespoon peeled minced fresh ginger
- 1 teaspoon <u>Chaat Masala</u> (Homemade or store-bought)
- 1 teaspoon cumin seeds, dry-roasted and crudely ground (See the dry-roasting section in Introduction)
- 1½ to 2 cups peanut oil for deep-frying

Directions:

1. Immerse the dal overnight in water to cover by 2-inches. In the meantime, ready the chaat masala and the cumin seeds. When ready, drain and place the dal Using a food processor, then process, adding the hot water as required to make a fluffy, semi-thick batter that can be shaped. Stir in all the rest of the ingredients (except the spinach and oil) and process once more. Move to a container and stir in the spinach, then allow to rest for approximately half an hour.
2. Heat the oil in a big wok or skillet to 350°F to 375°F on a frying thermometer, or until a pinch of batter dropped into the hot oil bubbles and instantly rises to the top. Pick up approximately 2 tablespoons of the batter with clean fingers or a spoon and push it cautiously into the hot oil. (Don't worry approximately the shape when you slide the croquettes into the oil.) Add as many as the wok will hold simultaneously without crowding, and fry, turning with a slotted spatula, until they are crisp and golden on all sides, approximately two to three minutes.

3. Using a slotted spatula, move croquettes to paper towels to drain. Repeat process with the rest of the batter. Move to a platter, garnish with chaat masala before you serve.

URAD CROQUETTES

This recipe is called "Urad dal kae bhallae" in Hindi

Yield: ten to twelve pieces

Ingredients:

- ¼ teaspoon baking soda
- ¼ teaspoon ground asafoetida
- ¼ to ⅓ cup hot water
- 1 (10-inch-square) piece of muslin or 4 layers of cheesecloth
- 1 cup dried split white urad beans (dhulli urad dal), sorted and washed in 3 to 4 changes of water
- 1 small 3-inch diameter container
- 1 tablespoon cumin seeds, dry-roasted and crudely ground (See the dry-roasting section in Introduction)
- 1 teaspoon salt, or to taste
- 1 to 3 fresh green chile peppers, such as serrano, stemmed
- 1½ to 2 cups peanut oil for deep-frying
- 5 to 7 quarter-size slices peeled fresh ginger

Directions:

1. Immerse the dal overnight in water to cover by 2 inches. In the meantime, ready the cumin. When ready, drain the dal. Using a food processor, combine and pulse the ginger and green chile peppers until minced. Put in the drained dal and process, adding the hot water as required to make a fluffy, thick batter that can be shaped.
2. Stir in the cumin, baking soda, asafoetida, and salt. Cover and keep in a warm, draft-free place, eight to ten hours to ferment. Next, using a whisk or a fork, whisk the batter to that it absorbs air and becomes fluffy, approximately one minute.

3. Heat the oil in a big wok or skillet to 350°F to 375°F on a frying thermometer, or until a pinch of batter dropped into the hot oil bubbles and instantly rises to the top.
4. In the meantime, have ready a small-sized container of water. Wet the cheesecloth with water, squeeze it out completely and wrap it tautly over the top of the container. There will be some overhang. Holding the overhang securely under the container, with a clean hand, place approximately 2 tablespoons of the batter on the cheesecloth and, with lightly moistened fingers, spread it into a 3-inch disc. With your forefinger, make a ½-inch hole in the center of the disc to make a doughnut. Gently push from one side to slide each doughnut into the hot oil. (Dip your fingers in the container of water as you work.) Add as many doughnuts as the wok can hold simultaneously without crowding and deep-fry, turning once in a while with a slotted spatula until they are crisp and golden on all sides, approximately two to three minutes. Remove croquettes to paper towels to drain. Repeat the process with the rest of the batter. Move to a platter and serve hot.

STEAMED RICE CAKES (IDLI)

These soft, spongy, and delicious rice cakes greatly enhance the taste of whatever curry or sauce they are eaten with. This snack is a South Indian staple, and is usually enjoyed with "sambar", a south Indian curry, or coconut chutney, or both!

To make authentic disc-shaped Idlis, dedicated cookware can be bought online, or from a nearby Indian store. These Idli molds make the job much easier.

BASIC STEAMED RICE CAKES

This recipe is called "Iddli" in Hindi

Yield: 16 to 20 pieces

Ingredients:

- ¼ to ½ cup plain yogurt

- ½ cup dried white urad beans (dhulli urad dal), sorted, washed in 3 or 4 changes of water
- ½ cup semolina
- ½ teaspoon baking powder
- ⅔ cup parboiled (converted) rice, sorted, washed in 3 or 4 changes of water
- 1 teaspoon salt, or to taste
- 4 tablespoons water

Directions:

1. Immerse the rice and the dal in separate containers overnight, in water to cover by 2 inches. Drain. Using a blender or a food processor, grind the rice, adding approximately 2 tablespoons water until the desired smoothness is achieved yet somewhat grainy. Move to a container and grind the dal with approximately 2 tablespoons water until as fine as possible.
2. Mix the dal into the rice, along with the semolina, yogurt, and salt. Using a whisk or a fork, whip well to incorporate air into the batter and make it fluffy, approximately one minute. Cover the container and set it in a warm, dry place approximately eight to ten hours to ferment.
3. Grease the idli molds (or coat with non-stick spray) and keep them ready. Put in the baking powder to the fermented batter and whisk thoroughly until it becomes fluffy. Little bubbles of air should be visible on the sides. Pour in additional water if the batter appears too thick. Next, pour ¼ to ⅓ cup batter into each mold and place the idli trays on the stand.
4. Put approximately 1 inch of water inside a pressure cooker or large pot, and place the idli stand in the pot. Cover the pot, leaving the vent open if you're using a pressure cooker or the cover askew if you're using a regular pot, to let the steam to escape. Cook using high heat until the idli are soft and spongy, approximately ten to twelve minutes. Allow the steam to escape from the sides, but do not remove the lid of the pot for ten to twelve minutes.
5. Allow to cool, then remove each idli from the mold using a spoon or clean fingers. Pry lightly with a knife or a small spatula if they get stuck. Serve.

QUICK SEMOLINA CAKES

This recipe is called "Sooji ki iddli" in Hindi

Yield: 16 to 20 pieces

Ingredients:

- ¼ cup water
- 1 teaspoon salt, or to taste
- 1½ teaspoons Eno fruit salt or ¾ teaspoon each of baking soda and citric acid
- 2 cups semolina
- 2 teaspoons melted butter
- 4¼ cups (18 ounces) non-fat plain yogurt
- 8 to 10 fresh curry leaves, chopped

Directions:

1. Put the semolina and butter in a wok or skillet and roast, stirring over moderate heat approximately five minutes. The semolina should not turn golden; if it does, reduce the heat or take the pan off the heat. Move to a large container.
2. Using a food processor, combine and pulse the yogurt, curry leaves, and salt. Put into the semolina. Using a whisk or a fork, whip well to incorporate air into the batter and make it fluffy, approximately one minute. Add approximately ¼ cup or more water, as required. Allow to rest approximately one hour.
3. Grease the idli molds (or coat with non-stick spray). Mix the fruit salt into the batter; it will bubble instantly. Swiftly, before it diminishes, pour ¼ to ⅓ cup of the batter into each mold and place each tray on the stand.
4. Put approximately 1 inch of water inside a pressure cooker or large pot, then place the idli stand in the pot. Cover the pot, leaving the vent open if you're using a pressure cooker pot or the cover askew if you're using a regular pot, to let the steam to escape. Cook using high heat until the idli are soft and spongy, approximately ten to twelve minutes. Allow the steam to escape from the sides, but do not remove the lid of the pot ten to twelve minutes.
5. Allow to cool and remove each idli from the mold using a spoon or with clean fingers. Pry lightly with a knife or a small spatula if they get stuck. Serve.

SPICY RICE CAKES

This recipe is called "Masala iddli" in Hindi

Yield: 16 to 20 pieces

Ingredients:

- ¼ cup finely chopped fresh cilantro, including soft stems
- ½ cup finely chopped onion
- ½ teaspoon ground asafoetida
- 1 recipe batter for Traditional Steamed Fermented Rice Cakes or Instant Steamed Semolina Cakes with Yogurt
- 1 tablespoon finely chopped fresh curry leaves
- 1 tablespoon peeled minced fresh ginger
- 1 teaspoon black mustard seeds
- 1 to 3 fresh green chile peppers, such as serrano, minced with seeds
- 2 tablespoons peanut oil
- 2 to 4 dried red chile peppers, such as chile de arbol, whole or broken

Directions:

1. Prepare either of the idli batters. When the fermented batter is ready (through step 2 in either recipe), stir in the onion, ginger, green chile peppers, cilantro, and half (¼ teaspoon) the asafoetida. Next, continue with Step 3 of the recipe.
2. When the idlis are steamed, move them to a serving plate. Heat the oil in a small-sized non-stick wok or saucepan using moderate to high heat and put in the red chile peppers and mustard seeds. They should splutter when they touch the hot oil, so cover the pan until the spluttering diminishes. Swiftly put in the rest of the asafoetida and curry leaves, and stir for approximately half a minute. Put into the idlis and toss lightly to mix. Serve.

BEAN AND RICE CAKES (DHOKLA)

Dhokla is a staple from the West Indian state of Gujarat, but is extremely popular all over India. These spicy and juicy cakes are healthy and insanely delicious.

CLASSIC CHICKPEA CAKES

This recipe is called "Khaman dhokla" in Hindi

Yield: 4 to 6 servings

Ingredients:

- ¼ cup peanut oil
- ¼ teaspoon ground asafoetida
- ½ cup non-fat plain yogurt, whisked until the desired smoothness is achieved
- ½ cup water, or more as required
- ½ teaspoon baking soda
- ½ teaspoon citric acid
- 1 cup dried yellow split chickpeas (channa dal), sorted and washed in 3 to 4 changes of water
- 1 tablespoon fresh or frozen grated coconut
- 1 teaspoon black mustard seeds
- 1 teaspoon salt, or to taste
- 1 to 3 fresh green chile peppers, such as serrano, whole or split in half lengthwise
- 2 tablespoons finely chopped fresh curry leaves
- 2 to 3 tablespoons finely chopped fresh cilantro, including soft stems
- 4 to 6 dried red chile peppers, such as chile de arbol, with stems

Directions:

1. Immerse the dal overnight in water to cover by 2 inches. Drain and process Using a food processor, adding the yogurt and the water to make a smooth semi-thick batter, yet with a soft grain. Move to a container and set in a warm, dry place at least 1two hours to ferment.
2. Stir in 2 tablespoons oil, asafoetida, and salt, and using a whisk or a fork, whip well to incorporate air into the batter, approximately one minute.
3. Put approximately a 1-inch layer of water into your pressure cooker or a large pot to be used for steaming the dhokla. Grease well the dhokla tray or trays, or a metal pie pan with raised edges. Mix the baking soda and citric acid into the batter, which will make it foam instantly. Working swiftly, move to the dhokla tray or pie pan and place the tray in the steaming pot, ensuring it sits approximately 1 inch above the water level. Cover the pot, leaving the

vent open if you're using a pressure cooker, or leaving the cover a little askew if you're using a regular pot, to let the steam to escape. Cook using high heat approximately fifteen to twenty minutes, or until a toothpick inserted in the center of the cake comes out clean. Remove trays from the pot.

4. Heat the rest of the 2 tablespoons oil in a small-sized non-stick wok or saucepan using moderate to high heat, and put in the red chile peppers and mustard seeds. They should splutter when they touch the hot oil, so reduce the heat and cover the pan until the spluttering diminishes. Swiftly put in the green chile peppers, curry leaves, cilantro, and coconut, and cook, stirring, approximately one minute. Spread the mixture uniformly over the dhokla cake. Allow to cool, cut into the desired size squares, rectangles or other shapes, place them on a serving platter and serve.

CHICKPEA FLOUR ROLLS

This recipe is called "Khandvi" in Hindi

Yield: 4 to 6 servings

These rolls are healthy, and were my favourite snack growing up as a kid. Maybe they are my favourite even now!

Ingredients:

- ⅛ teaspoon ground asafoetida
- ⅛ teaspoon ground paprika
- ¼ cup finely chopped fresh cilantro, including soft stems
- ¼ cup fresh or frozen grated coconut
- ¼ teaspoon ground turmeric
- ¾ teaspoon salt, or to taste
- 1 cup chickpea flour
- 1 fresh green chile pepper, such as serrano, stemmed
- 1 tablespoon black mustard seeds
- 1 tablespoon fresh lemon juice
- 2 cups non-fat plain yogurt, whisked until the desired smoothness is achieved
- 2 cups water

- 2 fresh green chile peppers, such as as serrano, quartered lengthwise, with or without seeds
- 2 tablespoons finely chopped fresh curry leaves
- 2 tablespoons peanut oil
- 4 to 6 dried red chile peppers, such as chile de arbol, with stems
- 5 to 6 quarter-size slices peeled fresh ginger

Directions:

1. Sieve the chickpea flour through a fine-mesh strainer to remove any lumps. Grease or lightly spray two 12-by-18-inch baking trays and set aside.
2. Using a blender mix together and pulse the whole green chile pepper, ginger, lemon juice, and 1 cup of the yogurt until the desired smoothness is achieved. Next, Put in the rest of the 1 cup yogurt, chickpea flour, salt, and turmeric, and blend again until the desired smoothness is achieved.
3. Move to a large non-stick wok or saucepan, stir in the water, and cook, stirring continuously and scraping the sides to stop any lumping, using moderate to high heat, approximately two to three minutes, then using moderate to low heat until it begins to splutter and turns into a very thick batter, three to five minutes.
4. Pour the batter into the 2 trays and, with a scraper or a spatula, spread it uniformly and as thinly as you can. Set aside to cool, for approximately half an hour. Using a knife or pizza cutter, cut each sheet of batter into 6-by-2-inch strips and roll each strip firmly like a jellyroll. Move the rolls to a serving platter and sprinkle the coconut and cilantro on top.
5. Heat the oil in a small saucepan using moderate to high heat and put in the green and red chile peppers. Stir a few minutes, then put in the mustard seeds; they will splutter when they touch the hot oil, so reduce the heat and cover the pan until the spluttering diminishes. Put in the asafoetida and curry leaves. When they sizzle, put in the paprika and instantly pour over the khandvi rolls. Serve warm or place in your fridge for a maximum of two hours and serve cold.

CHICKPEA FLOUR ROLLS- STUFFED

This recipe is called "Bharvan khandvi" in Hindi

Yield: 4 to 6 servings

Ingredients:

- ⅛ teaspoon ground asafoetida
- ⅛ teaspoon ground paprika
- ¼ cup finely chopped fresh cilantro, including soft stems + 2 tablespoons
- 1 recipe Gujarati Chickpea Flour Rolls
- 1 small or half large seedless cucumber, crudely chopped
- 1 small red bell pepper, crudely chopped
- 1 tablespoon black mustard seeds
- 2 fresh green chile peppers, such as serrano, quartered lengthwise, with or without seeds
- 2 tablespoons finely chopped fresh curry leaves
- 2 tablespoons fresh or frozen grated coconut
- 2 tablespoons peanut oil
- 4 to 6 whole dried red chile peppers, such as chile de arbol,

Directions:

1. Ready the chickpea flour roll recipe through Step 4—up to spreading the cooked batter on the trays.
2. Using a food processor, combine and pulse the cucumber, red bell pepper, and cilantro until minced. Move them to a moderate-sized non-stick skillet and cook over moderate heat until the vegetables first release their juices and then until the juices dry up, 2 to four minutes. Sprinkle over the batter in the trays and allow to cool down, for approximately half an hour.
3. Using a knife or pizza cutter, cut each sheet of batter into 6-by-2-inch strips then roll each strip firmly like a jellyroll. (Push seeping filling back in using your fingers.) Move the rolls to a serving platter and sprinkle the coconut and cilantro on top.
4. Heat the oil in a small saucepan using moderate to high heat and put in the green and red chile peppers. Stir a few minutes, then put in the mustard seeds; they will splutter when they touch the hot oil, so reduce the heat and cover the pan until the spluttering diminishes. Put in the asafoetida and the curry leaves. When they sizzle, put in the paprika, then instantly pour over the khandvi rolls. Serve warm or refrigerate at least two hours and serve cold.

CHICKPEA ZUCCHINI CAKE

This recipe is called "Handwa" in Hindi

Yield: 4 to 6 servings

Ingredients:

- ¼ teaspoon ground asafoetida
- ½ cup chickpea flour
- ½ cup grated zucchini
- ½ teaspoon ground turmeric
- ⅔ cup buttermilk
- 1 cup rice flour
- 1 tablespoon ground coriander
- 1 teaspoon black mustard seeds
- 1 teaspoon garam masala
- 1 teaspoon salt, or to taste
- 2 tablespoons Basic Ginger and Green Chile Pepper Paste
- 2 tablespoons finely chopped fresh curry leaves
- 2 to 3 tablespoons Basic Green Chutney
- 3 tablespoons vegetable oil
- About ⅔ cup water

Directions:

1. Ready the ginger-green chile pepper paste. In a container, combine the rice and chickpea flours, then put in the buttermilk, plus water as required to make a batter that will pour easily. Stir in the ginger-chile paste, coriander, garam masala, turmeric, and salt, and using a whisk or a fork, whip well to incorporate air into the batter and make it fluffy, approximately one minute. Stir in the zucchini.
2. Heat the oil in a small saucepan using moderate to high heat and put in the mustard seeds; they should splutter when they touch the hot oil, so cover the pan until the spluttering diminishes. Put in the asafoetida and curry leaves, and mix the spices into the batter. Cover and place in a warm, draft-free place eight to ten hours to ferment.
3. Heat your oven beforehand to 400°F. Grease a flat, ovenproof dish with raised edges (such as a shallow metal cake pan or pie pan). Pour the batter

into the dish and bake approximately forty five minutes, or until a knife inserted into the cake comes out clean.
4. In the meantime, ready the chutney. Slice the cake into pieces, top each one with a drop of chutney before you serve warm.

STEAMED CHICKPEA FLOUR CAKES

This recipe is slightly different version of "khaman dhokla"

Yield: 4 to 6 servings

Ingredients:

- ½ cup chopped fresh cilantro, including soft stems
- ½ cup fresh or frozen grated coconut
- ½ cup water
- ½ teaspoon baking soda
- ½ teaspoon citric acid
- ½ teaspoon salt, or to taste
- 1 cup chickpea flour (besan)
- 1 tablespoon Basic Ginger and Green Chile Pepper Paste
- 1 teaspoon black mustard seeds
- 1 teaspoon sugar, dissolved in ⅓ cup water
- 1 teaspoon white sesame seeds
- 2 fresh green chile peppers, such as serrano, quartered lengthwise
- 4 tablespoons vegetable oil
- ten to fifteen fresh curry leaves

Directions:

1. Ready the ginger-green chile paste. Next, in a container, combine the chickpea flour and water and, using a whisk or a fork, whip well to incorporate air and make a semi-thick batter, approximately one minute. Put in the ginger-green chile paste, salt, 2 tablespoons oil, and mix thoroughly.
2. Put approximately 1 inch of water into your pressure cooker or in a big pot that will be used for steaming the dhokla. Grease well 1 large or 2 small dhokla trays or metal pie pans with raised edges.

3. Mix the citric acid and baking soda into the batter, which will make it foam instantly. Working swiftly, move the batter to the trays and place the tray in the pot, ensuring it sits approximately 1 inch above the water level. Cover the pot, leaving the vent open if you're using a pressure cooker or leaving the cover a little askew if you're using a regular pot, to let the steam to escape. Cook using high heat approximately fifteen to twenty minutes, or until a toothpick inserted in the center of the dhokla comes out clean. Remove from the pot.
4. Heat the rest of the 2 tablespoons oil in a small-sized non-stick wok or saucepan using moderate to high heat and put in the mustard seeds. They should splutter when they touch the hot oil, so reduce the heat and cover the pan until the spluttering diminishes. Put in the sesame seeds, green chile peppers, and curry leaves, and cook approximately half a minute. Stir in the sugar-water and pour uniformly over the dhokla cake. Allow to cool and cut into the desired size squares, rectangles, or other shapes, and place them on a serving platter. Garnish with the cilantro and coconut before you serve.

STEAMED MUNG CAKES (V)

This recipe is called "Dhokla-iddli" in Hindi

Yield: 4 to 6 servings

Ingredients:

- ¼ cup any green chutney if your choice (Refer to the chutney recipes int his book)
- ¼ cup finely chopped fresh cilantro, including soft stems
- ¼ teaspoon ground asafoetida
- ½ cup each: dried yellow mung beans (dhulli mung dal), and dried yellow split chickpeas (channa dal), sorted and washed in 3 to 4 changes of water
- ½ cup finely chopped onions
- ½ teaspoon baking soda
- ½ teaspoon citric acid
- ¾ to 1 cup water
- 1 cup sev noodles
- 1 teaspoon salt, or to taste
- 2 tablespoons Basic Ginger and Green Chile Pepper Paste

- 2 tablespoons Garlic and Fresh Red Chile Pepper Chutney
- 2 to 3 tablespoons peanut oil

Directions:

1. In separate containers, soak both the dals overnight in water to cover by minimum two inches. Ready the ginger-green chile paste and the chutneys. When ready, drain and process each dal separately Using a food processor, adding up to ½ cup of water each, to make a paste as smooth as possible.
2. Move both the dals to a container and combine well. Put in the oil, ginger-green chile paste, asafoetida, and salt, and whip well using a whisk or a fork to incorporate air and make a batter, approximately one minute. The batter should be semi-thick, with the tiniest bit of a grain. If batter is thin, add 1 to 2 teaspoons of semolina.
3. Grease the idli molds (or coat with non-stick spray). Mix the citric acid and baking soda into the batter; it will bubble instantly. Working swiftly, before the bubbling diminishes, pour 2 tablespoons of the batter into each mold and place each tray on the stand.
4. Put approximately 1 inch of water into your pressure cooker or large pot then place the idli stand in the pot. Cover the pot, leaving the vent open if you're using a pressure cooker or leaving the cover a little askew if you're using a regular pot, to let the steam to escape. Cook using high heat until the cakes are soft and spongy, approximately ten to twelve minutes. Allow the steam to escape from the sides, but do not remove the lid from the pot for ten to twelve minutes. Allow to cool. Using a spoon or clean fingers, remove each dhokla-idli from the mold. Pry lightly with a knife or a small spatula if they stick.
5. Line a serving platter with a mixture of the sev noodles, onion, and cilantro, and place the small dhoklas over the mixture. Top each dhokla with a layer of green chutney, place a dollop of garlic chutney on top before you serve.

INDIAN STREET FOODS

CRISPY FLOUR CHIPS MIX

This recipe is called "Sev-poori" in Hindi

Yield: 4 to 6 servings

Ingredients:

- ¼ cup Basic Green Chutney
- ¼ cup Minty Sonth Chutney with Mango (or Tamarind) Powder and Jaggery
- ½ cup crunchy sev noodles
- ½ cup plain yogurt, whisked until the desired smoothness is achieved
- ½ cup sprouted green mung beans (saabut mung dal), (not compulsory)
- 1 cup finely chopped fresh cilantro, including soft stems
- 1 large russet (or any) potato
- 1 medium onion, finely chopped
- 1 to 3 tablespoons Garlic and Fresh Red Chile Pepper Chutney
- 20 to 24 flour chips, store-bought or homemade

Directions:

1. Ready the chutneys. Boil the potato in lightly salted boiling water to cover until tender, approximately twenty minutes. Drain, allow to cool down, then peel and cut finely. Lay out the poori chips on a serving platter.
2. combine the potato, onion, sprouted beans (if using), and cilantro, and place approximately 1 tablespoon on each chip, then place 2 teaspoons yogurt on top of that. Drizzle from 1 to 2 teaspoons of each of the chutneys over the yogurt and top with a sprinkling of sev. Serve instantly or they will get soggy.

CRUNCHY PUFFS WITH SPICY TAMARIND WATER Ⓥ

This recipe is called "Paani poori, or Gol Gappe" in Hindi

Yield: 4 to 6 servings

Ingredients:

- ¼ cup finely chopped fresh cilantro, including soft stems
- ½ cup canned chickpeas, drained and crudely mashed

- ½ cup Minty Sonth Chutney with Mango (or Tamarind) Powder and Jaggery
- ½ cup sprouted green mung beans (saabut mung dal) (not compulsory)
- ½ gallon Spicy Tamarind Water with Mint and Roasted Cumin
- 1 large russet (or any) potato
- 1 teaspoon New Delhi Street Food Masala, or Chaat Masala (Homemade or store-bought)
- 25 to 30 paani-poori puffs, store-bought

Directions:

1. Cook the potato in lightly salted boiling water to cover until tender, approximately twenty minutes. In the meantime, ready the chutney, tamarind water, and masala.
2. Drain the potatoes, allow to cool down, then peel and finely cut or mash them. In a large container, combine the potato, cilantro, chickpeas, sprouted dal (if using), and masala.
3. Using a clean thumb or forefinger, softly make a big hole on the thin side of the paani-poori puff and fill with up to 2 teaspoons of the potato mixture. Dunk each filled puff into a container full of tamarind water and eat instantly. Or, at large gatherings, set out the paani-poori puffs, the chutney, and the tamarind water like a salad bar and let everyone help themselves.

FLOUR CHIPS YOGURT MIX

This recipe is called "Papri chaat" in Hindi

Yield: 4 to 6 servings

Ingredients:

- ¼ cup finely chopped fresh cilantro, including soft stems
- ½ cup or more Sonth Chutney with Dried Mango Slices
- ½ teaspoon cayenne pepper, or to taste
- 1 cup canned chickpeas, drained, rinsed, and crudely mashed
- 1 large russet (or any) potato
- 1 to 3 fresh green chile peppers, such as serrano, minced with seeds
- 1½ to 2 cups plain non-fat yogurt, whisked until the desired smoothness is achieved

- 12 (8-inch) thin flour tortillas, if possible vegetarian style
- 2 teaspoons New Delhi Street Food Masala, or Chaat Masala (Homemade or store-bought)
- 2 to 3 cups peanut oil for deep-frying

Directions:

1. Ready the chutney and the masala. Boil the potato in lightly salted boiling water until tender, approximately twenty minutes. Drain, allow to cool down, then peel and crudely mash. Slice the flour tortillas into 1-inch pieces.
2. Heat the oil in a wok or skillet using high heat until it achieves 350°F to 375°F on a frying thermometer or until a tiny piece of the tortilla dropped into the hot oil bubbles and instantly rises to the top. Deep-fry the tortilla pieces in 3 or 4 batches, turning them with a slotted spatula, until a golden colour is achieved, approximately two minutes per batch.
3. Using a slotted spatula move to paper towels to drain. Allow to cool and use instantly, or store in airtight containers approximately one month.
4. To serve, spread the chips on a serving platter, then one at a time, top with the potato and chickpea mixture, pour the yogurt uniformly on the top and sides, ensuring that most of the chips are covered (with some peeking through), then drizzle the sonth chutney over the yogurt. Sprinkle the masala and cayenne pepper, then the green chile peppers and cilantro. Serve instantly or it will get soggy.

PUFFED RICE SPICY MIX Ⓥ

This recipe is called "Bhel poori" in Hindi

Yield: 4 to 6 servings

A speciality of Bombay, the home of Bollywood!

Ingredients:

- ½ cup shelled, chopped roasted peanuts
- 1 cup finely chopped fresh cilantro, including soft stems
- 1 large russet (or any) potato
- 1 medium onion, finely chopped

- 1 to 3 tablespoons Garlic and Fresh Red Chile Pepper Chutney
- 1 to 3 tablespoons Roasted Dal and Fresh Green Chile Pepper Chutney
- 2 to 4 tablespoons Sweet Sonth Chutney with Dates
- 4 cups bhel-poori mix, store-bought

Directions:

1. Ready the chutneys. Cook the potato in lightly salted boiling water to cover until tender, approximately twenty minutes, then peel and finely chop.
2. In a large container, combine the bhel-poori mix, mashed potato, onion, and cilantro. Add all the chutneys and toss to mix thoroughly. Scatter the peanuts on top and serve instantly or the mixture will get soggy.

STUFFED CRISPY PUFFS WITH

This recipe is called "Batata poori chaat" in Hindi

Yield: 4 to 6 servings

Ingredients:

- ¼ cup Cilantro-Lime Chutney (Homemade or store-bought)
- ¼ cup finely chopped fresh cilantro, including soft stems
- ¼ cup Minty Sonth Chutney with Mango (or Tamarind) Powder and Jaggery
- ½ teaspoon cayenne pepper, or to taste
- ½ teaspoon salt, or to taste
- 1 cup canned chickpeas, drained and crudely mashed
- 1 large russet (or any) potato
- 1 tablespoon New Delhi Street Food Masala, or Chaat Masala (Homemade or store-bought)
- 1 tablespoon peeled minced fresh ginger
- 1 teaspoon cumin seeds, dry-roasted and crudely ground (See the dry-roasting section in Introduction)
- 1 to 3 fresh green chile peppers, such as serrano, minced with seeds
- 2 cups non-fat plain yogurt, whisked until the desired smoothness is achieved
- 20 to 24 paani-poori puffs, store-bought

Directions:

1. Cook the potato in lightly salted boiling water to cover until tender, approximately fifteen minutes. Drain the potato, allow to cool down, then peel and mash it. In the meantime prepare both chutneys and the masala.
2. In a moderate-sized container, combine the mashed potato, chickpeas, cilantro, green chile peppers, ginger, and masala.
3. Using a clean thumb or forefinger, softly make a big hole on the thin side of each puffed poori and fill with approximately 1 tablespoon of the potato mixture. Put on a serving platter, and scatter whatever potato mixture is leftover on top of the poories.
4. Into the yogurt, stir in the cumin, salt, and cayenne pepper, and pour it over the stuffed poories. Drizzle the chutneys on top and serve.

KEBABS

This section is for all the meat lovers out there. These insanely delicious delicacies were brought to India by the Mughals, and are easily one of the most popular non-vegetarian street foods you can find in India. There are many ways of cooking these, but in the Indian streets you will usually see them being cooked on coal, and on skewers.

Tikkas are a kind of kebab where small chunks of marinated meat are cooked directly over hear, commonly using skewers.

If you're preparing a full course meal for meat lovers, kebabs and tikkas are served first. They are great appetizers. You can also add kebabs and Tikkas to chopped vegetables to make insanely delicious and nutritious salads.

KEBAB AND TIKKA FINISHING GLAZE

Before they are finished, all tandoor-cooked kebabs and tikkas are moistened with a special finishing glaze that is made with seasoned ghee, butter, or oil and, in some cases, lemon juice. Brushed on the foods during the last few minutes, while the meat is still cooking, this glaze really enhances the flavours and gives the food a radiant shine.

Directions:

1. Start with 1 to 2 tablespoons melted butter or any vegetable oil, mixed with ½ teaspoon Asian sesame oil or ghee.
2. Put in 2 tablespoons fresh lemon or lime juice/vinegar, ½ teaspoon dried fenugreek leaves, and ground black salt to taste.
3. Next, stir in any one of the two: ½ to 1 teaspoon dry-roasted and crudely ground cumin or black peppercorns (See the dry-roasting section in Introduction) OR 1 teaspoon Chaat Masala (Homemade or store-bought)

BLACK CHICKPEA KEBABS Ⓥ

This recipe is called "Kaala channa kebabs" in Hindi

Yield: 4 to 6 servings

Ingredients:

- ½ cup crudely chopped fresh cilantro, including soft stems
- ¾ to 1 cup chickpea flour
- 1 cup dried black chickpeas (kaalae channae), sorted and washed in 3 to 4 changes of water
- 1 teaspoon garam masala
- 1 teaspoon salt, or to taste
- 1 to 1½ cups peanut oil for deep-frying
- 1 to 3 fresh green chile peppers, such as serrano, crudely chopped
- 2 large cloves fresh garlic, peeled
- 2 to 3 cups water
- 5 to 6 quarter-size slices peeled fresh ginger

Directions:

1. Immerse the dal overnight in water to cover by 2 inches. Next, drain and place the dal, water, garam masala, and salt into your pressure cooker. Ensure that the lid is secure, and cook using high heat until the regulator

shows that the pressure is high, then cook approximately one minute more. Reduce the heat to low and continue to cook another 1 minute. Remove the pot from the heat and let the pressure release automatically, twelve to fifteen minutes. Next, cautiously open the lid and check to see if the chickpeas are very soft, with some of them broken; if not, cover, bring up to pressure, and cook under pressure another minute.

2. Another way is to place the dal, spices and water in a big pot, cover and boil until the chickpeas are soft and all the water has evaporated, for approximately half an hour.
3. Allow to cool, then move to a food processor along with garlic, ginger, chile peppers, and cilantro, and process until the desired smoothness is achieved. Add half the chickpea flour and process once again, adding more flour until everything begins to gather, almost like soft dough that can be shaped. Divide into 25 portions and shape into smooth patties or rolls.
4. Heat the oil in a wok or skillet using high heat until it registers 350°F to 375°F on a frying thermometer or until a small piece of the mixture dropped into the hot oil bubbles and instantly rises to the top. Fry the kebabs, as many as the wok can hold simultaneously without crowding, turning them with a slotted spatula a few times until a golden colour is achieved and crunchy on all sides, approximately three minutes per batch. Drain using paper towels. Move to a platter and serve hot.

CHICKEN DRUMSTICK KEBABS

This recipe is called "Tangdhi kebabs" in Hindi

Yield: 4 to 6 servings

Ingredients:

- ¼ teaspoon freshly ground nutmeg
- ¼ teaspoon ground turmeric
- ½ teaspoon cayenne pepper, or to taste
- 1 tablespoon ground coriander
- 1 tablespoon melted ghee
- 1 teaspoon cumin seeds, dry-roasted, crudely ground (See the dry-roasting section in Introduction)
- 1 teaspoon dried fenugreek leaves

- 1 teaspoon garam masala
- 1 teaspoon ground cumin
- 12 skinless chicken drumsticks
- 2 tablespoons Basic Ginger-Garlic Paste (Homemade or store-bought)
- 2 tablespoons fresh lime juice
- 2 tablespoons vegetable oil
- Lemon wedges, onion slivers, and split fresh green chile peppers, for garnish

Directions:

1. Ready the ginger-garlic paste and the cumin seeds. Next, with a sharp knife, make 2 to 3 deep cuts along the diagonal on each drumstick and place in a big non-reactive container.
2. In a container, combine all the rest of the ingredients (except the ghee, roasted cumin, and the garnishes) and add to the drumsticks. Mix well, ensuring that some of the marinade reaches inside the gashes and all the pieces are coated thoroughly. Cover and marinate in the fridge for minimum 8 and maximum 1two hours.
3. Preheat a grill to 375°F to 400°F, or preheat the broiler. Wrap the bone side of each drumstick with a piece of foil, and grill using moderate to high heat or broil on the top rack (about 6-inches away from the heating element), flipping regularly, until firm and mildly charred on all sides, approximately twenty minutes.
4. During the last two to three minutes, heat the ghee in a small saucepan using moderate to high heat, stir in the roasted cumin seeds, and baste over the drumsticks. Move to a serving platter, garnish with the lemon wedges, onion, and green chile peppers before you serve.

CHICKEN LIVER KEBABS

This recipe is called "Kalaeji kebabs" in Hindi

Yield: 4 to 6 servings

Ingredients:

- ¼ cup non-fat plain yogurt, whisked until the desired smoothness is achieved
- ½ cup canned tomato sauce

- 1 large onion, finely chopped
- 1 pound chicken livers, cut into 1-inch pieces
- 1 tablespoon dried fenugreek leaves
- 1 tablespoon ground coriander
- 1 teaspoon garam masala
- 1 teaspoon ground cumin
- 1 to 2 tablespoons vegetable oil
- 2 tablespoons Basic Ginger-Garlic Paste (Homemade or store-bought)
- 2 tablespoons fresh lime juice
- twelve to fifteen metal or bamboo skewers, soaked in water at least 30 minutes

Directions:

1. Put the liver pieces in a non-reactive container and stir in all the rest of the ingredients. Cover using plastic wrap and marinate in the fridge for minimum 4 and maximum one day.
2. Move the liver and all the marinade to a non-stick skillet and bring to a boil using high heat. Reduce the heat to moderate to low, cover the pan and simmer until the liver is tender and the sauce has almost evaporated, approximately fifteen minutes. Allow to cool.
3. Preheat a grill to 375°F to 400°F or preheat the broiler. Thread the meat onto the skewers and grill, or broil on the top rack (about 6 inches from the heating element), flipping regularly, until mildly charred on all sides, approximately ten minutes. Move to a platter and serve hot.

COTTAGE CHEESE AND VEGETABLE KEBABS

This recipe is called "Paneer shaslik kebabs" in Hindi

Yield: 4 to 6 servings

Ingredients:

- ¼ teaspoon ground turmeric
- ½ teaspoon cayenne pepper, or to taste

- 1 cup non-fat plain yogurt, whisked until the desired smoothness is achieved
- 1 teaspoon garam masala
- 1 teaspoon salt, or to taste
- 2 tablespoons Basic Ginger-Garlic Paste (Homemade or store-bought)
- 2 tablespoons chickpea flour
- 2 tablespoons fresh lemon juice
- 2 tablespoons peanut oil
- 4 to 6 metal or bamboo skewers, soaked in orange juice or water at least 30 minutes
- 8 ounces (1 recipe) Paneer Cheese, cut into 16 equal pieces
- About 1½ pounds mixed fresh vegetables of your choice, cut into 1½-inch pieces
- Shredded lettuce (not compulsory)

Directions:

1. Ready the paneer cheese. Ready the ginger-garlic paste. Put the paneer cheese and vegetables in a big non-reactive container. In a small-sized container combine the paneer, lemon juice, oil, chickpea flour, ginger-garlic paste, garam masala, cayenne pepper, turmeric, and salt. Put into the paneer cheese pieces and vegetables and mix thoroughly, ensuring that all the pieces are coated thoroughly. Cover and marinate in the fridge for minimum 8 hours or up to 12.
2. Preheat a grill to 375°F to 400°F or preheat the broiler. Thread the vegetables and paneer cheese onto the skewers and grill over medium-high heart coals, or broil on the top rack (about four to five inches from the heating element), flipping regularly, until lightly golden, approximately five to seven minutes. (Don't overcook, as paneer cheese will toughen.) Moisten once in a while with the marinade. Move to a serving platter and serve the shaslik on skewers, or slide the pieces off onto a bed of shredded lettuce, if using.

COTTAGE CHEESE KEBABS WITH POMEGRANATE SEEDS

This recipe is called "Anardana paneer kebabs" in Hindi

Yield: 4 to 6 servings

Ingredients:

- ½ teaspoon dry-roasted and crudely ground cumin seeds (See the dry-roasting section in Introduction)
- 1 cup sour cream, any kind
- 1 teaspoon salt, or to taste
- 1½ teaspoons garam masala
- 1½ teaspoons ground paprika
- 2 tablespoons peeled minced fresh ginger
- 2 teaspoons ground dried pomegranate seeds
- 2 to 3 large cloves fresh garlic, minced
- 8 ounces (1 recipe) <u>Paneer Cheese</u> (Homemade or store-bought), cut into 1-inch or larger pieces, each approximately ⅓-inch thick

Directions:

1. Ready the cumin seeds and paneer cheese. Next, place the paneer cheese in a flat dish. In a moderate-sized container, combine the sour cream, garlic, ginger, pomegranate seeds, garam masala, paprika, and salt. Put into the paneer cheese, ensuring that all the pieces are coated thoroughly. Cover and marinate in the fridge for minimum 8 hours or up to 12.
2. Preheat the broiler. Grease a broiler-safe tray or cover with foil. Leaving all the marinade behind, move the paneer cheese, piece by piece, to the broiling tray and broil on the top rack (four to five inches from the heating element) until the top side is golden, approximately five minutes. Flip over once and broil the other side until a golden colour is achieved, approximately three minutes. (Do not overcook; the paneer will toughen.) Move to a serving platter, sprinkle the roasted cumin on top before you serve.

DEEP-FRIED MUTTON KEBAB PATTIES

This recipe is called "Shaami kebabs" in Hindi

Yield: 4 to 6 servings

Ingredients:

- ½ cup dried yellow split chickpeas (channa dal), sorted and washed in 3 to 4 changes of water
- 1 large egg, lightly beaten
- 1 pound boneless leg of lamb, all visible fat trimmed, cut into small pieces
- 1 small onion, crudely chopped
- 1 tablespoon ground coriander
- 1 to 3 fresh green chile peppers, such as serrano, stemmed
- 1½ cups water
- 1½ to 2 cups peanut oil for deep-frying
- 2 (1-inch) sticks cinnamon
- 2 large cloves fresh garlic, peeled
- 4 black cardamom pods, crushed lightly to break the skin
- 6 green cardamom pods, crushed lightly to break the skin
- 6 to 8 quarter-size slices peeled fresh ginger
- 8 whole cloves
- Freshly ground black pepper, to taste

Directions:

1. Put the lamb, dal, ginger, garlic, onion, both cardamoms, cinnamon, cloves, and water into your pressure cooker. Ensure that the lid is secure, and cook using high heat until the regulator shows that the pressure is high, then cook approximately one minute more. Reduce the heat to low and continue to cook another 3 minutes. Next, remove from the heat and allow the pot to depressurize automatically, twelve to fifteen minutes.
2. Cautiously take the lid off and cook using moderate to high heat, stirring, until the lamb is completely dry, approximately seven to ten minutes. Allow to cool and remove all the whole spices.
3. Using a food processor, process the green chile peppers until minced. Stir in the cooked lamb, egg, coriander, and black pepper, and process to make a soft dough that can hold its shape, approximately fifteen seconds. Shape into 16 to 20 2-inch patties and set aside.
4. Heat the oil in a big wok or skillet until it reaches 350°F to 375°F on a frying thermometer or until a small piece of the mixture dropped into the hot oil bubbles and instantly rises to the top. Fry the kebabs, as many as the wok can hold simultaneously without crowding, turning a few times with a slotted spatula until a golden colour is achieved and crunchy on all sides,

approximately five minutes. Drain using paper towels. Move to a platter and serve hot.

EGG-STUFFED CHICKEN KEBABS

This recipe is called "Anda-bharae tangdhi kebabs" in Hindi

Yield: 4 to 6 servings

Ingredients:

- ¼ cup grated cheddar or Monterey Jack cheese
- ½ cup finely chopped fresh cilantro, including soft stems
- ½ teaspoon ground paprika
- 1 fresh green chile pepper, such as serrano, minced with seeds
- 1 small onion, cut into half along the length and thinly chopped
- 1 tablespoon ground coriander
- 1 teaspoon dried fenugreek leaves
- 1 teaspoon garam masala
- 12 skinless and boneless chicken drumsticks
- 2 large eggs
- 2 tablespoons fresh lime juice
- 2 tablespoons minced fresh mint leaves
- 2 tablespoons vegetable oil
- 2 to 3 tablespoons <u>Basic Ginger-Garlic Paste</u> (Homemade or store-bought)
- Salt and freshly ground black pepper, to taste

Directions:

1. Ready the ginger-garlic paste. In a moderate-sized saucepan, place the eggs in water to cover by 2 inches and bring to a boil using high heat. Reduce the heat to medium, cover the pan and simmer until hard-boiled, approximately ten to twelve minutes. Allow to cool or plunge into cold water, shell them, then mince them. Mix with the cheese, ¼ cup of the cilantro, and chile pepper, and season lightly with salt and black pepper if you wish. Divide into 12 portions.
2. Using a thin sharp knife, make several cuts in the drumstick meat. Butterfly (open up like a book) each boned drumstick and place one portion of the egg

filling in the center of each drumstick. Close it like a book, then secure with toothpicks along the opening and place in a non-reactive pan. Replicate the process for all the drumsticks.

3. In a small-sized container, combine the ginger-garlic paste, lime juice, mint, coriander, garam masala, fenugreek leaves, and paprika, and add to the drumsticks. Mix well, ensuring that some of it reaches inside the cuts in the meat and that all pieces are coated thoroughly. Cover and marinate in the fridge for minimum 8 and maximum 1two hours.

4. Heat the oil in a big non-stick skillet using moderate to high heat and cook the onion, stirring, until a golden colour is achieved, approximately four minutes. Put in the marinated drumsticks, plus the marinade, and cook, turning as required, until a golden colour is achieved on all sides, approximately ten minutes. Put in the rest of the ¼ cup of the cilantro, cook approximately two minutes, then move to a serving platter and serve hot.

FISH KEBABS

This recipe is called "Macchi kebabs" in Hindi

Yield: 4 to 6 servings

Ingredients:

- ⅛ teaspoon ground asafoetida
- ¼ teaspoon ground turmeric
- ¼ to ⅓ cup water
- ½ cup cornmeal
- ½ cup rice flour
- ½ teaspoon ground fenugreek seeds
- 1 tablespoon fresh lemon juice
- 1 teaspoon ground cumin seeds
- 1 teaspoon salt, or to taste
- 1 to 2 tablespoons finely chopped fresh cilantro, including soft stems
- 1½ pounds any firm white fish fillets, such as sea bass or cod, approximately 1-inch thick, cut into 3-inch pieces
- 1½ to 2 cups peanut oil for deep-frying
- 2 teaspoons hot red pepper flakes, or to taste
- Lemon wedges

Directions:

1. Put the fish pieces in a big non-reactive container, put in the salt and turmeric, and mix thoroughly. Cover and marinate in the fridge one to two hours.
2. In a moderate-sized container, combine the rice flour, red pepper flakes, cumin, fenugreek, asafoetida, and just sufficient water to form a thick paste.
3. Heat the oil in a wok or large skillet using high heat until it registers 350°F to 375°F on a frying thermometer or until a small piece of fish dropped into the hot oil bubbles and instantly rises to the top.
4. Smear each piece of fish with the rice flour paste, dredge it in the corn meal and cautiously add to the hot oil, adding as many pieces as the wok can hold simultaneously. Fry, turning as required, until they are golden and crisp, approximately two to three minutes. Move to paper towels to drain. Move to a serving dish, garnish with lemon wedges and cilantro before you serve.

GREEN CHUTNEY COTTAGE CHEESE KEBABS

This recipe is called "Hari chutney paneer kebabs" in Hindi

Yield: 4 to 6 servings

Ingredients:

- ¼ teaspoon garam masala
- ¼ teaspoon salt, or to taste
- ½ cup <u>Basic Green Chutney</u> (Homemade or store-bought)
- ½ cup non-fat plain yogurt or non-fat sour cream, whisked until the desired smoothness is achieved
- 1 tablespoon vegetable oil
- 2 to 3 scallions, green parts only, minced
- 8-ounces (1 recipe) <u>Paneer Cheese</u> (Homemade or store-bought), cut into 1-by-1½-inch pieces

Directions:

1. Ready the paneer and the green chutney. Put the paneer pieces in a big non-reactive container. In a small-sized container, combine the yogurt (or sour cream), green chutney, and salt. Put into the paneer cheese pieces and mix thoroughly, ensuring all the pieces are coated thoroughly. Cover and marinate in the fridge overnight.
2. Preheat the broiler. Oil or coat with foil a large broiler-safe tray and place the paneer cheese pieces on it in a single layer. Put the tray on the top rack, approximately four to five inches from the heating element, and broil until the pieces are barely golden, approximately five minutes. (Do not overcook; they will toughen.)
3. Turn off the broiler and turn on the oven to 500°F. Put the tray on the bottom rack bake until the pieces are just golden on the bottom, approximately five minutes. Another way is to leave the tray in the broiler, turn the paneer over using a spatula, and broil approximately three minutes more until a golden colour is achieved. Move to a serving platter, garnish with scallion greens and garam masala before you serve.

MARINATED LAMB KEBABS

This recipe is called "Boti kebabs" in Hindi

Yield: 4 to 6 servings

Ingredients:

- ¼ cup Basic Ginger-Garlic Paste (Homemade or store-bought)
- ¼ cup fresh lemon or lime juice
- ½ cup non-fat plain yogurt, whisked until the desired smoothness is achieved
- 1 tablespoon ground coriander
- 1 tablespoon ground cumin
- 1 tablespoon melted unsalted butter
- 1 tablespoon vegetable oil
- 1 teaspoon cayenne pepper, or to taste
- 1½ teaspoons salt, or to taste
- 1½ to 2 pounds boneless leg of lamb, all visible fat trimmed, cut into 1½-inch pieces
- 2 tablespoons finely chopped fresh cilantro, including soft stems
- 2 teaspoon garam masala

- 6 metal or bamboo skewers, soaked in water at least 30 minutes

Directions:

1. Ready the chaat masala. Using a fork, prick each piece of lamb all over and place in a big non-reactive container. In another container, combine the yogurt, ginger-garlic paste, lemon juice, oil, coriander, cumin, garam masala, cayenne pepper, and salt. Put in the yogurt mixture to the lamb pieces. Mix well, ensuring that all the pieces are coated with the marinade. Cover and marinate in the fridge for approximately one day.
2. Skewer the marinated pieces of chicken (four to five pieces per skewer) and discard the marinade. (If you absolutely must, instantly boil the marinade approximately five minutes and use it in sauces. Boiling kills any bacteria.)
3. Preheat a grill on medium-high heat (375°F to 400°F) and grill, flipping the skewered pieces over until they are mildly charred and super soft, approximately twenty minutes. During the last minute of the cook, baste with the melted butter. Transfer to a serving platter, garnish with the cilantro and serve.

MUTTON KEBAB WITH CARDAMOM SEEDS

This recipe is called "Pasindae illaichi" in Hindi

Yield: 4 to 6 servings

Ingredients:

- ½ cup non-fat plain yogurt, whisked until the desired smoothness is achieved
- ½ teaspoon ground black cardamom seeds
- 1 tablespoon ground unsweetened dried coconut
- 1 teaspoon garam masala
- 1 teaspoon ground green cardamom seeds
- 1 teaspoon ground paprika
- 1 teaspoon salt, or to taste
- 1½ pounds boneless leg of lamb, all visible fat trimmed
- 2 tablespoons Basic Ginger-Garlic Paste (Homemade or store-bought)

- 2 tablespoons fresh lemon or lime juice
- 6 to 8 metal or bamboo skewers, soaked in water at least 30 minutes
- Chopped cilantro, lemon wedges, and scallion whites

Directions:

1. Ready the ginger-garlic paste. Slice the lamb into thin 1-by-1½-inch pieces. Put the pieces on a cutting board, cover using plastic wrap and, with the flat side of a meat mallet, pound them until they are minimum two inches long and approximately ¼-inch thick. (These are the pasindas.)
2. In a small non-reactive container, mix the ginger-garlic paste, garam masala and salt, and rub it well into the lamb pieces. Cover using plastic wrap and marinate in the fridge for approximately two hours.
3. In another small-sized container, combine the yogurt, lime juice, coconut, paprika, and both the cardamom seeds, and put them in to the lamb. Mix well, cover using plastic wrap and marinate at least 4 more hours in a fridge.
4. To skewer, fold each pasinda in half and poke the skewer through the center. Next, pull both the sides away from one another to make a small curve.
5. Preheat a grill to high heat (400°F to 425°F) and grill, flipping the skewered lamb pieces until they are seared on all sides, approximately a minute or two. Next, move the skewers to the sides where the heat is a little less and carry on grilling, turning, until the lamb is golden brown and super soft, approximately ten minutes. Move to a serving platter, garnish with chopped cilantro, lemon wedges, and scallion whites before you serve.

MUTTON KEBAB WITH NUTS AND POPPY SEEDS

This recipe is called "Maeva-khaskhas pasindae" in Hindi

Yield: 4 to 6 servings

Ingredients:

- ½ cup non-fat plain yogurt, whisked until the desired smoothness is achieved
- ½ teaspoon cayenne pepper, or to taste

- ½ teaspoon garam masala
- 1 small onion, crudely chopped
- 1 tablespoon chickpea flour (besan), dry-roasted
- 1 tablespoon poppy seeds
- 1½ pounds boneless leg of lamb, all visible fat trimmed
- 2 tablespoons crudely chopped cashews
- 2 tablespoons Basic Ginger-Garlic Paste (Homemade or store-bought)
- 2 tablespoons blanched raw almonds
- 2 tablespoons fresh lime juice

Directions:

1. Ready the ginger-garlic paste. Slice the lamb into thin 1-by-1½-inch pieces. Put the pieces on a cutting board, cover using plastic wrap and, with the flat side of a meat mallet, pound them until they are minimum two inches long and approximately ¼-inch thick. (These are the pasindas.)
2. Dry-roast the chickpea flour. Next, Using a food processor, combine and pulse the cashews, almonds, poppy seeds, chickpea flour, garam masala, and cayenne pepper until finely ground. Put in the onion, yogurt, and lime juice, and process once more until a smooth paste is achieved.
3. Put the pasindas in a big non-reactive container, put in the marinade and mix thoroughly. Cover using plastic wrap or the lid of the container and marinate in the fridge for minimum 4 and maximum one day.
4. To skewer, fold each pasinda in half and poke the skewer through the center. Next, pull both the sides away from one another to make a small curve.
5. Preheat a grill to high heat (400°F to 425°F) and grill, flipping the skewered lamb pieces until they are seared on all sides, approximately a minute or two. Next, move the skewers to the sides where the heat is a little less and carry on grilling, turning, until the lamb is golden brown and super soft, approximately ten minutes. Move to a serving platter, garnish with chopped cilantro, lemon wedges, and scallion whites before you serve.

MUTTON KEBABS WITH FENUGREEK LEAVES

This recipe is called "Gosht kae methi kabaab" in Hindi

Yield: 4 to 6 servings

Ingredients:

- ¼ teaspoon ground turmeric
- ½ teaspoon ground cumin
- ½ teaspoon ground paprika
- 1 large egg, lightly beaten
- 1 pound minced leg of lamb
- 1 tablespoon ground coriander
- 1 teaspoon garam masala
- 1 teaspoon salt, or to taste
- 1 to 3 fresh green chile peppers, such as serrano, crudely chopped
- 1½ to 2 cups peanut oil for deep-frying
- 2 tablespoons Basic Ginger-Garlic Paste (Homemade or store-bought)
- 2 teaspoons dried fenugreek leaves
- 3 slices white bread, crusts removed

Directions:

1. Ready the ginger-garlic paste. Immerse the bread slices in water to cover until soft, approximately one minute. Drain, squeeze out all surplus water, and crumble finely. In a container, combine everything except the oil. Cover and marinate in the fridge for approximately 1 hour.
2. Heat the oil in a big wok or skillet using moderate to high heat until it achieves 325°F to 350°F on a frying thermometer or until a small piece of the mixture dropped into the hot oil takes about fifteen to twenty seconds to surge to the top.
3. Using clean hands, pinch approximately 1 tablespoon of the mixture, flatten lightly by pressing it between your fingers and thumb to make irregular-shaped patties, and cautiously put it into the oil. Add as many kebabs as the wok can hold simultaneously without crowding, and fry, turning them a few times with a slotted spatula, until a golden colour is achieved and crunchy on

all sides, approximately five minutes. Drain using paper towels. Move to a platter and serve.

PANEER KEBABS

This recipe is called "Paneer seekh kebabs" in Hindi

Yield: 4 to 6 servings

Ingredients:

- ½ cup crudely chopped fresh cilantro, including soft stems
- ½ cup chopped cashews, soaked in water to cover approximately one hour, then drained
- ½ small onion, crudely chopped
- 1 tablespoon ground coriander
- 1 tablespoon melted unsalted butter
- 1 teaspoon Chaat Masala (Homemade or store-bought) + ¼ teaspoon
- 1 teaspoon ground cumin
- 1 teaspoon mango powder
- 1 teaspoon salt, or to taste
- 1 to 3 fresh green chile peppers, such as serrano, crudely chopped
- 2 cups shredded lettuce, such as green or red leaf, or romaine
- 2 to 4 tablespoons all-purpose flour, as required
- 4 quarter-size slices peeled fresh ginger
- 8 ounces (1 recipe) Paneer Cheese (Homemade or store-bought), crumbled
- twelve to fifteen metal or bamboo skewers, soaked in water at least 30 minutes

Directions:

1. Ready the chaat masala and the paneer cheese. Next, Using a food processor, combine and pulse the cashews, green chile peppers, ginger, onion, and cilantro until fine. Next, Put in the paneer cheese and all the rest of the ingredients (except the flour, butter, chaat masala, and lettuce) and process until everything is well mixed and begins to gather together, approximately one minute.

2. Preheat a grill to 375°F to 400°F or preheat the broiler. Moisten your clean fingers with water, and divide the mixture into twelve to fifteen equivalent portions, making long, thin shapes, similar to hot dogs. If the mixture appears too soft to work with, stir in some all-purpose flour, using as much as required to make a soft dough that holds its shape.
3. Skewer them and grill or broil on the top rack (about 6 inches from the heating element), flipping regularly, until firm and lightly golden. (Do not overcook, or they will become tough.)
4. Heat the butter in a small saucepan using moderate to high heat, stir in 1 teaspoon chaat masala and lightly baste the kebabs just before removing them from the heat. Move to a platter lined with the lettuce, sprinkle the ¼ teaspoon chaat masala on top before you serve.

PAN-FRIED LAMB KEBABS

This recipe is called "Bhunnae boti kabaab" in Hindi

Yield: 4 to 6 servings

Ingredients:

- ½ cup finely chopped fresh cilantro, including soft stems
- ½ cup vegetable oil for pan-frying
- ½ teaspoon cayenne pepper, or to taste
- ½ teaspoon garam masala
- ¾ to 1 cup bread crumbs
- 1 (2-foot-long) piece of cheesecloth
- 1 tablespoon black peppercorns
- 1 teaspoon salt, or to taste
- 10 cloves
- 1½ to 2 pounds boneless leg of lamb, all visible fat trimmed, cut into 1-inch pieces
- 2 (1-inch) sticks cinnamon, broken into 2 to 3 pieces
- 2 large eggs, lightly beaten
- 3 tablespoons Basic Ginger-Garlic Paste (Homemade or store-bought)
- 4 bay leaves
- 4 black cardamom pods, crushed lightly to break the skin
- 5 to 6 cups water

- 6 to 8 green cardamom pods

Directions:

1. Fold the cheesecloth twice, so you have a 5- to 6-inch square with 4 layers. Put the bay leaves, peppercorns, cloves, cinnamon, and both kinds of cardamom pods on top. Tie the seasoning pouch closed with kitchen string. Crush the contents lightly with a pestle or meat pounder to crudely break all the spices.
2. Ready the ginger-garlic paste, and place in a big non-stick pan along with the lamb, seasoning pouch, water, and salt. Bring to a boil, and boil using high heat approximately five minutes. Reduce the heat to low, cover the pan and cook until all the water has been absorbed and the meat is super soft, 50 to 60 minutes. (If the meat is not tender, add up to 1 cup more water and continue cooking.) Watch cautiously that the pan doesn't boil over.
3. Allow to cool, then put in the eggs, cayenne pepper, garam masala, ¾ cup bread crumbs, and cilantro, and mix thoroughly. The meat should be completely dry. If not, stir in another ¼ cup bread crumbs.
4. Heat the oil in a big skillet using moderate to high heat and fry the lamb pieces, adding as many as the skillet can hold simultaneously, turning a few times with a slotted spatula, until a golden colour is achieved and crisp, approximately five minutes. Drain using paper towels and serve hot.

SKEWERED MINCED LAMB KEBABS

This recipe is called "Mutton Seekh kebabs" in Hindi

Yield: 4 to 6 servings

These look like sausages, but taste way different.

Ingredients:

- ½ cup Basic Onion Paste
- ½ teaspoon Chaat Masala or store-bought)
- ½ teaspoon saffron threads
- 1 tablespoon milk
- 1 teaspoon Kashmiri Garam Masala or garam masala

- 1 teaspoon salt, or to taste
- 1 to 3 tablespoons semolina or chickpea flour, if required
- 1½ pounds extra lean ground lamb
- 2 cups shredded lettuce, such as green or red leaf, to line a platter
- twelve to fifteen metal or bamboo skewers, soaked in water at least 30 minutes

Directions:

1. Ready the garam masala, chaat masala, and the onion paste. Roast the saffron in a small skillet, approximately one minute, then grind it using the back of a spoon and immerse it in milk for approximately half an hour.
2. Put the lamb in a big mixing container and stir in the onion and ginger-garlic pastes, garam masala, salt, and saffron milk. Cover and marinate in the fridge for approximately four hours.
3. Preheat the grill to 375°F to 400°F, or the broiler. Moisten your clean fingers with water and split the meat into twelve to fifteen equivalent portions. Mould each portion into a long and thin shape, like a sausage. If the mixture appears too soft to work with, stir in the semolina (or chickpea flour), using as much as required to make a soft dough that holds its shape.
4. Skewer them and grill on moderate to high heat or broil on the top rack (about 6 inches away from the heating element), flipping regularly until crunchy yet still moist. Move to a platter lined with lettuce, sprinkle mildly with the chaat masala before you serve.

SMOOTH MINCED CHICKEN KEBABS

This recipe is called "Murgh reshmi seekh kebabs" in Hindi

Yield: 4 to 6 servings

Ingredients:

- ¼ cup all-purpose flour, as required
- ¼ teaspoon freshly ground nutmeg
- ¼ teaspoon ground black salt or Chaat Masala (Homemade or store-bought)
- ½ cup crudely chopped cashews
- ½ cup Basic Green Chutney

- ½ cup finely chopped fresh cilantro, including soft stems
- ½ small onion, crudely chopped
- ½ teaspoon ground white pepper
- 1 small onion, cut in half along the length and thinly chopped
- 1 tablespoon fresh lime juice
- 1 tablespoon ground coriander
- 1 tablespoon melted unsalted butter
- 1 tablespoon vegetable oil
- 1 teaspoon garam masala
- 1 to 3 fresh green chile peppers, such as serrano, crudely chopped
- 1½ to 2 pounds boneless skinless chicken breasts, cut in small pieces
- 2 large egg whites, lightly beaten
- 3 to 4 large cloves fresh garlic, peeled
- 8 quarter-size slices peeled fresh ginger
- twelve to fifteen metal or bamboo skewers, soaked in water at least 30 minutes

Directions:

1. Ready the chutney. Next, in a small-sized container, combine the lime juice, butter, and black salt (or chaat masala), and reserve.
2. Using a blender or a food processor, combine and pulse the chicken, onion, cashews, garlic, ginger, chile peppers, egg whites, and all the spices until thoroughly smooth. Cover and marinate in the fridge for approximately four hours.
3. Preheat a grill to 375°F to 400°F, or preheat the broiler. Moisten your clean fingers with water, split the meat into 12 to 16 equivalent portions, and make each portion into a long, thin shape, similar to a hot dog. If the mixture appears too soft to work with, stir in the all-purpose flour, using as much as required to make a soft dough that holds its shape. Thread the chicken onto the skewers, brush with the lime-butter mixture and grill using moderate to high heat coals, or broil on the top rack (about 6-inches away from the heating element), flipping regularly, until firm and mildly charred on all sides, approximately ten minutes. Move to a platter.
4. Heat the oil in a small-sized non-stick skillet using moderate to high heat and cook the chopped onion until a golden colour is achieved, approximately three minutes. Put in the cilantro and stir approximately one minute, then scatter over kebabs. Dot with some of the chutney and serve the rest of the chutney on the side.

VEGETABLE KEBABS

This recipe is called "Sabzi-seekh kebabs" in Hindi

Yield: 4 to 6 servings

Ingredients:

- ¼ cup crudely chopped almonds
- ¼ cup crudely chopped cashews
- ½ teaspoon ajwain seeds
- ½ teaspoon cayenne pepper, or to taste
- 1 cup finely chopped fresh fenugreek leaves
- 1 cup Paneer Cheese (Homemade or store-bought), crudely crumbled
- 1 large russet (or any) potato
- 1 small orange-fleshed yam
- 1 teaspoon Chaat Masala (Homemade or store-bought)
- 1 teaspoon salt, or to taste
- 1 to 2 tablespoons melted unsalted butter
- 1 to 3 fresh green chile peppers, such as serrano, crudely chopped
- 16 to 20 metal or bamboo skewers, soaked in water at least 30 minutes
- 2 large cloves fresh garlic, peeled
- 2 to 3 tablespoons bread crumbs
- 3 cups crudely chopped mixed fresh vegetables, such as cauliflower, broccoli, carrots, green beans
- 6 quarter-size slices of peeled fresh ginger
- About 2 cups shredded green or red leaf lettuce

Directions:

1. Ready the chaat masala. Cook the potato and the yam in lightly salted boiling water to cover until tender, approximately twenty minutes. Drain, allow to cool down, then peel. Move to a moderate-sized container and mash together.
2. Using a food processor, combine and pulse the cashews, almonds, ginger, garlic, and green chile peppers, until minced. Put in the paneer cheese and fenugreek leaves and process once more until minced. Move to a large container.

3. Put the vegetables in your food processor and process until minced. Put into the processed nut mixture. Next, Put in the bread crumbs, mashed potato and yam, ajwain seeds, cayenne pepper, and salt, and mix thoroughly.
4. Preheat a grill to 375°F to 400°F or preheat the broiler. Moisten your clean fingers with water, and divide the mixture into twelve to fifteen equivalent portions, making long, thin shapes, similar to hot dogs. If the mixture appears too soft to work with, stir in some all-purpose flour, using as much as required to make a soft dough that holds its shape.
5. Skewer them and grill or broil on the top rack (about 6 inches from the heating element), flipping regularly, until firm and lightly golden. (Do not overcook, or they will become tough.)
6. Heat the butter in a small saucepan using moderate to high heat, stir in 1 teaspoon chaat masala and lightly baste the kebabs just before removing them from the heat. Move to a platter lined with the lettuce, sprinkle the ¼ teaspoon chaat masala on top before you serve.

TIKKA KEBABS AND MARINADES

In this section you fill find recipes of Tikkas, as well as marinades. Marinades greatly enhance the flavour of Tikka recipes, and feel free to try out different marinades with different recipes! At the end of the day, it is the marinades that determine how the meat will taste, as the meat itself won't change much.

MARINADES

For marinating time, lamb usually needs at least one day, chicken at least one to two hours, and fish at least two hours. All marinade recipes are sufficient to marinate approximately 2 pounds of tikka kebabs.

CHILE CHICKEN TIKKA MARINADE

This recipe is called "Murgh tikka—laal mirchi" in Hindi

Yield: 4 to 6 servings

Ingredients:

- ½ teaspoon black peppercorns
- 1 cup crudely chopped fresh cilantro, including soft stems
- 1 tablespoon peanut oil
- 1 teaspoon salt, or to taste
- 2 large cloves fresh garlic, peeled
- 2 tablespoons distilled white vinegar
- 4 to 6 dried red chile peppers, such as chile de arbol, broken
- 6 to 8 quarter-size slices peeled fresh ginger

Directions:

1. Heat the oil in a small-sized non-stick saucepan using moderate to high heat and cook the red chile peppers, peppercorns, ginger, and garlic, stirring until a golden colour is achieved, approximately one minute.
2. Move to a small food processor or a blender, stir in the cilantro, vinegar, and salt, and process until the desired smoothness is achieved.

CITRUS CHICKEN TIKKA MARINADE

This recipe is called "Murgh tikka—phal-rus" in Hindi

Yield: 4 to 6 servings

Ingredients:

- ¼ cup non-fat plain yogurt, whisked until the desired smoothness is achieved
- ¼ teaspoon cayenne pepper, or to taste
- ½ teaspoon ground dried oregano
- ½ teaspoon grounds cumin
- 1 large clove fresh garlic, minced

- 1 tablespoon olive oil
- 1 teaspoon salt, or to taste
- 1½ teaspoons garam masala
- 2 tablespoons frozen orange juice pulp
- 2 tablespoons peeled minced fresh ginger
- 3 to 4 tablespoons fresh lime juice

Directions:

Mix everything together in a big non-reactive container.

CREAMY CHICKEN TIKKA MARINADE

This recipe is called "Murgh tikka—malai" in Hindi

Yield: 4 to 6 servings

Use this if you want white, rich, and creay tikkas!

Ingredients:

- ⅛ teaspoon ground mace
- ⅛ teaspoon ground nutmeg
- ¼ cup grated pepper-Jack cheese
- ¼ cup heavy cream
- 1 large egg (or 2 egg whites), lightly beaten
- 1 tablespoon cornstarch
- 1 teaspoon freshly ground white pepper
- 1 teaspoon salt, or to taste
- 2 fresh green chile peppers, such as serrano, crudely chopped
- 2 tablespoons Hyderabadi Ginger-Garlic Paste

Directions:

1. Ready the ginger-garlic paste. In a large non-reactive container, mix the paste, white pepper, and salt, rub the chicken pieces with this mixture, and set aside 30 to 40 minutes.

2. Using a blender, mix together and pulse the cream, cheese, egg, chile peppers, cornstarch, mace, and nutmeg, and pulse until the desired smoothness is achieved. Put into the chicken and mix thoroughly.

GARLIC CHICKEN TIKKA MARINADE

This recipe is called "Murgh tikka—lussan" in Hindi

Yield: 4 to 6 servings

Ingredients:

- ½ teaspoon black freshly ground black pepper
- ½ teaspoon ground green cardamom seeds
- 1 tablespoon Basic Garlic Paste (Homemade or store-bought)
- 1 tablespoon ground coriander
- 1 tablespoon olive oil
- 1 teaspoon garam masala
- 1 teaspoon ground cumin
- 1 teaspoon salt, or to taste
- 3 to 4 tablespoons fresh lemon juice

Directions:

Ready the garlic paste. Next, mix everything together, in a large, non-reactive container.

GREEN CHUTNEY LAMB TIKKA MARINADE

This recipe is called "Gosht tikka—hari chutni" in Hindi

Yield: 4 to 6 servings

To use this marinade, first marinate the lamb with the ginger-garlic paste, then stir in the rest of the flavourings.

Ingredients:

- ¼ cup Basic Green Chutney
- ½ cup non-fat plain yogurt, whisked until the desired smoothness is achieved
- ¾ teaspoon salt, or to taste
- 1 tablespoon peanut oil
- 1 teaspoon Asian sesame oil
- 1 teaspoon Chaat Masala (Homemade or store-bought)
- 1 teaspoon garam masala
- 1 teaspoon ground paprika
- 1½ to 2 pounds boneless leg of lamb, all visible fat trimmed, cut into 1½-inch pieces
- 3 tablespoons Basic Ginger-Garlic Paste (Homemade or store-bought)

Directions:

1. Ready the chutney, ginger-garlic paste, and chaat masala. In a large non-reactive container, combine the ginger-garlic paste, salt, and the lamb, and place in your fridge for approximately two hours.
2. Put in the yogurt, green chutney, garam masala, and chaat masala to the lamb, and mix thoroughly. Next, heat both the oils in a small-sized non-stick saucepan using moderate to high heat, put in the paprika, swiftly pour into the container with the lamb, and mix thoroughly.

GRILLED FISH TIKKA MARINADE

This recipe is called "Macchi tikka—tandoori" in Hindi

Yield: 4 to 6 servings

Ajwain goes great with Fish!

Ingredients:

- ¼ cup non-fat plain yogurt, whisked until the desired smoothness is achieved
- ¼ teaspoon ground turmeric
- ½ teaspoon crudely ground ajwain seeds
- 1 teaspoon cayenne pepper, or to taste

- 1 teaspoon salt, or to taste
- 2 teaspoons garam masala
- 2 teaspoons ground cumin
- 2 to 3 tablespoons fresh lemon juice or distilled white vinegar
- 3 tablespoons Basic Ginger-Garlic Paste (Homemade or store-bought)

Directions:

Ready the ginger-garlic paste. Mix all the ingredients well in a big non-reactive container.

MINT CHICKEN TIKKA MARINADE

This recipe is called "Murgh tikka—pudina" in Hindi

Yield: 4 to 6 servings

Ingredients:

- ½ cup non-fat plain yogurt
- 1 cup lightly packed fresh mint leaves
- 1 medium onion, crudely chopped
- 1 small green bell pepper, crudely chopped
- 1 teaspoon garam masala
- 1 teaspoon salt, or to taste
- 1 to 2 tablespoons fresh lime juice
- 1 to 3 fresh green chile peppers, such as serrano, stemmed
- 3 large cloves fresh garlic, peeled
- 6 to 8 quarter-size slices peeled fresh ginger

Directions:

1. Using a food processor or blender, combine and pulse the onion, bell pepper, green chile peppers, garlic, ginger, and mint until minced.
2. Put in the yogurt, lime juice, garam masala, and salt, and process once more until the desired smoothness is achieved. Move to a large non-reactive container to marinate.

ROSEMARY LAMB TIKKA MARINADE

This recipe is called "Gosht tikka—rosemary" in Hindi

Yield: 4 to 6 servings

Ingredients:

- ½ cup crudely chopped fresh cilantro, including soft stems
- ½ cup non-fat plain yogurt, whisked until the desired smoothness is achieved
- ½ teaspoon cayenne pepper, or to taste
- 1 tablespoon minced fresh rosemary leaves
- 1 tablespoon peanut oil
- 1 teaspoon garam masala
- 1 teaspoon ground paprika
- 1 teaspoon salt, or to taste
- 2 tablespoons distilled white vinegar
- 2 to 3 tablespoons <u>Basic Ginger-Garlic Paste</u> (Homemade or store-bought)

Directions:

1. Ready the ginger-garlic paste. In a large non-reactive container, combine the yogurt, ginger-garlic paste, vinegar, cilantro, rosemary, garam masala, and salt.
2. Heat the oil in a small saucepan using moderate to high heat and put in the paprika and cayenne pep-per; they should sizzle when they touch the hot oil. Swiftly, before they burn, mix everything into the yogurt.

ROYAL LAMB TIKKA MARINADE

This recipe is called "Gosht tikka—shahi" in Hindi

Yield: 4 to 6 servings

Use this marinade if you like rich, exotic tasting meat!

Ingredients:

- ¼ cup grated Monterrey Jack cheese
- ¼ cup heavy cream
- ½ teaspoon ground mace
- 1 tablespoon white poppy seeds
- 1 teaspoon freshly ground black pepper, or to taste
- 1 teaspoon ground green cardamom seeds
- 1 teaspoon salt, or to taste
- 1 to 3 fresh green chile peppers, such as serrano, minced with seeds
- 2 tablespoons Almond and Poppy Seed Paste
- 2 tablespoons Basic Cashew Paste
- 2 tablespoons lemon juice
- 2 tablespoons vegetable oil
- 2 teaspoons ground black cumin seeds
- 3 tablespoons Basic Ginger-Garlic Paste (Homemade or store-bought)
- Green chile peppers, such as serrano, minced with seeds

Directions:

Prepare all the pastes, then mix all the ingredients together in a big container.

SESAME FISH TIKKA MARINADE

This recipe is called "Macchi tikkae—til" in Hindi

Yield: 4 to 6 servings

This marinade Is great for a big catch!

Ingredients:

- ¼ cup non-fat plain yogurt, whisked until the desired smoothness is achieved
- ¼ teaspoon ground asafoetida
- ½ teaspoon Asian sesame oil
- ½ teaspoon cayenne pepper, or to taste
- 1 teaspoon Chaat Masala (Homemade or store-bought)
- 1 teaspoon salt, or to taste
- 1 teaspoon sesame seeds, dry-roasted
- 2 tablespoons Basic Ginger-Garlic Paste (Homemade or store-bought)

- 2 tablespoons Tamarind Paste
- 2 teaspoons garam masala

Directions:

1. Ready the chaat masala, sesame seeds, ginger-garlic paste, and the tamarind paste.
2. In a large non-reactive container, combine all the ingredients, except the chaat masala and sesame seeds. Sprinkle the chaat masala and sesame seeds as a decoration, just before you serve.
3. Variation: Try this recipe adding <u>Indian Grilling Masala</u> instead of garam masala.

SMOOTH CHICKEN TIKKA MARINADE

This recipe is called "Murgh tikka—raeshmi" in Hindi

Yield: 4 to 6 servings

Cream and egg result in a smooth tikka recipe!

Ingredients:

- ½ cup crudely chopped cashew nuts or blanched almonds
- ½ teaspoon finely ground green cardamom seeds
- 1 large egg, white only
- 1 tablespoon heavy cream
- 1 teaspoon garam masala
- 1 teaspoon salt, or to taste
- 2 fresh green serrano or jalapeño peppers
- 3 scallions, white parts only, crudely chopped
- 3 tablespoons fresh lime or lemon juice
- 4 large cloves garlic, peeled
- 6 to 8 quarter-size slices peeled fresh ginger

Directions:

1. Immerse the cashews (or almonds) in water to cover approximately one hour. Drain. Using a blender or a small food processor, combine and pulse the cashews, scallions, peppers, garlic, and ginger until minced.
2. Put in the lime juice, cream, egg white, garam masala, cardamom seeds, and salt, and process until the desired smoothness is achieved.

TURMERIC LAMB TIKKA MARINADE

This recipe is called "Gosht tikka—haldi" in Hindi

Yield: 4 to 6 servings

Ingredients:

- ½ teaspoon cayenne pepper, or to taste
- ¾ cup non-fat plain yogurt, whisked until the desired smoothness is achieved
- 1 tablespoon peanut oil
- 1 teaspoon ground cumin
- 1 teaspoon ground turmeric
- 1 teaspoon salt, or to taste
- 2 teaspoons garam masala
- 2 to 3 tablespoons fresh lime juice
- 3 tablespoons Basic Ginger-Garlic Paste (Homemade or store-bought)

Directions:

1. Ready the ginger-garlic paste. In a large non-reactive container, combine the yogurt, ginger-garlic paste, lime juice, garam masala, cumin, and salt.
2. Heat the oil in a small saucepan using moderate to high heat and put in the turmeric and cayenne pepper; they should sizzle when they touch the hot oil. Swiftly, before they burn, mix everything into the yogurt.

BASIC TIKKA RECIPES

Now that we have taken a look at all the marinade recipes, we can move on to the base meat recipes which you will marinate in the marinades you saw above.

BASIC MUTTON TIKKA

This recipe is called "Gosht tikka" in Hindi

Yield: 4 to 6 servings

Ingredients:

- 1 recipe Kabaab and Tikka Finishing Glaze
- 1 recipe Tikka Marinade of your choice
- 1 to 2 fresh green chile peppers, such as serrano, stemmed, seeded, and thinly chopped
- 1½ to 2 pounds boneless leg of lamb, all visible fat trimmed, cut into 1½-inch pieces
- 8 to 10 metal or bamboo skewers soaked, in water at least 30 minutes
- Lemon and tomato wedges

Directions:

1. Ready the marinade. Next, place the lamb in a big non-reactive container. Put in the marinade (saving approximately ¼ cup to use for basting as you grill) and mix thoroughly, ensuring all the pieces are coated thoroughly. Cover the container and marinate the lamb in the fridge for minimum 12 and maximum 36 hours. (To prevent potential salmonella contamination, never marinate poultry, meats, or seafood at room temperature.)
2. When ready to cook, ready the finishing glaze. Next, skewer the lamb pieces (four to five per skewer), and discard the used marinade. (If you prefer, instantly boil the marinade approximately five minutes and use it as a sauce. Boiling kills any bacteria.)
3. Preheat a grill using high heat to 400°F to 425°F and grill the lamb skewers, turning and rotating as required, until they are seared on all sides, approximately five minutes. Next, move the skewers to the sides where the heat is lower and carry on grilling until the lamb is tender, 20 to 25 minutes. Moisten once in a while with the reserved marinade. During the last minute

of the cook, baste with the finishing glaze and move to a serving platter lined with lemon and tomato wedges. Top with green chile peppers and serve.

BASIC CHICKEN TIKKA KABAABS

This recipe is called "Murgh tikka" in Hindi

Yield: 4 to 6 servings

Ingredients:

- 1 recipe Kabaab and Tikka Finishing Glaze
- 1 recipe Tikka Marinade of your choice
- 1 to 2 fresh green chile peppers, such as serrano, stemmed, seeded, and thinly chopped
- 2 cups shredded greens, such as romaine or green leaf lettuce
- 2 pounds skinless boneless chicken breasts, cut into 1½-inch pieces
- 8 to 10 metal or bamboo skewers, soaked in water at least 30 minutes
- Lemon and tomato wedges
- Scallions, thinly chopped

Directions:

1. Ready the marinade. Next, place the chicken in a big non-reactive container, put in the marinade (saving approximately ¼ cup to use for basting as you grill), and mix thoroughly, ensuring all the pieces are coated thoroughly. Cover the container and marinate the chicken in the refrigerator, at least 6 and maximum one day. (To prevent potential salmonella contamination, never marinate poultry, meat, or seafood at room temperature.)
2. When ready to cook, ready the finishing glaze and save for later. Next, thread the marinated pieces of chicken on skewers (four to five pieces per skewer) and discard the used marinade. (If you prefer, instantly boil the marinade approximately five minutes and then use it as a sauce. Boiling kills any bacteria.)
3. Preheat a grill using moderate to high heat to 375°F to 400°F and grill, turning and rotating the chicken until mildly charred on all sides and tender, approximately twenty minutes. Moisten once in a while with the reserved marinade. During the last minute of the cook, baste with the finishing glaze.

Move to a platter lined shredded greens. Garnish with lemon and tomato wedges, chopped scallions, and green chile peppers before you serve.

BASIC FISH TIKKA KABAABS

This recipe is called "Macchi tikka" in Hindi

Yield: 4 to 6 servings

Fish is fragile, so handle with care.

Ingredients:

- 1 recipe Tikka Marinade of your choice
- 1 tablespoon melted butter
- 1 to 2 fresh green chile peppers, such as serrano, stemmed, seeded, and thinly chopped
- 1½ to 2 pounds firm white fish fillets, such as sea bass, halibut, or orange roughy, approximately ¾ to 1 inch thick, cut into 1½-inch pieces
- 8 to 10 metal or bamboo skewers, soaked in water at least 30 minutes
- Salad greens, lime or lemon, and tomato wedges, scallion whites, thinly chopped

Directions:

1. Ready the marinade. Next, place the fish pieces in a big non-reactive container, put in the marinade (saving approximately ¼ cup to use for basting as you grill), and mix thoroughly, ensuring all the pieces are coated thoroughly. Cover and marinate in the refrigerator, approximately two hours. (To prevent potential salmonella contamination, never marinate any poultry, meat, or seafood at room temperature.)
2. Thread fish pieces on skewers (four to five pieces per skewer) and discard the used marinade. (If you absolutely must, instantly boil the marinade approximately five minutes and then use it in sauces. Boiling kills any bacteria.)
3. Preheat a grill using moderate to high heat to 375°F to 400°F and grill, turning and rotating the skewers, until mildly charred and tender, approximately ten minutes. Moisten once in a while with the reserved

marinade. During the last minute of the cook, baste with the melted butter. Move to a platter lined with salad greens. Garnish with fresh lime or lemon and tomato wedges, scallion whites, and green chile peppers. Serve.

SOUPS

Indian soup recipes are easy to make, highly nutritious, and insanely delicious. These are almost always served steaming hot.

Ⓥ= Vegan Ⓟ= Quick Pressure Cooker Recipe

BASIC BROTHS

VEGETARIAN BROTH Ⓥ

This recipe is called "Akhni" in Hindi

Yield: Approximately 3 cups

Ingredients:

- ¼ teaspoon ajwain seeds
- 1 (1-inch) stick cinnamon
- 1 green bell pepper, chopped
- 1 large onion, chopped
- 1 tablespoon vegetable oil
- 1 teaspoon black peppercorns
- 1 teaspoon cumin seeds
- 1 teaspoon fennel seeds
- 10 whole cloves

- 2 large cloves fresh garlic, chopped
- 3 dried red chile peppers, such as chile de arbol, broken into pieces
- 4 black cardamom pods, crushed lightly to break the skin
- 4 quarter-size slices peeled fresh ginger
- 5 cups water
- 5 green cardamom pods, crushed lightly to break the skin

Directions:

1. Heat the oil in a big saucepan using moderate to high heat and cook the red chile peppers, cumin and black peppercorns, stirring, approximately half a minute. Next, Put in the garlic, ginger, black and green cardamom pods, cinnamon, cloves, fennel, and ajwain seeds, and stir approximately one minute.
2. Put in the onion and bell pepper, decrease the heat to medium, cover the pan and cook until tender, approximately five minutes.
3. Put in the water and bring to a boil using high heat. Decrease the heat to moderate to low, cover the pan, and simmer until the broth is reduced by approximately half, approximately one hour. Simmer longer for a more concentrated broth.
4. Strain to eliminate big spice particles.

SPICY CHICKEN BROTH

This recipe is called "Murgh yakhni" in Hindi

Yield: Approximately 3 cups

Ingredients:

- 1 (2½- to 3-pound) chicken, skin removed
- 1 teaspoon black peppercorns, crushed lightly
- 1 teaspoon salt, or to taste
- 10 cloves, crushed lightly
- 2 bay leaves
- 3 (2-inch) sticks cinnamon, broken in pieces
- 3 large cloves fresh garlic, peeled
- 4 black cardamom pods, crushed lightly to break the skin

- 5 to 6 cups water
- 6 green cardamom pods, crushed lightly to break the skin
- 8 quarter-size slices peeled fresh ginger
- 8 to 10 fresh lemon or lime leaves or 1 tablespoon of fresh lemon or lime juice

Directions:

1. Wash and put the whole chicken in a big saucepan. Put in the water and all the rest of the ingredients and bring to a boil using high heat. Decrease the heat to moderate to low, cover the pan and simmer until the meat is super soft, approximately forty five minutes.
2. With large tongs or a large slotted spoon, move the chicken to a container. Once cool sufficient to hold, take the meat off the bones and store the meat for another recipe. Return the bones to the pan and carry on simmering until the broth is reduced by at least half, approximately one hour. Simmer longer for a more concentrated broth.
3. Allow to cool. Next, secure a piece of muslin or 4 layers of cheesecloth over a big container and pour the broth through to collect a clear broth. Throw away the muslin or cheesecloth and chill the broth in the refrigerator, at least two hours. Using a spoon, skim off and eliminate the layer of fat that solidifies on the top. Reheat to serve as a soup or use as a flavoured broth in other recipes.

SPICY LAMB BROTH

This recipe is called "Gosht yakhni" in Hindi

Yield: Approximately 3 cups

Ingredients:

- 1 cup crudely chopped fresh cilantro, including soft stems
- 1 green bell pepper, finely chopped
- 1 large onion, finely chopped
- 1 teaspoon black peppercorns, crushed lightly using the back of a spoon to break
- 1 teaspoon salt, or to taste

- 1 to 3 fresh green chile peppers, such as serrano, chopped
- 10 cloves, crushed lightly
- 2 bay leaves
- 2 pounds leg of lamb with bone, all visible fat trimmed
- 2 small carrots, finely chopped
- 2 small turnips, finely chopped
- 2 tablespoons coriander seeds
- 3 (2-inch) sticks cinnamon, broken
- 3 large cloves fresh garlic, peeled
- 4 black cardamom pods, crushed lightly to break the skin
- 6 to 7 cups water
- 8 quarter-size slices peeled fresh ginger
- 8 to 10 fresh lemon or lime leaves or 2 lemongrass stalks (bottom 4 inches only), chopped (not compulsory)

Directions:

1. Rinse the lamb and put it in a large saucepan. Cover liberally with water and boil using high heat approximately three minutes. Drain and discard the water and wash the meat in cold water. Next, separate the bones from the meat, then cut the meat with a sharp knife into 1-inch pieces.
2. Put the meat and the bones, along with all the rest of the ingredients, in a big saucepan and bring to a boil using high heat. Decrease the heat to moderate to low, cover the pan and simmer until the meat is super soft, approximately one hour.
3. Take the pieces of meat out and store for a future recipe. Keep the bones in the pan and carry on simmering until the broth is reduced by at least half, approximately one hour. Simmer longer for a more concentrated broth.
4. Allow to cool. Secure a piece of muslin or 4 layers of cheesecloth around a big container and pour the broth through the cloth into the container. Throw away the cloth. Chill the clear broth in the refrigerator, at least two hours. Using a spoon, skim off and eliminate the layer of fat that solidifies on the top. Reheat to serve.

TOMATO SOUPS

CREAMY TOMATO SOUP

This recipe is called "Tamatar ka soop" in Hindi

Yield: 6 to 8 servings

Ingredients:

- ¼ teaspoon nutmeg (freshly grated preferred)
- ½ cup plain whole-milk or low-fat yogurt, whisked until the desired smoothness is achieved
- 1 cup milk, any kind
- 1 medium carrot, unpeeled, crudely chopped
- 1 small red onion, crudely chopped
- 1 small russet (or any) potato, unpeeled, crudely chopped
- 1 tablespoon cornstarch
- 1 tablespoon vegetable oil
- 1 teaspoon cumin seeds, dry-roasted and crudely ground (See the dry-roasting section in Introduction)
- 1 teaspoon salt
- 1 teaspoon sugar
- 1½ pounds ripe tomatoes, crudely chopped
- 2 quarter-size slices peeled fresh ginger
- 2 tablespoons finely chopped fresh cilantro
- 4 cups water
- Freshly ground black pepper, to taste

Directions:

1. Ready the cumin seeds. Next, place the onion and ginger into a food processor and pulse until minced. Move to a container. Next, Put in the carrot and potato and pulse until minced. Move to another container. Put in the tomatoes and pulse until crudely chopped. Leave in your food processor.
2. Heat the oil in a big non-stick saucepan over moderate heat and cook the onion and ginger, stirring, until translucent, approximately one minute. Put in the minced carrot and potato and cook, stirring, approximately one minute. stir in the tomatoes, increase the heat to high and cook, stirring, approximately two to three minutes. Put in the water, salt, and sugar, cover

the pan and bring to a boil. Decrease the heat to medium and cook approximately fifteen minutes.
3. Allow to cool, then if desired, pass the soup through a food mill or a fine-mesh strainer into a heatproof container. (If you prefer a chunky soup, do not strain.) Return to the pan and boil once more.
4. Dissolve the cornstarch in the milk and stir it into the boiling soup. Season with the cumin and nutmeg. Move to a serving container, swirl in the yogurt, garnish with the cilantro and black pepper before you serve.

TOMATO SOUP WITH CURRY LEAVES

This recipe is called "Kari pattae vaala tamatar ka soop" in Hindi

Yield: 6 to 8 servings

Ingredients:

- four to five quarter-size slices peeled fresh ginger
- ⅛ teaspoon ground asafoetida
- ½ cup crudely chopped broccoli or cauliflower stems (not compulsory)
- 1 cup crudely chopped fresh cilantro, including soft stems
- 1 large round white (or any kind) potato, unpeeled, crudely chopped
- 1 small onion, crudely chopped
- 1 tablespoon heavy or light cream
- 1 teaspoon salt, or to taste
- 1 teaspoon vegetable oil
- 1 to 3 fresh green chile peppers, such as serrano, crudely chopped
- 1½ pounds ripe tomatoes, crudely chopped
- 15 to 20 fresh curry leaves
- 2 small carrots, unpeeled, crudely chopped
- 3 to 5 cups water
- Freshly ground black pepper, to taste

Directions:

1. Heat the oil in a big saucepan using moderate to high heat and cook the curry leaves, ginger, and onion, stirring until a golden colour is achieved, approximately a minute or two.

2. Mix in first the asafoetida and then all the vegetables and 3 cups water, and bring to a boil using high heat. Decrease the heat to moderate to low, cover the pan, and simmer until the vegetables are very soft, for approximately half an hour.
3. Allow to cool off the heat, then pass the soup through a food mill or blend using a blender until the desired smoothness is achieved. If using a blender, pour through a fine-mesh strainer into a container, if you prefer a smoother consistency.
4. Return the soup to the saucepan, put in the salt and black pepper and more water as needed for the consistency you like. Boil using high heat approximately two minutes, or longer if you wish. Move to a serving container, swirl in the cream and serve. Or present in cups, with each cup of soup topped with a few drops of cream.

TOMATO SOUP WITH MUNG

This recipe is called "Dhulli moong aur tamatar ka soop" in Hindi

Yield: 4 to 6 servings

Ingredients:

- four to five quarter-size slices peeled fresh ginger
- ½ cup crudely chopped fresh cilantro, including soft stems
- ½ cup dried split yellow mung bean (dhulli mung dal), sorted and washed in 3 to 4 changes of water
- 1 large clove garlic, peeled
- 1 small onion, quartered
- 1 small russet (or any) potato, unpeeled, crudely chopped
- 1 tablespoon coriander seeds, crudely ground
- 1 tablespoon peanut oil
- 1 teaspoon cumin seeds, crudely ground
- 1 teaspoon freshly ground black pepper, or to taste
- 1 teaspoon salt, or to taste
- 1½ pounds vine-ripened tomatoes, crudely chopped
- 2 small carrots, crudely chopped
- 4 to 6 cups water

- Minced scallions, green parts only, or chives
- twelve to fifteen green beans, ends removed, crudely chopped

Directions:

1. Put everything except the oil, coriander and cumin seeds, and scallion greens in a big saucepan and bring to a boil using high heat. Decrease the heat to moderate to low and cook, uncovered, until the dal and the green beans become soft, approximately 35 minutes.
2. Allow to cool, then pour contents into a blender and pulse until the desired smoothness is achieved. If you prefer a smoother texture, pass soup through a food mill or a fine-mesh strainer into a container.
3. Return the soup to the pan and bring to a boil using high heat, pouring in additional water if you prefer a thinner soup. Decrease the heat to moderate to low, cover the pan and simmer 7 to ten minutes to blend the flavours. Move to a serving container, cover and keep warm.
4. Heat the oil in a small saucepan using moderate to high heat and put in the coriander and cumin seeds; they should sizzle when they touch the hot oil. Swiftly move them to the soup and stir mildly. Garnish with scallion greens and serve.

TOMATO SOUP WITH SAUTÉED VEGETABLES (V)

This recipe is called "Sabziyon vaala tamatar ka soop" in Hindi

Yield: 6 to 8 servings

Ingredients:

- ½ teaspoon ground paprika
- 1 bay leaf
- 1 cup crudely chopped fresh cilantro, including soft stems + more for garnish
- 1 cup finely chopped celery stems
- 1 large clove fresh garlic, minced
- 1 tablespoon ground coriander
- 1 tablespoon olive oil

- 1 tablespoon peeled minced fresh ginger
- 1 teaspoon freshly ground black pepper, or to taste
- 1 teaspoon salt, or to taste
- 1½ pounds ripe tomatoes, crudely chopped
- 2 teaspoons cumin seeds
- 2 to 3 cups water
- 3 cups mixed fresh or frozen vegetables, cut into 3/4-inch or smaller pieces, such as green beans, carrots, mixed bell peppers, broccoli, potatoes, peas
- 3 to 4 leeks, white parts only, cleaned and chopped

Directions:

1. Heat the oil in a big non-stick pan using moderate to high heat. Put in the bay leaf and cumin seeds; they should sizzle when they touch the hot oil. Swiftly put in the leeks and cook, stirring, until they begin to turn golden, approximately three to four minutes.
2. Put in the garlic, ginger, and celery, and cook, stirring, approximately two minutes, then stir in the coriander and paprika. Put in the vegetables and cook, stirring, until crisp-tender, approximately eight to ten minutes. Move to a container.
3. Using a food processor or a blender, combine and pulse the tomatoes and cilantro to make a fine purée and move to the pan in which the vegetables were cooked. Stir in the salt and black pepper and bring to a boil using high heat. Decrease the heat to moderate to low, put in the water, cover the pan, and simmer approximately ten minutes.
4. Stir in the reserved vegetables and bring to a rolling boil, then simmer approximately 5 more minutes, or a little longer if you prefer your vegetables to be soft. Move to a serving container, garnish with cilantro before you serve.

SOUTH INDIAN SOUPS (RASAM)

These are tangy and spicy legume soups highly popular in south India. Rasam is watery and served steaming hot.

CLASSIC SOUTH INDIAN SPLIT PIGEON PEA SOUP Ⓥ

This recipe is called "Toor dal rasam" in Hindi

Yield: 4 to 6 servings

Ingredients:

- ⅛ teaspoon ground asafoetida
- ¼ cup dried split pigeon peas (toor dal), sorted and washed in 3 to 4 changes of water
- ¼ cup finely chopped fresh cilantro, including soft stems
- ¼ teaspoon ground turmeric
- ½ teaspoon cumin seeds
- ½ teaspoon salt, or to taste
- 1 fresh green chile pepper, such as serrano, minced with seeds
- 1 large tomato, finely chopped
- 1 tablespoon minced fresh curry leaves
- 1 tablespoon minced peeled fresh ginger
- 1 teaspoon black mustard seeds
- 2 teaspoons peanut oil or melted ghee
- 2 whole dried red chile peppers, such as chile de arbol
- 3 tablespoons Tamarind Paste (Homemade or store-bought)
- 5 to 6 cups water

Directions:

1. Immerse the dal in 1 cup water until it absorbs the water and softens slightly, for approximately half an hour. In the meantime, ready the tamarind paste. Next, move the dal to a moderate-sized saucepan, put in the ginger, green chile pepper, turmeric, salt and another cup of water, and bring to a boil using high heat. Decrease the heat to moderate to low and simmer, watching cautiously and stirring, until the dal is very soft, for approximately half an hour.
2. In another saucepan, combine the tomatoes, tamarind, asafoetida, and the rest of the water and bring to a boil using high heat. Decrease the heat to moderate to low, cover the pan and simmer until the tomatoes are soft,

approximately five minutes. Put in the cooked dal mixture, pouring in additional water if you prefer a thinner soup, and bring to a boil once more. Move to a serving container.
3. Heat the oil (or ghee) in a small saucepan using moderate to high heat and put in the red chile peppers and the mustard and cumin seeds; they should splutter when they touch the hot oil, so cover the pan until the spluttering diminishes. Put in the curry leaves and cilantro and stir 1 minute. Move to the soup. Mix thoroughly and serve.

BUTTERMILK SOUP

This recipe is called "lussi rasam" in Hindi

Yield: 4 to 6 servings

Ingredients:

- ⅛ teaspoon ground asafoetida
- ¼ cup dried split pigeon peas (toor dal), sorted and washed in 3 to 4 changes of water
- ½ cup finely chopped fresh cilantro, including soft stems
- ½ teaspoon black peppercorns
- ½ teaspoon fenugreek seeds
- ½ teaspoon salt, or to taste
- 1 large tomato, crudely chopped
- 1 tablespoon coriander
- 1 tablespoon dried yellow split chickpeas (channa dal), sorted and washed in 3 to 4 changes of water
- 1 tablespoon peanut oil or melted ghee
- 1 teaspoon cumin seeds
- 1 teaspoon mustard seeds
- 1½ cups buttermilk
- 2 to 3 whole dried red chile peppers, such as chile de arbol
- 3 to 4 cups water
- 3 to 4 scallions, green parts only, finely chopped
- 5 to 6 fresh green curry leaves

Directions:

1. In a small saucepan, heat 2 teaspoons oil (or ghee) over moderate heat, put in the whole red chile peppers and stir until a golden colour is achieved, approximately half a minute, then put in the channa dal, coriander, fenugreek, peppercorns, and asafoetida, and cook, stirring, until the channa dal is golden, approximately one minute. Allow to cool, then move to a blender and blend, adding approximately ¼ cup water until a smooth paste is achieved.
2. In a moderate-sized saucepan, add toor dal, 3 cups water, tomato, and salt. Bring to a boil using high heat. Decrease the heat to moderate to low, cover the pan, and simmer until the toor dal is soft, for approximately half an hour. Stir in the cilantro and the spice paste and simmer until another 5 minutes to blend the flavours.
3. In a small saucepan, heat the rest of the 1 teaspoon of the ghee over moderate heat and put in the mustard and cumin seeds and the curry leaves; they should splutter when they touch the hot oil, so cover the pan and decrease the heat until the spluttering diminishes. Put in the spiced oil to the soup. Next, Put in the buttermilk and scallions and stir well to mix. Serve.

CHUNKY SOUTH INDIAN TOMATO SOUP Ⓥ

This recipe is called "Tamatar rasam" in Hindi

Yield: 4 to 6 servings

Ingredients:

- ⅛ teaspoon ground asafoetida
- ¼ cup finely chopped fresh cilantro, including soft stems
- ½ teaspoon salt, or to taste
- 1 tablespoon minced fresh curry leaves
- 1 tablespoon South Indian Soup Powder (Rasam Podi) or store-bought
- 1 teaspoon black mustard seeds
- 1 teaspoon black peppercorns
- 1 teaspoon cumin seeds
- 2 teaspoons peanut oil or melted ghee
- 4 large tomatoes (about 2 pounds), crudely chopped

- 5 to 6 cups water

Directions:

1. Ready the soup powder. Next, in a small skillet, roast the cumin seeds and peppercorns over moderate heat until fragrant and seems slightly darker, approximately two minutes. Move them to a cutting board and grind them crudely with the back of a big sized spoon.
2. Blend half the tomatoes using a blender until the desired smoothness is achieved. Move to a moderate-sized saucepan. Stir in the rest of the chopped tomatoes, and then add approximately 5 cups water, roasted cumin and black pepper, salt, and rasam powder, and bring to a boil using high heat. Decrease the heat to moderate to low, cover the pan, and simmer until the chopped tomatoes are soft, approximately five to seven minutes. (Pour in additional water for a thinner rasam.)
3. Heat the oil (or ghee) in a small-sized non-stick sauce-pan using moderate to high heat and put in the mustard seeds; they should splutter when they touch the hot oil, so cover the pan and decrease the heat until the spluttering diminishes. Put in the asafoetida, curry leaves, and cilantro and stir for approximately half a minute. Combine with the rasam. Bring to a boil again, then serve hot.

LEMON AND MUNG SOUP

This recipe is called "nimboo aur mung dal rasam" in Hindi

Yield: 4 to 6 servings

Ingredients:

- ⅛ teaspoon ground asafoetida
- ¼ teaspoon ground turmeric
- ½ cup dried split yellow mung beans (dhulli mung dal), sorted and washed in 3 to 4 changes of water
- ½ cup finely chopped fresh cilantro, including soft stems
- ½ teaspoon black mustard seeds
- ½ teaspoon cumin seeds
- ½ teaspoon freshly ground black pepper, or to taste

- ½ teaspoon salt, or to taste
- 1 to 2 tablespoons fresh lemon juice
- 1 to 3 fresh green chile peppers, such as serrano, stemmed
- 2 teaspoons peanut oil or melted ghee
- 2 whole dried red chile peppers, such as chile de arbol
- 4 quarter-size slices peeled fresh ginger
- 6 cups water
- 6 to 10 fresh curry leaves

Directions:

1. Immerse the dal in 1 cup water until it absorbs the water and softens slightly, for approximately half an hour. Next, move to a large saucepan, put in the turmeric, salt, and 2 cups water and bring to a boil using high heat. Decrease the heat to moderate to low and simmer, watching cautiously and stirring, until the dal is very soft, 20 to 30 minutes.
2. Using a hand-held beater or immersion blender, whip the dal in the pan, or stir it vigorously to make it as smooth as possible.
3. Using a blender, mix together and pulse the ginger and green chile peppers, adding some water until the desired smoothness is achieved, approximately half a minute. Move to the dal and add more water to make approximately 4 cups of soup. Bring to a boil using high heat. Decrease the heat to moderate to low, cover the pan, and simmer approximately five minutes.
4. Heat the oil (or ghee) in a small saucepan using moderate to high heat and put in the red chile peppers, and mustard and cumin seeds; they should splutter when they touch the hot oil, so cover the pan and decrease the heat until the spluttering diminishes. Put in the black pepper, asafoetida, and curry leaves, stir for approximately half a minute, and mix thoroughly into the dal. Put in the lemon juice and cilantro, bring to a boil once again before you serve.

MULLIGATAWNY SOUP Ⓥ

This recipe is called "Millagu-tanni" in Hindi

Yield: 4 to 6 servings

Ingredients:

- four to five cups water
- ¼ cup Tamarind Paste (Homemade or store-bought)
- ¼ teaspoon ground asafoetida
- ¼ teaspoon ground turmeric
- ½ teaspoon cumin seeds
- ½ teaspoon dried fenugreek seeds
- 1 large clove fresh garlic, minced
- 1 large tomato, crudely chopped
- 1 small onion, finely chopped
- 1 tablespoon coriander seeds
- 1 tablespoon peanut oil
- 1 teaspoon black mustard seeds
- 1 teaspoon black peppercorns
- 1 teaspoon cumin seeds
- 1 teaspoon salt, or to taste
- 1 to 2 fresh green chile peppers, such as serrano, chopped diagonally, with seeds
- 3 dried red chile peppers, such as chile de arbol, whole or broken

Directions:

1. Ready the tamarind paste. Next, heat a small skillet and dry-roast together the coriander and cumin seeds, peppercorns, and fenugreek over moderate heat until they are seems slightly darker, approximately three minutes. Allow to cool, then grind them finely.
2. Stir together the water, tamarind paste, and tomato in a big saucepan, bring to a boil using moderate to high heat, and boil approximately five minutes. Stir in the roasted spices and the salt, and boil another 5 minutes.
3. Heat the oil in a small saucepan using moderate to high heat and put in the red chile peppers, and the mustard and cumin seeds; they should splutter when they touch the hot oil, so reduce the heat and cover the pan until the spluttering diminishes. Put in the onion and green chile peppers and cook, stirring, until a mild brown colour is achieved and soft, approximately three minutes. Put in the garlic, turmeric, and asafoetida and stir another minute.
4. Mix these seasonings into the tomato soup base and simmer using low heat approximately ten minutes to blend the flavours. Adjust seasonings, if required before you serve.

MYSORE COCONUT SOUP (V)

This recipe is called "Mysore nariyal rasam" in Hindi

Yield: 4 to 6 servings

Ingredients:

- ¼ cup <u>Tamarind Paste</u> (Homemade or store-bought)
- ¼ teaspoon ground asafoetida
- ¼ teaspoon ground turmeric
- ½ cup finely chopped fresh cilantro, including soft stems
- ½ cup fresh or canned <u>Coconut Milk</u> (Homemade or store-bought)
- ½ teaspoon crudely ground black pepper, or to taste
- ½ teaspoon salt, or to taste
- 1 cup dried split pigeon peas (toor dal), sorted and washed in 3 to 4 changes of water
- 1 large tomato, finely chopped
- 1 tablespoon peanut oil or melted ghee
- 1 teaspoon black mustard seeds
- 1 teaspoon cumin seeds
- 2 tablespoons fresh or frozen grated coconut
- 2 whole dried red chile peppers, such as chile de arbol
- 5 to 6 cups water
- 6 to 10 fresh curry leaves

Directions:

1. Immerse the dal in 2 cups water until it absorbs the water and softens slightly, for approximately half an hour. Next, move to a large saucepan, put in the turmeric, salt and another cup of water and bring to a boil using high heat. Decrease the heat to moderate to low and simmer, watching cautiously and stirring, until the dal is very soft, for approximately half an hour. In the meantime, ready the tamarind paste and coconut milk.
2. When soft, whip the dal in the saucepan with a hand-held beater or immersion blender, or stir it vigorously to make it as smooth as possible.
3. Heat the oil (or ghee) in a big saucepan using moderate to high heat and put in the mustard and cumin seeds; they should splutter when they touch the hot oil, so cover the pan and decrease the heat until the spluttering

diminishes. Put in the black pepper, asafoetida, curry leaves, and grated coconut, and stir approximately one minute. Put in the tomato and cook, stirring, another two minutes.

4. Stir in the tamarind paste and the rest of the water and bring to a boil using high heat. Decrease the heat to moderate to low, cover the pan, and simmer until the tomato is very soft, approximately ten minutes.
5. **5. Stir in the dal and simmer approximately five minutes to blend the flavours. Next, stir in the coconut milk and cilantro, cook another two minutes before you serve.**

SOUTH INDIAN GINGER SOUP

This recipe is called "Adrak rasam" in Hindi

Yield: 4 to 6 servings

Ingredients:

- four to five cups water
- ¼ cup dried split pigeon peas (toor dal), sorted and washed in 3 to 4 changes of water
- ¼ cup finely chopped fresh cilantro, including soft stems
- ¼ teaspoon ground asafoetida
- ½ teaspoon salt, or to taste
- 1 teaspoon black peppercorns
- 1 teaspoon cumin seeds
- 1 teaspoon mustard seeds
- 1 teaspoon peanut oil or melted ghee
- 1 to 3 fresh green chile peppers, such as serrano, stemmed
- 1 whole dried red chile pepper, such as chile de arbol
- 5 quarter-size slices peeled fresh ginger
- 5 to 6 fresh green curry leaves

Directions:

1. Immerse the dal 30 minutes in ½ cup water. Next, in a blender, mix together and grind the dal and water, cumin seeds, black peppercorns, green chile peppers, and ginger to make as smooth a paste as possible.

2. Move to a moderate-sized saucepan. Stir in the water and salt and bring to a boil using high heat. Decrease the heat to moderate to low and simmer, approximately five minutes. Move to a container, cover, and keep warm.
3. Heat the oil (or ghee) in a small saucepan using moderate to high heat and put in the mustard seeds; they should splutter when they touch the hot oil, so cover the pan and reduce the heat until the spluttering diminishes. Swiftly put in the asafoetida, red chile pepper, and curry leaves. Stir approximately half a minute and mix thoroughly into the soup. Garnish with the cilantro and serve.

SOUTH INDIAN TAMARIND SOUP

This recipe is called "imli rasam" in Hindi

Yield: 4 to 6 servings

Ingredients:

- four to five cups water
- ⅛ teaspoon ground asafoetida
- ¼ teaspoon ground turmeric
- ⅓ cup seedless tamarind pulp
- ½ teaspoon black mustard seeds
- ½ teaspoon cumin seeds
- 1 tablespoon grated jaggery (gur), or brown sugar
- 1 tablespoon minced fresh curry leaves
- 1 tablespoon peanut oil or melted ghee
- 1 teaspoon salt, or to taste
- 2 tablespoons dried split chickpeas (channa dal), sorted and washed in 3 to 4 changes of water
- 2 to 3 tablespoons South Indian Soup Powder (Rasam Podi) or store-bought
- 3 whole dried red chile peppers, such as chile de arbol

Directions:

1. Immerse the tamarind in 1 cup water approximately two hours. Mash with clean fingers or a wooden spoon and pass through a fine-mesh strainer into a container to extract the pulp. Add another ½ cup water to the leftover

pulp, mash and pass through the strainer again to extract more pulp. Throw away the residue.
2. Immerse the dal in approximately ½ cup water for approximately half an hour, then drain. In the meantime, ready the soup powder.
3. Heat the oil (or ghee) in a big saucepan and put in the red chile peppers, mustard and cumin seeds; they should splutter when they touch the hot oil, so reduce the heat and cover the pan until the spluttering diminishes. Stir in the soaked dal and curry leaves and cook, stirring, approximately three minutes. Next, Put in the asafoetida, turmeric, and salt, and stir for approximately half a minute.
4. Stir in the tamarind extract, jaggery, soup powder, and the rest of the water, and bring to a boil using high heat. Decrease the heat to moderate to low, cover the pan and simmer until the dal is soft, approximately fifteen minutes. Taste, adjust the seasonings before you serve.

SOUTH INDIAN VEGETABLE AND TAMARIND SOUP Ⓥ

This recipe is called "Tarkari rasam" in Hindi

Yield: 4 to 6 servings

Ingredients:

- ⅛ teaspoon ground asafoetida
- ¼ cup Tamarind Paste (Homemade or store-bought)
- ½ cup dried split pigeon peas (toor dal), sorted and washed in 3 to 4 changes of water
- ½ cup finely chopped fresh cilantro, including soft stems
- 1 small onion, finely chopped
- 1 tablespoon Basic Ginger-Garlic Paste (Homemade or store-bought)
- 1 tablespoon minced fresh curry leaves
- 1 tablespoon peanut oil or melted ghee
- 1 teaspoon black mustard seeds
- 1 teaspoon cumin seeds
- 1 teaspoon salt, or to taste
- 1 to 2 tablespoons South Indian Soup Powder (Rasam Podi) or store-bought

- 3 cups crudely chopped fresh or frozen mixed vegetables, such as eggplant, okra, carrots, drumsticks, and green beans
- 5 to 6 cups water

Directions:

1. Immerse the dal in 1 cup water until it absorbs the water and softens slightly, for approximately half an hour. In the meantime ready the ginger-garlic paste and the tamarind paste.
2. When soft, move the dal to a moderate-sized saucepan, add another cup of water, and bring to a boil using high heat. Decrease the heat to moderate to low and simmer, watching cautiously and stirring, until the dal is very soft, 20 to 30 minutes. In the meantime, ready the soup powder.
3. Heat the oil (or ghee) in a big non-stick saucepan using moderate to high heat and put in the mustard and cumin seeds and the asafoetida; they should splutter when they touch the hot oil, so cover the pan and decrease the heat until the spluttering diminishes. Swiftly put in the onion and stir approximately one minute.
4. Add vegetables, the soup powder, and salt and cook, stirring, approximately five minutes. Next, Put in the cooked dal, the rest of the water, tamarind paste, ginger-garlic paste, curry leaves, and cilantro, and bring to a boil using high heat. Decrease the heat to moderate to low, cover the pan, and simmer until the vegetables become soft, approximately ten to twelve minutes. (Pour in additional water if you prefer a thinner soup.) Serve hot.

BEAN AND LENTIL SOUPS

BLACK BEAN SOUP Ⓟ

This recipe is called "Kaalae rajma ka soop" in Hindi

Yield: 4 to 6 servings

Ingredients:

- ⅛ teaspoon ground asafoetida
- ¼ teaspoon ground turmeric
- ½ cup finely chopped fresh cilantro, including soft stems
- ½ cup finely chopped onion
- ½ cup non-fat plain yogurt, whisked until the desired smoothness is achieved
- ½ teaspoon garam masala
- 1 (15-ounce) can tomato sauce
- 1 cup dried black beans, sorted and washed in 3 to 4 changes of water
- 1 large clove fresh garlic, minced
- 1 large tomato, finely chopped
- 1 tablespoon ground coriander
- 1 tablespoon peanut oil
- 1 tablespoon peeled minced fresh ginger
- 1 teaspoon cumin seeds
- 1 teaspoon ground cumin
- 1 teaspoon salt, or to taste
- 1 to 3 fresh green chile peppers, such as serrano, minced with seeds
- 4 cups water

Directions:

1. Put the beans into your pressure cooker along with the water, chile peppers, and salt. Ensure that the lid is secure, and cook using high heat until the regulator shows that the pressure is high, then cook approximately 1½ minutes more. Turn off the heat and let the pressure release automatically, twelve to fifteen minutes. Cautiously take the lid off and check if the beans are soft. If not, secure lid, bring back up to high pressure and cook another half a minute, or cover with another lid and cook over moderate heat until tender.
2. Heat the oil in a moderate-sized non-stick wok or saucepan using moderate to high heat and put in the cumin seeds; they should sizzle when they touch the hot oil. Swiftly put in the onion and cook, stirring, until a golden colour is achieved, approximately three minutes. Put in the ginger, garlic, and tomato, and cook until all the fluids vaporize, approximately five to seven minutes.
3. Put in the coriander, cumin, turmeric, and asafoetida, stir and cook half a minute, then stir in the yogurt, slowly and gradually, to stop it from curdling. Cook approximately one minute, then Combine with the beans. Put in the cilantro, tomato sauce, and more water if the soup appears thick, and cook

another 5 minutes. Trans-fer to a serving container, garnish with garam masala before you serve.

BLACK CHICKPEA SOUP Ⓥ Ⓟ

This recipe is called "Kaalae channae ka soop" in Hindi

Yield: 4 to 6 servings

Ingredients:

- ¼ cup finely chopped fresh cilantro, including soft stems
- ¼ teaspoon ground turmeric
- ½ teaspoon salt, or to taste
- 1 (15-ounce) can tomato sauce
- 1 (1-inch) piece peeled fresh ginger, cut into thin matchsticks
- 1 cup dried black chickpeas (kaalae channae), sorted and washed in 3 to 4 changes of water
- 1 large tomato, finely chopped
- 1 tablespoon Basic Ginger-Garlic Paste or store-bought
- 1 tablespoon ground coriander
- 1 teaspoon cumin seeds
- 1 teaspoon melted ghee (not compulsory)
- 2 (1-inch) sticks cinnamon
- 2 tablespoons vegetable oil
- 4 black cardamom pods, crushed lightly to break the skin
- 6 to 7 cups water

Directions:

1. Ready the ginger-garlic paste. Next, soak the chickpeas overnight in water to cover by 2 inches, then drain. Put the chickpeas, water, cinnamon, cardamom pods, ginger-garlic paste, and salt into your pressure cooker, secure the lid, cook using high heat until the regulator shows that the pressure is high, then cook 3 more minutes. Turn off the heat and allow the pressure to depressurize automatically, fifteen to twenty minutes. Open the lid cautiously and check the chickpeas; they should be soft and watery. If not, reseal the lid, bring back up to high pressure, and cook 1 more minute.

2. Move to a large cast-iron wok (if possible) or skillet, stir in the tomato sauce and cook using high heat, stirring intermittently, approximately five minutes, then using moderate to low heat approximately one hour. When you're done, you should have at least 4 cups of soup. if required, add more water and bring to a boil.
3. Heat the oil and the ghee in a big non-stick wok or saucepan using moderate to high heat and cook the ginger sticks, stirring frequently, until a golden colour is achieved, approximately one minute. Put in the cumin seeds; they should sizzle when they touch the hot oil. Swiftly put in the coriander and turmeric, stir for approximately half a minute, then stir in the chopped tomato and cilantro and cook until the tomatoes are slightly soft. Mix everything into the soup.
4. Move the soup to a serving container, leaving the chickpeas in the pan. Remove approximately ½ cup of the chickpeas, crudely mash them, and put them in to the soup. Reserve the rest for another purpose. (Eat them as is, or toss into salads or over rice pullaos.)

CHICKPEA CHICKEN SOUP

This recipe is called "Murgh yakhni aur channae ka soop" in Hindi

Yield: 4 to 6 servings

Ingredients:

- ¼ teaspoon ground asafoetida
- ¼ to ½ cup whipping cream (not compulsory)
- ½ teaspoon freshly ground black pepper
- ½ teaspoon salt, or to taste
- 1 (15½-ounce) can chickpeas, drained and rinsed
- 1 cup lowfat milk, at room temperature
- 1 tablespoon peanut oil
- 1 teaspoon black mustard seeds
- 1 to 2 tablespoons fresh lime juice
- 1 to 3 fresh green chile peppers, such as serrano, stemmed, seeded, and cut into thin diagonal slices
- 2 tablespoons all-purpose flour
- 2 tablespoons unsalted butter

- 3 cups canned reduced-fat low-sodium chicken broth or 1 recipe Spicy Chicken Broth
- 3 quarter-size slices peeled fresh ginger

Directions:

1. Using a food processor or a blender, combine and pulse ginger, chickpeas, and broth until the desired smoothness is achieved.
2. Melt the butter in a big non-stick saucepan using moderate to low heat, put in the flour and cook, stirring and watching, until a golden colour is achieved and fragrant, approximately two minutes. Increase the heat to medium-high and put in the milk in a thin stream, stirring continuously to stop the formation of any lumps, until the sauce is smooth, approximately two minutes.
3. **3.** Stir in the processed chickpea blend, then the salt, black pepper, and lime juice. Bring to a boil using high heat. Decrease the heat to moderate to low, cover the pan, and simmer approximately five minutes to blend the flavours, adding more broth or water if you prefer a thinner soup. Stir in the cream (if using) and boil once more. Move to a serving container.
4. Heat the oil in a small-sized non-stick saucepan using moderate to high heat and cook the red chile peppers, stirring until tender, approximately half a minute. Put in the mustard seeds and asafoetida; they should splutter when they touch the hot oil, so cover the pan and decrease the heat until the spluttering diminishes. Swiftly put in the spiced oil to the soup and stir mildly to combine, with parts of it visible as a decoration. Serve hot or let soup cool. Refrigerate for at least two hours and serve chilled.

CHILLED CHICKPEA SOUP

This recipe is called "Channae ka thanda soop" in Hindi

Yield: 4 to 6 servings

Ingredients:

- ¼ teaspoon salt, or to taste
- ½ cup crudely chopped fresh cilantro, including soft stems
- ½ teaspoon ajwain seeds, crudely ground

- ½ teaspoon freshly ground black pepper
- 1 fresh green chile pepper, such as serrano, stemmed
- 1 large clove fresh garlic, peeled
- 1 tablespoon peanut oil
- 1 teaspoon cumin seeds, crudely ground
- 2 (15½-ounce) cans chickpeas, drained and rinsed
- 2 to 3 dried red chile peppers, such as chile de arbol, with stems
- 3 cups non-fat plain yogurt
- 4 quarter-size slices peeled fresh ginger

Directions:

1. Using a food processor or a blender, combine and pulse the ginger, garlic, green chile pepper, chickpeas, and ¼ cup cilantro until the desired smoothness is achieved. Next, stir in the yogurt, salt, and black pepper and process once more until the desired smoothness is achieved. Move to a serving container.
2. Heat the oil in a small-sized non-stick saucepan using moderate to high heat and cook the red chile peppers, stirring until tender, approximately half a minute. Next, Put in the cumin and ajwain seeds; they should sizzle when they touch the hot oil. Swiftly put in the other ¼ cup cilantro and stir until wilted, approximately one minute. Move to the soup and stir mildly to combine, with parts of the spiced oil visible as a decoration.

LENTIL, BARLEY, AND VEGETABLE SOUP ℗

This recipe is called "Dal, jau aur sabziyon ka soop" in Hindi

Yield: 4 to 6 servings

Ingredients:

- four to five cups water
- ⅛ teaspoon ground asafoetida
- ¼ cup pearl barley

- ½ cup dried lentils (masoor dal), sorted and washed in 3 to 4 changes of water
- ½ teaspoon freshly ground black pepper
- ½ teaspoon garam masala
- 1 (15-ounce) can tomato sauce
- 1 cup finely chopped onion
- 1 tablespoon melted ghee
- 1 tablespoon peeled minced fresh ginger
- 1 tablespoon vegetable oil
- 1 teaspoon cumin seeds
- 1 teaspoon dried fenugreek leaves
- 1 teaspoon salt, or to taste
- 1 to 3 fresh green chile peppers, such as serrano, minced with seeds
- 2 bay leaves
- 2 teaspoons minced garlic
- 2 to 3 tablespoons fresh lime juice
- 3 cups finely chopped fresh or frozen mixed vegetables, such as bell peppers, green beans, carrots, celery, peas, corn and others

Directions:

1. Immerse the lentils and barley in a moderate-sized container of water to cover until they absorb some water and soften slightly, approximately one hour. Next, pour through a fine-mesh strainer over another container, saving the water to use as part of the soup.
2. Heat the oil and ghee into your pressure cooker using moderate to high heat and put in the bay leaves and cumin seeds; they should sizzle when they touch the hot oil. Swiftly put in the asafoetida and onions and cook, stirring, until the onions are golden, approximately five minutes. Stir in the ginger, garlic, and green chile peppers and stir momentarily, then put in the lentils and barley. Cook, stirring, using moderate to high heat approximately five minutes. Put in the vegetables and cook another 5 minutes.
3. **3.** Stir in the water, tomato sauce, salt, and black pepper. Secure the lid of the pressure cooker and cook using high heat until the regulator shows that the pressure is high, then cook 1 minute more. Turn off the heat and let the pressure release automatically, twelve to fifteen minutes. Cautiously take the lid off and check to see if the lentils become soft. If not, reseal the lid, bring back up to high pressure and cook another half a minute, or cover with another lid and cook until tender.

4. Cautiously open the pressure cooker, put in the lime juice and fenugreek leaves, and bring to a boil using high heat. Adjust seasonings and remove the bay leaves, if required, then move to a serving container, stir in the garam masala before you serve.

MUNG AND SPINACH SOUP

This recipe is called "Mung dal aur palak ka soop" in Hindi

Yield: 4 to 6 servings

Ingredients:

- ¼ teaspoon ground paprika
- ¼ teaspoon ground turmeric
- ¼ teaspoon hot red pepper flakes, or to taste
- ¾ teaspoon salt, or to taste
- 1 cup dried split yellow mung beans (dhulli mung dal), sorted and washed in 3 to 4 changes of water
- 1 cup finely chopped fresh cilantro, including soft stems
- 1 medium russet (or any) potato, peeled and cut into small pieces
- 1 tablespoon Basic Ginger-Garlic Paste (Homemade or store-bought)
- 1 tablespoon ground coriander
- 1 teaspoon cumin seeds
- 1 teaspoon melted ghee (not compulsory)
- 2 cups firmly packed finely chopped fresh spinach (from 1 small bunch)
- 2 tablespoons peanut oil
- 5 to 6 cups water
- Freshly ground black pepper, to taste

Directions:

1. Ready the ginger-garlic paste. Put the dal and potato with 5 cups water, the ginger-garlic paste, turmeric, red pepper flakes, and salt in a moderate-sized saucepan and boil using high heat approximately five minutes. Decrease the heat to moderate to low and cook until the dal is soft and creamy, approximately 40 minutes. For a thinner soup, add another cup of water and boil once more.

2. Put in the spinach and cilantro during the last 5 to ten minutes. Move to a serving container.
3. Heat the oil (and ghee, if using) in a small saucepan over medium-medium-high heat and put in the cumin seeds; they should sizzle when they touch the hot oil. Swiftly put in the coriander. Take the pan off the heat stir in the paprika, then mix the spiced oil into the hot dal. Sprinkle the black pepper on top and serve.

SINDHI SPLIT PIGEON PEA SOUP

This recipe is called "Sindhi toor dal ka soop" in Hindi

Yield: 4 to 6 servings

Ingredients:

- ⅛ teaspoon ground asafoetida
- ¼ teaspoon ground turmeric
- ½ teaspoon ground paprika
- ½ teaspoon salt, or to taste
- 1 cup dried yellow split pigeon peas (toor dal), sorted and washed in 3 to 4 changes of water
- 1 large tomato, crudely chopped
- 1 tablespoon peeled minced fresh ginger
- 1 tablespoon vegetable oil
- 1 teaspoon cumin seeds
- 1 teaspoon mustard seeds
- 1 to 3 fresh green chile peppers, such as serrano, crudely chopped
- 2 tablespoons chickpea flour
- 2 to 3 tablespoons Tamarind Paste or lemon juice
- 5 cups water, or more as required
- twelve to fifteen fresh curry leaves

Directions:

1. Ready the tamarind paste. Next, place the dal, ginger, green chile peppers, tomato, turmeric, salt, and water into your pressure cooker. Ensure that the lid is secure, and cook using high heat until the regulator shows that the

pressure is high, then cook approximately half a minute more. Turn off the heat and let the pressure release automatically, twelve to fifteen minutes. Cautiously take the lid off, allow to cool down, then pass everything through a food mill or a fine-mesh strainer and place in a container.
2. Heat the oil in a big non-stick wok or saucepan using moderate to high heat and put in the cumin and mustard seeds; they should splutter when they touch the hot oil, so cover the pan and decrease the heat until the spluttering diminishes. Swiftly put in the curry leaves, stir a few seconds, then put in the chickpea flour, paprika, and asafoetida and stir until the chickpea flour is fragrant and golden, approximately a minute or two.
3. **3.** Stir in the dal soup, the tamarind, and more water if you want, bring to a boil, and continue to boil, using moderate to high heat the first two to three minutes and then over moderate heat, approximately five to seven minutes, to blend the flavours. Move to a serving container and serve hot.

VEGETABLE SOUPS

CABBAGE AND VEGETABLE SOUP

This recipe is called "Bandh gobhi aur sabziyon ka soop" in Hindi

Yield: 8 to 10 servings

Ingredients:

- four to five cups finely chopped fresh vegetables, such as celery, beets, green beans, cauliflower, carrots, bell peppers, and any others
- four to five cups water
- ½ cup finely chopped fresh curry leaves
- ½ teaspoon freshly ground black peppercorns, or to taste
- 1 cup finely chopped fresh cilantro, including soft stems
- 1 small head green cabbage, shredded
- 1 small onion, thinly chopped
- 1 tablespoon vegetable oil

- 1 teaspoon garam masala
- 1 teaspoon salt, or to taste
- 1 to 3 fresh green chile peppers, such as serrano, stemmed
- 2 cups finely chopped greens, such as spinach, mustard, turnip, or beet greens, or any others
- 2 large round white (or any) potatoes, finely chopped
- 2 large tomatoes, crudely chopped
- 2 teaspoons dried mint leaves
- 3 tablespoons fresh lemon juice

Directions:

1. Heat the oil in a big stockpot or saucepan over moderate heat and cook the onions and green chile peppers approximately five minutes. Put in the potatoes, chopped vegetables, cabbage, greens, and tomatoes and cook, stirring, another 5 minutes.
2. Put in the water and bring to a boil using high heat. Next, cover the pan and cook until the vegetables become soft, approximately fifteen minutes. Stir in all the rest of the ingredients and cook until everything is nice and soft, approximately fifteen minutes more, then serve.

CARROT AND GINGER SOUP

This recipe is called "Gajjar-adrak ka soop" in Hindi

Yield: 4 to 6 servings

Ingredients:

- 1 cup crudely chopped fresh cilantro, including soft stems
- 1 cup finely chopped onion
- 1 cup light cream or plain yogurt (any kind), whisked until the desired smoothness is achieved
- 1 pound carrots, unpeeled, crudely chopped
- 1 teaspoon cumin seeds
- 1 teaspoon dry-roasted and crudely ground black pepper (See the dry-roasting section in Introduction)
- 1 teaspoon salt, or to taste

- 1 to 2 tablespoons fresh lemon juice
- 2 bay leaves
- 2 tablespoons vegetable oil
- 5 to 6 cups water
- 8 to 10 quarter-size slices peeled fresh ginger

Directions:

1. Ready the black pepper. Next, heat the oil in a big non-stick wok or saucepan using moderate to high heat and cook the bay leaves and cumin seeds, stirring frequently; they should sizzle when they touch the hot oil. Swiftly put in the onion and cook, stirring, until a golden colour is achieved, approximately five minutes. Put in the ginger and cook another minute.
2. Put in the carrots and cilantro and cook, stirring, until the carrots are golden, approximately seven minutes. Add 5 cups water and the salt and bring to a boil using high heat. Decrease the heat to moderate to low, cover the pan and simmer until the carrots are soft, approximately ten minutes.
3. Allow to cool, remove the bay leaves, then purée the carrots with all the juices using a blender until the desired smoothness is achieved. Return to the pan and boil until the soup is reduced by approximately one quarter (For a thinner soup, put in the rest of the 1 cup water and boil once more.) stir in the cream or yogurt and bring to a quick boil. Move to a serving container, stir in the lemon juice, garnish with black pepper before you serve.

CHILLED POTATO SOUP

This recipe is called "Aalu ka thanda soop" in Hindi

Yield: 4 to 6 servings

Ingredients:

- ¼ cup crudely chopped fresh cilantro, including soft stems
- ¼ teaspoon ground asafoetida
- ½ teaspoon freshly ground black pepper
- 1 large onion, finely chopped
- 1 pound russet (or any) potatoes
- 1 tablespoon ground coriander

- 1 tablespoon minced fresh curry leaves
- 1 tablespoon peeled minced fresh ginger
- 1 teaspoon minced fresh mint
- 1 teaspoon mustard seeds
- 1 teaspoon salt, or to taste
- 2 cups non-fat plain yogurt or 1 cup light cream and 1 cup yogurt
- 2 cups water
- 2 tablespoons peanut oil

Directions:

1. Boil the potatoes in lightly salted water to cover until tender, then peel and crudely cut them. Heat the oil in a big saucepan over moderate heat and put in the mustard seeds; they should splutter when they touch the hot oil, so cover the pan and decrease the heat until the spluttering diminishes. Swiftly put in the onion and cook, stirring until a golden colour is achieved, approximately five minutes.
2. Put in the asafoetida, ginger, curry leaves, mint, and cilantro, and stir 1 minute. Put in the coriander, salt, and potatoes, and cook, stirring, until the potatoes are golden, approximately eight to ten minutes. Put in the water and bring to a boil using high heat. Decrease the heat to moderate to low, cover the pan and simmer until the potatoes start to break, approximately five minutes.
3. Allow to cool, then move to a blender or food processor and process until the desired smoothness is achieved. Move to a serving container, stir in the yogurt (or cream and yogurt), adjust the seasoning, and refrigerate at least two hours or until ready to serve. Garnish with the black pepper and serve.

CURRIED GREEN PEA SOUP

This recipe is called "Muttar ka soop" in Hindi

Yield: 4 to 6 servings

Ingredients:

- ¼ teaspoon freshly ground black pepper
- 1 cup plain yogurt, any kind

- 1 large clove fresh garlic, peeled
- 1 small crudely chopped onion
- 1 tablespoon ground coriander
- 1 teaspoon cornstarch
- 1 teaspoon ground cumin
- 1 teaspoon salt, or to taste
- 1 to 2 fresh green chile peppers, such as serrano, stemmed
- 1 to 2 tablespoons peanut oil
- 2½ cups fresh or thawed frozen green peas
- 4 quarter-size slices peeled fresh ginger
- 6 to 7 cups water

Directions:

1. Put the peas and 2 cups water in a moderate-sized saucepan and bring to a boil using high heat. Decrease the heat to moderate to low, cover the pan, and simmer until the peas become soft, approximately twenty minutes. Allow to cool, then move along with the water to a blender or food processor and process until the desired smoothness is achieved. Move to a container.
2. In the same blender, mix together and pulse the yogurt, cornstarch and another cup of water. Move to a container and save for later. Next, combine and pulse the onion, green chile peppers, ginger, and garlic until the desired smoothness is achieved.
3. Heat the oil in a big non-stick wok or sauce-pan over moderate heat, put in the processed onion-garlic mixture and cook, stirring, until a golden colour is achieved, approximately five minutes. Put in the coriander and cumin, then put in the puréed peas, salt, and the rest of the 3 cups water and bring to a boil using high heat. Decrease the heat to moderate to low, cover the pan, and simmer approximately ten minutes.
4. Stir in the puréed yogurt, raise the heat to medium-high, and boil until the soup is smooth, approximately three minutes. Move to a serving container, garnish with the black pepper before you serve.

GOAN CAULIFLOWER SOUP

This recipe is called "Goa ka gobhi soop" in Hindi

Yield: 4 to 6 servings

Ingredients:

- 1 large clove fresh garlic, peeled
- 1 medium onion, crudely chopped
- 1 pound russet (or any) potatoes, peeled and chopped
- 1 tablespoon grated pepper Jack cheese
- 1 teaspoon salt, or to taste
- 2 cups cauliflower florets (from approximately a 1-pound head)
- 2 cups shredded cauliflower leaves or any other greens
- 2 teaspoons olive oil
- 7 to 8 cups water

Directions:

1. Put the potatoes, onion, cauliflower, garlic, and 6 cups water in a big saucepan and bring to a boil using high heat. Decrease the heat to moderate to low, cover the pan and simmer until the vegetables are soft, for approximately half an hour.
2. Let the vegetables cool, then purée using a blender or a food processor until the desired smoothness is achieved. Return to the saucepan. Put in the rest of the water, olive oil, cauliflower leaves, and salt. Cover and simmer over moderate heat, stirring as needed, until the greens are soft, approximately twenty minutes. Move to a serving container, garnish with the cheese before you serve.

PUMPKIN SOUP Ⓥ

This recipe is called "Pethae ka soop" in Hindi

Yield: 4 to 6 servings

Ingredients:

- ¼ teaspoon ground turmeric
- ¼ teaspoon kalonji seeds

- ½ pound pumpkin, peeled, seeded, and crudely chopped, or 1 (15-ounce) can pumpkin (not pumpkin pie filling)
- ½ pound round white (or any) potatoes, crudely chopped
- ½ teaspoon fenugreek seeds, crudely ground
- ½ teaspoon salt, or to taste
- 1 large clove fresh garlic, peeled
- 1 large onion, crudely chopped
- 1 tablespoon vegetable oil
- 1 teaspoon cumin seeds
- 1 teaspoon fennel seeds, crudely ground
- 1 teaspoon fresh lime or lemon juice
- 1 to 3 fresh green chile peppers, such as serrano, stemmed
- 4 to 6 quarter-size slices peeled fresh ginger
- 5 to 6 cups water

Directions:

1. Put the pumpkin (if using fresh), potatoes, onion, ginger, garlic, green chile peppers, turmeric, salt, and 4 cups water in a big saucepan and bring to a boil using high heat. Decrease the heat to moderate to low, cover the pan and simmer, until the vegetables are soft, for approximately half an hour. (If using canned pumpkin, mix it into the soup in step 2, after it has been passed through the food mill or processed.)
2. Allow to cool, and pass soup through a food mill into a container or process Using a food processor. Return to the pan and stir in the lime juice. Stir in 1 to 2 cups water and boil using high heat approximately two minutes. Tweak the seasonings to your taste.
3. Heat the oil in a small-sized non-stick wok or saucepan using moderate to high heat and add all the seeds; they should sizzle when they touch the hot oil. Swiftly mix the spiced oil into the soup and simmer approximately five minutes to blend the flavours. Serve.

ROOT VEGETABLE SOUP

This recipe is called "Jadhi sabziyon ka soop" in Hindi

Yield: 4 to 6 servings

Ingredients:

- four to five cups crudely chopped root vegetables, such as beets, kohlrabi, potatoes, turnips, and carrots
- four to five cups water
- ½ teaspoon ajwain seeds, crudely crushed
- ½ teaspoon freshly ground black pepper
- ½ teaspoon garam masala
- 1 cup crudely chopped fresh cilantro, including soft stems
- 1 large tomato, crudely chopped
- 1 small onion, crudely chopped
- 1 tablespoon ground coriander
- 1 tablespoon peanut oil
- 1 teaspoon cumin seeds
- 1 teaspoon salt, or to taste
- 1 to 2 tablespoons fresh lime or lemon juice
- 1 to 3 fresh green chile peppers, such as serrano, stemmed
- 5 quarter-size slices peeled fresh ginger
- Snipped chives

Directions:

1. Put the all the root vegetables into your pressure cooker. Put in the onion, tomato, green chile peppers, ginger, cilantro, and 3 cups water. Secure the lid of the pressure cooker and cook using high heat until the regulator shows that the pressure is high, then cook 1 minute. Turn off the heat and let the pressure release automatically, twelve to fifteen minutes. Cautiously take the lid off.
2. Allow to cool, then blend everything using a blender in 2 to 3 batches until the desired smoothness is achieved. For a very smooth texture, pass the blended soup through a food mill, adding the rest of the water as needed for desired consistency.
3. Return the soup to the pressure cooker, stir in the salt, black pepper, and lemon juice and bring to a boil using high heat. Decrease the heat to moderate to low and simmer another 5 minutes to blend the flavours. Move to a serving container.
4. Heat the oil in a small saucepan using moderate to high heat and put in the cumin and ajwain seeds; they should sizzle when they touch the hot oil. Swiftly put in the coriander and garam masala and move the seasoned oil to

the soup. Swirl lightly to combine, with parts of it visible as a decoration. Sprinkle the chives on top and serve.

SPINACH SOUP

This recipe is called "Palak ka soop" in Hindi

Yield: 4 to 6 servings

Ingredients:

- ½ cup plain yogurt (any kind), whisked until the desired smoothness is achieved
- 1 cup crudely chopped fresh cilantro, including soft stems
- 1 cup milk (any kind)
- 1 large clove fresh garlic, peeled
- 1 medium onion, crudely chopped
- 1 small (8- to 10-ounce) bunch fresh spinach, trimmed, washed, and crudely chopped
- 1 tablespoon all-purpose flour
- 1 teaspoon garam masala
- 2 tablespoons crudely chopped fresh mint
- 2 tablespoons vegetable oil
- 4 cups water
- 4 quarter-size slices peeled fresh ginger

Directions:

1. Put the spinach, cilantro, mint, onion, ginger, and garlic in a big saucepan. Put in the water and bring to a boil using high heat. Decrease the heat to moderate to low, cover the pan and simmer, until the onions are soft, approximately ten minutes. Allow to cool, then purée using a blender or food processor until the desired smoothness is achieved.
2. Heat the oil in separate large non-stick wok or saucepan using moderate to high heat, put in the flour and cook, stirring, until a golden colour is achieved and very fragrant, approximately one minute. Put in the milk in a thin stream, stirring continuously to ensure no lumps form. Slowly, while stirring constantly, put in the puréed spinach and the garam masala, and mix

thoroughly. Move soup to a serving container, put in the yogurt, stir mildly to combine with parts of it visible as a decoration before you serve.

YOGURT SOUPS

BASIC YOGURT SOUP

This recipe is called "Dahi ka soop" in Hindi

Yield: 4 to 6 servings

Ingredients:

- ¼ teaspoon ground asafoetida
- ¼ teaspoon ground turmeric
- ½ teaspoon salt, or to taste
- 1 large clove fresh garlic, peeled
- 1 tablespoon dried split yellow mung beans (dhulli mung dal), sorted and washed in 3 to 4 changes of water
- 1 tablespoon dried yellow urad beans (dhulli urad dal), sorted and washed in 3 to 4 changes of water
- 1 tablespoon peanut oil
- 1 teaspoon black mustard seeds
- 1 teaspoon ground cumin
- 1 to 3 fresh green chile peppers, such as serrano, stemmed
- 1½ cups water
- 2 tablespoons finely chopped fresh cilantro, including soft stems
- 3 cups plain yogurt (any kind), whisked until the desired smoothness is achieved
- 3 quarter-size slices peeled fresh ginger
- 3 tablespoons long grain white rice
- 6 to 8 fresh curry leaves

Directions:

1. In a small-sized non-stick or cast-iron skillet over moderate heat, dry-roast together the rice, both the dals, and the cumin seeds, stirring and shaking the skillet until the mixture is fragrant and golden, approximately three minutes. Move to a spice or a coffee grinder and grind to make it as fine as possible.
2. Using a blender or food processor, mix together and pulse the yogurt, water, green chile peppers, ginger, and garlic until the desired smoothness is achieved. Stir in the turmeric, salt, and the ground rice-dal mixture, and blend again until thoroughly smooth.
3. Heat the oil in a big non-stick wok or saucepan using moderate to high heat and put in the mustard seeds and curry leaves; they should splutter when they touch the hot oil, so cover the pan and decrease the heat until the spluttering diminishes.
4. Put in the asafoetida and the yogurt mixture and bring to a boil, stirring constantly, using high heat. Decrease the heat to moderate to low and simmer approximately ten minutes. Move to a serving dish, stir in the cilantro before you serve.

ALMOND–POPPY SEED SOUP

This recipe is called "Badaam aur khas-khas ka soop" in Hindi

Yield: 4 to 6 servings

Ingredients:

- ¼ cup dry-roasted almonds (Homemade or store-bought)
- ½ cup Almond and Poppy Seed Paste
- ½ teaspoon salt, or to taste
- 1 (1-inch) stick cinnamon
- 1 cup finely chopped onion
- 1 cup non-fat plain yogurt, whisked until the desired smoothness is achieved
- 1 cup water
- 1 teaspoon freshly ground black pepper
- 1 teaspoon garam masala
- 2 bay leaves
- 2 cups lowfat milk
- 2 tablespoons vegetable oil

- 3 black cardamom pods, crushed lightly to break the skin
- 6 whole cloves

Directions:

1. Ready the nut-seed paste. Next, heat the oil in a big non-stick wok or saucepan using moderate to high heat and cook the cinnamon, cloves, cardamom pods, and bay leaves, stirring frequently, for 1 minute. Put in the onion and continue to cook until browned, approximately seven minutes. Put in the almond and poppy seed paste, black pepper, and garam masala, and cook, stirring, until a golden colour is achieved, approximately five minutes.
2. Put in the water and bring to a boil using high heat. Decrease the heat to moderate to low, put in the milk and simmer, stirring, until the soup is thick, approximately ten minutes. In the meantime roast the almonds.
3. Allow to cool, remove the bay leaves, then stir in the yogurt and salt. Move to a serving container, refrigerate at least two hours or up to two days before you serve. Garnish with the roasted almonds and serve.

CHILLED ROASTED VEGETABLE SOUP

This recipe is called "Bhuni sabziyon ka thanda soop" in Hindi

Yield: 4 to 6 servings

Ingredients:

- ½ cup crudely chopped fresh cilantro, including soft stems
- ½ teaspoon freshly ground black pepper
- 1 large red onion, thinly chopped
- 1 teaspoon cumin seeds, dry-roasted and crudely ground (See the dry-roasting section in Introduction)
- 2 large cloves fresh garlic, peeled
- 2 large tomatoes, halved
- 3 cups non-fat plain yogurt, whisked until the desired smoothness is achieved
- 3 large red bell peppers, stemmed, halved lengthwise, and seeded
- 4 small Chinese or Japanese eggplants, halved lengthwise

- 5 quarter-size slices peeled fresh ginger

Directions:

1. Ready the cumin seeds. Preheat the broiler. Put the bell pepper halves, eggplants, tomatoes, onion, ginger, and garlic on a baking tray and roast on the center rack of the oven broiler, turning once in a while until the peppers and tomatoes are charred and the onion, ginger, and garlic are golden, approximately five minutes. Remove the pieces as they turn golden.
2. Move everything to a blender, including accumulated juices. (Deglaze the baking tray with ½ cup water, taking care to dissolve the browned juices, then add to the blender also.) Put in the cilantro and pulse until the desired smoothness is achieved. Move to a large serving container.
3. Stir in the yogurt, garnish with the roasted cumin and black pepper, refrigerate for at least 1 hour and maximum 1two hours before you serve chilled.

MUSHROOM YOGURT SOUP

This recipe is called "Khumbi soop" in Hindi

Yield: 4 to 6 servings

Ingredients:

- ½ teaspoon dry-roasted and crudely ground black peppercorns
- 1 cup lowfat milk
- 1 large clove fresh garlic, minced
- 1 pound white or brown mushrooms, quartered
- 1 teaspoon dry-roasted and crudely ground cumin seeds (See the dry-roasting section in Introduction)
- 1 teaspoon salt, or to taste
- 1 to 2 tablespoons fresh lemon juice
- 1 to 3 fresh green chile peppers, such as serrano, minced with seeds
- 2 cups non-fat plain yogurt, whisked until the desired smoothness is achieved
- 2 tablespoons vegetable oil
- 3 to 4 medium leeks, white parts only, rinsed and finely chopped

- 3 to 4 scallions, green parts only, minced

Directions:

1. Ready the cumin seeds and peppercorns. Next, heat the oil in a big non-stick wok or saucepan using moderate to high heat and cook the leeks and green chile peppers, stirring, until a golden colour is achieved, approximately five minutes. Put in the mushrooms and garlic, and cook, stirring, until a golden colour is achieved, approximately seven minutes. (The mushrooms will first release their juices and then dry out.) Allow to cool, move to a food processor or a blender, and process until the desired smoothness is achieved.
2. Put the yogurt in a big serving container and stir in the milk, mushrooms, lemon juice, the prepared cumin and black pepper, and the salt. Store, covered, in the fridge for minimum two hours or until ready to serve. Garnish with scallion greens and serve.

SPINACH YOGURT SOUP

This recipe is called "Palak aur dahi ka soop" in Hindi

Yield: 4 to 6 servings

Ingredients:

- ½ cup milk (any kind)
- ½ cup water
- ½ teaspoon black mustard seeds
- ½ teaspoon cumin seeds
- ½ teaspoon dried ground fenugreek leaves
- ½ teaspoon salt, or to taste
- 1 small (8- to 10-ounce) bunch fresh spinach, trimmed, washed, and crudely chopped
- 1 tablespoon peanut oil
- 1 teaspoon dried mint leaves
- 1 to 3 fresh green chile peppers, such as serrano, stemmed
- 3 cups non-fat plain yogurt, whisked until the desired smoothness is achieved

Directions:

1. In a saucepan, cover and cook the spinach with the water until wilted, approximately five minutes. Move to a food processor and process until the desired smoothness is achieved. With the spinach still in your food processor, put in the green chile peppers, yogurt, milk, and salt, and process once more until blended and smooth. Move to a serving container.
2. Heat the oil in a small-sized non-stick wok or saucepan using moderate to high heat and cook the cumin and mustard seeds; they should splutter when they touch the hot oil, so cover the pan and decrease the heat until the spluttering diminishes. Swiftly put in the mint and fenugreek leaves and move the seasoned oil to the soup. Swirl lightly to combine, with parts of it visible as a decoration before you serve.

VEGETABLE, YOGURT, AND COCONUT SOUP

This recipe is called "Avial" in Hindi

Yield: 4 to 6 servings

Ingredients:

- four to five cups crudely chopped fresh vegetables, such as eggplant, bell peppers, carrots, zucchini, potatoes, onions, cauliflower, pumpkin, kohlrabi
- ¼ cup finely chopped fresh cilantro, including soft stems + 2 tablespoons for garnish
- ¼ teaspoon ground asafoetida
- ½ teaspoon ground turmeric
- ½ teaspoon salt, or to taste
- 1 (4-inch) piece of fresh coconut, shelled, peeled, and crudely chopped, or ½ cup canned coconut milk
- 1 tablespoon fresh curry leaves
- 1 tablespoon peanut oil
- 1 teaspoon black mustard seeds
- 1 to 3 fresh green chile peppers, such as serrano, stemmed
- 1½ cups plain yogurt (any kind)

- 3 cups water

Directions:

1. Put the vegetables, water, turmeric, and salt in a big non-stick saucepan. Cover and bring to a boil using high heat. Decrease the heat to medium and simmer until the vegetables are crisp-tender, 20 to 25 minutes.
2. Using a food processor or a blender, combine and pulse the coconut (or coconut milk), chile peppers, and yogurt until the desired smoothness is achieved, and then mix it into the vegetable soup, along with the cilantro. Cover the pan and simmer approximately ten minutes to blend the flavours. Move to a serving container.
3. Heat the oil in a small-sized non-stick saucepan using moderate to high heat and put in the mustard seeds; they should splutter when they touch the hot oil, so cover the pan and decrease the heat until the spluttering diminishes. Put in the curry leaves and asafoetida, stir a few seconds, then mix the spiced oil into the soup. Garnish with chopped cilantro and serve.

YOGURT AND ROASTED EGGPLANT SOUP

This recipe is called "Bhunae baigan aur dahi ka soop" in Hindi

Yield: 4 to 6 servings

Ingredients:

- ½ cup lowfat milk
- ½ teaspoon salt, or to taste
- 1 pound small thin eggplants
- 1 teaspoon sesame seeds
- 1½ teaspoons cumin seeds
- 3 cups non-fat plain yogurt, whisked until the desired smoothness is achieved

Directions:

1. Roast and mash the eggplants according to the directions in the "Roasting and Grilling Vegetables" section near the start of this book. Next, place the roasted eggplant pulp using a blender or a food processor, put in the yogurt, milk, and salt, and pulse until the desired smoothness is achieved. Move to a serving container.
2. Put the cumin seeds in a small-sized non-stick skillet and dry-roast, stirring over moderate heat until fragrant and seems slightly darker, approximately two minutes. Allow to cool, then grind crudely with the back of a big sized spoon. Combine with the yogurt.
3. Same way, place the sesame seeds in the skillet and dry-roast them until a golden colour is achieved, approximately one minute. Sprinkle them over the soup as a decoration. Serve hot, or refrigerate at least two hours and serve chilled.

FISH AND CHICKEN SOUPS

CASHEW CORN-CHICKEN BROTH SOUP

This recipe is called "Kaaju-makki soop" in Hindi

Yield: 4 to 6 servings

Ingredients:

- ten to twelve scallions, white and light green parts, minced (to make 1 cup)
- ¼ cup finely chopped fresh cilantro, including soft stems
- ¼ teaspoon ground ginger
- ¼ teaspoon salt, or to taste
- ½ teaspoon garam masala
- 1 cup crudely chopped raw cashews
- 1 cup frozen corn kernels, thawed
- 1 cup lowfat milk
- 1 cup water
- 1 large clove fresh garlic, minced

- 1 tablespoon peanut oil
- 1 teaspoon crudely ground black pepper
- 2 to 3 tablespoons fresh lemon juice
- 3 cups reduced-fat low-sodium chicken broth, or 1 recipe Spicy Chicken Broth

Directions:

1. Put the cashews and milk in a microwave-safe container and cook on high 3 minutes. Remove from the microwave and set aside to soak and soften, ten minutes.
2. Heat the oil in a big saucepan using moderate to high heat, put in the scallions and garlic and cook, stirring, until barely golden, approximately two minutes. Put in the broth and simmer, approximately five minutes.
3. Using a food processor, combine and pulse the cashews, milk, and corn to make a coarse purée. Move to the pan with the broth. Rinse the processor with the 1 cup water and add to the soup. Stir in the rest of the ingredients (except the cilantro) and simmer another ten minutes to blend the flavours. Move to a serving container, garnish with the cilantro before you serve.

CHICKEN AND CORN SOUP

This recipe is called "Murgh aur makki ka soop" in Hindi

Yield: 4 to 6 servings

Ingredients:

- four to five cups water
- ¼ teaspoon freshly ground black pepper, or to taste
- ⅓ cup cornstarch
- 1 (15½-ounce) can cream-style corn
- 1 (2½- to 3-pound) chicken, skinned
- 1 teaspoon salt, or to taste
- 1 to 3 fresh green chile peppers, such as serrano, diagonally chopped or split in half along the length and seeded (not compulsory)
- 2 large egg whites, lightly beaten
- 2 to 4 tablespoons distilled white vinegar

Directions:

1. Wash and put the chicken in a big saucepan. Put in the water and salt and bring to a boil using high heat. Decrease the heat to moderate to low, cover the pan, and simmer until the meat is super soft, approximately forty five minutes.
2. With large tongs or a slotted spoon move the chicken to a container. Once cool sufficient to hold, shred approximately 1 cup of the meat and reserve for the soup. (Cover and refrigerate the rest of the chicken for another use.) Using a slotted spoon, remove any scum from the broth, then stir in the corn and bring to a boil using high heat. Decrease the heat to moderate to low and simmer approximately five minutes.
3. Dissolve the cornstarch in approximately ⅓ cup water and add it to the soup, stirring continuously to stop the formation of lumps. carry on stirring until the soup thickens, approximately two minutes.
4. Mix the egg whites with 2 to 3 tablespoons water and stir them into the soup slowly. Keep stirring as you Put in the egg, or it will coagulate into big lumps. Stir in the vinegar and the green chile peppers, if using, sprinkle the black pepper on top and serve hot.

CHICKEN SOUP WITH CHAYOTE SQUASH

This recipe is called "Murgh aur chow-chow ka soop" in Hindi

Yield: 4 to 6 servings

Ingredients:

- four to five small tomatoes (about 1 pound), crudely chopped
- ½ cup finely chopped fresh cilantro, including soft stems
- ½ cup thinly chopped scallions, green parts only
- ½ teaspoon freshly ground black pepper, or to taste
- 1 large onion, halved along the length and thinly chopped
- 1 pound skinless, boneless chicken thighs
- 1 tablespoon fresh lemon juice
- 1 tablespoon melted butter

- 1 tablespoon olive oil
- 1 teaspoon garam masala
- 1 teaspoon salt, or to taste
- 1 to 3 fresh green chile peppers, such as serrano, minced with seeds
- 2 bay leaves
- 2 medium chayote squash, peeled or unpeeled, crudely chopped
- 2 tablespoons cumin seeds
- 2 to 3 tablespoons peeled minced fresh ginger
- 4 small russet (or any) potatoes, peeled or unpeeled, quartered
- 5 to 6 cups water

Directions:

1. Heat the oil and butter in a big non-stick wok or saucepan using moderate to high heat and put in the ginger, cumin seeds, bay leaves, black pepper, and green chile peppers. Cook, stirring, approximately one minute.
2. Put in the onion, tomatoes, squash, potatoes, chicken, salt, and water, and bring to a boil using high heat. Decrease the heat to moderate to low, cover the pan, and simmer until the chicken is opaque and fork-tender, 30 to 40 minutes.
3. Remove the bay leaves. Mash some of the potatoes and squash pieces against the inside of the pot to thicken the soup. Put in the lemon juice and garam masala and cook another few minutes. Move to a serving container, stir in the cilantro and scallion greens before you serve.

GINGER AND COCONUT MILK CHICKEN SOUP

This recipe is called "Adrak aur nariyal vala murgh soup" in Hindi

Yield: 4 to 6 servings

Ingredients:

- four to five cups water
- ⅛ teaspoon ground asafoetida
- ½ cup crudely chopped fresh cilantro, including soft stems

- 1 (2½- to 3-pound) chicken, skinned
- 1 cup Coconut Milk (Homemade or store-bought)
- 1 cup plain yogurt (any kind), whisked until the desired smoothness is achieved
- 1 fresh green chile pepper, such as serrano, stemmed
- 1 tablespoon ground coriander
- 1 teaspoon cumin seeds
- 1 teaspoon ground cumin
- 1 teaspoon salt, or to taste
- 2 cups water
- 2 tablespoons vegetable oil
- 2 teaspoons peeled minced fresh ginger
- 20 fresh curry leaves + 10 for final seasoning
- 4 dried red chile peppers, such as chile de arbol, with stems
- 6 quarter-size slices peeled fresh ginger

Directions:

1. Rinse the chicken, then put it in a large saucepan. Add 4 cups water and salt and bring to a boil using high heat. Decrease the heat to moderate to low, cover the pan, and simmer until the meat is super soft, approximately forty five minutes. In the meantime, ready the coconut milk.
2. Using a slotted spoon, remove the chicken to a container. Once cool sufficient to hold, cut the breast meat into ½-inch pieces and reserve for the soup. (Use the rest of the chicken for another recipe.) Using a slotted spoon, remove any scum from the broth.
3. Using a food processor or a blender, combine and pulse the cilantro, green chile pepper, ginger, 20 curry leaves, coriander, and cumin until a smooth paste is achieved. Put in the yogurt and process once more until the desired smoothness is achieved. Stir the mixture into broth and bring to a boil using high heat. Decrease the heat to moderate to low, cover the pan, and simmer approximately ten minutes to blend the flavours.
4. Stir in the reserved chicken pieces and the coconut milk and simmer using moderate to low heat approximately five minutes. Move to a serving container, cover, and keep warm.
5. Heat the oil in a small-sized non-stick wok or saucepan using moderate to high heat and put in the cumin seeds; they should sizzle when they touch the hot oil. Swiftly put in the red chile peppers, 10 curry leaves, and asafoetida,

and put in the seasoning to the soup. Swirl lightly to combine, with parts of it visible as a decoration. Serve.

GOAN SHRIMP SOUP

This recipe is called "Goa ka jhinga soop" in Hindi

Yield: 4 to 6 servings

Ingredients:

- ¼ cup finely chopped fresh cilantro, including soft stems
- ¼ teaspoon ground turmeric
- ½ teaspoon freshly ground black pepper
- ½ teaspoon salt, or to taste
- 1 large onion, finely chopped
- 1 large tomato, finely chopped
- 1 pound medium (about 30) fresh or thawed frozen shrimp, shell on, rinsed
- 1 tablespoon minced fresh garlic
- 2 tablespoons olive oil
- 2 to 3 fresh green chile peppers, such as serrano, halved lengthwise
- 5 to 6 cups water

Directions:

1. Rinse shrimp well and place them and the water, ground turmeric, and garlic in a big saucepan using high heat. Bring to a boil, then decrease the heat to moderate to low, cover the pan, and simmer until the shrimp are pink and opaque, approximately five to seven minutes. Leaving the water in the pan, remove the shrimp using a slotted spoon to a container. Allow to cool, then shell and devein each shrimp and allow to sit until the soup is ready.
2. Heat the oil in a small-sized non-stick wok or saucepan using moderate to high heat and cook the onion, stirring, until a golden colour is achieved. Put in the tomatoes and cook until tender, approximately five minutes. Move to the pan with the shrimp-cooking water, put in the green chile peppers, and simmer approximately five minutes to blend flavours.
3. Return shrimp to the pan, season with salt and black pepper, garnish with cilantro before you serve.

SHRIMP, COCONUT MILK, AND TOMATO SOUP

This recipe is called "Jhinga, nariyal doodh, aur tamatar ka soop" in Hindi

Yield: 4 to 6 servings

Ingredients:

- ¼ teaspoon ground turmeric
- ½ teaspoon salt, or to taste
- 1 cup crudely chopped fresh cilantro, including soft stems
- 1 cup canned coconut milk
- 1 large onion, crudely chopped
- 1 large tomato, crudely chopped
- 1 pound large (about 20) fresh or thawed frozen shrimp, shell on, rinsed
- 1 tablespoon ground coriander
- 1 tablespoon tamarind powder or 1 to 2 tablespoons fresh lemon juice
- 1 tablespoon vegetable oil
- 1 to 3 fresh green chile peppers, such as serrano, chopped along the diagonal or split in half along the length and seeded
- 2 large cloves fresh garlic, minced
- 2 tablespoons finely chopped scallion greens, chives, or cilantro
- 5 to 6 cups water

Directions:

1. Put the shrimp, 5 cups water, garlic, and salt in a big saucepan and bring to a boil using high heat. Decrease the heat to moderate to low, cover the pan, and simmer until the shrimp are pink and opaque, approximately three minutes. Remove the shrimp from the soup with a slotted spoon, let them cool, then shell and devein them, leaving the tails intact on half (reserve the tailed shrimp for garnish).
2. Using a food processor or a blender, process the onion until a smooth paste is achieved. Move to a container. Process the tomato and cilantro until a smooth purée is achieved and move to a separate container. Next, Put in the shrimps without the tails to the work container and pulse a few times until they are minced. Mix the shrimp pieces into the soup.

3. Heat the oil in a small-sized non-stick saucepan using moderate to high heat and cook the onion paste, stirring, until a golden colour is achieved, approximately five minutes. Put in the coriander and turmeric and stir another minute. Next, stir in the puréed tomato and cilantro and the green chile peppers and cook, stirring, until most of the fluids vaporize, approximately five minutes.
4. Move to the soup. Put in the tamarind powder and coconut milk and bring to a boil using high heat. Decrease the heat to moderate to low and simmer approximately five minutes. Move to a serving container, stir in the reserved tails-on shrimp, garnish with your choice of greens before you serve.

SALADS

Salads are enjoyed all over the world, and India is no exception. Indians usually enjoy a salad as a side dish with a curry, but these also make great meals on their own.

Ⓥ= Vegan Ⓟ= Quick Pressure Cooker Recipe

FRESH CHOPPED SALADS (KACHUMBAR)

These salads are super easy to make. Just finely chop stuff up and mix!

ARMENIAN CUCUMBER AND PEANUT SALAD Ⓥ

This recipe is called "Kakri ka Kachumbar" in Hindi

Yield: 4 to 6 servings

Ingredients:

- ⅛ teaspoon ground asafoetida
- ¼ teaspoon salt, or to taste
- ½ cup finely chopped fresh cilantro, including soft stems
- ½ cup roasted and lightly salted peanuts, crudely chopped
- 1 fresh green chile pepper, such as serrano, minced with seeds
- 1 pound Armenian or any seedless cucumbers, finely chopped
- 1 tablespoon minced fresh curry leaves
- 1 tablespoon peanut oil
- 1 teaspoon black mustard seeds
- 2 teaspoons Marathi Curry Powder with Coconut and Sesame Seeds (Homemade or store-bought)

Directions:

1. Ready the curry powder. In a serving container, combine the cucumbers, peanuts, cilantro, green chile pepper and salt.
2. Heat the oil in a small-sized non-stick saucepan using moderate to high heat and put in the mustard seeds; they should splutter when they touch the hot oil, so cover the pan and decrease the heat until the spluttering diminishes.
3. Swiftly put in the curry powder, asafoetida, and curry leaves, and stir for a few seconds. Move to the salad. Mix thoroughly and serve. If you wish to serve the salad chilled, mix only the cucumbers, peanuts, cilantro, and green chile pepper, and chill up to one day. Put in the spices just before you serve, or the salt will draw out the juices from the ingredients and make the salad too liquid.

CUCUMBER AND RED LENTIL SALAD

This recipe is called "Kheera aur laal dal ra salaad" in Hindi

Yield: 4 to 6 servings

Ingredients:

- ½ cup red lentils (dhulli masoor dal), sorted, washed and soaked in water to cover approximately two hours, then drained
- ½ teaspoon crudely ground black pepper
- ½ teaspoon black mustard seeds
- ½ teaspoon cumin seeds
- ½ teaspoon salt, or to taste
- 1 tablespoon vegetable oil
- 1 teaspoon peeled minced fresh ginger
- 1 to 2 tablespoons fresh lemon juice
- 1¼ pounds pickling or seedless cucumbers, finely chopped
- 2 tablespoons finely chopped fresh cilantro, with soft stems
- 4 scallions, white and light green parts only, finely chopped

Directions:

1. In a serving container, combine the dal, cucumbers, scallions, and cilantro.
2. Heat the oil in a small-sized non-stick saucepan using moderate to high heat and add all the spices; they should sizzle when they touch the hot oil. Swiftly put in the ginger, stir for a few seconds, then put in the lemon juice and salt. Move to the salad, mix thoroughly and serve.

DAIKON, MUNG, PEANUT SALAD

This recipe is called "Mooli, phooti mung dal aur moong-phalli ka salaad" in Hindi

Yield: 4 to 6 servings

Ingredients:

- ½ cup raw shelled peanuts, red skin on
- 1 cup finely chopped daikon or red radish leaves
- 1 cup finely chopped daikon radishes
- 1 fresh green chile pepper, such as serrano, minced with seeds or to taste
- 1 tablespoon fresh lime or lemon juice
- 1½ cups <u>sprouted</u> green mung beans (saabut mung dal) or store-bought
- 1½ teaspoons <u>Chaat Masala</u> (Homemade or store-bought), or more to taste
- 8 to 10 scallions, white parts only, thinly chopped

Directions:

1. Ready the chaat masala. Next, in a small-sized cast-iron or non-stick skillet, roast the peanuts, stirring and swaying the pan, over moderate heat until they are golden. Allow to cool, then grind crudely with a mortar and pestle or a spice grinder.
2. In a serving container, combine the radishes, radish leaves, mung dal, scallions, chile pepper, and ground peanuts. Put in the chaat masala and lime juice and toss to mix. Serve, if possible at room temperature.

GINGERED TOMATO CUCUMBER SALAD Ⓥ

This recipe is called "Adrak vaala tamatar-kheerae ka salaad" in Hindi

Yield: 4 to 6 servings

Ingredients:

- ¼ cup finely chopped fresh cilantro, including soft stems
- ¼ teaspoon ground ajwain seeds
- ½ pound Armenian or any seedless cucumbers, finely chopped
- 1 fresh green chile pepper, minced with seeds
- 1 pound yellow tomatoes, finely chopped
- 1 to 2 tablespoon fresh lime or lemon juice
- 1 to 2 tablespoons peeled minced fresh ginger
- 1½ teaspoons Chaat Masala (Homemade or store-bought), or more to taste
- 2 cups finely chopped romaine lettuce or fresh spinach leaves

Directions:

1. Ready the chaat masala. Next, mix everything in a big container. Tweak the seasonings to your taste and serve. If you wish to serve the salad chilled, combine all the ingredients except the chaat masala and ajwain seeds, and chill up to one day.
2. Put in the spices just before you serve, or the salt in the chaat masala will draw out the juices from the ingredients and make the salad too liquidy.

TOMATO SALADS

COLOURFUL TOMATO SALAD (V)

This recipe is called "Rang-birangae tamatar ka salaad" in Hindi

Yield: 4 to 6 servings

Ingredients:

- ⅛ teaspoon ground asafoetida
- 1 fresh green chile pepper, such as serrano, minced with seeds
- 1 tablespoon olive oil
- 1 teaspoon black mustard seeds
- 1 teaspoon cumin seeds
- 1½ pounds firm vine-ripened tomatoes of mixed colors, crudely chopped
- 2 tablespoons fresh lemon juice
- 2 tablespoons minced fresh curry leaves
- 2 to 3 cups mixed baby lettuce, mesclun, or other mixed greens
- 5 to 7 cherry or pear-shaped tomatoes of mixed colors

Directions:

1. Line a serving platter with the lettuce. Keeping a large non-stick wok or saucepan tilted to one side, heat the oil and put in the cumin and mustard seeds; they should sizzle instantly when they touch the hot oil. Lay the pan flat, and swiftly Put in the green chile pepper, curry leaves, asafoetida and lemon juice and cook 1 minute.
2. Put in the tomatoes and stir softly until heated through, but still firm, approximately a minute or two. Move to the lettuce-lined platter and serve.

PAN-FRIED GREEN TOMATO SALAD (V)

This recipe is called "Bhunnae harae tamatar ka salaad" in Hindi

Yield: 4 to 6 servings

Ingredients:

- ¼ cup finely chopped fresh cilantro, with soft stems
- ½ teaspoon Chaat Masala (Homemade or store-bought)
- ½ teaspoon salt, or to taste
- 1 tablespoon fresh lemon juice
- 1 tablespoon ground coriander
- 1 tablespoon peanut oil
- 3 to 4 large unripe green tomatoes (about 1½ pounds), each cut into 8 wedges

Directions:

1. Ready the chaat masala. Next, lay the tomato wedges in a single layer in a big non-stick skillet. Drizzle the oil over them and cook using moderate to high heat until the bottoms are golden, approximately four minutes.
2. Turn each piece over, sprinkle the coriander and salt over them, and cook until the other side is golden, approximately two minutes.
3. Put in the lemon juice and cilantro, very cautiously mix everything together, and cook approximately half a minute. Move to a serving dish, sprinkle with the chaat masala before you serve.

TOMATO, SCALLION, SEV SALAD

This recipe is called "Tamatar, harae pyaz, aur sev ka salaad" in Hindi

Yield: 4 to 6 servings

Ingredients:

- Crudely ground black pepper, to taste
- ten to twelve scallions, white and light green parts only, thinly chopped
- ¼ cup packaged fine sev noodles
- ¼ teaspoon salt, or to taste
- 1 small lime
- 1 tablespoon minced fresh mint leaves

- 2 tablespoons minced fresh cilantro leaves
- 6 to 8 small, firm, vine-ripened tomatoes, cut into thin wedges

Directions:

1. Put the tomato wedges on a large serving platter and scatter the scallions over them.
2. Slice the lime in half and microwave on high approximately half a minute. Squeeze 1 or both the halves over the tomatoes. Top with salt, black pepper, cilantro, mint, and sev noodles before you serve.

CABBAGE SALADS

CABBAGE AND BROCCOLI SALAD

This recipe is called "Bundh gobhi aur kaali mirch ka salaad" in Hindi

Yield: 4 to 6 servings

Ingredients:

- ¼ cup finely chopped fresh cilantro, with soft stems
- ½ cup grated daikon radish
- ½ cup non-fat plain yogurt, whisked until the desired smoothness is achieved
- ½ teaspoon salt, or to taste
- 1 cup ½- to 1-inch broccoli florets
- 1 cup finely shredded romaine lettuce
- 1 tablespoon peeled minced fresh ginger
- 1 teaspoon fresh lime juice
- 1½ teaspoons multi-colored peppercorns, <u>dry-roasted</u>, crudely ground + more for garnish
- 2 cups finely shredded green cabbage
- 8 to 10 small cherry or pear-shaped tomatoes, halved

Directions:

1. In a large serving container, combine the cabbage, lettuce, broccoli, tomatoes, daikon radish, and cilantro. In a small-sized container, combine the yogurt, ginger, lime juice, salt, and pepper, and add to the salad.
2. Roast the peppercorns. Toss the salad well then garnish with a few coarse grindings from the peppermill. Serve.

KERAL CABBAGE AND RED ONION SALAD Ⓥ

This recipe is called "Kerala ka bundh gobhi aur laal pyaz ka salaad" in Hindi

Yield: 4 to 6 servings

Ingredients:

- ten to twelve fresh curry leaves
- ¼ teaspoon salt, or to taste
- 1 green bell pepper, cut into thin matchsticks
- 1 small red onion, cut in half along the length and thinly chopped
- 1 tablespoon coconut or peanut oil
- 1 tablespoon distilled white vinegar
- 1 tablespoon sesame seeds, dry-roasted
- 1 teaspoon mustard seeds
- 2 cups shredded green cabbage
- 4 small tomatoes, cut into thin wedges
- 4 whole dried red chile peppers, such as chile de arbol

Directions:

1. Roast the sesame seeds. Next, in a big serving container, combine the onion, cabbage, bell pepper, and tomatoes.
2. Heat the oil in a small-sized non-stick wok or saucepan using moderate to high heat and put in the mustard seeds; they should splutter when they touch the hot oil, so cover the pan and decrease the heat until the spluttering diminishes. Swiftly put in the red chile peppers and curry leaves

and cook, stirring, approximately half a minute. Put in the vinegar and salt and move the mixture to the salad. Toss well, and garnish with sesame seeds. Refrigerate up to two hours before you serve chilled.

LEMONY CABBAGE SALAD

This recipe is called "Dakshini bundh gobhi salaad" in Hindi

Yield: 4 to 6 servings

Ingredients:

- ½ teaspoon black mustard seeds
- ½ teaspoon cumin seeds
- ½ teaspoon salt, or to taste
- 1 tablespoon peanut oil
- 2 cups finely shredded green cabbage
- 2 tablespoons fresh lemon juice
- 2 whole dried red chili peppers, such as chile de arbol
- 5 fresh curry leaves

Directions:

1. Heat the oil in a big non-stick wok or skillet over moderate heat and put in the mustard and cumin seeds; they should sizzle when they touch the hot oil.
2. Swiftly put in the red chili peppers and the fresh curry leaves and stir a few seconds, then, put in the cabbage and cook briefly—maximum ten to fifteen seconds. If you see the cabbage wilting, move it to a big container instantly. Put in the lemon juice and salt.
3. Toss and serve instantly, or refrigerate one to two hours to serve chilled.

YOGURT COLESLAW

This recipe is called "Dahi-bundh gobhi ka salaad" in Hindi

Yield: 4 to 6 servings

Ingredients:

- ten to twelve scallions, white and light green parts only, minced
- ¼ cup almond slivers, dry-roasted
- ½ cup finely chopped fresh cilantro, including soft stems
- ½ teaspoon freshly ground black pepper, or to taste
- ½ teaspoon salt, or to taste
- 1 cup finely diced bell peppers of mixed colors
- 1 cup plain yogurt (any kind), whisked until the desired smoothness is achieved
- 1 fresh serrano pepper, minced, with seeds
- 1 tablespoon fresh lime or lemon juice
- 1 tablespoon minced fresh mint leaves
- 1 tablespoon peeled minced fresh ginger
- 1 teaspoon Chaat Masala (Homemade or store-bought)
- 2 cups finely shredded green cabbage
- 2 cups finely shredded purple cabbage
- 2 pickling cucumbers, grated
- Ground paprika

Directions:

1. Ready the almonds and the chaat masala. In a moderate-sized container, combine the yogurt, lime juice, serrano pepper, ginger, chaat masala, black pepper, and salt.
2. Put the green and purple cabbage, bell pepper, cucumbers, scallions, cilantro, and mint in a big container. Put in the yogurt dressing and toss to mix thoroughly. Move to a wide serving container, garnish with the paprika and almonds before you serve.

MARINATED SALADS

CARROT AND CASHEW SALAD

This recipe is called "Gajjar aur kajju ka salaad" in Hindi

Yield: 4 to 6 servings

Ingredients:

- ⅛ teaspoon ground asafoetida
- ¼ cup grated fresh or frozen coconut or 2 tablespoons shredded unsweetened dried coconut
- ½ cup finely chopped fresh cilantro, including soft stems
- ½ teaspoon salt, or to taste
- ¾ to 1 pound carrots, peeled and grated
- 1 tablespoon finely chopped fresh curry leaves
- 1 teaspoon black mustard seeds
- 1 teaspoon cumin seeds
- 1 teaspoon peanut oil
- 1 to 2 tablespoons fresh lemon juice
- 15 to 20 raw cashews, crudely chopped
- 2 fresh green chile peppers, such as serrano, halved lengthwise

Directions:

1. In a large serving container, combine the carrots, coconut, cashews, cilantro, salt, and lemon juice.
2. In a small saucepan, heat the oil over moderate heat and put in the mustard and cumin seeds; they should splutter when they touch the hot oil, so cover the pan until the spluttering diminishes.
3. Put in the curry leaves, asafoetida, and green chile peppers and cook, stirring, approximately one minute. Move to the carrots, stirring softly to mix. Serve at room temperature or refrigerate at least two hours to serve chilled.

LEMONY RED ONION RINGS

This recipe is called "Nimboo vaalae pyaz" in Hindi

Yield: 4 to 6 servings

Ingredients:

- ¼ to ½ cup finely chopped fresh cilantro, including soft stems
- ½ teaspoon hot red pepper flakes, or to taste
- 1 teaspoon Basic Ginger Paste (Homemade or store-bought)
- 2 tablespoons fresh lemon or lime juice
- 2 teaspoons salt, or to taste
- 4 to 6 small red onions, cut into rings

Directions:

1. Ready the ginger paste. Next, in a non-reactive container, place the onions, put in the salt, and toss well. Cover and let marinate approximately two hours at room temperature. Next, pour into a fine-mesh strainer and drain all the juices and salt (or wash under running water and then drain).
2. Move to a serving container and stir in the cilantro, lemon juice, ginger paste, and red pepper flakes. Cover and place in your fridge for approximately two hours in the fridge to marinate. Serve chilled.

MARINATED PEANUT SALAD Ⓥ

This recipe is called "Moong-phalli ka salaad" in Hindi

Yield: 4 to 6 servings

Ingredients:

- ¼ teaspoon salt, or to taste
- ½ cup finely chopped fresh cilantro, including soft stems
- ½ cup orange juice
- 1 cup finely chopped, firm tomato
- 1 teaspoon ground dried mint leaves
- 2 cups raw peanuts, red skins removed
- 2 tablespoons fresh lemon juice
- 2 teaspoons Chaat Masala (Homemade or store-bought)

- 3 to 4 scallions, finely chopped

Directions:

1. Ready the chaat masala. Next, in a moderate-sized container mix the orange juice, 1 teaspoon chaat masala, mint, salt, and peanuts. Cover and marinate in the refrigerator, 2 to four hours.
2. Move the peanuts to a large non-stick skillet and cook using moderate to high heat, stirring, approximately two to three minutes, then decrease the heat to medium and cook until most of the liquid evaporates. Move to a serving container and allow to cool down. Next, stir in the tomato, scallions, cilantro, and lemon juice. Sprinkle the rest of the chaat masala on top and serve.

OKRA AND RADISH SALAD (V)

This recipe is called "Bhindi aur mooli ka salaad" in Hindi

Yield: 4 to 6 servings

Ingredients:

- ten to twelve small red radishes, thinly chopped
- ¼ cup finely chopped fresh cilantro, including soft stems
- ¼ teaspoon salt, or to taste
- ½ small onion, crudely chopped
- ½ teaspoon Chaat Masala (Homemade or store-bought)
- ½ teaspoon freshly ground black pepper, or to taste
- 1 clove fresh garlic, peeled
- 1 fresh green chili pepper, such as serrano, stemmed
- 1 pound fresh tender okra, rinsed and patted dry
- 1 quarter-sized slice peeled fresh ginger
- 1 small tomato, crudely chopped
- 1 tablespoon fresh lime juice

Directions:

1. Ready the chaat masala. Next, cut a thin slice off the stem end of a piece of okra. Next, working from the stem down, make a partial slit into the okra, stopping ½ inch from the tip. (This forms a pocket for the marinade to penetrate but keeps the okra intact.) Replicate the process for all the okra.
2. Bring a medium pot of water to a boil using high heat and put in the okra. Cover the pan and turn off the heat. Remove the okra after 1 minute, drain well and lay flat on a kitchen towel to air-dry for a few minutes. Move to a work container, toss in the radishes, and set aside.
3. Using a food processor or a blender, mix together and pulse the onion, tomato, ginger, garlic, lime juice, and chile pepper until minced. (Do not purée.) Put into the okra, put in the salt and black pepper, and mix thoroughly. Cover and let the okra marinate in the refrigerator, 2 to four hours. Move to a serving platter, sprinkle with the chaat masala and serve.

ZUCCHINI PINEAPPLE SALAD

This recipe is called "Zucchini aur annanas ka salaad" in Hindi

Yield: 4 to 6 servings

Ingredients:

- ⅛ teaspoon ground asafoetida
- ¼ teaspoon ajwain seeds
- ½ cup non-fat plain yogurt, whisked until the desired smoothness is achieved
- ½ teaspoon salt, or to taste
- 1 tablespoon peeled minced fresh ginger
- 1 tablespoon vegetable oil
- 1 teaspoon crudely ground black pepper, or to taste
- 1 teaspoon cumin seeds
- 1 to 3 fresh green chile peppers, such as serrano, minced with seeds
- 2 cups canned pineapple pieces, plus ¼ cup juice
- 2 tablespoons fresh lemon juice
- 4 to 6 zucchini, cut into ½-inch pieces

Directions:

1. Put the zucchini in a microwave-safe container. Cover and cook in the microwave on high power approximately two minutes. Allow to cool, then drain and move to a serving container. Put in the pineapple and juice, green chile peppers, yogurt, salt, and black pepper, and mix thoroughly.
2. Heat the oil in a small saucepan using moderate to high heat and put in the cumin and ajwain seeds; they should sizzle when they touch the hot oil. Swiftly put in the ginger and asafoetida, cook another half a minute, and put in the lemon juice. Move to the zucchini, stirring softly to mix. Serve at room temperature or refrigerate at least two hours to serve chilled.

BEAN AND LEGUME SALADS

BLACK-EYED PEA SALAD

This recipe is called "Lobia ka salaad" in Hindi

Yield: 4 to 6 servings

Ingredients:

- four to five scallions, white parts only, minced
- ¼ teaspoon ground black salt (not compulsory)
- ¼ teaspoon ground turmeric
- ½ cup plain yogurt (any kind), whisked until the desired smoothness is achieved
- ½ teaspoon Chaat Masala (Homemade or store-bought)
- ½ teaspoon ground cumin
- ½ teaspoon ground paprika
- 1 cup black-eyed peas (lobia), sorted, washed, and soaked overnight in 2 cups water
- 1 fresh green chile pepper, such as serrano, minced with seeds
- 1 large firm tomato, finely chopped
- 1 tablespoon ground coriander
- 1 tablespoon minced fresh mint leaves

- 1 tablespoon peanut oil
- 1 tablespoon peeled minced fresh ginger
- 1 teaspoon cumin seeds
- 1 teaspoon salt, or to taste
- 1 to 2 tablespoons fresh lime juice
- Several outer leaves of radicchio or butter lettuce, or approximately 3 cups shredded greens

Directions:

1. Ready the chaat masala. Next, place the black-eyed peas and soaking water, turmeric, and salt in a moderate-sized non-stick saucepan and bring to a boil using high heat. Decrease the heat to moderate to low, cover the pan, and simmer until all the water evaporates, leaving behind beans that are soft and tender but not broken, approximately one hour. (Pour in additional water during cooking, if needed.)
2. Move to a container and stir in the tomato, scallions, ginger, mint, green chile pepper, and lime juice. Allow to cool, then stir in the yogurt.
3. Heat the oil in a small-sized non-stick saucepan using moderate to high heat and put in the cumin seeds; they should sizzle when they touch the hot oil. Swiftly put in the coriander, ground cumin, black salt, and paprika, stir for approximately half a minute, and move to the black-eyed peas. Mix well. Present the salad in radicchio or butter lettuce cups, or mounded over a bed of shredded greens. Garnish with chaat masala before you serve at room temperature or chilled.

CHICKPEA CHAAT SALAD Ⓥ

This recipe is called "Channa chaat" in Hindi

Yield: 4 to 6 servings

Ingredients:

- four to five scallions, white parts only, thinly chopped
- ¼ cup water
- ½ cup finely chopped fresh cilantro, including soft stems
- ½ cup fresh pomegranate seeds

- 1 fresh green chile pepper, such as serrano, minced with seeds
- 1 large, firm vine-ripened tomato, finely chopped
- 1 small seedless cucumber, such as Armenian or Japanese, finely chopped
- 1 tablespoon peeled minced fresh ginger
- 1 teaspoon minced fresh garlic
- 1½ tablespoons ground coriander
- 1½ tablespoons Tamarind Paste
- 2 (15½-ounce) cans chickpeas, rinsed and drained well
- 2 tablespoons peanut oil
- 2 teaspoons Chaat Masala (Homemade or store-bought)

Directions:

1. Ready the chaat masal and tamarind paste. Next, in a moderate-sized container, combine the tomato, cucumber, scallions, ¼ cup of the cilantro and ½ teaspoon of the chaat masala.
2. Heat the oil in a big non-stick skillet using moderate to high heat then cook the garlic, ginger, and green chile pepper, stirring, until a golden colour is achieved, approximately one minute. Put in the ground coriander, the rest of the chaat masala, and the rest of the cilantro, and stir for approximately half a minute.
3. Put in the chickpeas, water, and tamarind, and cook, stirring as needed, until the chickpeas become soft and all the fluids vaporize, approximately four minutes.
4. Move to a serving platter. Lightly stir in the tomato mixture and scatter the pomegranate seeds on top. Serve at room temperature or chilled.

DEW BEAN SALAD Ⓥ

This recipe is called "Moth dal ki chaat" in Hindi

Yield: 4 to 6 servings

Ingredients:

- four to five scallions, finely chopped
- ¼ cup any sonth chutney of your choice (Homemade or store-bought)
- ⅓ cup finely chopped fresh cilantro, including soft stems

- ⅓ teaspoon ground turmeric
- ½ cup dried split yellow chickpeas (channa dal), sorted and washed in 3 to 4 changes of water
- ½ teaspoon cayenne pepper, or to taste
- ½ teaspoon salt, or to taste
- 1 medium tomato, finely chopped
- 1½ teaspoons Chaat Masala (Homemade or store-bought), or to taste1 cup dried dew beans (muth dal), sorted and washed in 3 to 4 changes of water
- 2 tablespoons peeled minced fresh ginger
- 2 to 3 tablespoons fresh lime juice
- 3 to 4 cups water

Directions:

1. Ready the sonth chutney and the chaat masala. Next, place both dals, the turmeric, cayenne pepper, salt, and water in a moderate-sized saucepan and bring to a boil using high heat. Decrease the heat to moderate to low, cover the pan, and simmer until all the water has evaporated, approximately 25 minutes, leaving behind a soft-cooked, dry dal. Stir in the ginger and allow to cool down.
2. When cool, stir in the tomato, scallions, lime juice, cilantro, and chaat masala. Move to a serving dish, drizzle with sonth chutney before you serve, if possible at room temperature.

MIXED SPROUTED BEAN & POTATO VERMICELLI SALAD Ⓥ

This recipe is called "Phooti mung dal aur aalu bhujia ki chaat" in Hindi

Yield: 4 to 6 servings

Ingredients:

- ¼ cup finely chopped fresh cilantro, including soft stems
- 1 cup packaged potato vermicelli (aalu bhujia), store-bought
- 1 fresh green chile pepper, such as serrano, minced with seeds
- 1 teaspoon New Delhi Street Food Masala or store-bought Chaat Masala

- 1 to 2 tablespoons fresh lime juice
- 3 cups sprouted mixed dals and grains, such as green mung beans, green and red lentils, and whole-wheat kernels

Directions:

1. Ready the sprouted dals and grains in advance. Ready the masala.
2. Next, mix everything in a big serving container and serve instantly, before the vermicelli gets soggy.

PARSI SPROUTED BEAN SALAD

This recipe is called "Parsi phooti dal ka salaad" in Hindi

Yield: 4 to 6 servings

Ingredients:

- ½ cup finely chopped fresh cilantro, including soft stems
- 1 fresh green chile pepper, such as serrano, minced with seeds
- 1 small onion, finely chopped
- 1 tablespoon Parsi Garam Masala with Star Anise or store-bought garam masala
- 1 tablespoon sprouted fenugreek seeds
- 1 teaspoon salt or to taste
- 1 to 2 tablespoons fresh lime juice
- 1 tomato, cut into wedges
- 2 tablespoons peanut oil
- 2 tablespoons water
- 3 to 4 cups sprouted mixed dals, such as mung beans and green lentils (Homemade or store-bought)

Directions:

1. Ready the sprouted beans in advance. Next, ready the masala and the fenugreek seeds. Next, heat the oil in a moderate-sized non-stick wok or saucepan using moderate to high heat and cook the onion, stirring, until a golden colour is achieved, approximately five minutes. Put in the garam

masala, green chile pepper, and cilantro, and cook, stirring, approximately one minute.

2. Put in the sprouted dals, fenugreek seeds, salt, and water, and decrease the heat to moderate to low. Cover the pan and cook from 3 to ten minutes, depending on the desired softness. Stir in the lime juice. Move to a serving platter, garnish with tomato wedges and serve warm or at room temperature.

RED BEAN SALAD

This recipe is called "Chotae rajma ka salaad" in Hindi

Yield: 4 to 6 servings

Ingredients:

- ¼ cup finely chopped fresh cilantro, including soft stems
- ¼ cup non-fat plain yogurt, whisked until the desired smoothness is achieved
- ½ teaspoon cumin seeds, <u>dry-roasted</u> and crudely ground
- 1 (1-inch) stick cinnamon, broken lengthwise
- 1 cup dried red (chotae rajma) or pinto beans, sorted, washed and soaked overnight in 2 cups water
- 1 fresh green chile pepper, such as serrano, minced with seeds
- 1 large clove fresh garlic, minced
- 1 tablespoon minced fresh mint leaves
- 1 teaspoon <u>Chaat Masala</u> (Homemade or store-bought)
- 1 teaspoon salt, or to taste
- 2 black cardamom pods, pounded lightly to break the skin
- 2 tablespoons peeled minced fresh ginger
- 2 tablespoons <u>Tamarind Paste</u> or 1 tablespoon tamarind powder

Directions:

1. Ready the cumin seeds, tamarind paste, and chaat masala. Next, place the dal and the soaking water, garlic, cardamom pods, cinnamon, and salt in a moderate-sized non-stick saucepan and bring to a boil using high heat. Decrease the heat to moderate to low, cover the pan, and simmer until all the water evaporates, leaving behind beans that are soft and tender but not

broken, approximately one hour. (Pour in additional water during cooking, if needed.) Move to a serving container.
2. In a small-sized container, combine the cumin seeds, yogurt, tamarind, ginger, green chile pepper, and chaat masala. Put into the cooked beans and mix thoroughly, adjusting the seasonings, if needed. Move to a serving dish, stir in the cilantro and mint leaves before you serve, if possible at room temperature.

SOYBEAN-TOMATO SALAD

This recipe is called "Soyabean aur tamatar ka salaad" in Hindi

Yield: 4 to 6 servings

Ingredients:

- ¼ teaspoon crudely ground black pepper, or to taste
- ½ cup water
- ½ teaspoon salt, or to taste
- 1 (1-inch) piece fresh ginger, cut into thin matchsticks
- 1 large clove fresh garlic, minced
- 1 large, firm tomato, finely chopped
- 1 tablespoon ground coriander
- 1 tablespoon peanut oil
- 1 teaspoon Chaat Masala (Homemade or store-bought)
- 1 teaspoon cumin seeds
- 1 to 2 tablespoons fresh lemon juice
- 1½ cups frozen shelled soybeans, thawed
- 2 cups finely chopped dark green lettuce, such as romaine, green leaf or red leaf
- 4 scallions, white and light green parts only, minced

Directions:

1. Ready the chaat masala. Next, place the soybeans and water in a microwave-safe dish. Cook in the microwave on high power 5 to 6 minutes, or until the beans are very soft to the touch. Put the lettuce, tomato, and scallion in a big serving container.

2. Heat the oil in a moderate-sized non-stick saucepan using moderate to high heat and put in the ginger and cumin seeds; they should sizzle when they touch the hot oil. Swiftly add first the garlic, coriander, and black pepper, then the soybeans, the rest of the cooking water, and salt. Cover and cook, stirring and swaying the pan, until the soybeans are coated thoroughly, approximately five minutes.
3. Move to the container with the lettuce, tomato and scallion, and put in the lemon juice and chaat masala. Toss and serve warm or at room temperature.

SPROUTED MUNG AND CABBAGE SALAD (V)

This recipe is called "Phooti mung dal aur bundh gobhi ka salaad" in Hindi

Yield: 4 to 6 servings

Ingredients:

- ¼ cup crudely chopped roasted peanuts
- ¼ cup fresh orange juice
- ½ cup finely chopped fresh cilantro, including soft stems
- ½ teaspoon salt, or to taste
- 1 cup finely chopped onion
- 1 cup thinly shredded green cabbage
- 1 cup thinly shredded red cabbage
- 1 fresh green chile pepper, such as serrano, minced with seeds
- 1 tablespoon peeled minced fresh ginger
- 1 tablespoon sesame seeds, <u>dry-roasted</u>
- 1 teaspoon <u>Chaat Masala</u> (Homemade or store-bought)
- 2 cups mixed baby greens, or any other lettuce
- 2 cups <u>sprouted</u> green mung beans (Homemade or store-bought)
- 2 tablespoons fresh lime juice
- 4 small tomatoes, each cut into 6 to 8 wedges
- Freshly ground black pepper, to taste

Directions:

1. Ready the sprouted beans in advance. Ready the sesame seeds and the chaat masala. Next, in a container, mix everything except the sesame seeds, baby greens, and peanuts. Cover and marinate at least two hours in a fridge.
2. Mound the mixture over a bed of baby greens, scatter the sesame seeds and peanuts on top before you serve.

POTATO AND ROOT VEGETABLE SALADS

POTATO SALAD WITH YOGURT

This recipe is called "Aalu aur dahi ka salaad" in Hindi

Yield: 4 to 6 servings

Ingredients:

- ¼ cup finely chopped fresh cilantro, including soft stems
- ¼ teaspoon freshly ground black pepper, or to taste
- ¼ teaspoon salt, or to taste
- ½ teaspoon salt, or to taste
- 1 cup non-fat plain yogurt, whisked until the desired smoothness is achieved
- 1 tablespoon peeled minced fresh ginger
- 1 to 2 fresh green chile peppers, such as serrano, minced with seeds
- 1½ pounds russet, red, or Yukon gold potatoes, peeled or unpeeled
- 1½ teaspoons cumin seeds, dry-roasted and crudely ground
- 2 tablespoons peanut oil
- 6 to 8 scallions, white parts only, finely chopped

Directions:

1. Ready the cumin seeds. Next, in a medium pan, cover the potatoes with water, bring to a boil, and cook until tender, approximately fifteen minutes.

Drain, Allow to cool, then cut into 3/4-inch pieces. Ready the cumin seeds. In a moderate-sized container, combine the yogurt, salt, black pepper, and scallions.
2. Heat the oil in a big skillet using moderate to high heat and lightly cook the potatoes, stirring, approximately three minutes. Put in the ginger, green chile peppers, cilantro, and salt, and cook, turning as required, until the potatoes are golden on all sides, approximately five minutes.
3. Move to a serving dish and drizzle the yogurt sauce and half the roasted cumin over the potatoes. Mix lightly. Garnish with the rest of the cumin and serve.

POTATO, SWEET POTATO, AND PEA SALAD Ⓥ

This recipe is called "Aalu, shakkar-kandi, aur muttar ki chaat" in Hindi

Yield: 4 to 6 servings

Ingredients:

- ½ cup finely chopped fresh cilantro, including soft stems
- ½ cup finely chopped sweet onion or white parts of scallions
- ½ pound small, pale-fleshed sweet potatoes
- ½ teaspoon cayenne pepper, or to taste
- ½ teaspoon salt, or to taste
- ½ to 1 teaspoon Chaat Masala (Homemade or store-bought)
- 1 cup frozen peas, thawed
- 1 pound small white potatoes
- 2 to 3 tablespoons peanut oil
- 3 to 4 tablespoons Tamarind Paste

Directions:

1. Ready the tamarind paste and chaat masala. Next, in separate pots, cover the white potatoes and sweet potatoes in lightly salted water, bring to a boil, and cook until tender, approximately fifteen minutes for the potatoes and fifteen to twenty minutes for the sweet potatoes (depending on their

thickness). Drain and allow to cool down, then peel all the potatoes. Cut each white potato in half lengthwise, and cut the sweet potatoes into thick rounds.

2. In a large cast-iron or non-stick skillet, heat the oil using moderate to high heat and cook the white potatoes and sweet potatoes until a golden colour is achieved-brown on both sides, approximately seven minutes, turning as required. As you cook them, press each piece with the back of the spatula to flatten it as much as possible. Move to a plate, and when they are cool sufficient to handle, use clean fingers to crudely break each piece into 2 or 3 smaller pieces.
3. Put in the peas to the same skillet and cook using moderate to high heat, stirring, until barely golden, approximately four minutes.
4. Mix the potatoes and sweet potatoes into the peas. Next, Put in the tamarind paste, salt, cayenne pepper, chaat masala, and cilantro and cook, turning a few times as required, approximately two minutes. Adjust seasonings, adding more salt, chaat masala, or tamarind, if required. Move to a serving platter, top with the chopped onions before you serve.

RED POTATO CHAAT SALAD

This recipe is called "Laal aalu ki chaat" in Hindi

Yield: 4 to 6 servings

Ingredients:

- ½ cup finely chopped fresh cilantro, including soft stems
- ½ teaspoon salt, or to taste
- 1 fresh green chile pepper, such as serrano, minced with seeds
- 1 tablespoon minced fresh mint leaves
- 1 teaspoon cumin seeds
- 1½ pounds small red potatoes, unpeeled
- 1½ teaspoons grated lemon peel (zest)
- 1½ to 2 teaspoons Chaat Masala (Homemade or store-bought)
- 2 tablespoons olive oil
- 2 to 3 tablespoons fresh lemon juice

Directions:

1. Ready the chaat masala. In a medium pot, cover the potatoes with water, bring to a boil, and cook until tender, approximately fifteen minutes. Drain, allow to cool down, then cut into ½-inch pieces. (Do not remove the skin.)
2. In a large skillet, heat the oil using moderate to high heat and add first the cumin seeds, then the lemon peel, mint, and green chile pepper. Cook, shaking the skillet, approximately half a minute. Put in the potatoes and salt and cook, flipping the potatoes as required, until a golden colour is achieved on all sides, approximately seven minutes. Decrease the heat if they begin to brown too swiftly.
3. Put in the cilantro and lemon juice, cook another minute, then stir in half the chaat masala. Move to a serving dish. Sprinkle with the rest of the chaat masala and serve warm or at room temperature.

SWEET POTATO SALAD

This recipe is called "Shakkar-kandi ki chaat" in Hindi

Yield: 4 to 6 servings

Ingredients:

- ¼ cup finely chopped fresh cilantro, including soft stems
- ½ teaspoon salt, or to taste
- 1 fresh green chile pepper, such as serrano, minced with seeds
- 1 tablespoon brown sugar
- 1 tablespoon peeled minced fresh ginger
- 1 teaspoon cumin seeds, <u>dry-roasted</u> and crudely ground
- 2 tablespoons Tamarind Paste
- 4 small sweet potatoes (about 1 pound)

Directions:

1. Ready the cumin seeds and tamarind paste. In a large pot, cover the sweet potatoes with water, bring to a boil, and cook until tender, approximately fifteen minutes. Allow to cool, then peel and cut into 3/4-inch pieces.
2. Put in a serving container and stir in all the rest of the ingredients. Cover and refrigerate approximately one hour to serve chilled.

TARO ROOT SALAD Ⓥ

This recipe is called "Arbi ki chaat" in Hindi

Yield: 4 to 6 servings

Ingredients:

- ¼ teaspoon salt, or to taste
- ½ teaspoon ajwain seeds, crudely ground
- ½ teaspoon Chaat Masala (Homemade or store-bought), or to taste
- 1 fresh green chile pepper, such as serrano, minced with seeds
- 1 tablespoon minced fresh mint leaves
- 1 to 1½ tablespoons fresh lime juice
- 2 to 3 tablespoon finely chopped fresh cilantro, including soft stems
- 6 to 8 small taro roots (about 1 pound)

Directions:

1. Ready the chaat masala. Next, in a medium pot, cover the taro root with water, bring to boil, and cook until tender, approximately fifteen minutes. Allow to cool slightly, then peel and cut into ½-inch pieces.
2. Put in a serving container and stir in all the rest of the ingredients. Serve warm or at room temperature.

GREEN SALADS

COTTAGE CHEESE SALAD WITH BABY GREENS

This recipe is called "Paneer Ka hara salaad" in Hindi

Yield: 4 to 6 servings

Ingredients:

- ½ cup any sonth chutney of your choice
- ½ cup non-fat plain yogurt, whisked until the desired smoothness is achieved
- 1 cup peanut oil for deep-frying
- 2 teaspoons Chaat Masala (Homemade or store-bought)
- 4 cups mixed baby greens
- 8 ounces (1 recipe) Paneer Cheese (Homemade or store-bought), cut into ½-by-3-inch pieces

Directions:

1. Ready the paneer, sonth chutney, and chaat masala. Heat the oil in a big non-stick skillet using moderate to high heat until it achieves 325°F to 350°F on a frying thermometer or a small piece of paneer cheese dropped into the hot oil surges to the surface of the oil in fifteen to 20 seconds. Put in the paneer cheese, 2 to 4 pieces at a time, and fry until barely golden, 30 to 40 seconds.
2. Move to a plate, allow to cool down, then when cool sufficient to handle, crudely break them into ½-inch pieces. Mix the pieces with ¼ cup sonth chutney and 1 teaspoon chaat masala. Cover and keep warm.
3. In a small-sized container, combine the yogurt and the rest of the sonth chutney. Toss the baby greens with this mixture and spread them on a serving platter. Put the paneer cheese over the greens, garnish with the rest of the chaat masala before you serve.

PAN-ROASTED TOMATO MIX SALAD

This recipe is called "Bhunae tamatar ka hara salaad" in Hindi

Yield: 4 to 6 servings

Ingredients:

- four to five cups crudely broken mixed sweet and bitter greens, such as iceberg, romaine, green oak, endive, and arugula, rinsed and drained
- ¼ teaspoon salt, or to taste
- ½ cup buttermilk

- 1 tablespoon peanut oil
- 1 tablespoon peeled minced fresh ginger
- 1½ teaspoons Chaat Masala (Homemade or store-bought)
- 4 to 6 small firm vine-ripened tomatoes, crudely chopped
- Freshly ground black pepper, to taste

Directions:

1. Ready the chaat masala. Put the lettuce in a big salad container. Heat the oil in a big non-stick skillet using moderate to high heat, put in the tomatoes, ginger and salt, and cook, shaking the skillet and turning the tomato pieces once or twice, until they are soft but retain their shape, approximately three minutes. Sprinkle half the chaat masala on top and move to the lettuce container. Do not mix.
2. Put in the buttermilk and the rest of the chaat masala to the skillet and stir, being sure to scrape the bottom of the skillet to incorporate any tomato bits and juices into the buttermilk. Bring to a boil using high heat. Allow to cool, then add it to the salad and toss to mix. Top with freshly ground black pepper and serve.

SPINACH SALAD

This recipe is called "Palak ka salaad" in Hindi

Yield: 4 to 6 servings

Ingredients:

- ½ teaspoon ground ginger
- ½ teaspoon salt, or to taste
- 1 cup non-fat plain yogurt, whisked until the desired smoothness is achieved
- 1 tablespoon fresh lemon juice
- 1 tablespoon melted honey
- 1 teaspoon peanut oil
- 2 teaspoons cumin seeds, dry-roasted and crudely ground
- 5 cups firmly packed baby spinach leaves, trimmed, washed well and spin-dried
- Freshly ground black pepper, to taste

Directions:

1. Ready the cumin seeds. Next, place the spinach leaves in a salad container.
2. Heat the oil in a small saucepan and add first the ginger, then the lemon juice and honey, and stir to mix. Turn off the heat and allow to cool down. Stir in the yogurt, 1 teaspoon cumin seeds, salt, and black pepper. Put into the spinach and toss lightly to mix. Sprinkle the rest of the cumin seeds on top and serve.

FRUIT SALADS

SAVORY SUMMER FRUIT SALAD

This recipe is called "Phallon ki chaat" in Hindi

Yield: 4 to 6 servings

Ingredients:

- ½ cup finely chopped fresh cilantro, including soft stems
- 1 cup cherries, pitted and halved
- 1 cup strawberries, crudely chopped
- 1 fresh green chile pepper, such as serrano, minced with seeds
- 1 large mango, peeled and crudely chopped
- 1 tablespoon minced fresh mint leaves
- 1 tablespoon peeled minced fresh ginger
- 1 to 2 tablespoons fresh lime or lemon juice
- 1 to 2 teaspoons Chaat Masala (Homemade or store-bought)
- 2 pounds mixed fruits, such as peaches, nectarines, and apricots, pitted and crudely chopped

Directions:

1. Ready the chaat masala. Next, in a big serving container, combine the peaches, nectarines, apricots, and mango. Remove approximately 1 cup of the mixed fruits, mash coarsely, and return to the container.
2. Stir in the cherries and strawberries, then put in the ginger, cilantro, mint, chili pepper, lime juice, and chaat masala. Mix thoroughly and serve.

SPICY MIXED BERRY SALAD

This recipe is called "Berriyon ki chaat" in Hindi

Yield: 4 to 6 servings

Ingredients:

- 1 teaspoon Chaat Masala (Homemade or store-bought), or more to taste
- 2 to 3 cups fresh mixed berries, such as raspberries, blackberries, and boysenberries
- Finely chopped fresh mint leaves

Directions:

1. Rinse and drain the berries, blot with paper towels, then place on a towel and allow to air-dry until as dry as possible.
2. In the meantime, ready the chaat masala. Move to a serving container, put in the chaat masala, and toss lightly. Garnish with mint leaves and serve.

NON-VEGETARIAN SALADS

EGG SALAD

This recipe is called "Andae ka salaad" in Hindi

Yield: 4 to 6 servings

Ingredients:

- ¼ cup finely chopped fresh cilantro, including soft stems
- ¼ teaspoon salt, or to taste
- ½ cup plain Yogurt Cheese
- 1 tablespoon dry-roasted sesame seeds
- 1 tablespoon peeled minced fresh ginger
- 1 teaspoon Basic Curry Powder (Homemade or store-bought)
- 1 teaspoon dry-roasted and crudely ground cumin seeds
- 1 to 2 fresh green chile peppers, such as serrano, minced with seeds
- 4 large eggs

Directions:

1. Ready the yogurt cheese. Next, ready the cumin, the sesame seeds, and the curry powder. In a moderate-sized saucepan, place the eggs in water to cover by 2 inches and bring to a boil using high heat. Decrease the heat to medium, cover the pan and simmer until hard-boiled, approximately ten to twelve minutes. Allow to cool or plunge into cold water, shell them, then cut finely.
2. Put the eggs in a big serving container, stir in all the rest of the ingredients and serve.

GINGER-SHRIMP SALAD

This recipe is called "Adrak-jhinga ka salaad" in Hindi

Yield: 4 to 6 servings

Ingredients:

- ¼ teaspoon cayenne pepper, or to taste
- ½ teaspoon freshly ground black pepper, or to taste
- ½ teaspoon salt, or to taste
- 1 (1-inch) piece fresh ginger, peeled and cut into thin matchsticks
- 1 each of red and yellow bell peppers, cut into thin 1½-inch matchsticks
- 1 large clove fresh garlic, minced

- 1 pound extra-large shrimp (about 20), shelled and deveined, with tails left on
- 1 small seedless cucumber, such as Armenian or Japanese, cut into thin 1½-inch matchsticks
- 1 teaspoon crudely ground ajwain seeds
- 1 teaspoon Chaat Masala (Homemade or store-bought)
- 2 cups mixed baby greens
- 2 tablespoons fresh lime or lemon juice
- 2 tablespoons minced fresh mint leaves
- 2 tablespoons vegetable oil
- 3 to 4 scallions, white parts only, thinly chopped

Directions:

1. Ready the chaat masala. Put the shrimp in a big non-reactive container. Put in the ginger, garlic, lime juice, ajwain seeds, salt, cayenne and black peppers and mix thoroughly, ensuring all the shrimp are coated thoroughly with the marinade. Refrigerate approximately two hours.
2. Heat the oil in a big non-stick wok or saucepan using moderate to high heat and cook the mint leaves, stirring, approximately half a minute. Put in the shrimp and the marinade and cook until the shrimp are pink, approximately three minutes.
3. In a large container, combine the greens, bell peppers, and cucumber, and toss with the chaat masala. Move to a serving platter. Scatter the cooked shrimp over the greens, top with the scallions before you serve.

MINCED CHICKEN AND LENTIL WAFER SALAD

This recipe is called "Murgh keema aur paapad ki chaat" in Hindi

Yield: 4 to 6 servings

Ingredients:

- ½ cup finely chopped fresh cilantro, including soft stems
- ½ cup non-fat plain yogurt, whisked until the desired smoothness is achieved

- 1 fresh green chile pepper, such as serrano, minced with seeds
- 1 large clove fresh garlic, minced
- 1 large onion, finely chopped
- 1 large russet potato, unpeeled
- 1 pound boneless, skinless chicken breasts, minced
- 1 red bell pepper, finely chopped
- 1 tablespoon peeled minced fresh ginger
- 1 teaspoon dried fenugreek leaves
- 1 teaspoon garam masala
- 1 teaspoon salt, or to taste
- 1 to 2 tablespoons fresh lime juice
- 2 tablespoons vegetable oil
- 4 to 6 <u>Spicy Lentil Wafers</u>, microwaved for 1 minute each

Directions:

1. In a small pan, cover the potato with water, bring to a boil, and cook until tender, approximately ten minutes. Allow to cool, then peel, finely chop, and save for later. In a non-stick saucepan, heat the oil using moderate to high heat and cook the chicken, onion, ginger, garlic, green chile pepper, garam masala, fenugreek leaves, and salt, stirring to break most of the lumps, until the chicken is golden, approximately five minutes.
2. Add all the yogurt at once, and cook until most of the liquid has evaporated and the yogurt is absorbed, approximately five minutes.
3. Stir in the lime juice, red bell pepper, potato, and cilantro, and cook another 3 minutes. Allow to cool. In the meantime, ready the paapads.
4. Move the chicken and vegetables to a serving platter. Break the paapads into small pieces and place them around the chicken. Serve.

TANDOORI CHICKEN SALAD

This recipe is called "Tandoori murgh ki chaat" in Hindi

Yield: 4 to 6 servings

Ingredients:

- ¼ cup finely chopped fresh cilantro, including soft stems

- 1 (1-inch) piece peeled fresh ginger, cut into thin matchsticks
- 1 (2- to 2½-pound) (1 recipe) <u>Grilled Tandoori Chicken</u>
- 1 large tomato, cut into ½-inch pieces
- 1 teaspoon <u>Chaat Masala</u> (Homemade or store-bought), or to taste
- 1 teaspoon cumin seeds, <u>dry-roasted</u> and crudely ground
- 1 to 2 fresh green chile peppers, such as serrano, minced with seeds
- 1½ tablespoons vegetable oil
- 2 tablespoons minced fresh mint leaves
- 2 to 3 small seedless cucumbers, such as Armenian or Japanese, cut into ½-inch pieces
- 2 to 3 tablespoons fresh lemon or lime juice
- 6 to 8 scallions, white parts only, thinly chopped

Directions:

1. Ready the tandoori chicken, then pull the meat off the bone and shred it. Ready the cumin seeds and the chaat masala. In a serving container, combine the shredded chicken, tomato, cucumbers, scallions, and cilantro.
2. Heat the oil in a small-sized non-stick saucepan using moderate to high heat and cook the ginger, stirring, until a golden colour is achieved, approximately three minutes. Stir in the green chile peppers and mint and stir approximately one minute. Next, Put in the lemon juice and chaat masala and stir a few seconds. Put into the chicken and mix thoroughly. Taste and adjust the seasonings. Sprinkle with the roasted cumin and serve.

YOGURT RAITAS AND PACHADIS

Most of the Indian recipes are quite spicy, even for the average Indian. This makes yogurt an indispensable part of Indian cuisine. We Indians fire up our tongues with something spicy, and then eat a spoonful of "raita" to soothe our tongues. The feeling is heavenly, and if you haven't tried doing this yourself, what are you waiting for?

Not just the taste, yogurt is an insanely nutritious pro-biotic food that enhances digestion, and overall health. Yogurt is converted into "raita" by mixing it with seasonings, or fibrous foods, or both (usually both). Yogurt by itself is quite nutritious, but when enriched and converted into raita, its health benefits skyrocket!

BASIC RAITAS

SIMPLE SALT AND PEPPER RAITA

This recipe is called "Namak aur Kaali mirch ka raita" in Hindi

Yield: 4 to 6 servings

Ingredients:

- ⅓ teaspoon salt, or to taste
- 3 cups non-fat plain yogurt, whisked until the desired smoothness is achieved
- Freshly ground mixed peppercorns, such as red, black, green, and white, to taste

Directions:

1. In a serving container, combine the yogurt, salt, and half the mixed peppercorns.
2. Sprinkle the rest of the pepper on top as a decoration, and refrigerate until ready to serve.

GINGER AND SCALLION RAITA

This recipe is called "Adrak aur harae pyaz ka raita" in Hindi

Yield: 4 to 6 servings

Ingredients:

- ⅓ teaspoon salt, or to taste
- ½ teaspoon ground paprika
- 1 fresh green chile pepper, such as serrano, minced with seeds
- 1 teaspoon sugar
- 1 to 2 tablespoons minced fresh mint leaves
- 1½ tablespoons peeled minced fresh ginger
- 3 cups non-fat plain yogurt, whisked until the desired smoothness is achieved
- 5 to 6 scallions, white and light green parts, minced

Directions:

1. In a serving container, combine the yogurt, ginger, scallions, sugar, and salt.
2. Garnish with paprika and mint before you serve.

ICED RAITA

This recipe is called "Mattha" in Hindi

Yield: 4 to 6 servings

Ingredients:

- ¼ teaspoon salt, or to taste
- 1 cup crushed ice (kept chilled)
- 3 cups non-fat plain yogurt, whisked until the desired smoothness is achieved
- Freshly ground black pepper, to taste

Directions:

1. Mix everything together in a big container and serve instantly.

LEMON PICKLE RAITA

This recipe is called "Nimboo achaar ka raita" in Hindi

Yield: 4 to 6 servings

Ingredients:

- 1 tablespoon Crushed Lemon and Fresh Red Chile Pepper Pickle
- 2 to 3 tablespoons snipped chives
- 3 cups non-fat plain yogurt, whisked until the desired smoothness is achieved

Directions:

1. Ready the pickle. Next, place the yogurt in a serving container and stir in the lemon pickle. Add salt and pepper, if required.
2. Put in the chives and stir mildly to combine, with some of them visible as a decoration.

VEGETABLE RAITAS

BEET AND SCALLION RAITA

This recipe is called "Chukandar aur harae pyaz ka raita" in Hindi

Yield: 4 to 6 servings

Ingredients:

- four to five scallions, minced
- ½ teaspoon freshly ground black pepper, or to taste
- ½ teaspoon salt, or to taste
- 1 fresh green chile pepper, such as serrano, minced with seeds
- 1 teaspoon minced fresh garlic
- 2 cups non-fat plain yogurt, whisked until the desired smoothness is achieved

- 2 tablespoons finely chopped cilantro
- 3 medium beets

Directions:

1. Put the beets in a small pan with water to cover by 2 inches and bring to a boil using high heat. Decrease the heat to moderate to low, cover the pan, and simmer until tender, approximately fifteen minutes. Turn off the heat, allow to cool down, then peel and cut finely. Let sit for about 1 tablespoon for garnish.
2. Put the yogurt in a serving dish and stir in the beets, scallions, garlic, green chile pepper, salt, and black pepper. Garnish with the reserved beets and the cilantro before you serve.

CUCUMBER AND RADISH RAITA

This recipe is called "Kheera aur mooli ka raita" in Hindi

Yield: 4 to 6 servings

Ingredients:

- ½ teaspoon freshly ground black pepper, or to taste
- ½ teaspoon ground paprika
- ½ teaspoon salt, or to taste
- 1 fresh green chile pepper, such as serrano, minced with seeds
- 1 large firm tomato, finely chopped
- 1 teaspoon Chaat Masala (Homemade or store-bought)
- 2 cups non-fat plain yogurt, whisked until the desired smoothness is achieved
- 2 to 4 seedless cucumbers, grated (peeled or unpeeled)
- Cilantro or mint leaves
- twelve to fifteen red radishes, grated and squeezed

Directions:

1. Ready the chaat masala. Put the yogurt in a serving container. Put in the cucumbers, radishes, tomato, green chile pepper, chaat masala, salt, and pepper and stir to mix thoroughly.
2. Garnish with the paprika and cilantro or mint leaves before you serve.

KASHMIRI MOREL MUSHROOM RAITA

This recipe is called "Kashmiri gucchiyon ka raita" in Hindi

Yield: 4 to 6 servings

Ingredients:

- ¼ cup finely chopped fresh cilantro
- 1 medium onion, cut in half along the length and thinly chopped
- 1 medium russet potato
- 1 tablespoon vegetable oil
- 2½ teaspoons Kashmiri Raita Masala
- 3 cups non-fat plain yogurt, whisked until the desired smoothness is achieved
- 8 to 10 large fresh or dried reconstituted morel mushrooms, thinly chopped
- Salt, to taste

Directions:

1. Boil the potato in lightly salted water to cover until tender, then peel it and finely cut it. While it's cooking, ready the raita masala. Next, place the yogurt in a big serving container and stir in 2 teaspoons raita masala. Add salt, if required (there is already some in the masala).
2. Heat the oil in a small-sized non-stick skillet using moderate to high heat and cook the onion, stirring, until a golden colour is achieved, approximately two to three minutes. Put in the potato and cook, stirring, approximately one minute, then put in the morel mushrooms and cilantro and cook another minute. Move to the yogurt, and mix thoroughly. Garnish with the rest of the ½ teaspoon raita masala and serve.

MUSTARD SEED RAITA

This recipe is called "Raayi ka raita" in Hindi

Yield: 4 to 6 servings

Ingredients:

- ¼ cup finely chopped fresh cilantro
- ½ teaspoon salt, or to taste
- 1 small red onion, finely chopped
- 1 tablespoon black mustard seeds
- 1 tablespoon yellow or brown mustard seeds
- 1 to 2 teaspoons mustard oil or peanut oil
- 3 to 4 pickling cucumbers, peeled and finely chopped
- 4 cups non-fat plain yogurt, whisked until the desired smoothness is achieved

Directions:

1. In a mortar and pestle or a spice grinder, crudely grind all the mustard seeds. Transfer to a small non-reactive container and stir in approximately ½ cup yogurt and the salt. Set aside to ferment at least 4 and maximum 1two hours at room temperature.
2. Put the yogurt in a big serving container and stir in the fermented mustard seed mixture. Stir in the cucumbers and onions. Swirl in the mustard oil, garnish with the cilantro before you serve.

POTATO AND BEET RAITA

This recipe is called "Aalu aur chukandar ka raita" in Hindi

Yield: 4 to 6 servings

Ingredients:

- ⅓ teaspoon salt, or to taste
- 1 tablespoon peeled minced fresh ginger

- 1 tablespoon sesame seeds
- 1 teaspoon cumin seeds
- 1 teaspoon sugar
- 1 to 2 tablespoons fresh lemon juice
- 2 cups non-fat plain yogurt, whisked until the desired smoothness is achieved
- 2 small beets
- 3 small russet potatoes

Directions:

1. Put the potatoes and beets in a small sauce-pan with water to cover and bring to a boil using high heat. Decrease the heat to moderate to low, cover the pan, and simmer until tender, approximately fifteen minutes. Turn off the heat, allow to cool down, then peel and cut them finely.
2. While the beets and potatoes are cooking, place the sesame and cumin seeds in a small-sized non-stick saucepan and dry-roast using moderate to high heat until they are fragrant and seems slightly darker, approximately two minutes. Allow to cool, then grind crudely in a mortar and pestle or a spice grinder.
3. Put the yogurt in a big serving container. Stir in the lemon juice, ginger, sugar, salt, and half the sesame seeds. Stir in the potatoes and fold in the beets. Sprinkle the rest of the sesame seeds and the cumin seeds on top and serve.

POTATO AND CUMIN RAITA

This recipe is called "Jeerae aur aalu ka raita" in Hindi

Yield: 4 to 6 servings

Ingredients:

- ⅓ teaspoon salt, or to taste
- ½ cup minced chives or scallion greens
- ½ red bell pepper, finely chopped
- ½ teaspoon black peppercorns, or to taste
- 1 large russet potato

- 1¼ teaspoons cumin seeds
- 2½ cups non-fat plain yogurt, whisked until the desired smoothness is achieved

Directions:

1. Boil the potato in lightly salted water to cover until tender, then peel it, and cut it finely. Next, place the cumin and black peppercorns in a small-sized non-stick saucepan and dry-roast using moderate to high heat until they are fragrant and seems slightly darker, approximately two minutes. Allow to cool, then grind crudely in a mortar and pestle or a spice grinder.
2. Put the yogurt in a serving container, stir in the potato, salt, and half the ground cumin-pepper mixture.
3. Put in the chives and stir mildly to combine, with a few of them visible as a decoration. Top with the rest of the cumin-pepper mixture, scatter the red bell pepper over everything before you serve.

POTATO-MUSTARD RAITA

This recipe is called "Aalu aur saag ka raita" in Hindi

Yield: 4 to 6 servings

Ingredients:

- ¼ teaspoon salt, or to taste
- 1 cup crudely chopped fresh cilantro, including soft stems
- 1 cup crudely chopped fresh spinach leaves
- 1 large russet potato
- 1 teaspoon cumin seeds
- 1 teaspoon ground pomegranate seeds
- 2 cups non-fat plain yogurt, whisked until the desired smoothness is achieved
- 3 to 4 scallions, crudely chopped

Directions:

1. Boil the potato in lightly salted water to cover until tender, then peel it, and cut it finely. Next, place the cumin in a small-sized non-stick saucepan and dry-roast using moderate to high heat until they are fragrant and seems slightly darker, approximately two minutes. Allow to cool, then grind crudely in a mortar and pestle or a spice grinder. Next, place the yogurt in a big serving container; stir in the potato.
2. Using a food processor a blender, combine and pulse the spinach, cilantro, and scallions until puréed. Move to the yogurt. Put in the salt, pomegranate seeds, and half the cumin and mix thoroughly. Sprinkle the rest of the cumin on top and stir mildly with a fork, with most of it visible as a decoration. Serve.

SPROUTED BEANS AND VEGETABLE RAITA

This recipe is called "Phooti dalon aur sabziyon ka raita" in Hindi

Yield: 4 to 6 servings

Ingredients:

- ¼ cup finely chopped fresh cilantro, including soft stems
- ½ cup sprouted split mung beans (mung dal) (Homemade or store-bought)
- ½ teaspoon freshly ground black pepper, or to taste
- ½ teaspoon salt, or to taste
- 1 cup sprouted red lentils (Homemade or store-bought)
- 1 fresh green chile pepper, such as serrano, minced with seeds
- 1 small tomato, finely chopped
- 1 teaspoon Chaat Masala (Homemade or store-bought)
- 1 teaspoon dry-roasted sesame seeds
- 1 to 4 seedless cucumbers, grated (peeled or unpeeled)
- 2 cups non-fat plain yogurt, whisked until the desired smoothness is achieved

Directions:

1. Ready the beans and lentils in advance. Ready the sesame seeds and chaat masala.
2. Put the yogurt in a big serving container. Stir in everything except 2 tablespoons of the red lentils, the sesame seeds, and the chaat masala. Sprinkle the reserved red lentils and sesame seeds on top, top with the chaat masala before you serve.

TOMATO AND MINT LEAVES RAITA

This recipe is called "Tamatar aur pudinae ka raita" in Hindi

Yield: 4 to 6 servings

Ingredients:

- ¼ cup finely chopped fresh mint leaves
- ¼ teaspoon crudely ground black pepper
- ½ teaspoon cumin seeds
- ½ teaspoon salt, or to taste
- 1 large tomato, finely chopped
- 1 teaspoon minced fresh garlic
- 2 cups non-fat plain yogurt, whisked until the desired smoothness is achieved
- 3 to 4 scallions, green parts only, thinly chopped

Directions:

1. Put the sesame and cumin seeds in a small-sized non-stick saucepan and dry-roast using moderate to high heat until they are fragrant and seems slightly darker, approximately two minutes. Allow to cool, then grind crudely in a mortar and pestle or a spice grinder.
2. Put the yogurt in a serving dish and stir in the mint, tomato, scallions, garlic, and salt. Sprinkle black pepper and cumin on top and stir mildly to combine, with parts of them visible as a decoration. Serve.

RAITAS WITH HERBS AND GREENS

FRESH SPINACH RAITA WITH GINGER-LIME PICKLE

This recipe is called "Palak ka khatta raita" in Hindi

Yield: 4 to 6 servings

Ingredients:

- ⅓ teaspoon freshly ground black pepper, or to taste
- ⅓ teaspoon salt, or to taste
- 1 small bunch (8 to 10 ounces) fresh spinach, trimmed of roots only, washed and finely chopped
- 1 tablespoon Minced Ginger-Lime Pickle
- 1 teaspoon <u>dry-roasted</u> and crudely ground cumin seeds
- 2½ cups non-fat plain yogurt, whisked until the desired smoothness is achieved

Directions:

1. Ready the ginger-lime pickle in advance. Ready the cumin seeds. Next, place the yogurt in a serving container. Put in the spinach, ginger-lime pickle, salt, and black pepper, and stir to mix.
2. Lightly swirl in the cumin seeds, with parts of them visible as a decoration before you serve.

FROZEN SPINACH RAITA

This recipe is called "Barafeela palak raita" in Hindi

Yield: 4 to 6 servings

Ingredients:

- ¼ teaspoon black mustard seeds
- ¼ teaspoon ground black salt (not compulsory)
- ¼ teaspoon salt, or to taste
- ¼ teaspoon whole cumin seeds + 1 teaspoon <u>dry-roasted</u> and crudely ground cumin seeds
- 1 (10-ounce) package thawed frozen spinach (reserve all juices)
- 1 small onion, finely chopped
- 1 teaspoon olive oil
- 1 teaspoon peeled minced fresh ginger
- 3 cups non-fat plain yogurt, whisked until the desired smoothness is achieved
- A scant pinch ground asafoetida

Directions:

1. Ready the roasted cumin seeds. Next, place the yogurt in a serving container. Stir in the salt and black salt.
2. Heat the oil in a small saucepan using moderate to high heat. Put in the mustard seeds and ¼ teaspoon whole cumin seeds; they should sizzle when they touch the hot oil. Swiftly stir in the asafoetida, then the onion and ginger, and cook, stirring, until a golden colour is achieved, approximately three minutes.
3. Put in the spinach plus all the juices and cook until most of the fluids vaporize, approximately four minutes. Allow to cool, then stir well into the yogurt. Mix half the roasted cumin into the yogurt, sprinkle the rest of the on top before you serve.

GREEN RAITA

This recipe is called "Hara raita" in Hindi

Yield: 4 to 6 servings

Ingredients:

- ½ cup crudely chopped fresh cilantro, including soft stems

- ½ teaspoon salt, or to taste
- 1 cup finely chopped yellow and red tomatoes
- 1 cup firmly packed fresh watercress leaves
- 1 fresh green chile pepper, such as serrano, stemmed
- 1 teaspoon dry-roasted and crudely ground cumin seeds
- 2 to 3 cups non-fat plain yogurt, whisked until the desired smoothness is achieved
- 3 large scallions, crudely chopped
- Freshly ground black pepper, to taste

Directions:

1. Ready the cumin seeds. Next, Using a food processor or a blender, combine and pulse the scallions, green chile pepper, cilantro, and watercress until a smooth purée is achieved.
2. Put the yogurt in a serving container and stir in the puréed greens and salt. Pile up the tomatoes in the center. (Do not mix them into the raita.) Sprinkle the roasted cumin and black pepper on top before you serve.

SAUTÉED SPINACH RAITA

This recipe is called "Bhuni palak ka raita" in Hindi

Yield: 4 to 6 servings

Ingredients:

- ¼ cup roasted peanuts, crudely chopped
- ½ teaspoon salt, or to tasteFreshly ground black pepper, to taste
- 1 small bunch fresh spinach (8 to 10 ounces), trimmed of roots only, washed and finely chopped,
- 1 tablespoon peeled minced fresh ginger
- 1 tablespoon vegetable oil
- 1 teaspoon dry-roasted and crudely ground cumin seeds (See the dry-roasting section in Introduction)
- 1 teaspoon minced fresh garlic
- 1 teaspoon sesame seeds, dry-roasted (See the dry-roasting section in Introduction)

- 3 cups non-fat plain yogurt, whisked until the desired smoothness is achieved

Directions:

1. Ready the cumin and sesame seeds. Next, heat the oil in a big non-stick wok or saucepan using moderate to high heat and cook the ginger and garlic, stirring, until a golden colour is achieved, approximately one minute. Put in the spinach and cook, stirring, until completely wilted and slightly golden, three to five minutes. Set aside to cool.
2. Put the yogurt in a serving container. Put in the salt, then stir in the cooled spinach, plus any juices that may have accumulated.
3. Lightly swirl in the cumin and sesame seeds, and the black pepper, with parts of them visible as a decoration. Sprinkle the peanuts on top andserve.

SPICY RAITA WITH LAMB'S QUARTERS

This recipe is called "Bathuae ka raita" in Hindi

Yield: 4 to 6 servings

Ingredients:

- ¼ teaspoon salt, or to taste
- 1 fresh green chile pepper, such as serrano, minced with seeds
- 1 teaspoon cumin seeds
- 1 to 2 teaspoons olive oil
- 2 cups finely chopped lamb's quarters leaves
- 2 cups non-fat plain yogurt, whisked until the desired smoothness is achieved
- 3 to 4 scallions, green parts only, finely chopped
- Freshly ground black pepper, to taste

Directions:

1. Put the leaves in a big saucepan of water to cover using high heat and bring to a boil. Boil until soft, about four to five minutes. Another way is to cover

and cook in a microwave-safe dish on high, approximately two to three minutes.
2. Allow to cool. Move to a food processor and pulse until crudely chopped, or cut by hand.
3. Put the yogurt in a serving dish and softly stir in the greens. Put in the scallions, salt, and black pepper, and mix once more.
4. Heat the oil in a small saucepan using moderate to high heat and put in the chile pepper and cumin seeds; they should sizzle when they touch the hot oil. Swiftly put them in to the yogurt, swirl lightly before you serve.

TOFU AND GREENS MIX RAITA

This recipe is called "Tofu ka hara raita" in Hindi

Yield: 4 to 6 servings

Ingredients:

- ¼ teaspoon salt, or to taste
- ½ cup crudely chopped fresh cilantro, including soft stems
- ½ teaspoon Roasted Cumin-Pepper Masala
- 1 (10½-ounce) package firm tofu, towel-dried and crudely crumbled
- 1 cup crudely chopped fresh dry spinach leaves, rinsed and blotted
- 1 fresh green chile pepper, such as serrano, minced with seeds
- 1 tablespoon peeled minced fresh ginger
- 1½ cups non-fat plain yogurt, whisked until the desired smoothness is achieved
- 4 to 6 scallions, white parts only, minced

Directions:

1. Ready the masala. Next, Using a food processor or blender, combine and pulse the tofu, spinach, and cilantro until the desired smoothness is achieved.
2. Move to a serving container, stir in the yogurt, ginger, scallions, chile pepper, and salt. Garnish with the cumin-pepper masala and serve.

TOFU AND MINT CHUTNEY RAITA

This recipe is called "Tofu aur pudina chutni ka raita" in Hindi

Yield: 4 to 6 servings

Ingredients:

- ½ teaspoon salt, or to taste
- 1 (10½-ounce) package firm tofu, towel-dried and crudely crumbled
- 1 large red bell pepper, stemmed, seeded, and finely chopped
- 1 teaspoon Chaat Masala (Homemade or store-bought)
- 1½ cups non-fat plain yogurt, whisked until the desired smoothness is achieved
- 2 tablespoons Mint Chutney with Pomegranate Seeds

Directions:

1. Ready the chutney and the chaat masala. Next, place the yogurt in a big serving container and stir in the chutney, chaat masala, and salt.
2. Put in the tofu and mix once more. Garnish with the red bell pepper and serve.

GRILLED OR ROASTED VEGETABLE RAITAS

EGGPLANT AND SESAME RAITA

This recipe is called "Baigun-til ka raita" in Hindi

Yield: 4 to 6 servings

Ingredients:

- ½ teaspoon salt, or to taste
- 1 small oval eggplant, cut into 1-inch pieces
- 1 tablespoon <u>dry-roasted</u> sesame seeds
- 1 tablespoon vegetable oil
- 1 teaspoon crudely crushed ajwain seeds
- 1 teaspoon minced fresh garlic
- 3 cups non-fat plain yogurt, whisked until the desired smoothness is achieved
- 3 to 4 drops sesame oil

Directions:

1. Ready the sesame seeds. Next, heat both the oils in a big non-stick wok or saucepan using moderate to high heat and cook the garlic and ajwain seeds, stirring, until a golden colour is achieved, approximately half a minute. Put in the eggplant and cook, stirring, until a golden brown colour is achieved, approximately five to seven minutes. Cover the pan and cook using low heat until the eggplant pieces are very soft, approximately eight to ten minutes. Allow to cool.
2. Put the yogurt in a serving container. Put in the salt, then stir in the cooled eggplant, plus any juices that may have accumulated. Stir in the sesame seeds, with some of them visible as a decoration. Serve.

GARLICK CHINESE EGGPLANT RAITA

This recipe is called "Lambae baigan-lussan ka raita" in Hindi

Yield: 4 to 6 servings

Ingredients:

- ¼ cup finely chopped fresh cilantro, including soft stems
- ¼ teaspoon ground paprika
- ½ teaspoon cayenne pepper, or to taste
- ½ teaspoon dry-roasted and crudely ground cumin seeds (See the dry-roasting section in Introduction)
- ½ teaspoon freshly ground black pepper, to taste
- ½ teaspoon salt, or to taste

- 1 pound long, thin Chinese eggplants, cut into ¼-inch diagonal slices
- 1 teaspoon minced fresh garlic
- 1 teaspoon olive oil
- 2 cups non-fat plain yogurt, whisked until the desired smoothness is achieved

Directions:

1. Ready the cumin seeds. Next, preheat the oven to 500°F. Put the eggplant in a container and toss with the oil, garlic, and cayenne pepper. Move to a broiler tray and roast on the center rack until browned on the underside, approximately five to seven minutes. Leaving the tray on the same rack, switch to the broiler heat (or raise the heat to broil and move the tray to the broiler, if required). Broil until the tops of the vegetables are soft and mildly charred, three to five minutes. Allow to cool.
2. Put the yogurt in a big serving container and stir in the salt and black pepper. Put in the roasted eggplant and cilantro, and mix thoroughly. Garnish with the roasted cumin and paprika before you serve.

GRILLED EGGPLANT RAITA

This recipe is called "Bhunae baigan ka raita" in Hindi

Yield: 4 to 6 servings

Ingredients:

- ¼ cup finely chopped fresh cilantro, with soft stems
- ½ teaspoon freshly ground black pepper, or to taste
- ½ teaspoon ground cayenne pepper
- ½ teaspoon salt, or to taste
- 1 tablespoon dry-roasted sesame seeds (See the dry-roasting section in Introduction)
- 1 teaspoon minced fresh garlic
- 2 cups non-fat plain yogurt, whisked until the desired smoothness is achieved
- 2 teaspoons dry-roasted and crudely ground cumin seeds (See the dry-roasting section in Introduction)

- 2 to 3 (1¼ pounds) small eggplants, roasted, any method, peeled, and mashed (See the "Roasting and Grilling Vegetables" section in Introduction)

Directions:

1. Ready the cumin and sesame seeds. Ready the eggplants.
2. Put the yogurt in a serving container and stir in the mashed eggplant. Put in the garlic, cilantro, cumin, cayenne pepper, salt, and black pepper. Garnish with the sesame seeds and serve.

GRILLED ZUCCHINI AND ONION RAITA

This recipe is called "Bhuna ghia aur chotae pyaz ka raita" in Hindi

Yield: 4 to 6 servings

Ingredients:

- ½ cup finely chopped fresh cilantro, including soft stems
- ½ teaspoon salt, or to taste
- 1 tablespoon Roasted Cumin-Pepper Masala
- 2 cups non-fat plain yogurt, whisked until the desired smoothness is achieved
- 20 pearl onions, peeled
- 3 small zucchini

Directions:

1. Ready the cumin-pepper masala. Next, preheat a grill using moderate to high heat, and grill the zucchini and onions according to Roasting and Grilling Vegetables directions. Set aside the onions. Let the zucchini cool, then lightly remove the charred skin (leave some of the charred bits on for flavour), and mash the zucchini.
2. Put the yogurt in a big serving container and stir in the zucchini pulp, onions, cilantro, salt, and half the cumin-pepper masala. Lightly swirl in the rest of the masala, with some of it visible as a decoration. Serve.

ROASTED BELL PEPPER RAITA

This recipe is called "Bhuni shimla mirch ka raita" in Hindi

Yield: 4 to 6 servings

Ingredients:

- ½ teaspoon ajwain seeds, crudely ground
- ½ teaspoon salt, or to taste
- 1 teaspoon minced fresh garlic
- 1 teaspoon olive oil
- 2 cups non-fat plain yogurt, whisked until the desired smoothness is achieved
- 3 to 4 bell peppers of different colors, stemmed, seeded, and cut into 3/4-inch pieces
- Fresh mint leaves
- Freshly ground black pepper, to taste

Directions:

1. Preheat your oven to 500°F. Put the bell peppers in a container and toss with the oil, garlic, and ajwain seeds. Move to a broiler tray and roast on the center rack until browned on the underside, approximately five to seven minutes. Leaving the tray on the same rack, switch the oven to broiler heat (and move the tray to the broiler, if required). Broil until the tops of the vegetables are soft and mildly charred, three to five minutes.
2. Put the yogurt in a big serving container, stir in the salt and black pepper, then put in the roasted bell peppers. Garnish with mint and serve.

FRESH AND DRIED FRUIT RAITAS

BANANA RAITA

This recipe is called "Kaelae ka raita" in Hindi

Yield: 4 to 6 servings

Ingredients:

- ¼ cup any sonth chutney of your choice
- ¼ cup chopped raw almonds
- ¼ teaspoon salt, or to taste
- ½ teaspoon dry-roasted and crudely ground cumin seeds (See the dry-roasting section in Introduction)
- ½ teaspoon freshly ground black pepper, or to taste
- 1 tablespoon sugar
- 2 cups non-fat plain yogurt, whisked until the desired smoothness is achieved
- 2 small ripe bananas, peeled and chopped diagonally

Directions:

1. Ready the chutney and the cumin seeds. Next, place the yogurt in a container and stir in the sugar, salt, black pepper, and half the almonds.
2. Gently stir in the bananas. Next, swirl in the sonth chutney, sprinkle the cumin seeds and the rest of the almonds on top before you serve.

DRIED FRUIT RAITA

This recipe is called "Sookhae phallon ka raita" in Hindi

Yield: 4 to 6 servings

Ingredients:

- ¼ cup any sonth chutney of your choice
- ½ cup finely chopped fresh cilantro, including soft stems
- ½ cup lowfat milk
- ½ teaspoon freshly ground black pepper
- ½ teaspoon salt, or to taste
- 1 cup finely chopped mixed dried fruit, such as peaches, plums, apricots, and raisins

- 1 teaspoon Chaat Masala (Homemade or store-bought)
- 2 cups non-fat plain yogurt, whisked until the desired smoothness is achieved

Directions:

1. Ready the chutney and the masala. Next, place the milk and the dried fruits in a microwave-safe container and cook on high, approximately one minute. Cover the container and allow the dried fruits to soften, approximately one hour. Allow to cool, then move them, with the liquid, to a serving container.
2. Put in the yogurt, salt, pepper, and cilantro, and mix thoroughly. Lightly swirl in the sonth chutney, with parts of it visible as a decoration. Sprinkle the chaat masala on top and serve.

MANDARIN ORANGE RAITA

This recipe is called "Suntarae ka raita" in Hindi

Yield: 4 to 6 servings

Ingredients:

- ¼ cup shelled and crudely chopped raw peanuts, without the red skin
- ¼ teaspoon salt, or to taste
- 1 cup canned mandarin orange segments, drained well
- 1 tablespoon peeled minced fresh ginger
- 1 teaspoon Chaat Masala (Homemade or store-bought)
- 2 cups non-fat plain yogurt, whisked until the desired smoothness is achieved
- 2 tablespoons finely chopped fresh mint leaves
- 2 teaspoons Chile Pepper Paste, or to taste

Directions:

1. Ready the chile paste and the chaat masala. Next, place the yogurt in a serving container and stir in the chile paste, chaat masala, and salt. Fold in the mandarin segments, ginger, and mint leaves.

2. Put the peanuts in a small skillet and roast using moderate heat until it begins to look golden and releases its fragrance, approximately two minutes. Scatter over the yogurt mixture and serve.

MANGO CHUTNEY RAITA

This recipe is called "Aam ki chutni ka raita" in Hindi

Yield: 4 to 6 servings

Ingredients:

- ½ cup Fragrant Mango Chutney Preserve
- 2 cups non-fat plain yogurt, whisked until the desired smoothness is achieved
- 2 tablespoons Dessert Masala

Directions:

1. Ready the mango chutney and the dessert masala. Next, Using a food processor or blender, combine and pulse the chutney and 1 cup yogurt until the desired smoothness is achieved.
2. Transfer to a serving container and stir in the rest of the yogurt. Put in the dessert masala and stir mildly to combine, with parts of it visible as a decoration.

MANGO-GINGER RAITA

This recipe is called "Aam-adrak ka raita" in Hindi

Yield: 4 to 6 servings

Ingredients:

- ½ teaspoon freshly ground black pepper, or to taste
- ½ teaspoon salt, or to taste
- 1 fresh green chile pepper, such as serrano, minced with seeds

- 1 tablespoon fresh lemon juice
- 1 tablespoon peeled minced fresh ginger
- 2 cups non-fat plain yogurt, whisked until the desired smoothness is achieved
- 2 large soft ripe mangoes

Directions:

1. Cut or peel off the skin of the mangoes, then cut around the seed to make 2 cheeks of the flesh. Cut this fruit and the other fruit left near the seed into ½-inch pieces. Put three-quarters of the pieces in a shallow serving dish. Crudely mash the rest of the quarter with a fork to make a textured, chunky sauce, and set the sauce aside.
2. To the mango chunks, put in the yogurt, ginger, lemon juice, green chile pepper, salt, and black pepper, and mix gently. Drizzle the mango sauce on top and serve.

DUMPLING RAITAS

Tiny droplets of chickpea flour batter, deep-fried until a golden colour is achieved and crisp, are called boondi. Many Indian home cooks rely on them, sometimes as a main ingredient to make special raitas (in this chapter) or curries, etc.

"Crispy Chickpea Batter Drops" or "boondi" can be made at home, but are much more convenient to buy from a market because of the ultra-cheap price and easy availability. Search for them in a nearby Indian store, or you can always buy them online from amazon.

CRISPY CHICKPEA BATTER DROPS RAITA

This recipe is called "Sookhi boondi ka raita" in Hindi

Yield: 4 to 6 servings

Ingredients:

- ¼ cup finely chopped fresh cilantro, including soft stems
- ¼ teaspoon salt, or to taste
- ½ teaspoon freshly ground black pepper, or to taste
- ½ teaspoon ground paprika for garnish
- 1 teaspoon dry-roasted and crudely ground cumin seeds
- 2 cups non-fat plain yogurt, whisked until the desired smoothness is achieved
- 2 cups savory Crispy Chickpea Batter Drops (Boondi) or store-bought

Directions:

1. Ready the boondi and the cumin. Next, place the yogurt in a serving container and stir in the salt, black pepper, cumin, and paprika.
2. Lightly stir in the boondi with some of them visible as garnish (or just mound them all on top). Sprinkle the cilantro on top and serve instantly (or the boondi will get soggy).

CRISPY URAD DAL CROQUETTES IN YOGURT

This recipe is called "Sookhae dahi bhallae" in Hindi

Yield: 4 to 6 servings

Ingredients:

- ¼ cup any sonth chutney of your choice, such as Minty Sonth Chutney with Mango Powder and Jaggery
- ¼ teaspoon salt, or to taste
- ½ cup lowfat milk
- ½ teaspoon cayenne pepper, or to taste
- ½ teaspoon freshly ground black pepper, or to taste
- ½ to 1 cup Fresh Coconut Chutney with Cilantro
- 1 tablespoon minced fresh cilantro, including soft stems
- 1 tablespoon minced fresh green mint leaves

- 1 teaspoon cumin seeds, dry-roasted and crudely ground (See the dry-roasting section in Introduction)
- 1 to 2 fresh green chile peppers, such as serrano, minced with seeds
- 2 teaspoons New Delhi Street Food Masala (Papri Masala)or to taste
- 3 cups non-fat plain yogurt, whisked until the desired smoothness is achieved
- 5 to 6 (½ recipe) Mung Bean Croquettes

Directions:

1. Ready the croquettes, cumin, masala, and chutneys in advance, if possible. Put the yogurt in a big serving dish, stir in the coconut chutney, milk, salt, black pepper, cayenne pepper, and roasted cumin, and refrigerate until needed.
2. An hour before you serve, cut each croquette in half across the width and add to the yogurt. Mix softly until all of the croquettes are coated thoroughly with yogurt. Drizzle the sonth chutney on top. Garnish with the masala, green chile peppers, mint, and cilantro before you serve.

MUNG BEAN CROQUETTES RAITA

This recipe is called "Pakaudhiyon ka raita" in Hindi

Yield: 4 to 6 servings

Ingredients:

- ½ teaspoon freshly ground pepper, or to taste
- ½ teaspoon salt, or to taste
- 1 fresh green chile pepper, such as serrano, minced with seeds
- 16 to 20 (1 recipe) Mung Bean Croquettes
- 2 tablespoons finely chopped fresh cilantro, with soft stems
- 2 teaspoons dry-roasted and crudely ground cumin seeds (See the dry-roasting section in Introduction)
- 3 cups water for soaking the croquettes
- 3 to 4 cups non-fat plain yogurt, whisked until the desired smoothness is achieved

Directions:

1. Ready the cumin seeds and the croquettes. Next, place the yogurt in a big serving container, stir in the salt, black pepper, and 1 teaspoon cumin seeds, and refrigerate until needed.
2. An hour before you serve, put the water in a big saucepan, bring to a boil, then remove from the heat and soak the croquettes until they absorb the water and become soft, approximately two to three minutes. Press lightly to see if the center is soft; if not, add more water (if needed) and bring to a boil again using high heat. When the croquettes are soft, remove them from water; allow to cool down. Once cool sufficient to hold, press each croquette between the palms of your hands to squeeze out all the surplus water.
3. Put in the croquettes to the yogurt and mix softly until all croquettes are coated thoroughly with the yogurt. Garnish with the rest of the 1 teaspoon cumin, green chile pepper, and cilantro before you serve.

RAITA WITH CHICKPEA FLOUR PANCAKES

This recipe is called "Doiyon ka raita" in Hindi

Yield: 4 to 6 servings

Ingredients:

- ⅛ teaspoon baking soda
- ⅛ teaspoon salt, or to taste
- ¼ cup chickpea flour
- ¼ cup water
- 1 fresh green chile pepper, such as serrano, minced with seeds
- 1 tablespoon finely chopped fresh cilantro, including soft stems
- 1 tablespoon minced fresh mint leaves
- 1 to 2 tablespoons peanut oil
- 2 cups non-fat plain yogurt, whisked until the desired smoothness is achieved
- 2 tablespoons minced scallions, white parts only
- 2 teaspoons Punjabi Raita and Buttermilk Masala

Directions:

1. Ready the masala. Next, in a small-sized container, combine the chickpea flour, baking soda, salt, scallions, cilantro, and green chile pepper. Put in the water to make a semi-thin batter. Set aside for approximately half an hour to rest.
2. Heat 1 teaspoon of the oil in a moderate-sized non-stick skillet over moderate heat. Add approximately 2 tablespoons of the batter and spread it using a spatula to make a 3-inch pancake. When the bottom turns golden, approximately one minute, turn it over and slide it toward the side of the pan, making room for others. Make similar pancakes with the rest of the batter, starting in the center and moving out the side after the first side turns golden. Add more oil, as needed.
3. When the bottoms of the pancakes at the side of the pan brown, approximately one minute, turn them over and let the other side brown, approximately half a minute, then remove to a plate. Break each pancake into ½-inch pieces and set aside.
4. In a serving container, combine the yogurt, raita masala, and the pancake pieces. Garnish with the mint and serve.

SOFTENED CHICKPEA BATTER DROPS RAITA

This recipe is called "Bheegi boondi ka raita" in Hindi

Yield: 4 to 6 servings

Ingredients:

- ¼ cup lowfat milk
- ½ teaspoon freshly ground black pepper
- ½ teaspoon ground paprika
- ½ teaspoon salt, or to taste
- 1 tablespoon finely chopped scallion, green parts only
- 1 tablespoon fresh cilantro
- 1 teaspoon dry-roasted and crudely ground cumin seeds (See the dry-roasting section in Introduction)

- 2 cups non-fat plain yogurt, whisked until the desired smoothness is achieved
- 2½ cups Crispy Chickpea Batter Drops (Boondi) or store-bought
- 3 cups boiling water for soaking the boondi

Directions:

1. Ready the boondi drops and cumin. Next, in a serving container, whisk together the yogurt and milk until the desired smoothness is achieved.
2. Immerse the boondi in boiling water, approximately 1 min-ute, then move to a fine-mesh strainer and drain. Press lightly on the boondi to squeeze out all the surplus water.
3. Put in the boondi to the yogurt, then stir in the salt, black pepper, and half the cumin. Garnish with the rest of the cumin, paprika, cilantro, and scallions before you serve.

SPICY MUNG BEAN CROQUETTES RAITA WITH SONTH CHUTNEY

This recipe is called "Pakaudhiyon ki chaat" in Hindi

Yield: 4 to 6 servings

Ingredients:

- ¼ cup any sonth chutney of your choice, such as Minty Sonth Chutney with Mango Powder and Jaggery
- ½ teaspoon freshly ground black pepper, or to taste
- ½ teaspoon ground paprika or cayenne pepper
- ½ teaspoon salt, or to taste
- 1 tablespoon finely chopped fresh cilantro
- 1 tablespoon peeled minced fresh ginger
- 1 teaspoon dry-roasted and crudely ground cumin seeds (See the dry-roasting section in Introduction)
- 1 to 3 fresh green chile peppers, such as serrano, minced with seeds
- 16 to 20 (1 recipe) Mung Bean Croquettes
- 2 tablespoons finely chopped fresh mint leaves

- 2 teaspoons New Delhi Street Food Masala
- 2 to 3 tablespoons Mint Chutney with Pomegranate Seeds
- 3 cups water for soaking the croquettes
- 3 to 4 cups non-fat plain yogurt, whisked until the desired smoothness is achieved

Directions:

1. Ready the cumin and the masala, the sonth and mint chutneys, and the croquettes—in advance, if possible.
2. Put the yogurt in a container, stir in the salt, black pepper, cumin, ginger, and mint leaves, and refrigerate until needed.
3. An hour before you serve, put the water in a big saucepan, bring to a boil, then remove from the heat and soak the croquettes until they absorb the water and become soft, approximately two to three minutes. Press lightly to see if the center is soft; if not, add more water (if needed) and bring to a boil again using high heat. When the croquettes are soft, remove them from water; allow to cool down. Once cool sufficient to hold, press each croquette between the palms of your hands to squeeze out all the surplus water.
4. Put croquettes in a big flat serving dish and cautiously pour the yogurt over the croquettes until they are coated thoroughly. Add more yogurt than you think is necessary, because the croquettes will absorb some of it. Drizzle the sonth chutney over the yogurt, then scatter the mint chutney on top. Garnish with the chile peppers, cilantro, chaat masala, and paprika or cayenne pepper before you serve.

URAD DAL CROQUETTES RAITA

This recipe is called "Dahi-vadae" in Hindi

Yield: 4 to 6 servings

Ingredients:

- ten to twelve (1 recipe) Punjabi-Style Fermented Urad Bean Croquettes
- ⅛ teaspoon ground asafoetida
- ¼ cup any sonth chutney of your choice, such as Minty Sonth Chutney with Mango Powder and Jaggery

- ¼ cup finely chopped fresh cilantro
- ½ cup lowfat milk
- ½ teaspoon cayenne pepper, or to taste
- ½ teaspoon ground black salt
- 1 tablespoon ground cumin
- 1 teaspoon ground paprika
- 1 to 3 fresh green chile peppers, such as serrano, stemmed +1 fresh green chile pepper, minced with seeds
- 3 cups water to soak croquettes
- 3 to 4 cups non-fat plain yogurt, whisked until the desired smoothness is achieved
- 4 quarter-size slices peeled fresh ginger

Directions:

1. Ready the croquettes and the sonth chutney. Next, in a small skillet, dry-roast together the cumin, cayenne pepper, black salt, and asafoetida over moderate heat, stirring and swaying the pan until fragrant and seems slightly darker, approximately two minutes. Allow to cool.
2. In a small food processor or blender, combine and pulse the ginger and stemmed green chile peppers with 1 to 2 tablespoons of the yogurt until a smooth paste is achieved.
3. In a moderate-sized container, whisk together the rest of the yogurt and milk until the desired smoothness is achieved. Stir in the ginger-chile pepper mixture and most of the roasted cumin-cayenne pepper mixture (save some for garnish), and refrigerate.
4. An hour before you serve, put the water in a big saucepan, bring to a boil, then remove from the heat and soak the croquettes until they absorb the water and become soft, approximately two to three minutes. Press lightly to see if the center is soft; if not, add more water (if needed) and bring to a boil again using high heat. When the croquettes are soft, remove them from water; allow to cool down. Once cool sufficient to hold, press each croquette between the palms of your hands to squeeze out all the surplus water.
5. Put the croquettes in a serving dish and pour the yogurt on top, ensuring that each croquette is coated thoroughly with yogurt. Add more yogurt than you think is needed, because the croquettes will absorb some of it. Drizzle the sonth chutney over the yogurt, then sprinkle the reserved cumin-cayenne pepper mixture, paprika, minced green chile pepper, and cilantro on top and serve.

MEAT RAITAS

GROUND LAMB RAITA

This recipe is called "Gosht ka raita" in Hindi

Yield: 4 to 6 servings

Ingredients:

- ¼ cup dried yellow split chickpeas (channa dal), sorted and washed in 3 to 4 changes of water
- ¼ teaspoon salt, or to taste
- ½ cup finely chopped fresh cilantro, including soft stems
- 1 cup finely chopped onion
- 1 cup trimmed and ground leg of lamb
- 1 fresh green chile pepper, such as serrano, minced with seeds
- 1 large clove fresh garlic, minced
- 1 tablespoon peeled minced fresh ginger
- 2 teaspoons ground coriander
- 2 teaspoons Kashmiri Raita Masala
- 4 cups non-fat plain yogurt, whisked until the desired smoothness is achieved

Directions:

1. Immerse the dal in water to cover, 1 hour. In the meantime, ready the raita masala. Next, place 3 cups of the yogurt in a big serving container. Stir in 1½ teaspoons of the raita masala. Reserve.
2. Drain the dal, then place it and the lamb, onion, garlic, cilantro, ginger, green chile pepper, coriander, and salt in a small-sized non-stick skillet and cook, stirring, using moderate to high heat until the lamb and onions brown, approximately five minutes. Put in the rest of the 1 cup yogurt and cook, stirring until the lamb and dal become soft, approximately twenty minutes.
3. Allow to cool, move to the container with the yogurt and masala, and mix thoroughly. Garnish with the rest of the ½ teaspoon raita masala and serve.

SHREDDED CHICKEN RAITA

This recipe is called "Murgh ka raita" in Hindi

Yield: 4 to 6 servings

Ingredients:

- ½ recipe Pan-Cooked Chile-Chicken Thighs
- 2 cups non-fat plain yogurt, whisked until the desired smoothness is achieved
- 2 to 3 tablespoons Crushed Lemon and Fresh Red Chile Pepper Pickle
- 2 to 3 tablespoons snipped chives

Directions:

1. Ready the pickle in advance. Ready the chicken. Shred the chicken pieces by hand or simply mince them into a food processor and set aside.
2. Put the yogurt in a big serving container and stir in the lemon pickle. Put in the chicken and mix thoroughly. Put in the chives and stir mildly to combine, with some of them visible as a decoration. Serve.

SOUTH INDIAN PACHADIS

These are raitas with South Indian seasonings, and taste quite different compared to the raitas we saw above.

CHOPPED SALAD YOGURT

This recipe is called "Cachumbar pachadi" in Hindi

Yield: 4 to 6 servings

Ingredients:

- ½ cup finely chopped fresh cilantro, including soft stems
- 1 fresh green chile pepper, such as serrano, minced with seeds
- 1 tablespoon grated fresh coconut or shredded unsweetened dried coconut
- 1 tablespoon peeled minced fresh ginger
- 1 teaspoon black mustard seeds
- 1 teaspoon cumin seeds
- 1 teaspoon dried white urad beans (dhulli urad dal)
- 1 teaspoon dried yellow split chickpeas (channa dal)
- 1 teaspoon salt, or to taste
- 2 cups non-fat plain yogurt (do not whisk)
- 2 tablespoons minced fresh curry leaves
- 2 teaspoons peanut oil
- 3 cups finely chopped mixed fresh vegetables, such as tomato, red and daikon radishes, cucumber, scallion, jicama, and zucchini
- A scant pinch ground asafoetida

Directions:

1. Put the chopped vegetables in a flat serving dish and stir in the cilantro, ginger, coconut, green chile pepper, and salt. Next, lightly fold in the yogurt.
2. Heat the oil in a small-sized non-stick saucepan using moderate to high heat and put in the cumin and mustard seeds; they should splatter when they touch the hot oil, so cover the pan and reduce the heat until the spluttering diminishes. Swiftly add both the dals, the asafoetida, and the curry leaves, and stir until the dals are golden, approximately one minute. Move the seasonings to the yogurt and stir mildly to combine, leaving most of it visible as a decoration. Serve.

CUCUMBER PACHADI

This recipe is called "kheera pachadi" in Hindi

Yield: 4 to 6 servings

Ingredients:

- ¼ teaspoon salt, or to taste
- ½ cup finely chopped fresh cilantro, including soft stems

- ½ teaspoon black mustard seeds
- ½ teaspoon cumin seeds
- 1 to 2 teaspoons peanut oil
- 2 cups non-fat plain yogurt (do not whisk)
- 2 to 3 fresh green chile peppers, such as serrano, cut in half along the length and seeded
- 3 small seedless cucumbers, peeled and grated
- 8 fresh green curry leaves

Directions:

1. Put the cucumbers, cilantro, and salt in a serving container, and fold in the yogurt until just incorporated.
2. Heat the oil in a small-sized non-stick saucepan using moderate to high heat and put in the cumin and mustard seeds; they should splutter when they touch the hot oil, so cover the pan and reduce the heat until the spluttering diminishes. Add 5 of the curry leaves and the green chile peppers and stir approximately one minute. Move the seasonings to the yogurt container and fold in gently. Lightly crumble the rest of the 3 curry leaves to release their aroma, and put them in to the pachadi as a decoration. Serve.

GREEN PAPAYA AND COCONUT PACHADI

This recipe is called "Hara papita aur nariyal pachadi" in Hindi

Yield: 4 to 6 servings

Ingredients:

- ⅛ teaspoon ground asafoetida
- ⅛ teaspoon ground paprika
- ¼ teaspoon ground black mustard seeds
- ½ cup crudely chopped fresh cilantro, including soft stems
- ½ cup grated fresh or frozen coconut
- ½ teaspoon salt, or to taste
- 1 small seedless cucumber, grated

- 1 small unripe green papaya, peeled and grated to make 1 cup
- 1 teaspoon black mustard seeds
- 1 teaspoon peanut oil
- 1 teaspoon sugar
- 1 to 2 dried red chile peppers, such as chile de arbol, crudely broken
- 1 to 3 fresh green chile peppers, such as serrano, crudely chopped
- 2 cups non-fat plain yogurt (do not whisk)
- 2 quarter-size slices peeled fresh ginger
- 2 small carrots, grated

Directions:

1. In a small food processor, combine and pulse the coconut, cilantro, ginger, green chile peppers, sugar, salt, and ground mustard seeds, adding approximately ¼ cup of the yogurt until a smooth paste is achieved.
2. Put the yogurt in a serving dish and very lightly stir in first the coconut paste, then the papaya, cucumber, and carrots, leaving a few vegetables showing their color through the yogurt.
3. Heat the oil in a small saucepan using moderate to high heat and cook the red chile peppers and mustard seeds; they should splutter when they touch the hot oil, so reduce the heat and cover the pan until the spluttering diminishes. Put in the asafoetida and paprika, then move the seasonings to the pachadi and stir it in, leaving some visible as a decoration. Serve.

GREEN TOMATO CHUTNEY PACHADI

This recipe is called "Harae-tamatar ki chutni ki pachadi" in Hindi

Yield: 4 to 6 servings

Ingredients:

- 1 small onion, crudely chopped
- 1 tablespoon black mustard seeds
- 1 tablespoon peanut oil
- 1 teaspoon salt, or to taste
- 1 teaspoon <u>South Indian Sambar Powder</u> (Homemade or store-bought)

- 1 to 3 fresh green chile peppers, such as serrano, crudely chopped with seeds
- 2 cups non-fat plain yogurt (do not whisk)
- 2 large firm green tomatoes, crudely chopped
- 2 tablespoons Tamarind Paste (Homemade or store-bought)
- 8 to 10 fresh curry leaves

Directions:

1. Ready the tamarind paste and sambar powder. Next, heat the oil in a big non-stick wok or saucepan using moderate to high heat and put in the mustard seeds; they should splutter when they touch the hot oil, so cover the pan and reduce the heat until the spluttering diminishes. Swiftly put in the green chile peppers, tomatoes, and onion, and cook, stirring, until the tomatoes are golden, approximately three minutes. Turn off the heat and allow to cool down.
2. Move to a food processor or blender, put in the tamarind, curry leaves, and salt, and process to make a smooth chutney.
3. Put the yogurt in a serving container and fold in the chutney, with parts of it visible as a decoration. Top with the sambar powder and serve.

MANGO AND COCONUT PACHADI

This recipe is called "Aam aur nariyal ki pachadi" in Hindi

Yield: 4 to 6 servings

Ingredients:

- ½ teaspoon salt, or to taste
- 1 fresh green chile pepper, such as serrano, minced with seeds
- 1 large semi-ripe mango, peeled and cut into ½-inch pieces
- 1 tablespoon dried coconut powder (kopra) or unsweetened shredded dried coconut
- 1 tablespoon peeled minced fresh ginger
- 1 teaspoon black mustard seeds
- 1 teaspoon peanut oil
- 1½ cups non-fat plain yogurt (do not whisk)

- 2 dried red chile peppers, such as chile de arbol, broken
- 5 to 7 fresh curry leaves
- A scant pinch ground asafoetida

Directions:

1. Put the mango pieces in a serving container and cautiously stir in the coconut powder (or dried coconut), ginger, green chile pepper, and salt. Next, fold in the yogurt.
2. Heat the oil in a small-sized non-stick saucepan using moderate to high heat and put in the red chile peppers and mustard seeds; they should splutter when they touch the hot oil, so cover the pan and reduce the heat until the spluttering diminishes. Swiftly put in the asafoetida and curry leaves and stir for approximately half a minute. Move to the yogurt and stir mildly to combine, leaving most of it visible on top as a decoration. Serve.

MASHED POTATO AND CILANTRO PACHADI

This recipe is called "Masslae aalu aur dhaniyae ki pachadi" in Hindi

Yield: 4 to 6 servings

Ingredients:

- ⅛ teaspoon ground asafoetida
- ¼ teaspoon ground turmeric
- ½ cup finely chopped fresh cilantro, including soft stems
- ½ teaspoon crudely ground black pepper
- ½ teaspoon fenugreek seeds, crudely ground
- 1 cup non-fat plain yogurt (do not whisk)
- 1 fresh green chile pepper, such as serrano, minced with seeds
- 1 pound russet (or boiling) potatoes
- 1 tablespoon peanut oil
- 1 teaspoon black mustard seeds
- 1 teaspoon cumin seeds
- 1 teaspoon dried yellow split chickpeas (channa dal)

- 1 teaspoon salt, or to taste
- 3 dried red chile peppers, such as chile de arbol, with stems
- 5 to 7 fresh curry leaves

Directions:

1. Boil the potatoes in lightly salted water to cover until soft, approximately twenty minutes. Allow to cool, then peel and mash them crudely with a fork.
2. Heat 1 teaspoon oil in a moderate-sized non-stick wok or saucepan using moderate to high heat and put in the cumin, fenugreek, black pepper, and asafoetida. Stir approximately half a minute. Put in the mashed potatoes, green chile pepper, turmeric, and salt, and cook, stirring, using moderate to high heat until heated through, approximately two minutes. Decrease the heat to low, cover the pan, and cook, stirring intermittently, approximately ten minutes.
3. Allow to cool to room temperature. Move to a serving container and fold in the yogurt until just incorporated. Lightly stir in the cilantro.
4. Heat the rest of the oil in a small-sized non-stick saucepan using moderate to high heat and put in the red chile peppers and mustard seeds; they should splutter when they touch the hot oil, so cover the pan and reduce the heat until the spluttering diminishes. Swiftly put in the dal and curry leaves and stir until a golden colour is achieved, approximately half a minute. Move to the yogurt container and stir mildly to combine, leaving most of it visible as a decoration. Serve.

PUMPKIN AND TAMARIND PACHADI

This recipe is called "Imli-petha ki pachadi" in Hindi

Yield: 4 to 6 servings

Ingredients:

- ⅛ teaspoon ground asafoetida
- ½ cup finely chopped fresh cilantro, including soft stems
- ½ teaspoon black peppercorns, crudely ground
- 1 cup non-fat plain yogurt, whisked until the desired smoothness is achieved
- 1 fresh green chile pepper, such as serrano, minced with seeds

- 1 pound pumpkin or any other orange squash, peeled and cut into ½-inch pieces
- 1 tablespoon peanut oil
- 1 teaspoon black mustard seeds
- 1 teaspoon dried coconut powder
- 1 teaspoon fenugreek seeds, crudely ground
- 1 teaspoon melted ghee
- 1 teaspoon salt, or to taste
- 2 teaspoons dried tamarind powder
- 3 whole dried red chile peppers, such as chile de arbol

Directions:

1. Heat the oil in a moderate-sized non-stick saucepan using moderate to high heat then put in the fenugreek, black peppercorns, and asafoetida; stir for approximately half a minute. Stir in the pumpkin, green chile pepper, and salt, and cook, stirring, using moderate to high heat until heated through, approximately two minutes. Decrease the heat to low, cover the pan and cook, stirring intermittently, until the pumpkin is soft, 20 to 30 minutes.
2. Put in the tamarind and coconut during the last 5 minutes of cooking. When completely cooked, stir in the cilantro and allow to cool down to room temperature. Move to a serving container and fold in the yogurt until just incorporated.
3. Heat the ghee in a small-sized non-stick saucepan using moderate to high heat and put in the red chile peppers and mustard seeds; they should splutter when they touch the hot oil, so cover the pan and reduce the heat until the spluttering diminishes. Swiftly move to the yogurt container, mix lightly before you serve.

RICE FLAKES PACHADI

This recipe is called "Poha pachadi" in Hindi

Yield: 4 to 6 servings

Ingredients:

- ⅛ teaspoon ground asafoetida

- ¼ cup finely chopped fresh cilantro, including soft stems
- ¼ teaspoon ground paprika
- ¼ teaspoon salt, or to taste
- ½ teaspoon black mustard seeds
- 1 cup pressed rice flakes (poha), sorted
- 1 fresh green chile pepper, such as serrano, minced with seeds
- 1 tablespoon grated fresh or frozen coconut or shredded unsweetened dried coconut
- 1 teaspoon coconut or peanut oil
- 2 cups non-fat plain yogurt, whisked until the desired smoothness is achieved
- 6 to 8 fresh curry leaves

Directions:

1. In a skillet, dry-roast the rice flakes, coconut, cilantro, and green chile pepper over moderate heat until it begins to look golden and releases its fragrance, approximately two minutes. Put the yogurt in a serving container and stir in the roasted rice flakes mixture and salt.
2. Heat the oil in a small saucepan using moderate to high heat and put in the curry leaves and mustard seeds; they should splutter when they touch the hot oil, so reduce the heat and cover the pan until the spluttering diminishes. Mix in the paprika and asafoetida, then instantly move the seasonings to the yogurt and stir mildly to combine, with parts of it visible as a decoration. Serve.

SAUTÉED BANANA PACHADI

This recipe is called "Bhunae kaelae ki pachadi" in Hindi

Yield: 4 to 6 servings

Ingredients:

- ⅛ teaspoon ground asafoetida
- ¼ cup grated fresh or frozen coconut
- ¼ teaspoon + ½ teaspoon salt, or to taste
- ½ teaspoon fenugreek seeds

- ½ teaspoon freshly ground black pepper, or to taste
- 1 tablespoon dried curry leaves
- 1 tablespoon peanut oil
- 1 teaspoon black mustard seeds
- 1 teaspoon cumin seeds
- 1 teaspoon hot red pepper flakes, or to taste
- 2 medium firm ripe bananas, peeled and cut into ¼-inch pieces
- 2 to 3 tablespoons fresh lemon juice
- 3 cups non-fat plain yogurt, whisked until the desired smoothness is achieved

Directions:

1. In a serving container, combine the yogurt, coconut, ¼ teaspoon salt, and black pepper. In a spice or a coffee grinder, mix together and grind the mustard, cumin, and fenugreek seeds, and the asafoetida, curry leaves, and red pepper flakes until fine.
2. Heat the oil in a big non-stick wok or saucepan using moderate to high heat and put in the ground spice mixture; it should sizzle instantly. Swiftly put in the bananas and ½ teaspoon salt and cook, flipping the pieces carefully, until a golden colour is achieved on both sides, approximately three minutes.
3. **3.** Stir in the lemon juice and cook another minute. Move the seasoned bananas to the yogurt and stir mildly to combine, with parts of them visible as a decoration. Refrigerate at least two hours to chill, then serve.

SAUTÉED TOMATOES AND COCONUT PACHADI

This recipe is called "Bhunae tamatar aur nariyal ki pachadi" in Hindi

Yield: 4 to 6 servings

Ingredients:

- ¼ cup finely chopped fresh cilantro, including soft stems
- ¼ cup fresh or frozen grated coconut or unsweetened shredded coconut
- ½ cup Coconut Milk (Homemade or store-bought)

- ½ teaspoon salt, or to taste
- 1 tablespoon peanut or coconut oil
- 1 tablespoon peeled minced fresh ginger
- 1 teaspoon black mustard seeds
- 1 teaspoon cumin seeds
- 1 teaspoon dried yellow split chickpeas (channa dal)
- 1 to 3 fresh green chile peppers, such as serrano, minced with seeds
- 2 cups non-fat plain yogurt (do not whisk)
- 2 large tomatoes, crudely chopped
- 3 dried red chile peppers, such as chile de arbol, with stems
- 8 to 10 fresh curry leaves

Directions:

1. Ready the coconut milk. Next, in a serving container, lightly combine the yogurt, coconut milk, ginger, cilantro, green chile peppers, coconut, and salt. (It should not be smooth.)
2. Heat the oil in a small-sized non-stick saucepan using moderate to high heat and put in the red chile peppers, dal, mustard and cumin seeds; they should splutter when they touch the hot oil, so cover the pan and reduce the heat until the spluttering diminishes. Swiftly put in the curry leaves and stir for approximately half a minute. Put in the tomatoes and cook, stirring, until tender, approximately two minutes, then fold everything into the yogurt. Serve.

TOMATO AND CUCUMBER PACHADI

This recipe is called "Tamatar aur kheera pachadi" in Hindi

Yield: 4 to 6 servings

Ingredients:

- four to five small seedless cucumbers, peeled and finely chopped
- ¼ teaspoon salt, or to taste
- ½ cup finely chopped fresh cilantro, including soft stems
- ½ teaspoon cumin seeds
- 1 large tomato, finely chopped

- 1 teaspoon black mustard seeds
- 1 teaspoon dried yellow split chickpeas (channa dal)
- 1 teaspoon peanut oil
- 2 cups non-fat plain yogurt (do not whisk)
- 2 tablespoons minced fresh curry leaves
- 2 to 3 fresh green chile peppers, such as serrano, cut in half along the length and seeded
- A few fresh cilantro leaves
- A scant pinch ground asafoetida

Directions:

1. Put the cucumbers, tomato, cilantro, and salt in a serving container and fold in the yogurt until just incorporated.
2. Heat the oil in a small-sized non-stick saucepan using moderate to high heat and put in the mustard seeds; they should splutter when they touch the hot oil, so cover the pan and reduce the heat until the spluttering diminishes. Swiftly put in the dal and stir until a golden colour is achieved, approximately half a minute, then put in the cumin seeds, curry leaves, and asafoetida and stir another half a minute. Move the seasonings into the yogurt container and fold in gently. Garnish with the green chile peppers and cilantro leaves before you serve.

TOMATO, CUCUMBER, AND ONION YOGURT

This recipe is called "Tamatar, kheera, aur pyaz ki pachadi" in Hindi

Yield: 4 to 6 servings

Ingredients:

- four to five small seedless cucumbers, peeled and finely chopped
- ½ cup finely chopped fresh cilantro, including soft stems + extra for garnish
- ½ teaspoon salt, or to taste
- 1 large tomato, finely chopped
- 1 small white onion, cut in half along the length and thinly chopped

- 1 tablespoon minced fresh curry leaves
- 1 tablespoon peeled minced fresh ginger
- 1 teaspoon black mustard seeds
- 1 teaspoon cumin seeds
- 1 teaspoon dried yellow split chickpeas (channa dal)
- 1 teaspoon dried yellow split pigeon peas (toor dal)
- 1 teaspoon peanut oil
- 1½ cups non-fat plain yogurt (do not whisk)
- 2 dried red chile peppers, such as chile de arbol, crudely broken
- 2 fresh green chile peppers, such as serrano, diagonally chopped thin ½ teaspoon ground fenugreek seeds
- 2 tablespoons finely chopped fresh cilantro, including soft stems

Directions:

1. Put the cucumbers, tomato, onion, cilantro, and salt in a serving container and fold in the yogurt until just incorporated.
2. Heat the oil in a small-sized non-stick saucepan using moderate to high heat and put in the red chile peppers and ginger, stir a few seconds, then put in the cumin and mustard seeds; they should splutter when they touch the hot oil, so cover the pan and reduce the heat until the spluttering diminishes. Swiftly add both dals, curry leaves, green chile peppers, and fenugreek, and stir until a golden colour is achieved, approximately one minute. Move seasoning into the yogurt container and fold it in gently. Garnish with the cilantro leaves and serve.

PANEER CHEESE

The most widely eaten and easily available cheese of India is called "Paneer". In India, most of the paneer is made from buffalo's milk, and in the USA, it is made from cow's milk. Paneer is easily available in stores all across the world, and it can also be made quite easily at home. If you're living in the USA and are having a hard time finding paneer, just grab some "**Ricotta Cheese**". Ricotta cheese is basically paneer, and can be used instead of traditional Indian paneer in every recipe in this section. If you're a vegan, use tofu instead of paneer.

Paneer is basically the solid component of milk. It is obtained by separating it from the liquid whey component of milk. This can be done by a number of sour agents like lemon juice, vinegar, yogurt, citric acid, etc. Once the milk has broken down, the paneer can be separated from the whey by draining the whey with the help of something like a cheesecloth.

Paneer is a plain canvas- both in taste, and appearance. It appears pure white, and has a very mild taste. It pretty much takes the appearance and taste depending on how you cook it, and what kind of seasoning you use. It is also a great source of protein for vegetarians.

Paneer is a very versatile food. It can be cooked like you cook meat kebabs, it can be cooked into a curry, or just eaten by itself with or without seasoning. It is due to this versatility I had to dedicate a whole section to this one particular ingredient. So, without much ado, let us jump right into the recipes!

Ⓥ= Vegan Ⓟ= Quick Pressure Cooker Recipe

HOMEMADE PANEER CHEESE

Yield: About 8 ounces Paneer Cheese

Ingredients:

- ½ gallon milk
- ½ teaspoon salt, or to taste
- 1 (2-foot-square) piece fine muslin or 8-foot-piece cheesecloth folded in 4 layers
- 2 cups plain yogurt, whisked until the desired smoothness is achieved, or 3 to 4 tablespoons fresh lime or lemon juice

Directions:

1. Pour the milk in a big and heavy pan, add the salt, and bring to a boil using high heat, stirring slowly. Immediately before the milk boils and the bubbles spill over, stir in the yogurt or the lemon juice and stir slowly, until the milk curdles and divides into curds and translucent green liquid whey, approximately a minute or two. Remove pan from the heat.

2. Pour the curdled milk into a big container through a cheesecloth or muslin. The whey will pass through, and paneer cheese will be left behind in the muslin/cheesecloth. When you're done pouring, pick up the muslin by all 4 corners and tie the 4 ends into a knot over the sink in your kitchen. Allow to drain, three to five minutes.

PANEER CHEESE APPETIZERS

PANEER KEBABS

This recipe is called "Paneer seekh kebabs" in Hindi

Yield: 4 to 6 servings

Ingredients:

- ½ cup crudely chopped fresh cilantro, including soft stems
- ½ cup chopped cashews, soaked in water to cover approximately one hour, then drained
- ½ small onion, crudely chopped
- 1 tablespoon ground coriander
- 1 tablespoon melted unsalted butter
- 1 teaspoon Chaat Masala (Homemade or store-bought) + ¼ teaspoon
- 1 teaspoon ground cumin
- 1 teaspoon mango powder
- 1 teaspoon salt, or to taste
- 1 to 3 fresh green chile peppers, such as serrano, crudely chopped
- 2 cups shredded lettuce, such as green or red leaf, or romaine
- 2 to 4 tablespoons all-purpose flour, as required
- 4 quarter-size slices peeled fresh ginger
- 8 ounces (1 recipe) Paneer Cheese (Homemade or store-bought), crumbled

- twelve to fifteen metal or bamboo skewers, soaked in water at least 30 minutes

Directions:

5. Ready the chaat masala and the paneer cheese. Next, Using a food processor, combine and pulse the cashews, green chile peppers, ginger, onion, and cilantro until fine. Next, Put in the paneer cheese and all the rest of the ingredients (except the flour, butter, chaat masala, and lettuce) and process until everything is well mixed and begins to gather together, approximately one minute.
6. Preheat a grill to 375°F to 400°F or preheat the broiler. Moisten your clean fingers with water, and divide the mixture into twelve to fifteen equivalent portions, making long, thin shapes, similar to hot dogs. If the mixture appears too soft to work with, stir in some all-purpose flour, using as much as required to make a soft dough that holds its shape.
7. Skewer them and grill or broil on the top rack (about 6 inches from the heating element), flipping regularly, until firm and lightly golden. (Do not overcook, or they will become tough.)
8. Heat the butter in a small saucepan using moderate to high heat, stir in 1 teaspoon chaat masala and lightly baste the kebabs just before removing them from the heat. Move to a platter lined with the lettuce, sprinkle the ¼ teaspoon chaat masala on top before you serve.

CHICKPEA FLOUR PANEER

This recipe is called "Besan paneer" in Hindi

Yield: 4 to 6 servings

Ingredients:

- ¼ cup finely chopped fresh cilantro
- ½ teaspoon ground turmeric
- ½ teaspoon hot red pepper flakes, or to taste
- 1 tablespoon peeled minced fresh ginger
- 1 teaspoon cumin seeds
- 1 teaspoon ground cumin

- 1 teaspoon mango powder
- 1 teaspoon salt, or to taste
- 2 tablespoons dried fenugreek leaves
- 2 tablespoons peanut oil
- 2 to 3 tablespoons chickpea flour
- 8 ounces (1 recipe) Paneer Cheese (Homemade or store-bought)

Directions:

1. Ready the paneer cheese then cut it into 1-inch wedges or rectangles. Heat the oil in a big non-stick wok or saucepan over moderate heat and put in the cumin seeds; they should sizzle when they touch the hot oil.
2. Swiftly put in the ginger, stir for approximately half a minute, then stir in the cumin, red pepper flakes, and turmeric. Put in the fenugreek leaves, mango powder, and salt, then stir in the paneer cheese pieces. Cook, turning, until a mild brown colour is achieved, about fifteen to twenty seconds per side.
3. Sprinkle the chickpea flour uniformly over the paneer cheese, and cook, flipping the pieces, approximately two minutes. The chickpea flour will roast and form a fragrant coating over the pieces. Move to a serving dish, sprinkle the cilantro on top before you serve.

LIGHTLY SEARED SOUR PANEER

This recipe is called "Halka-bhoona khatta paneer" in Hindi

Yield: 4 to 6 servings

Ingredients:

- ¼ cup heavy cream or plain yogurt, whisked until the desired smoothness is achieved
- ¼ cup minced chives
- ½ teaspoon crudely ground black pepper
- ½ teaspoon salt, or to taste
- 1 fresh green chile pepper, such as serrano, minced with seeds
- 1 tablespoon unsalted butter
- 1 tablespoon vegetable oil
- 1 teaspoon Chaat Masala (Homemade or store-bought), or to taste

- 1½ tablespoons peeled minced fresh ginger
- 2 tablespoons fresh lemon juice
- 8 ounces (1 recipe) <u>Paneer Cheese</u> (Homemade or store-bought)

Directions:

1. Ready the masala. Ready the paneer cheese then cut it into 4 long flat pieces, each approximately ¼-inch thick. Season lightly with chives, salt, and black pepper.
2. Heat the oil in a big non-stick skillet or griddle using moderate to high heat and swiftly sear the paneer cheese pieces until lightly golden, approximately about fifteen to twenty seconds per side. Move to a serving dish, cover, and keep warm.
3. Heat the butter in a small saucepan over moderate heat until it just begins to bubble. Put in the ginger and green chile pepper and cook, stirring, until a golden colour is achieved, approximately one minute. Put in the lemon juice and chaat masala and bring to a quick boil.
4. Put in the cream (or yogurt) and stir until just heated through. (If you're using yogurt, don't heat for a long period or the yogurt will separate.) Drizzle over the paneer cheese and serve.

ONION CRUNCHY PANEER

This recipe is called "Pyaz vaala paneer ka gol tukra" in Hindi

Yield: 6 to 8 servings; approximately 8 ounces

Ingredients:

- ¼ teaspoon salt
- ½ cup minced red bell pepper
- ½ teaspoon crudely ground black pepper
- ½ to 1 teaspoon <u>Chaat Masala</u> (Homemade or store-bought)
- 1 small onion, finely chopped
- 1 tablespoon peeled minced fresh ginger
- 1 teaspoon cumin seeds
- 1 to 3 fresh green chile peppers, such as serrano, minced with seeds
- 2 tablespoons vegetable oil

- 8 ounces (1 recipe) Paneer Cheese (Homemade or store-bought)

Directions:

1. Ready the masala. Ready the paneer cheese. Next, crumble the cheese coarsely, put it in a food processor and pulse a few times until the desired smoothness is achieved. Move to a large container.
2. Heat the oil in a small-sized non-stick wok or saucepan using moderate to high heat and put in the cumin seeds and black pepper; they should sizzle when they touch the hot oil. Swiftly put in the onion and cook, stirring, until a golden colour is achieved, approximately three minutes. Put in the ginger, green chile peppers, red bell pepper, and salt, and stir approximately two minutes. Allow to cool.
3. Put in the vegetables to the paneer cheese and mix thoroughly with clean fingers or a spoon. Next, shape into a ball (or any shape you prefer), garnish with chaat masala before you serve.

PANEER BALLS

This recipe is called "Paneer koftas" in Hindi

Yield: 4 to 6 servings

Ingredients:

- ¼ cup finely chopped fresh cilantro, including soft stems
- ½ teaspoon ajwain seeds, crudely ground
- ½ teaspoon garam masala
- ¾ teaspoon salt, or to taste
- 1 small potato (any kind), boiled in water to cover until tender, then peeled and grated
- 1 tablespoon peeled minced fresh ginger
- 1 teaspoon Chaat Masala (Homemade or store-bought)
- 1 to 1½ cups peanut oil for deep-frying
- 1 to 3 fresh green chile peppers, such as serrano, minced with seeds
- 8 ounces (1 recipe) Paneer Cheese (Homemade or store-bought)

Directions:

1. Ready the chaat masala. Ready the paneer, then grate the cheese by hand or briefly Using a food processor. Move to a container, then put in the potato, cilantro, ginger, chile peppers, ajwain seeds, garam masala, and salt. Combine until the mixture resembles a soft dough.
2. Divide the cheese dough into fifteen to 20 portions, each approximately 1¼-inches, and shape each portion into a smooth ball.
3. Line a tray or cookie sheet with paper towels. Heat the oil in a wok until it reaches 325°F to 350°F on a frying thermometer, or until a small piece of dough dropped into the hot oil surges to the surface of the oil in fifteen to 20 seconds. Put the paneer balls into the hot oil carefully, to avoid splattering, adding as many as the wok can hold simultaneously without crowding. Fry, flipping over once or twice, until a golden colour is achieved on all sides, approximately two to three minutes. Using a slotted spoon, move to the lined tray to drain. Put on a serving platter, sprinkle the chaat masala on top and serve.

PANEER WRAPS

This recipe is called "Paneer kaathi kabaab" in Hindi

Yield: ten to twelve rolls

Ingredients:

- ½ cup (¼ recipe) Yogurt Cheese, whisked until the desired smoothness is achieved
- ½ cup finely chopped fresh cilantro, including soft stems
- 1 large white onion, cut in half along the length and thinly chopped
- 1 recipe Griddle-Cooked Flour and Potato Bread for Spicy Wraps
- 1 tablespoon ground cumin
- 1 teaspoon cayenne pepper, or to taste
- 1 teaspoon Chaat Masala (Homemade or store-bought)
- 1 teaspoon salt, or to taste
- 1 to 3 fresh green chile peppers, such as serrano, minced with seeds
- 2 tablespoons fresh lemon juice
- 2 to 3 teaspoons mustard or peanut oil
- 3 tablespoons Basic Ginger-Garlic Paste (Homemade or store-bought)
- 8 ounces (1 recipe) Paneer Cheese (Homemade or store-bought)

Directions:

1. Ready the paneer cheese, potato bread wraps, yogurt cheese, ginger-garlic paste, and chaat masala. Next, cut the paneer into ½-inch pieces.
2. In a large non-reactive container, combine the yogurt cheese, oil, ginger-garlic paste, cumin, cayenne pepper, and salt. Put in the paneer pieces and mix thoroughly. Cover and marinate at least two hours at room temperature or up to one day in a fridge.
3. Preheat your oven to 400°F and mildly grease a baking sheet. Remove the paneer cheese pieces from the marinade and place them in a single layer on the baking sheet. (Throw away mayonnaise.) Bake, flipping the pieces once or twice, until barely golden, approximately five to seven minutes. (Do not overbake, or the pieces will toughen.) Move to a container, cover, and keep warm.
4. In another container, combine the onion, green chile peppers, cilantro, lemon juice, and chaat masala. Adjust seasoning, adding salt if you wish.
5. To assemble, lay out all the potato rotis. Put the paneer cheese pieces along the center length of each roti, top with the onion-chile pepper mixture and roll tightly. Serve instantly or wrap each one in foil and place in your fridge for a maximum of two days.

SAFFRON PANEER

This recipe is called "Kesari paneer" in Hindi

Yield: 4 to 6 servings

Ingredients:

- ¼ cup finely chopped fresh cilantro
- ¼ teaspoon cayenne pepper, or to taste
- ¼ teaspoon ground green cardamom seeds
- ¼ teaspoon ground paprika
- ¼ teaspoon saffron, dry-roasted and ground (See the dry-roasting section in Introduction)
- ½ cup plain yogurt (any kind), whisked until the desired smoothness is achieved
- ½ teaspoon ajwain seeds

- 1 cup water
- 1 tablespoon ground coriander
- 1 teaspoon cumin seeds
- 1 teaspoon garam masala
- 1 teaspoon salt, or to taste
- 2 tablespoons Basic Ginger-Garlic Paste (Homemade or store-bought)
- 2 teaspoons cornstarch
- 3 tablespoons vegetable oil
- 8 ounces (1 recipe) Paneer Cheese (Homemade or store-bought)

Directions:

1. Ready the ginger-garlic paste and the saffron. Ready the paneer cheese, then cut it into triangles approximately ½ inch thick. In a large container, combine the yogurt and saffron and allow to steep at least 30 minutes. Next, add in the ginger-garlic paste, garam masala, ajwain seeds, cayenne pepper, paprika, and salt. Put in the paneer cheese pieces and mix thoroughly. Cover and marinate at least 4 and maximum 8 hours in a fridge.
2. Heat 2 tablespoons oil in a big non-stick skillet using moderate to high heat. Fry the paneer pieces until lightly golden, about fifteen to twenty seconds per side. Move to a serving platter and keep warm.
3. combine the water and cornstarch and stir it into the marinade left sticking to the pan.
4. In a small-sized non-stick wok or skillet, heat the rest of the 1 tablespoon oil using moderate to high heat then put in the cumin seeds; they should sizzle when they touch the hot oil. Swiftly stir in the coriander and the cornstarch mixture and bring to a quick boil using high heat. The sauce should thicken instantly. Stir in the cardamom seeds. Drizzle the sauce over the paneer cheese, garnish with the cilantro before you serve.

SEARED PANEER WITH CAPER SAUCE

This recipe is called "bhoona kair vaala paneer" in Hindi

Yield: 4 to 6 servings

Ingredients:

- ¼ cup drained brine-packed capers (with 1 tablespoon brine reserved)
- ¼ cup minced red or orange bell pepper
- ½ teaspoon crudely ground black pepper
- ½ teaspoon Chaat Masala (Homemade or store-bought), or to taste
- ½ teaspoon salt, or to taste
- 1 tablespoon peeled minced fresh ginger
- 1 tablespoon vegetable oil
- 1 to 3 fresh green chile peppers, such as serrano, minced with seeds
- 1½ tablespoons unsalted butter
- 8 ounces (1 recipe) Paneer Cheese (Homemade or store-bought)

Directions:

1. Ready the masala. Ready the paneer cheese then cut it into ten to twelve large pieces, each approximately ½-inch thick. Season lightly with salt and black pepper.
2. Heat the oil in a big non-stick skillet or griddle using moderate to high heat and swiftly sear the paneer cheese pieces until a golden colour is achieved, approximately one minute per side. Move to a serving dish, cover, and keep warm.
3. Heat the butter in a small saucepan over moderate heat until it starts bubbling. Put in the capers, bell pepper, ginger, and green chile peppers and cook, stirring, approximately two minutes. Put in the reserved brine and bring to a quick boil. Next, drizzle everything over the paneer pieces, garnish with chaat masala before you serve.

SPICY PEPPERED PANEER

This recipe is called "Kaali mirch vaala paneer" in Hindi

Yield: 6 to 8 servings

Ingredients:

- ½ gallon milk
- ½ teaspoon salt, or to taste
- 1 (2-foot-square) piece fine muslin or 8-foot-piece cheesecloth folded in 4 layers

- 1 (8-ounce) package cream cheese, at room temperature
- 1 tablespoon black peppercorns, dry-roasted and crudely ground (See the dry-roasting section in Introduction)
- 1 tablespoon peanut oil
- 1 to 3 fresh green chile peppers, such as serrano, stemmed
- 2 cups plain yogurt, whisked until the desired smoothness is achieved, or 3 to 4 tablespoons fresh lime or lemon juice
- 2 tablespoons fine plain bread crumbs
- 2 tablespoons peeled minced fresh ginger

Directions:

1. Pour the milk in a big and heavy pan, add the salt, and bring to a boil using high heat, stirring slowly. Immediately before the milk boils and the bubbles spill over, stir in the yogurt or the lemon juice and stir slowly, until the milk curdles and divides into curds and translucent green liquid whey, approximately a minute or two. Remove pan from the heat.
2. Pour the curdled milk into a big container through a cheesecloth or muslin. The whey will pass through, and paneer cheese will be left behind in the muslin/cheesecloth. When you're done pouring, pick up the muslin by all 4 corners and tie the 4 ends into a knot over the sink in your kitchen. Allow to drain, three to five minutes.
3. While the cheese drains, heat the oil in a small saucepan over moderate heat and cook, the ginger, stirring, until a golden colour is achieved, approximately one minute. Put in the black pepper and bread crumbs and stir until the seasonings are dry but not scorched. Turn off the heat and spread the mixture uniformly on a plate.
4. Move the paneer curds from the muslin to a food processor, then put in the cream cheese and chile peppers and process until thoroughly mixed.
5. With lightly buttered clean hands, or using a piece of waxed paper, shape the cheese mixture into a ball, then roll the ball uniformly in the bread crumb mixture, ensuring it is coated thoroughly. Keep it as a ball or push softly using your hands to flatten it into a patty, an oval, a rectangle, or a log. Serve as you would any other cheese balls or spreads, such as with an assortment of crackers or with crudités.

PANEER CHEESE SNACKS AND SIDE DISHES

APPLE-GINGER SCRAMBLED PANEER

This recipe is called "Saeb aur adrak chutni vaala paneer" in Hindi

Yield: 4 to 6 servings

Ingredients:

- ½ cup finely chopped, fresh cilantro, including soft stems
- ½ teaspoon salt, or to taste
- 1 cup (½ recipe) Tart Apple-Ginger Chutney with Green Tomatoes
- 1 small onion, finely chopped
- 2 tablespoons vegetable oil
- 2 teaspoons ground coriander
- 8 ounces (1 recipe) Paneer Cheese (Homemade or store-bought)
- Freshly ground black pepper, to taste

Directions:

1. Ready the paneer cheese and crumble it coarsely. Ready the chutney. Heat the oil in a moderate-sized non-stick wok or skillet using moderate to high heat and cook the onion, stirring, until lightly brown, approximately ten minutes. Put in the paneer cheese and cook, stirring, approximately two minutes. Next, stir in the chutney and cook, stirring intermittently, approximately five minutes.
2. Put in the coriander and salt, decrease the heat to medium, and cook until the paneer is barely golden, approximately seven minutes. Stir in the cilantro, move to a serving dish, season with black pepper before you serve.

BASIC SCRAMBLED PANEER

This recipe is called "Paneer ki bhurji" in Hindi

Yield: 4 to 6 servings

Ingredients:

- ¼ teaspoon ground turmeric
- ½ cup finely chopped fresh cilantro, including soft stems
- ½ teaspoon ground cumin
- 1 teaspoon salt, or to taste
- 1 to 3 fresh green chile peppers, such as serrano, minced with seeds
- 2 cups finely chopped onions
- 2 large tomatoes, finely chopped
- 2 tablespoons vegetable oil
- 2 teaspoons ground coriander
- 8 ounces (1 recipe) <u>Paneer Cheese</u> (Homemade or store-bought)
- Freshly ground black pepper, to taste

Directions:

1. Ready the paneer cheese and crudely crumble. Heat the oil in a moderate-sized non-stick wok or skillet using moderate to high heat, put in the onions and cook, stirring, until a golden colour is achieved, three to five minutes.
2. Put in the tomatoes and green chile peppers and cook, stirring as required, until most of the fluids vaporize, approximately seven minutes. Add all the spices and the salt, then stir in the paneer cheese. Cook, stirring, using moderate to high heat for the first 3 to four minutes and then over moderate heat until a golden colour is achieved, approximately ten minutes. Stir in the cilantro. Move to a serving dish, sprinkle the black pepper on top before you serve.

CHILLI PANEER AND FRIED GINGER

This recipe is called "Mirchi paneer aur tala adrak" in Hindi

Yield: 4 to 6 servings

Ingredients:

- ¼ cup fresh orange juice
- ½ cup Crispy Fried Fresh Ginger
- ½ cup finely chopped fresh cilantro, including soft stems
- ½ teaspoon black peppercorns, dry-roasted and crudely crushed (See the dry-roasting section in Introduction)
- ½ teaspoon Chaat Masala (Homemade or store-bought)
- ¾ teaspoon salt, or to taste
- 1 cup finely chopped red bell pepper
- 1 large clove fresh garlic, minced
- 1 to 3 fresh green chile peppers, such as serrano, minced with seeds
- 2 to 3 tablespoons distilled white vinegar
- 2 to 3 tablespoons peanut oil
- 4 to 6 dried red chile peppers, such as chile de arbol, with stems
- 5 to 6 scallions, white parts only, thinly chopped
- 8 ounces (1 recipe) Paneer Cheese (Homemade or store-bought)

Directions:

1. Ready the peppercorns and the masala. Ready the paneer cheese and cut into 1-inch squares. Ready the fried ginger and save for garnish (reserve the oil).
2. Heat (or reheat) the oil (used for frying the ginger) in a big non-stick skillet using moderate to high heat and cook the red chile peppers, stirring, approximately one minute. Put in the paneer cheese pieces and cook (in 2 to 3 batches, if required), turning them once, until barely golden on both sides, approximately one to two minutes per batch.
3. Put in the garlic, scallions, green chile peppers, black pepper, and salt and cook approximately two minutes. Put in the cilantro, orange juice, and vinegar and cook until most of the juices are absorbed by the paneer cheese, approximately five minutes.
4. Put in the red bell pepper and cook approximately two minutes, then decrease the heat to low, cover the pan, and cook another 5 minutes to blend the flavours. Move to a serving dish, garnish with the fried ginger and chaat masala before you serve.

DICED PANEER WITH AJWAIN SEEDS

This recipe is called "Paneer ajwaini" in Hindi

Yield: 4 to 6 servings

Ingredients:

- ¼ teaspoon ajwain seeds, crudely ground
- ¼ teaspoon garam masala
- ½ cup finely chopped fresh cilantro, including soft stems
- ½ teaspoon salt, or to taste
- ¾ teaspoon black peppercorns, dry-roasted and crudely ground (See the dry-roasting section in Introduction)
- 1 to 3 fresh green chile peppers, such as serrano, chopped diagonally
- 2 small onions, cut in half along the length and thinly chopped
- 2 tablespoons fresh lemon juice
- 2 tablespoons peanut oil
- 2 tablespoons peeled minced fresh ginger
- 8 ounces (1 recipe) <u>Paneer Cheese</u> (Homemade or store-bought)

Directions:

1. Ready the peppercorns. Ready the paneer cheese then cut it into ½-inch pieces.
2. Heat the oil in a big non-stick wok or saucepan using moderate to high heat and cook the onions, stirring, until a golden colour is achieved, approximately ten minutes. Put in the green chile peppers and cook another 1 minute.
3. Put in the paneer cheese, ginger, ajwain seeds, salt, and black pepper, and cook, flipping the pieces very carefully, until barely golden, approximately five minutes. Stir in the lemon juice and cilantro and cook another two minutes. Move to a serving dish, garnish with the garam masala before you serve.

PANEER WITH CAULIFLOWER AND BROCCOLI

This recipe is called "Gobhi aur hari gobhi ka paneer" in Hindi

Yield: 4 to 6 servings

Ingredients:

- ¼ cup finely chopped fresh cilantro, including soft stems (reserve some for garnish)
- ½ teaspoon dry-roasted and crudely ground black pepper (See the dry-roasting section in Introduction), or to taste
- ½ teaspoon ground cumin
- ½ teaspoon salt, or to taste
- 1 cup finely chopped mixed red and yellow bell peppers
- 1 cup fresh cauliflower florets
- 1 to 3 fresh green chile peppers, such as serrano, stemmed
- 1½ tablespoons ground coriander
- 2 cups fresh broccoli florets
- 2 to 3 tablespoons vegetable oil
- 5 to 7 quarter-size slices peeled fresh ginger
- 8 ounces (1 recipe) <u>Paneer Cheese</u> (Homemade or store-bought)

Directions:

1. Ready the pepper. Ready the paneer cheese then cut it into ½-inch pieces.
2. In a small food processor, combine and pulse the ginger and green chile peppers until minced, approximately half a minute. Heat the oil in a big non-stick wok or saucepan, then put in the ginger and green chile peppers and cook using moderate to high heat, stirring, until a golden colour is achieved, approximately a minute or two.
3. Put in the paneer cheese, coriander, cumin, and ¼ teaspoon salt and cook, turning carefully, until a golden colour is achieved, approximately five minutes. Put in the cilantro and cook another two minutes. Move to a serving dish.
4. To the same pan, put in the cauliflower and broccoli florets, bell peppers, and the rest of the ¼ teaspoon salt and stir until crisp-tender, approximately five minutes. Move to the serving dish and mix lightly with the paneer. Garnish with cilantro, sprinkle the black pepper on top before you serve.

PANEER-CILANTRO BAKE

This recipe is called "Dhania-paneer bake" in Hindi

Yield: 4 to 6 servings

Ingredients:

- ½ cup plain yogurt, whisked until the desired smoothness is achieved
- 1 cup crudely chopped fresh cilantro, including soft stems
- 1 tablespoon fresh lemon juice
- 1 teaspoon Chaat Masala (Homemade or store-bought)
- 1 teaspoon salt, or to taste
- 1 to 3 fresh green chile peppers, such as serrano, stemmed
- 2 large cloves fresh garlic, peeled
- 2 to 3 teaspoons mustard or peanut oil
- 6 quarter-size slices peeled fresh ginger
- 8 ounces (1 recipe) Paneer Cheese (Homemade or store-bought)

Directions:

1. Ready the masala. Ready the paneer cheese then cut into ½-inch pieces. Using a food processor or a blender, combine and pulse the ginger, garlic, green chile peppers, lemon juice, and cilantro until a smooth purée is achieved.
2. Move to an ungreased flat ovenproof dish and stir in the yogurt, oil, and salt. Put in the paneer cheese pieces and marinate at least two hours at room temperature or up to one day in a fridge.
3. Preheat your oven to 450°F. Bake the paneer cheese, flipping the pieces once or twice, until barely golden, approximately ten minutes. (Do not overcook or the paneer will become tough.) Sprinkle the chaat masala on top and serve.

QUICK & EASY SPINACH PANEER

This recipe is called "Jaldi ka saag paneer" in Hindi

Yield: 4 to 6 servings

Ingredients:

- ¼ teaspoon crudely ground fenugreek seeds
- ½ teaspoon black mustard seeds
- ¾ teaspoon garam masala
- ¾ teaspoon salt, or to taste
- 1 fresh green chile pepper, such as serrano, minced with seeds
- 1 large clove fresh garlic, minced
- 1 large tomato, crudely chopped
- 1 teaspoon cumin seeds
- 2 small bunches fresh spinach (about 1 pound), trimmed of roots only, washed well, and crudely chopped
- 2 tablespoons olive or vegetable oil
- 2 teaspoons ground coriander
- 8 ounces (1 recipe) Paneer Cheese (Homemade or store-bought) or tofu
- Freshly ground black pepper, to taste

Directions:

1. Ready the paneer cheese and crumble it coarsely. Heat the oil in a big non-stick wok or saucepan using moderate to high heat and put in the cumin, mustard seeds, and fenugreek; they should sizzle when they touch the hot oil. Swiftly put in the tomato, garlic, and chile pepper and cook, stirring, approximately one minute.
2. Put in the spinach. Cover the pan and cook, stirring once or twice until wilted, approximately three minutes. Put in the paneer cheese, coriander, garam masala, and salt and cook over moderate heat, uncovered, stirring as required, until all the liquids vaporize and the dish is quite dry, approximately five minutes. Move to a serving dish, garnish with freshly ground black pepper before you serve.

SAUTÉED PANEER WITH GREEN CHUTNEY

This recipe is called "Paneer hari chutni" in Hindi

Yield: 4 to 6 servings

Ingredients:

- ¾ teaspoon cumin seeds, dry-roasted and crudely ground (See the dry-roasting section in Introduction)
- 1 cup crudely chopped fresh cilantro, including soft stems
- 1 large tomato, cut into ½-inch pieces
- 1 teaspoon salt, or to taste
- 1 to 1½ teaspoons <u>Chaat Masala</u> (Homemade or store-bought)
- 1½ tablespoons ground coriander
- 1½ teaspoons ground cumin
- 2 tablespoons fresh lemon juice
- 2 to 3 tablespoons peanut oil
- 8 ounces (1 recipe) <u>Paneer Cheese</u> (Homemade or store-bought)

Directions:

1. Ready the chaat masala and the cumin. Ready the paneer cheese and cut it into 1½-by-½-inch pieces. Using a food processor or blender, combine and pulse the cilantro, lemon juice, coriander, cumin, and salt to make a smooth chutney.
2. Put the paneer cheese in a flat dish and cautiously stir in the chutney, ensuring that all the pieces are coated thoroughly. Cover and marinate in the refrigerator, 1 to four hours.
3. Heat the oil in a big non-stick wok or skillet using moderate to high heat and cook the paneer pieces (in 2 batches, if needed), stirring, until just heated through, approximately a minute or two per batch. Move to a serving platter, cover, and keep warm.
4. Add the rest of the marinade to the skillet along with the tomato and cook, stirring, until the tomato is soft, approximately one minute. Move to the paneer platter. Garnish with the chaat masala and cumin seeds and serve.

SCRAMBLED GINGER-LIME PANEER

This recipe is called "Adrak-nimboo vaala paneer" in Hindi

Yield: 4 to 6 servings

Ingredients:

- ½ cup finely chopped fresh cilantro, including soft stems
- 1 tablespoon vegetable oil
- 1 to 1½ tablespoons Minced Ginger-Lime Pickle
- 8 ounces (1 recipe) Paneer Cheese (Homemade or store-bought)
- Freshly ground black pepper, to taste

Directions:

1. Ready the ginger-lime pickle in advance. Ready the paneer cheese then cut it into ½-inch pieces.
2. Put the paneer cheese in a medium non-reactive container. Stir in the ginger-lime pickle, cover and marinate at room temperature or in the refrigerator, 1 to four hours.
3. Heat the oil in a moderate-sized non-stick wok or skillet using moderate to high heat and put in the marinated paneer cheese. Cook, stirring lightly, until heated through, approximately a minute or two. Put in the cilantro and cook, turning as required, until the paneer is golden, approximately two to three minutes. Move to a serving dish, garnish with black pepper before you serve.

SCRAMBLED MUSHROOM PANEER

This recipe is called "Sookha gucchi paneer" in Hindi

Yield: 4 to 6 servings

Ingredients:

- ¼ cup finely chopped fresh cilantro, including soft stems
- ¼ teaspoon garam masala
- ¼ teaspoon salt, or to taste
- 1 cup (about fifteen medium) fresh or reconstituted dried morel mushrooms, chopped along the diagonal into thin rounds
- 1 large onion, finely chopped
- 1 red bell pepper, cut into ¼-inch pieces
- 1 teaspoon black mustard seeds
- 1 teaspoon cumin seeds
- 1 to 3 fresh green chile peppers, such as serrano, minced with seeds
- 3 tablespoons vegetable oil

- 8 ounces (1 recipe) Paneer Cheese (Homemade or store-bought)

Directions:

1. Ready the paneer and cut into ½-inch pieces. Heat 2 tablespoons oil in a moderate-sized non-stick wok or skillet using moderate to high heat and cook the onion and green chile peppers, stirring, until a mild brown colour is achieved and soft, approximately ten minutes. Move to a container.
2. Put in the red bell pepper and mushrooms to the pan and cook approximately one minute. Move to the container with the onion and green chile peppers.
3. Heat the rest of the 1 tablespoon oil in the pan and put in the cumin and mustard seeds; they should splatter when they touch the hot oil, so reduce the heat and cover the pan until the splattering diminishes. Swiftly put in the paneer cheese and salt and cook, stirring lightly, until a golden colour is achieved. Stir in the mushroom mixture and cook over moderate heat, stirring, approximately five minutes to blend the flavours. Stir in the cilantro. Move to a serving dish, sprinkle the garam masala on top before you serve.

SCRAMBLED PANEER AND CAULIFLOWER

This recipe is called "Sookha gobhi paneer" in Hindi

Yield: 4 to 6 servings

Ingredients:

- ¼ teaspoon ground turmeric
- ½ cup finely chopped fresh cilantro
- ½ teaspoon hot red pepper flakes, or to taste
- 1 small head cauliflower, minced to make 2 cups
- 1 small tomato, finely chopped
- 1 tablespoon peeled minced fresh ginger
- 1 teaspoon cumin seeds
- 1 teaspoon ground cumin
- 1 teaspoon salt, or to taste

- 1 to 3 fresh green chile peppers, such as serrano, minced with seeds
- 2 tablespoons vegetable oil
- 8 ounces (1 recipe) <u>Paneer Cheese</u> (Homemade or store-bought)
- Tomato wedges

Directions:

1. Ready the paneer cheese and grate it, if possible by hand. Heat 1 tablespoon oil in a big non-stick wok or skillet using moderate to high heat and stir-fry the cauliflower and cilantro until the cauliflower is golden, approximately three minutes. Move to a container.
2. Heat the rest of the 1 tablespoon oil using high heat. Put in the cumin seeds; they should sizzle when they touch the hot oil. Swiftly put in the ginger and green chile peppers, cook 1 minute, then stir in the turmeric, red pepper flakes, salt, and cumin.
3. Put in the chopped tomato and grated paneer cheese and cook, stirring, until heated through, approximately two minutes. Move to a serving dish and spoon in the cauliflower. Garnish with tomato wedges and serve.

SOYBEANS SCRAMBLED PANEER

This recipe is called "Soyabeans vaali paneer bhurji" in Hindi

Yield: 4 to 6 servings

Ingredients:

- ¼ teaspoon garam masala
- ¼ teaspoon ground turmeric
- ¼ teaspoon hot red pepper flakes, or to taste
- ½ cup finely chopped fresh cilantro, including soft stems
- ½ teaspoon fenugreek seeds, crudely ground
- ½ teaspoon ground cumin
- 1 cup shelled frozen soybeans, thawed
- 1 large onion, finely chopped
- 1 large tomato, finely chopped
- 1 tablespoon minced fresh mint leaves
- 1 teaspoon cumin seeds

- 1 teaspoon salt, or to taste
- 1 to 3 fresh green chile peppers, such as serrano, minced with seeds
- 1½ tablespoons ground coriander
- 2 tablespoons vegetable oil
- 8 ounces (1 recipe) <u>Paneer Cheese</u> (Homemade or store-bought)

Directions:

1. Ready the paneer cheese and crumble it coarsely. Put the soybeans in a microwave-safe dish. Cover and cook in the microwave on high power 3 to four minutes or until the soybeans are very soft.
2. Another way is to put them in a saucepan in water to cover and boil until tender.
3. Heat the oil in a moderate-sized non-stick wok or skillet using moderate to high heat and put in the cumin and fenugreek seeds; they should sizzle when they touch the hot oil. Swiftly put in the onion and cook, stirring, until a golden colour is achieved, approximately ten minutes. Put in the tomato and green chile peppers and cook, stirring as required, until most of the fluids vaporize, approximately seven minutes.
4. Add all the coriander, cumin, turmeric, red pepper flakes, and salt to the pan, then stir in the soy beans and stir approximately five minutes. Put in the paneer cheese and cook, stirring, using moderate to high heat the first two to three minutes and then over moderate heat until a golden colour is achieved, ten minutes. Stir in the cilantro and mint. Move to a serving dish, garnish with garam masala before you serve.

SUN-DRIED TOMATO-PANEER

This recipe is called "Dhoop mein sookhae tamatar ka paneer" in Hindi

Yield: 4 to 6 servings

Ingredients:

- ½ teaspoon crudely ground black peppercorns
- ½ teaspoon dried fenugreek leaves
- ½ teaspoon salt, or to taste

- 1 cup chopped drained oil-packed sun-dried tomatoes (with 3 tablespoons olive oil reserved)
- 1 fresh green chile pepper, such as serrano, minced with seeds
- 1 large onion, cut in half along the length and thinly chopped
- 1 small bunch snipped chives
- 1½ tablespoons ground coriander
- 1½ teaspoons cumin seeds
- 8 ounces (1 recipe) <u>Paneer Cheese</u> (Homemade or store-bought)

Directions:

1. Ready the paneer cheese and cut it into ½-inch pieces. Heat the oil in a big non-stick wok or saucepan using moderate to high heat and put in the cumin seeds and peppercorns; they should sizzle when they touch the hot oil. Swiftly put in the onion and cook, stirring, until a golden colour is achieved, approximately five minutes.
2. Put in the paneer cheese, green chile pepper, coriander, fenugreek leaves, and salt, and cook, stirring and turning cautiously until a golden colour is achieved, approximately five minutes. Put in the sun-dried tomatoes and continue to cook, turning a few times, approximately five minutes. Move to a serving dish, sprinkle the snipped chives on top before you serve.

TOMATO DRY PANEER

This recipe is called "Tamatar vaala sookha paneer" in Hindi

Yield: 4 to 6 servings

Ingredients:

- ¼ teaspoon garam masala
- ½ teaspoon ajwain seeds, crudely crushed
- ½ teaspoon freshly ground black pepper
- ¾ cup crudely ground mixed nuts, such as cashews, almonds, or peanuts
- 1 cup crudely chopped fresh cilantro, including soft stems
- 1 fresh green chile pepper, such as serrano, minced with seeds
- 1 large clove fresh garlic, peeled
- 1 large onion, crudely chopped

- 1 large tomato, crudely chopped
- 1 tablespoon cumin seeds, dry-roasted and crudely ground (See the dry-roasting section in Introduction)
- 1 teaspoon salt, or to taste
- 2 to 3 tablespoons vegetable oil
- 3 quarter-size slices peeled fresh ginger
- 8 ounces (1 recipe) <u>Paneer Cheese</u> (Homemade or store-bought)
- A few sprigs fresh cilantro

Directions:

1. Ready the cumin. Ready the paneer cheese then cut it into 1-by-2-inch pieces. Put the onion, garlic, ginger, and green chile pepper into a food processor and pulse a few times until just minced. (Do not overprocess or the onion will become watery.) Move to a container, then process the tomato and cilantro until puréed.
2. Heat the oil in a big non-stick wok or saucepan using moderate to high heat and cook the onion mixture, stirring, using moderate to high heat the first two to three minutes and then over moderate heat until the onions are a nicely browned, approximately ten minutes. Add ½ cup nuts and stir approximately two minutes. (Reserve the rest of the nuts for garnish.)
3. Put in the paneer cheese, cumin, salt, pepper, and ajwain seeds and cook, stirring carefully, approximately five minutes. Put in the puréed tomatoes and cook, stirring as required, until all the liquids vaporize and cling to the paneer cheese, approximately ten minutes. Move to a serving dish, sprinkle the reserved nuts and garam masala on top, garnish with the cilantro sprigs before you serve.

PANEER CHEESE MAIN COURSES AND CURRIES

These are traditionally enjoyed with Indian griddle flatbreads, but will taste absolutely amazing with pretty much any bread you can get your hands on!

GRIDDLE-FRIED PANEER

This recipe is called "Tava-paneer" in Hindi

Yield: 4 to 6 servings

Ingredients:

- ¼ cup finely chopped fresh cilantro, including soft stems
- ¼ cup heavy cream
- ½ cup canned tomato sauce
- ½ teaspoon Chaat Masala (Homemade or store-bought)
- ½ teaspoon salt, or to taste
- 1 (1-inch) piece peeled fresh ginger, cut into thin matchsticks + 1 tablespoon peeled and minced ginger
- 1 tablespoon ground coriander
- 1 teaspoon ajwain seeds, crudely crushed
- 1 teaspoon cumin seeds
- 1 teaspoon garam masala
- 1 to 3 fresh green chile peppers, such as serrano, minced with seeds
- 2 small onions, cut in half along the length and thinly chopped
- 3 tablespoons melted ghee or vegetable oil
- 8 ounces (1 recipe) Paneer Cheese (Homemade or store-bought)

Directions:

1. Ready the chaat masala. Ready the paneer cheese then cut it into 3/4-inch pieces. In a container, combine the tomato sauce, cream, and garam masala.
2. Heat the ghee or oil on a large tava griddle or a skillet using moderate to high heat and put in the cumin and ajwain seeds; they should sizzle when they touch the hot oil. Swiftly put in the onion and ginger matchsticks and cook, stirring, until a golden colour is achieved, approximately five to seven minutes.
3. Put in the minced ginger, green chile peppers, and coriander, stir for approximately half a minute, then put in the paneer cheese pieces and salt. Cook, cautiously turning the pieces, until lightly golden, approximately two minutes.
4. Put in the tomato-cream mixture and cook, stirring and turning the pieces carefully, until the liquid evaporates completely, leaving behind a lovely red

glaze, approximately two to three minutes. Stir in the cilantro and stir another minute. Sprinkle the chaat masala on top and serve straight from the tava or move to a serving dish.

NINE-JEWEL PANEER CURRY

This recipe is called "Navrattan korma" in Hindi

Yield: 6 to 8 servings

Ingredients:

- ¼ cup crudely chopped raw almonds
- ¼ cup crudely chopped raw cashews
- ¼ cup raisins
- ½ cup finely chopped fresh cilantro, including soft stems
- 1 cup fresh or canned Coconut Milk (Homemade or store-bought)
- 1 cup plain yogurt, whisked until the desired smoothness is achieved
- 1 large onion, finely chopped
- 1 tablespoon ground coriander
- 1 tablespoon peeled minced fresh ginger
- 1 teaspoon garam masala + more for garnish
- 1 teaspoon ground cumin
- 1 teaspoon salt, or to taste
- 1 to 3 fresh green chile peppers, such as serrano, minced with seeds
- 1½ cups water
- 2 (1-inch) sticks cinnamon
- 2 bay leaves
- 2 teaspoons fresh garlic, minced
- 3 cups finely chopped mixed fresh or (thawed) frozen vegetables, such as carrots, potatoes, cauliflower, beans, and peas
- 3 tablespoons vegetable oil
- 4 whole cloves
- 5 black cardamom pods, pounded lightly to break the skin
- 8 ounces (1 recipe) Paneer Cheese (Homemade or store-bought)

Directions:

1. Ready the coconut milk. Ready the paneer cheese then cut into 3/4-inch thick pieces. Using a blender, mix together and pulse the yogurt, coconut milk, water, and salt until the desired smoothness is achieved.
2. Heat 1 tablespoon oil in a big non-stick saucepan using moderate to high heat and cook the cashews, almonds, and raisins, stirring, until the raisins expand, approximately one minute. Move to a container. Add 1 more tablespoon oil to the same pan and cook the vegetables, stirring, until a golden colour is achieved, approximately ten minutes. Move to a different container.
3. Put in the rest of the 1 tablespoon oil to the same pan and cook the bay leaves, cardamom pods, cinnamon, and cloves, stirring, approximately one minute. Put in the onion and cook, stirring, until thoroughly browned, ten minutes. Put in the ginger, garlic, and green chile peppers and stir approximately one minute. Next, Put in the coriander, cumin, and 1 teaspoon garam masala and stir another minute.
4. Put in the yogurt-coconut milk mixture and cook, stirring approximately five minutes. Stir in the paneer cheese pieces and the cooked vegetables, cover the pan, decrease the heat to moderate to low, and simmer until the vegetables become soft and the sauce is very thick, approximately fifteen minutes. Stir in the cilantro during the last 5 minutes of cooking. Move to a serving dish, garnish with the nut-raisin mixture, sprinkle on some garam masala before you serve.

PANEER AND RED CHILE PEPPER CURRY

This recipe is called "Paneer, laal mirchi" in Hindi

Yield: 4 to 6 servings

Ingredients:

- ¼ teaspoon garam masala
- ¼ teaspoon ground turmeric
- ¼ to ½ cup heavy cream
- ½ cup finely chopped fresh cilantro, including soft stems
- ½ teaspoon hot red pepper flakes, or to taste

- 1 tablespoon Basic Ginger-Garlic Paste (Homemade or store-bought)
- 1 tablespoon ground coriander
- 1 teaspoon cumin seeds
- 1 teaspoon salt, or to taste
- 2 medium tomatoes, finely chopped
- 2 tablespoons vegetable oil
- 4 to 6 whole dried red chile peppers, such as chile de arbol
- 8 ounces (1 recipe) Paneer Cheese (Homemade or store-bought)

Directions:

1. Ready the ginger-garlic paste. Ready the paneer cheese and cut it into 1-inch-by-½-inch pieces. Heat the oil in a big non-stick wok or saucepan using moderate to high heat and cook the red chile peppers, stirring, until a golden colour is achieved brown, approximately one minute. Put in the cumin seeds; they should sizzle when they touch the hot oil. Swiftly put in the ginger-garlic paste and cook, stirring, approximately one minute. Next, Put in the tomatoes and cook until the fluids vaporize, approximately five minutes.
2. Put in the cream and cook, stirring, over moderate heat until it is well completely blended with the sauce, approximately five minutes. Stir in the coriander, red pepper flakes, turmeric, and salt, then put in the paneer cheese and cook, stirring carefully, approximately five minutes. Stir in the cilantro and cook approximately two minutes. Move to a serving dish, sprinkle the garam masala on top before you serve.

PANEER ONION CURRY

This recipe is called "Do-pyaza paneer" in Hindi

Yield: 4 to 6 servings

Ingredients:

- ¼ cup finely chopped fresh cilantro, including soft stems
- ¼ teaspoon ground turmeric
- ½ teaspoon garam masala
- ½ teaspoon hot red pepper flakes, or to taste
- 1 (1-inch) stick cinnamon

- 1 cup finely chopped white or yellow onions
- 1 tablespoon ground coriander
- 1 teaspoon fresh garlic, minced
- 1½ teaspoons cumin seeds
- 2 black cardamom pods, crushed lightly to break the skin
- 2 tablespoons vegetable oil
- 3 green cardamom pods, crushed lightly to break the skin
- 3 to 4 small red onions, quartered (cut the larger ones into eighths)
- 3 to 4 small tomatoes, quartered
- 8 ounces (1 recipe) <u>Paneer Cheese</u> (Homemade or store-bought)

Directions:

1. Ready the paneer cheese and cut into 1¼-inch pieces.
2. Heat the oil in a big non-stick wok or saucepan using moderate to high heat and put in the cinnamon, green and black cardamom pods, and cumin seeds; they should sizzle when they touch the hot oil. Swiftly put in the chopped onion and cook, stirring, until a golden colour is achieved, approximately five minutes.
3. **3.** Stir in the garlic, red pepper flakes, and turmeric, then put in the quartered red onions and the coriander and cook, stirring, using moderate to low heat until a mild brown colour is achieved, approximately five minutes. Put in the tomatoes and paneer cheese pieces and cook, stirring and turning carefully, until the paneer cheese is very soft, approximately five to seven minutes. Put in the cilantro during the last two minutes of cooking. Move to a serving dish, lightly stir in the garam masala before you serve.

PANEER-COCONUT CURRY

This recipe is called "Paneer korma" in Hindi

Yield: 4 to 6 servings

Ingredients:

- ⅛ teaspoon ground mace
- ⅛ teaspoon ground nutmeg
- ¼ cup Dessert Masala

- 1 (1-inch) stick cinnamon
- 1 cup Coconut Milk (Homemade or store-bought)
- 1 cup frozen peas, thawed
- 1 large tomato, crudely chopped
- 1 small onion, crudely chopped
- 1 teaspoon cumin seeds
- 1 teaspoon garam masala
- 1 teaspoon ground coriander
- 1 teaspoon salt, or to taste
- 1 to 3 fresh green chile peppers, such as serrano, stemmed
- 10 raw cashews, crudely chopped
- 2 bay leaves
- 2 tablespoons vegetable oil
- 2 to 3 large cloves fresh garlic, peeled
- 4 cloves
- 4 green cardamom pods, pounded lightly to break the skin
- 5 to 6 quarter-size slices peeled fresh ginger
- 8 ounces (1 recipe) Paneer Cheese (Homemade or store-bought)
- Freshly ground black pepper, for garnish

Directions:

1. Ready the coconut milk. Ready the paneer cheese then cut into 1½-by-½-inch thick rectangles. Ready the dessert masala.
2. Using a food processor or a blender, combine and pulse the onion, garlic, ginger, green chile peppers, and cashews approximately one minute until a smooth paste is achieved. Move to a container, put in the tomato to your food processor, and process until puréed.
3. Heat the oil in a big non-stick wok or saucepan using moderate to high heat and cook the bay leaves, cumin, cinnamon, cardamom pods, and cloves, stirring, until fragrant, approximately one minute. Decrease the heat to medium and add, the nutmeg and mace, then the coriander and garam masala. Stir approximately half a minute, then put in the onion paste and cook, stirring, until thoroughly browned, approximately ten minutes.
4. Put in the puréed tomato and cook, stirring constantly, until the fluids vaporize, approximately three minutes. Put in the paneer cheese, peas, salt, and coconut milk. Cover the pan, lower the heat, and simmer until the paneer pieces are soft and the sauce is thick, ten to fifteen minutes. Move to a serving dish, garnish with black pepper before you serve.

PANEER-PEA-POTATO CURRY

This recipe is called "Paneer, mutter aur aalu ki kari" in Hindi

Yield: 6 to 8 servings

Ingredients:

- ⅛ teaspoon ground nutmeg
- ¼ cup finely chopped fresh cilantro, including soft stems
- ¼ cup heavy cream (not compulsory)
- ¼ cup non-fat plain yogurt, whisked until the desired smoothness is achieved
- ¼ teaspoon cayenne pepper, or to taste
- ¼ teaspoon garam masala
- ¼ teaspoon ground paprika
- ¼ teaspoon ground turmeric
- ¾ cup (½ recipe) Boiled Onion Paste
- ¾ teaspoon salt, or to taste
- 1 (1-inch) stick cinnamon
- 1 cup frozen peas, thawed
- 1 large tomato, finely chopped
- 1 tablespoon ground coriander
- 1 teaspoon dried fenugreek leaves
- 1 to 1½ cups peanut oil for deep-frying
- 1½ teaspoons cumin seeds
- 3 black cardamom pods, crushed lightly to break the skin
- 3 to 5 fresh green chile peppers, such as serrano, skin punctured to stop bursting
- 4 cups water
- 4 small russet potatoes (or any kind), peeled and cut into 4 wedges each
- 8 ounces (1 recipe) <u>Paneer Cheese</u> (Homemade or store-bought)

Directions:

1. Ready the paneer cheese then cut into 1-inch pieces. Ready the onion paste.
2. Line a tray with paper towels. Heat the oil in a big wok until it reaches 325°F to 350°F on a frying thermometer, or until a small piece of paneer cheese dropped into the hot oil bubbles and surges to the surface of the oil instantly. Standing far from the wok (because the paneer cheese will splatter

from the moisture), cautiously Put in the paneer cheese pieces, one at a time, adding as many as the wok will hold without crowding. Fry the paneer, flipping over once or twice, until just golden on both sides, approximately half a minute. (This happens very swiftly, so work fast.) Using a slotted spoon, move to paper towels to drain.

3. Remove all but 2 tablespoons of the oil from the wok and heat it using moderate to high heat. Put in the green chile peppers, cinnamon, cardamom pods, and cumin seeds; they should sizzle when they touch the hot oil. Swiftly put in the coriander, turmeric, cayenne pepper, paprika, and nutmeg, and stir for approximately half a minute. Put in the tomato and cook, stirring, until all the fluids vaporize, approximately five minutes. Put in the yogurt, slowly and gradually, stirring continuously to stop it from curdling.
4. Put in the potatoes and cook, stirring, approximately five minutes. Next, Put in the water and salt and bring to a boil using high heat. Decrease the heat to moderate to low, cover the pan, and simmer until the potatoes tender, approximately twenty minutes. Stir in the peas and paneer cheese, cover the pan, and simmer until the peas and paneer cheese pieces are soft and the sauce is thick, approximately ten minutes. Put in the cream (if using) and fenugreek leaves and simmer approximately five minutes to blend the flavours. Move to a serving dish. Stir in the cilantro and garam masala and serve.

PANEER-POTATO CURRY

This recipe is called "Paneer aalu ki kari" in Hindi

Yield: 4 to 6 servings

Ingredients:

- ⅛ teaspoon ground asafoetida
- ¼ teaspoon garam masala
- ¼ teaspoon ground paprika
- ¼ teaspoon ground turmeric
- ¼ teaspoon hot red pepper flakes
- ½ cup finely chopped fresh cilantro, including soft stems
- ½ teaspoon dried fenugreek leaves
- 1 large russet potato, peeled and cut into 3/4-inch pieces

- 1 tablespoon ground coriander
- 1 tablespoon minced fresh mint
- 1 tablespoon peeled and chopped fresh ginger
- 1 teaspoon cumin seeds
- 1 teaspoon salt, or to taste
- 2 tablespoons melted ghee or vegetable oil
- 3 to 4 cups water
- 3 to 4 medium tomatoes, finely chopped
- 5 to 7 fresh green chile peppers, such as serrano, skin punctured to stop bursting
- 8 ounces (1 recipe) <u>Paneer Cheese</u> (Homemade or store-bought)

Directions:

1. Ready the paneer cheese and cut it into 1-inch or larger pieces.
2. Heat the ghee (or oil) in a big non-stick saucepan using moderate to high heat and put in the green chile peppers, cumin seeds, and ginger; they should sizzle when they touch the hot oil. Swiftly put in the asafoetida, coriander, fenugreek leaves, paprika, turmeric, red pepper flakes, and salt, and stir for approximately half a minute.
3. Put in the tomatoes and cilantro and cook until most of the liquid tomatoes evaporates, approximately ten minutes. Put in the potato and cook, stirring, approximately five minutes. Put in the water, cover the pan, and cook using moderate to high heat the first two to three minutes and then over moderate heat until the potatoes become soft, 20 to 25 minutes. Stir occasionally. When the potatoes are soft, using the back of a ladle or a wooden spoon, mash a few of them against the sides of the pan to thicken the gravy.
4. Put in the paneer cheese, cover the pan and simmer, stirring intermittently, approximately five minutes. (Add another ½ cup water if the sauce gets too thick.) Move to a serving dish, lightly stir in the mint and garam masala before you serve.

ROYAL PANEER CURRY

This recipe is called "Shahi paneer" in Hindi

Yield: 4 to 6 servings

Ingredients:

- ¼ cup crudely chopped shelled raw pistachios
- ¼ cup raw almond slivers
- ½ cup golden raisins
- 1 (1-inch) piece peeled fresh ginger, cut into thin matchsticks
- 1 teaspoon cumin seeds
- 1 teaspoon ground dried fenugreek leaves
- 1 to 3 fresh green chile peppers, such as serrano, each split along the length in half, with or without seeds
- 1½ tablespoons melted ghee
- 2 tablespoons heavy cream
- 4 cups (1 recipe) Butter-Cream Sauce with Fresh Tomatoes
- 8 ounces (1 recipe) <u>Paneer Cheese</u> (Homemade or store-bought)

Directions:

1. Ready the paneer cheese then cut into thick 1½-inch squares. Ready the cream sauce.
2. Heat 1 tablespoon ghee in a big non-stick wok or saucepan using moderate to high heat and cook the ginger and green chile peppers, stirring, until a golden colour is achieved, approximately two minutes. Put in the cumin seeds; they should sizzle when they touch the hot oil. Swiftly put in the raisins, pistachios, and almond slivers and stir until the raisins start to expand, approximately one minute. Remove everything to a container and reserve.
3. Put in the rest of the ½ tablespoon ghee to the pan and cook the paneer cheese pieces, stirring, approximately two minutes. Put in the cream sauce and fenugreek leaves and simmer approximately ten minutes to blend the flavours. Move to a serving dish, swirl in the heavy cream, garnish with the raisin-nut mixture before you serve.

SPINACH AND FENUGREEK PANEER

This recipe is called "Palak aur methi paneer" in Hindi

Yield: 6 to 8 servings

Ingredients:

- ¼ cup Crispy Fried Fresh Ginger
- ¼ teaspoon ground turmeric
- ½ cup plain yogurt, whisked until the desired smoothness is achieved
- 1 large clove fresh garlic, peeled
- 1 tablespoon melted ghee
- 1 teaspoon salt, or to taste
- 1 to 3 fresh green chile peppers, such as serrano, stemmed
- 2 cups packed fresh fenugreek leaves (or ¼ cup dried)
- 2 tablespoons peanut oil
- 4 cups packed (2 small bunches) fresh baby spinach
- 4 quarter-size slices peeled fresh ginger
- 8 ounces (1 recipe) <u>Paneer Cheese</u> (Homemade or store-bought)

Directions:

1. Ready the paneer cheese and cut it into thick 3/4-inch pieces. Ready the crunchy fried ginger.
2. Trim and wash the spinach. If using fresh fenugreek, pick out the leaves and the softest stems and discard the hard and fibrous parts. Rinse well. Move the spinach, prepared fresh or dried fenugreek, fresh ginger, garlic, and green chile peppers to a food processor and process until minced, approximately one minute.
3. Heat the oil and ghee in a big cast-iron or non-stick wok or a saucepan using moderate to high heat and cook the greens, stirring and scraping the sides of the wok, using moderate to high heat the first two to three minutes and then over moderate heat until well-roasted and deep green in color, fifteen to twenty minutes.
4. Stir in the paneer cheese, salt, and turmeric and cook, stirring, approximately two to three minutes. Put in the yogurt, slowly and gradually, stirring continuously to stop it from curdling, and continue to cook until all the liquids vaporize and paneer pieces are soft, three to five minutes. Move to a serving dish, garnish with the fried ginger before you serve.

SPINACH PANEER

This recipe is called "Saag paneer" in Hindi

Yield: 4 to 6 servings

Ingredients:

- ¼ cup plain yogurt (any kind), whisked until the desired smoothness is achieved
- ¼ cup water
- ½ teaspoon ground paprika
- ½ teaspoon salt, or to taste
- 1 large onion, crudely chopped
- 1 tablespoon ground coriander
- 1 tablespoon melted ghee
- 1 teaspoon dried fenugreek leaves
- 1 teaspoon garam masala
- 1 to 2 tablespoons unsalted butter, at room temperature
- 2 (1-inch) sticks cinnamon
- 2 small bunches (about 1 pound) fresh spinach, trimmed of roots only, washed well and crudely chopped
- 2 tablespoons vegetable oil
- 3 large cloves fresh garlic, peeled + 1 clove minced
- 4 quarter-size slices peeled fresh ginger + 1 (1-inch) piece peeled and cut into thin matchsticks
- 4 whole dried red chile peppers, such as chile de arbol
- 5 green cardamom pods, crushed lightly to break the skin
- 8 ounces (1 recipe) <u>Paneer Cheese</u> (Homemade or store-bought)

Directions:

1. Ready the paneer cheese and cut it into 1-by-½-inch squares.
2. Put the spinach, onion, ginger slices, whole garlic, and water in a big non-stick saucepan. Cover and bring to a boil using high heat. Decrease the heat to moderate to low, cover the pan, and simmer until the spinach is wilted and the onion tender, approximately ten minutes. Allow to cool, then pulse lightly Using a food processor until just minced (do not make a smooth purée). Return to the pan.

3. Heat the oil and ghee in a small saucepan using moderate to high heat and cook the cinnamon, cardamom pods, and ginger matchsticks, stirring, until the ginger is golden, approximately a minute or two. Put in the minced garlic, coriander, garam masala, fenugreek leaves, and salt and stir a few seconds. Next, Put in the yogurt, slowly and gradually, stirring continuously to stop curdling. Immediately move to the spinach, cover, and simmer over moderate heat, ten to fifteen minutes.
4. Put in the paneer cheese to the pan and stir softly to combine, trying not to break the pieces. Cover and simmer, stirring intermittently, approximately ten minutes to blend the flavours. Move to a serving dish.
5. Heat the butter in a small saucepan, put in the dried chile peppers, and cook, stirring, until a golden colour is achieved, approximately half a minute. Remove the pan from the heat, put in the paprika, then instantly add to the spinach dish and stir mildly to combine, with parts of the chile peppers visible as a decoration. Serve hot.

STIR-FRIED PANEER WITH ONIONS AND BELL PEPPERS

This recipe is called "Kadhai paneer" in Hindi

Yield: 4 to 6 servings

Ingredients:

- Crudely ground black pepper, to taste
- four to five small bell peppers of assorted colors, cut into thin matchsticks
- ¼ cup finely chopped fresh cilantro, including soft stems
- ¼ teaspoon ground black salt
- ½ teaspoon ground anise or fennel seeds
- ½ teaspoon ground black cardamom seeds
- ½ teaspoon hot red pepper flakes, or to taste
- ½ teaspoon salt, or to taste
- 1 (1-inch) piece peeled fresh ginger, cut into thin matchsticks
- 1 teaspoon ground cumin
- 1 teaspoon ground dried pomegranate seeds
- 1½ tablespoons ground coriander

- 2 large cloves garlic, thinly chopped
- 2 small onions, cut in half along the length and thinly chopped
- 2 teaspoons ground dried fenugreek leaves
- 3 tablespoons peanut oil
- 4 ounces (½ recipe) <u>Paneer Cheese</u> (Homemade or store-bought)
- 4 small tomatoes, cut into wedges

Directions:

1. Ready the paneer cheese and cut it into thick 1½-by-½-inch rectangles.
2. Heat the oil in a big non-stick wok or skillet using moderate to high heat, put in the ginger and garlic, and cook, stirring, until a golden colour is achieved, approximately one minute. Put in the onions and cook, stirring, until barely golden, approximately two to three minutes. Using a slotted spoon, move the mixture to a container, leaving all the oil behind.
3. In the wok, put in the coriander, fenugreek, cumin, anise or fennel, pomegranate and cardamom seeds, red pepper flakes, salt, and black salt, and stir over moderate heat approximately two minutes. Put in the tomatoes and bell peppers, cover the wok, and cook until slightly softened, approximately five minutes. Cautiously stir in the paneer cheese, cover the wok, and continue to cook, flipping over once or twice, until the pieces are soft and the dish is somewhat saucy, approximately five minutes.
4. Put in the reserved onions and the cilantro and cook using moderate to high heat, uncovered, approximately five minutes. Move to a serving platter (or serve straight from the wok), top with black pepper before you serve.

STUFFED PANEER BALLS CURRY

This recipe is called "Malai kofta curry" in Hindi

Yield: 6 to 8 servings

Ingredients:

- ¼ cup finely chopped fresh cilantro, including soft stems
- ½ cup crudely chopped cashews
- ½ cup finely chopped onion
- ½ teaspoon freshly ground black pepper, or to taste

- 1 medium russet potato (or any kind)
- 1 tablespoon melted ghee or unsalted butter
- 1 teaspoon salt, or to taste
- 1½ to 2 cups peanut oil for deep-frying
- 2 tablespoons crudely chopped raw almonds
- 2 tablespoons crudely chopped raw pistachios
- 2 tablespoons chopped raisins
- 4 cups (1 recipe) Butter-Cream Sauce with Fresh Tomatoes
- 5 to 6 quarter-size slices peeled fresh ginger
- 8 ounces (1 recipe) <u>Paneer Cheese</u> (Homemade or store-bought)
- 8 scallions, white parts only, crudely chopped

Directions:

1. Ready the paneer cheese and crumble it coarsely. Ready the cream sauce and keep it ready. While you're making either the cheese or the sauce, also boil the potato in water to cover until tender, then peel and grate it.
2. Using a food processor, combine and pulse the cashews, ginger, and scallions until minced. Put in the paneer cheese, black pepper, and salt, and process until it begins to gather like a dough, approximately half a minute. Move to a container, put in the potato, then mix with clean hands to make a soft dough. Cover and reserve.
3. for the filling. Heat the ghee in a small saucepan using moderate to high heat and cook the onion, stirring, until a golden colour is achieved, approximately two minutes. Put in the pistachios, almonds, and raisins and stir another two minutes. Allow to cool.
4. Divide the paneer dough and the raisin-nut filling each into fifteen to 20 portions. Working with each paneer portion separately, flatten into a disk, place the nuts in the center, then close the disk around the filling and shape into 1½-inch smooth balls.
5. Heat the oil in a big wok using moderate to high heat until it achieves 325°F to 350°F on a frying thermometer, or a small bit of the dough dropped into the hot oil bubbles and surges to the surface of the oil instantly. Fry the paneer balls, as many as the wok can hold simultaneously without crowding, turning them a few times until a golden colour is achieved and crunchy on all sides, approximately five minutes. Using a slotted spoon, move to paper towels to drain.
6. Preheat your oven to 400°F. Move the paneer balls an oven-proof baking dish and pour in the prepared cream sauce. Cover and bake approximately

twenty minutes. Do not stir at any time. Take out of the oven, spoon the sauce over the paneer balls if they seem dry, garnish with the cilantro before you serve.

COCONUT AND CORN PANEER

This recipe is called "Nariyal aur makki ka paneer" in Hindi

Yield: 4 to 6 servings

Ingredients:

- ⅛ teaspoon ground asafoetida
- ¼ cup Coconut Milk (Homemade or store-bought)
- ½ cup finely chopped fresh cilantro, including soft stems
- ½ teaspoon freshly ground black pepper, or to taste
- ¾ teaspoon salt, or to taste
- 1 (3-inch-piece) fresh coconut, peeled and crudely chopped, or 1 tablespoon unsweetened shredded dried coconut
- 1 large onion, crudely chopped
- 1 pasilla pepper or green bell pepper, crudely chopped
- 1 tablespoon ground coriander
- 1 teaspoon black mustard seeds
- 1 teaspoon cumin seeds
- 1½ cups frozen corn (unthawed)
- 15 to 20 fresh curry leaves (or 1 teaspoon dried)
- 2 tablespoons vegetable oil
- 4 to 6 quarter-size slices peeled fresh ginger
- 8 ounces (1 recipe) Paneer Cheese (Homemade or store-bought)

Directions:

1. Ready the coconut milk. Ready the paneer cheese then cut into thin 1-inch pieces. Using a food processor or a blender, combine and pulse the ginger, coconut, and pasilla pepper until minced. Put in the onion and curry leaves and pulse a few times, until just minced. (Do not overprocess or the onion will become watery.)

2. Heat the oil in a big non-stick wok or saucepan using moderate to high heat and put in the cumin and mustard seeds; they should splatter when they touch the hot oil, so cover the pan and reduce the heat until the splattering diminishes. Swiftly put in the ginger-onion mixture and cook, stirring, until browned, approximately ten minutes.
3. Put in the asafoetida, coriander, and salt, then put in the paneer cheese and coconut milk, and cook over moderate heat, flipping the pieces carefully, until lightly golden, approximately five to seven minutes.
4. Put in the frozen corn, cover the wok, and cook, stirring carefully, using moderate to low heat, until the corn is tender and all the moisture is absorbed into the paneer, approximately ten minutes. Stir in the black pepper and cilantro, move to a serving dish before you serve.

BREADS AND CREPES

Indian breads taste great, are easy to make, and are highly nutritious since most of them are made using whole-grain flours. In India, a minicourse almost always contains an Indian flatbread, or rice, or both.

Whole-wheat flour (gehun ka atta or atta) is the most popular flour for flatbreads in India by a mile. The most common variety of wheat used to create whole-wheat flour in India is "durum" which is the hardest variety of wheat out there. It has a high protein and gluten content which is perfect for the texture of Indian flatbreads. Typical American whole-wheat flour is not ideal for making Indian flatbreads, so **make sure you find a source of Stone-Ground Durum** near you. It is easily available in Indian markets, and you can easily find it online on amazon.

Indian flatbreads can be broadly classified into the following categories:

- **Griddle Breads:** Made using a tava (concave Indian griddle), these are usually non-leavened, round, triangular, or square flatbreads called roti, chapati, phulka, rotli, and parantha.
- **Deep-Fried Breads:** Fried using an Indian wok or deep skillet, these breads can be leavened or un-leavened, andare called poori, kulcha, lucchi, or baati. They come in all shapes and sizes, pretty much.

- **Tandoori Breads:** Baked by sticking them on the inside wall of a tandoor oven, these breads, called tandoori roti, parantha, naan, or kulcha, can be round or triangular.
- **Crepes and Pancakes**: Griddle-fried and made with batters rather instead of a dough, and eaten in place of standard breads; these breads, called dosas, uthapam, pudhas, and chillas, are generally round, and originate in South India.

If you don't have a tava for making Indian flatbreads in your kitchen, you can always use something that resembles it until you decide to invest in a tava. Omelette pans get the job done nicely. At the same time, a tava is great for making omelettes too, so if you do invest in one, just know that it can be useful for much more than Indian cooking. You can easily find a tava in an Indian market, or you can always get one online on amazon.

All right, lets jump into the recipes!

Ⓥ= Vegan Ⓟ= Quick Pressure Cooker Recipe

SIMPLE GRIDDLE BREADS

These simple griddle breads are the most basic and commonly eaten breads in India. They are commonly enjoyed with a bit of "Ghee" (Indian clarified butter) smeared on one side, but if you're trying to cut your calories, you can skip the ghee. Do know that if you omit the ghee, you're missing out on the ultimate combo.

If you're cooking for a big gathering, you can always prepare these breads in advance, and then store them in the fridge up to five days and in the freezer for as long as sixty days. To do this, cook the breads mildly on both sides, alow them to cool to room temperature. Next, stack them one on top of the other and wrap using an aluminium foil or place in zip closure bags, and refrigerate or freeze. When its time to eat them, take them out of the fridge and cook again on the griddle for a short while, until cooked through.

WORKING WITH WHOLE-WHEAT DOUGH

Traditionally in India, the dough is worked with hand. Today, however, we have technology to make the work easier. Food processor and mixers come in handy. Chapati presses are also quite popular today, even in India. These make the job of flattening the dough really easy. All you need to do is make a ball of dough, place it in the chapati press, and... well, press. You can find these easily in an Indian store, or online on amazon.

Tips and Tricks for Working the Dough:

- Make a semi-firm dough that doesn't cling to your fingers. If the dough is too hard, the bread made from it will be hard too, and if it is too soft, it will cling to your fingers and you will be unable to work with it.
- Cover the dough using plastic wrap or the lid of the container and allow it to rest one to four hours to let the gluten to develop. This makes breads that are crunchy on the outside and soft on the inside.
- Whole-wheat dough stores well approximately 3 days in an airtight vessel in a fridge. Use it if possible at room temperature, or chilled straight from the refrigerator. Chilled dough will be firm and slightly tougher to use.
- Dough can be frozen up to sixty days. Thaw at room temperature. Never microwave. This cooks the dough, ruining it for bread making.

BASIC WHOLE-WHEAT DOUGH

This recipe is called "Gundha hua atta" in Hindi

Yield: ten to twelve breads

This will give you the most basic moist dough ready for making breads.

Ingredients:

- 2 cups stone-ground durum whole-wheat flour

- About 1 cup water, or non-fat plain yogurt, whisked until the desired smoothness is achieved

Directions To make Using a food processor:

1. Put the flour in the work container of your food processor fitted with the metal S-blade. Turn the machine on, put in the water or yogurt in a thin stream, and process until it just gathers into a ball.
2. Continue to process until the sides of the container look clean, 20 to half a minute. (Add 1 or 2 tablespoons more flour if the dough sticks to the sides of the work container, and some water if the dough appears hard.) Stop the machine, remove the dough to a container, cover using plastic wrap or the lid of the container, and allow to rest for minimum 1 and maximum four hours. (This lets the gluten develop.) If keeping for a longer period, place the dough in your fridge.

Directions To make by hand:

1. Put the flour in a container and add ¾ cup water. Stir lightly in round circular movements with clean fingers until it begins to gather. (Add 1 or 2 tablespoons more flour if the dough appears sticky, or some water if it appears too firm.)
2. Knead for approximately a minute, pushing your knuckles gently into the dough, flattening the dough outward, then pick up the ends of the flattened dough using your hands, and fold them so that all the ends meet in the center. Replicate this kneading process a few times until a tender and flexible dough is attained that does not cling to your fingers. If the dough gets too sticky while you work it, coat your hands with a little oil or water.
3. Cover using plastic wrap or the lid of the container and allow to rest for minimum one and maximum four hours at room temperature. (This lets the gluten develop.) If keeping for a longer period, place the dough in your fridge.

WHOLE-WHEAT GRIDDLE BREADS

This recipe is called "Chapati, roti, aur phulka" in Hindi

Yield: ten to twelve breads

This is the most commonly enjoyed bread in India. This bread sustains more than a billion people, and can be enjoyed in multiple ways. Throw some ghee and salt over it, and you're good to go. It is enjoyed with Indian curries, or just with a chutney or pickle. In India, these are almost always cooked immediately before consumption. Left over chapatis can be stored in hot cases if you wish to consume a few hours later.

Ingredients:

- 1 recipe Basic Whole-Wheat Dough
- 1 cup stone-ground durum whole-wheat flour in a moderate-sized container or a pie dish, for coating and dusting
- Rolling pin
- 3 to 4 tablespoons melted ghee or butter, for basting (not compulsory)

Directions:

1. Heat the tava or griddle using moderate to high heat until a sprinkling of the flour instantly turns dark brown. Wipe off the flour and continue. While the tava heats up, use mildly oiled hands to split the dough into ten to twelve identical balls and cover using a foil to stop drying.
2. Work with each ball one at a time, and put it in the container with the dry flour, flatten it using your fingertips and cover thoroughly with the flour. Next, move it to a cutting board or any other clean flat surface, and, use a rolling pin to roll it into a 6- to 7-inch evenly thick circle. If the dough sticks to the rolling surface, sprinkle mildly with more flour. (Chapatis can be rolled on a mildly floured surface also, though this is not a common practice in India.)
3. Put the rolled chapati on the hot tava and flip it over when small golden dots appear on the side being heated, approximately half a minute. Once the other side is covered with larger brown dots, flip it over once more. Soon the chapati will start to puff up. Use a crumpled kitchen towel to push softly on the puffed parts and softly guide and push the air into the flatter parts until the whole chapati puffs up into a round ball. (You will get used to this soon enough, even if you don't get it right on the frist try.) Move to a plate, baste lightly with the ghee, if using (and crumple it if you wish) before you serve hot.

MULTI-FLOUR GRIDDLE BREADS

This recipe is called "Millae-julle aatton ki roti" in Hindi

Yield: ten to twelve breads

A blend of flours is better than one.

Ingredients:

- ¼ cup ground flax seeds
- ¼ teaspoon freshly ground black pepper, or to taste
- ¼ teaspoon salt, or to taste
- ⅓ cup fine-grain semolina
- ⅓ cup oat flour
- ⅓ cup soy flour
- ⅓ cup whole-wheat flour
- ½ teaspoon crudely ground carom seeds
- ⅔ to ¾ cup water or non-fat plain yogurt, whisked until the desired smoothness is achieved
- 1 cup finely chopped fresh spinach, or any other greens
- 1 teaspoon dried fenugreek leaves
- 1 teaspoon dried mint leaves

Directions:

1. In a large container, combine everything except the water (or yogurt). Next, Put in the water (or yogurt), slowly and gradually, mixing lightly with clean fingers in round circular movements until the flour begins to gather. (Add 1 or 2 tablespoons more flour if the dough appears sticky, or some water if it appears too firm.)
2. Knead for approximately a minute, pushing your knuckles gently into the dough, flattening the dough outward, then gathering the ends together toward the center using your fingers. Push down the center, then repeat pressing and gathering a few times until a tender and flexible dough is attained that does not cling to your fingers. If the dough gets too sticky while you work it, coat your hands with a little oil or water.
3. Cover using plastic wrap or the lid of the container and allow it to rest at least 1 and maximum four hours at room temperature. This lets the gluten develop. If keeping for a longer period, place the dough in your fridge.

4. To make the chapati breads, with lightly oiled hands divide the dough equally into ten to twelve round balls, cover using a foil to stop drying, then follow the directions for <u>Whole-Wheat Griddle Breads</u> from Step 2.

GRIDDLE-FRIED BREADS (PARANTHAS)

Paranthas taste insanely delicious, and we Indians just can't live without them. They contain more calories than simple griddle breads as paranthas have a fat (usually butter, ghee, or oil) mixed into the dough. So, if you're watching your calories, or your heart health, paranthas are probably not your best bet. If you're healthy, feel free to indulge in moderation!

Stuffed paranthas require a little more effort to make, but are complete meals on their own, and can be eaten without any sides, or with pickle, yogurt, chutney, or other sides. Non-stuffed paranthas are usually enjoyed with a curry on the side.

BASIC PARANTHA BREADS

Paranthas have multiple layers, are crispy on the outside and soft on the inside. To make sure the parantha you make comes out as it is intended, you might need a bit of practice with the dough.

SHAPING PARANTHAS

In India, parathas are served in one of the three shapes- square, triangle, and circle. I will teach you how to make each shape here.

Directions to Make a Layered Triangle:

1. Sanitize your hands, lightly oil them, and split the dough into equivalent portions and cover using a foil to stop drying. Work one portion at a time,

flatten into a disc using your fingertips, liberally coat with flour, and roll into a 5- to 6-inch circle.
2. Coat the top surface mildly with oil, sprinkle on the spices, herbs, or vegetables, if you are using them, then sprinkle approximately 1 teaspoon dry flour over the spices and fold in half, making a semi-circle.
3. Coat the top of the semi-circle with oil and fold in half once more, making a triangle. Flatten this triangle into a larger triangle using your fingertips, coat it with flour once again, and roll it into a 6- to 7-inch triangle, making sure it retains its shape.

Directions To Make a Layered Square:

1. Split the dough into equivalent portions. Work one portion at a time, flatten into a disc using your fingertips, coat liberally with flour, and roll into a 5- to 6-inch circle.
2. Coat the top surface mildly with oil, sprinkle on the spices, herbs, or vegetables, if you are using them, then sprinkle approximately 1 teaspoon dry flour on top.
3. Mentally imagine splitting the circle into 3 portions lengthwise. Fold ⅓ over the center portion (you should get a D-shape), then fold the exposed portion toward the center, placing it on top of the first one. You should get a long, triple-folded rectangle.
4. Cover the top surface of this rectangle lightly with oil and fold it one more time, bringing the two smaller edges toward the center, placing one over the other, to make a small square. Flatten this square into a larger square using your fingertips, coat it with flour, and roll it out into a 6- to 7-inch square, making sure it retains its shape.

Directions To Make a Layered Circle :

1. Split the dough into equivalent portions. Work one portion at a time, flatten into a disc using your fingertips, coat with flour, and roll it into a 5- to 6-inch circle.
2. Coat the top surface mildly with oil, sprinkle on the spices, herbs, or vegetables, if you are using them, then sprinkle approximately 1 teaspoon dry flour over the spices, and roll it into a rope 7 to 8 inches long and ½ inch in diameter. Cover the rope lightly with oil.
3. Starting from one end, wind the rope into a spiral coil, with all sides touching. Flatten this coil using your fingertips and coat it with flour, then roll it out into a 6- to 7-inch circle.

BASIC PARANTHA Ⓥ

This recipe is called "Saada parantha" in Hindi

Yield: ten to twelve breads

The most basic parantha you can make. A good recipe to start making paranthas with.

Ingredients:

- 2 cups stone-ground durum whole-wheat flour + 1 cup for coating and dusting
- 3 to 4 tablespoons oil or melted ghee or butter, for basting
- About 1 cup water or non-fat plain yogurt, whisked until the desired smoothness is achieved
- Rolling pin

Directions:

1. Put the 2 cups flour in a mixing container, add ¾ cup water or yogurt, and mix with your clean fingers in round circular movements, until it begins to gather. (Add 1 or 2 tablespoons more flour if the dough appears sticky, or some water if it appears too firm.)
2. Knead for approximately a minute, pushing your knuckles gently into the dough, flattening the dough outward, then gathering the ends together toward the center using your fingers. Push down the center, then repeat pressing and gathering a few times until a tender and flexible dough is attained that does not stick to the fingers. Cover and allow it to rest at least 1 and maximum four hours at room temperature. (This gives time to the gluten develop.) If keeping for a longer period, place the dough in your fridge.
3. Preheat the tava or griddle using moderate to high heat until a sprinkling of the flour instantly turns dark brown. Wipe off the flour and continue. While the tava heats up, with lightly oiled hands divide the dough into ten to twelve round balls (depending on the size of the parantha you like). Cover with foil to stop drying.
4. Working with each ball of dough separately, place in the container with the dry flour, flatten it using your fingertips, and cover thoroughly with the dry flour. Move to a cutting board or any other clean flat surface and, use a

rolling pin to roll into a 6- to 7-inch evenly thick circle. (If the dough sticks to the rolling surface, dust with more flour.) Moisten the top of the dough with ghee and fold into the shape of your choice according to the directions in "Shaping Paranthas" at the start of this section.
5. Put the rolled parantha on the hot tava or griddle. Turn over when it is slightly cooked and dotted with tiny golden spots on the bottom, approximately one minute. When the other side is covered with larger brown dots, turn it over, and brush lightly with oil. Flip it over again and fry the oiled side approximately half a minute. Same way, baste and fry the other side another half a minute. There should be a total of 4 turns.
6. Take off the griddle and serve hot.

GREEN CHILE PEPPER PARANTHA

This recipe is called "Mirchi ka lachaedar paranthae" in Hindi

Yield: ten to twelve breads

Ingredients:

- ¼ cup finely chopped fresh cilantro, including soft stems
- ¼ teaspoon salt, or to taste
- 1 cup stone-ground durum whole-wheat flour in a moderate-sized container or a pie dish, for dusting
- 1 pound (1 recipe) dough for "Basic Parantha"
- 1 teaspoon Chaat Masala (Homemade or store-bought)
- 1 teaspoon ground dried fenugreek leaves
- 1 to 3 fresh green chile peppers, such as serrano, minced with seeds
- 2 tablespoons peeled minced fresh ginger
- 2 to 3 tablespoons vegetable oil
- 3 scallions, white parts only, minced

Directions:

1. Ready the chaat masala. Ready the dough. Next, in a small-sized container, combine the cilantro, ginger, scallions, green chile peppers, fenugreek leaves, and salt.

2. To roll the paranthas, divide the dough and the herb mixture into ten to twelve portions. Working with each dough portion separately, make a layered triangle, square, or circle as per the directions for Shaping Paranthas.
3. To cook the paranthas, proceed as per the directions for "Basic Parantha", from Step 5.

LEGUME PARANTHAS Ⓥ

This recipe is called "Dal kae paranthae" in Hindi

Yield: ten to twelve breads

Ingredients:

- ¼ cup finely chopped fresh cilantro, including soft stems
- ¼ teaspoon crudely ground ajwain seeds
- ¼ teaspoon freshly ground black pepper, or to taste
- ¼ teaspoon hot red pepper flakes, or to taste
- ¼ teaspoon salt, or to taste
- 1 cup any leftover cooked dal, such as Yellow Mung Beans with Sautéed Onion and Ginger, or Yellow Split Chickpeas with Spinach, or more as required
- 1 to 2 tablespoons peeled minced fresh ginger
- 1 to 3 fresh green chile peppers, such as serrano, minced with seeds
- 1½ cups stone-ground durum whole-wheat flour
- 2 scallions, minced

Directions:

1. Put all the ingredients except the dal in a moderate-sized container and mix thoroughly with your clean fingers. Add ⅔ cup dal and stir in round circular movements until it begins to gather into a dough. (Add 1 or 2 tablespoons more flour if the dough appears sticky, or some water if it appears too firm.)
2. Knead for approximately a minute, pushing your knuckles gently into the dough, flattening the dough outward, then gathering then ends together toward the center using your fingers. Push down the center, then repeat pressing and gathering a few times until a tender and flexible dough is

attained that does not cling to your fingers. If the dough gets too sticky while you work it, coat your hands with a little oil or water.
3. Cover using plastic wrap or the lid of the container and set aside at least 1 and maximum four hours. (This gives time to the gluten develop.) If keeping for a longer period, place the dough in your fridge.
4. Roll and cook according to the directions for the "Basic Parantha" from step 3.

MASHED POTATO PARANTHA

This recipe is called "Kuchle Aalu ke paranthe" in Hindi

Yield: ten to twelve breads

Ingredients:

- ¼ cup all-purpose flour
- ¼ cup non-fat plain yogurt, whisked until the desired smoothness is achieved, if required
- ¼ teaspoon crudely ground ajwain seeds
- ¼ teaspoon freshly ground black pepper, or to taste
- ½ teaspoon salt, or to taste
- 1 cup stone-ground durum whole-wheat flour
- 1 cup stone-ground durum whole-wheat flour in a moderate-sized container or a pie dish, for dusting
- 1 fresh green chile pepper, such as serrano, minced with seeds
- 1 tablespoon dried mint leaves
- 1 tablespoon peeled minced fresh ginger
- 1 teaspoon dried fenugreek leaves
- 2 large russet (or any kind) potatoes
- 2 tablespoons Basic Ginger and Green Chile Pepper Paste
- 2 tablespoons vegetable oil
- Chilled butter, to taste

Directions:

1. Boil the potatoes in lightly salted water to cover until tender, approximately twenty minutes. Drain, allow to cool down, then peel and grate them. In the meantime, ready the ginger-chile paste.
2. In a large container, with clean fingers, combine the whole-wheat and all-purpose flours, mint and fenugreek leaves, green chile pepper, salt, black pepper, and ajwain seeds. Next, stir in the potatoes, oil, and ginger. (By now there should be sufficient moisture to make the dough. If not, add up to ¼ cup yogurt to make a semi-firm dough that does not stick to the fingers.) This dough does not require resting time, nor should it be kneaded.
3. With lightly oiled hands, divide the dough into ten to twelve identical balls and cover using a foil to stop drying. Working with each ball of dough separately, coat with the dry flour, move to a cutting board or any other clean flat surface, and, use a rolling pin to roll into a thin 6- to 7-inch circle. (If the dough sticks to the rolling surface, dust with more flour.)
4. Heat a tava or a griddle using moderate to high heat and cook the breads, turning them once or twice until they are speckled with golden dots on both sides, approximately one minute per side. Remove from the griddle, lightly baste with butter before you serve.

MINT, AJWAIN, AND BLACK PEPPER PARANTHA

This recipe is called "Pudina, ajwain aur kaali mirch kae paranthae" in Hindi

Yield: ten to twelve breads

Ingredients:

- ¼ cup fine-grain semolina
- ⅓ teaspoon salt, or to taste
- ½ cup non-fat plain yogurt, whisked until the desired smoothness is achieved, or more if needed
- ½ teaspoon crudely ground ajwain seeds
- 1 tablespoon ground dried mint leaves + more for garnish
- 1 teaspoon black pepper, <u>dry-roasted</u> and crudely ground
- 1 to 3 fresh green chile peppers such as serrano, minced with seeds
- 1¼ cups stone-ground durum whole-wheat flour

- 2 to 3 tablespoons canola oil

Directions:

1. In a container, combine the whole-wheat flour and semolina with clean fingers, then put in the green chile peppers, black pepper, mint, ajwain, and salt. Rub in the oil. Put in the yogurt and mix again using your fingers in round circular movements until it begins to gather into a dough.
2. Knead approximately a minute, pushing your knuckles gently into the dough, flattening the dough outward, then gathering the ends together toward the center using your fingers. Repeat pressing and gathering a few times until a tender and flexible dough is attained that does not cling to your fingers. If the dough gets too sticky while you work it, coat your hands with a little oil or water.
3. Cover using plastic wrap or the lid of the container and allow it to rest at least 1 and maximum four hours. (This gives time to the gluten develop.) If keeping for a longer period, place the dough in your fridge.
4. Roll and cook according to the directions for the "Basic Parantha" from step 3. As each parantha is made, sprinkle approximately ¼ teaspoon dried mint, then serve.

MUGHLAI PARANTHA Ⓥ

This recipe is called "Khastae mughlai paranthae" in Hindi

Yield: ten to twelve breads

Ingredients:

- ½ cup stone-ground durum whole-wheat flour
- ½ teaspoon salt, or to taste
- 1 teaspoon crudely ground black pepper, or to taste
- 1 to 3 fresh green chile peppers, such as serrano, stemmed
- 1½ cups all-purpose flour
- 2 teaspoons ground dried fenugreek leaves
- 2 to 3 tablespoons vegetable oil
- 25 to 30 raw almonds, shelled
- 3 tablespoons black poppy seeds

- About ¾ cup water

Directions:

1. Immerse the almonds in water to cover overnight. Next, with clean hands, peel the softened brown skin off the almonds. Using a food processor, add all the ingredients except the water and process until everything is smooth. Next, with the motor running, put in the water in a slow, steady stream until the dough gathers into a smooth ball and cleans the sides of the work container. (Add more flour if the dough appears sticky and more water if it appears too dry.)
2. cover your hands with a thin layer of oil and move the dough to a container. Cover using plastic wrap or the lid of the container and allow it to rest for one to four hours. (This lets the gluten develop.) If keeping for a longer period, place the dough in your fridge.
3. Roll and cook according to the directions for the "Basic Parantha" from step 3.

OAT AND AJWAIN PARANTHA

This recipe is called "Jaee aur ajwain kae paranthae" in Hindi

Yield: ten to twelve breads

Ingredients:

- ¼ cup oat bran
- ⅓ teaspoon salt, or to taste
- ½ cup oat flour
- ½ cup water, or more if needed
- ½ teaspoon crudely crushed ajwain seeds
- ½ teaspoon cayenne pepper, or to taste
- ¾ cup stone-ground durum whole-wheat flour
- 2 tablespoons olive oil

Directions:

1. In a container, combine the whole-wheat and oat flours, oat bran, oil, ajwain seeds, cayenne pepper, and salt.
2. Put in the water and mix again with your clean fingers in round circular movements until it begins to gather. Knead for approximately a minute, pushing your knuckles gently into the dough, flattening the dough outward, then gathering then ends together toward the center using your fingers. Push down the center, then repeat pressing and gathering a few times until a tender and flexible dough is attained that does not cling to your fingers. If the dough gets too sticky while you work it, coat your hands with a little oil or water.
3. Cover using plastic wrap or the lid of the container and set aside at least 1 and maximum four hours. (This gives time to the gluten develop.) If keeping for a longer period, place the dough in your fridge.
4. Roll and cook according to the directions for the "Basic Parantha" from step 3.

ONION PARANTHA

This recipe is called "Pyaz ka parantha" in Hindi

Yield: ten to twelve breads

Ingredients:

- ¼ cup finely chopped fresh cilantro
- ½ teaspoon ground fenugreek seeds
- ½ teaspoon kalonji seeds
- ½ teaspoon salt, or to taste
- ⅔ cup non-fat plain yogurt, whisked until the desired smoothness is achieved
- 1 cup finely chopped red onion
- 1 teaspoon crudely ground fennel seeds
- 1 to 3 fresh green chile peppers, such as serrano, minced with seeds
- 2 cups stone-ground durum whole-wheat flour
- 3 tablespoons vegetable oil, melted ghee, or butter

Directions:

1. Put the flour and oil (or ghee or butter) in a container and rub with clean fingers to mix. Next, add all the rest of the ingredients, except the yogurt, and again, mix thoroughly using your fingers. Put in the yogurt and mix again using your fingers in round circular movements until it begins to gather into a dough. (Add 1 or 2 tablespoons more flour if the dough appears sticky, or some more yogurt if it appears too firm.)
2. Knead approximately a minute, pushing your knuckles gently into the dough, flattening the dough outward, then gathering the ends together toward the center using your fingers. Repeat pressing and gathering a few times until a tender and flexible dough is attained that does not cling to your fingers. (If the dough gets too sticky while you work it, coat your hands with a little oil or water.)
3. Cover using plastic wrap or the lid of the container and set aside at least 1 and maximum four hours. (This gives time to the gluten develop.) If keeping for a longer period, place the dough in your fridge.
4. To roll and cook the paranthas, proceed as per directions for "Basic Parantha", from Step 3.

SPINACH AND RED BELL PEPPER PARANTHA Ⓥ

This recipe is called "Palak aur laal shimla mirch kae paranthae" in Hindi

Yield: ten to twelve breads

Ingredients:

- ½ teaspoon crudely ground ajwain seeds
- ½ teaspoon salt, or to taste
- ⅔ to ¾ cup water
- 1 red bell pepper, cut into ¼-inch pieces
- 1 small bunch fresh spinach (8 to 10 ounces), trimmed, washed, and finely chopped
- 1 tablespoon peeled minced fresh ginger
- 1 teaspoon ground dried fenugreek leaves
- 1 to 3 fresh green chile peppers, such as serrano, minced with seeds

- 1½ cups stone-ground durum whole-wheat flour, or 1 cup whole-wheat flour and ½ cup oat bran
- 3 to 4 scallions, finely chopped
- Freshly ground black pepper, to taste

Directions:

1. Put everything except the water in a big mixing container and mix lightly with clean fingers. Put in the water, slowly and gradually, and mix using your fingers in round circular movements until it begins to gather into a dough. (Add 1 or 2 tablespoons more flour if the dough appears sticky or some water if it appears too firm.)
2. Knead approximately a minute, pushing your knuckles gently into the dough, flattening the dough outward, then gathering the ends together toward the center using your fingers. Repeat pressing and gathering a few times until a tender and flexible dough is attained that does not cling to your fingers.
3. Cover using plastic wrap or the lid of the container and allow it to rest at least 1 and maximum four hours at room temperature. (This gives time to the gluten develop.) If keeping for a longer period, place the dough in your fridge.
4. Roll and cook according to the directions for the "Basic Parantha" from step 3.

STUFFED GRIDDLE-FRIED FLATBREADS

BASIC STUFFED PARANTHA Ⓥ

This recipe is called "Bharae huae paranthae" in Hindi

Yield: ten to twelve breads

Ingredients:

- ¼ cup vegetable oil, or melted butter or ghee, for basting
- 1 cup whole-wheat flour in a moderate-sized container or pie dish, for coating and dusting
- 1 pound (1 recipe) Basic Whole-Wheat Dough
- 1 recipe stuffing (below this recipe) of your choice

Directions:

1. Ready the stuffing. Ready the dough. Heat the tava or griddle using moderate to high heat until a sprinkling of flour instantly turns dark brown. Wipe off the flour and continue. While the tava heats up, with lightly oiled clean hands, divide the dough equally into ten to twelve balls and cover using a foil to stop drying. Divide it into ten to twelve portions, approximately 3 to 4 tablespoons each.
2. Working with each ball of dough separately, move to the container with the dry flour, push softly to form a disc, coat liberally with dry flour, and roll into a 4- to 5-inch circle. Put the stuffing in the center. Bring the edges together, pinch to secure, then shape into a ball once more.
3. Flatten and coat this stuffed ball with flour and roll it into a 7- to 8-inch circle of uniform thickness. As you roll, keep turning and dusting the dough with flour or it may stick to the rolling surface. If the stuffing has surplus moisture, the paranthas may develop tiny (or large) holes as they stretch while rolling. If that happens, patch the holes by putting a little dry flour over them (or by pinching them together).
4. Put the rolled parantha on the hot tava. Flip it over when it is slightly cooked and dotted with tiny golden spots on the bottom, approximately one minute. When the other side is covered with larger brown dots, flip it over and brush lightly with oil. Flip it over again and fry the oiled side approximately half a minute. Same way, baste and fry the other side another half a minute. There should be a total of 4 turns. Take off the griddle and serve hot.

STUFFINGS FOR PARANTHA BREADS

Paranthas can be easily be stuffed with a variety of dry ingredients. If the stuffing is too moist, the dough will absorb it and become too moist and sticky to work. Some juicy vegetables can be used as stuffing after drying them a little by salting and grating, and then squeezing out the moisture.

After you prepare the stuffing below, continue with "Basic Stuffed Parantha" recipe just above this section.

POTATO PARANTHA STUFFING

This recipe is called "Aalu kae paranthae" in Hindi

Yield: sufficient for ten to twelve breads

- four to five scallions, white parts only, minced (not compulsory)
- ¼ cup finely chopped fresh cilantro, including soft stems
- ½ teaspoon garam masala
- ½ teaspoon ground cumin
- ¾ teaspoon salt, or to taste
- 1 teaspoon ground dried fenugreek leaves
- 1 to 2 fresh green chile peppers, such as serrano, minced with seeds
- 1 to 2 tablespoons peeled minced fresh ginger
- 2 tablespoons ground coriander
- 2 teaspoons ground dried pomegranate seeds
- 3 large russet (or any) potatoes (about 1¼ pounds)

Directions:

1. Boil the potatoes in lightly salted water to cover until tender, approximately twenty minutes. Next, peel and grate or mash them in a moderate-sized container.
2. Mix all the ingredients together. Continue with "Basic Stuffed Parantha" recipe just above this section.

CAULIFLOWER PARANTHA STUFFING

This recipe is called "Gobhi kae paranthae" in Hindi

Yield: sufficient for ten to twelve breads

- ½ cup crudely chopped fresh cilantro, including soft stems
- ½ teaspoon crudely ground ajwain seeds
- ½ teaspoon ground cumin
- ½ teaspoon salt, or to taste
- 1 small cauliflower (about ¾ pound), cut into florets
- 1 tablespoon ground coriander
- 1 to 3 fresh green chile peppers, such as serrano, stemmed
- 2 teaspoons ground pomegranate seeds
- 5 quarter-size slices peeled fresh ginger

Directions:

1. Using a food processor, combine and pulse the ginger, green chile peppers, cilantro, and cauliflower until minced.
2. Move to a container and stir in the spices, but not the salt. Put in the salt only to the individual paranthas as you roll them. (Mixing the salt will cause the cauliflower to release its juices and make it harder to use.)
3. Continue with "Basic Stuffed Parantha" recipe just above this section.

GROUND LAMB PARANTHA STUFFING

This recipe is called "Keemae kae paranthae" in Hindi

Yield: sufficient for ten to twelve breads

- ½ teaspoon salt, or to taste
- 1 fresh green chile pepper, such as serrano, stemmed
- 1 large clove fresh garlic, peeled
- 1 pound ground lamb, chicken, or turkey

- 1 small onion, crudely chopped
- 1 teaspoon garam masala
- 4 quarter-size slices peeled fresh ginger
- A few fresh mint leaves

Directions:

1. Cook the lamb (or poultry) over moderate heat until a golden colour is achieved, approximately five to seven minutes.
2. Allow to cool and move to a food processor. Put in the rest of the ingredients and process until minced. If the stuffing appears too moist from the onion, stir in up to 2 tablespoons chickpea or whole-wheat flour.
3. Continue with "Basic Stuffed Parantha" recipe just above this section.

PANEER PARANTHA STUFFING

This recipe is called "Paneer kae paranthae" in Hindi

Yield: sufficient for ten to twelve breads

- ¼ cup grated Monterey Jack or mild cheddar cheese
- ¼ teaspoon salt, or to taste
- ½ cup finely chopped fresh cilantro, with soft stems
- ½ teaspoon garam masala
- 1 large clove fresh garlic, peeled
- 1 tablespoon ground coriander
- 1 to 2 fresh green chile peppers, such as serrano, stemmed
- 3 quarter-size slices peeled fresh ginger
- 8 ounces (1 recipe) <u>Paneer Cheese</u> (Homemade or store-bought), crumbled

Directions:

1. Ready the paneer, then crumble and place Using a food processor along with the cheese, ginger, garlic, green chile peppers, and cilantro and process until minced.
2. Put in the coriander, garam masala, and salt and pulse until blended.
3. Continue with "Basic Stuffed Parantha" recipe just above this section.

RADISH PARANTHA STUFFING

This recipe is called "Mooli kae paranthae" in Hindi

Yield: sufficient ten to twelve breads

- ¼ cup finely chopped fresh cilantro, including soft stems
- ½ teaspoon crudely ground ajwain seeds
- 1 tablespoon peeled minced fresh ginger
- 1 teaspoon salt, or to taste
- 1 to 3 fresh green chile peppers, such as serrano, minced with seeds
- 1½ pounds white daikon radishes

Directions:

1. Using a food processor, grate or mince the radishes. Move to a container, stir in the salt and leave the radishes to sweat, for approximately half an hour.
2. Next, squeeze out as much water as you can. (This removes much of the strong and bitter juice from the daikons, making them much sweeter. If you wish, use these juices to make the dough for paranthas.) Put in the rest of the ingredients and mix thoroughly.
3. Continue with "Basic Stuffed Parantha" recipe just above this section.

PUFFED DEEP-FRIED BREADS (POORIYAN)

Poori (or poodhi) breads—crisp, balloon-like breads—are one of the many pleasures of Indian culinary life. They are deep-fried, puffed whole-wheat unleavened breads, light and crunchy, and best consumed as soon as they come out of the kadhai (Indian wok). Pooris are kinda oily, but are really easy to make, and hence the go-to bread in India if food needs to be served to hundreds of people. They also keep well at room temperature, and are great for journeys.

Pooris are typically eaten for breakfast, lunch, and brunch. They are almost never eaten for dinner.

BASIC POORI Ⓥ

This recipe is called "Saaddi pooriyan" in Hindi

Yield: 14 to 16 breads

Ingredients:

- ⅓ to ½ cup water
- ½ cup all-purpose flour
- 1 cup stone-ground durum whole-wheat flour
- 3 tablespoons vegetable oil

TO MAKE THE DOUGH

Directions To make dough using a food processor:

1. Put both the flours in the work container of a food processor and process approximately half a minute to mix. While the motor runs, put in the oil and then the water in a thin stream, and process until the dough gathers into a ball.
2. Continue to process until the sides of the container look clean, 20 to half a minute. (Add 1 to 2 tablespoons more flour if the dough sticks to the sides of the work container, or some water if the dough appears hard.) Stop the machine, move the dough to a container, cover using plastic wrap or the lid of the container, and allow to rest for minimum 1 and maximum four hours. (This gives time to the gluten develop.) If keeping for a longer period, place the dough in your fridge.

Directions To make dough by hand:

1. Put both the flours in a big container, combine, add I of the water and mix again with your clean fingers in round circular movements until it begins to

gather into a dough. (Add 1 or 2 tablespoons more flour if the dough appears sticky, or some more water if it appears too firm.)
2. Knead approximately a minute, pushing your knuckles gently into the dough, flattening the dough outward, then gathering the ends together toward the center using your fingers. Push down the center and repeat pressing and gathering a few times until a tender and flexible dough is attained that does not cling to your fingers. (If the dough gets too sticky while you work it, coat your hands with a little oil or water.)
3. Cover using plastic wrap or the lid of the container and set aside at least 1 and maximum four hours. (This gives time to the gluten develop.) If keeping for a longer period, place the dough in your fridge.

TO SHAPE AND FRY THE POORIES

- 1 cup stone-ground durum whole-wheat flour or all-purpose flour in a moderate-sized container or a pie dish, for dusting
- 1 recipe <u>Basic Deep-Fried Puffed Breads</u>, or any other poori bread dough
- 2 to 3 cups peanut oil for deep-frying
- Rolling pin

Directions:

1. Heat the frying oil in a wok or skillet using high heat until it achieves 350°F to 375°F on a frying thermometer, or until a little piece of the dough dropped into the hot oil bubbles and surges to the surface of the oil instantly.
2. While the oil is heating, lightly oil your clean hands and divide the dough equally into 14 to 16 balls. Cover with foil to stop drying, and set aside.
3. Working with each ball of dough separately, place in the container with the dry flour, flatten it using your fingertips and cover thoroughly with the dry flour. Move to a cutting board or any other clean flat surface and, use a rolling pin to roll into a thin 4- to 5-inch circle. (If the dough sticks to the rolling surface, dust with more flour.)
4. Cautiously place the rolled poori into the hot oil. Almost instantly the poori will rise to the top and start to puff up. With the back of a large slotted spatula, swiftly push softly on the puffed top surface, submerge the poori back into the oil, then release. This will guide the air toward the flatter portions and cause the poori to balloon into a complete round in approximately ten to fifteen seconds.

5. Turn the poori over once to cook the other side until a golden colour is achieved. (Perfectly fried poories should be crisp and golden, not brown.) Using a slotted spatula, remove to paper towels to drain and serve instantly.

FLAVORED DEEP-FRIED PUFFED BREADS

Now that we know how to make the basic poori, we can try making flavoured ones!

AJWAIN POORI Ⓥ

This recipe is called "Ajwaini pooriyan" in Hindi

Yield: 14 to 16 breads

- ⅓ to ½ cup water
- ½ cup all-purpose flour
- ½ teaspoon crudely ground ajwain seeds
- ½ teaspoon salt, or to taste
- 1 cup stone-ground durum whole-wheat flour
- 1 teaspoon dried mint leaves
- 3 tablespoons vegetable oil

Directions:

1. Ready the dough Using a food processor or by hand (refer to directions given in the "Basic Poori" recipe before this section), mixing together all the dry ingredients, then adding the oil to blend, followed by the water, until a dough is formed.
2. Shape and fry the poories (refer to directions given in the "Basic Poori" recipe before this section).

DEEP-FRIED BENGALI BREADS

This recipe is called "Lucchiyan" in Hindi

Yield: 8 to 10 breads

Ingredients:

- 1 cup all-purpose flour
- 2 to 3 tablespoons peanut oil or melted ghee
- A pinch of salt
- About ½ cup water

Directions:

1. Put the flour, salt, and oil (or ghee) in the work container of a food processor and process approximately half a minute to mix. While the motor runs, put in the water in a thin stream, and process until it gathers into a ball. Continue to process until the sides of the container look clean, 20 to half a minute. (Add 1 or 2 tablespoons more flour if the dough sticks to the sides of the work container, and some water if the dough appears hard.)
2. Move the dough to a large container, cover using plastic wrap or the lid of the container, and let rest for at least 1 and maximum four hours. (This gives time to the gluten develop.) If keeping for a longer period, place the dough in your fridge.
3. Shape and fry the poories (refer to directions given in the "Basic Poori" recipe before this section).

DEEP-FRIED LEAVENED BREAD

This recipe is called "Bhaturaae" in Hindi

Yield: 14 to 16 breads

Ingredients:

- ½ cup fine-grain semolina
- ½ teaspoon salt, or to taste

- ¾ to 1 cup non-fat plain yogurt, whisked until the desired smoothness is achieved
- 1 cup all-purpose flour in a moderate-sized container or a pie dish for coating and dusting
- 1 teaspoon sugar
- 1½ to 2 cups peanut oil for deep-frying
- 1¾ cups all-purpose flour
- 2 teaspoons active dry yeast

Directions:

1. Put the flour, semolina, sugar, salt, and yeast into a food processor and process until mixed, approximately half a minute.
2. While the motor runs, add yogurt through the feeder tube until the dough gathers into a ball and the sides of the work container look clean, 20 to half a minute. (If the dough appears too sticky, add some more flour through the feeder tube.) Move to a large container, cover using plastic wrap or the lid of the container, and place in a warm draft-free spot until it doubles in volume, at least 4 and maximum 8 hours. (This allows the yeast to ferment and multiply, causing the dough to rise.) If keeping for a longer period, place the dough in your fridge.
3. Sanitize your hands, lightly oil them, and divide the dough equally into 14 to 16 round balls and cover using a foil to stop drying. Working with each ball of dough separately, place in the container with the dry flour, flatten it using your fingertips, and cover thoroughly with the dry flour. Next, move to a cutting board or any other clean flat surface and, use a rolling pin to roll into 6 to 7-inch circle. (If the dough sticks to the rolling surface, dust with more flour.)
4. Heat the oil in a wok or skillet using high heat until it achieves 350°F to 375°F on a frying thermometer, or until a piece of dough dropped into the hot oil bubbles and surges to the surface of the oil instantly. Cautiously place the rolled bhatura into the hot oil. Almost instantly it will rise to the top and start to puff up. With the back of a large slotted spatula, swiftly push softly on the puffed top surface and submerge it back into the oil, then release. This will guide the air towards the flatter portions, and cause it to balloon into a complete round, ten to fifteen seconds.
5. Turn the bhatura over once to cook the other side until a golden colour is achieved. Bhaturas should be lightly golden on both sides, not brown.

Remove with a slotted spoon, move to paper towels to drain before you serve instantly.

FERMENTED SAFFRON POORI

This recipe is called "Khameeri kesar pooriyan" in Hindi

Yield: 14 to 16 breads

Ingredients:

- ¼ teaspoon saffron threads
- ½ cup warm milk (any kind), approximately 110°F
- ½ teaspoon salt, or to taste
- ¾ cup all-purpose flour
- ¾ cup stone-ground durum whole-wheat flour
- 1 cup all-purpose flour in a moderate-sized container or a pie dish, for coating and dusting
- 1 tablespoon fennel seeds, finely ground
- 1 teaspoon active dry yeast
- 1 teaspoon white poppy seeds
- 2 tablespoons non-fat plain yogurt, whisked until the desired smoothness is achieved
- 2 tablespoons sugar
- 2 tablespoons vegetable oil or melted ghee

Directions:

1. In a small-sized container, combine the milk, yeast, and 1 teaspoon sugar and set aside approximately five minutes, or until frothy. Put both the flours, the fennel seeds, the rest of the sugar, and the salt into a food processor and process until mixed, approximately half a minute.
2. While the motor runs, add first the oil (or ghee) and then the yeast-milk mixture through the feeder tube until the flours gather into a ball and the sides of the work container look clean. (If the dough appears too sticky, add some more flour through the feeder tube.) Move to a large container, cover using plastic wrap or the lid of the container, and place in a warm draft-free spot until it doubles in volume, at least 4 and maximum 8 hours. (This allows

the yeast to ferment and multiply, causing the dough to rise.) If keeping for a longer period, place the dough in your fridge.
3. Heat the frying oil (Step 1 refer to directions given in the "Basic Poori" recipe before this section). In a small-sized container, combine the yogurt, saffron, and poppy seeds. Next, with lightly oiled clean hands, divide the dough equally into 14 to 16 round balls and cover using a foil to stop drying. Working with each ball of dough separately, place in the container with the dry flour, flatten it using your fingertips and cover thoroughly with the dry flour from the container. Move to a cutting board or any other clean flat surface and, use a rolling pin to roll into a thin 4- to 5-inch circle. (If the dough sticks to the rolling surface, dust with more flour.)
4. Next, with a basting brush, lightly coat the top of the rolled poori with the yogurt mixture and fry the poories (Steps 4 and 5).

MINT (OR FENUGREEK) POORI Ⓥ

This recipe is called "Pudina (ya methi) ki pooriyan" in Hindi

Yield: 14 to 16 breads

- ten to twelve fresh mint leaves, or 1 tablespoon dried fenugreek leaves
- ¼ teaspoon crudely ground ajwain seeds
- ¼ teaspoon salt, or to taste
- ⅓ to ½ cup water
- ½ cup all-purpose flour
- 1 cup stone-ground durum whole-wheat flour
- 1 to 2 tablespoons dried mint leaves
- 3 tablespoons vegetable oil

Directions:

1. Ready the dough Using a food processor or by hand (refer to directions given in the "Basic Poori" recipe before this section), mixing together all the dry ingredients and the fresh mint leaves (or fenugreek leaves), then adding the oil to blend, followed by the water, until a dough is formed.
2. Heat the frying oil and shape each poori (Steps 1 to 3 refer to directions given in the "Basic Poori" recipe before this section). For each poori, dust

one of the sides with the dried mint leaves and push softly with the rolling pin to ensure that they adhere, then fry the poories (Steps 4 and 5).

SPINACH POORI Ⓥ

This recipe is called "Palak ki pooriyan" in Hindi

Yield: 14 to 16 breads

- ¼ teaspoon salt, or to taste
- ⅓ to ½ cup water
- ½ cup all-purpose flour
- ½ teaspoon freshly ground black pepper
- 1 cup stone-ground durum whole-wheat flour
- 1 large clove fresh garlic, peeled
- 1 small bunch fresh spinach (8 to 10 ounces), trimmed, washed, and crudely chopped
- 1 teaspoon dried fenugreek leaves
- 1 to 3 fresh green chile peppers, such as serrano, stemmed
- 3 tablespoons peanut oil

Directions:

1. Using a food processor, combine and pulse the spinach, garlic, and green chile peppers until minced, then add all the dry ingredients and process approximately half a minute to mix.
2. Next, Put in the oil to blend, followed by the water, and process until a dough is formed. Shape and fry the poories (refer to directions given in the "Basic Poori" recipe before this section).

STUFFED AND PUFFED POORI Ⓥ

This recipe is called "Bhari hui pooriyan" in Hindi

Yield: 14 to 16 breads

Ingredients:

- ¼ cup crudely chopped fresh cilantro, including soft stems
- ¼ teaspoon salt, or to taste
- ½ cup any skinless dried beans, such as green split pea (muttar dal), yellow split chickpea (channa dal), yellow mung (dhulli mung dal), or white urad (dhulli urad dal), sorted and washed in 3 to 4 changes of water
- 1 clove fresh garlic, peeled
- 1 cup stone-ground durum whole-wheat flour in a moderate-sized container or a pie dish, for coating and dusting
- 1 fresh green chile pepper, such as serrano, stemmed
- 1 recipe dough for Deep-Fried Puffed Breads with Ajwain Seeds
- 1 teaspoon garam masala
- 3 quarter-size slices peeled fresh ginger

Directions:

1. Immerse the dal in water to cover, approximately two hours, then drain. In the meantime, ready the dough and set aside at least 30 minutes. In a small food processor or a grinder, combine and pulse all the rest of the ingredients (except the flour for dusting) to make a paste that is as smooth as possible.
2. Heat the frying oil (Step 1 refer to directions given in the "Basic Poori" recipe before this section). Sanitize your hands, lightly oil them, and divide the dough equally into 14 to 16 balls and cover using a foil to stop drying.
3. Working with each ball of dough separately, move to the container with the dry flour, push softly to form a disc, cover thoroughly with dry flour and then roll it into a thin 2- to 3-inch circle. Put approximately 1 teaspoon filling in the center, then bring the edges together and pinch to secure. Shape into a ball and roll into a thin four to five-inch circle once more. (If the dough sticks to the rolling surface, dust with more flour.)
4. Fry the poories (Steps 4 and 5 refer to directions given in the "Basic Poori" recipe before this section).

OVEN-GRILLED NAAN AND OTHER BREADS

Naan breads are leavened breads traditionally made by sticking the dough to the inner wall of a tandoor. They cook really fast, and as a result, the moisture and flavour remain pretty much intact. Although a tandoor still remains the best way to cook these, you can also use an oven or boiler as a compromise. A tandoor or an authentic Indian restaurant with a tandoor remains your best option to experience truly authentic naan, though.

In this section, I will assume you don't have a tandoor at home, and will teach you how to make naan breads using appliances that can be found in an average American kitchen.

BASIC OVEN-GRILLED NAAN

This recipe is called "Tandoori naan" in Hindi

Yield: ten to twelve breads

Ingredients:

- ¼ cup melted butter or ghee, for basting (not compulsory)
- ¼ cup warm water (about 110°F)
- ¼ teaspoon salt, or to taste
- ½ cup non-fat plain yogurt, whisked until the desired smoothness is achieved
- 1 cup all-purpose flour in a moderate-sized container or a pie dish, for coating and dusting
- 1 teaspoon sugar
- 2 cups all-purpose flour, or bread flour
- 2 tablespoons vegetable oil
- 2 teaspoons active dry yeast

Directions:

1. For the dough, dissolve the yeast and sugar in warm water and allow to sit until frothy, approximately five minutes. Stir in the yogurt and oil.
2. Put the flour and salt in your food processor and process until mixed. While the motor runs, pour the yeast mixture into the work container in a thin stream and process until the flour gathers into a ball and the sides of the processor are clean. (If the dough appears too sticky, add some more flour

through the feeder tube, or add some more yogurt if the dough is dry and hard.) Move to a large container, cover using plastic wrap or the lid of the container, and place in a warm draft-free spot until it doubles in volume, three to four hours. (This allows the yeast to ferment and multiply, causing the dough to rise.) If keeping for a longer period, place the dough in your fridge.

3. To roll and grill the naan breads, with clean, lightly oiled hands, divide the dough equally into ten to twelve balls and cover using a foil to stop drying. Working with each ball of dough separately, place in the container with the dry flour, flatten it using your fingertips and cover thoroughly with the dry flour. Next, move to a cutting board or any other clean flat surface and, use a rolling pin to roll into a 7- to 8-inch triangle. (If the dough sticks to the rolling surface, dust with more flour.)
4. Put on large baking trays or, if you have a separate broiler, place on the broiler trays—3 to 4 per tray. Using a basting brush or your fingers, lightly baste the top of each naan with water. (This prevents them from drying out.)
5. Preheat your oven to broil or preheat the broiler, and place the trays, one at a time, four to five inches below the heating element and broil until small brown spots appear on the top surface, approximately one minute. Using a spatula, carefully, turn each naan over and cook until the other side is golden, approximately half a minute. Move the naan breads to a platter, baste lightly with butter, if you wish before you serve hot.

OVEN-GRILLED BREADS WITH DIFFERENT FLAVORS

Using the recipe of the basic Naan bread above, we will make flavoured naan in this section!

BAKED SEMOLINA BREADS

This recipe is called "Kulchae" in Hindi

Yield: ten to twelve breads

Ingredients:

- ¼ cup warm water (about 110°F)
- ¼ teaspoon salt, or to taste
- ¾ cup non-fat plain yogurt, whisked until the desired smoothness is achieved
- 1 cup all-purpose flour
- 1 cup all-purpose flour in a moderate-sized container or a pie dish, for coating and dusting
- 1 cup fine-grain semolina
- 1 teaspoon sugar
- 2 tablespoons unsalted butter, at room temperature
- 2 teaspoons active dry yeast

Directions:

1. For the dough, dissolve the yeast and sugar in warm water in a small-sized container and allow to sit until frothy, approximately five minutes. Stir in the yogurt.
2. Put the semolina, flour, butter, and salt into a food processor and process until mixed. While the motor runs, pour the yeast mixture into the work container in a thin stream and process until the flour gathers into a ball and the sides of the processor are clean. (If the dough appears too sticky, add some more flour through the feeder tube, or add some more yogurt if the dough is dry and hard).
3. Move to a large container, cover using plastic wrap or the lid of the container, and place in a warm draft-free spot until it doubles in volume, three to four hours. (This allows the yeast to ferment and multiply, causing the dough to rise.) If keeping for a longer period, place the dough in your fridge.
4. Lightly grease 2 or 3 large baking trays. Preheat your oven to the lowest setting, approximately ten minutes, then turn it off. Next, with lightly oiled clean hands, divide the dough equally into ten to twelve balls and cover using a foil to stop drying. Working with each ball of dough separately, place in the container with the dry flour, flatten it using your fingertips, and cover thoroughly with the dry flour. Move to a cutting board or any other clean flat surface and, use a rolling pin to roll into 5 to 6-inch circle and place on the baking trays. (If the dough sticks to the rolling surface, dust with more flour.)

5. Using a basting brush or your fingers, lightly baste the top surface of each bread with water. (This prevents them from drying out.) Cover with foil and place the trays in the turned-off oven to rise once more, approximately one hour.
6. Remove the baking trays and preheat the oven to 350°F. Bake until the kulcha breads are still white, but firm, approximately ten minutes. They should not brown. Serve.

CHEESE NAAN

This recipe is called "Cheese vaalae naan" in Hindi

Yield: ten to twelve breads

Ingredients:

- 1 cup grated Pepper Jack cheese, or more as required
- Basic Oven-Grilled Naan

Directions:

1. Ready the bread dough through Step 3 of Basic Oven-Grilled Naan, rolling them out using a rolling pin into 4- to 5-inch rounds and place approximately 1½ tablespoons of grated Pepper Jack cheese in the center.
2. Pick up the edges of the dough, bring them together, and pinch to secure. Next, roll out once again and broil the breads as described in Step 5.

DRIED HERB AND SPICE NAAN

This recipe is called "Sookhae masalae kae naan" in Hindi

Yield: ten to twelve breads

Ingredients:

- ¼ teaspoon crudely ground ajwain seeds
- ¼ teaspoon cayenne pepper or paprika

- 1 tablespoon melted ghee or butter
- 1 teaspoon ground dried curry leaves
- 1 teaspoon ground dried fenugreek
- 1 teaspoon ground dried mint
- Basic Oven-Grilled Naan

Directions:

1. Ready the bread dough through Step 4 of Basic Oven-Grilled Naan. Before you put the breads in the oven, combine all the ingredients except the ghee in a small-sized container.
2. Broil the breads as described in Step 5. Next, as soon as the breads come out of the oven, baste them liberally with melted ghee or butter and sprinkle some of the seasoning mixture on them before you serve.

KALONJI/SESAME NAAN

This recipe is called "Kalonji ya til kae naan" in Hindi

Yield: ten to twelve breads

Ingredients:

- 1 small onion, crudely chopped
- 1 tablespoon kalonji or sesame seeds
- 1 to 2 fresh green chile peppers, such as serrano, stemmed
- Basic Oven-Grilled Naan

Directions:

1. Ready the bread dough through Step 3 of Basic Oven-Grilled Naan. Next, Using a food processor, combine and pulse the onion and green chile pepper until minced, then add to the ingredients to make the dough.
2. Continue with Step 4 of Basic Oven-Grilled Naan, after the naans are rolled out and set on trays, sprinkle each one with approximately ¼ teaspoon kalonji or sesame seeds and press them into the dough to ensure they adhere to the naan. Broil the breads, as described in Step 5.

OVEN-GRILLED GARLIC AND TURMERIC BREADS

This recipe is called "Lussan haldi kae naan" in Hindi

Yield: ten to twelve breads

Ingredients:

- ¼ teaspoon turmeric
- 1 teaspoon melted butter or ghee
- 3 large cloves fresh garlic, peeled
- Basic Oven-Grilled Naan

Directions:

1. Ready the bread dough through Step 4 of Basic Oven-Grilled Naan. Next, in a small food processor, combine and pulse the garlic, butter (or ghee), and turmeric until a smooth paste is achieved.
2. Continue with Step 5 of Basic Oven-Grilled Naan, basting each rolled-out naan with this paste.

TOFU NAAN

This recipe is called "Tofu aur jaee kae naan" in Hindi

Yield: ten to twelve breads

Ingredients:

- ¼ cup non-fat plain yogurt, whisked until the desired smoothness is achieved
- ¼ cup warm lowfat milk (about 130°F)
- ¼ cup warm water (about 110°F)
- ¼ teaspoon salt, or to taste
- ½ cup oat bran
- ½ cup soft tofu, crumbled
- ½ cup soy flour

- 1 teaspoon sugar
- 2 cups all-purpose flour
- 2 tablespoons vegetable oil + 1 tablespoon if making dough by hand
- 2 teaspoons active dry yeast
- Chaat Masala (Homemade or store-bought), to taste
- Melted butter, for basting

Directions:

1. For the dough, dissolve the yeast and sugar in warm water in a small-sized container and allow to sit until frothy, approximately five minutes. In a moderate-sized container, combine the yogurt and milk. (The milk may curdle, but don't be concerned.)
2. Using a food processor, combine and pulse the flours, oat bran, tofu, 2 tablespoons oil, and salt until mixed. Next, with the motor running, pour through the feeder tube, first the yeast mixture, then the yogurt-milk mixture, and process until the flour gathers into a ball and the sides of the processor are clean. (If the dough appears too sticky, add some more flour through the feeder tube, or add some more yogurt if the dough is dry and hard.)
3. Move to a large container, cover using plastic wrap or the lid of the container, and place in a warm draft-free spot until it doubles in volume, three to four hours. (This allows the yeast to ferment and multiply, causing the dough to rise.) If keeping for a longer period, place the dough in your fridge. In the meantime, ready the chaat masala.
4. To roll and grill the naan breads, follow directions for Basic Oven-Grilled Naan, from Step 3. Remove the naan breads to a platter, baste lightly with the butter, sprinkle a generous pinch of chaat masala on top before you serve.

SPECIAL BREADS

In this section we will look at some special regional breads of India.

PUNJABI WHITE CORN FLATBREAD

This recipe is called "Safed makki ki roti" in Hindi

Yield: 8 to 10 breads

Ingredients:

- ¼ cup stone-ground durum whole-wheat flour
- ¾ to 1 cup hot water (only as hot as your hands can tolerate)
- 1¼ cups white corn flour
- 3 to 4 tablespoons corn oil or melted ghee, for basting

Directions:

1. In a container, combine the flours, then add sufficient hot water to make a semi-soft dough that does not cling to your fingers. (Coat your fingers with some oil if it does stick.) This dough does not require resting time, nor should it be kneaded.
2. Sanitize your hands, lightly oil them, and divide the dough equally into 8 to 10 balls and cover using a foil to stop drying. Work with each ball one at a time, and place between 2 sheets of wax paper, aluminium foil, or plastic wrap and softly press using your fingertips or a rolling pin to spread it into a 5- to 6-inch circle. If the dough breaks, pinch it together to secure.
3. Heat the tava on medium heat (do not make it too hot—these breads are thicker than the whole-wheat ones and need to cook longer), baste the tava lightly with oil (or ghee), then cautiously put the bread on it. Cook until the bottom is flecked with golden dots, approximately one minute, and turn it over.
4. When the other side is golden, flip it once more. Next, baste the top with ½ teaspoon oil (or ghee), put that side down onto the tava, and fry until crisp, a few seconds. Same way, baste and fry the other side until crisp. Replicate the process for all the other breads. Move to a serving plate and serve as hot as possible, topped with a dollop of whipped butter, if you wish.

BASIC RAJASTHANI ROLLS

This recipe is called "Baati" in Hindi

Yield: ten to twelve rolls

Ingredients:

- ¼ cup melted ghee (or butter or vegetable oil) + 1 tablespoon ghee for basting
- ½ teaspoon baking soda
- ½ teaspoon salt, or to taste
- ⅔ to 1 cup water
- 1 cup fine-grain semolina or chickpea flour (besan)
- 1 teaspoon ajwain seeds
- 1 teaspoon sugar
- 2 cups stone-ground durum whole-wheat flour

Directions:

1. Put the whole-wheat flour and semolina (or chickpea flour) in a big container and stir in the baking soda, ajwain seeds, salt, and sugar. Using your sanitized fingers, rub in the ghee (or butter or oil), then put in the water slowly and gradually to make a firm but pliable dough that does not cling to your fingers. Cover using plastic wrap or the lid of the container and let rest approximately one hour. (This lets the gluten develop.)
2. With lightly oiled hands, divide the dough equally into ten to twelve balls and cover using a foil to stop drying. Working with each ball of dough separately, flatten it to make a 3- to 3½-inch disc, then bring the edges up toward the center and pinch together to secure. Press down lightly on the seal with your thumb to make a slight depression, then flatten the rest of the dough once again to make a 2½-inch disc (the depression must show). Replicate the process for all the rest of the balls.
3. To steam: Put the baaties in a metal or bamboo steamer set over or in a pot half-filled with water. (The bottom of the steamer shouldn't touch the water.) Steam them (in 2 batches, if needed) 7 to ten minutes, or until a knife inserted in a baati comes out clean.
4. To boil: Half fill a large pot with water and bring it to a boil. Next, place as many of the baaties in the water as will fit comfortably. Cover and simmer until they float to the top, approximately ten minutes.
5. Lightly grease a large, heavy baking sheet. Cautiously remove the rolls from the steamer or the water and set them on the baking sheet.

6. To brown in the oven: Pre-heat the oven to 400°F. Put the baking sheet on the center rack and bake until the rolls are lightly golden, fifteen minutes. After fifteen minutes, turn the baaties over using tongs and bake until a golden colour is achieved-brown, another ten minutes. Take out of the oven and place each one individually on a clean pot holder or kitchen towel. Crumple lightly to break open and expose the insides. Return to the oven and bake another 5 to seven minutes, or until the insides are lightly golden, baste liberally with the ghee before you serve.
7. To brown on a grill: Preheat a grill to medium-high heat (400°F) and grill the baaties, turning them occasionally, until crunchy and lightly browned, approximately five minutes. Moisten liberally with the ghee and serve.

CHICKPEA FLOUR FLATBREAD

This recipe is called "Missi roti" in Hindi

Yield: 8 to 10 breads

Ingredients:

- ¼ teaspoon ajwain seeds, crudely ground
- ¼ teaspoon salt, or to taste
- ½ cup non-fat plain yogurt, or as required
- ½ cup stone-ground durum whole-wheat flour
- ½ teaspoon hot red pepper flakes, or to taste
- 1 cup chickpea flour (besan)
- 1 to 2 tablespoons water, as required

Directions:

1. In a large container, combine the chickpea and whole-wheat flours with clean fingers. Put in the salt, red pepper flakes, and ajwain seeds and mix once more. Put in the yogurt and mix using your fingers, in round circular movements, until it gathers into a soft, pliable ball that does not cling to your fingers. (Use the water only if you need to.)
2. Knead for approximately a minute, pushing your knuckles gently into the dough, flattening the dough outward, then gathering the ends together toward the center using your fingers. Push down the center, then repeat

pressing and gathering a few times until a tender and flexible dough is attained that does not cling to your fingers. If, while kneading, the dough sticks to your hands, scrape off the dough, put some oil on them, and continue kneading. Cover using plastic wrap or the lid of the container and let the dough rest at least 1 and maximum four hours at room temperature. (This gives time to the gluten develop.)
3. To roll and fry the breads, use mildly oiled hands to split the dough equally into 8 to 10 balls and cover using a foil to stop drying. Next, follow the directions for "Basic Parantha", starting from Step 4.

FERMENTED LEAVENED FLATREAD

This recipe is called "Khameeri roti" in Hindi

Yield: 8 to 10 breads

Ingredients:

- ¼ cup non-fat plain yogurt
- ¼ cup warm water (about 130°F)
- ½ teaspoon freshly ground black pepper
- ½ teaspoon salt, or to taste
- 1 teaspoon active dry yeast
- 1 teaspoon sugar
- 1½ cups stone-ground durum whole-wheat flour

Directions:

1. In a small-sized container, combine the yeast and sugar in the water and allow to sit until frothy, approximately five to seven minutes.
2. Put the flour, salt, and black pepper into a food processor and process until mixed. While the motor runs, slowly Put in the yeast mixture, then the yogurt, through the feeder tube until the flour gathers into a ball and the sides of the work container look clean, approximately one minute. (If the dough appears too sticky, add some more dry flour through the feeder tube.) Move to a large container, cover using plastic wrap or the lid of the container, and place in a warm draft-free spot until it doubles in volume, at least 4 and maximum 1two hours.

3. With lightly oiled hands, divide the dough equally into 8 to 10 balls and cover using a foil to stop drying.
4. Preheat a tava or griddle using moderate to high heat until a sprinkling of flour instantly turns dark brown. Wipe off the flour and continue. While the tava heats up, working with each ball separately, press into a flat disc in a container or pie tin with dry flour, and coat completely with flour. Using a rolling pin, on a cutting board or any clean flat work surface, roll each disc into 6- to 7-inch circles.
5. Cook the breads according to directions for "Basic Parantha", starting from Step 5.

FLOUR AND POTATO FLATBREAD

This recipe is called "Kathi kabaab ki aalu roti" in Hindi

Yield: 12 to 16 breads

This recipe is mostly used to make delicious wraps.

Ingredients:

- ½ cup all-purpose flour in a small-sized container or a pie dish, for dusting
- 1 cup self-rising flour
- 1 teaspoon vegetable oil
- 2 large russet potatoes (about ¾ pounds)

Directions:

1. Boil the potatoes in lightly salted water to cover until tender, approximately twenty minutes. Allow to cool, then peel them. Crudely cut them and place them Using a food processor along with the flour, and pulse 8 to 10 times (do not process continuously, the potatoes will become starchy) until you have a semi-firm dough, adding 1 to 2 tablespoons hot water only if needed. This dough does not require resting time, nor should it be kneaded.
2. Move to a container, put in the oil, and mix lightly with clean fingers. Next, use mildly oiled hands to split the dough equally into 12 to 16 balls and cover using a foil to stop drying. Work one portion at a time, coat with the dry flour and roll into a thin 6- to 8-inch circle.

3. Preheat a tava or a griddle using moderate to high heat until a little flour dropped on the surface turns brown. Wipe off the flour and continue. Cook the roti breads until lightly speckled with golden dots, approximately one minute per side. (These are not like well-cooked breads that are browned.)

GUJARATI FENUGREEK FLATBREAD

This recipe is called "Methi thepla" in Hindi

Yield: 12 to 16 breads

Ingredients:

- ⅛ teaspoon ground asafoetida
- ¼ cup chickpea flour (besan)
- ½ teaspoon ground turmeric
- ½ to ¾ cup non-fat plain yogurt, whisked until the desired smoothness is achieved
- 1 bunch fresh fenugreek leaves, trimmed and finely chopped
- 1 tablespoon Basic Ginger and Green Chile Pepper Paste
- 1 teaspoon salt, or to taste
- 1 teaspoon sugar
- 1¼ cups stone-ground durum whole-wheat flour
- 2 to 3 tablespoons peanut oil

Directions:

1. Ready the ginger-chile paste. Next, in a container, add all the ingredients except the yogurt and mix thoroughly with clean fingers. Add ½ cup yogurt and mix using your fingers in round circular movements until the dough begins to gather. (Add 1 or 2 tablespoons more flour if the dough appears sticky, or some water if it appears too firm.)
2. Knead for approximately a minute, pushing your knuckles gently into the dough, flattening the dough outward, and gathering the ends together toward the center using your fingers. Push the center down and repeat pressing and gathering a few times until a tender and flexible dough is attained that does not stick to the fingers. (If the dough gets too sticky while you work it, coat your hands with a little oil or water.)

3. Cover and allow to rest for minimum 1 and maximum four hours at room temperature. (This lets the gluten develop.) If keeping for a longer period, place the dough in your fridge.
4. To make the breads, preheat the tava or griddle using moderate to high heat until a sprinkling of the flour instantly turns dark brown. Wipe off the flour and continue. While the tava heats up, use mildly oiled hands to split the dough equally into 12 to 16 balls and cover using a foil to stop drying.
5. To roll and cook the breads, follow the directions for "Basic Parantha", starting from Step 4.

MILLET FLATBREAD ⓥ

This recipe is called "Bajrae ki roti" in Hindi

Yield: 8 to 10 breads

Ingredients:

- ⅓ cup finely chopped fresh cilantro, including soft stems
- ½ teaspoon salt, or to taste
- 1 fresh green chile pepper, such as serrano, stemmed
- 1 tablespoon ground coriander
- 2 cups millet flour
- 2 large russet (or any kind) potatoes
- 2 teaspoons ground pomegranate seeds
- 3 tablespoons vegetable oil
- 4 quarter-size slices peeled fresh ginger
- 6 to 8 scallions, white and light green parts only, crudely chopped

Directions:

1. Boil the potatoes in lightly salted water to cover until tender, approximately twenty minutes. Allow to cool, then peel and mash. Using a food processor, combine and pulse the scallions, ginger, and green chile pepper until minced.
2. Put in the flour, mashed potatoes, coriander, salt, pomegranate seeds, and oil, and pulse 8 to 10 times (do not process continuously or the potatoes with turn starchy) until everything begins to gather into a ball. Move to a container.

3. Put in the cilantro and mix with clean fingers to make a semi-soft dough that does not stick to them. (Coat your fingers with some oil if that happens.) There is no need to knead this dough or allow for any resting time.
4. Roll and cook the breads according to the directions for "Punjabi white corn flatbread", starting from Step 2.

OPO SQUASH FLATBREAD

This recipe is called "Lauki ka thepla" in Hindi

Yield: 12 to 16 breads

Ingredients:

- ⅛ teaspoon ground asafoetida
- ¼ cup chickpea flour (besan)
- ¼ teaspoon ajwain seeds
- ¼ teaspoon turmeric
- ½ small opo squash (about 1 pound), grated
- ½ teaspoon cayenne pepper, or to taste
- ½ teaspoon salt, or to taste
- 1 cup stone-ground whole-wheat flour
- 1 large clove fresh garlic, minced
- 1 to 3 fresh green chile peppers, such as serrano, minced with seeds
- 2 tablespoons vegetable oil

Directions:

1. In a large container, add all the dry ingredients and mix thoroughly with clean fingers. Put in the squash, garlic, oil, and green chile peppers and mix using your fingers in round circular movements, until it begins to gather into a dough. (Add 1 or 2 tablespoons more flour if the dough appears sticky, or some water if it appears too firm.)
2. Knead for approximately a minute, pushing your knuckles gently into the dough, flattening the dough outward, and gathering the ends together toward the center using your fingers. Push the center down and repeat pressing and gathering a few times until a tender and flexible dough is

attained that does not cling to your fingers. (If the dough gets too sticky while you work it, coat your hands with a little oil or water.)
3. Cover and allow to rest for minimum 1 and maximum four hours at room temperature. (This lets the gluten develop.) If keeping for a longer period, place the dough in your fridge.
4. To make the breads, preheat the tava or griddle using moderate to high heat until a sprinkling of the flour instantly turns dark brown. Wipe off the flour and continue. While the tava heats up, use mildly oiled hands to split the dough equally into 12 to 16 balls and cover using a foil to stop drying.
5. To roll and cook the breads, follow the directions for "Basic Parantha", starting from Step 4.

POTATO BAATI ROLLS

This recipe is called "Aalu bhari baati" in Hindi

Yield: ten to twelve rolls

Ingredients:

- ¼ cup fine-grain semolina
- ¼ cup melted warm ghee or butter + 1 tablespoon ghee for basting
- ½ recipe Rajasthani Potatoes with Cashews and Raisins
- ½ teaspoon ajwain seeds
- ½ teaspoon salt, or to taste
- 1 tablespoon crudely ground coriander seeds
- 2 cups stone-ground durum whole-wheat flour
- About ⅔ cup water

Directions:

1. Ready the potatoes. Next, place the whole-wheat flour and semolina in a big container and stir in the coriander, ajwain seeds, and salt. Using your sanitized fingers, stir in the ghee, then put in the water, slowly and gradually, to make a firm but pliable dough that does not cling to your fingers. Cover using plastic wrap or the lid of the container and let rest approximately one hour. (This lets the gluten develop.)

2. With lightly oiled hands, divide the dough equally into ten to twelve balls and cover using a foil to stop drying. Divide the potato filling into an equal number of portions.
3. Grease a large, heavy baking sheet. Working with each ball of dough separately, press it to make a thick 4- to 5-inch disc and place 1 portion of the filling in the center. Bring the edges up over the filling and push them together to secure. Pinch off the spare dough above the seal, then shape into a ball once more. Flatten the ball into a thick, 2½-inch disc and press down lightly on the seal with your thumb to make a slight depression (the depression must show). Put on the baking sheet. Replicate the process for all remain-ing portions.
4. To bake: Pre-heat the oven to 450°F. Put the baking sheet on the center rack and bake until the rolls are lightly golden, fifteen minutes. After fifteen minutes, turn the baaties over using tongs and bake until a golden colour is achieved-brown, another ten minutes. Take out of the oven, place each one individually on a clean pot holder or kitchen towel, and crumple lightly to break open and expose the insides. Return to the oven and bake another 5 to seven minutes, or until the cracked portions are lightly golden before you serve.
5. To grill: Preheat a grill to high heat (450°F) and grill the baaties, turning them occasionally, until crunchy and lightly browned, approximately five minutes.
6. Moisten liberally with the ghee and serve.

SORGHUM FLATBREAD Ⓥ

This recipe is called "Jowar ka rotla" in Hindi

Yield: 8 to 10 breads

Ingredients:

- ¼ cup stone-ground durum whole-wheat flour
- ½ cup water, as required
- ½ teaspoon salt, or to taste
- 1 cup finely chopped onions
- 1 teaspoon cumin seeds
- 1 to 3 fresh green chile peppers, such as serrano, minced with seeds
- 1½ cups sorghum flour

- 2 tablespoons vegetable oil or melted ghee
- Whipped butter

Directions:

1. In a container, combine the flours, oil (or ghee), onions, green chile peppers, cumin seeds, and salt and then put in the water to make to make a semi-soft dough that does not cling to your fingers. (If the dough sticks to your hands, put a little oil or water on them.) This dough does not require resting time, nor should it be kneaded.
2. With lightly oiled hands, divide the dough equally into 8 to 10 balls and cover using a foil to stop drying.
3. To cook, follow the directions for "Punjabi white corn flatbread", but make the roti into small 4- to 5-inch circles. Everything else remains the same. Serve with a dollop of whipped butter.

CREPES AND PANCAKES

These are the breads of South India, and are quite different than the breads we saw above.

BASIC RICE AND BEAN DOSA

This recipe is called "Saada dosa" in Hindi

Yield: 12 to 16 crepes

Ingredients:

- ½ cup water
- ½ teaspoon fenugreek seeds
- ½ teaspoon salt, or to taste
- ⅔ cup dried white urad beans (dhulli urad dal), sorted and washed in 3 to 4 changes of water

- 2 cups long-grain white or parboiled rice, sorted and washed in 3 to 4 changes of water
- About 3 tablespoons peanut oil

Directions:

1. Put the rice in one container and the dal and fenugreek seeds in another. Immerse both overnight in water to cover by approximately 2 inches. Drain and grind each one separately using a blender, blending to make a smooth and semi-thick batter, adding up to ¼ cup water to each mixture, as required.
2. In a large container, mix both the batters together and put in the salt. Cover and place in a warm, dry spot to ferment until fluffy and full of tiny bubbles, at least one day. Stir in up to ⅔ cup water—just sufficient to make a semi-thick batter of pouring consistency—then whip with a fork to make it fluffier.
3. To make the dosa, heat a large cast-iron tava or a non-stick griddle or skillet using moderate to high heat until a sprinkling of water sizzles instantly. Wipe the tava and baste it lightly with oil. Using a metal soup ladle, pour approximately ½ cup of batter onto the hot tava and spread it uniformly into a 6- to 7-inch circle by lightly pushing the batter outwards in round, circular movements with the back of the ladle.
4. As the dosa sets and turns lightly golden on the bottom (which happens very swiftly), drizzle ½ to 1 teaspoon oil around the edges and a few drops over the top and cook until the bottom takes on a rich golden hue, approximately fifteen seconds. Turn over once and cook until the other side is barely golden, approximately half a minute. Replicate the process for rest of the batter. Serve as is, or fill in some dry-cooked vegetables or meats.

SEMOLINA DOSA

This recipe is called "Rava dosa" in Hindi

Yield: 12 to 16 crepes

Ingredients:

- ¼ teaspoon ground fenugreek seeds
- ½ cup finely chopped fresh cilantro, including soft stems

- ½ cup non-fat plain yogurt, whisked until the desired smoothness is achieved
- ½ cup rice flour
- ½ teaspoon cumin seeds
- ½ teaspoon salt, or to taste
- 1 cup medium-grain semolina
- 1 tablespoon dried curry leaves
- 1 to 1½ cups water, as required
- 1 to 2 fresh green chile peppers, such as serrano, minced with seeds
- 2 tablespoons all-purpose flour
- 2 tablespoons grated fresh or frozen coconut

Directions:

1. In a moderate-sized container combine the semolina, rice flour, all-purpose flour, yogurt, 1 cup water, and salt and allow to sit until the semolina absorbs all the water, for approximately half an hour.
2. **2.** Stir in the rest of the ingredients and whisk for a few seconds, adding sufficient of the rest of the water to make a thin batter of pouring consistency. (If the batter becomes too thin, stir in some rice flour.)
3. Cook as per the directions for "Basic Rice and Bean Dosa", starting with Step 3.

STUFFED DOSA Ⓥ

This recipe is called "Masala dosa" in Hindi

Yield: 12 to 16 crepes

Ingredients:

- ⅛ teaspoon ground asafoetida
- ½ teaspoon ground turmeric
- 1 cup finely chopped fresh cilantro, including soft stems
- 1 tablespoon dried white urad beans (dhulli urad dal), sorted
- 1 tablespoon dried yellow split chickpeas (channa dal), sorted
- 1 teaspoon cumin seeds
- 1 teaspoon ground fenugreek seeds

- 1 teaspoon salt, or to taste
- 1 to 3 fresh green chile peppers, such as serrano, minced with seeds
- 1½ pounds russet (or any) potatoes
- 1½ teaspoons black mustard seeds
- 12 to 16 (1 recipe) "Basic Rice and Bean Dosa" or Semolina Crepes
- 2 tablespoons dried curry leaves
- 2 tablespoons peanut oil
- 2 tablespoons peeled minced fresh ginger
- 2 to 3 tablespoons fresh lemon juice
- 2 to 4 dried red chile peppers, such as chile de arbol, with stems

Directions:

1. Ready the dosa batter. Next, boil the potatoes in lightly salted water to cover until tender, approximately twenty minutes. Allow to cool, peel, and crudely mash.
2. Heat the oil in a big non-stick wok or saucepan using moderate to high heat, put in the red chile peppers and ginger and cook, stirring, until a golden colour is achieved, approximately one minute. Decrease the heat to medium and put in the green chile peppers, both the dals, mustard seeds, cumin, fenugreek, asafoetida, curry leaves, turmeric, and salt, and stir until a golden colour is achieved, approximately one minute.
3. Put in the potatoes and cook, stirring lightly, using moderate to high heat until heated through. Put in the cilantro and lemon juice and cook approximately five minutes to blend the flavours.
4. Cook as per the directions for "Basic Rice and Bean Dosa", starting with Step 3. As you make each dosa, place approximately ½ cup filling in the center of the softer (whiter) side, then serve open-faced, folded in half, or shaped into a cone.

CHICKPEA FLOUR CREPES Ⓥ

This recipe is called "Besan kae pudhae" in Hindi

Yield: 12 to 16 crepes

Ingredients:

- ¼ cup peanut oil
- ¼ teaspoon baking soda
- ½ cup finely chopped fresh cilantro, including soft stems
- 1 small onion, minced
- 1 tablespoon ground coriander
- 1 tablespoon peeled minced fresh ginger
- 1 teaspoon salt, or to taste
- 1 to 3 fresh green chile peppers, such as serrano, minced with seeds
- 1½ cups chickpea flour (besan)
- 1½ to 2 cups water, as required

Directions:

1. In a small-sized container, combine everything except the water and oil. Next, Put in the water as required to make a semi-thick batter of pouring consistency. Whip with a fork a few seconds to make it fluffy. Set aside for approximately half an hour.
2. Heat approximately 2 teaspoons oil in a tava or a moderate-sized non-stick skillet over moderate heat until a sprinkling of water sizzles instantly. Using a metal soup ladle, pour approximately ¼ cup batter onto the hot tava and spread it uniformly into a 5- to 6-inch circle by lightly pushing the batter outwards in round, circular movements with the back of the ladle.
3. As the pancake sets and turns lightly golden on the bottom (which happens very swiftly), drizzle ½ to 1 teaspoon oil around the edges and a few drops on top and cook until the bottom takes on a rich golden hue, approximately half a minute. Turn over once and cook until the other side takes on a similar color, approximately half a minute. Move to a serving platter, repeat with the rest of the batter before you serve hot.

CLASSIC LENTIL PANCAKES

This recipe is called "Addai" in Hindi

Yield: 12 to 16 pancakes

Ingredients:

- ¼ cup crudely chopped fresh cilantro, including soft stems

- ¼ teaspoon ground asafoetida
- ½ teaspoon salt, or to taste
- ⅔ cup long-grain white rice, sorted
- 1 ⅓ cups water, plus more for soaking the dals
- 1 small onion, crudely chopped
- 1 to 2 fresh green chile peppers, such as serrano, stemmed
- 3 tablespoons dried split pigeon peas (toor dal), sorted
- 3 tablespoons dried white urad beans (dhulli urad dal), sorted
- 3 tablespoons dried yellow mung beans (dhulli mung dal), sorted
- 3 tablespoons dried yellow split chickpeas (channa dal), sorted
- 3 to 4 tablespoons peanut oil

Directions:

1. Rinse the rice and dals in 3 to 4 changes of water. Next, place together in a container and soak overnight in water to cover by approximately 2 inches.
2. Drain and move to a blender, put in the onion, cilantro, green chile peppers, salt, and asafoetida, and pulse until the desired smoothness is achieved, adding up to 1 ⅓ cups water, as required, to make a thick and smooth batter. Whip with a fork a few seconds to make the batter fluffy. Set aside three to four hours. If the batter is too thick, add more water, as required, to make a semi-thick batter of pouring consistency.
3. Heat a cast-iron tava or a non-stick griddle or skillet using moderate to high heat until a sprinkling of water sizzles instantly. Wipe the tava and put approximately 1 teaspoon in the center. Next, using a metal soup ladle, pour approximately ½ cup batter onto the hot tava and spread it uniformly into a 5- to 6-inch circle by lightly pushing the batter outwards in round, circular movements with the back of the ladle.
4. As the pancake sets and turns lightly golden on the bottom (which happens very swiftly), drizzle ½ to 1 teaspoon oil around the edges and a few drops on top and cook until the bottom takes on a rich golden hue, approximately one minute. Turn over once and cook until the other side is takes on a similar color, approximately one minute. Move to a serving platter, repeat with the rest of the batter before you serve hot.

MUNG BEAN PANCAKES Ⓥ

This recipe is called "Mung dal kae chillae" in Hindi

Yield: 12 to 16 pancakes

Ingredients:

- ⅛ teaspoon ground asafoetida
- ¼ cup dried white urad beans (dhulli urad dal), sorted
- ¼ cup peanut oil
- ¼ teaspoon baking soda
- ¼ teaspoon freshly ground black pepper, or to taste
- ¼ teaspoon ground turmeric
- ¼ teaspoon salt, or to taste
- 1 cup dried yellow mung beans (dhulli mung dal), sorted
- 1 to 2 fresh green chile peppers, such as serrano, minced with seeds
- 1½ cups water, as required
- 3 to 4 quarter-size slices peeled fresh ginger

Directions:

1. Rinse both the dals in 3 to 4 changes of water. Put together in a container and immerse in water to cover by 2 inches, approximately 3 hours. Drain and move to a food processor, put in the ginger, green chile peppers, and 1 cup water and process to make a thick, smooth batter. (It will still have a bit of a grain.) Move to a container.
2. Put in the rest of the ½ cup water to your food processor and swirl to remove any batter left in the work container and mix it into the batter. Put in the asafoetida, turmeric, black pepper, baking soda, and salt, and mix thoroughly. Set aside three to four hours. If the batter is too thick, add more water, as is needed, to make a semi-thick batter of pouring consistency.
3. Cook the pancakes as described in "Classic Lentil Pancakes", starting from Step 3.

RICE FLOUR PANCAKES

This recipe is called "Gajjar utthapam" in Hindi

Yield: 12 to 16 pancakes

Ingredients:

- ¼ cup peanut oil
- ¼ to ½ cup water, as required
- ½ cup finely chopped fresh cilantro, including soft stems
- ½ cup urad bean flour
- ½ teaspoon salt, or to taste
- 1 cup rice flour
- 1 small red onion, finely chopped
- 1 to 3 fresh green chile peppers, such as serrano, minced with seeds
- 1½ to 2 cups non-fat plain yogurt, whisked until the desired smoothness is achieved
- 2 tablespoons finely chopped fresh dill leaves
- 2 to 3 small carrots, grated

Directions:

1. In a container, combine the rice flour, urad bean flour, and yogurt and mix to make a smooth batter. Whip with a fork a few seconds to make the batter fluffy. Set aside three to four hours. If the batter is too thick, add more water, as is needed, to make a semi-thick batter of pouring consistency. Stir in the onion, carrots, cilantro, green chile peppers, dill leaves, and salt.
2. Heat approximately ½ teaspoon oil in a non-stick tava or skillet over medium medium-high heat until, until a drop of batter sizzles lightly.
3. Next, using a metal soup ladle, pour approximately ½ cup batter onto the hot tava and spread it uniformly into a 5- to 6-inch circle by lightly pushing the batter outwards in round, circular movements with the back of the ladle.
4. As the pancake sets and turns lightly golden on the bottom (which happens very swiftly), drizzle ½ to 1 teaspoon oil around the edges and a few drops on top and cook until the bottom takes on a rich golden hue, approximately one minute. Turn over once and cook until the other side is takes on a similar color, approximately one minute. Move to a serving platter, repeat with the rest of the batter before you serve hot.

STUFFED PANEER CHEESE PANCAKE ROLLS Ⓥ

This recipe is called "Paneer-bharae chillae" in Hindi

Yield: 12 to 16 pancake rolls

Ingredients:

- ½ cup crudely chopped fresh cilantro, including soft stems
- ½ teaspoon kalonji seeds
- ½ teaspoon salt, or to taste
- 1 recipe Yellow Mung Bean Pancakes
- 1 small onion, crudely chopped
- 1 tablespoon peanut oil
- 1 to 3 fresh green chile peppers, such as serrano, stemmed
- 1½ cups <u>Paneer Cheese</u> (Homemade or store-bought), crudely crumbled
- Cilantro sprigs

Directions:

1. Ready the paneer cheese. Ready the pancakes. Next, Using a food processor, combine and pulse the paneer cheese, onion, green chile peppers, and cilantro until minced.
2. Heat the oil in a small-sized non-stick wok or saucepan using moderate to high heat and put in the kalonji seeds; they should sizzle when they touch the hot oil. Swiftly put in the processed paneer cheese mixture and the salt and cook, stirring, until lightly golden, approximately three minutes.
3. Working with each chilla separately, place approximately 2 tablespoons of the filling along one edge of the chilla, then roll it up into a long tube. Cut each roll along the diagonal into 2 pieces, place on a serving platter, garnish with cilantro sprigs before you serve.

TOMATO SEMOLINA PANCAKES

This recipe is called "Tamatar utthapam" in Hindi

Yield: 12 to 16 pancakes

Ingredients:

- ¼ cup peanut oil

- ¾ to 1 cup water, as required
- 1 cup finely chopped fresh cilantro, including soft stems
- 1 green bell pepper, finely chopped
- 1 large tomato, finely chopped
- 1 medium zucchini, grated
- 1 small onion, finely chopped
- 1 tablespoon fresh lemon juice
- 1 teaspoon salt, or to taste
- 1 to 3 fresh green chile peppers, such as serrano, minced with seeds
- 1½ cups fine-grain semolina
- 1½ cups non-fat plain yogurt, whisked until the desired smoothness is achieved
- 2 tablespoons peeled minced fresh ginger

Directions:

1. In a large container, combine the semolina flour, yogurt, ¾ cup water, salt, and lemon juice to make a smooth batter, then whip with a fork a few seconds to make it fluffy. Set aside three to four hours.
2. When ready to cook, if the batter is too thick, add up to ¼ cup more water to make a semi-thick batter of pouring consistency. Stir in the green chile peppers, onion, cilantro, and ginger.
3. In a separate container, combine the tomato, bell pepper, and zucchini. Heat approximately ½ teaspoon oil in a non-stick skillet using moderate to high heat, until a drop of batter sizzles lightly. Using a metal soup ladle, pour approximately ½ cup batter in the skillet and spread it uniformly by tilting and rotating the pan or with the back of the ladle, to make a 5- to 6-inch pancake.
4. Scatter approximately ⅓ cup mixed vegetables over the pancake. As the pancake sets and turns lightly golden on the bottom (which happens very swiftly), drizzle ½ to 1 teaspoon oil around the edges and a few drops on top and cook until the bottom takes on a rich golden hue, approximately one minute. Making sure the vegetables don't fall off, turn over the pancake with 2 large spatulas and cook until the other side takes on a similar color, approximately one minute. Move to a serving platter, repeat with the rest of the batter before you serve hot or warm.

RICE

Rice is an indispensable staple in India. It is eaten with curries, in pilafs (called pullao in Hindi), in biryanis, and in many other ways.

The most popular variety of rice consumed in India is called "Basmati" rice. Basmati rice is easily available in Indian markets, and online on amazon.

Rice can be cooked using three basic ways:

1. Boil it in water, then drain out the water (like you cook pasta);
2. Steam it in measured amounts of water (also known as the absorption method)
3. Cook it using your pressure cooker.

All the rice recipes that follow start with cooked rice, so make sure you know how it is done. Also, make sure you wash the rice before cooking. The best way to wash is to put all the rice is a big container and then add and drain water multiple times.

If you're using the seaming method to cook rice, make sure you immerse the rice in water for at least half an hour before cooking.

When cooking using your pressure cooker, you can soak the rice prior to cooking for better rice texture, but you can skip that step if you're in a rush.

Rice can be cooked ahead of time and re-heated before eating. Here's how—cook the rice completely, move it to a serving dish, cover it with the lid, and set it aside up to four hours at room temperature or up to one day in a fridge. Reheat in the microwave oven three to five minutes on high power or in a preheated 375°F oven for approximately half an hour. Sprinkle 1 to 2 tablespoons water over the rice, if you reheat it using your oven.

If you do not wish to pre-cook and re-heat the rice, combine everything that needs to go in the rice, then cook it minutes before you serve. Here's how—in a non-stick saucepan, sauté your herbs and spices (if using) until a golden colour is achieved, take the pan off the heat, and stir in the rice and the water. Allow the rice to soak in this up to 8 hours. Next, finish cooking the rice approximately ½ hour before you serve. (In this case, do not pre-soak the rice in a separate container.) The rice soaks in the pan in which it is to be cooked.

In general, one cup of uncooked rice makes 3 cups of cooked rice. Now that we have covered the basics of rice cooking, we can jump right into the recipes!

Ⓥ= Vegan Ⓟ= Quick Pressure Cooker Recipe

PLAIN AND STEAMED RICE DISHES

BOILED BASMATI RICE Ⓥ

This recipe is called "Khullae paani mein ooblae chaval" in Hindi

Yield: 4 to 6 servings, or approximately 4 cups

One of the easiest recipes in the world.

Ingredients:

- 1¼ cups basmati rice, sorted and washed in 3 to 4 changes of water
- 5 to 6 cups water

Directions:

1. Put the rice and the water in a big pot and bring to a rolling boil using high heat. Decrease the heat to medium, and carry on boiling until the rice is cooked, approximately seven minutes. Now we will need to train any surplus water from the rice. Use a fine-mesh strainer to drain the rice and throw away the water, or use it as a base for another watery recipe like soup.
2. Once thoroughly drained, transfer the rice back into the pot, use a sanitized ktichen towel to cover the pot (ensuring that the overhang is 1 inch or less, or it may burn on the stove), then place the lid of the pot back on, over the towel.
3. Place the pot back on your stove and cook using the lowrmost heat setting, heat until each grain of rice is fluffy and separate, ten to fifteen minutes. Turn off the heat and allow the rice to rest without interruption for

approximately five minutes. Move to a serving platter, fluff lightly using a fork before you serve.

STEAMED BASMATI RICE

This recipe is called "Ooblae chaval" in Hindi

Yield: 4 to 6 servings, or approximately 4 cups

This is the best method of making basmati rice, although slightly harder.

Ingredients:

- 1¼ cups basmati rice, sorted and washed in 3 to 4 changes of water
- 2 ⅓ cups water
- Cilantro sprig, for garnish (not compulsory)

Directions:

1. In a moderate-sized container, soak the rice in the water, for approximately half an hour.
2. Put the rice and the water in a moderate-sized saucepan and bring to a boil using high heat. Decrease the heat to the lowermost setting, cover the pan (partially at first, until the foam diminishes, then snugly), and cook until the rice is done, ten to fifteen minutes. Do not stir the rice at all. Take the pan off the heat and allow the rice to rest without interruption for approximately five minutes. Move to a serving platter, fluff lightly with a fork before you serve with a sprig of cilantro, if you like.

STEAMED GREEN RICE

This recipe is called "Harae ooblae chaval" in Hindi

Yield: 4 to 6 servings

A delicious rice recipe with the goodness of greens!

Ingredients:

- ¼ teaspoon garam masala
- ½ teaspoon crudely ground black pepper
- ¾ teaspoon salt, or to taste
- 1 cup fresh fenugreek or watercress leaves, washed and dried
- 1 fresh green chile pepper, such as serrano, stemmed
- 1 large bunch fresh spinach, trimmed, washed, dried, and crudely chopped
- 1½ cups basmati rice, sorted and washed in 3 to 4 changes of water
- 2¾ cups water

Directions:

1. In a moderate-sized container, soak the rice in the water, for approximately half an hour.
2. Put the spinach, fenugreek leaves, and green chile pepper into a food processor and pulse until minced. Transfer to a large non-stick saucepan and cook, stirring, using moderate to high heat until seems slightly darker, two to five minutes.
3. Put in the rice with the water it was soaking in, and the salt and black pepper. Mix lightly and bring to a boil using high heat. Decrease the heat to lowermost setting, cover the pan (partially at first, until the foam diminishes, then snugly), and cook until the rice is done, ten to fifteen minutes. Do not stir the rice while it cooks. Turn off the heat and allow the rice to rest without interruption for approximately five minutes. Move to a serving dish, sprinkle the garam masala on top before you serve.

STEAMED SPICY RICE (V)

This recipe is called "Bhunae masalae ke ooblae chaval" in Hindi

Yield: 4 to 6 servings

A nutritious and highly aromatic rice recipe!

Ingredients:

- ¼ cup finely chopped fresh cilantro, including soft stems

- ¼ teaspoon saffron threads
- ½ teaspoon crudely ground black pepper
- ½ teaspoon salt, or to taste
- 1½ cups basmati rice, sorted and washed in 3 to 4 changes of water
- 1½ teaspoons cumin seeds
- 2¾ cups water
- 5 to 7 green cardamom pods, crushed lightly to break the skin

Directions:

1. In a moderate-sized container, soak the rice in the water, for approximately half an hour. Drain, saving the water in a container.
2. Put the cumin, black pepper, saffron, and cardamom pods in a moderate-sized saucepan and roast, stirring and swaying the pan, using moderate to high heat until they are seems slightly darker and highly fragrant, approximately one minute. Put in the drained rice and continue to roast another two to three minutes, swaying the pan or turning the rice with a wooden spoon very cautiously (washed rice tends to break easily).
3. Put in the reserved rice-water and the salt, and bring to a boil using high heat. Decrease the heat to the lowermost setting, cover the pan (partially at first, until the foam diminishes, then snugly), and cook until the rice is done, ten to fifteen minutes. Do not stir the rice while it cooks. Turn off the heat and allow the rice to rest without interruption for approximately five minutes. Move to a serving platter, softly stir in the cilantro before you serve.

STEAMED TUMERIC RICE Ⓥ

This recipe is called "Haldi kae ooblae chaval" in Hindi

Yield: 4 to 6 servings, or 4 cups

This recipe looks spectacular and is highly beneficial for health!

Ingredients:

- ¼ teaspoon ground turmeric
- ½ teaspoon salt, or to taste

- 1 teaspoon dried mint leaves (or 1 tablespoon minced fresh)
- 1 teaspoon red or black peppercorns
- 1¼ cups basmati rice, sorted and washed in 3 to 4 changes of water
- 2 ⅓ cups water
- 5 black cardamom pods, crushed lightly to break the skin

Directions:

1. In a moderate-sized container, soak the rice in the water, for approximately half an hour.
2. Put the rice with the water it was soaking in, along with all the other ingredients (except the mint) in a moderate-sized saucepan and bring to a boil using high heat. Decrease the heat to the lowermost setting, cover the pan (partially at first, until the foam diminishes, then snugly), and cook until the rice is done, ten to fifteen minutes. Do not stir the rice while it cooks. Turn off the heat and allow the rice to rest without interruption for approximately five minutes. Move to a serving platter, garnish with the mint leaves before you serve.

SIMPLE HERBS AND SPICES PILAFS (PULLAOS)

CILANTRO-GARLIC-PEA PILAF Ⓥ Ⓟ

This recipe is called "Hara dhaniya lassan, aur muttar ka pullao" in Hindi

Yield: 4 to 6 servings

Ingredients:

- ½ teaspoon garam masala
- 1 (1-inch) stick cinnamon
- 1 cup frozen peas

- 1 small onion, cut in half along the length and thinly chopped
- 1 teaspoon salt, or to taste
- 1 to 3 fresh green chile peppers, such as serrano, minced with seeds
- 1¼ cups basmati rice, sorted and washed in 3 to 4 changes of water
- 1½ cups finely chopped fresh cilantro, including soft stems + 2 tablespoons for garnish
- 1½ teaspoons cumin seeds
- 2 ⅓ cups water
- 2 large cloves fresh garlic, minced
- 2 tablespoons canola oil
- 3 to 4 whole red chile peppers, such as such as chile de arbol
- 3 to 5 black cardamom pods, crushed lightly to break the skin

Directions:

1. Heat the oil into your pressure cooker using moderate to high heat and put in the cumin seeds, red chile peppers, cinnamon, and cardamom pods; they should sizzle when they touch the hot oil. Swiftly put in the onion and cook, stirring, until a golden colour is achieved, approximately three minutes.
2. Put in the garlic, green chile peppers, peas, cilantro, garam masala, and salt and cook using high heat, stirring, approximately two minutes.
3. Put in the rice and the water, secure the lid of the pressure cooker, place it using high heat and cook until the pressure gauge indicates high pressure. Next, remove from the heat and allow the pot to depressurize automatically, twelve to fifteen minutes. Cautiously open the lid. Do not stir or cook any more, or you will break the rice grains.

GINGER-MINT PILAF Ⓥ

This recipe is called "Adrak-pudina pullao" in Hindi

Yield: 4 to 6 servings

Ingredients:

- ¾ teaspoon salt, or to taste
- 1 fresh green chile pepper, such as serrano, minced with seeds

- 1 small onion, cut in half along the length and thinly chopped
- 1 small potato (any kind), finely chopped
- 1¼ cups basmati rice, sorted and washed in 3 to 4 changes of water
- 1½ tablespoons peeled minced fresh ginger
- 2 ⅓ cups water
- 2 tablespoons minced fresh mint leaves
- 2 tablespoons vegetable oil
- 2 teaspoons cumin seeds

Directions:

1. In a moderate-sized container, soak the rice in the water, for approximately half an hour.
2. Put the cumin seeds in a small skillet and roast, shaking the skillet, over moderate heat until fragrant and seems slightly darker, approximately one minute. Next, crudely crush the seeds using the back of a spoon and reserve.
3. Heat the oil in a big saucepan using moderate to high heat and sauté the onion over moderate heat until brown, approximately seven minutes. Put in the potato, ginger, half the mint, and the green chile pepper and cook, stirring, approximately two minutes.
4. Put in the rice with the water it was soaking in, and the salt, and bring to a boil using high heat. Decrease the heat to the lowermost setting, cover the pan (partially at first, until the foam diminishes, then snugly), and cook until the rice is done, ten to fifteen minutes. Do not stir the rice while it cooks. Turn off the heat and allow the rice to rest without interruption for approximately five minutes. Move to a serving platter, sprinkle the roasted cumin and the rest of the mint leaves on top before you serve.

ROASTED SAFFRON PILAF Ⓥ

This recipe is called "Kesari pullao" in Hindi

Yield: 4 to 6 servings

Ingredients:

- ¼ teaspoon garam masala
- ⅓ teaspoon saffron threads

- ½ teaspoon black cumin seeds (or 1 teaspoon cumin seeds)
- ¾ teaspoon salt, or to taste
- 1 (1-inch) stick cinnamon, bruised
- 1 tablespoon vegetable oil or melted ghee
- 1½ cups basmati rice, sorted and washed in 3 to 4 changes of water
- 2 bay leaves
- 2¾ cups water
- 5 to 7 green cardamom pods, lightly crushed to break the skin

Directions:

1. In a moderate-sized container, soak the rice in the water for approximately half an hour. Put the saffron in a small skillet and roast using moderate heat, shaking the skillet until the saffron is fragrant and seems slightly darker, approximately one minute. Move to a container and crush lightly using a spoon.
2. Heat the oil (or ghee) in a big saucepan using moderate to high heat and cook the cinnamon, bay leaves, and cardamom pods, stirring, until a golden colour is achieved, approximately one minute. Put in the cumin seeds, then the rice with the water it was soaking in. Stir in the roasted saffron and salt and bring to a boil using high heat. Decrease the heat to the lowermost setting, cover the pan (partially at first, until the foam diminishes, then snugly), and cook until the rice is done, ten to fifteen minutes. Do not stir the rice while it cooks. Turn off the heat and allow the rice to rest without interruption for approximately five minutes. Move to a serving platter, sprinkle the garam masala on top before you serve.

SAFFRON AND ALMOND PILAF

This recipe is called "Kesar-badaam pullao" in Hindi

Yield: 4 to 6 servings

Ingredients:

- ¼ cup warm milk (any kind)
- ¼ teaspoon garam masala
- ½ cup chopped or slivered raw almonds

- ½ teaspoon black cumin seeds (or 1 teaspoon cumin seeds)
- ½ teaspoon freshly ground black pepper, or to taste
- ½ teaspoon saffron threads
- 1 tablespoon melted ghee, or vegetable oil
- 1 tablespoon peeled minced fresh ginger
- 1 teaspoon salt, or to taste
- 1¼ cups basmati rice, sorted and washed in 3 to 4 changes of water
- 2 tablespoons shelled, raw pistachios, thinly chopped
- 2¼ cups water
- 6 green cardamom pods, shelled and ground

Directions:

1. In a moderate-sized container, soak the rice in the water, for approximately half an hour. Put the almonds in a small skillet and roast, stirring and shaking the skillet, over moderate heat until seems slightly darker, approximately one minute. Reserve for garnish. Immerse the saffron in the milk approximately fifteen minutes.
2. Heat the ghee (or oil) in a big non-stick saucepan using moderate to high heat and sauté the ginger, cumin, cardamom, and black pepper, approximately one minute. Put in the rice with the water it was soaking in. Stir in the salt and bring to a boil using high heat. Decrease the heat to lowermost setting, cover the pan (partially at first, until the foam diminishes, then snugly), and cook until the rice is almost done, 8 to ten minutes.
3. Uncover the pan, sprinkle the saffron milk over the rice, then cover the pan and cook another 5 minutes to blend the flavours. Do not stir the rice while it cooks. Turn off the heat and allow the rice to rest without interruption for approximately five minutes. Move to a serving platter, lightly stir in the garam masala, then scatter the roasted almonds and the pistachios on top and serve.

SIMPLE CUMIN PILAF Ⓥ

This recipe is called "Jeera chaval" in Hindi

Yield: 4 to 6 servings

The most basic and easiest Indian Pilaf you can make!

Ingredients:

- ½ teaspoon crudely ground black pepper, or to taste
- ¾ teaspoon salt, or to taste
- 1 tablespoon peanut oil or melted ghee
- 1½ cups basmati rice, sorted and washed in 3 to 4 changes of water
- 1½ teaspoons cumin seeds
- 2¾ cups water
- Finely chopped fresh cilantro

Directions:

1. In a moderate-sized container, soak the rice in the water for approximately half an hour.
2. Heat the oil (or ghee) in a big saucepan using moderate to high heat and put in the cumin seeds and black pepper; they should sizzle when they touch the hot oil. Swiftly put in the rice with the water it was soaking in. Stir in the salt and bring to a boil using high heat. Decrease the heat to the lowermost setting, cover the pan (partially at first, until the foam diminishes, then snugly), and cook until the rice is done, ten to fifteen minutes. Do not stir the rice while it cooks. Turn off the heat and allow the rice to rest without interruption for approximately five minutes. Move to a serving platter, garnish with cilantro before you serve.

WHOLE SPICE PILAF Ⓥ

This recipe is called "Khadha masala chaval" in Hindi

Yield: 4 to 6 servings

Ingredients:

- ½ teaspoon crudely ground black pepper, or to taste
- ¾ teaspoon salt, or to taste
- 1 (2-inch) stick cinnamon, broken
- 1 teaspoon cumin seeds
- 1½ cups basmati rice, sorted and washed in 3 to 4 changes of water
- 1½ tablespoons peanut oil or melted ghee

- 2 bay leaves
- 2¾ cups water
- 4 black cardamom pods, crushed lightly to break the skin
- 5 green cardamom pods, crushed lightly to break the skin
- 8 to 10 whole cloves
- Finely chopped fresh cilantro

Directions:

1. In a moderate-sized container, soak the rice in the water for approximately half an hour.
2. Heat the oil (or ghee) in a big saucepan using moderate to high heat and put in the cumin seeds; they should sizzle when they touch the hot oil. Reduce the heat to medium, then swiftly add all the rest of the spices and cook, stirring, approximately one minute.
3. Put in the rice plus the water it was soaking in. Stir in the salt and bring to a boil using high heat. Decrease the heat to low, cover the pan (partially at first, until the foam diminishes, then snugly), and cook until the rice is done, ten to fifteen minutes. Do not stir the rice while it cooks. Turn off the heat and allow the rice to rest without interruption for approximately five minutes. Move to a serving platter, garnish with the cilantro before you serve.

SOUTH AND WEST INDIAN VEGETARIAN RICE DISHES

COORGI YOGURT RICE

This recipe is called "Coorg ka dahi-bhath" in Hindi

Yield: 4 to 6 servings

Ingredients:

- ¼ cup finely chopped fresh cilantro, including soft stems
- ¼ teaspoon freshly ground black pepper, or to taste
- ¼ teaspoon ground paprika
- ¾ teaspoon salt, or to taste
- 1 cup long-grain white rice, sorted
- 1 fresh green chile pepper, such as serrano, minced with seeds
- 1 small sweet onion, such as Vidalia or Maui, finely chopped
- 1 tablespoon peanut oil
- 1 teaspoon peeled minced fresh ginger
- 1½ to 2 cups non-fat plain yogurt, whisked until the desired smoothness is achieved
- 2 cups water

Directions:

1. Bring the rice and water to a boil in a moderate-sized non-stick saucepan using moderate to high heat. Decrease the heat to the lowermost setting, cover the pan (partially at first, until the foam diminishes, then snugly), and cook until all the water has been absorbed and the rice is tender, twelve to fifteen minutes.
2. Heat the oil in a moderate-sized non-stick wok or skillet using moderate to high heat and cook the onion, ginger, and green chile pepper until heated through, approximately one minute. Put in the rice and salt and cook, stirring to break any clumps, until thoroughly mixed. Stir in the yogurt and the cilantro and remove from the heat. Move to a serving dish, garnish with black pepper and paprika before you serve (if possible) at room temperature.

GOAN COCONUT MILK PILAF Ⓥ

This recipe is called "Goan nariyal doodh ka pullao" in Hindi

Yield: 4 to 6 servings

Ingredients:

- ½ to 1 teaspoon Goan Vindaloo Powder (Homemade or store-bought) or garam masala
- 1 (1-inch) stick cinnamon
- 1 cup Coconut Milk (Homemade or store-bought)
- 1 large onion, finely chopped
- 1 teaspoon salt, or to taste
- 1 to 2 tablespoons peanut oil
- 1½ cups basmati rice, sorted and washed in 3 to 4 changes of water
- 1¾ cups water
- 2 tablespoons finely chopped fresh cilantro
- 2 tablespoons grated fresh coconut or shredded unsweetened dried coconut
- 5 whole cloves
- 6 green cardamom pods, lightly crushed to break the skin

Directions:

1. Ready the vindaloo masala and the coconut milk. Next, dry-roast the coconut in a small skillet or tava over moderate heat until fragrant, but just barely darker, approximately a minute or two.
2. Heat the oil in a moderate-sized non-stick saucepan using moderate to high heat, put in the cinnamon, cloves, and cardamom pods, and cook, stirring, until fragrant, approximately one minute.
3. Put in the onion and cook until a golden colour is achieved, approximately five minutes. Next, stir in the rice, coconut milk, water, and salt and bring to a boil using high heat. Decrease the heat to low, cover the pan (partially at first until the foam diminishes, and then snugly), and cook until all the water has been absorbed and the rice is tender, twelve to fifteen minutes. Do not stir the rice while it is cooking. Turn off the heat and allow the rice to rest approximately five minutes. Next, move to a serving platter, lightly stir in the roasted coconut, vindaloo powder (or garam masala), and cilantro before you serve.

LEMON RICE

This recipe is called "Nimboo bhath" in Hindi

Yield: 4 to 6 servings

Ingredients:

- ¼ cup finely chopped fresh cilantro, including soft stems
- ¼ teaspoon ground turmeric
- 1 tablespoon dried white urad beans (dhulli urad dal), sorted
- 1 tablespoon dried yellow split chickpeas (channa dal), sorted
- 1 teaspoon salt, or to taste
- 1/16 teaspoon ground asafoetida
- 1½ cups long-grain white rice, sorted
- 1½ tablespoons minced fresh curry leaves
- 1½ teaspoons brown mustard seeds
- 2 (1-inch) sticks cinnamon
- 2 tablespoons fresh lemon juice
- 2 tablespoons peanut oil
- 3 cups water
- 3 to 5 dried red chili peppers, such as chile de arbol, broken
- 6 to 8 whole cloves

Directions:

1. In a large container, put the rice, water, turmeric, and salt in a moderate-sized non-stick saucepan and bring to a boil using moderate to high heat. Decrease the heat to low, cover the pan (partially at first until the foam diminishes, and then snugly), and cook until all the water has been absorbed and the rice is tender, twelve to fifteen minutes. Cautiously stir in the lemon juice and move the rice to a serving platter. Cover and keep warm.
2. Heat the oil in a small-sized non-stick saucepan using moderate to high heat and put in the red chile peppers, both the dals, cinnamon, and cloves. Cook, stirring, until the dals are golden, approximately one minute. (Stand away from the pan in case the peppers burst.) Put in the mustard seeds, asafoetida, cilantro, and curry leaves and cook, stirring, another minute. Move to the rice platter and cautiously Combine with the rice, taking care that some of this mixture is visible as a decoration. Serve hot.

MADRASI EGGPLANT RICE Ⓥ

This recipe is called "Vangi bhath" in Hindi

Yield: 4 to 6 servings

Ingredients:

- ⅛ teaspoon ground asafoetida
- ¼ cup Tamarind Paste
- ¼ teaspoon ground cinnamon
- ¼ teaspoon ground cloves
- ¼ teaspoon ground turmeric
- ½ teaspoon black peppercorns
- ½ teaspoon green cardamom seeds
- 1 cup grated fresh or frozen coconut or shredded unsweetened dried coconut
- 1 large eggplant (about 1 pound), cut in 1-inch pieces
- 1 tablespoon black mustard seeds
- 1 tablespoon dried white urad beans (dhulli urad dal), sorted
- 1 tablespoon dried yellow split chickpeas (channa dal), sorted
- 1 tablespoon minced fresh curry leaves
- 1 teaspoon cumin seeds
- 1 teaspoon salt, or to taste
- 1½ tablespoons coriander seeds
- 2 tablespoons peanut oil
- 2 teaspoons sesame seeds
- 4 cups (1 recipe) Steamed Basmati Rice (Absorption Method)
- 8 to 10 dried red chile peppers, such as chile de arbol, broken

Directions:

1. Ready the tamarind paste and then the rice. Next, place the coconut, red chile peppers, coriander, both the dals, cumin, sesame seeds, cardamom seeds, and black peppercorns in a medium skillet and dry-roast, stirring and shaking the skillet, over moderate heat until a golden colour is achieved and fragrant, approximately two minutes. Allow to cool, then and grind using a spice or coffee grinder until fine. Stir in the turmeric, cloves, and cinnamon.
2. Heat the oil in a big non-stick wok or saucepan using moderate to high heat and put in the mustard seeds; they should splutter when they touch the hot oil, so cover the pan until the spluttering diminishes. Swiftly put in the curry leaves, asafoetida, eggplant, salt, and half the ground spice mixture. Cover the pan and cook using moderate to high heat the first two to three minutes,

then decrease the heat to medium and cook until the eggplant is quite soft, approximately ten minutes.
3. Put in the tamarind paste and cook approximately five minutes. Gently stir in the cooked rice and most of the rest of the ground spice mixture (save some for garnish). Cover and cook over low heat, approximately five to seven minutes, to blend the flavours. Move to a serving dish, sprinkle the reserved spice mixture on top before you serve.

POTATO-COCONUT-YOGURT RICE

This recipe is called "Aalu-nariyal ka dahi bhath" in Hindi

Yield: 4 to 6 servings

Ingredients:

- ⅛ teaspoon ground asafoetida
- ¼ teaspoon ground turmeric
- ⅓ cup fresh, frozen, or unsweetened dried grated coconut
- ½ cup finely chopped fresh cilantro, with soft stems
- ½ teaspoon crudely ground fenugreek seeds
- ½ teaspoon salt, or to taste
- 1 cup non-fat plain yogurt, whisked until the desired smoothness is achieved
- 1 tablespoon melted ghee or vegetable oil
- 1 teaspoon black mustard seeds
- 1 teaspoon cumin seeds
- 1 to 3 fresh green chile peppers, such as serrano, minced with seeds
- 2 medium potatoes (any kind)
- 3 tablespoons peeled minced fresh ginger
- 4 cups (1 recipe) Steamed Basmati Rice (Absorption Method)

Directions:

1. Ready the rice. In the meantime, boil the potatoes in lightly salted water to cover until tender, approximately twenty minutes, then peel and cut them into ½-inch pieces.

2. Put the coconut in a big non-stick wok or saucepan and stir over moderate heat golden, approximately one minute. Next, Put in the ginger and green chile peppers and stir another minute. Remove from the pan.
3. To the pan, put in the ghee (or oil), then put in the cumin, mustard seeds, and fenugreek seeds; they should splutter when they touch the hot oil, so cover the pan until the spluttering diminishes. Swiftly put in the asafoetida, potatoes, cilantro (save some for garnish), turmeric, and salt and stir approximately five minutes.
4. Stir in the cooked rice and yogurt, cover, and cook until all the yogurt is absorbed by the rice, 5 minutes. Move to a serving dish, garnish with the reserved cilantro before you serve.

ROASTED PEANUT RICE

This recipe is called "Moong-phalli bhath" in Hindi

Yield: 4 to 6 servings

Ingredients:

- ⅛ teaspoon ground asafoetida
- ¼ teaspoon ground turmeric
- ½ cup shelled raw peanuts, red skin on or removed
- 1 tablespoon dried white urad beans (dhulli urad dal), sorted
- 1 teaspoon salt, or to taste
- 1¼ cups long-grain white rice, sorted
- 1½ tablespoons minced fresh curry leaves
- 1½ teaspoons black mustard seeds
- 2 tablespoons dried yellow split chickpeas (channa dal), sorted
- 2 tablespoons finely chopped fresh cilantro, including soft stems
- 2 tablespoons finely chopped scallions, green parts only
- 2 tablespoons peanut oil
- 2 to 3 tablespoons fresh lemon juice
- 2½ cups water
- 3 to 5 whole dried red chile peppers, such as chile de arbol

Directions:

1. In a small-sized container, soak the 2 dals in water to cover by 2 inches, for approximately half an hour. Drain thoroughly and spread on paper towels to dry.
2. Put the rice, water, turmeric, and salt in a moderate-sized non-stick saucepan and bring to a boil using moderate to high heat. Decrease the heat to low, cover the pan (partially at first until the foam diminishes, then snugly), and cook until all the water has been absorbed and the rice is tender, twelve to fifteen minutes.
3. In a small-sized non-stick skillet, roast the peanuts, stirring and swaying the pan, over moderate heat until a golden colour is achieved, approximately two minutes. Move to a container. In the same skillet, heat the oil over moderate heat and cook the red chile peppers and the 2 dals, stirring, until a golden colour is achieved, approximately one minute. (Stand away from the pan in case the peppers burst.) Put in the mustard seeds, asafoetida, and curry leaves and cook, stirring, another half a minute.
4. Put in the roasted peanuts, cook approximately one minute, then move everything to the rice pan. Put in the lemon juice and mix thoroughly. Move to a serving platter, garnish with the chopped cilantro and scallion greens before you serve hot. Or place in your fridge for a maximum of two days and serve cold.

SOUTHERN MUSTARD-ASAFOETIDA PILAF Ⓥ Ⓟ

This recipe is called "Dakshini raayi aur hing ka pullao" in Hindi

Yield: 4 to 6 servings

Ingredients:

- ⅛ teaspoon ground asafoetida
- ¼ teaspoon ground turmeric
- ½ teaspoon crudely ground black pepper
- ½ teaspoon dried fenugreek leaves
- ½ teaspoon ground fenugreek seeds
- ¾ teaspoon salt, or to taste
- 1 tablespoon canola oil

- 1 tablespoon dried curry leaves
- 1 teaspoon black mustard seeds
- 1 teaspoon cumin seeds
- 1 teaspoon dried mint leaves
- 1¼ cups basmati rice, sorted and washed in 3 to 4 changes of water
- 2 ⅓ cups water
- Finely chopped fresh cilantro

Directions:

1. In a moderate-sized container, soak the rice in the water for approximately half an hour.
2. Heat the oil in a big saucepan using moderate to high heat and put in the cumin, mustard seeds, and black pepper; they should splutter when they touch the hot oil, so reduce the heat and cover the pan until the spluttering diminishes. Swiftly stir in the fenugreek seeds, asafoetida, and curry, mint and fenugreek leaves, and then put in the rice with the water it was soaking in. Stir in the salt and turmeric and bring to a boil using high heat.
3. Decrease the heat to the lowermost setting, cover the pan (partially at first, until the foam diminishes, then snugly), and cook until the rice is done, ten to fifteen minutes. Do not stir the rice while it cooks. Turn off the heat and allow the rice to rest without interruption for approximately five minutes. Move to a serving platter, garnish with cilantro before you serve.

SOUTHERN SESAME RICE Ⓥ

This recipe is called "Dakshinitil bhath" in Hindi

Yield: 4 to 6 servings

Ingredients:

- ten to twelve raw cashews, crudely broken
- ¼ cup white sesame seeds
- ½ teaspoon Asian sesame oil
- 1 tablespoon dried split black urad beans (chilkae vaali urad dal), sorted
- 1 teaspoon salt, or to taste

- 1½ cups long-grain white rice, sorted
- 2 scallions, green parts only, finely chopped
- 2 tablespoons peanut oil
- 2 to 5 dried red chile peppers, such as chile de arbol, broken
- 3 cups water
- 8 to 10 fresh curry leaves

Directions:

1. Put the rice, water, and salt in a moderate-sized non-stick saucepan and bring to a boil using moderate to high heat. Decrease the heat to low, cover the pan (partially at first until the foam diminishes, and then snugly), and cook until all the water has been absorbed and the rice is tender, twelve to fifteen minutes. Let the rice rest without interruption for approximately five minutes.
2. In a small skillet, over moderate heat, dry-roast the sesame seeds until a golden colour is achieved, remove to a container, and allow to sit for approximately 2 teaspoons for garnish. Next, dry-roast the dal and red chile peppers until a golden colour is achieved. Move to a spice or coffee grinder, along with the sesame seeds, and grind coarsely.
3. Heat both oils in a big non-stick skillet over moderate heat and cook the cashews and curry leaves, stirring, until a golden colour is achieved, approximately one minute. Put in the scallion greens and stir for approximately half a minute.
4. Put in the cooked rice and ground sesame-red chile mixture and mix thoroughly. Cover and cook using low heat three to five minutes. Move to a serving dish, garnish with the reserved sesame seeds before you serve.

SOUTHERN TAMARIND RICE Ⓥ

This recipe is called "Puliyodarai" in Hindi

Yield: 4 to 6 servings

Ingredients:

- ¼ teaspoon ground turmeric
- ½ cup shelled raw peanuts, without red skin

- ½ cup Tamarind Paste, or to taste
- ½ teaspoon crudely ground fenugreek seeds
- 1 tablespoon dried yellow split chickpeas (channa dal), sorted
- 1 teaspoon black mustard seeds
- 1 teaspoon salt, or to taste
- 1 teaspoon white sesame seeds
- 1¼ cups long-grain white rice, sorted
- 1½ tablespoons coriander seeds
- 15 to 20 raw cashews, crudely chopped
- 2 tablespoons vegetable oil or melted ghee
- 2 to 4 dried red chile peppers, such as chile de arbol, broken
- 2½ cups water
- ten to fifteen fresh curry leaves

Directions:

1. Ready the tamarind paste. Next, put the rice, water, and salt in a moderate-sized non-stick saucepan and bring to a boil using moderate to high heat. Decrease the heat to low, cover the pan (partially at first until the foam diminishes, and then snugly), and cook until all the water has been absorbed and the rice is tender, twelve to fifteen minutes. Let the rice rest without interruption for approximately five minutes, then move to a serving platter. Cover and keep warm.
2. In a small skillet, over moderate heat, dry-roast—separately and in order—coriander seeds (approximately one minute), sesame seeds (about half a minute), and red chile peppers (about 1½ minutes), until a mild brown colour is achieved, moving each to a container as it is done. Allow to cool, then grind them all together as fine as possible. Combine with the rice.
3. Heat 1 tablespoon oil in a small-sized non-stick skillet using moderate to high heat and cook the peanuts, cashews, and curry leaves until fragrant and lightly browned. Put into the rice.
4. Put in the rest of the 1 tablespoon oil to the skillet and put in the mustard and fenugreek seeds; they should splutter when they touch the hot oil, so cover the pan and decrease the heat until the spluttering diminishes. Swiftly put in the chickpea dal and turmeric, and cook, stirring, until a golden colour is achieved, then put in the tamarind paste and cook, stirring, approximately a minute or two. Move this sauce to the rice platter and mix it into the rice, taking care that some of it is visible as a decoration. Serve.

TANGY SOUTHERN RICE

This recipe is called "Bise bele bhath" in Hindi

Yield: 4 to 6 servings

Ingredients:

- ⅛ teaspoon ground asafoetida
- ¼ cup crudely chopped raw cashews
- ¼ cup finely chopped fresh cilantro, including soft stems
- ¼ cup Tamarind Paste
- ¼ teaspoon fenugreek seeds
- ¼ teaspoon ground turmeric
- ¾ cup dried split pigeon peas (toor dal), sorted and washed in 3 to 4 changes of water
- 1 cup long-grain white rice, sorted
- 1 tablespoon coriander seeds
- 1 teaspoon black mustard seeds
- 1 teaspoon dried white urad beans (dhulli urad dal), sorted
- 1 teaspoon dried yellow split chickpeas (channa dal), sorted
- 1 teaspoon garam masala
- 1 teaspoon salt, or to taste
- 2 tablespoons unsweetened grated or shredded dried coconut
- 2 tablespoons vegetable oil or melted ghee
- 2 to 4 dried red chile peppers, such as chile de arbol, crudely broken
- 3 cups finely chopped mixed fresh or frozen vegetables, such as potatoes, green beans, eggplants, and peas
- 4 cups water
- 8 to 10 fresh curry leaves

Directions:

1. Ready the tamarind paste. Put the toor dal and 2 cups water in a big saucepan and bring to a boil using high heat. Decrease the heat to moderate to low and simmer, uncovered, stirring intermittently, until the toor dal is very soft and creamy, approximately twenty minutes.

2. In the meantime, in a small skillet, dry-roast together the red chile peppers, coriander seeds, channa and urad dals, and fenugreek seeds over moderate heat until fragrant and seems slightly darker, approximately two minutes. Put in the coconut and stir until the coconut is golden, approximately a minute or two. Move to a small spice or coffee grinder and grind until thoroughly smooth.
3. To the cooked toor dal, put in the rice and vegetables, along with the turmeric, asafoetida, salt, tamarind, and the rest of the 2 cups water and bring to a boil using high heat. Decrease the heat to low, cover the pan, and cook until the rice and vegetables become soft, twelve to fifteen minutes. Stir in the roasted spice mixture and move to a serving dish.
4. Heat the ghee (or oil) in a small-sized non-stick saucepan using moderate to high heat and put in the mustard seeds; they should splutter when they touch the hot oil, so cover the pan until the spluttering diminishes. Swiftly put in the curry leaves, cashews, and the garam masala and cook, stirring, until the cashews are golden, approximately one minute. Put into the rice and stir mildly to combine, with parts of it visible as a decoration. Sprinkle the cilantro on top and serve.

YOGURT-CASHEW RICE

This recipe is called "Dahi-kaaju bhath" in Hindi

Yield: 4 to 6 servings

Ingredients:

- ⅛ teaspoon ground asafoetida
- ½ cup crudely chopped raw cashews
- 1 fresh green chile pepper, such as serrano, minced with seeds
- 1 tablespoon black mustard seeds
- 1 tablespoon peanut oil
- 1 tablespoon peeled minced fresh ginger
- 1 teaspoon salt, or to taste
- 1¼ cups long-grain white rice, such as jasmine rice, sorted
- 1½ tablespoons minced fresh curry leaves
- 1½ to 2 cups non-fat plain yogurt, whisked until the desired smoothness is achieved

- 2 tablespoons finely chopped fresh cilantro
- 2 to 4 seedless cucumber (about ⅓ pound), peeled and grated
- 2½ cups water
- 5 to 7 whole dried red chile peppers, such as chile de arbol

Directions:

1. Bring the rice, water, and salt to a boil in a moderate-sized non-stick saucepan using moderate to high heat. Decrease the heat to low, cover the pan (partially at first, until the foam diminishes, then snugly), and cook until all the water has been absorbed and the rice is tender, twelve to fifteen minutes.
2. In a moderate-sized container, mix the yogurt, cucumber, ginger, and green chile pepper and mix thoroughly. Next, Combine with the rice. Cover and keep warm.
3. Heat the oil in a small saucepan over moderate heat and cook the red chile peppers, stirring, approximately one minute. Next, Put in the mustard seeds; they should splutter when they touch the hot oil, so cover the pan and decrease the heat until the spluttering diminishes. Swiftly put in the cashews, asafoetida, and curry leaves and stir approximately two minutes over moderate heat. Move to the rice and mix thoroughly. Put the rice on a serving platter, garnish with cilantro before you serve.

VEGETABLE PILAFS (SABZI KAE PULLAO)

CAULIFLOWER PILAF (V)

This recipe is called "gobhi pullao" in Hindi

Yield: 4 to 6 servings

Ingredients:

- ¼ cup finely chopped fresh cilantro, including soft stems
- ¼ head finely shredded green cabbage
- ¼ teaspoon hot red pepper flakes, or to taste
- ½ teaspoon freshly ground black pepper
- ½ teaspoon salt, or to taste
- 1 cup finely chopped kohlrabi
- 1 cup thinly chopped broccoli florets, stems discarded
- 1 cup thinly chopped cauliflower florets, stems discarded
- 1 small onion, cut in half along the length and thinly chopped
- 1 teaspoon garam masala
- 2 tablespoons vegetable oil
- 4 cups (1 recipe) Simple Cumin Basmati Rice

Directions:

1. Ready the rice and allow to cool down to room temperature. Next, heat the oil in a big non-stick skillet using moderate to high heat and cook the onion, stirring, until a golden colour is achieved, approximately five minutes.
2. Put in the kohlrabi, cauliflower, broccoli, and cabbage, along with the salt, black pepper, red pepper flakes, and half the garam masala, and stir approximately two minutes. Decrease the heat to medium, cover the pan, and cook until the vegetables are crisp-tender, three to five minutes.
3. Put in the rice and the cilantro and mix carefully, trying not to break the rice. Move to a serving dish, sprinkle the rest of the garam masala on top before you serve.

CORN-PEAS-TOMATO PILAF Ⓥ

This recipe is called "Makki, muttar, aur tamatar ka pullao" in Hindi

Yield: 4 to 6 servings

Ingredients:

- ⅛ teaspoon ground asafoetida
- ¼ teaspoon ground turmeric
- ½ cup finely chopped fresh cilantro, including soft stems

- 1 large clove fresh garlic, minced
- 1 large tomato, crudely chopped
- 1 small onion, finely chopped
- 1 tablespoon ground dried curry leaves
- 1 teaspoon black mustard seeds
- 1 teaspoon cumin seeds
- 1 teaspoon ground dried fenugreek leaves
- 1 teaspoon ground dried mint leaves
- 1 teaspoon peanut oil
- 1 teaspoon salt or to taste
- 1 to 3 fresh green chile peppers, such as serrano, minced with seeds
- 1½ cups frozen corn kernels, thawed
- 1½ cups frozen peas, thawed,
- 2 tablespoons peeled minced fresh ginger
- 4 cups (1 recipe) Steamed Basmati Rice (Absorption Method)

Directions:

1. Ready the rice. Next, heat the oil in a big non-stick wok or skillet using moderate to high heat and cook the ginger, garlic, and green chile peppers, stirring, approximately one minute. Put in the cumin and mustard seeds; they should splutter when they touch the hot oil, so cover the pan until the spluttering diminishes. Swiftly put in the curry leaves, fenugreek leaves, mint leaves, turmeric, and asafoetida and stir for approximately half a minute.
2. Put in the peas, corn, onion, and salt and stir until a golden colour is achieved, approximately five minutes. Put in the tomato and cilantro, then cautiously stir in the cooked rice. Cover and cook using low heat approximately five minutes to blend the flavours. Move to a platter and serve.

CRANBERRY PILAF

This recipe is called "Karonda pullao" in Hindi

Yield: 4 to 6 servings

Ingredients:

- ¼ cup finely chopped fresh cilantro, including soft stems
- ½ teaspoon crudely ground black pepper
- 1 large onion, cut in half along the length and thinly chopped
- 1 tablespoon Basic Ginger-Garlic Paste (Homemade or store-bought)
- 1 tablespoon Bengali 5-Spices (Panch-Phoran) or store-bought
- 1¼ cups basmati rice, sorted and washed in 3 to 4 changes of water
- 2 (1-inch) sticks cinnamon
- 2 ⅓ cups water
- 2 cups fresh or frozen thawed cranberries
- 2 tablespoons grated jaggery (gur), or brown sugar
- 2 tablespoons peanut oil
- 3 black cardamom pods, crushed lightly to break the skin

Directions:

1. Ready the ginger-garlic paste and 5-spices. In a moderate-sized container, soak the rice in the water, for approximately half an hour.
2. Heat the oil in a big non-stick saucepan using moderate to high heat and cook the cinnamon, cardamom pods, panch-phoran, and black pepper until fragrant, approximately one minute. Put in the onion and cook, stirring, until a golden colour is achieved, approximately five minutes.
3. **3.** Stir in the ginger-garlic paste and cranberries and stir approximately two minutes. Next, Put in the rice with the water it was soaking in and bring to a boil using high heat. Decrease the heat to the lowermost setting, cover the pan (partially at first until the foam diminishes, and then snugly), and cook until all the water has been absorbed and the rice is done, twelve to fifteen minutes.
4. Lightly fork in the jaggery and cilantro, and allow the rice to rest without interruption for approximately five minutes. Move to a serving platter, fluff with a fork before you serve.

GREEN CHICKPEA PILAF Ⓥ

This recipe is called "Chholia ka pullao" in Hindi

Yield: 4 to 6 servings

Ingredients:

- ¼ teaspoon ground turmeric
- ½ teaspoon garam masala + ¼ teaspoon for garnish
- 1 (1-inch) stick cinnamon
- 1 large clove fresh garlic, minced
- 1 large tomato, finely chopped
- 1 tablespoon ground coriander
- 1 tablespoon peanut oil
- 1 tablespoon peeled minced fresh ginger
- 1 teaspoon cumin seeds
- 1 teaspoon salt, or to taste
- 1¼ cups basmati rice, sorted and washed in 3 to 4 changes of water
- 1½ cups shelled fresh green chickpeas (chholia)
- 2 ⅓ cups water
- 2 small onions, finely chopped
- 3 to 5 black cardamom pods, crushed lightly to break the skin

Directions:

1. In a moderate-sized container, soak the rice in the water, for approximately half an hour.
2. Heat the oil in a big saucepan using moderate to high heat and cook the cardamom pods and cinnamon, stirring, approximately half a minute. Put in the cumin seeds; they should sizzle when they touch the hot oil. Swiftly put in the onions and cook, stirring, until a golden colour is achieved, approximately five minutes. Put in the ginger, garlic, coriander, garam masala, and turmeric, stir for approximately half a minute, then put in the tomato and green chickpeas and cook, stirring, approximately five minutes.
3. Put in the rice with the water it was soaking in, and the salt, and bring to a boil using high heat. Decrease the heat to the lowermost setting, cover the pan (partially at first, until the foam diminishes, then snugly), and cook until the rice is done, ten to fifteen minutes. Do not stir the rice while it cooks. Turn off the heat and allow the rice to rest without interruption for approximately five minutes. Move to a serving platter, sprinkle the garam masala on top before you serve.

GRILLED BELL PEPPER PILAF (V)

This recipe is called "Bhuni shimla mirch ka pullao" in Hindi

Yield: 4 to 6 servings

Ingredients:

- four to five small red and yellow bell peppers, washed
- ½ cup finely chopped fresh cilantro, including soft stems
- ¾ teaspoon salt, or to taste
- 1 large clove fresh garlic, minced
- 1 pasilla chile or green bell pepper, washed
- 1 small onion, cut in half along the length and thinly chopped
- 1 tablespoon ground coriander
- 1¼ cups basmati rice, sorted and washed in 3 to 4 changes of water
- 2 ⅓ cups water
- 2 tablespoons olive oil
- Finely chopped scallion, green parts only

Directions:

1. Roast the peppers according to the directions in the "Roasting and Grilling Vegetables" section near the start of this book. Move to a container, cover using plastic wrap or foil, and set aside to cool, approximately 5 to seven minutes. While they are still a little warm, peel off only the highly charred skin. Throw away the stems and seeds and cut the peppers coarsely. Strain and save any juices that may have accumulated in the container.
2. Heat the oil in a big non-stick saucepan using moderate to high heat and cook the onion, stirring, until a golden colour is achieved, 5 minutes. Put in the garlic, rice, coriander, and cilantro and cook over moderate heat, stirring carefully, until a golden colour is achieved, approximately five minutes.
3. Put in the water, salt, and any reserved juices from the peppers and bring to a boil using moderate to high heat. Decrease the heat to low, cover the pan, and cook until all the water has been absorbed and the rice is tender, twelve to fifteen minutes. Gently stir in the roasted peppers, cover the pan, and allow the rice to rest without interruption for approximately five minutes. Move to a serving dish, fluff with a fork, garnish with the scallion greens before you serve.

KASHMIRI MIXED VEG PILAF Ⓥ

This recipe is called "Kashmiri sabzi pullao" in Hindi

Yield: 4 to 6 servings

Ingredients:

- ⅛ teaspoon ground asafoetida
- ½ cup finely chopped fresh cilantro, including soft stems
- ½ small cauliflower, cut into florets
- ½ teaspoon ground turmeric
- 1 cup frozen peas, thawed
- 1 fresh green chile pepper, such as serrano, minced with seeds
- 1 tablespoon ground coriander
- 1 teaspoon black cumin seeds
- 1 teaspoon fennel seeds
- 1 teaspoon <u>Kashmiri Garam Masala</u> or garam masala
- 1 teaspoon salt, or to taste
- 1¼ cups basmati rice, sorted and washed in 3 to 4 changes of water
- 1½ cups finely chopped tomatoes
- 2 bay leaves
- 2 small carrots, cut into ½-inch slices
- 2 tablespoons vegetable oil or melted ghee
- 2¼ cups water
- 3 small white potatoes, cut into wedges
- 6 whole cloves

Directions:

1. Ready the Kashmiri masala. Heat the oil (or ghee) in a big non-stick saucepan using moderate to high heat and put in the cumin, cloves, fennel, bay leaves, and asafoetida; they should sizzle when they touch the hot oil. Swiftly put in the potatoes and cook, stirring until a golden colour is achieved, approximately two minutes.
2. Put in the rice and cook, stirring, approximately three minutes, then put in the carrots, cauliflower, and peas. Cook a few minutes, then stir in the

tomatoes, green chile pepper, coriander, garam masala, turmeric, and salt and cook, stirring, another three to five minutes.
3. Put in the water and bring to a boil using high heat. Decrease the heat to the lowermost setting, cover the pan (partially at first, until the foam diminishes, then snugly), and cook until the rice is done, ten to fifteen minutes, pouring in additional water if required. Do not stir the rice while it is cooking. Turn off the heat, lightly stir in the cilantro, then allow the rice to rest approximately five minutes. Move to a serving platter, fluff with a fork before you serve.

MIXED VEG PILAF

This recipe is called "Sabzi pullao" in Hindi

Yield: 4 to 6 servings

Ingredients:

- ¼ cup non-fat plain yogurt, whisked until the desired smoothness is achieved
- ½ teaspoon garam masala
- 1 cup basmati rice, sorted and washed in 3 to 4 changes of water
- 1 small onion, cut in half along the length and thinly chopped
- 1 tablespoon peeled minced fresh ginger
- 1 teaspoon salt, or to taste
- 1 to 3 fresh green chile peppers, such as serrano, minced with seeds
- 1½ teaspoons cumin seeds
- 1¾ cups water
- 2 cups finely chopped fresh or frozen mixed vegetables
- 2 tablespoons canola oil
- 2 tablespoons finely chopped fresh cilantro
- 3 to 5 black cardamom pods, crushed lightly to break the skin

Directions:

1. In a moderate-sized container, soak the rice in the water, for approximately half an hour.
2. Heat the oil in a big non-stick saucepan using moderate to high heat and put in the cumin seeds and black cardamom pods; they should sizzle when they

touch the hot oil. Swiftly put in the onion and cook, stirring, until a mild brown colour is achieved, approximately five to seven minutes.
3. Put in the ginger and green chile peppers, stir in the vegetables, garam masala, and salt and cook, stirring, using high heat, approximately two minutes. Stir in the yogurt and cook another minute.
4. Put in the rice with the water it was soaking in and bring to a boil using high heat. Decrease the heat to the lowermost setting, cover the pan (partially at first, until the foam diminishes, then snugly), and cook until the rice is done, ten to fifteen minutes. Do not stir the rice while it is cooking. Turn off the heat and allow the rice to rest without interruption for approximately five minutes. Move to a serving platter, fluff with a fork, garnish with the cilantro before you serve.

MUSHROOM-PISTACHIO PILAF

This recipe is called "Gucchi-pista pullao" in Hindi

Yield: 4 to 6 servings

Ingredients:

- ten to twelve dried morel mushrooms
- ¼ cup finely chopped fresh cilantro, including soft stems
- ¼ teaspoon garam masala
- ½ cup blanched raw pistachios (Blanching Raw Nuts)
- ½ teaspoon black peppercorns
- 1 medium onion, cut in half along the length and thinly chopped
- 1 tablespoon Basic Ginger-Garlic Paste (Homemade or store-bought)
- 1 teaspoon black cumin seeds
- 1 teaspoon dried mint leaves
- 1¼ cups basmati rice, sorted and washed in 3 to 4 changes of water
- 2 (1-inch) sticks cinnamon, broken
- 2 ⅓ cups water
- 2 bay leaves
- 2 tablespoons vegetable oil or melted ghee
- 3 black cardamom pods, crushed lightly to break the skin
- 5 to 7 green cardamom pods, crushed lightly to break the skin

- 6 (4-inch) squares silver leaves (not compulsory)

Directions:

1. Ready the ginger-garlic paste. Rinse then soak the morel mushrooms in water to cover by 2 inches, 1 hour or longer. Drain (saving the water) and wash under running water to remove any loosened dirt. Next, slice each mushroom into thin ¼-inch rings. In the meantime, blanch the pistachios.
2. Strain the mushroom water through paper towels and use it, cup for cup, in place of plain water to soak and cook the rice. In a moderate-sized container, soak the rice in the strained mushroom water, for approximately half an hour.
3. Heat the ghee (or oil) in a big non-stick saucepan using moderate to high heat and stir-fry the cinnamon, cardamom pods, bay leaves, and black peppercorns until fragrant, approximately one minute. Put in the cumin, then stir in the onion and cook, stirring, until a golden colour is achieved, three to five minutes.
4. Put in the ginger-garlic paste and mint leaves, then stir in the rice with the water it was soaking in, and bring to a boil using high heat. Decrease the heat to low, cover the pan (partially at first until the foam diminishes, and then snugly), and cook until all the water has been absorbed but the rice is still not fully cooked, 8 to ten minutes.
5. Cautiously stir in the mushroom rings, cilantro, and half the pistachios, cover the pan, and cook using low heat until the rice is done, approximately five to seven minutes. Turn off the heat and allow the rice to rest without interruption for approximately five minutes. Move to a serving platter, fluff with a fork, garnish with the silver leaves (if using), the reserved pistachios and the garam masala before you serve.

MUSHROOMS-CHARD PILAF Ⓥ

This recipe is called "Khumb aur laal saag ka pullao" in Hindi

Yield: 4 to 6 servings

Ingredients:

- ¼ teaspoon salt, or to taste

- 1 bunch (about 1 pound) finely chopped red chard or beet greens, trimmed, washed, and finely chopped
- 1 large clove fresh garlic, minced
- 1 pound medium mushrooms, such as white button, washed and quartered
- 1 to 3 fresh green chile peppers, such as serrano, minced with seeds
- 2 tablespoons vegetable oil
- 4 cups (1 recipe) Simple Cumin Basmati Rice
- Freshly ground black pepper

Directions:

1. Ready the rice. Next, place the mushrooms in a big non-stick skillet (with no oil) and cook, stirring, using moderate to high heat until they release their juices. Continue cooking until the fluids vaporize and the mushrooms are golden, approximately five to seven minutes. Move to a container.
2. To the same skillet, put in the oil and red chard and cook, stirring, using moderate to high heat until wilted, approximately three minutes. Put in the garlic, green chile peppers, and salt, decrease the heat to medium, cover the skillet, and cook until the leaves are soft, approximately eight to ten minutes. Stir in the mushrooms.
3. To serve, arrange the rice in 3 to 4 diagonal rows on a platter, each approximately 2 inches apart. Fill the empty rows with the mushrooms and chard. Garnish with black pepper and serve.

ONION AND BROCCOLI PILAF Ⓥ

This recipe is called "Bhunna pyaz aur hari gobhi ka pullao" in Hindi

Yield: 4 to 6 servings

Ingredients:

- 1 (1-inch) stick cinnamon
- 1 small head broccoli, cut into ½-inch florets, stems cut into ¼-inch pieces
- 1 teaspoon black mustard seeds
- 1 teaspoon cumin seeds
- 1 teaspoon salt, or to taste

- 1½ cups basmati rice, sorted and washed in 3 to 4 changes of water
- 2 teaspoons sugar
- 2¾ cups water
- 3 to 4 small onions, cut in half along the length and thinly chopped
- 4 tablespoons peanut oil or melted ghee
- 6 to 8 green cardamom pods, crushed lightly to break the skin
- 6 to 8 whole cloves

Directions:

1. In a moderate-sized container, soak the rice in the water, for approximately half an hour.
2. Heat 3 tablespoons oil (or ghee) in a moderate-sized non-stick saucepan using moderate to high heat and cook the cardamom pods, cinnamon, and cloves, stirring, approximately half a minute. Put in the onions and cook, stirring as required, until a golden colour is achieved, approximately five minutes. Sprinkle the sugar over the onions, decrease the heat to moderate to low, and continue to cook until they are dark brown. Using a slotted spatula, remove half the onions, drain them on paper towels (to make them crisp), and reserve for garnish.
3. To the pan, put in the rice, the water it was soaking in, and the salt and bring to a boil using moderate to high heat. Decrease the heat to low, cover the pan (partially at first until the foam diminishes, and then snugly), and cook until all the water has been absorbed and the rice is tender, twelve to fifteen minutes. Do not stir the rice while it is cooking. Turn off the heat and allow the rice to rest approximately five minutes.
4. In the meantime in a small saucepan, heat the rest of the 1 tablespoon oil and put in the cumin and mustard seeds; they should splutter when they touch the hot oil, so reduce the heat and cover the pan until the spluttering diminishes. Swiftly put in the broccoli florets and stir approximately two minutes. Move the rice to a serving platter and lightly stir in the broccoli, with some of it visible as a decoration, top with the reserved onions before you serve.

ROASTED FENUGREEK PILAF Ⓥ

This recipe is called "Bhuni methi ka pullao" in Hindi

Yield: 4 to 6 servings

Ingredients:

- ¼ teaspoon garam masala
- ¼ teaspoon ground turmeric
- ½ teaspoon salt, or to taste
- 1 large russet potato
- 2 tablespoons vegetable oil
- 2 to 3 bunches fresh fenugreek leaves (about 4 cups), trimmed and finely chopped
- 4 cups (1 recipe) Simple Cumin Basmati Rice

Directions:

1. Ready the rice and keep warm. In the meantime, boil the potato in lightly salted water to cover until soft, approximately twenty minutes. Allow to cool, then peel and cut finely.
2. Put the oil and the fenugreek leaves in a big cast-iron or non-stick skillet and cook, over moderate heat, stirring, approximately five minutes. Put in the potato, turmeric, and salt and continue to cook until the leaves are dark brown and crisp, approximately twenty minutes. Move the rice to a serving platter and cautiously stir in the fenugreek and potatoes. Sprinkle the garam masala on top and serve.

ROYAL PILAF

This recipe is called "Shahi pullao" in Hindi

Yield: 4 to 6 servings

Ingredients:

- ¼ cup each raisins and finely chopped dried peaches, dried nectarines, and dried dates
- ¼ teaspoon ground green cardamom seeds
- ¼ teaspoon saffron threads
- ½ cup each finely chopped fresh apples, pineapple, and bananas

- ¾ teaspoon salt, or to taste
- 1 cup shelled, raw mixed nuts (such as almonds, walnuts, cashews, peanuts, and pistachios), chopped
- 1 large clove fresh garlic, minced
- 1 tablespoon Mughlai Garam Masala with Nutmeg and Mace or garam masala
- 1 tablespoon peeled minced fresh ginger
- 1½ cups basmati rice, sorted and washed in 3 to 4 changes of water
- 2 drops rose essence (not compulsory)
- 2 tablespoons <u>Dessert Masala</u> or crudely ground raw pistachios and almonds
- 2 tablespoons melted ghee or vegetable oil
- 2 tablespoons milk (any kind)
- 2¾ cups water
- 6 to 8 silver leaves (not compulsory)

Directions:

1. In a small-sized container, soak the saffron threads in the milk at least 30 minutes. In the meantime, in a moderate-sized container, soak the rice in the water, for approximately half an hour. Ready the garam masala and dessert masala.
2. Heat 1 tablespoon ghee (or oil) in a big saucepan using moderate to high heat and cook the nuts, stirring, until a golden colour is achieved. Using a slotted spatula, remove the nuts to a container, leaving as much of the ghee as possible behind in the pan. In the same ghee, cook all the dried fruits. Move to the container with the nuts. Next, cook the fresh fruits until a golden colour is achieved, approximately one minute, and Combine with the nuts.
3. Heat the rest of the 1 tablespoon ghee to the pan and cook the ginger, garlic, and garam masala, stirring, until fragrant, approximately half a minute. Put in the rice with the water it was soaking in, and the salt, and bring to a boil using moderate to high heat. Decrease the heat to the lowermost setting, cover the pan (partially at first until the foam diminishes, and then snugly), and cook until all the water has been absorbed and the rice is almost tender, approximately ten to twelve minutes. Do not stir the rice while it is cooking.
4. Lightly mix the fried nuts and fruits, into the cooked rice, then drizzle the saffron milk and the rose essence (if using) over the rice. Cover and cook using moderate to low heat until the rice is done, approximately ten to twelve minutes.

5. Turn off the heat and allow the rice to rest approximately five minutes. Move to a serving platter, garnish with the silver leaves (if using), sprinkle the saffron, ground cardamom seeds, and dessert masala (or chopped nuts) on top before you serve.

SOYBEAN PILAF ⓟ

This recipe is called "Soyabeans ka pullao" in Hindi

Yield: 4 to 6 servings

Ingredients:

- ⅛ teaspoon ground asafoetida
- ¼ teaspoon garam masala
- ¼ teaspoon ground paprika
- ½ teaspoon crudely crushed fenugreek seeds
- 1 large clove fresh garlic, minced
- 1 large red bell pepper, finely chopped
- 1 large tomato, finely chopped
- 1 tablespoon ground coriander
- 1 teaspoon cumin seeds
- 1 teaspoon salt, or to taste
- 1¼ cups basmati rice, sorted and washed in 3 to 4 changes of water
- 1½ cups shelled frozen soybeans
- 2 ⅓ cups water
- 2 tablespoons vegetable oil

Directions:

1. In a moderate-sized container, soak the rice in the water, for approximately half an hour.
2. Heat the oil into your pressure cooker using moderate to high heat and put in the cumin, fenugreek seeds, and garlic; they should sizzle when they touch the hot oil. Swiftly put in the coriander, soybeans, tomato, paprika, garam masala, asafoetida, salt, and cook, stirring, until lightly roasted, approximately five to seven minutes.

3. Put in the rice with the water with was soaking in, and the red bell pepper. Secure the lid, cook using high heat until the regulator shows that the pressure is high, then cook approximately half a minute more. Turn off the heat and allow the pot to depressurize automatically, twelve to fifteen minutes. Cautiously open the lid, move to a serving platter, fluff with a fork before you serve.

SPINACH-BELL PEPPER PILAF

This recipe is called "Palak aur shimla mirch ka pullao" in Hindi

Yield: 4 to 6 servings

Ingredients:

- ¼ teaspoon garam masala
- ½ teaspoon salt, or to taste
- 1 large bunch fresh spinach, washed, trimmed, and crudely chopped
- 1 large clove garlic, minced
- 1 large red bell pepper, cut into 3/4-inch dice
- 1 tablespoon minced fresh mint leaves
- 1 tablespoon peanut oil
- 1 teaspoon Chaat Masala (Homemade or store-bought)
- 1 teaspoon ground dried fenugreek leaves
- 1 to 3 fresh green chile peppers, such as serrano, minced with seeds
- 4½ cups (1 recipe) Simple Cumin Basmati Rice

Directions:

1. Ready the chaat masala and the rice. Next, heat the oil in a big non-stick wok or saucepan using moderate to high heat. Put in the garlic, green chile peppers, fenugreek, and spinach and cook, stirring, until the spinach is wilted.
2. Reduce the heat to medium, put in the bell pepper, cover the pan, and cook, stirring intermittently, until the bell pepper is crisp-tender, approximately two to three minutes. Stir in the salt.

3. Put in the cooked rice and chaat masala and cook, stirring carefully, to mix. Cover and set aside three to five minutes to blend the flavours. Move to a serving platter, sprinkle the mint and garam masala on top before you serve.

TOFU/PANEER AND CHICKPEA PILAF

This recipe is called "Tofu aur channae ka pullao" in Hindi

Yield: 6 to 8 servings

Ingredients:

- ½ teaspoon crudely ground ajwain seeds
- 1 (1-inch) stick cinnamon
- 1 small tomato, finely chopped
- 1 teaspoon cumin seeds, dry-roasted and crudely ground (See the dry-roasting section in Introduction) + 1 teaspoon
- 1 teaspoon salt, or to taste
- 1¼ cups basmati rice, sorted and washed in 3 to 4 changes of water
- 1½ cups extra-firm tofu, or paneer cheese, cut into ½-inch pieces
- 2 ⅓ cups water
- 2 cups canned chickpeas, drained and rinsed
- 2 large cloves fresh garlic, thinly chopped
- 2 tablespoons peanut oil
- 2 to 3 scallions, thinly chopped
- 3 black cardamom pods, crushed lightly to break the skin
- 4 whole dried red chile peppers, such as chile de arbol

Directions:

1. In a moderate-sized container, soak the rice in the water, for approximately half an hour. Prepare 1 teaspoon cumin seeds.
2. Heat the oil in a big non-stick saucepan using moderate to high heat and stir the red chile peppers, garlic, cinnamon, and cardamom pods, approximately one minute. Put in the rest of the 1 teaspoon cumin seeds and ajwain seeds, then stir in the chickpeas and cook until a golden colour is achieved, approximately three minutes.

3. Put in the tofu (or paneer cheese) and salt, and cook, stirring, another two minutes. Next, stir in the rice with the water it was soaking in. Bring to a boil using high heat. Decrease the heat to the lowermost setting, cover the pan (partially at first, until the foam diminishes, then snugly), and cook until the rice is done, ten to fifteen minutes. Do not stir the rice while it cooks.
4. Turn off the heat and allow the rice to rest without interruption for approximately five minutes. Move to a serving platter, then cautiously stir in the scallions and tomatoes, sprinkle the dry-roasted cumin seeds on top before you serve.

NON-VEGETARIAN PILAFS (PULLAO)

BASIC LAMB PILAF

This recipe is called "Gosht pullao" in Hindi

Yield: 4 to 6 servings

Ingredients:

- ½ teaspoon ground green cardamom seeds
- 1 cup milk (any kind)
- 1 large clove fresh garlic, minced
- 1 large onion, crudely chopped
- 1 large russet potato, peeled and cut into 1-inch pieces
- 1 large tomato, finely chopped
- 1 tablespoon ground coriander
- 1 teaspoon salt, or to taste
- 1 to 3 fresh green chile peppers, such as serrano, minced with seeds
- 1¼ cups basmati rice, sorted and rinsed in 3 to 4 changes of water
- 1½ pounds boneless leg of lamb, all visible fat trimmed, cut into 1-inch pieces
- 2 tablespoons peanut oil
- 2 tablespoons peeled minced fresh ginger

- 2 teaspoons garam masala

Directions:

1. Immerse the rice in water to cover by 2 inches, 30 minutes or longer. Drain, saving 1¼ cups of the water.
2. Heat the oil in a big non-stick saucepan using moderate to high heat and sauté the onion until a golden colour is achieved, approximately five minutes. Put in the lamb, ginger, garlic, green chile peppers, tomato, coriander, garam masala, and salt and cook over moderate heat the first three to five minutes, then over moderate heat until the lamb pieces are golden brown and almost done, approximately twenty minutes.
3. Put in the potato and cook, stirring, approximately two minutes. Next, Put in the rice, the reserved 1¼ cups water, and the milk, and bring to a boil using high heat. Decrease the heat to moderate to low, cover the pan, and simmer until the rice is done and the lamb and potatoes become soft, twelve to fifteen minutes. Move to a serving dish, sprinkle the cardamom seeds on top before you serve.

CHICKEN PILAF

This recipe is called "Murgh pullao" in Hindi

Yield: 4 to 6 servings

Ingredients:

- ½ cup finely chopped fresh cilantro, including soft stems
- ½ teaspoon ground turmeric
- 1 cup non-fat plain yogurt, whisked until the desired smoothness is achieved
- 1 large onion, cut in half along the length and thinly chopped
- 1 large tomato, finely chopped
- 1 pound skinless boneless chicken breasts, cut into 1½-inch pieces
- 1 tablespoon ground coriander
- 1 teaspoon dried fenugreek leaves
- 1 teaspoon garam masala + ¼ teaspoon for garnish
- 1 teaspoon ground cumin
- 1 teaspoon salt, or to taste

- 1 to 3 fresh green chile peppers, such as serrano, minced with seeds
- 1¼ cups basmati rice, sorted and washed in 3 to 4 changes of water
- 2 (1-inch) sticks cinnamon
- 2 ⅓ cups water
- 2 large cloves fresh garlic, minced
- 2 tablespoons peeled minced fresh ginger
- 3 black cardamom pods, crushed lightly to break the skin
- 3 tablespoons vegetable oil
- 5 to 7 green cardamom pods, crushed lightly to break the skin

Directions:

1. In a moderate-sized container, soak the rice in the water, for approximately half an hour.
2. Heat the oil in a big saucepan using moderate to high heat and cook the green and black cardamom pods, and cinnamon, stirring, half a minute. Put in the onion and cook, stirring, until a golden colour is achieved, approximately five minutes.
3. Put in the garlic, ginger, and green chile peppers, stir approximately one minute, then put in the coriander, cumin, fenugreek leaves, 1 teaspoon garam masala, turmeric, and ½ teaspoon salt, and stir another minute.
4. Put in the chicken, tomato, and cilantro, then put in the yogurt, slowly and gradually, stirring continuously to stop it from curdling until it comes to a boil. Decrease the heat to medium, cover the pan, and cook until the chicken is tender and the sauce is thick, ten to fifteen minutes. Leaving approximately ½ cup of the sauce in the pan, remove the chicken pieces to a container and keep warm.
5. **5.** Stir in the rice with the water it was soaking in, and the rest of the ½ teaspoon salt, and bring to a boil using high heat. Decrease the heat to the lowermost setting, cover the pan (partially at first, until the foam diminishes, then snugly), and cook until most of the water has been absorbed but the rice is not yet fully cooked, approximately ten minutes.
6. Cautiously stir in the cooked chicken. Cover and cook using low heat until the rice is tender, approximately ten to twelve minutes. Turn off the heat and allow the rice to rest without interruption for approximately five minutes. Move to a serving platter, fluff with a fork, sprinkle the ¼ teaspoon garam masala on top before you serve.

GROUND LAMB PILAF

This recipe is called "Keema pullao" in Hindi

Yield: 4 to 6 servings

Ingredients:

- ¼ cup blanched almond slivers
- ½ cup finely chopped fresh cilantro, including soft stems
- ½ teaspoon ground cumin
- ½ teaspoon ground turmeric
- 1 large onion, finely chopped
- 1 large tomato, finely chopped
- 1 pound ground extra lean lamb or beef
- 1 tablespoon ground coriander
- 1 teaspoon dried fenugreek leaves
- 1 teaspoon garam masala
- 1 teaspoon salt, or to taste
- 1 to 3 fresh green chile peppers, such as serrano, minced with seeds
- 1½ cups non-fat plain yogurt, whisked until the desired smoothness is achieved
- 1½ tablespoons peeled minced fresh ginger
- 2 large cloves fresh garlic, minced
- 4 cups (1 recipe) Steamed Basmati Rice (Absorption Method)
- Freshly ground black pepper, or to taste

Directions:

1. Ready the rice. Next, place the ground lamb and everything else (except the cooked rice, yogurt, cilantro, black pepper, and almonds) into a large non-stick saucepan and cook, stirring as required, using moderate to high heat the first two to three minutes and then over moderate heat until all the liquids vaporize and the lamb is golden, 25 to 30 minutes.
2. Put in the yogurt, slowly and gradually, stirring continuously to stop it from curdling, and cook until most of it is absorbed, approximately five minutes.
3. Put in the cooked rice and cilantro. Cover the pan and cook over low heat, approximately five to seven minutes, to blend the flavours. Move to a serving platter, garnish with black pepper and almonds before you serve.

SHRIMP PILAF

This recipe is called "Jhinga pullao" in Hindi

Yield: 4 to 6 servings

Ingredients:

- ¼ teaspoon garam masala
- ¼ teaspoon salt, or to taste
- ½ cup Coconut Milk (Homemade or store-bought)
- ½ cup finely chopped fresh cilantro, including soft stems
- ½ teaspoon ajwain seeds
- 1 fresh green chile pepper, such as serrano, minced with seeds
- 1 large onion, cut in half along the length and thinly chopped
- 1 teaspoon cumin seeds
- 2 large cloves fresh garlic, minced
- 2 tablespoons fresh lime or lemon juice
- 2 tablespoons vegetable oil
- 25 to 30 fresh large shrimp (about 1¼ pounds), shelled, deveined and tails removed
- 3 to 4 scallions, green parts only, finely chopped
- 4 cups (1 recipe) Steamed Turmeric and Red Peppercorn Basmati Rice

Directions:

1. Ready the coconut milk. Next, ready the rice and keep warm. Heat the oil in a big non-stick saucepan using moderate to high heat and put in the cumin seeds; they should sizzle when they touch the hot oil. Swiftly put in the onion and cook, stirring, until a golden colour is achieved, approximately seven minutes.
2. Put in the cilantro, green chile pepper, and garlic, and stir until the cilantro is completely wilted, approximately two minutes. Next, Put in the shrimp, ajwain seeds, garam masala, and salt and cook, stirring, until the shrimp are pink and opaque, approximately two minutes. Put in the coconut milk and simmer using moderate to low heat, approximately five minutes.
3. Move the cooked rice to a serving platter. Very cautiously stir in the cooked shrimp, plus any sauce in the pan. Drizzle the lime juice on top, garnish with

the scallion greens, cover the platter, and keep warm approximately five minutes before you serve.

LAYERED RICE DISHES (BIRYANIS)

Biryanis need no introduction. Basically, these dishes are prepared by layering cooked lice with a protein usually. Historically, biryanis have almost always been meat-based, but various vegetarian versions are cropping up too these days. Still, biryani tastes best with meat. I will still give one vegan biryani recipe below, just in case.

Enjoy biryani with a "Raita" recipe on the side. There are plenty of raita recipes in this book, so find your favourite combinations! Have fun!

EGGPLANT BIRYANI (V)

This recipe is called "Baingan biryani" in Hindi

Yield: 4 to 6 servings

Ingredients:

- ½ cup finely chopped fresh cilantro, including soft stems
- ½ cup grated fresh or frozen coconut
- ½ teaspoon ground turmeric
- 1 large clove fresh garlic, peeled
- 1 large tomato, finely chopped
- 1 small onion, crudely chopped
- 1 teaspoon garam masala + ¼ teaspoon for garnish
- 1 teaspoon ground coriander
- 1 to 3 dried red chile peppers, such as chile de arbol, broken into pieces
- 1 to 3 fresh green chile peppers, such as serrano, minced with seeds
- 1¼ cups basmati rice, sorted and washed in 3 to 4 changes of water
- 1¼ teaspoons salt, or to taste
- 1¾ cups water

- 2 cups Coconut Milk (Homemade or store-bought)
- 2 tablespoons finely chopped fresh mint leaves
- 2 to 3 Chinese eggplants (about 1 pound), cut into 3/4-inch pieces
- 2 to 3 tablespoons fresh lemon juice
- 3 tablespoons peanut oil
- 5 quarter-size slices peeled fresh ginger

Directions:

1. Ready the coconut milk. Next, in a moderate-sized container, soak the rice in the water, 30 minutes or longer.
2. In the meantime, place the grated coconut and red chile peppers in a small-sized non-stick skillet and dry-roast, stirring and swaying the pan, over moderate heat until a mild golden colour and fragrance is achieved, approximately a minute or two. Allow to cool, then move to a blender or food processor and process along with the garlic, ginger, green chile peppers, and onion until everything is finely ground. Stir in the coriander, garam masala, and turmeric and process once more. Move to a large non-stick saucepan. Add 2 tablespoons oil and cook, stirring, using moderate to high heat until a golden colour is achieved, approximately five minutes.
3. Put in the eggplants, half the salt, and ½ cup coconut milk and cook using high heat approximately three minutes. Decrease the heat to medium, cover the pan, and cook until the eggplants are soft, fifteen to twenty minutes. Move to a container.
4. To the same pan, put in the rest of the 1 tablespoon oil, tomato, mint, and cilantro and cook over moderate heat, stirring, until most of the juice from the tomato evaporates, approximately two minutes. Put in the rice with the water it was soaking in, along with the rest of the salt and coconut milk, and bring to a boil using high heat. Decrease the heat to low, cover the pan (partially at first until the foam diminishes, and then snugly), and cook until most the water has been absorbed but the rice is not yet fully cooked, approximately ten minutes.
5. To assemble the biryani: Remove approximately half the rice to a container. Spread the cooked eggplant mixture over the rice that remains in the saucepan. Cover the eggplant mixture with the reserved rice. Drizzle the lemon juice over the rice, cover the pan, and cook over lowest heat setting, ten to fifteen minutes, to blend the flavours. Sprinkle the garam masala on top and serve from the pan itself, or move to a serving platter, fluff the top of the rice with a fork before you serve.

HYDERABADI CHICKEN BIRYANI

This recipe is called "Murgh biryani" in Hindi

Yield: 4 to 6 servings

Ingredients:

- ¼ cup finely chopped fresh cilantro, including soft stems
- ¼ teaspoon saffron threads
- ½ recipe Hyderabadi Chicken Curry
- ½ teaspoon ground green cardamom seeds
- 1 cup Crispy Fried Onions
- 1 tablespoon fresh lime juice
- 1 teaspoon finely chopped fresh mint leaves
- 1 teaspoon salt
- 1¼ cups basmati rice, sorted and washed in 3 to 4 changes of water
- 2 tablespoons milk (any kind)
- 4 cups water

Directions:

1. Ready the chicken. In the meantime, in a small-sized container, soak the saffron in the milk, 30 minutes or longer. Ready the fried onions.
2. In a moderate-sized container, soak the rice in the water and salt, 30 minutes or longer. Drain over a container and save the drained water. Put the drained water in a big pot and bring to a rolling boil. Stir in the rice and cook using moderate to high heat, uncovered, until most of the water has been absorbed but the rice is not yet fully cooked, approximately ten minutes. Drain the rice and discard the water (or use it for soups).
3. Preheat your oven to 350°F. To assemble the biryani, baste the bottom of a large oven-safe dish using a spoonful or two of the sauce from the chicken dish and spread half the rice in the dish. Layer all the chicken over the rice. Top with the lime juice, cilantro, and mint, then spread the rest of the rice over the chicken.
4. Drizzle the saffron milk on top, scatter the crunchy onions on the rice, and cover well with aluminium foil. Bake until the chicken literally falls off the bone, the rice grains are soft, and the flavours are well-blended,

approximately one hour. Take out of the oven, fluff the top of the rice lightly with a fork, sprinkle the cardamom seeds on top before you serve hot.

HYDERABADI MARINATED CHICKEN BIRYANI

This recipe is called "Kacchi murgh biryani" in Hindi

Yield: 4 to 6 servings

Ingredients:

- ¼ cup milk (any kind)
- ½ teaspoon ground green cardamom seeds
- ½ teaspoon saffron threads
- 1 (1-inch) stick cinnamon
- 1 (2- to 2½-pound) chicken, skinned and cut into serving pieces (discard back and wings)
- 1 cup crudely chopped fresh cilantro, including soft stems + ½ cup finely chopped
- 1 tablespoon garam masala
- 1 teaspoon salt, or to taste
- 1 to 3 fresh green chile peppers, such as serrano, stemmed
- 1½ cups (½ recipe) Crispy Fried Onions
- 1½ cups basmati rice, sorted and washed in 3 to 4 changes of water
- 2 cups non-fat plain yogurt, whisked until the desired smoothness is achieved
- 2 large tomatoes, crudely chopped
- 2 tablespoons finely chopped fresh mint
- 2 tablespoons vegetable oil or melted ghee
- 2 teaspoons black cumin seeds
- 2 to 3 tablespoons fresh lime juice
- 2 whole bay leaves
- 4 black cardamom pods, crushed lightly to break the skin
- 4 cups water
- 4 large cloves fresh garlic, peeled

- 6 green cardamom pods, crushed lightly to break the skin
- 8 to 10 quarter-size slices peeled fresh ginger

Directions:

1. Using a food processor or a blender, combine and pulse the garlic, ginger, and green chile peppers until minced. Put in the tomatoes, crudely chopped cilantro, and lime juice and process once more until a smooth purée is achieved. Move to a large non-reactive container and stir in the yogurt, garam masala, and salt. Put in the chicken and mix thoroughly, ensuring all the pieces are coated thoroughly with the marinade. Cover and marinate at least 8 and maximum one day in a fridge.
2. In a small-sized container, soak the saffron in the milk, 30 minutes or longer. In a moderate-sized container, soak the rice in the water, 30 minutes or longer. Ready the fried onions.
3. Put the rice and water in a big non-stick saucepan and bring to a boil using high heat. Decrease the heat to moderate to low, and cook, uncovered, until the most of the water has been absorbed but the rice is not yet fully cooked, approximately ten minutes. Drain the rice and discard the water (or use it for soups).
4. Heat the ghee (or oil) in a big nonstick, oven-safe saucepan (such as a Dutch oven) using moderate to high heat. Put in the black and green cardamom pods, cinnamon, bay leaves, and cumin seeds; they should sizzle when they touch the hot oil. Swiftly put in the marinated chicken, plus all the marinade, and stir well. Turn off the heat.
5. Spread the fried onions (save some for garnish), chopped cilantro, and mint on top of the chicken, then cover everything well with the partially cooked rice. Top the rice with the saffron milk, seal the pan well using aluminium foil and place the lid over the foil. Cook using moderate to high heat approximately ten minutes. Reduce the heat to medium and cook approximately fifteen minutes. Reduce the heat further to low, and continue to cook until the chicken literally falls off the bone, the rice grains are soft, and the flavours are well-blended, approximately one hour. Take out of the oven, fluff the top of the rice lightly with a fork, sprinkle the cardamom seeds and the reserved fried onions on top before you serve.

HYDERABADI MIXED VEG BIRYANI

This recipe is called "Sabz biryani" in Hindi

Yield: 4 to 6 servings

Ingredients:

- ¼ cup milk (any kind)
- ¼ teaspoon saffron threads
- ½ cup crudely chopped mixed raw nuts, such as almonds, pistachios, cashews, and walnuts
- ½ cup finely chopped fresh cilantro, including soft stems
- ½ teaspoon ground green cardamom seeds
- 1 cup non-fat plain yogurt, whisked until the desired smoothness is achieved
- 1 medium onion, cut in half along the length and thinly chopped
- 1 tablespoon Hyderabadi Ginger-Garlic Paste
- 1 to 2 tablespoons fresh lime juice
- 1 to 3 fresh green chile peppers, such as serrano, minced with seeds
- 2 (1-inch) sticks cinnamon
- 2 bay leaves
- 2 tablespoons finely chopped fresh mint leaves
- 2 tablespoons melted ghee, or 1 tablespoon each ghee and peanut oil
- 3 to 4 cups washed and chopped mixed fresh vegetables, such as green beans, carrots, potatoes, eggplant, and peas
- 4 cups (1 recipe) Steamed Basmati Rice (Absorption Method)
- 5 green cardamom pods, crushed lightly to break the skin
- 6 whole cloves

Directions:

1. Ready the ginger-garlic paste and the rice. In the meantime, soak the saffron in milk 30 minutes or longer. Put the nuts in a small skillet and dry-roast them over moderate heat, stirring and swaying the pan, until a golden colour is achieved, approximately three minutes. Reserve.
2. Heat the ghee (or ghee and oil) in a big non-stick wok or saucepan using moderate to high heat and put in the cinnamon, cloves, cardamom pods, and bay leaves and cook, stirring, until fragrant, approximately one minute. Put in the onion and cook, stirring, until browned, approximately seven minutes. Stir in the ginger-garlic paste and green chile peppers and cook, stirring, approximately one minute.

3. Put in the vegetables and cook, stirring, approximately five to seven minutes. Next, Put in the yogurt, slowly and gradually, stirring continuously to stop it from curdling, and cook until most of it is absorbed, approximately five minutes. Remove from heat.
4. Preheat your oven to 350°F. To assemble the biryani, baste the bottom of a clear oven-safe dish with some of the juices from the vegetables and spread half the rice in the pan. Layer all the vegetables over the rice and top with the lime juice, cilantro, and mint. Next, spread the rest of the half of the rice over the vegetables.
5. Drizzle the saffron milk over the rice and cover well with aluminium foil. Bake the rice until the grains are soft and the flavours are well-blended, for approximately half an hour. Take out of the oven, fluff the rice lightly with a fork, garnish with the roasted nuts and cardamom seeds before you serve.

LAMB CHOP BIRYANI

This recipe is called "Chaamp ki biryani" in Hindi

Yield: 4 to 6 servings

Ingredients:

- ⅛ teaspoon ground asafoetida
- ¼ teaspoon ground cinnamon
- ¼ teaspoon ground mace
- ¼ teaspoon ground nutmeg
- ½ cup milk (any kind)
- ½ teaspoon ground black cardamom seeds
- ½ teaspoon ground cloves
- ½ teaspoon saffron threads
- 1 cup non-fat plain yogurt, whisked until the desired smoothness is achieved
- 1 teaspoon garam masala
- 1 teaspoon ground cumin
- 1 teaspoon rosewater or 2 drops rose essence
- 1 teaspoon salt, or to taste
- 1 to 3 fresh green chile peppers, such as serrano, minced with seeds
- 1½ tablespoons Basic Ginger-Garlic Paste (Homemade or store-bought)

- 2 pounds lamb rib chops with bone, all visible fat trimmed
- 2 tablespoons finely chopped fresh mint
- 2 tablespoons melted ghee or peanut oil
- 4 cups (1 recipe) Simple Cumin Basmati Rice

Directions:

1. Immerse the saffron in the milk at least 30 minutes or longer. In the meantime, ready the ginger-garlic paste and the rice.
2. Heat the ghee (or oil) in a big non-stick wok or saucepan using moderate to high heat and put in the lamb chops, ginger-garlic paste, green chile peppers, garam masala, asafoetida, and salt and cook, flipping over once or twice, until the chops are golden, approximately two to three minutes per side.
3. Put in the yogurt, slowly and gradually, stirring continuously to stop it from curdling, until all the yogurt is absorbed, approximately seven minutes. Next, Put in the cumin, cardamom seeds, cloves, cinnamon, nutmeg, and mace and continue to cook over moderate heat the first two to three minutes, then over moderate heat until the lamb is super soft, for approximately half an hour.
4. Preheat your oven to 350°F. To make the biryani, spread half the rice in a big ovenproof covered dish, spread the lamb chops and all the sauce uniformly over the rice, then cover the chops well with the rest of the half of the rice.
5. Mix the rosewater into the saffron milk and drizzle over the rice. Cover well using aluminium foil and then with the lid of the dish. Bake the rice approximately one hour. Take out of the oven, fluff the top of the rice lightly with a fork, sprinkle the mint leaves on top before you serve.

MIXED NUTS AND SAFFRON BIRYANI

This recipe is called "Dry-fruit ki biryani" in Hindi

Yield: 4 to 6 servings

Ingredients:

- ¼ cup Crispy Fried Fresh Ginger
- ¼ cup raisins
- ¼ teaspoon saffron threads

- ½ cup light cream, half and half, or whole milk
- 1 teaspoon crudely ground green cardamom seeds
- 1 teaspoon salt, or to taste
- 1¼ cups basmati rice, sorted and washed in 3 to 4 changes of water
- 1½ cups Crispy Fried Onions
- 1½ teaspoons Mughlai Garam Masala with Nutmeg and Mace, or garam masala
- 2 cups crudely chopped mixed nuts, such as almonds, pistachios, walnuts, peanuts, cashews, and pine nuts
- 2 tablespoons peanut oil
- 2¼ cups water

Directions:

1. Ready the garam masala. Immerse the saffron in the cream or milk for approximately half an hour. In the meantime, ready the fried onions and ginger.
2. Heat 1 tablespoon oil in a big non-stick saucepan over moderate heat and cook the nuts and the raisins, stirring, until the nuts are golden, approximately two to three minutes. Move to a container. In the same pan, heat the rest of the 1 tablespoon oil using moderate to high heat and put in the garam masala; it should sizzle when they touch the hot oil. Swiftly put in the rice and cook using high heat, stirring cautiously by swaying the pan, until lightly golden, three to five minutes.
3. Put in the water and salt and bring to a boil using high heat. Decrease the heat to low, cover the pan (partially at first until the foam diminishes, and then snugly), and cook until most of the water has been absorbed but the rice is not yet fully cooked, approximately ten minutes.
4. Preheat your oven to 350°F. To assemble the biryani, mildly grease the bottom of a clear oven-safe dish with some ghee (or butter or oil) and spread half the rice in the dish. Layer the roasted nuts and raisins over the rice, then spread the rest of the half of the rice over the nuts.
5. Drizzle the saffron cream over the rice, garnish with the fried onions and ginger, and cover well with aluminium foil. Bake the rice until the grains are soft and the flavours well-blended, for approximately half an hour. Take out of the oven, fluff the top of the rice lightly with a fork, ensuring that some of the nuts are visible, sprinkle the cardamom seeds on top before you serve.

MUTTON-APRICOT BIRYANI

This recipe is called "Gosht aur khubani ki biryani" in Hindi

Yield: 4 to 6 servings

Ingredients:

- four to five large cloves fresh garlic, peeled
- ¼ cup milk (any kind)
- ¼ teaspoon saffron threads
- ½ cup crudely chopped raw cashews
- 1 cup crudely chopped fresh cilantro, including soft stems
- 1 tablespoon cumin seeds
- 1 tablespoon garam masala
- 1¼ cups basmati rice, sorted and washed in 3 to 4 changes of water
- 1½ cups non-fat plain yogurt, whisked until the desired smoothness is achieved
- 1½ teaspoons salt, or to taste
- 1½ to 2 pounds boneless leg of lamb, all visible fat trimmed, cut into 1½-inch pieces
- 2 (1-inch) sticks cinnamon
- 2 ⅓ cups water
- 2 large potatoes (any kind), peeled and cut into 1-inch pieces
- 2 large tomatoes, crudely chopped
- 2 tablespoons melted ghee or peanut oil
- 2 to 3 tablespoons fresh lime juice
- 20 to 25 fresh curry leaves
- 3 bay leaves
- 3 to 5 fresh green chile peppers, such as serrano, stemmed
- 6 to 8 green cardamom pods, crushed lightly to break the skin
- 6 to 8 quarter-size slices peeled fresh ginger
- 8 to 10 dried apricots, crudely chopped

Directions:

1. Put the meat on a clean cutting board, cover with plastic wrap, then, with the flat side of a meat mallet, lightly pound each piece of lamb a few times to break the fibers.
2. Using a food processor or a blender, combine and pulse the cashews, garlic, ginger, cilantro, curry leaves, green chile peppers, tomatoes, lime juice, garam masala, and salt until a smooth paste is achieved. Move to a large non-reactive container, put in the yogurt, and mix thoroughly. Put in the lamb, potatoes, and apricots and mix thoroughly, ensuring everything is coated thoroughly with the marinade. Cover and marinate at least 4 and maximum one day in a fridge.
3. In a moderate-sized container, soak the rice in the water at least 30 minutes. Immerse the saffron in the milk at least 30 minutes or longer. Preheat your oven to 450°F. Put the rice in a big non-stick saucepan and bring to a boil using high heat. Decrease the heat to low, cover the pan, and cook until most of the water is absorbed but the rice is not yet fully cooked, approximately ten minutes.
4. Lightly grease the bottom of large oven-safe covered dish. Spread half the rice in the dish, spread all the marinated meat, plus the marinade, over the rice, then cover the meat with the rest of the rice.
5. Heat the ghee (or oil) in a small-sized non-stick saucepan using moderate to high heat and put in the cinnamon, cardamom pods, bay leaves, and cumin seeds; they should sizzle when they touch the hot oil. Turn off the heat, put in the saffron milk, then drizzle everything over the rice. Cover well with aluminium foil, and then with the lid of the dish. Bake the rice approximately fifteen minutes, then reduce the heat to 350°F and continue to bake until the lamb is very soft and the flavours are well-blended, approximately one hour. Take out of the oven, fluff the top of the rice lightly with a fork before you serve.

KHICHADIS (RICE AND GRAIN RECIPES)

Kichadi is a popular Indian rice recipe typically made with rice and lentils, but the combinations can be endless.

MUNG KHICHADI Ⓟ

This recipe is called "Mung dal ki khichadi" in Hindi

Yield: 4 to 6 servings

Ingredients:

- ⅓ cup dried green split mung beans (chilkae vaali mung dal), sorted and washed in 3 to 4 changes of water
- ¾ teaspoon salt, or to taste
- 1 cup basmati rice, sorted and washed in 3 to 4 changes of water
- 1 teaspoon black peppercorns
- 1½ teaspoons cumin seeds
- 2 (1-inch) sticks cinnamon
- 2 tablespoons melted ghee or olive oil
- 4 black cardamom pods, crushed lightly to break the skin
- 5½ to 6 cups water

Directions:

1. Put the rice and the dal into your pressure cooker along with 5½ cups water, the cardamom pods, peppercorns, cinnamon, and salt. Ensure that the lid is secure, and cook using high heat until the regulator shows that the pressure is high, then cook approximately one minute more. Turn off the heat and allow the pot to depressurize automatically, twelve to fifteen minutes. Cautiously open the lid and stir the rice. The khichadi should be soft and creamy; if not, then add more water, if required, cover and boil, stirring a few times, until it is soft and creamy, approximately five minutes. Move to a serving dish.
2. Heat the ghee (or oil) in a small saucepan using moderate to high heat and put in the cumin seeds; they should sizzle when they touch the hot oil. Swiftly put in the tarka to the khichadi and mix lightly, with parts of it visible as a decoration. Serve.

MIXED VEG-SPINACH KHICHADI Ⓟ

This recipe is called "Sabzi aur palak ki khichadi" in Hindi

Yield: 4 to 6 servings

Ingredients:

- ⅛ teaspoon ground asafoetida
- ⅓ cup dried yellow mung beans (dhulli mung dal), sorted and washed in 3 to 4 changes of water
- ½ teaspoon crudely ground fenugreek seeds
- ⅔ cup basmati rice, sorted and washed in 3 to 4 changes of water
- ¾ teaspoon salt, or to taste
- 1 black cardamom pod, seeds only, crudely ground
- 1 small bunch fresh spinach (8 to 10 ounces), trimmed, washed, and cut into thin ribbons
- 1 tablespoon peeled minced fresh ginger
- 1 teaspoon crudely ground black pepper
- 1 teaspoon minced garlic
- 1½ teaspoons cumin seeds
- 2 (1-inch) sticks cinnamon
- 2 tablespoons ghee or olive oil
- 3 cups finely chopped fresh or frozen vegetables, such as carrots, potatoes, green beans, cauliflower, peas, or others
- 4 black cardamom pods, crushed lightly to break the skin
- 5 to 5½ cups water

Directions:

1. Put the rice and dal into your pressure cooker. Put in the vegetables, ginger, garlic, cardamom pods, cinnamon, salt, and water. Ensure that the lid is secure, and cook using high heat until the regulator shows that the pressure is high, then cook approximately one minute more. Turn off the heat and allow the pot to depressurize automatically, twelve to fifteen minutes. Cautiously, open the lid, stir in the spinach, and cook using low heat until the spinach is wilted, approximately two minutes. Move to a serving dish.
2. To make the tarka, heat the ghee in a small saucepan using moderate to high heat and put in the cumin seeds; they should sizzle when they touch the hot oil. Swiftly put in the black pepper, fenugreek seeds, and asafoetida and stir a few seconds. Move to the khichadi in the serving dish, stir mildly to

combine, with parts of it visible as a decoration, sprinkle the cardamom seeds on top and serve.

TAPIOCA KHICHADI

This recipe is called "Sabudana khichadi" in Hindi

Yield: 4 to 6 servings

Ingredients:

- ⅓ cup shelled raw peanuts, with or without red skin
- ½ cup finely chopped fresh cilantro, with soft stems
- ½ teaspoon salt, or to taste
- 1 cup medium-grain tapioca, sorted and washed in 3 to 4 changes of water
- 1 fresh green chile pepper, such as serrano, minced with seeds
- 1 tablespoon fresh lime juice
- 1 tablespoon peeled and minced or crudely chopped fresh ginger
- 1 tablespoon vegetable oil or melted ghee
- 1½ teaspoons cumin seeds
- 2 small russet potatoes

Directions:

1. Immerse the tapioca in the water to cover approximately two hours. Drain thoroughly through a fine-mesh strainer and spread on a tray coated using paper towels to dry it completely. (This step is essential, or the khichadi will be soggy.) In the meantime, boil the potatoes in lightly salted water to cover, approximately twenty minutes. Allow to cool, then peel and finely chop.
2. Heat the ghee in a big non-stick wok or skillet and put in the cumin seeds; they should sizzle when they touch the hot oil. Swiftly put in the peanuts, decrease the heat to moderate to low, and cook until a golden colour is achieved, approximately three minutes.
3. Put in the potatoes, ginger, and green chile pepper and stir 2 more minutes. Next, Put in the tapioca, salt, cilantro, and lime juice, cover the pan, and cook, stirring as required, approximately two minutes. Turn off the heat and set aside approximately five minutes. Move to a serving container and serve.

WHEAT, RICE, AND MUNG KHICHADI

This recipe is called "Gehun, chaval, aur mung ki khichadi" in Hindi

Yield: 4 to 6 servings

Ingredients:

- ⅛ teaspoon ground asafoetida
- ½ cup basmati rice, sorted
- ½ cup dried yellow mung beans (dhulli mung dal), sorted
- ½ teaspoon ajwain seeds
- 1 cup cracked wheat or pearl barley, sorted
- 1 teaspoon salt, or to taste
- 1 to 2 tablespoons fresh lime or lemon juice
- 1½ teaspoons cumin seeds
- 2 tablespoons minced fresh mint leaves
- 2 to 3 tablespoons vegetable oil or melted ghee
- 6 to 7 cups water

Directions:

1. Combine the cracked wheat (or barley), rice, and dal and wash in 3 to 4 changes of water. Next, soak everything overnight in the 6 cups of the water.
2. Move the grains and water to a pressure cooker. Stir in the salt, then secure the lid and cook using high heat until the regulator shows that the pressure is high, and cook approximately half a minute more. Decrease the heat to low and continue to cook another minute. Turn off the heat and allow the pot to depressurize automatically, twelve to fifteen minutes. Cautiously open the lid and check to see if the khichadi is soft and creamy; if not, add more water if required, cover, bring up to pressure, and cook under pressure another minute. Or cover and boil until soft, approximately ½ hour. Stir well and move to a serving container.
3. Heat the oil (or ghee) in a small saucepan using moderate to high heat and put in the cumin and ajwain seeds; they should sizzle when they touch the hot oil. Swiftly put in the asafoetida, mint, and lime juice and move to the

khichadi. Swirl lightly to combine, with parts of it visible as a decoration before you serve.

WHEAT-LENTIL-BEAN KHICHADI

This recipe is called "Gehun aur dal ki khichadi" in Hindi

Yield: 4 to 6 servings

Ingredients:

- ¼ cup vegetable oil or melted ghee
- ½ teaspoon cayenne pepper, or to taste
- ½ teaspoon garam masala
- ½ teaspoon ground turmeric
- ¾ cup cracked wheat, sorted
- 1 teaspoon salt, or to taste
- 2 tablespoons Basic Ginger-Garlic Paste (Homemade or store-bought)
- 2 tablespoons each: split pigeon peas (toor dal), yellow split chickpeas (channa dal), white urad beans (dhulli urad dal), yellow mung beans (dhulli mung dal) and red lentils (red masoor dal), sorted and washed in 3 to 4 changes of water
- 3 small onions, cut in half along the length and thinly chopped
- 3 to 4 cups water

Directions:

1. combine the cracked wheat and dals and soak them in 3 cups of the water overnight. In the meantime, ready the ginger-garlic paste.
2. Move the softened grains and water to a pressure cooker, put in the salt and more water if all of it has been absorbed. Ensure that the lid is secure, and cook using high heat until the regulator shows that the pressure is high, then cook approximately one minute more. Turn off the heat and allow the pot to depressurize automatically, twelve to fifteen minutes. Cautiously open the lid and check to see if the khichadi is soft and creamy; if not, add more water if required, cover, bring up to pressure, and cook under pressure another minute. Or cover and boil until soft, approximately ½ hour. Stir well and move to a serving dish.

3. Heat the oil (or ghee) in a big non-stick wok or saucepan over moderate heat and cook the onions until dark brown, approximately fifteen minutes. Set aside some of them for garnish.
4. Add ginger-garlic paste, cayenne pepper, turmeric, and garam masala and stir another minute. Add to dish and stir mildly to combine, with parts of it visible as a decoration. Top with the reserved fried onions and serve.

YELLOW MUNG AND GINGER KHICHADI ⓟ

This recipe is called "Sookhi dhulli mung ki khichadi" in Hindi

Yield: 4 to 6 servings

Ingredients:

- ½ cup dried yellow mung beans (dhulli mung dal), sorted and washed in 3 to 4 changes of water
- ⅔ cup basmati rice, sorted and washed in 3 to 4 changes of water
- ¾ teaspoon salt, or to taste
- 1 black cardamom pod, seeds only, crudely ground
- 1 tablespoon peeled minced fresh ginger
- 1 teaspoon crudely ground black pepper
- 1½ teaspoons cumin seeds
- 2 (1-inch) sticks cinnamon
- 2 tablespoons ghee or olive oil
- 3 black cardamom pods, crushed lightly to break the skin
- 5 to 5½ cups water

Directions:

1. Put the rice and dal into your pressure cooker along with 5 cups water, cardamom pods, cinnamon, and salt. Ensure that the lid is secure, and cook using high heat until the regulator shows that the pressure is high, then cook approximately half a minute more. Turn off the heat and allow the pot to depressurize automatically, twelve to fifteen minutes. Cautiously open the lid and stir the rice and dal. If the rice and dal are not soft, put in the rest of

the ½ cup water and cook using low heat another 5 to seven minutes. (The rice grains should be separate; don't stir to make it creamy.) Move to a serving dish.
2. Heat the ghee in a small saucepan using moderate to high heat and put in the cumin seeds; they should sizzle when they touch the hot oil. Swiftly put in the ginger, black pepper, and cardamom seeds and stir a few seconds, then add to the khichadi and mix lightly, with parts of it visible as a decoration. Serve.

OTHER GRAIN PILAFS

ASAFOETIDA BROWN BASMATI Ⓥ Ⓟ

This recipe is called "Hing vaali brown basmati" in Hindi

Yield: 4 to 6 servings

Ingredients:

- ⅛ teaspoon ground asafoetida
- ½ teaspoon salt, or to taste
- 1 large onion, finely chopped
- 1 large tomato, finely chopped
- 1 tablespoon Basic Ginger-Garlic Paste (Homemade or store-bought)
- 1 teaspoon black mustard seeds
- 1 teaspoon cumin seeds
- 1 teaspoon dried fenugreek leaves
- 1¼ cups brown basmati rice, sorted and washed in 3 to 4 changes of water
- 2 tablespoons finely chopped fresh cilantro
- 2 tablespoons finely chopped fresh curry leaves
- 2 tablespoons peanut oil
- 3 cups water

Directions:

1. In a moderate-sized container, soak the rice in the water, 2 to 3 hours. In the meantime, ready the ginger-garlic paste.
2. Heat the oil in a moderate-sized saucepan using moderate to high heat and put in the cumin and mustard seeds; they should splutter when they touch the hot oil, so cover the pan until the spluttering diminishes. Swiftly put in the onions and cook, stirring, until a golden colour is achieved, approximately five minutes. Put in the tomato, ginger-garlic paste, curry leaves, fenugreek leaves, asafoetida, and salt and stir a few minutes. Move to a pressure cooker.
3. Put in the rice with the water it was soaking in. Ensure that the lid is secure, and cook using high heat until the regulator shows that the pressure is high, then cook approximately one minute more. Decrease the heat to low and continue to cook another 3 minutes. Next, remove from the heat and allow the pot to depressurize automatically, twelve to fifteen minutes. Cautiously open the lid and check to see if the rice is very soft; if not, cover, bring up to pressure, and cook under pressure another minute. Or cover and boil until soft, approximately ½ hour. Move to a serving dish, garnish with chopped cilantro before you serve.

PEAS-POTATO RICE FLAKES

This recipe is called "Muttar-aalu poha" in Hindi

Yield: 6 to 8 servings

Ingredients:

- ⅛ teaspoon ground asafoetida
- ¼ cup shelled raw peanuts, with red skin
- ¼ teaspoon ground turmeric
- ½ cup finely chopped fresh cilantro, including soft stems
- 1 cup frozen peas, thawed
- 1 medium onion, cut in half along the length and thinly chopped
- 1 tablespoon ground coriander
- 1 teaspoon salt, or to taste
- 1 to 3 fresh green chile peppers, such as serrano, minced with seeds
- 2 small russet (or any) potatoes

- 2 teaspoons black mustard seeds
- 2 to 3 tablespoons fresh lime or lemon juice
- 3 cups thick pressed rice flakes, sorted
- 3 tablespoons peanut oil
- Lime or lemon slices

Directions:

1. Boil the potatoes in lightly salted water to cover until tender, approximately twenty minutes. Drain, allow to cool down, then peel and cut into 6 wedges each. Put the rice flakes in a big fine-mesh strainer and wash well under running water. With the rice flakes still in the strainer, soak in a container of water approximately one minute, then drain and set aside.
2. Heat the oil in a big non-stick skillet using moderate to high heat and cook the peanuts, stirring, until lightly golden. Use a slotted spatula to remove the peanuts to a container, leaving all the oil behind.
3. Put in the mustard seeds to the oil; they should splutter when they touch the hot oil, so decrease the heat and cover the pan until the spluttering diminishes. Swiftly put in the onion and cook, stirring, until a golden colour is achieved, approximately three to four minutes. Put in the asafoetida and green chile peppers, then stir in the peas and potatoes and cook, stirring, until the potatoes are golden, approximately four minutes.
4. Put in the turmeric, coriander, and salt, then put in the rice flakes and stir softly to mix. Cover and cook using moderate to low heat until fluffy and yellow, about four to five minutes. Stir in the cilantro and lime (or lemon) juice. Move to a platter, garnish with lime (or lemon) slices before you serve.

SPICY SEMOLINA Ⓥ

This recipe is called "Rava uppma" in Hindi

Yield: 4 to 6 servings

Ingredients:

- ½ cup finely chopped fresh cilantro, including soft stems
- 1 small onion, finely chopped

- 1 tablespoon each: yellow split chickpeas (channa dal), split black urad beans (chilkae vaali urad dal), white urad beans (dhulli urad dal), sorted and washed in 3 to 4 changes of water
- 1 tablespoon peeled minced fresh ginger
- 1 teaspoon black mustard seeds
- 1 teaspoon salt, or to taste
- 1 to 2 tablespoons fresh lime or lemon juice
- 1 to 3 fresh green chile peppers, such as serrano, minced with seeds
- 1½ cups semolina
- 2 tablespoons chopped raw cashews
- 2 tablespoons shelled raw peanuts, with red skin
- 2 tablespoons vegetable oil
- 3 to 3½ cups water
- ten to fifteen fresh curry leaves

Directions:

1. Immerse the dals in water to cover for approximately half an hour. Drain. Put the semolina in a big wok or saucepan and dry-roast, stirring using moderate to high heat until heated through. Decrease the heat to medium and continue to roast until a golden colour is achieved, approximately five minutes. Move to a container.
2. In the same pan, heat the oil and put in the mustard seeds; they should splutter when they touch the hot oil, so reduce the heat and cover the pan until the spluttering diminishes. Swiftly put in the drained dals and stir for approximately half a minute.
3. With the heat still on medium, put in the peanuts and cashews, and cook, stirring, until a golden colour is achieved, approximately one minute. Put in the onion, ginger, green chile peppers, and curry leaves, and cook, stirring, until the onions are golden, approximately five minutes.
4. Stir in the roasted semolina, salt, and water and bring to a boil using high heat. Decrease the heat to moderate to low and simmer until all the water is absorbed and the semolina is soft and fluffy, approximately five minutes. Stir in the cilantro and lime (or lemon) juice, allow to rest approximately five minutes before you serve.

STIR-FRIED VERMICELLI

This recipe is called "Sevai uppma" in Hindi

Yield: 4 to 6 servings

Ingredients:

- ¼ cup finely chopped fresh cilantro, including soft stems
- ¼ teaspoon ground asafoetida
- ½ cup semolina
- 1 cup Indian vermicelli
- 1 small onion, finely chopped
- 1 tablespoon grated fresh or frozen coconut
- 1 tablespoon peanut oil or melted ghee
- 1 tablespoon peeled minced fresh ginger
- 1 teaspoon black mustard seeds
- 1 teaspoon salt, or to taste
- 1 to 2 cups finely chopped fresh or frozen mixed vegetables, such as carrots, peas, corn, and cauliflower florets
- 1 to 2 tablespoons fresh lime or lemon juice
- 1 to 3 fresh green chile peppers, such as serrano, minced with seeds
- 3 to 3½ cups water
- ten to fifteen fresh curry leaves

Directions:

1. In a large non-stick wok or skillet over moderate heat, dry-roast the semolina until it begins to look golden and releases its fragrance, approximately five minutes. Move to a container. In the same pan, heat 1 teaspoon oil (or ghee) and roast the vermicelli until a golden colour is achieved, approximately five minutes. Put into the semolina container.
2. In the same pan, heat the rest of the ghee (or oil) and put in the mustard seeds; they should splutter when they touch the hot oil, so cover the pan until the spluttering diminishes. Swiftly stir in the asafoetida, onion, ginger, green chile peppers, curry leaves, and coconut, and cook, stirring, until the onions are golden, approximately three minutes.
3. Put in the vegetables and salt and cook, stirring, 3 more minutes, then put in the water and bring to a boil using high heat.
4. Stir in the roasted semolina and vermicelli, decrease the heat to moderate to low, cover the pan and simmer, until the vegetables become soft and all the water has been absorbed, approximately ten minutes. Stir every few

minutes. Stir in the cilantro and lime or lemon juice, allow to rest approximately five minutes, then serve.

TAMARIND RICE FLAKES

This recipe is called "Imli poha" in Hindi

Yield: 4 to 6 servings

Ingredients:

- ⅛ teaspoon ground asafoetida
- ¼ teaspoon ground turmeric
- ½ cup finely chopped fresh cilantro, including soft stems
- ½ cup water
- ½ teaspoon salt
- 1 tablespoon dried white urad beans (dhulli urad dal), sorted
- 1 tablespoon dried yellow split chickpeas (channa dal), sorted
- 1 tablespoon finely chopped fresh curry leaves
- 1 tablespoon sesame seeds, dry-roasted (See the dry-roasting section in Introduction)
- 1 to 3 fresh green chile peppers, such as serrano, minced or split in half lengthwise
- 2 teaspoons black mustard seeds
- 2 to 5 dried red chile peppers, such as chile de arbol, broken
- 3 cups thick pressed rice flakes, sorted
- 3 tablespoons peanut oil
- 3 tablespoons <u>Tamarind Paste</u> (Homemade or store-bought)

Directions:

1. Ready the sesame seeds and the tamarind paste. Next, in a small-sized container, combine the tamarind paste, water, turmeric, and salt.
2. Put the rice flakes in a fine-mesh strainer and wash well under running water. Move to a large container, stir in the tamarind-water, and allow to sit until all the water is absorbed and the grains stand separate, approximately five minutes.

3. Heat the oil in a big non-stick skillet using moderate to high heat and put in the red chile peppers and mustard seeds; they should splutter when they touch the hot oil, so cover the pan and decrease the heat until the spluttering diminishes. Swiftly add both the dals, curry leaves, asafoetida, and green chile peppers and cook, stirring, until the dals are golden, approximately one minute.
4. Put in the rice flakes and stir softly to mix. Cover and cook using moderate to low heat until completely dry and fluffy, about four to five minutes. Stir in the cilantro, sprinkle the sesame seeds on top before you serve.

WILD RICE PILAF (V)

This recipe is called "Junglee pullao" in Hindi

Yield: 4 to 6 servings

Ingredients:

- ¼ cup crudely broken raw peanuts, without red skin, dry-roasted
- ¼ cup chopped raw almonds, dry-roasted
- ⅓ cup wild rice, sorted and washed in 3 to 4 changes of water
- 1 cup basmati rice, sorted and washed in 3 to 4 changes of water
- 1 tablespoon white sesame seeds, dry-roasted
- 1 teaspoon cumin seeds
- 1 teaspoon salt, or to taste
- 1 to 2 tablespoons peanut oil
- 2 (1-inch) sticks cinnamon
- 2 bay leaves
- 2 large cloves fresh garlic, minced
- 3 black cardamom pods, crushed lightly to break the skin
- 3 whole dried red chile peppers, such as chile de arbol
- 3¼ cups water

Directions:

1. Put the wild rice in a moderate-sized saucepan, add 1¼ cups water, and bring to a boil using high heat. Decrease the heat to moderate to low, cover the

pan, and cook until the all the water is absorbed and the rice is soft, approximately 40 minutes.
2. In the meantime, in a moderate-sized container, soak the basmati rice in the rest of the 2 cups water for approximately half an hour. In a small skillet, dry-roast the peanuts, almonds, and sesame seeds, roasting each separately because they cook at different rates. Next, mix them all together and save for garnish.
3. Heat the oil in a big saucepan using moderate to high heat and put in the cumin seeds; they should sizzle when they touch the hot oil. Swiftly put in the cinnamon, cardamom pods, and red chile peppers and cook, stirring, approximately one minute.
4. Put in the bay leaves and the garlic and cook, stirring, another minute. Put in the cooked wild rice, the basmati rice, plus all the water it was soaking in, and the salt and bring to a boil using high heat. Decrease the heat to lowest heat setting, cover the pan (partially at first, until the foam diminishes, then snugly), and cook until the rice is done, ten to fifteen minutes. (Do not stir the rice while it cooks.) Let the rice rest approximately five minutes. Move to a serving platter, softly stir in the roasted nuts and sesame seeds, with some of them visible as a decoration before you serve.

DRIED BEANS, LENTILS, AND PEAS (DAL)

Dals are a staple in the Indian kitchen. They are super inexpensive, easy to cook, nutritious, and delicious! If I told you how much dal I've eaten in my lifetime, you'd probably not believe it. Everyone has a recipe they cook when nothing comes to mind. Dal is that food for Indian housewives and cooks. If nothing comes to mind, cook dal. You can't go wrong with dal.

So, if you're an Indian, you probably don't need an introduction to Dal. If, however, you're not an Indian, you could use a bit of information. Dal is a Hindi word which means dried, split pulses that do not require pre-soaking. These pulses can be lentils, beans, or peas.

Dals come in all shapes and sizes, and are complete nutritious meals as they have the perfect balance of fiber, carbohydrates, protein, minerals, and vitamins. They generally have little to no fat. In India, Dal recipes are usually enjoyed with Indian Rice recipes, or Indian breads. They can also be eaten all on their own.

The variety of dals enjoyed in India is actually a little insane, and I will try my best to do justice to this variety in this section.

Ⓥ= Vegan Ⓟ= Quick Pressure Cooker Recipe

KNOW YOUR DAL

Before we jump into the recipes, it would be useful to learn a little about the dals that the recipes call for. If you're not living in India, it would be useful to learn the English names of Indian dals. You can always google a dal's name and find out more about it though. Pretty much every dal here has a Wikipedia page.

MUNG DAL

The mung bean, also known as the green gram, maash, or moong, is a plant species in the legume family. The mung bean is mainly cultivated in East Asia, Southeast Asia and the Indian subcontinent. It is used as an ingredient in both savory and sweet dishes.

MASOOR, OR MASSAR DAL

The lentil is a staple in Indian cuisine. These green-brown discs come in two sizes, with the common American variety being larger then the Indian ones. Both work just fine in recipes.

TOOR, TUAR, ARHAR DAL

Also known as pigeon peas or red gram, this dal is the most popular Dal in South India. It can easily be found in Indian markets, or online.

CHANNA, CHOLA DAL

Also called yellow split chickpeas or split Bengal gram, this dal is made using black chickpeas, and takes a while to digest, keeping you full for quite a while.

URAD, MAAS, MAANH DAL

Also known as Urad beans or black gram. These small, dull-black beans look like green mung dal in appearance. They are dense, and hard to digest. Their recipes require a lot of seasoning.

MOTH, MUTH DAL

Also known as dew beans, this dal is small, and is sold with skin still on. It makes great snacks.

SOOKHAE MUTTAR AND MUTTAR KI DAL

Also known as dried peas and green and yellow split peas, this dal can be bought whole or split without the skin. They are easy to digest, and are used in a variety of recipes in India.

CHORI DAL

Also known as Adzuki beans, this dal appears reddish-brown, and is slightly bigger than mung beans. It is easy to digest.

LOBIA

Also known as black-eyed peas or cow peas, this dal takes a long time to cook, and takes a long time to digest too.

RAAJMA

Also known as Kidney or red beans, this dal is my personal favourite, and I'm sure I share the love for Raajma with millions of Indians.

CHANNAE, CHOLAE

Also known as Chickpeas, garbanzo beans, or Bengal gram, this dal is one of the most nutritious ingredients out there.

SOYABEANS BHATMAS

Also known as Soy beans, these are loaded with protein, and are quickly gaining popularity all over the world.

BASICS OF COOKING DAL

Before you start to cook, place the dals (of any variety or form) in a big container and wash them in 3 to 4 changes of water. All the husks and hollow grains float to the top and can be poured out with the water. You will not be able to do this if you wash them using a fine-mesh strainer under running water.

Next, cook them using your pressure cooker or saucepan. Smaller dals can be cooked using a saucepan, but it is still better to use a pressure cooker, as that is how most Indian cooks do it. It is quicker, and safer.

If you don't have a pressure cooker, and don't wish to invest in one yet, you can use a saucepan to cook dals. It will take longer, but it will work. Just boil the dal in your saucepan until it becomes soft. Make sure you add more water as needed.

All cooked beans stay fresh in the fridge for approximately 5 days. Reheat with additional water in the microwave or over moderate heat. For maximum flavour, reheat any previously cooked or leftover dal and then add a fresh tarka (sizzling flavour topping), which was used in the main recipe, just before you serve.

Know that Dals can also also used as seasonings or to add texture to a dish. They are regularly processed with herbs and spices, or are simply dry-roasted before being added to a dish. They do not need to be soaked if you're using them as a seasoning.

MUNG BEANS (MUNG DAL) RECIPES

YELLOW MUNG DAL (V)

This recipe is called "Dhulli mungi ki dal" in Hindi

Yield: 4 to 6 servings

One of the most popular recipes on North India.

Ingredients:

- ¼ cup finely chopped fresh cilantro, including soft stems
- ¼ teaspoon ground paprika
- ¼ teaspoon ground turmeric
- ½ small onion, finely chopped
- ½ teaspoon ground cumin
- ¾ teaspoon salt, or to taste
- 1 cup yellow mung beans (dhulli mung dal), sorted and washed in 3 to 4 changes of water
- 1 tablespoon ground coriander
- 1 tablespoon peeled minced fresh ginger
- 1 teaspoon cumin seeds
- 1 teaspoon melted ghee (not compulsory)
- 2 tablespoons peanut or canola oil
- 3 to 5 whole fresh green chile peppers, such as serrano
- 3½ to 4 cups water
- Freshly ground black pepper

Directions:

1. Put the dal, 3½ cups water, green chile peppers, turmeric, and salt in a moderate-sized saucepan and bring to a boil using high heat. Decrease the heat to medium and cook the dal, uncovered, stirring intermittently and watching cautiously that it doesn't boil over, approximately ten minutes. Decrease the heat to low, put in the rest of the water, if required, and simmer until the dal is soft and creamy, approximately fifteen minutes. Stir in the cilantro during the last 5 minutes of cooking. Move to a serving container, cover, and keep warm.
2. Heat the oil (and the ghee, if using) in a small saucepan using moderate to high heat and put in the cumin seeds; they should sizzle when they touch the hot oil. Swiftly put in the onion and cook, stirring, until a golden colour is achieved, approximately one minute. Put in the ginger and cook another minute. Next, Put in the coriander and cumin and stir for approximately half a minute. Take the pan off the heat and put in the paprika. Immediately pour the tarka over the warm dal and stir mildly to combine, with parts of it visible as a decoration. Top with black pepper and serve.

GUJARATI GREEN MASALA MUNG DAL

This recipe is called "Gujarati hara masala saabut mung dal" in Hindi

Yield: 4 to 6 servings

Ingredients:

- ⅛ teaspoon ground asafoetida
- ¼ teaspoon garam masala
- ½ teaspoon ground turmeric
- 1 teaspoon salt, or to taste
- 1¼ cups green mung beans (saabut mung dal), sorted and washed in 3 to 4 changes of water
- 1½ teaspoons Gujarati Green Paste
- 2 tablespoons finely chopped fresh cilantro
- 2 tablespoons peanut oil

- 4 to 6 dried red chile peppers, such as chile de arbol, broken
- 4½ to 5 cups water

Directions:

1. Ready the masala paste. Next, place the dal, water, masala paste, turmeric, and salt into your pressure cooker. Secure the lid of the pressure cooker and cook it using high heat until the regulator shows that the pressure is high, then cook approximately half a minute more. Remove the pot from the heat and let the pressure release automatically, twelve to fifteen minutes. Cautiously open the lid and check to see if the dal is very soft and creamy; if not, cover and simmer until soft, approximately ten minutes. Move to a serving dish, cover, and keep warm.
2. Heat the oil in a small-sized non-stick saucepan using moderate to high heat, put in the red chile peppers and cook, stirring, until they are seems slightly darker. (If using the chiles whole, stand back from the pan in case they burst.) Turn off the heat, put in the asafoetida, then lightly Combine with the dal, with parts of it visible as a decoration. Sprinkle the garam masala and cilantro on top and serve.

PUNJABI DRY-COOKED MUNG DAL

This recipe is called "Sookhi dhulli mung dal" in Hindi

Yield: 4 to 6 servings

Ingredients:

- ¼ cup finely chopped cilantro, including soft stems
- ¼ teaspoon garam masala
- ¼ teaspoon ground turmeric
- ½ teaspoon ground paprika
- ½ teaspoon mango powder
- ½ teaspoon salt, or to taste
- 1 cup yellow mung beans (dhulli mung dal), sorted and washed in 3 to 4 changes of water
- 1 fresh green chile pepper, such as serrano, minced with seeds
- 1 small onion, cut in half along the length and thinly chopped

- 1 small tomato, crudely chopped
- 1 tablespoon ground coriander
- 1 tablespoon peeled minced fresh ginger
- 1 teaspoon cumin seeds
- 2 cups water
- 2 tablespoons canola oil or melted ghee

Directions:

1. Immerse the dal in water to cover by 2 inches, approximately two hours. Drain and move to a moderate-sized saucepan. Put in the water, turmeric, and salt and bring to a boil using high heat. Decrease the heat to moderate to low and cook, stirring once or twice, until the dal is soft and all the water has been absorbed, approximately ten to twelve minutes. Very gently, trying not to break the dal, stir in the cilantro and mango powder. Move to a serving dish, cover, and keep warm.
2. To make the tarka, heat the oil (or ghee) using moderate to high heat and put in the cumin seeds; they should sizzle upon contact with the hot ghee. Swiftly put in the onion and cook, stirring, until a golden colour is achieved, approximately two to three minutes. Put in the ginger and green chile pepper, then put in the tomato and cook, stirring, until the tomato is slightly soft, approximately one minute. Put in the coriander and paprika and stir for approximately half a minute. Move to the dal and stir mildly to combine, with parts of it visible as a decoration, sprinkle the garam masala on top before you serve.

PUNJABI GREEN MUNG DAL ℗

This recipe is called "Punjabi saabut mung dal" in Hindi

Yield: 4 to 6 servings

Ingredients:

- ¼ teaspoon garam masala
- ¼ teaspoon ground turmeric
- ¼ teaspoon hot red pepper flakes, or to taste
- ¼ teaspoon paprika

- ½ teaspoon ground cumin
- 1 (1-inch) piece fresh ginger, peeled and cut into thin matchsticks
- 1 cup green mung beans (saabut mung dal), sorted and washed in 3 to 4 changes of water
- 1 large tomato, crudely chopped
- 1 tablespoon ground coriander
- 1 tablespoon peeled and minced (or ground) fresh ginger
- 1 teaspoon cumin seeds
- 1 teaspoon salt, or to taste
- 1 to 3 fresh green chile peppers, such as serrano, minced with seeds
- 1small onion, finely chopped
- 2 nickel-size slices peeled fresh ginger
- 2 tablespoons peanut oil
- 4½ to 5 cups water

Directions:

1. Put the dal, water, ginger slices, minced or ground ginger, green chile peppers, salt, turmeric, and red pepper flakes into your pressure cooker. Ensure that the lid is secure, and cook using high heat until the regulator shows that the pressure is high, then cook half a minute more. Turn off the heat and allow the pot to depressurize automatically, twelve to fifteen minutes. Cautiously open the lid and stir the dal; it should be very soft and creamy. If not, simmer over moderate heat until done. Transfer to a serving dish, cover, and keep warm.
2. Heat the oil in a small-sized non-stick saucepan over moderate heat and cook the ginger matchsticks until a golden colour is achieved, approximately two minutes. Put in the cumin seeds; they should sizzle when they touch the hot oil. Swiftly put in the onion and cook, stirring, until a golden colour is achieved, approximately two minutes. Put in the tomato and cook until soft, approximately two minutes.
3. Mix in the coriander, cumin, and paprika, then move to the dal and swirl lightly, with bits of it visible as a decoration. Sprinkle the garam masala on top and serve.

This recipe is called "Chilkae vaali mung dal" in Hindi

Yield: 4 to 6 servings

Ingredients:

- ⅛ teaspoon ground asafoetida
- ¼ cup finely chopped scallions, white parts only
- ¼ teaspoon garam masala
- ¼ teaspoon ground turmeric
- ½ cup finely chopped fresh cilantro, including soft stems
- ½ teaspoon ground cumin
- ¾ teaspoon salt, or to taste
- 1 (1-inch) stick cinnamon
- 1 tablespoon ground coriander
- 1 teaspoon dried fenugreek leaves
- 1 to 3 fresh green chile peppers, such as serrano, minced with seeds
- 1½ cups split green mung beans (chilkae vaali mung dal), sorted and washed in 3 to 4 changes of water
- 1½ teaspoons cumin seeds
- 2 large tomatoes, finely chopped
- 2 tablespoons peeled and finely chopped fresh ginger
- 2 tablespoons vegetable oil
- 3 black cardamom pods, crushed lightly to break the skin
- 3½ to 4 cups water
- Fresh lime juice, to taste

Directions:

1. Immerse the dal in water to cover by 2 inches, approximately two hours. Drain. Heat the oil in a moderate-sized saucepan using moderate to high heat. Put in the cumin seeds, cinnamon, and cardamom pods; they should sizzle when they touch the hot oil. Swiftly put in the ginger, green chile peppers, and tomatoes and stir approximately one minute.
2. Put in the coriander, fenugreek leaves, cumin, turmeric, asafoetida, and salt, then put in the dal plus all the water. Bring to a boil using high heat, then decrease the heat to moderate to low, cover the pan, and cook until all the water has been absorbed and the dal is tender, for approximately half an hour. Add extra water, if required. Stir in the lime juice, cilantro, and

scallions, move to a serving dish, sprinkle the garam masala on top before you serve.

ROASTED MUNG AND POTATOES

This recipe is called "Bhuni mung dal aur aalu" in Hindi

Yield: 4 to 6 servings

Ingredients:

- ⅛ teaspoon ground asafoetida
- ¼ cup finely chopped fresh cilantro, including soft stems
- ¼ teaspoon cayenne pepper, or to taste
- ¼ teaspoon ground turmeric
- ½ teaspoon kalonji seeds
- 1 cup yellow mung beans (dhulli mung dal), sorted and washed in 3 to 4 changes of water
- 1 large clove fresh garlic, minced
- 1 large russet potato (or any kind), peeled and cut into ½-inch pieces
- 1 tablespoon mustard oil
- 1 tablespoon vegetable oil
- 1 teaspoon cumin seeds
- 1 teaspoon salt, or to taste
- 1 to 2 tablespoons fresh lemon juice
- 1 to 3 teaspoons sugar
- 4 to 4½ cups water

Directions:

1. Heat the mustard oil in a big non-stick wok or saucepan using moderate to high heat and roast the dal and potato, stirring and swaying the pan, until the dal is golden, approximately three minutes.
2. Add 4 cups water, salt, cayenne pepper, and turmeric and bring to a boil using high heat. Decrease the heat to medium and cook the dal, stirring intermittently and watching cautiously that it doesn't boil over, approximately ten minutes. Decrease the heat to low, put in the rest of the ½ cup water, and simmer until the dal is soft and creamy, approximately

fifteen minutes. Stir in the sugar, lemon juice, and cilantro, and move to a serving dish. Cover and keep warm.

3. Heat the vegetable oil in a small-sized non-stick saucepan using moderate to high heat and put in the cumin and kalonji seeds; they should sizzle when they touch the hot oil. Swiftly put in the garlic and asafoetida, stir a few seconds, and add to the dal. Swirl lightly to combine, with parts of it visible as a decoration. Serve.

SINDHI DRY-COOKED MUNG DAL

This recipe is called "Sindhi sookhi mung dal" in Hindi

Yield: 4 to 6 servings

Ingredients:

- ¼ teaspoon cayenne pepper, or ground paprika
- ¼ teaspoon ground turmeric
- ½ small onion, finely chopped
- ½ teaspoon mango powder
- ½ teaspoon salt, or to taste
- 1 cup yellow mung beans (dhulli mung dal), sorted and washed in 3 to 4 changes of water
- 1 fresh green chile pepper, such as serrano, minced with seeds
- 1 large tomato, finely chopped
- 1 tablespoon ground coriander
- 1 teaspoon cumin seeds
- 2 cups water
- 2 tablespoons vegetable oil or melted ghee
- 3 tablespoons finely chopped cilantro, including soft stems

Directions:

1. Immerse the dal in water to cover by 2 inches, approximately two hours. Drain and move to a moderate-sized saucepan. Put in the water, turmeric, and salt and cook using moderate to high heat, stirring once or twice, until the dal is soft and all the water has been absorbed, approximately ten to twelve minutes.

2. Super cautiously, trying not to break the dal, stir in the mango powder and cilantro, then move to a serving dish. Scatter the tomato, onion, and green chile pepper over the dal and mix lightly with a fork.
3. Heat the oil (or ghee) using moderate to high heat and put in the cumin seeds; they should sizzle when they touch the hot oil. Swiftly put in the coriander and cayenne pepper (or paprika), pour over the dal before you serve.

SOUTHERN MUNG DAL Ⓥ

This recipe is called "South ki mung dal" in Hindi

Yield: 4 to 6 servings

Ingredients:

- ⅛ teaspoon ground asafoetida
- ¼ cup finely chopped fresh cilantro, including soft stems
- ¼ teaspoon ground paprika
- ¼ teaspoon ground turmeric
- ½ teaspoon cumin seeds
- ½ teaspoon ground fenugreek seeds
- ¾ teaspoon salt, or to taste
- 1 cup yellow mung beans (dhulli mung dal), sorted and washed in 3 to 4 changes of water
- 1 teaspoon black mustard seeds
- 1 teaspoon ghee (not compulsory)
- 2 tablespoons minced fresh curry leaves
- 2 tablespoons peanut or canola oil
- 3½ to 4 cups water
- 4 to 6 whole dried red chile peppers, such as chile de arbol

Directions:

1. Put the dal, 3½ cups water, turmeric, and salt in a moderate-sized saucepan and bring to a boil using high heat. Decrease the heat to medium and cook the dal, uncovered, stirring intermittently and watching cautiously that it doesn't boil over, approximately ten minutes. Decrease the heat to low, put

in the rest of the ½ cup water, and simmer until the dal is soft and creamy, approximately fifteen minutes. Stir in the cilantro during the last 5 minutes of cooking. Transfer to a serving container, cover, and keep warm.

2. Heat the oil (and the ghee, if using) in a small-sized non-stick saucepan over moderate heat and cook the red chile peppers, stirring, approximately half a minute (stand back in case they burst). Put in the mustard and cumin seeds; they should splutter when they touch the hot oil, so reduce the heat and cover the pan until the spluttering diminishes. Put in the curry leaves, fenugreek seeds, and asafoetida, and cook approximately one minute. Remove from heat, put in the paprika and instantly pour the tarka over the warm dal. Swirl lightly to combine, with parts of it visible as a decoration. Serve.

ZUCCHINI MUNG DAL Ⓥ Ⓟ

This recipe is called "Zucchini vaali dhulli mung dal" in Hindi

Yield: 4 to 6 servings

Ingredients:

- ¼ teaspoon garam masala
- ¼ teaspoon ground paprika
- ¼ teaspoon ground turmeric
- ½ teaspoon ground cumin
- ¾ teaspoon salt, or to taste
- 1 (1-inch) stick cinnamon
- 1 cup yellow mung beans (dhulli mung dal), sorted and washed in 3 to 4 changes of water
- 1 fresh green chile pepper, such as serrano, minced with seeds
- 1 small onion, cut in half along the length and thinly chopped
- 1 tablespoon <u>Basic Ginger-Garlic Paste</u> (Homemade or store-bought)
- 1 tablespoon fresh lime juice
- 1 tablespoon ground coriander
- 1 tablespoon peeled minced fresh ginger
- 1 teaspoon cumin seeds
- 2 black cardamom pods, crushed lightly to break the skin

- 2 tablespoons finely chopped cilantro
- 2 tablespoons peanut oil
- 3 to 3½ cups water
- 3 to 4 small zucchini, cut into 3/4-inch slices

Directions:

1. Ready the ginger-garlic paste. Next, place the dal, water, zucchini, ginger-garlic paste, green chile pepper, cardamom pods, cinnamon, turmeric, and salt into your pressure cooker. Ensure that the lid is secure, and cook the using high heat until the regulator to indicates high pressure, then cook approximately half a minute. Turn off the heat and allow the pot to depressurize automatically, twelve to fifteen minutes. Cautiously take the lid off, stir in the lime juice, and move to a serving container. Cover the container and keep warm.
2. To make the tarka, heat the oil in a small saucepan using moderate to high heat and put in the cumin seeds; they should sizzle when they touch the hot oil. Swiftly put in the onion and cook, stirring, until a golden colour is achieved, approximately two minutes. Next, Put in the minced ginger, stir a few seconds and put in the coriander and cumin and stir for approximately half a minute.
3. Remove the pan from the heat, put in the paprika, and instantly pour over the hot dal and stir mildly to combine, with parts of it visible as a decoration. Sprinkle the cilantro and garam masala on top and serve.

LENTIL (MASOOR DAL) RECIPES

BENGALI SPICED RED LENTILS Ⓥ

This recipe is called "Bengali dhulli masoor dal" in Hindi

Yield: 4 to 6 servings

Ingredients:

- ¼ teaspoon ground paprika or cayenne pepper
- ¼ teaspoon ground turmeric
- ½ teaspoon ground cumin
- ¾ teaspoon salt, or to taste
- 1 cup red lentils (dhulli masoor dal), sorted and washed in 3 to 4 changes of water
- 1 fresh green chile pepper, such as serrano, minced with seeds
- 1 small onion, finely chopped
- 1 tablespoon Basic Ginger-Garlic Paste (Homemade or store-bought)
- 1 tablespoon ground coriander
- 1 to 2 teaspoon sugar
- 2 tablespoons mustard or peanut oil
- 2 teaspoons Bengali 5-Spices (Panch-Phoran) or store-bought
- 4 to 6 whole dried red chile peppers, such as chile de arbol
- 4½ cups water

Directions:

1. Ready the ginger-garlic paste and the 5-spices mixture. Next, place the dal, water, turmeric, and salt in a moderate-sized saucepan and bring to a boil using high heat. Decrease the heat to medium and cook the dal, stirring intermittently and watching cautiously that it doesn't boil over, approximately ten minutes.
2. Put in the onion, ginger-garlic paste, green chile pepper, coriander, cumin, paprika (or cayenne pepper), and sugar, decrease the heat to low, and simmer until the dal is soft and creamy, approximately fifteen minutes. Transfer to a serving dish, cover, and keep warm.
3. Heat the oil in a small saucepan using moderate to high heat and cook the red chile peppers, stirring, approximately half a minute (stand back in case they burst). Next, Put in the panch-phoran; they should sizzle when they touch the hot oil. Immediately, pour over the hot dal and stir mildly to combine, with parts of it visible as a decoration before you serve.

DRY-COOKED RED LENTILS Ⓥ

This recipe is called "Sookhi dhulli masoor dal" in Hindi

Yield: 4 to 6 servings

Ingredients:

- ¼ cup cooked and minced fresh or drained canned beets
- ¼ cup finely chopped cilantro, including soft stems
- ½ teaspoon garam masala
- ½ teaspoon ground cumin
- ½ teaspoon salt, or to taste
- 1 cup red lentils (dhulli masoor dal), sorted and washed in 3 to 4 changes of water
- 1 tablespoon fresh lime or lemon juice
- 1 tablespoon peeled minced fresh ginger
- 1½ teaspoons cumin seeds
- 2 cups water
- 2 tablespoons vegetable oil
- 2 teaspoons ground coriander
- 3 to 5 dried red chile peppers, such as chile de arbol
- 4 scallions, finely chopped

Directions:

1. Put the dal, water, and beets in a container and allow to soak approximately two hours or longer.
2. Heat the oil in a moderate-sized non-stick saucepan using moderate to high heat and cook the red chile peppers until a golden colour is achieved, approximately one minute. (Stand away from the pan, in case they burst.) Put in the cumin seeds; they should sizzle when they touch the hot oil. Swiftly put in the ginger and stir, approximately one minute.
3. Put in the coriander, cumin, garam masala, and then stir in the dal plus all the water, and the salt, and cook using high heat until the water evaporates and the dal is tender, approximately five minutes. Stir a few times with a fork just to fluff it, taking care not to break the dal.
4. Using a fork, softly stir in the cilantro and lime juice, cover the pan, and set using low heat approximately two minutes to blend the flavours. Move to a serving dish, lightly stir in the scallions before you serve.

ONION AND GREEN LENTILS

This recipe is called "Saabut masoor dal" in Hindi

Yield: 4 to 6 servings

Ingredients:

- ¼ teaspoon cayenne pepper, or to taste
- ¼ teaspoon garam masala
- ¼ teaspoon ground turmeric
- ½ teaspoon ground cumin
- ½ teaspoon ground paprika
- 1 (1-inch) stick cinnamon
- 1 fresh green chile pepper, such as serrano, minced with seeds
- 1 large clove fresh garlic, crudely chopped
- 1 teaspoon cumin seeds
- 1 teaspoon salt, or to taste
- 1¼ cups green lentils (saabut masoor dal), sorted and washed in 3 to 4 changes of water
- 1½ tablespoons ground coriander
- 1½ tablespoons peeled minced fresh ginger
- 1 medium onion, finely chopped
- 2 black or 4 green cardamom pods, crushed lightly to break the skin
- 2 tablespoons peanut oil
- 4 to 4½ cups water

Directions:

1. Put the dal, water, cinnamon, cardamom pods, garlic, turmeric, cayenne pepper, and salt into your pressure cooker. Ensure that the lid is secure, and cook using high heat until the regulator shows that the pressure is high, then cook half a minute more. Turn off the heat and allow the pot to depressurize automatically, twelve to fifteen minutes. Cautiously open the lid and check to see if the beans are very soft and some of them are broken; if not, cover, bring up to high pressure again, and cook another half a minute. Or cover and boil until soft, for approximately half an hour more. Transfer to a serving dish, cover, and keep warm.

2. Heat the oil in a small-sized non-stick saucepan using moderate to high heat and put in the cumin seeds; they should sizzle when they touch the hot oil. Swiftly put in the onion and cook, stirring, until a golden colour is achieved, approximately three minutes. Put in the ginger and green chile pepper and cook approximately one minute, then put in the coriander, cumin, and paprika and stir a few seconds. Move to the dal and stir mildly to combine, with parts of it visible as a decoration. Sprinkle the garam masala on top and serve.

ROASTED GREEN LENTILS

This recipe is called "Bhunni saabut masoor dal" in Hindi

Yield: 4 to 6 servings

Ingredients:

- ⅛ teaspoon ground asafoetida
- ¼ cup finely chopped fresh cilantro, including soft stems
- ¼ teaspoon ground fenugreek seeds
- ½ teaspoon garam masala
- ½ teaspoon ground paprika
- ¾ teaspoon salt, or to taste
- 1 fresh green chile peppers, such as serrano, minced with seeds
- 1 tablespoon ground coriander
- 1 tablespoon mustard oil
- 1¼ cups green lentils (saabut masoor dal), sorted and washed in 3 to 4 changes of water
- 1½ teaspoons minced garlic
- 2 medium tomatoes, crudely chopped
- 2 tablespoons peeled minced fresh ginger
- 4 whole dried red chile peppers, such as chile de arbol
- 4½ to 5 cups water

Directions:

1. Put the dal in a big non-stick saucepan and stir over moderate heat until dry. Put in the oil, red chile peppers, garam masala, fenugreek, and asafoetida

and cook, stirring, until the dal is golden, approximately three minutes. Decrease the heat if too much smoke arises. Put in the ginger, garlic, green chile pepper, coriander, and paprika and stir another 5 minutes.
2. Put in the water and salt and bring to a boil using high heat. Decrease the heat to low, cover the pan, and cook, stirring intermittently, until the dal is soft and creamy, approximately one hour, pouring in additional water if it dries too swiftly. Stir in the tomatoes and cook until they are quite soft, approximately five minutes. Move to a serving dish, stir in the cilantro before you serve.

SPLIT PIGEON PEAS (TOOR DAL) RECIPES

BASIC SOUTH INDIAN SAMBAR Ⓥ Ⓟ

This recipe is called "Sambar" in Hindi

Yield: 4 to 6 servings

The most popular thing in South India!

Ingredients:

- ¼ teaspoon ground asafoetida
- ¼ teaspoon ground turmeric
- ½ cup finely chopped fresh cilantro, including soft stems
- 1 cup split pigeon peas (toor dal), sorted and washed in 3 to 4 changes of water
- 1 small onion, finely chopped
- 1 tablespoon minced fresh curry leaves
- 1 tablespoon peeled minced fresh ginger
- 1 teaspoon black mustard seeds
- 1 teaspoon salt, or to taste

- 2 tablespoons finely chopped cilantro
- 2 tablespoons South Indian Sambar Powder (Homemade or store-bought)
- 2 to 3 tablespoons peanut oil
- 2 to 3 tablespoons Tamarind Paste
- 4½ to 5 cups water
- 5 to 7 fresh green chile peppers, such as serrano
- 8 to 10 whole dried red chile peppers, such as chile de arbol

Directions:

1. Ready the tamarind paste and the sambar powder. Next, place the dal, water, green chile peppers, curry leaves, turmeric, and salt into your pressure cooker. Ensure that the lid is secure, and cook using high heat until the regulator shows that the pressure is high, then cook 1 minute more. Turn off the heat and allow the pot to depressurize automatically, twelve to fifteen minutes. Cautiously open the lid and stir in the tamarind and cilantro. Stir vigorously to mash the dal, then move to a serving container, cover, and keep warm.
2. Heat the oil in a small-sized non-stick saucepan over moderate heat. Put in the red chile peppers, stirring approximately half a minute (stand back in case they burst), then the onion, and cook, stirring, until a mild brown colour is achieved, approximately five minutes. Put in the ginger, fry a few seconds, then put in the asafoetida and mustard seeds; they should splutter when they touch the hot oil, so reduce the heat and cover the pan until the spluttering diminishes. Put in the sambar powder and cook, approximately half a minute. Move to the dal and stir mildly to combine, with parts of it visible as a decoration. Top with the cilantro and serve.

DRY PIGEON PEA CAKE Ⓥ

This recipe is called "Sookhi toor dal" in Hindi

Yield: 4 to 6 servings

Ingredients:

- ⅛ teaspoon ground asafoetida
- ¼ teaspoon ground turmeric

- ½ teaspoon salt, or to taste
- 1 cup split pigeon peas (toor dal), sorted and washed in 3 to 4 changes of water
- 1 tablespoon dried curry leaves
- 1 teaspoon black mustard seeds
- 1¾ cups water
- 2 dried red chile peppers, such as chile de arbol, broken
- 3 tablespoons peanut oil

Directions:

1. Immerse the dal in the water approximately one hour or longer. Move the dal and water to a small, non-stick saucepan, put in the salt and turmeric, and bring to a boil using high heat. Decrease the heat to moderate to low, cover the pan, and simmer until all water is absorbed.
2. Decrease the heat further and drizzle 2 tablespoons oil into the dal along the circumference of the pan. Cover and allow the dal to develop a thin crust at the bottom (do not stir), 30 to 40 minutes. Using a rubber spatula lightly dislodge the edges, then invert the cake onto a serving platter.
3. Heat the rest of the 1 tablespoon oil in a small-sized non-stick saucepan. Put in the red chile peppers and mustard seeds; they should splutter when they touch the hot oil, so cover the pan and decrease the heat until the spluttering diminishes. Put in the asafoetida and curry leaves, stir a few seconds, then pour everything over the dal as a decoration. Serve.

GUJARATI SPLIT PIGEON PEAS

This recipe is called "Gujarati toor dal" in Hindi

Yield: 4 to 6 servings

Ingredients:

- ¼ cup finely chopped fresh cilantro
- ¼ teaspoon cayenne pepper, or to taste
- ¼ teaspoon ground asafoetida
- ½ teaspoon ground turmeric
- 1 (1-inch) stick cinnamon

- 1 cup split pigeon peas (toor dal), sorted and washed in 3 to 4 changes of water
- 1 tablespoon ground coriander
- 1 teaspoon black mustard seeds
- 1 teaspoon cumin seeds
- 1 teaspoon ground cumin
- 1 teaspoon salt, or to taste
- 1 to 3 fresh green chile peppers, such as serrano, stemmed
- 2 tablespoons ground jaggery
- 2 tablespoons vegetable oil
- 3 large tomatoes, crudely chopped
- 4 pieces dried kokum halves, washed
- 4 whole cloves
- 5 to 7 whole dried red chile peppers, such as chile de arbol
- 6 cups water
- 6 to 8 quarter-size slices peeled fresh ginger
- ten to fifteen fresh curry leaves

Directions:

1. Put the dal with 3 cups water in a big saucepan (not nonstick) and boil using high heat approximately five minutes. Decrease the heat to medium, cover the pan, and cook until the dal is very soft and broken, for approximately half an hour. Allow to cool, then with an electric hand-held mixer, beat it on medium speed until a smooth purée is achieved, approximately one minute. Stir in the rest of the 3 cups water, kokum, jaggery, coriander, cumin, turmeric, cayenne pepper, half the asafetida, and salt.
2. Using a food processor, combine and pulse the tomatoes, green chile peppers, ginger, and curry leaves until a smooth purée is achieved, approximately half a minute, and add it to the dal.
3. Boil the soupy dal using high heat approximately five minutes, then decrease the heat to moderate to low, cover the pan, and simmer the dal approximately twenty minutes. Move to a serving dish, stir in the cilantro, cover, and keep warm.
4. Heat the oil in a small saucepan using moderate to high heat and cook the cinnamon, cloves, and red chile peppers approximately half a minute. Next, Put in the mustard and cumin seeds, and the rest of the ⅛ teaspoon asafoetida; they should splutter when they touch the hot oil, so reduce the

heat and cover the pan until the spluttering diminishes. Move to the dal and stir mildly to combine, with parts of it visible as a decoration. Serve.

MADRASI VEGETABLE SAMBAR

This recipe is called "Madras ka sabzi sambar" in Hindi

Yield: 4 to 6 servings

Ingredients:

- ⅛ teaspoon ground asafoetida
- ¼ cup finely chopped fresh cilantro, including soft stems
- ¼ cup ground fresh coconut
- ¼ cup Tamarind Paste
- ¼ teaspoon ground turmeric
- ½ teaspoon Asian sesame oil
- ½ teaspoon ground fenugreek seeds
- 1 cup split pigeon peas (toor dal), sorted and washed in 3 to 4 changes of water
- 1 large clove fresh garlic, minced
- 1 tablespoon peeled minced fresh ginger
- 1 teaspoon black mustard seeds
- 1 to 3 fresh green chile peppers, such as serrano, split along the length into 2 pieces
- 1½ teaspoons salt, or to taste
- 2 tablespoons minced fresh curry leaves
- 3 cups mixed fresh vegetables, such as onions, eggplant, green beans, okra, and summer squash, cut into 1-inch pieces
- 3 tablespoons peanut oil
- 4 to 6 whole dried red chile peppers, such as chile de arbol
- 6 cups water

Directions:

1. Ready the tamarind paste. Next, soak the dal in water to cover by 2 inches, approximately two hours. Drain and place in a big saucepan along with the

water, turmeric, and sesame oil, and bring to a boil using high heat. Decrease the heat to low, cover the saucepan, partially at first and then completely, and cook, stirring intermittently, until creamy, 25 to 30 minutes. (As the dal cooks, some of it may foam and rise to the top. Mix the foam back into the dal.) Stir vigorously to mash the dal. Keep using low heat while you proceed with the next steps.

2. Heat 2 tablespoons peanut oil in a moderate-sized non-stick saucepan using moderate to high heat and put in the red chile peppers, mustard seeds, fenugreek, coconut, and asafoetida. Cover and cook, swaying the pan, approximately one minute. Put in the green chile peppers and curry leaves, cook approximately one minute, then put in the ginger and garlic and cook approximately two minutes. Combine with the dal.

3. To the same pan, put in the rest of the 1 tablespoon oil, vegetables, and salt and cook, stirring, using moderate to high heat until a golden colour is achieved, approximately five minutes. Put in the tamarind paste, cover the pan, and cook until the vegetables become soft, approximately five minutes. Move to the dal and cook, stirring intermittently, approximately ten minutes to blend the flavours. (Pour in additional water if you desire a soupier sambar.) Move to a serving container, stir in the cilantro before you serve.

PUNJABI-STYLE SPLIT PIGEON PEAS

This recipe is called "Punjabi toor dal" in Hindi

Yield: 4 to 6 servings

Ingredients:

- ¼ teaspoon ground turmeric
- ½ teaspoon ground cumin
- ½ teaspoon ground paprika
- 1 fresh green chile pepper, such as serrano, minced with seeds
- 1 tablespoon ground coriander
- 1 tablespoon peeled minced fresh ginger
- 1 teaspoon cumin seeds
- 1 teaspoon salt
- 1 to 2 tablespoon fresh lime or lemon juice, or to taste
- 1 to 2 tablespoons minced fresh curry leaves

- 1½ cups split pigeon peas (toor dal), sorted and washed in 3 to 4 changes of water
- 1 small onion, finely chopped
- 2 tablespoons vegetable oil
- 4 to 4½ cups water
- Finely chopped fresh cilantro

Directions:

1. Put the dal in a big saucepan and add water, salt, and turmeric. Bring to a boil using high heat. Decrease the heat to low, cover the saucepan (partially at first, then completely), and cook, stirring intermittently, until the dal is creamy, approximately thirty to forty minutes. As the dal cooks, some of it may foam and rise to the top. Stir the foam back into the dal. Stir in the lime juice and move to a serving dish. Cover and keep warm.
2. Heat the oil in a small saucepan and cook the onion, curry leaves and green chile pepper, stirring, until a golden colour is achieved, approximately two minutes. Put in the cumin seeds and ginger and stir approximately one minute. Put in the coriander, ground cumin, and paprika and stir approximately one minute, then move to the dal and stir mildly to combine, with parts of it visible as a decoration. Top with the cilantro and serve.

SWEET SPLIT PIGEON PEAS

This recipe is called "Gur vaali toor dal" in Hindi

Yield: 4 to 6 servings

Ingredients:

- ten to twelve fresh curry leaves
- ⅛ teaspoon ground asafoetida
- ¼ cup finely chopped fresh cilantro, including soft stems
- ¼ cup grated jaggery (gur)
- ½ teaspoon cayenne pepper, or to taste
- ½ teaspoon fenugreek seeds
- ½ teaspoon ground turmeric

- 1 cup split pigeon peas (toor dal), sorted and washed in 3 to 4 changes of water
- 1 teaspoon black mustard seeds
- 1 teaspoon cumin seeds
- 1 teaspoon salt, or to taste
- 1½ tablespoons Gujarati Curry Powder with Coriander and Cumin (dhana-jeera masala)
- 2 tablespoons fresh lime or lemon juice
- 2 tablespoons peanut oil
- 6 cups water

Directions:

1. Ready the masala, then place the dal, water, and curry leaves into your pressure cooker. Ensure that the lid is secure, and cook using high heat until the regulator shows that the pressure is high, then cook half a minute more. Turn off the heat and allow the pot to depressurize automatically, twelve to fifteen minutes. Cautiously open the lid. Allow to cool, then blend in the pot with a hand-held immersion mixer or move to a blender and purée, then return it to the pressure cooker.
2. In a small-sized container, mix the curry powder, turmeric, cayenne pepper, and salt. Reserve 1 teaspoon of the mixture and put in the rest to the processed dal. Stir in the lime juice and jaggery.
3. To make the tarka, heat the oil in a small saucepan using moderate to high heat and put in the mustard, cumin, and fenugreek seeds; they should sizzle when they touch the hot oil. Take the pan off the heat and put in the reserved 1 teaspoon curry powder mixture and the asafoetida. Immediately Put in the tarka to the dal and mix thoroughly. Move to a serving container, stir in the cilantro before you serve.

VEGGIES COCONUT SAMBAR Ⓥ Ⓟ

This recipe is called "Sabzi aur nariyal sambar" in Hindi

Yield: 4 to 6 servings

Ingredients:

- ⅛ teaspoon ground asafoetida
- ¼ cup grated fresh coconut or unsweetened dried shredded coconut
- ¼ cup Tamarind Paste
- ¼ teaspoon cayenne pepper, or to taste
- ½ cup Coconut Milk (Homemade or store-bought)
- ½ cup finely chopped fresh cilantro, including soft stems
- ½ teaspoon ground turmeric
- ¾ to 1 cup split pigeon peas (toor dal), sorted and washed in 3 to 4 changes of water
- 1 tablespoon coriander seeds
- 1 tablespoon white urad beans (dhulli urad dal), sorted
- 1 tablespoon yellow split chickpeas (channa dal), sorted
- 1 teaspoon black mustard seeds
- 1 teaspoon cumin seeds
- 1 teaspoon fenugreek seeds
- 1 teaspoon salt, or to taste
- 2 tablespoons minced fresh curry leaves
- 2 tablespoons peanut oil
- 3 to 5 whole dried red chile peppers, such as chile de arbol
- 4 cups fresh vegetables, such as tomatoes, okra, potatoes, zucchini, eggplant, cauliflower, carrots, and bell peppers, cut into 1-inch pieces
- 4 to 4½ cups water

Directions:

1. Ready the tamarind paste and coconut milk. Next, place the dal, water, salt, turmeric, and vegetables into your pressure cooker. Ensure that the lid is secure, and cook using high heat until the regulator shows that the pressure is high, then cook 1 minute more. Turn off the heat and allow the pot to depressurize automatically, twelve to fifteen minutes. Cautiously open the lid and stir mildly.
2. Heat the oil in a small-sized non-stick saucepan using moderate to high heat and cook the red chile peppers and coconut until the coconut is golden, approximately one minute. Put in the mustard, cumin, fenugreek, and coriander seeds and the channa and urad dals and cook until a golden colour is achieved, approximately one minute. Put in the cayenne pepper, asafoetida, and curry leaves and stir another 1 minute.
3. Allow to cool, move the spice mixture to a blender or a food processor, and process to make a paste, adding up to 3 tablespoons water, as required. Mix

the paste into the dal, then put in the tamarind and coconut milk and bring to a boil using high heat. Decrease the heat to medium and simmer approximately ten minutes. Move to a serving container, stir in the cilantro before you serve.

URAD BEANS (URAD DAL)

CHICKPEAS-URAD DAL (V) (P)

This recipe is called "Urad-channae ki dal" in Hindi

Yield: 4 to 6 servings

Ingredients:

- ⅓ cup yellow split chickpeas (channa dal), sorted and washed in 3 to 4 changes of water
- ½ cup finely chopped fresh cilantro, including soft stems
- ½ teaspoon garam masala
- ½ teaspoon ground paprika
- ½ teaspoon ground turmeric
- 1 (1-inch) piece fresh ginger, peeled and cut into thin matchsticks
- 1 (1-inch) stick cinnamon, broken lengthwise
- 1 cup split black urad beans (chilkae vaali urad dal), sorted and washed in 3 to 4 changes of water
- 1 small onion, finely chopped
- 1 tablespoon ground coriander
- 1 tablespoon peeled minced fresh ginger
- 1 teaspoon ground cumin
- 1 teaspoon salt, or to taste
- 1 to 2 fresh green chile peppers, such as serrano, minced with seeds
- 2 tablespoons vegetable oil
- 4 black cardamom pods, crushed lightly to break the skin
- 4½ to 5 cups water

Directions:

1. Put the dals, minced ginger, green chile pep-pers, cardamom pods, cinnamon, turmeric, salt, and 4½ cups water into your pressure cooker. Ensure that the lid is secure, and cook using high heat until the regulator shows that the pressure is high, then cook 1 minute more. Turn off the heat and allow the pot to depressurize automatically, twelve to fifteen minutes. Cautiously open the lid and check to see if the beans are very soft, with some of them broken; if not, cover, bring up to pressure, and cook under pressure another fifteen to 20 seconds. Or, cover and boil until soft, for approximately half an hour, adding water if required. Move to a serving dish, cover, and keep warm.
2. Heat the oil in a small saucepan using moderate to high heat and cook the onion and ginger matchsticks until a golden colour is achieved, three to five minutes. Put in the coriander and cumin, stir a few seconds, then remove from the heat and put in the paprika. Lightly swirl everything into the dal, with parts of it visible as a decoration. Sprinkle the garam masala and cilantro on top before you serve.

KASHMIRI BLACK URAD DAL

This recipe is called "Kashmiri saabut urad dal" in Hindi

Yield: 4 to 6 servings

Ingredients:

- ¼ teaspoon ground turmeric
- ¼ teaspoon Kashmiri Garam Masala or garam masala
- 1 cup non-fat plain yogurt, whisked until the desired smoothness is achieved
- 1 tablespoon ground fennel seeds
- 1 tablespoon unsalted butter, at room temperature
- 1 teaspoon ground ginger
- 1 teaspoon salt, or to taste
- 1¼ cups black urad beans (saabut urad dal), sorted and washed in 3 to 4 changes of water
- 5 to 6 cups water

Directions:

1. Immerse the dal overnight in water to cover by 2 inches. In the meantime ready the kashmiri garam masala. When ready, drain and place the dal in a big saucepan. Add 5 cups water and salt, cover the pan, and boil using high heat approximately five minutes. Decrease the heat to moderate to low and continue to cook until the dal is soft and very little water remains in the pan, approximately 1½ hours. If the dal softens sooner, uncover and cook using high heat until most of the water evaporates. Pour in additional water if the dal dries out sooner.
2. Put in the butter, yogurt, fennel seeds, ginger, and turmeric and bring to a boil using high heat, stirring continuously to stop the yogurt from curdling. Decrease the heat to moderate to low, cover the pan, and simmer until each bean bursts open to reveal its white interior and begins to break apart, 25 to 30 minutes. Move to a serving dish, sprinkle the garam masala on top before you serve.

PUNJABI BLACK URAD DAL

This recipe is called "Punjabi saabut urad dal" in Hindi

Yield: 4 to 6 servings

Ingredients:

- ¼ cup red or pinto beans, sorted and washed in 3 to 4 changes of water
- ¼ cup yellow split chickpeas (channa dal), sorted and washed in 3 to 4 changes of water
- ¼ teaspoon garam masala
- ½ teaspoon ground turmeric
- 1 cup black urad beans (saabut urad dal), sorted and washed in 3 to 4 changes of water
- 1 large red onion, crudely chopped
- 1 tablespoon dried mint leaves
- 1 teaspoon cayenne pepper, or to taste
- 1 teaspoon salt, or to taste
- 1 to 3 fresh green chile peppers, such as serrano, minced with seeds
- 2 (1-inch) pieces peeled fresh ginger, cut into thin matchsticks

- 2 (1-inch) sticks cinnamon, broken lengthwise
- 2 large cloves fresh garlic, minced
- 2 tablespoons unsalted butter, at room temperature
- 6 black cardamom pods, crushed lightly to break the skin
- 8 cups water or more, as required

Directions:

1. Immerse the dals and beans overnight, in water to cover by minimum two inches. Drain and place in a big cast-iron or other heavy saucepan. Add 6 cups water and all the rest of the ingredients (except the mint, butter, and garam masala), cover the pan and boil using high heat, approximately ten minutes. Decrease the heat to medium and cook, stirring intermittently, approximately one hour.
2. Decrease the heat to moderate to low and continue to cook until the dal is very soft, thick, and creamy, approximately three to four hours, adding 2 cups or more water as required. Put in the mint leaves and the butter and cook for another half an hour. Move to a serving dish, sprinkle the garam masala on top before you serve.

ROASTED FENUGREEK URAD DAL

This recipe is called "Bhuni methi vaali dhulli urad dal" in Hindi

Yield: 4 to 6 servings

Ingredients:

- ¼ teaspoon ground turmeric
- ½ teaspoon ground cumin
- ½ teaspoon ground paprika
- 1 fresh green chile pepper, such as serrano, minced with seeds
- 1 small bunch fresh fenugreek leaves (about ¼ pound)
- 1 tablespoon ground coriander
- 1 teaspoon salt, or to taste
- 1¼ cups dried white urad beans (dhulli urad dal), sorted and washed in 3 to 4 changes of water
- 1½ teaspoons cumin seeds

- 2 tablespoons peanut oil
- 2 tablespoons peeled minced fresh ginger
- 3½ to 4 cups water

Directions:

1. Put the dal, 3½ cups water, turmeric, and salt in a moderate-sized saucepan and bring to a boil using high heat. Decrease the heat to medium and cook the dal, stirring intermittently but watching cautiously that it doesn't boil over, approximately ten minutes. Decrease the heat to low, put in the rest of the ½ cup water, if required, and simmer until each bean is soft but not broken and very little water remains in the pan, approximately fifteen minutes. Cover and keep warm.
2. In the meantime, discard the hard and fibrous part of the fenugreek greens, pick out the leaves and the softest stems, and wash them well. Slice thinly in your food processor or by hand.
3. Heat 1 tablespoon oil in a moderate-sized cast-iron or non-stick wok or a saucepan and cook the fenugreek greens using moderate to high heat, stirring and scraping the sides of the wok, approximately three minutes. Decrease the heat to medium low and cook until the leaves are completely dry and deep green, ten to fifteen minutes. Mix lightly into the dal.
4. Heat the rest of the 2 tablespoons oil in a small saucepan using moderate to high heat and put in the cumin seeds; they should sizzle when they touch the hot oil. Swiftly put in the ginger and green chile pepper and stir approximately one minute. Put in the coriander, cumin, and paprika, stir a few seconds, then put in the seasonings to the dal. Swirl lightly to combine, with parts of it visible as a decoration. Serve.

SLOW COOKED BLACK URAD DAL

This recipe is called "Dheere Paki saabut urad dal" in Hindi

Yield: 4 to 6 servings

Ingredients:

- ⅛ teaspoon ground asafoetida
- ¼ cup non-fat plain yogurt, whisked until the desired smoothness is achieved

- ¼ cup red or kidney beans, sorted and washed in 3 to 4 changes of water
- ¼ teaspoon ground paprika
- ¼ teaspoon ground turmeric
- 1 (1½-inch) piece fresh ginger, peeled and cut into thin matchsticks
- 1 (15-ounce) can tomato sauce
- 1 large clove fresh garlic, minced
- 1 medium onion, finely chopped
- 1 tablespoon peeled minced fresh ginger
- 1 teaspoon dried fenugreek leaves
- 1 teaspoon salt, or to taste
- 1 to 3 fresh green chile peppers, such as serrano, minced with seeds
- 1¼ cups black urad beans (saabut urad dal), sorted and washed in 3 to 4 changes of water
- 1½ tablespoons olive oil, melted butter, or ghee
- 1½ teaspoons cumin seeds
- 2 (1-inch) sticks cinnamon, broken
- 2 bay leaves
- 3 to 5 whole dried red chile peppers, such as chile de arbol
- 5 black cardamom pods, crushed lightly to break the skin
- 7 to 8 cups water

Directions:

1. Put the dal, beans, green chile peppers, minced ginger, garlic, onion, cardamom pods, cinnamon, bay leaves, turmeric, salt, and 5 cups water in a big saucepan and boil using high heat approximately five minutes.
2. Move to a slow cooker. Choose the highest setting and cook the dal until soft and creamy, 10 to 1two hours. Stir every once in awhile. Once most of the water has been absorbed by the dal, boil the rest of the water and add it to the pot. Stir in the tomato sauce during the last hour of cooking. Move to a serving dish, swirl in the yogurt, and keep warm.
3. Heat the oil in a small-sized non-stick saucepan using moderate to high heat and cook the ginger matchsticks and red chile peppers until a golden colour is achieved, approximately one minute. (Stand back from the pan just in case the peppers burst.) Put in the cumin seeds; they should sizzle when they touch the hot oil. Swiftly put in the fenugreek leaves, then remove from the heat, put in the paprika and asafoetida, and instantly Put in the tarka to the dal. Swirl lightly to combine, with parts of it visible as a decoration. Serve.

SMOKED BLACK URAD DAL ⓟ

This recipe is called "Dhuandar urad saabut" in Hindi

Yield: 4 to 6 servings

Ingredients:

- ⅛ teaspoon ground asafoetida
- ¼ cup non-fat plain yogurt, whisked with ½ cup water
- ¼ cup yellow split chickpeas (channa dal), sorted and washed in 3 to 4 changes of water
- ¼ teaspoon garam masala
- ¼ teaspoon ground fenugreek seeds
- ¼ teaspoon ground turmeric
- ¼ teaspoon liquid hickory smoke
- ½ cup finely chopped fresh cilantro, including soft stems
- ½ teaspoon ground cumin
- ½ teaspoon ground oregano leaves
- 1 (15-ounce) can tomato sauce
- 1 cup black urad beans (saabut urad dal), sorted and washed in 3 to 4 changes of water
- 1 large clove fresh garlic, minced
- 1 tablespoon ground coriander
- 1 tablespoon peanut oil
- 1 tablespoon peeled minced fresh ginger
- 1 teaspoon dried fenugreek leaves
- 1 teaspoon salt, or to taste
- 2 tablespoons kidney beans, sorted and washed in 3 to 4 changes of water
- 4 to 6 fresh green chile peppers, such as serrano, skin punctured to stop bursting
- 5 whole dried red chile peppers, such as chile de arbol
- 7 to 8 cups water

Directions:

1. In a container, combine the dals and the kidney beans. Next, heat the oil in a moderate-sized cast-iron or non-stick saucepan using moderate to high heat and cook the green and red chile peppers, stirring, until a golden colour is

achieved, approximately one minute. (Stand back from the pan in case they burst.) Put in the ginger and garlic, then the coriander, cumin, oregano, fenugreek seeds, turmeric, asafoetida, salt, and liquid smoke. Stir approximately half a minute.

2. Put in the dals and beans and stir continuously using moderate to low heat until fragrant and well roasted, approximately five minutes. Move to a pressure cooker, add 6 cups water, secure the lid and cook using high heat until the regulator shows that the pressure is high, then cook 1 minute more. Decrease the heat to low and continue to cook another 3 minutes. Turn off the heat and allow the pot to depressurize automatically, twelve to fifteen minutes. Cautiously open the lid and check to see if the beans are very soft with some of them broken; if not, add rest of the 2 cups water, cover, bring back up to high pressure, and cook under pressure another 1 minute. Or cover and boil until soft, for approximately half an hour.

3. **3.** Stir in the tomato sauce, cilantro, fenugreek leaves, and yogurt-water, and cook, stirring intermittently, using low heat until the dal is thick and creamy, 45 to 60 minutes. Move to a serving dish, sprinkle the garam masala on top before you serve.

STIR-FRIED BLACK URAD DAL

This recipe is called "Bhuni saabut urad dal" in Hindi

Yield: 4 to 6 servings

Ingredients:

- ⅛ teaspoon ground asafoetida
- ⅛ teaspoon ground turmeric
- ¼ cup finely chopped cilantro
- ¼ teaspoon black cumin seeds
- ½ cup finely chopped scallions
- ½ teaspoon cumin seeds
- ½ teaspoon salt, or to taste
- 1 cup finely chopped tomato
- 1 fresh green chile pepper, such as serrano, minced with seeds
- 1 large clove fresh garlic, minced
- 1 tablespoon fresh lemon juice

- 1 tablespoon ground coriander
- 1 tablespoon olive oil
- 1 tablespoon peeled minced fresh ginger
- 1¼ cups black urad beans (saabut urad dal), sorted and washed in 3 to 4 changes of water
- 5 to 6 cups water

Directions:

1. Immerse the beans overnight in water to cover by 2 inches. Drain and place them in a big saucepan. Add 5 cups of water, salt, and turmeric, cover the pan, and boil using high heat, approximately five minutes. Decrease the heat to moderate to low and continue to cook until the dal is very soft, each bean bursts open to reveal its white interior, and most of the water has evaporated, approximately 1½ hours. (Pour in additional water if the dal dries out sooner.)
2. Heat the oil in a big non-stick wok or skillet using moderate to high heat and put in the cumin seeds; they should sizzle when they touch the hot oil. Swiftly put in the ginger, garlic, and green chile pepper and cook approximately one minute. Put in the asafoetida and coriander and stir a few seconds.
3. Put in the tomato and stir until most of the fluids vaporize, approximately two minutes. Next, Put in the dal and lemon juice, cover the pan, reduce the heat, and simmer using low heat approximately five minutes to blend the flavours. Move to a serving dish, lightly stir in the scallions and cilantro before you serve.

WHITE URAD DAL Ⓥ

This recipe is called "Dhulli urad dal" in Hindi

Yield: 4 to 6 servings

Ingredients:

Ingredients:

- ¼ teaspoon ground turmeric

- ½ cup finely chopped fresh cilantro, including soft stems
- ½ teaspoon ground cumin
- ½ teaspoon ground paprika
- 1 fresh green chile pepper, such as serrano, minced with seeds
- 1 small onion, finely chopped
- 1 tablespoon ground coriander
- 1 tablespoon minced red bell pepper
- 1 teaspoon ghee (not compulsory)
- 1 teaspoon salt, or to taste
- 1¼ cups white urad beans (dhulli urad dal), sorted and washed in 3 to 4 changes of water
- 1½ tablespoons fresh lemon juice, or more to taste
- 1½ teaspoons cumin seeds
- 2 tablespoons peeled minced fresh ginger
- 2 tablespoons vegetable oil
- 3½ to 4 cups water

Directions:

1. Immerse the dal in water to cover by 2 inches, approximately two hours. Next, place the dal, 3½ cups water, turmeric, and salt in a moderate-sized saucepan and bring to a boil using high heat. Decrease the heat to medium and cook the dal, stirring intermittently and watching cautiously that it doesn't boil over, approximately ten minutes. Decrease the heat to low, put in the rest of the water, if required, and simmer until each bean is soft but not broken and very little water remains in the pan, approximately fifteen minutes. Cautiously, stir in the lemon juice and cilantro and move to a serving container. Cover and keep warm.
2. Heat the oil (and ghee, if using) in a small saucepan using moderate to high heat and put in the cumin seeds; they should sizzle when they touch the hot oil. Swiftly put in the onion, decrease the heat to medium, and cook until a golden colour is achieved, approximately four minutes.
3. Put in the ginger, green chile pepper, and bell pepper and stir approximately one minute. Put in the coriander, cumin, and paprika, stir a few seconds, and add to the dal. Swirl lightly to combine, with parts of it visible as a decoration. Serve.

SPLIT CHICKPEAS AND SPLIT PEAS (CHANNA DAL AND MUTTAR DAL) RECIPES

DRY-COOKED GREEN SPLIT PEA DAL

This recipe is called "Sookhi muttar dal" in Hindi

Yield: 4 to 6 servings

Ingredients:

- ⅛ teaspoon ground asafoetida
- ¼ teaspoon garam masala
- ½ teaspoon ground fenugreek seeds
- ¾ teaspoon salt, or to taste
- 1 fresh green chile peppers, such as serrano, minced with seeds
- 1 small tomato, finely chopped
- 1 tablespoon peeled minced fresh ginger
- 1 to 2 tablespoons fresh lemon juice
- 1¼ cups green split peas (muttar dal), sorted and washed in 3 to 4 changes of water
- 1½ tablespoons dried curry leaves
- 1½ teaspoons black mustard seeds
- 2 tablespoons vegetable oil
- 3 to 3½ cups water

Directions:

1. Immerse the dal in water to cover by 2 inches, approximately two hours, then drain. Heat the oil in a big non-stick wok or saucepan using moderate to high heat and put in the mustard seeds; they should splutter when they touch the hot oil, so cover the pan until the spluttering diminishes. Put in the fenugreek seeds and asafoetida, then stir in the curry leaves and stir

approximately one minute. Put in the ginger and green chile peppers, stir approximately one minute, then stir in the dal, 2 cups water, and salt, and bring to a boil using high heat.

2. Decrease the heat to moderate to low, cover the pan, and simmer, stirring as required, until the dal is tender, approximately seven minutes. Add ½ cup more water if the dal sticks to the pan. Stir in the tomato and lemon juice, cover, and cook over low heat, approximately five minutes. Transfer to a serving dish, sprinkle the garam masala on top before you serve.

OPO SQUASH AND YELLOW SPLIT CHICKPEAS Ⓥ Ⓟ

This recipe is called "Channa dal aur lavki" in Hindi

Yield: 4 to 6 servings

Ingredients:

- ¼ cup finely chopped fresh cilantro, including soft stems
- ¼ teaspoon ajwain seeds
- ¼ teaspoon garam masala
- ¼ teaspoon ground turmeric
- ½ teaspoon ground paprika
- 1 cup yellow split chickpeas (channa dal), sorted and washed in 3 to 4 changes of water
- 1 fresh green chile pepper, such as serrano, minced with seeds
- 1 medium tomato, finely chopped
- 1 small onion, finely chopped
- 1 small opo squash (about ¾ pound), peeled and cut into 1-inch pieces
- 1 teaspoon cumin seeds
- 1 teaspoon salt, or to taste
- 2 large cloves fresh garlic, chopped
- 2 tablespoons vegetable oil
- 4½ cups water

Directions:

1. Put the dal, water, turmeric, salt, green chile pepper, squash, and garlic into your pressure cooker. Ensure that the lid is secure, and cook using high heat until the regulator shows that the pressure is high, then cook half a minute more. Turn off the heat and allow the pot to depressurize automatically, twelve to fifteen minutes. Cautiously open the lid; the dal should be thick and creamy and the squash should be soft. Move to a serving dish, cover, and keep warm.
2. Heat the oil in a small saucepan using moderate to high heat and put in the cumin and ajwain seeds; they should sizzle when they touch the hot oil. Swiftly put in the onion and cook until a golden colour is achieved, approximately five minutes. Put in the tomato and paprika and cook until most of the fluids vaporize, 2 to four minutes. Move everything to the dal and stir mildly to combine, with parts of it visible as a decoration. Stir in the cilantro, sprinkle the garam masala on top before you serve.

QUICK DRY COOKED GREEN PEAS

This recipe is called "Sookhae muttar" in Hindi

Yield: 4 to 6 servings

Ingredients:

- four to five cups water
- ⅛ teaspoon ground asafoetida
- ¼ cup dried whole green peas (sookhae harae muttar), sorted and washed in 3 to 4 changes of water
- ¼ teaspoon ground turmeric
- 1 medium onion, finely chopped
- 1 teaspoon black mustard seeds
- 1 teaspoon cumin seeds
- 1 teaspoon melted coconut oil, melted ghee, or vegetable oil
- 1 teaspoon salt, or to taste
- 2 large tomatoes, finely chopped
- 2 tablespoons peanut oil
- 3 dried red chile peppers, such as chile de arbol, broken or whole with stems 2 large cloves fresh garlic, minced

Directions:

1. Immerse the peas overnight in water to cover by 2 inches, then drain. Heat the oil in a big non-stick wok or saucepan using moderate to high heat and put in the cumin and mustard seeds; they should splutter when they touch the hot oil, so reduce the heat and cover the pan until the spluttering diminishes. Swiftly put in the red chile peppers, garlic, tomatoes, onion, asafoetida, and turmeric, and cook, stirring, until most of the fluids vaporize, approximately fifteen minutes.
2. Put in the drained peas, salt, and 4 cups water, and bring to a boil using high heat. Decrease the heat to moderate to low, cover the pan, and simmer until the peas become soft and the sauce thick, approximately one hour, adding the rest of the 1 cup water as required. Move to a serving container, stir in the coconut oil (or ghee or vegetable oil) before you serve.

SPICY DRY YELLOW PEAS Ⓥ Ⓟ

This recipe is called "Masaladar sookhae peelae muttar" in Hindi

Yield: 4 to 6 servings

Ingredients:

- four to five cups water
- ⅛ teaspoon ground asafoetida
- ¼ cup dried whole yellow peas (sookhae peelae muttar), sorted and washed in 3 to 4 changes of water
- ¼ teaspoon ajwain seeds, crudely ground
- ¼ teaspoon ground black salt
- ¼ teaspoon ground turmeric
- ½ cup finely chopped fresh cilantro, including soft stems
- ½ teaspoon salt, or to taste
- 1 (1-inch) stick cinnamon, broken lengthwise
- 1 fresh green chile pepper, such as serrano, minced with seeds
- 1 large clove fresh garlic, peeled
- 1 large tomato, crudely chopped
- 1 small onion, crudely chopped

- 1 tablespoon ground coriander
- 1 teaspoon cumin seeds, dry-roasted and crudely ground (See the dry-roasting section in Introduction)
- 1 teaspoon ground cumin
- 2 tablespoons vegetable oil
- 2 to 3 tablespoons fresh lemon or lime juice
- 4 black cardamom pods, crushed lightly to break the skin
- 6 quarter-size slices peeled fresh ginger
- twelve to fifteen fresh mint leaves

Directions:

1. Immerse the peas overnight in water to cover by 2 inches. In the meantime, ready the cumin seeds. Drain the dried peas and place them into your pressure cooker, along with 4 cups water, salt, cardamom pods, and cinnamon. Ensure that the lid is secure, and cook using high heat until the regulator shows that the pressure is high, then cook 1 minute more. Turn off the heat and allow the pot to depressurize automatically, twelve to fifteen minutes. Cautiously open the lid and check to see if the peas are soft; if not, put in the rest of the water, cover, bring up to high pressure, and cook under pressure approximately half a minute. Or, cover and boil until soft, for approximately half an hour.
2. Using a food processor, combine and pulse the tomato, onion, ginger, garlic, green chile pepper, and mint leaves until the desired smoothness is achieved. Put in the coriander, ground cumin, turmeric, and asafoetida, and process once more to mix thoroughly. Move to the cooked peas and cook, stirring as required until most of the juices are absorbed and the sauce is thick, approximately twenty minutes. Stir in the cilantro and lemon juice.
3. Heat the oil in a small saucepan using moderate to high heat and put in the ajwain seeds and black salt; they should sizzle when they touch the hot oil. Swiftly add to the peas and cook another 5 minutes. Move to a serving dish, sprinkle the roasted cumin seeds on top before you serve.

SPINACH AND YELLOW SPLIT CHICKPEAS Ⓥ Ⓟ

This recipe is called "Channa dal sai-bhaji" in Hindi

Yield: 4 to 6 servings

Ingredients:

- ½ bunch (¼ cup) fresh dill, finely chopped
- ½ cup yellow split chickpeas (channa dal), sorted and washed in 3 to 4 changes of water
- ½ teaspoon cayenne pepper, or to taste
- 1 (8-ounce) package frozen spinach, thawed
- 1 cup water
- 1 large clove fresh garlic, minced
- 1 large tomato, finely chopped, or ½ cup canned tomato sauce
- 1 medium onion, finely chopped
- 1 small carrot, peeled and finely chopped
- 1 small russet potato (or any kind), peeled and finely chopped
- 1 tablespoon fresh lime or lemon juice
- 1 tablespoon peeled minced fresh ginger
- 1 teaspoon cumin seeds
- 1 teaspoon salt, or to taste
- 2 tablespoons olive oil
- Finely chopped fresh cilantro

Directions:

1. Heat the oil in a big pressure cooker using moderate to high heat and put in the cumin seeds; they should sizzle when they touch the hot oil. Swiftly put in the onion, garlic, and ginger and cook, stirring, until a golden colour is achieved, approximately five minutes. Put in the dal and cook, stirring, approximately five minutes. Next, Put in the tomato (or tomato sauce), salt, and cayenne pepper, and stir approximately two minutes.
2. Put in the spinach, dill, potato, and carrot, stir approximately five minutes then put in the water. Ensure that the lid is secure, and cook using high heat until the regulator shows that the pressure is high, then cook half a minute more. Turn off the heat and allow the pot to depressurize automatically, twelve to fifteen minutes. Cautiously open the lid, put in the lemon juice, and stir well, mashing some of the dal and vegetables with a ladle or a spatula. Move to a serving dish, garnish with the cilantro before you serve.

MIXED BEANS AND LENTILS

FIVE JEWELS DAL Ⓥ Ⓟ

This recipe is called "Panchrattani dal" in Hindi

Yield: 4 to 6 servings

Ingredients:

- four to five cups water
- ⅛ teaspoon ground asafoetida
- ¼ cup each: black split urad beans (chilkae vaali urad dal), green mung beans (saabut mung dal), green lentils (saabut masoor dal), split pigeon peas (toor dal) and yellow split chickpeas (channa dal), sorted and washed in 3 to 4 changes of water
- ½ teaspoon garam masala
- ½ teaspoon ground paprika
- ½ teaspoon ground turmeric
- 1 small onion, finely chopped
- 1 tablespoon ground coriander
- 1 tablespoon vegetable oil or melted ghee
- 1 teaspoon cumin seeds
- 1 teaspoon minced fresh garlic
- 1 teaspoon salt, or to taste
- 1 to 3 fresh green chile peppers, such as serrano, split lengthwise, with or without seeds
- 2 tablespoons peeled minced fresh ginger
- 2 teaspoon ground cumin

Directions:

1. Heat the oil in a moderate-sized cast-iron or non-stick saucepan using moderate to high heat, put in the dals and onion, and stir continuously using moderate to low heat until fragrant and well roasted, approximately five minutes. Stir in the ginger and garlic, then the coriander, cumin, garam

masala, turmeric, asafoetida, and salt, and stir for approximately half a minute.
2. Move to a pressure cooker, add 4 cups water. Ensure that the lid is secure, and cook using high heat until the regulator shows that the pressure is high, then cook 1 minute more. Turn off the heat and allow the pot to depressurize automatically, twelve to fifteen minutes. Cautiously open the lid and check to see if the dal is very soft and creamy; if not, put in the rest of the 1 cup water, cover, bring up to pressure, and cook under high pressure approximately half a minute. Or cover and boil until soft, for approximately half an hour.
3. Uncover and simmer using moderate to low heat approximately ten minutes, then remove to a serving dish, cover, and keep warm.
4. Heat the oil (or ghee) in a small saucepan and cook the green chile peppers approximately half a minute. Put in the cumin seeds; they should sizzle when they touch the hot oil. Turn off the heat, put in the paprika, and put in the tarka to the cooked dal. Swirl lightly to combine, with parts of it visible as a decoration before you serve.

RAJASTHANI FIVE IN ONE DAL

This recipe is called "Panch bheli dal" in Hindi

Yield: 4 to 6 servings

Ingredients:

- ⅛ teaspoon ground asafoetida
- ¼ cup white urad beans (dhulli urad dal), sorted and washed in 3 to 4 changes of water
- ¼ teaspoon ground paprika
- ¼ teaspoon ground turmeric
- ¼ teaspoon salt, or to taste
- ⅓ cup yellow mung beans (dhulli mung dal), sorted and washed in 3 to 4 changes of water
- 1 (1-inch) stick cinnamon, broken lengthwise
- 1 bay leaf
- 1 tablespoon dried curry leaves
- 1 teaspoon cumin seeds

- 2 green cardamom pods, crushed lightly to break the skin
- 2 tablespoons Basic Ginger and Green Chile Pepper Paste
- 2 tablespoons finely chopped fresh cilantro
- 2 tablespoons split green mung beans (chilkae vaali mung dal), sorted and washed in 3 to 4 changes of water
- 2 tablespoons split pigeon peas (toor dal), sorted and washed in 3 to 4 changes of water
- 2 tablespoons yellow split chickpeas (channa dal), sorted and washed in 3 to 4 changes of water
- 2 to 3 tablespoons vegetable oil or melted ghee
- 2 whole dried red chile peppers, such as chile de arbol
- 4 to 4½ cups water
- 4 whole cloves

Directions:

1. Ready the ginger-chile paste. Put the dals into your pressure cooker, along with the salt, turmeric, 2 cloves, and water. Ensure that the lid is secure, and cook using high heat until the regulator shows that the pressure is high, then cook 1 minute more. Turn off the heat and allow the pot to depressurize automatically, twelve to fifteen minutes. Cautiously open the lid and check to see if the dal is soft and creamy; if not, cover and boil until soft, approximately ten minutes. Move to a serving dish, cover, and keep warm.
2. Heat the oil (or ghee) in a big non-stick wok or saucepan using moderate to high heat and cook the cardamom pods, the rest of the 2 cloves, red chile peppers, cinnamon, and bay leaf approximately half a minute. Put in the cumin seeds and asafoetida; they should sizzle upon contact with the hot ghee. Swiftly put in the curry leaves and then stir in the ginger-chile paste and stir approximately one minute.
3. Put in the paprika and instantly stir in approximately ¼ cup water and bring to a boil using high heat. Move to the dal and stir mildly to combine, with parts of it visible as a decoration. Garnish with the cilantro and serve.

SPINACH-URAD DAL Ⓥ Ⓟ

This recipe is called "Urad channae ki dal aur palak" in Hindi

Yield: 4 to 6 servings

Ingredients:

- four to five cups water
- ¼ teaspoon cayenne pepper, or to taste
- ¼ teaspoon ground turmeric
- ½ cup yellow split chickpeas (channa dal), sorted and washed in 3 to 4 changes of water
- ½ teaspoon garam masala
- ½ teaspoon ground paprika
- ¾ cup split urad beans (chilkae vaali urad dal), sorted and washed in 3 to 4 changes of water
- 1 cup finely chopped fresh cilantro, including soft stems
- 1 large bunch fresh spinach (about 1 pound), trimmed of roots only, washed, and finely chopped
- 1 large clove fresh garlic, minced
- 1 large tomato, finely chopped
- 1 small onion, finely chopped
- 1 tablespoon ground coriander
- 1 teaspoon ground cumin
- 1 teaspoon ground dried fenugreek seeds
- 1 teaspoon salt, or to taste
- 1 to 3 fresh green chile peppers, such as serrano, minced with seeds
- 1½ teaspoons cumin seeds
- 2 tablespoons peeled minced fresh ginger
- 3 tablespoons vegetable oil

Directions:

1. Put the dals, 4 cups water, turmeric, cayenne pepper, and salt into your pressure cooker. Ensure that the lid is secure, and cook using high heat until the regulator shows that the pressure is high, then cook 1 minute more. Turn off the heat and allow the pot to depressurize automatically, twelve to fifteen minutes. Cautiously open the lid, stir the dal, and simmer using moderate to low heat, approximately ten minutes, pouring in additional water, if required.

2. Put in the spinach, cilantro, and ginger and carry on simmering until the spinach is wilted and the dal is creamy, approximately fifteen minutes. Move to a serving dish, cover, and keep warm.
3. Heat the oil in a small saucepan using moderate to high heat and put in the cumin seeds; they should sizzle when they touch the hot oil. Swiftly put in the onion and cook, stirring, until a golden colour is achieved, approximately three minutes. Put in the garlic, tomato, and green chile peppers, stir 1 minute, then put in the coriander, cumin, fenugreek, and paprika. Move to the dal and stir mildly to combine, with parts of it visible as a decoration. Sprinkle the garam masala on top and serve.

VEGGIE AND LEGUME DAL Ⓥ Ⓟ

This recipe is called "Dhansak dal" in Hindi

Yield: 4 to 6 servings

Ingredients:

- ¼ cup crudely chopped fresh cilantro, including soft stems, + more for garnish
- ¼ cup each, red lentils (dhulli masoor dal), and split pigeon peas (toor dal), sorted and washed in 3 to 4 changes of water
- ¼ teaspoon ground turmeric
- 1 (3-inch) piece pumpkin, finely chopped
- 1 cup crudely chopped fresh fenugreek leaves, or ¼ cup dried
- 1 large tomato, chopped
- 1 medium russet (or any) potato, chopped (peeled or unpeeled)
- 1 small Chinese or Japanese eggplant, finely chopped
- 1 tablespoon Basic Ginger-Garlic Paste (Homemade or store-bought)
- 1 tablespoon chopped fresh mint leaves
- 1 teaspoon cayenne pepper, or to taste
- 1 teaspoon salt, or to taste
- 1 to 2 tablespoons ground jaggery (gur)
- 1½ tablespoons ground coriander
- 2 small onions, 1 crudely chopped and 1 cut in half along the length and thinly chopped

- 2 tablespoons each, yellow mung beans (dhulli mung dal), yellow split chickpeas (channa dal), and white urad beans (dhulli urad dal), sorted and washed in 3 to 4 changes of water
- 2 tablespoons Gujarati Lentil Masala (Dhansak Masala) or store-bought
- 2 teaspoons garam masala
- 2 teaspoons ground cumin
- 2 to 3 tablespoons <u>Tamarind Paste</u>
- 3 cups water
- 3 tablespoons vegetable oil
- 3 to 5 fresh green chile peppers, such as serrano, minced with seeds

Directions:

1. Ready the tamarind paste. Next, place all the dals into your pressure cooker along with the potato, tomato, pumpkin, eggplant, chopped onion, fenugreek leaves, cilantro, mint, green chile peppers, turmeric, salt, and water. Ensure that the lid is secure, and cook using high heat until the regulator shows that the pressure is high, then cook half a minute more. Turn off the heat and allow the pot to depressurize automatically, twelve to fifteen minutes. Cautiously open the lid, allow to cool down, then blend in the pot with a hand-held immersion mixer or move to a food processor or blender, process to make a thick and smooth purée, then return to the pot.
2. In the meantime, ready the ginger-garlic paste and lentil masala. Next, in a small-sized container combine the ginger-garlic paste, coriander, cumin, cayenne pepper and garam masala with 1 to 2 tablespoons water to make a thick paste.
3. Heat the oil in a big non-stick wok or saucepan using moderate to high heat and cook the chopped onions, stirring, until a golden colour is achieved, approximately five to seven minutes. Put in the spice paste and Gujarati masala and stir until fragrant, approximately a minute or two. Combine with the dal along with the tamarind and jaggery, and simmer over low heat, approximately five to seven minutes. (Add some water if the dal appears too thick.) Move to a serving dish, garnish with the cilantro before you serve.

WHOLE DRIED BEAN DISHES

BLACK RAJMA CURRY Ⓥ Ⓟ

This recipe is called "Rassadar kaalae rajma" in Hindi

Yield: 4 to 6 servings

Ingredients:

- ¼ cup finely chopped fresh cilantro, including soft stems
- ¼ teaspoon cayenne pepper, or to taste
- ¼ teaspoon ground turmeric
- ½ teaspoon ground turmeric
- 1 (15-ounce) can tomato sauce
- 1 large clove fresh garlic, minced
- 1 small onion, finely chopped
- 1 tablespoon ground fenugreek leaves
- 1 tablespoon peeled minced fresh ginger
- 1 teaspoon garam masala + ¼ teaspoon for garnish
- 1 teaspoon ghee
- 1 teaspoon ground cumin
- 1 teaspoon salt, or to taste
- 1½ cups black beans, sorted and washed in 3 to 4 changes of water
- 1½ tablespoons ground coriander
- 2 tablespoons peanut oil
- 2 teaspoons cumin seeds
- 4 to 4¼ cups water

Directions:

1. Immerse the beans overnight in water to cover by 2 inches. Next, drain and place them into your pressure cooker along with the water, turmeric, and salt. Ensure that the lid is secure, and cook using high heat until the regulator shows that the pressure is high, then cook half a minute more. Turn off the heat and allow the pot to depressurize automatically, twelve to fifteen minutes. Cautiously open the lid and check to see if the beans are very soft with some of them broken; if not, cover, bring up to pressure, and cook under high pressure another minute. Or cover and boil until the dal is soft and creamy, for approximately half an hour. Put in the tomato sauce and simmer using moderate to low heat approximately fifteen minutes.

2. Heat the oil and ghee in a small saucepan using moderate to high heat and put in the cumin seeds; they should sizzle when they touch the hot oil. Swiftly put in the onion and stir until a golden colour is achieved, approximately five minutes. Next, Put in the ginger and garlic and stir approximately one minute.
3. Put in the coriander, fenugreek leaves, ground cumin, garam masala, turmeric, and cayenne pepper, stir for approximately half a minute, and move to the cooked beans. Stir in the cilantro and simmer approximately ten minutes. Move to a serving dish, sprinkle the garam masala on top before you serve.

BLACK-EYED PEAS CURRY ℗

This recipe is called "Rassaedar lobia" in Hindi

Yield: 4 to 6 servings

Ingredients:

- ¼ teaspoon garam masala
- ¼ teaspoon ground turmeric
- ½ cup finely chopped fresh cilantro, including soft stems + more for garnish
- ½ cup non-fat plain yogurt, whisked until the desired smoothness is achieved
- ½ teaspoon ground cumin
- 1 fresh green chile pepper, such as serrano, minced with seeds
- 1 large tomato, finely chopped
- 1 small clove fresh garlic, minced
- 1 tablespoon ground coriander
- 1 tablespoon peeled minced fresh ginger
- 1 teaspoon cumin seeds
- 1 teaspoon ground dried fenugreek leaves
- 1 teaspoon salt, or to taste
- 1¼ cups dried black-eyed peas (lobia), sorted and washed in 3 to 4 changes of water
- 2 tablespoons peanut oil
- 3 to 3½ cups water

Directions:

1. Immerse the black-eyed peas overnight in water to cover by 2 inches. Next, place them into your pressure cooker along with the water and salt. Ensure that the lid is secure, and cook using high heat until the regulator shows that the pressure is high, then cook 1 minute more. Turn off the heat and allow the pot to depressurize automatically, twelve to fifteen minutes. Cautiously open the lid and check to see if the beans are very soft with some of them broken; if not, cover, bring up to pressure, and cook under high pressure another minute. Or cover and boil until the dal is soft and creamy, for approximately half an hour.
2. In the meantime, ready the sauce. Heat the oil in a moderate-sized non-stick wok or saucepan using moderate to high heat. Put in the cumin seeds; they should sizzle when they touch the hot oil. Swiftly put in the ginger, garlic, and green chile pepper and stir until a golden colour is achieved, half a minute.
3. Put in the tomato and cilantro and cook, stirring, until all the liquids vaporize and the mixture is completely dry, three to five minutes. Stir in the coriander, fenugreek leaves, ground cumin, and turmeric and stir for approximately half a minute.
4. Put in the yogurt, slowly and gradually, stirring continuously to stop it from curdling. Next, move everything to the black-eyed peas and simmer over moderate heat approximately fifteen minutes to blend the flavours. Pour in additional water if you prefer a thinner sauce, or cook longer if you favor a thicker sauce. Move to a serving dish, garnish with garam masala and cilantro before you serve.

CLASSIC ONION-FREE RAJMA ⓟ

This recipe is called "Bina pyaz kae rajma" in Hindi

Yield: 4 to 6 servings

Ingredients:

- four to five cups water
- ¼ cup non-fat plain yogurt, whisked until the desired smoothness is achieved
- ¼ teaspoon ground turmeric
- ½ cup finely chopped fresh cilantro, including soft stems
- ½ teaspoon garam masala + more for garnish

- ½ teaspoon ground cumin
- 1 (2-inch) stick cinnamon, broken lengthwise
- 1 large clove fresh garlic, minced
- 1 tablespoon ground coriander
- 1 tablespoon melted ghee
- 1 tablespoon peeled minced fresh ginger
- 1 teaspoon cumin seeds
- 1 teaspoon dried fenugreek leaves
- 1 teaspoon salt, or to taste
- 1¼ cups dried kidney beans, sorted and washed in 3 to 4 changes of water
- 2 large tomatoes, finely chopped
- 2 tablespoons vegetable oil
- 4 black cardamom pods, crushed lightly to break the skin

Directions:

1. Immerse the beans overnight in water to cover by 2 inches. Next, drain and place them into your pressure cooker, along with the cardamom pods, cinnamon, turmeric, salt, and 4 cups water. Secure the lid of the pressure cooker, place using high heat, and cook until the gauge indicates high pressure, then cook approximately one minute more. Decrease the heat to low and continue to cook another 3 minutes. Next, remove from the heat and allow pot to depressurize automatically, fifteen to twenty minutes. Cautiously open the lid and check to see if the beans are very soft, with some of them broken; if not, cover, bring up to pressure again, and cook under pressure another minute. Or cover and boil until soft, approximately ½ hour.
2. In the meantime, ready the sauce. Heat the oil and ghee in a small saucepan using moderate to high heat and put in the cumin seeds, they should sizzle when they touch the hot oil. Swiftly, put in the ginger and garlic and stir a few seconds. Put in the tomatoes and cilantro (reserve some for garnish) and cook, stirring intermittently, until the fluids vaporize, 8 to ten minutes.
3. **3.** Stir in the yogurt, slowly and gradually, stirring continuously to stop it from curdling. Put in the coriander, fenugreek leaves, cumin, and garam masala, and stir approximately one minute. Move to the pot with the kidney beans and simmer, stirring intermittently, over low heat, another fifteen to twenty minutes. Add up to 1 cup more water if you prefer a thinner dish. Move to a serving dish, sprinkle the garam masala and cilantro on top before you serve.

CLASSIC SPICED RAJMA Ⓥ Ⓟ

This recipe is called "Masalaedaar rajma" in Hindi

Yield: 4 to 6 servings

Ingredients:

- four to five cups water
- ¼ cup finely chopped fresh cilantro, including soft stems + more for garnish
- ¼ teaspoon ground turmeric
- ½ cup (1 recipe) Basic Curry Paste with Onion
- ½ teaspoon garam masala + more for garnish
- ½ teaspoon ground cumin
- 1 (2-inch) stick cinnamon, broken lengthwise
- 1 tablespoon ground coriander
- 1 teaspoon dried fenugreek leaves
- 1 teaspoon salt, or to taste
- 1¼ cups dried kidney beans, sorted and washed in 3 to 4 changes of water
- 4 black cardamom pods, crushed lightly to break the skin

Directions:

1. Immerse and cook the kidney beans along with the cardamom pods, cinnamon, turmeric, salt, and 4 cups water, until they become soft, as per Step 1 of Classic Onion-free Rajma.
2. In the meantime, ready the onion paste and then stir in the coriander, fenugreek leaves, cumin, and garam masala and stir, approximately two minutes. Move to the cooked kidney beans, put in the cilantro, and simmer over low heat, stirring intermittently, fifteen to twenty minutes. Add up to 1½ cups more water as it cooks if you prefer a thinner, saucier dish. Move to a serving dish, sprinkle the garam masala and cilantro on top before you serve.

KASHMIRI SMALL RAJMA Ⓟ

This recipe is called "Kashmiri chottae raajma" in Hindi

Yield: 4 to 6 servings

Ingredients:

- ⅛ teaspoon ground asafoetida
- ¼ teaspoon ground turmeric
- ½ cup finely chopped fresh cilantro, including soft stems
- ½ teaspoon garam masala
- ½ teaspoon ground dried ginger
- ½ teaspoon hot red pepper flakes, or to taste
- ½ teaspoon salt, or to taste
- 1 cup non-fat plain yogurt, whisked until the desired smoothness is achieved
- 1 tablespoon peeled minced fresh ginger
- 1 teaspoon ground fennel seeds
- 1 teaspoon minced fresh garlic cloves
- 1 teaspoon vegetable oil
- 1¼ cups dried small red beans, sorted and washed in 3 to 4 changes of water
- 2 bay leaves
- 5 black cardamom pods, crushed lightly to break the skin
- 5 cups water

Directions:

1. Heat the oil into your pressure cooker using moderate to low heat. Put in the beans, bay leaves, cardamom pods, ginger, garlic, fennel seeds, red pepper, dried ginger, turmeric, asafoetida, and salt, and stir continuously until fragrant and well roasted, approximately five minutes.
2. Cautiously, standing far from the pan, add 4 cups water. (The heated metal pan causes the water to sizzle and steam upon contact.) Or let the pan cool down before adding the water. Ensure that the lid is secure, and cook using high heat until the regulator shows that the pressure is high, then cook 1 minute more. Decrease the heat to low and continue to cook another 3 minutes. Turn off the heat and allow the pot to depressurize automatically, twelve to fifteen minutes.
3. Cautiously open the lid and check to see if the beans are very soft with some of them broken; if not, then cover, bring up to pressure, and cook under high pressure another minute. Or cover and boil until the dal is soft and creamy, approximately forty five minutes.

4. In the meantime, using a blender or a food processor, combine and pulse the yogurt, the rest of the 1 cup water and the cilantro, and add to the beans. Cook using moderate to high heat until the sauce is thick, approximately ten minutes. Move to a serving dish, sprinkle the garam masala on top before you serve.

PUNJABI PICKLE MASALA RAAJMA ℗

This recipe is called "Punjab kae achaari raajma" in Hindi

Yield: 4 to 6 servings

Ingredients:

- ¼ teaspoon garam masala
- ¼ teaspoon ground paprika
- ¼ teaspoon ground turmeric
- ½ cup crudely chopped fresh cilantro, including soft stems + more for garnish
- ½ cup water
- ½ teaspoon ground cumin
- ½ teaspoon salt, or to taste
- ¾ cup non-fat plain yogurt, whisked until the desired smoothness is achieved
- 1 fresh green chile pepper, such as serrano, stemmed
- 1 large clove fresh garlic, peeled
- 1 small onion, crudely chopped
- 1 tablespoon ground coriander
- 1 teaspoon ground dried fenugreek leaves
- 1¼ cups dried red or kidney beans, sorted and washed in 3 to 4 changes of water
- 2 to 3 tablespoons peanut oil
- 2 to 3 teaspoons any mango pickle (Homemade or store-bought)
- 3 to 4 small tomatoes, crudely chopped
- 4½ cups hot water
- 5 quarter-size slices peeled fresh ginger

Directions:

1. In a pressure cooker, soak the red beans, mango pickle masala, and salt in the hot water approximately 6 hours, or until the beans swell up and become much lighter in color. Ensure that the lid is secure, and cook using high heat until the regulator shows that the pressure is high, then cook half a minute more. Turn off the heat and allow the pot to depressurize automatically, twelve to fifteen minutes. Cautiously open the lid and check to see if the beans are very soft with some of them broken; if not, cover, bring up to pressure, and cook under high pressure another minute. Or cover and boil until the dal is soft and creamy, for approximately half an hour.
2. In the meantime, ready the sauce. Using a food processor, combine and pulse the onion, ginger, and garlic until a fine paste is achieved. Move to a container and process the tomatoes, cilantro, and green chile pepper until puréed. Transfer to a separate container, then process the yogurt and water until the desired smoothness is achieved.
3. Heat the oil in a moderate-sized non-stick wok or saucepan over moderate heat and cook the onion-garlic paste, stirring, until thoroughly browned, approximately ten minutes. Put in the puréed tomato mixture and stir until all the liquids vaporize and traces of oil are visible on the sides, approximately five minutes. Stir in the coriander, cumin, turmeric, paprika and fenugreek leaves, and stir for approximately half a minute. Put in the yogurt-water and cook, stirring continuously, until it is thoroughly blended with the dish and the mixture is dry, approximately two minutes.
4. Move everything to the softened beans and simmer over moderate heat, approximately fifteen minutes, to blend the flavours. Pour in additional water if you prefer a thinner sauce, or cook longer if you favor thicker sauce. (The beans will thicken as the dish cools, so add your water accordingly.) Move to a serving dish, garnish with garam masala and cilantro before you serve.

ROASTED ADZUKI BEANS

This recipe is called "Bhuni laal chori dal" in Hindi

Yield: 4 to 6 servings

Ingredients:

- ⅛ teaspoon ground asafoetida

- ¼ cup finely chopped fresh cilantro, including soft stems
- ½ cup non-fat plain yogurt, whisked until the desired smoothness is achieved
- ½ teaspoon ground cumin
- 1 cup dried adzuki beans (red chori dal), sorted and washed in 3 to 4 changes of water
- 1 large clove fresh garlic, peeled
- 1 large tomato, finely chopped
- 1 tablespoon ground coriander
- 1 tablespoon mustard oil
- 1 tablespoon peeled minced fresh ginger
- 1 teaspoon black mustard seeds
- 1 teaspoon salt, or to taste
- 5 to 6 cups water
- twelve to fifteen fresh curry leaves

Directions:

1. Heat the oil in a big non-stick wok or saucepan using moderate to high heat and put in the mustard seeds; they should splutter when they touch the hot oil, so cover the pan and decrease the heat until the spluttering diminishes.
2. Add everything except the water, cilantro, and yogurt, and stir to roast the dal until it is fragrant and lightly golden, approximately ten minutes. Add approximately 4 cups water and bring to a boil using high heat. Decrease the heat to moderate to low, cover the pan, and simmer until the dal is soft and creamy, approximately one hour. Stir once in a while and add more water as required. Move to a serving dish, stir in the cilantro, then swirl in the yogurt with parts of it visible as a decoration. Serve.

SPICED ADZUKI BEANS

This recipe is called "Laal chori dal" in Hindi

Yield: 4 to 6 servings

Ingredients:

- ¼ cup finely chopped fresh cilantro
- ¼ teaspoon garam masala

- ½ teaspoon ground cumin
- ½ teaspoon ground paprika
- ½ teaspoon ground turmeric
- 1 large tomato, finely chopped
- 1 tablespoon ground coriander
- 1 tablespoon minced peeled fresh ginger
- 1 teaspoon cumin seeds
- 1 teaspoon salt, or to taste
- 1 to 3 fresh green chile peppers, such as serrano, minced with seeds
- 1¼ cups dried adzuki beans (laal chori dal), sorted and washed in 3 to 4 changes of water
- 2 tablespoons peanut oil
- 5 to 6 cups water

Directions:

1. Put the dal, 4 cups water, tomato, ginger, green chile peppers, salt, and turmeric into your pressure cooker. Ensure that the lid is secure, and cook using high heat until the regulator shows that the pressure is high, then cook 1 minute more. Turn off the heat and allow the pot to depressurize automatically, twelve to fifteen minutes. Cautiously open the lid and check to see if the beans are very soft, with some of them broken; if not, add more water as required, cover, bring up to pressure, and cook under high pressure approximately half a minute. Or cover and boil until the dal is soft and creamy, for approximately half an hour.
2. Heat the oil in a small-sized non-stick saucepan using moderate to high heat and put in the cumin seeds; they should sizzle when they touch the hot oil. Swiftly put in the coriander and cumin, cook 5 to 10 seconds, and remove from the heat. Stir in the paprika and then lightly swirl everything into the dal, with parts of it visible as a decoration. Sprinkle the garam masala on top and serve.

WHITE RAJMA Ⓥ Ⓟ

This recipe is called "Sufaid rajma" in Hindi

Yield: 4 to 6 servings

Ingredients:

- ¼ teaspoon garam masala
- ½ cup finely chopped fresh cilantro, including soft stems
- ½ cup non-fat plain yogurt, whisked until the desired smoothness is achieved
- ½ teaspoon ground turmeric
- ½ teaspoon ground, dried fenugreek leaves
- 1 (1-inch) stick cinnamon
- 1 cup white beans, washed
- 1 large clove fresh garlic, minced
- 1 teaspoon ground cumin
- 1 teaspoon salt, or to taste
- 1 to 3 fresh green chile peppers, such as serrano, minced with seeds
- 1½ tablespoons peeled minced fresh ginger
- 1½ teaspoon cumin seeds
- 2 bay leaves
- 2 black cardamom pods, crushed lightly to break the skin
- 2 large tomatoes, finely chopped
- 2 tablespoons ground coriander
- 3 tablespoons vegetable oil
- 4 to 4½ cups water

Directions:

1. Immerse the beans in water to cover by 2 inches at least four hours. Drain, then place them into your pressure cooker along with 4 cups water, salt, bay leaves, cardamom pods, and cinnamon. Ensure that the lid is secure, and cook using high heat until the regulator shows that the pressure is high, then cook 1 minute more. Decrease the heat to low and continue to cook another minute. Turn off the heat and allow the pot to depressurize automatically, twelve to fifteen minutes. Cautiously open the lid and check to see if the beans are very soft with some of them broken; if not, cover, bring up to pressure, and cook under high pressure another minute. Or cover and boil until the dal is soft and creamy, for approximately half an hour.
2. In the meantime, heat the oil in a moderate-sized non-stick saucepan, and cook the garlic until barely golden, approximately half a minute. Put in the cumin seeds; they should sizzle when they touch the hot oil. Swiftly put in the tomatoes, green chile peppers, and ginger and cook, stirring as required,

initially over high and then over moderate heat until all the fluids vaporize, approximately ten minutes.
3. Put in the coriander, ground cumin, and turmeric and cook, stirring, approximately one minute. Next, Put in the yogurt, slowly and gradually, stirring continuously to stop it from curdling, until it is absorbed. Stir in the fenugreek leaves and cilantro, and simmer another 5 minutes. Move to the pressure cooker. Stir well and bring to a boil using high heat. Decrease the heat to low and simmer approximately fifteen minutes, uncovered, pouring in additional water, if needed. Move to a serving dish, sprinkle the garam masala on top before you serve.

YOGURT SOYBEANS Ⓥ

This recipe is called "Dahi vaalae soyabeans" in Hindi

Yield: 4 to 6 servings

Ingredients:

- ¼ teaspoon garam masala
- ¼ teaspoon ground turmeric
- ½ cup crudely chopped fresh cilantro, including soft stems
- ½ teaspoon crudely ground fenugreek seeds
- ¾ cup non-fat plain yogurt
- 1 (16-ounce) package frozen shelled soybeans (edamame), thawed
- 1 large clove fresh garlic, minced
- 1 small onion, finely chopped
- 1 tablespoon ground coriander
- 1 tablespoon peeled minced fresh ginger
- 1 teaspoon cumin seeds
- 1 teaspoon salt, or to taste
- 1 to 3 fresh green chile peppers, such as serrano, stemmed
- 2 cups water
- 2 large tomatoes, crudely chopped
- 2 tablespoons vegetable oil

Directions:

1. Using a food processor or a blender, combine and pulse the tomatoes, green chile peppers, and cilantro. Move to a container and process the yogurt and water until the desired smoothness is achieved.
2. Heat the oil in a big saucepan using moderate to high heat and put in the cumin and fenugreek seeds; they should sizzle when they touch the hot oil. Swiftly put in the onion, ginger, and garlic and cook until a golden colour is achieved, approximately four minutes. Put in the coriander, turmeric, and salt, then stir in the processed tomatoes and cook until most of the fluids vaporize, approximately five minutes.
3. Put in the soybeans and stir approximately five minutes. Stir in the yogurt-water mixture, and bring to a boil using high heat. Decrease the heat to moderate to low, cover the pan, and simmer until the beans are soft and the sauce is thick, for approximately half an hour. Move to a serving container, sprinkle garam masala on top before you serve.

YOGURT-BLACK-EYED PEAS CURRY ⓟ

This recipe is called "Dahi ka lobia" in Hindi

Yield: 4 to 6 servings

Ingredients:

- ¼ cup finely chopped fresh cilantro, including soft stems + more for garnish
- ¼ teaspoon garam masala
- ¼ teaspoon ground turmeric
- ½ teaspoon crudely ground fenugreek seeds
- ½ teaspoon ground cumin
- ½ teaspoon ground green cardamom seeds
- 1 (1-inch) stick cinnamon, broken lengthwise
- 1 cup dried black-eyed peas (lobia), sorted and washed in 3 to 4 changes of water
- 1 cup non-fat plain yogurt, whisked until the desired smoothness is achieved
- 1 small onion, cut in half along the length and thinly chopped
- 1 tablespoon Basic Ginger-Garlic Paste (Homemade or store-bought)
- 1 tablespoon ground coriander
- 1 teaspoon cumin seeds
- 1 teaspoon salt, or to taste

- 1 to 3 fresh green chile peppers, such as serrano, minced with seeds
- 2 black cardamom pods, crushed lightly to break the skin
- 3 cups water
- 3 tablespoons vegetable oil

Directions:

1. Immerse the black-eyed peas overnight in water to cover by 2 inches. In the meantime, ready the ginger-garlic paste. When ready, place the peas into your pressure cooker along with the water, cardamom pods, cinnamon, and salt. Ensure that the lid is secure, and cook using high heat until the regulator shows that the pressure is high, then cook 1 minute more. Turn off the heat and allow the pot to depressurize automatically, twelve to fifteen minutes. Cautiously open the lid and check to see if the beans are very soft with some of them broken; if not, cover, bring up to pressure, and cook under high pressure another minute. Or cover and boil until the dal is soft and creamy, for approximately half an hour.
2. In the meantime, ready the sauce. In a moderate-sized non-stick saucepan, heat the oil over moderate heat and put in the cumin and fenugreek seeds; they should sizzle when they touch the hot oil. Swiftly put in the onion and cook, stirring, until a golden colour is achieved, approximately three minutes, then stir in the green chile peppers and the ginger-garlic paste and stir for approximately half a minute. Put in the coriander, ground cumin, and turmeric and stir another minute.
3. Put in the yogurt, slowly and gradually, stirring continuously to stop it from curdling. Move everything to the black-eyed peas, stir in the ground cardamom seeds and cilantro, cover, and bring to a boil using high heat (no need to secure the lid). Decrease the heat to low and simmer approximately fifteen minutes, pouring in additional water, if needed. Move to a serving dish, sprinkle the garam masala and cilantro on top before you serve.

WHOLE CHICKPEA DISHES

CHICKPEA CHAAT MASALA

This recipe is called "Channa-chaat masala" in Hindi

Yield: 4 to 6 servings

Ingredients:

- ⅓ cup water
- ½ cup finely chopped fresh cilantro, including soft stems
- ½ teaspoon dried fenugreek leaves
- ½ teaspoon ground cumin
- 1 large clove fresh garlic, minced
- 1 teaspoon Chaat Masala (Homemade or store-bought), or more to taste
- 1 to 2 tablespoons fresh lime or lemon juice
- 1½ tablespoons ground coriander
- 2 tablespoons peanut oil
- 2 tablespoons peeled minced fresh ginger
- 2 teaspoons cumin seeds
- 4 (15½-ounce) cans chickpeas, drained and rinsed well
- 5 to 7 fresh green chile peppers, such as serrano, skin punctured to stop bursting
- Tomato wedges, chopped scallions, and chopped cilantro, for garnish

Directions:

1. Ready the chaat masala. Next, heat the oil in a big non-stick wok or skillet using moderate to high heat and cook the green chile peppers, stirring slowly, approximately half a minute (stand back in case they burst). Put in the cumin seeds; they should sizzle when they touch the hot oil. Swiftly put in the ginger and garlic and stir for approximately half a minute.
2. Put in the coriander, cumin, and fenugreek leaves, stir momentarily, then stir in the chickpeas and water. Cover and cook over moderate heat until the chickpeas are soft, approximately four minutes. Put in the lime juice, chaat masala, and cilantro and cook, stirring, another 5 minutes. Move to a serving dish, stir in the tomato wedges, scallions, and cilantro before you serve.

CHICKPEA-POMEGRANATE

This recipe is called "Pindi channae—anardana" in Hindi

Yield: 4 to 6 servings

Ingredients:

- ¼ teaspoon ground black salt
- ½ cup finely chopped fresh cilantro, including soft stems
- ½ cup finely chopped scallions
- ½ cup water
- ½ teaspoon cayenne pepper or ground paprika
- ½ teaspoon garam masala
- 1 (1-inch) piece peeled fresh ginger, cut into thin matchsticks
- 1 large clove garlic, peeled
- 1 tablespoon ground coriander
- 1 tablespoon ground dried pomegranate seeds
- 1 tablespoon vegetable oil or melted ghee
- 1 teaspoon Chaat Masala (Homemade or store-bought)
- 1 teaspoon cumin seeds
- 1 teaspoon mango powder
- 1 to 3 fresh green chile peppers, such as serrano, stemmed
- 1½ teaspoons ground cumin
- 2 tablespoons peanut oil
- 2 to 3 small tomatoes, cut into wedges
- 4 (15½-ounce) cans chickpeas, drained and rinsed well
- 6 quarter-size slices peeled fresh ginger

Directions:

1. Ready the chaat masala. Put the pomegranate seeds, cumin, mango powder, garam masala, and cayenne pepper (or paprika) in a small skillet and roast, stirring and shaking the skillet, over moderate heat until the spices are fragrant and dark brown (almost like the color of instant coffee), approximately three minutes. Move to a container. Using a food processor or a blender, combine and pulse the ginger slices, garlic, and green chile peppers until minced.
2. Heat the oil (or ghee, if using) in a big non-stick skillet using moderate to high heat and cook the ginger-garlic mixture, stirring, until a golden colour is achieved, approximately one minute. Put in the coriander, chaat masala, and black salt, then stir in the chickpeas and water and cook, stirring as required

until tender and almost dry, approximately five minutes. Put in the roasted spices, decrease the heat to medium and cook another 5 minutes to blend the flavours. Move to a serving dish and keep warm.
3. Heat the ghee in a small saucepan using moderate to high heat and put in the cumin seeds; they should sizzle when they touch the hot oil. Swiftly put in the ginger matchsticks and cook until a golden colour is achieved, approximately three minutes. Put in the cilantro and stir 1 minute, then put in the scallions and tomato wedges. Stir approximately one minute and add to the chickpeas. Mix lightly, with parts of it visible as a decoration before you serve.

CHICKPEAS IN A CAN Ⓥ Ⓟ

This recipe is called "Peepae vaalae chholae" in Hindi

Yield: 4 to 6 servings

Ingredients:

- four to five cups water
- ¼ cup Tamarind Paste
- ¼ teaspoon baking soda
- ¼ teaspoon ground turmeric
- ½ cup finely chopped fresh cilantro, including soft stems
- ½ teaspoon cayenne pepper
- ½ teaspoon garam masala
- 1 (1-inch) piece fresh ginger, cut into thin matchsticks
- 1 (1-inch) stick cinnamon
- 1 fresh green chile pepper, such as serrano, minced with seeds
- 1 large russet (or any) potato, peeled and cut into 3/4-inch pieces
- 1 small onion, chopped
- 1 tablespoon ground coriander
- 1 tablespoon vegetable oil or melted ghee
- 1 teaspoon ground cumin
- 1 teaspoon salt, or to taste
- 1 to 3 fresh green chile peppers, such as serrano, split in half lengthwise

- 1¼ cups dried chickpeas (or yellow peas), sorted and washed in 3 to 4 changes of water
- 1½ tablespoons Basic Ginger-Garlic Paste (Homemade or store-bought)
- 2 bay leaves
- 2 large tomatoes, finely chopped
- 3 to 5 black cardamom pods, crushed lightly to break the skin
- 5 to 7 green cardamom pods, crushed lightly to break the skin
- 5 to 7 whole cloves
- 8 scallions, white parts only, halved lengthwise

Directions:

1. Immerse the chickpeas overnight in water to cover by 2 inches. In the meantime, ready the tamarind paste and ginger-garlic paste, then drain and place the chickpeas into your pressure cooker along with all the other ingredients (except the tamarind paste, cilantro, scallions, and green chile peppers). Ensure that the lid is secure, and cook using high heat until the regulator shows that the pressure is high, then cook 1 minute more. Decrease the heat to low and continue to cook another two minutes. Turn off the heat and allow the pot to depressurize automatically, twelve to fifteen minutes.
2. Cautiously open the lid and check to see if the beans are very soft with some of them broken; if not, add more water, as required, cover, bring up to pressure, and cook under high pressure another minute. Or cover and boil until the chickpeas are soft and creamy, approximately forty five minutes.
3. **3.** Stir in the tamarind paste and cilantro. Using a ladle, mash some of the chickpeas and simmer another fifteen minutes. Move to a serving dish, garnish with the scallions and green chile peppers before you serve.

CLASSIC CHICKPEAS IN CURRY ⓟ

This recipe is called "Rassaedar channae" in Hindi

Yield: 4 to 6 servings

Ingredients:

- ¼ cup finely chopped fresh cilantro, including soft stems

- ¼ cup plain non-fat yogurt, whisked until the desired smoothness is achieved
- ¼ teaspoon baking soda
- ¼ teaspoon ground paprika
- ¼ teaspoon ground turmeric
- ½ teaspoon garam masala + ¼ teaspoon for garnish
- 1 large clove fresh garlic, peeled
- 1 small onion, crudely chopped
- 1 tablespoon fresh lime juice
- 1 teaspoon cumin seeds
- 1 teaspoon ground coriander
- 1 teaspoon salt or to taste
- 1 to 3 fresh green chile peppers, such as serrano, stemmed
- 1¼ cups dried chickpeas, sorted and washed in 3 to 4 changes of water
- 2 large tomatoes, crudely chopped
- 2 tablespoons peanut oil
- 4 to 4½ cups water
- 5 quarter-size slices peeled fresh ginger

Directions:

1. Immerse the chickpeas overnight in water to cover by 2 inches. Next, drain and place them into your pressure cooker along with the water, baking soda, and salt. Ensure that the lid is secure, and cook using high heat until the regulator shows that the pressure is high, then cook 1 minute more. Decrease the heat to low and continue to cook another 3 minutes. Turn off the heat and allow the pot to depressurize automatically, twelve to fifteen minutes. Cautiously open the lid and check to see if the beans are very soft with some of them broken; if not, cover, bring up to pressure, and cook under high pressure another minute. Or cover and boil until the chickpeas are soft and creamy, for approximately half an hour.
2. In the meantime, Using a food processor or a blender, combine and pulse the onion, green chile peppers, garlic, and ginger to make a paste. Move to a container, then purée the tomatoes.
3. Heat the oil in a small-sized non-stick saucepan using moderate to high heat and put in the cumin seeds; they should sizzle when they touch the hot oil. Swiftly put in the onion-garlic paste and cook, stirring, over moderate heat until browned, approximately five minutes. Put in the tomatoes and cook until the fluids vaporize, approximately seven minutes.

4. Put in the coriander, garam masala, turmeric, paprika, and lime juice, then put in the yogurt slowly and gradually, stirring continuously to stop it from curdling. Combine with the chickpeas and simmer approximately fifteen minutes to blend the flavours. Pour in additional water for a thinner curry. Move to a serving dish, stir in the cilantro and garam masala before you serve.

DRY CHICKPEAS, SPINACH, AND POTATOES

This recipe is called "Sookhae channae, palak, aur aalu" in Hindi

Yield: 4 to 6 servings

Ingredients:

- ¼ teaspoon garam masala
- ¼ teaspoon ground turmeric
- ½ cup finely chopped fresh cilantro, including soft stems
- 1 large bunch (12 to 14 ounces) fresh spinach, trimmed, washed and finely chopped
- 1 tablespoon Basic Ginger-Garlic Paste (Homemade or store-bought)
- 1 tablespoon chickpea flour
- 1 tablespoon Chickpea Masala with Pomegranate Seeds (Homemade or store-bought)
- 1 tablespoon ground coriander
- 1 teaspoon fenugreek seeds, crudely ground
- 1½ cups water
- 1½ teaspoons cumin seeds
- 2 (15½-ounce) cans chickpeas, drained and rinsed well
- 2 small tomatoes, cut into 6 wedges each
- 2 tablespoons Tamarind Paste
- 3 tablespoons peanut oil
- 3 to 4 small (about 1 pound) unpeeled red or Yukon gold potatoes
- 3 to 5 dried red chile peppers, such as chile de arbol, broken

Directions:

1. Ready the tamarind paste, the chickpea masala, and the ginger-garlic paste. Boil the potatoes in lightly salted water to cover until soft, approximately twenty minutes. Let cook, then cut into wedges. Heat the oil in a big non-stick wok or skillet using moderate to high heat and put in the red chile peppers, cumin, and fenugreek seeds; they should sizzle when they touch the hot oil. Swiftly put in the turmeric and chickpea flour and stir over moderate heat until fragrant, approximately one minute.
2. Put in the ginger-garlic paste and stir 1 minute. Next, Put in the spinach and cook, stirring, until wilted, approximately three minutes. Put in the potatoes, chickpeas, water, tamarind paste, and cilantro, and bring to a boil using high heat. Cover the pan, decrease the heat to medium, and cook until the chickpeas are soft, approximately seven minutes. Stir in the coriander, chickpea masala, and garam masala during the last 5 minutes of cooking. Move to a serving dish, garnish with the tomato wedges before you serve.

GINGER-CUMIN BLACK CHICKPEAS

This recipe is called "Adrak-jeera vaalae kaalae channae" in Hindi

Yield: 4 to 6 servings

Ingredients:

- ¼ cup finely chopped fresh cilantro
- ¼ teaspoon ground black salt
- ½ teaspoon ground paprika
- ½ teaspoon salt, or to taste
- 1 (1-inch) piece peeled fresh ginger, cut into thin matchsticks
- 1 fresh green chile pepper, such as serrano, minced with seeds
- 1 tablespoon <u>Basic Ginger-Garlic Paste</u> (Homemade or store-bought)
- 1 tablespoon ground coriander
- 1 teaspoon cumin seeds
- 1 teaspoon melted ghee (not compulsory)
- 1½ cups dried black chickpeas, sorted and washed in 3 to 4 changes of water
- 2 (1-inch) sticks cinnamon
- 2 black cardamom pods, crushed lightly to break the skin

- 2 tablespoons vegetable oil
- 5 cups water

Directions:

1. Immerse the chickpeas overnight in water to cover by 2 inches. In the meantime, ready the ginger-garlic paste. When ready, drain the chickpeas then place them into your pressure cooker, along with 4½ cups water, the cinnamon, cardamom podes, green chile pepper, ginger-garlic paste, salt, and black salt. Ensure that the lid is secure, and cook using high heat until the regulator shows that the pressure is high, then cook 1 minute more. Decrease the heat to low and continue to cook another 3 minutes. Turn off the heat and allow the pot to depressurize automatically, twelve to fifteen minutes.
2. Cautiously open the lid and check to see if the beans are very soft with some of them broken; unlike other beans, black chickpeas do not become soft to the point of disintegrating. If not sufficiently cooked, cover, bring up to pressure, and cook under high pressure another minute. Or cover and boil until soft, for approximately half an hour.
3. Move to a large cast-iron wok or skillet and cook using high heat approximately five minutes, then using moderate to low heat until all the water evaporates and the chickpeas are glazed with a dark brown coating, approximately 40 minutes. Stir occasionally.
4. Heat the oil (and the ghee, if using) in a big non-stick wok or saucepan using moderate to high heat and cook the ginger matchsticks, stirring, until a golden colour is achieved, approximately one minute. Put in the cumin seeds; they should sizzle when they touch the hot oil. Swiftly put in the coriander and paprika, stir for approximately half a minute, then Combine with the chickpeas. Move to a serving dish, stir in the cilantro before you serve.

GREEN CHICKPEAS WITH LENTILS

This recipe is called "Rassaedar vadi-chholia" in Hindi

Yield: 4 to 6 servings

Ingredients:

- ¼ teaspoon ground turmeric
- ¼ teaspoon hot red pepper flakes, or to taste
- ½ cup non-fat plain yogurt, whisked until the desired smoothness is achieved
- 1 cup finely chopped onion
- 1 cup finely chopped tomatoes
- 1 large lentil nugget (badiyan)
- 1 large potato, peeled and cut into ½-inch pieces
- 1 tablespoon ground coriander
- 1 tablespoon peeled minced fresh ginger
- 1 teaspoon ground cumin
- 1 to 3 fresh green chile peppers, such as serrano, minced with seeds
- 2 cups shelled fresh green chickpeas
- 2 to 3 cups water
- 3 tablespoons peanut oil
- Chopped cilantro and garam masala

Directions:

1. Using a rolling pin or the back of a small saucepan, break the lentil nugget into half-inch pieces. (The nugget is very soft and easy to break; if it breaks into smaller piece, that's fine.) Heat 1½ tablespoons oil in a moderate-sized non-stick saucepan over moderate heat and fry the nugget pieces in 2 to 3 batches, frying similar-size pieces at one time and removing them as they brown, which happens very swiftly.
2. To the same pan, add rest of the 1½ tablespoons oil and the onion, and cook, stirring, until a golden colour is achieved, approximately five minutes. Put in the ginger and green chile peppers and cook, stirring, another two minutes. Next, stir in the tomatoes and cook, stirring, until all the fluids vaporize, approximately five minutes.
3. Put in the coriander, ground cumin, turmeric, and red pepper flakes, stir briefly, then put in the green chickpeas and the fried nuggets. Cook, stirring, over moderate heat approximately five minutes to roast them. Put in the yogurt slowly and gradually, stirring continuously to stop it from curdling, until absorbed. Put in the water and bring to a boil using high heat. Decrease the heat to moderate to low, cover the pan and cook until the chickpeas become soft, for approximately half an hour. Move to a serving dish, garnish with cilantro and garam masala before you serve.

PICKLEY CHICKPEAS (V)

This recipe is called "Achaari channae" in Hindi

Yield: 4 to 6 servings

Ingredients:

- ⅛ teaspoon ground asafoetida
- ¼ teaspoon garam masala
- ¼ teaspoon ground turmeric
- ½ cup finely chopped fresh cilantro, including soft stems
- ½ cup water
- 1 fresh green chile pepper, such as serrano, minced with seeds
- 1 large clove fresh garlic, minced
- 1 large russet (or any) potato
- 1 tablespoon Bengali 5-Spices (Panch-Phoran) or store-bought
- 1 tablespoon ground coriander
- 1 tablespoon mustard oil
- 1 tablespoon peanut oil
- 1 to 2 tablespoons Tamarind Paste
- 2 tablespoons peeled minced fresh ginger
- 3 (15½-ounce) cans chickpeas, drained and rinsed well

Directions:

1. Boil the potato in lightly salted water to cover until tender, approximately twenty minutes. In the meantime, ready the tamarind paste, then in a mortar and pestle, or with the back of a big sized spoon, crudely grind the panch-phoran seeds. When the potato is cooked, allow to cool down, then peel and finely cut it.
2. Heat both the oils in a big non-stick skillet using moderate to high heat and put in the panch-phoran; they should sizzle when they touch the hot oil. Swiftly put in the ginger, garlic, and green chile pepper, then put in the coriander, turmeric, and asafoetida.
3. Stir in the chickpeas, potato, and water and cook, stirring carefully, until they become soft and most of the liquid evaporates, approximately five minutes. Put in the tamarind paste and cilantro and cook another two minutes. Move to a large platter, sprinkle the garam masala on top before you serve.

SPICED BLACK CHICKPEAS

This recipe is called "Masaladar kaalae channae" in Hindi

Yield: 4 to 6 servings

Ingredients:

- ¼ cup finely chopped fresh cilantro, including soft stems
- ½ cup finely chopped tomatoes
- ½ teaspoon ground paprika
- ¾ teaspoon salt, or to taste
- 1 tablespoon ground coriander
- 1 tablespoon peeled minced fresh ginger
- 1 teaspoon cumin seeds
- 1 teaspoon melted ghee (not compulsory)
- 1 to 3 fresh green chile peppers, such as serrano, split along the length in half or minced
- 1½ cups dried black chickpeas, sorted and washed in 3 to 4 changes of water
- 2 tablespoons peanut oil
- 3 to 4 tablespoons Chickpea Masala with Pomegranate Seeds (Channa Masala) or store-bought
- 4 scallions, white parts only, finely chopped
- 5 cups water

Directions:

1. Immerse the chickpeas overnight in water to cover by 2 inches. In the meantime, ready the channa masala. When ready, drain the chickpeas, then place them into your pressure cooker, along with 4½ cups water and salt. Ensure that the lid is secure, and cook using high heat until the regulator shows that the pressure is high, then cook 1 minute more. Decrease the heat to low and continue to cook another 3 minutes. Turn off the heat and allow the pot to depressurize automatically, twelve to fifteen minutes. Cautiously open the lid and check to see if the beans are very soft with some of them broken; unlike other beans, black chickpeas do not become soft to the point of disintegrating. If not sufficiently cooked, add more water, cover, bring up to pressure, and cook under high pressure another minute. Or cover and boil until soft, approximately forty five minutes.

2. Move the softened chickpeas to a cast-iron wok or saucepan and cook using moderate to high heat approximately five minutes, then using moderate to low heat until all the water evaporates and the chickpeas are glazed with a dark brown coating, approximately 40 minutes. Stir occasionally. Stir in half the chickpea masala, then put in the tomatoes, scallions, and cilantro and cook, stirring slowly, approximately two minutes. Move to a serving dish and sprinkle the rest of the chickpea masala uniformly on top.
3. Heat the oil (and ghee, if using) in a small saucepan using moderate to high heat and put in the cumin seeds; they should sizzle when they touch the hot oil. Swiftly put in the ginger and green chile peppers and cook until a golden colour is achieved, approximately one minute. Stir in the coriander and paprika and instantly pour everything over the chickpeas. Stir lightly to combine and serve.

TAMARIND-CHICKPEAS Ⓥ Ⓟ

This recipe is called "Imli-channae" in Hindi

Yield: 6 to 8 servings

Ingredients:

- ¼ cup Tamarind Paste
- ¼ teaspoon baking soda
- ¼ teaspoon ground black salt
- ¼ teaspoon ground turmeric
- ½ cup finely chopped fresh cilantro, including soft stems
- ½ teaspoon ajwain seeds
- ½ teaspoon garam masala
- 1 (1-inch) stick cinnamon
- 1 large onion, finely chopped
- 1 tablespoon ground coriander
- 1 teaspoon cumin seeds
- 1 teaspoon ground cumin
- 1 teaspoon salt, or to taste
- 1 to 3 fresh green chile peppers, such as serrano, split along the length in half

- 1½ cups finely chopped tomatoes
- 1½ tablespoons <u>Basic Ginger-Garlic Paste</u> (Homemade or store-bought)
- 1¾ cups dried chickpeas, sorted and washed in 3 to 4 changes of water
- 2 bay leaves
- 2 tablespoons minced fresh mint leaves
- 3 tablespoons peanut oil
- 3 to 5 black cardamom pods, crushed lightly to break the skin
- 5 to 6 cups water

Directions:

1. Immerse the chickpeas overnight in water to cover by 2 inches. In the meantime, ready the tamarind paste and the ginger-garlic paste. When ready, drain the chickpeas and place them into your pressure cooker along with 5 cups water, baking soda, salt, cardamom pods, cinnamon, and bay leaves. Ensure that the lid is secure, and cook using high heat until the regulator shows that the pressure is high, then cook two minutes. Turn off the heat and allow the pot to depressurize automatically, twelve to fifteen minutes.
2. Cautiously open the lid and check to see if the beans are very soft with some of them broken; if not, add more water as required, cover, bring up to pressure, and cook under high pressure another minute. Or, cover and boil until the chickpeas are soft and creamy, approximately forty five minutes.
3. Heat the oil in a small-sized non-stick saucepan using moderate to high heat and put in the cumin and ajwain seeds; they should sizzle when they touch the hot oil. Swiftly put in the onion and cook, stirring, until a golden colour is achieved, approximately five minutes. Put in the ginger-garlic paste and stir approximately one minute. Put in the tomatoes and continue to cook until the tomatoes are soft and all the fluids vaporize, approximately five minutes.
4. Put in the coriander, ground cumin, garam masala, turmeric, and black salt, then put in the tamarind paste and bring to a quick boil. Combine with the chickpeas along with the green chile peppers, cilantro, and mint, and simmer until the sauce is very thick, approximately fifteen minutes. Stir vigorously and smash some of the chickpeas to further thicken the dish. Serve.

ENDNOTE

Thank you for the valuable time you spend on my book. I hope it helped you at least a little, making you a slightly better Indian cook. Every little bit counts! If you liked this book, don't forget to check out other books on Indian Cooking by Rekha Sharma!

Printed in Great Britain
by Amazon